on ne peut plus cultiver les c

St Laurent

ANGLAISE
P.A. 1.100.000.h.

Quebec

Lac Supérieur

CANADA

et qui partage

New Hamshire

Plymouth où abordès
les puritains en 162

MICHIGAN T.
P.A. 30.000.h.

L. Michigan

L. Huron

Lac Ontario

NEW-YORK

se confédérerent en 17

Quebec

Island

Illinois R.

Lac Erie

le continent en deux

qui se

PENSYLVANIE

Hudson R.

ÉTATS

OHIO
F.1802 P.A. 937.000

Alleghani

ILLINOIS
F.1818 P.A. 157.000.h.

INDIANA
F. 1816
P.A.

UNIS

Ohio R.

Washington

Jamestown où les Anglais
fondèrent leur première colonie
en 1607

MISSOURI
F. P.A. 140.000.h.

KENTUCKI
F.1796 P.A. 688.000.h.

VIRGINIE

ÉTATS

ARKANSAS T.
P.A. 20.000 h

TENNESSE
F. 1796 P.A. 684.000.h.

CAROLINE
DU NORD

Limites des treize états

ESCLAVES

CAROLINE
DU SUD

MISSISSIPI
F.1817
P.A.136.000.h.

ALABAMA
F. 1818
P.A. 508.000 h.

GEORGIE

LOUISANE
F.1812
P.A.153.000.h

Nlle Orleans

FLORIDE T.
P.A. 34.000.h.

DEMOCRACY IN AMERICA

Alexis de

Democracy

TRANSLATED, EDITED, AND WITH AN INTRODUCTION BY

Tocqueville
in America

HARVEY C. MANSFIELD AND DELBA WINTHROP

THE UNIVERSITY OF CHICAGO PRESS • CHICAGO AND LONDON

University of Chicago Press, Chicago 60637

The University of Chicago Press, Ltd., London

© 2000 by The University of Chicago

All rights reserved. Published 2000

Paperback edition 2002

Printed in the United States of America

09 08 07 06 05 04 03   7 8 9

ISBN: 0–226-80532-8 (cloth)

ISBN: 0–226-80536-0 (paper)

The French text on which this translation is based has been licensed to the University of Chicago Press by Éditions Gallimard and is protected by French and international copyright laws and agreements. © Éditions Gallimard, 1992

Library of Congress Cataloging-in-Publication Data

Tocqueville, Alexis de, 1805–1859.

[De la démocratie en Amérique. English]

Democracy in America / translated, edited, and with an introduction by Harvey C. Mansfield and Delba Winthrop.

p.   cm.

Includes bibliographical references and index.

ISBN 0-226-80532-8 (hardcover)

1. United States—Politics and government. 2. United States—Social conditions. 3. Democracy—United States. I. Mansfield, Harvey Claflin, 1932– II. Winthrop, Delba. III. Title.

JK216 .T713 2000b

320.473—DC21

00-008418

♾ The paper used in this publication meets the minimum requirements of the American National Standard for Information Sciences—Permanence of Paper for Printed Library Materials, ANSI Z39.48–1992.

CONTENTS

Volume One

PART ONE

v

PART TWO

Volume Two

PART ONE
INFLUENCE OF DEMOCRACY
ON INTELLECTUAL MOVEMENT
IN THE UNITED STATES

PART TWO
INFLUENCE OF DEMOCRACY ON THE
SENTIMENTS OF THE AMERICANS

PART THREE
INFLUENCE OF DEMOCRACY ON MORES PROPERLY SO-CALLED

PART FOUR

ON THE INFLUENCE THAT DEMOCRATIC
IDEAS AND SENTIMENTS EXERT ON
POLITICAL SOCIETY

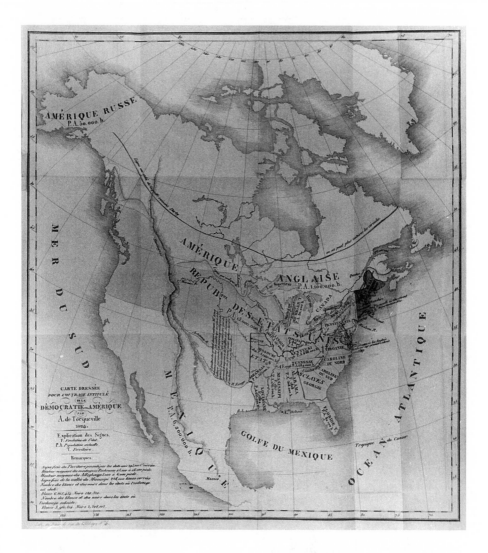

Map of the United States appearing in the first edition of *Democracy in America* (1835). Courtesy of the Department of Special Collections, Joseph Regenstein Library, University of Chicago.

E D I T O R S ' I N T R O D U C T I O N

Harvey C. Mansfield and Delba Winthrop

Democracy in America is at once the best book ever written on democracy and the best book ever written on America. Tocqueville connects the two subjects in his Introduction, and in his title, by observing that America is the land of democracy. It is the country where democracy is least hindered and most perfected, where democracy is at its most characteristic and at its best. Today that claim might be contested, but it is at least arguable. If the twentieth century has been an American century, it is because the work of America—not altogether unsuccessful—has been to keep democracy strong where it is alive and to promote it where it is weak or nonexistent. Somehow, after 165 years, democracy is still in America.

Tocqueville went to America, he said, to see what a great republic was like, and what struck him most was its equality of conditions, its *democracy*. Long ago began a democratic revolution, and it continues today, gathering speed as resistance to it declines. He sets forth the "point of departure" in Puritan America and the origin of self-government in the towns of New England. He analyzes the federal constitution that was meant to facilitate democratic self-government and keep it moderate. He shows that the people are sovereign, whether through the Constitution or despite it, and he warns of the tyranny of the majority. In the very long last chapter of the first volume he examines aspects of American democracy peculiar to America, especially the juxtaposition of the three races there, and he speculates about what these portend for America's future.

In the second volume Tocqueville turns the argument from the natural rise of democracy in America to the influence of democracy on America, beginning with its intellectual movements. Americans have a philosopher unknown to them—Descartes—whose precepts they follow and whose books

they never read. Descartes endorses their reliance on their own judgment, which tells them they can do without his help. Americans suffer, consequently, from "individualism," a lamentable condition—which Tocqueville was the first to depict—in which democratic men and women are thrown on their own resources and consequently come to feel themselves overpowered by impersonal, external forces. But individualism is not the fated consequence of democracy: there are remedies against it, above all the capability of Americans to associate with one another voluntarily in accordance with their own will and reason instead of relying on a centralized, "schoolmaster" government to take care of them. Tocqueville dubs this government an "immense being" and says that it brings on a "mild despotism," which he describes with uncomfortably accurate foresight. To these few highlights one might easily add others, but let these suffice for a welcome to this marvelous work.

Tocqueville's book has acquired the authority of a classic. It is cited with approval by politicians—by all American presidents since Eisenhower—as well as by professors in many fields.[1] Universal accord in its praise suggests that it has something for everyone. But it also suggests that readers tolerate, or perhaps simply overlook, the less welcome passages that their political and scholarly opponents are citing. It is quite striking that both Left and Right appeal to *Democracy in America* for support of their contrary policies. Tocqueville seems to have achieved the goal, expressed at the end of his Introduction, of standing above the parties of the day. Yet his widespread appeal should not mask the controversial and unsettling character of the work.

When Tocqueville wrote his book, it was to speak reprovingly, and sometimes severely, to the partisans of his day for and against democracy. Although the Old Regime has now faded into unremembered history and everyone has followed Tocqueville's advice to accept democracy, partisans remain within it, and they still divide over whether to restrain democracy or push it further. Tocqueville has something dismaying, but instructive, to say to both parties. He knows the extent of democracy in America because he sees better than we the resistances to it in America. He came to America to examine democracy up close and to be sure of what he thought he might find. Unlike other visitors he knew that America was not merely derivative of Europe. It was not behind but ahead of Europe and in that sense exceptional. Tocqueville takes the measure of America's boast, repeated on the first page of *The Federalist*, to set an example for all mankind. He makes his ambition the study of America's ambition, in both cases an ambition that leaves others

---

1. "America is great because America is good"—a mushy sentiment unworthy of the author—is persistently attributed to him.

free. It is open to any country to surpass America if it can, and it is possible that some writer, some day, will write a better book on democracy in America than this one.

Before we survey the marvels of *Democracy in America* and the difficulties of interpreting what it means, let us look at Tocqueville the man to see from whence he came, the conditions of life imposed on him, and the influences he chose to accept.

WHO WAS TOCQUEVILLE?[2]

Alexis de Tocqueville was born on July 29, 1805, and died in his fifty-fourth year on April 16, 1859: not a long life, and one often afflicted with ill health. He was born a French aristocrat and lived as one; and he was also a liberal who both rejected the old regime of aristocracy and doubted the revolution that overturned it. An aristocratic liberal he was, and if we knew everything contained in that difficult combination, we could stop here. But since we do not, the formula will serve as a beginning. In thought as in life Tocqueville always held to freedom and to nobility, and his question, his concern was how to keep them together.

Tocqueville was born into a very old Norman family named Clérel; one of his ancestors had fought in the company of William the Conqueror at the Battle of Hastings. Through marriage, negotiation and action at law, the Clérels acquired the fief of Tocqueville in Normandy, and in 1661 took that name. Alexis's grandfather was a chevalier; his father Hervé became a count in 1820. In 1793 Hervé had married the granddaughter of Malesherbes, a great figure late in the Old Regime: botanist, correspondent of Jean-Jacques Rousseau, both minister and critic of Louis XVI, and courageous defender of the king at his trial in 1792–1793. Malesherbes and Hervé de Tocqueville were imprisoned during the Terror, the former guillotined together with a sister, a daughter, a son-in-law, and a granddaughter and her husband. Hervé was spared and released in 1794, his hair having turned snow white at the age of twenty-two. Hervé became the guardian of the two orphans of Malesherbes's son-in-law, who was the elder brother of the great writer François-René de Chateaubriand. In his *Memoirs* Chateaubriand speaks of seeing his nephews growing up with Alexis, future author of *Democracy in America*. He remarks in one of his epigrams: "Alexis de Tocqueville went through civilized America while I visited its forests."[3] Here is the hauteur of the aristocrat that Tocque-

2. The following account is based on André Jardin, *Tocqueville: A Biography*, L. Davis trans. (New York: Farrar Straus Giroux, 1988).

3. Chateaubriand, *Mémoires d'outre-tombe*, 2 vols. (Paris: Gallimard, éd. Pléiade, 1951), 1: 576; cf. 2: 1053–1054.

ville could have imitated but did not. If he remained in any powerful sense an aristocrat, it was only after having concluded that all partisan sentiment in favor of aristocracy is now vain and nostalgic. He himself had no children and no particular wish to sustain his own noble family. He once said that he would passionately desire to have children as he could imagine them but had "no very keen desire to draw from the great lottery of paternity."[4] However sharp his sympathetic appreciation for aristocratic society—and it was considerable—this was not a man of aristocratic feeling, ready to make sacrifices as *père de famille* on behalf of aristocratic illusions.

The irresistible democratic revolution is the theme of Tocqueville's three great books. It is set forth in his Introduction to *Democracy in America* (the first volume of which was published in 1835, the second in 1840). It is applied to his own time in his *Souvenirs* (written in 1851 but not for publication; first published only in 1893), in which he recounts the (ultimately) socialist revolution that he witnessed in 1848. And he uncovers its remote origins in *The Old Regime and the Revolution,* published in 1856 with a promise he could not fulfill to write further on the events of the Revolution and to provide a judgment on its result.

Unlike other aristocrats of his time, Tocqueville did not despair of democracy. He neither scorned it nor opposed it. On the whole, he approved of it—or at least accepted it with every appearance of willingness. Readers of *Democracy in America* have always disagreed over how democratic he was both in mind and in heart, but it is fair to say that he directed much of his energy to warning the reactionaries in his country that democracy was irreversible as well as irresistible, and to showing them that it was wrong to hate the consequences of the French Revolution. He believed that the beginnings of democracy antedated the Revolution, and that its worst aspects—which were not violence and disruption—were even initiated by the Old Regime of the monarchy.

So, far from hiding or sulking, like a displaced refugee of the old order, or from reluctantly accepting duties that were pressed upon him, Tocqueville sought out opportunities for engagement in politics. In 1837, when, perhaps, he should have been working without interruption on the second volume of *Democracy in America,* he ran for the Chamber of Deputies in the regime of Louis-Philippe, and was defeated. In 1839 he ran again and was elected; he was reelected in 1842, and again in 1846. He became a leading figure of the liberal newspaper *Le commerce* in 1844; then, as the Chamber turned to the Right, he helped create a group called the "Young Left." On January 27, 1848,

4. Letter to his brother Edouard, September 2, 1840; Alexis de Tocqueville, *Selected Letters on Politics and Society,* Roger Boesche ed. (Berkeley, Calif.: University of California Press, 1985), 148.

he gave a famous speech in the Chamber warning, with an accuracy that surprised even him, of the "wind of revolution" that was in the air;[5] here, in addition to the more general predictions of *Democracy in America*, was an instance of his uncanny ability to sense the drifts and trends of politics. Later in that year, after the fall of Louis-Philippe's monarchy, he was elected to the constituent assembly of the Second Republic and served on the committee that prepared its constitution. Then, in 1848, he was elected to the new Assembly and served briefly, honorably, and unsuccessfully as Minister of Foreign Affairs in a cabinet that lasted from June 2 to October 31. By the following spring he had been stricken with the illness, probably tuberculosis, that would eventually claim his life.

Tocqueville did his best to govern, as he said, "in a regular, moderate, conservative, and quite constitutional way," but he was in a situation in which "everyone wanted to depart from the constitution."[6] In such a predicament a consistent line of conduct is almost impossible, and in any case the French had put their new republic on borrowed time by electing Louis Napoleon as its president. His coup d'état putting an end to the republic came in December, 1851, at which time Tocqueville, as a protesting deputy, was imprisoned for two days, then released. Suffering under an illiberal regime and from ill health, he was now free to write his book on the Old Regime. Yet for him, the freedom to write and publish was not enough. He also wanted political freedom, and he wanted to taste it for himself by holding office. He seems to have understood the desire to distinguish oneself as essentially political because the goods of this world, even the intellectual joys of understanding, never give satisfaction or repose. Theory itself is a sort of activity fraught with restiveness, and as such not surely superior to action. Writing in 1840 to his older brother Edouard, he explained himself:

> What moves the soul is different, but the soul is the same—this restive and insatiable soul that despises all goods of the world and which, nonetheless, incessantly needs to be stirred in order to seize them, so as to escape the grievous numbness that is experienced as soon as it relies for a moment on itself. This is a sad story. It is a little bit the story of all men, but of some more than others, and of myself more than anyone I know.[7]

---

5. See Alexis de Tocqueville, *Oeuvres complètes* (hereafter *OC*), 18 vols. (Paris: Gallimard, 1961–1998), 3.2: 745–758. This speech was published by AT in the last edition of *DA* printed in his lifetime.

6. *Recollections of Alexis de Tocqueville* [*Souvenirs*], J. P. Mayer ed. (Garden City, N.Y.: Doubleday, 1971), 228; *OC* 12: 202. For the general difficulty, see Aristotle, *Politics*, 1294b35–40.

7. *Selected Letters*, 148–149; *OC* 14: 214.

Tocqueville did not bask in the triumphant success of *Democracy in America* but went elsewhere in search of new distinction.

It cannot be said, however, that Tocqueville was successful as a politician. He woefully lacked the common touch, as he confessed in his *Souvenirs:*

> Every time that a person does not strike me by something rare in his mind or sentiments, I so to speak do not see him. I have always thought that mediocre men, as well as men of merit, have a nose, a mouth, and eyes, but I have never been able to fix in my memory the particular form of these features in each one of them. I am constantly asking the names of these unknowns whom I see every day, and I constantly forget them; yet I do not despise them, only I consort with them little, I treat them as commonplace. I honor them, for they lead the world, but they bore me profoundly.[8]

This avowal, he further admits, arises not from true modesty but from "great pride" [*grand orgueil*].[9] Yet Tocqueville is not merely being fastidious with his fellow men, his fellow democrats whom he cannot tell apart. Political freedom in republics does more than provide security to multitudes; it clears the way for those few who desire to distinguish themselves and sharpens their hunger for greatness.

So Tocqueville set his hand as well as put his mind to politics, examining the democratic revolution from up close and as it affected him. All the while he was aware that he did not duly appreciate mediocre men: he could not be one of them, and he was unwilling either to know them individually or to master them as a class. In politics he learned about politics and about himself, or better to say, he learned about both together. In addition to his three wonderful books are volumes of letters, especially (but not only) to his friends Gustave de Beaumont and Louis de Kergorlay, which are of surpassing interest to readers of his books. He also wrote reports on slavery, poverty, the colonies, and penitentiaries—his inquiry into the latter being the "pretext" (as he called it) for the trip to America that led to, or in any case preceded, the writing of *Democracy in America*.[10] He also wrote diaries of his voyages, including the one to America but also to England, Switzerland, Ireland, and Algeria.

In recognition of his writings, Tocqueville was made a member of the *Académie des sciences morales et politiques* in 1838 and then elected in 1841, when only thirty-six years old, to the *Académie française*. For twenty years

---

8. *Recollections,* 93; *OC* 12: 103.

9. *OC* 12: 104.

10. Letter to Louis de Kergorlay, January 1835. *Selected Letters,* 95; *OC* 13.1: 374.

his social life was spent at the *Institut de France,* which under the Second Empire became a kind of refuge for liberals like himself who were kept out of politics by Louis Napoleon. On entering the *Académie française* he had the duty of eulogizing the deceased member whose seat he was taking. It was the Comte de Cessac, a minister and admirer of Napoleon I, selfless builder of the very French state that Tocqueville deplored, criticized, and opposed all his life.[11] At the *Académie des sciences morales et politiques* Tocqueville gave a speech in 1852 on the nature of political science in which he concluded that political science and the art of governing were "two very distinct things." Political science, identified with the art of writing, serves the logic of ideas and gives a taste for "the fine, the delicate, the ingenious, the original," whereas the world obeys its passions and is led by gross commonplaces.[12] Tocqueville admits that France has seen eminent statesmen who wrote beautiful books, but their books were no help to their deeds. Here is a comment, perhaps, on his own experience. But failure in the art of governing cannot be inferred from a short term in a post subject to others and under the ominous presidency of a Napoleon. A writer has his own command, and a powerful one, because political science, Tocqueville asserts, gives birth or form to the general ideas of society out of which emerge particular facts and laws.[13] For all the opposition between governing and writing, Tocqueville was always unusually detached for a politician, and unusually engaged for a philosopher.

TOCQUEVILLE'S CONTEXT

The reason for Tocqueville's detachment and for his engagement could be the same: his love of greatness. It was having his eye out for distinctive and remarkable men that kept him from entering wholeheartedly into the concerns of mediocre politicians and even, as he says, from learning to recognize their faces. Yet a certain unphilosophical pride in himself, arising from love of greatness, made politics attractive to him despite the cares and burdens of treating with mediocrity that always attend the desire for outstanding distinction. "My imagination easily climbs to the summit of human greatness,"[14] he said, not because he could see himself on top of the world but because he was dissatisfied with worldly things, yet uncertain of God. Back and forth he went between disdain for ordinary politics and anguished doubt of the

11. Alexis de Tocqueville, *Oeuvres,* 2 vols., A. Jardin ed. (Paris: Gallimard, éd. Pléiade, 1991–1992), 1: 1199–1213.

12. AT, *Oeuvres,* 1: 1217.

13. AT, *Oeuvres,* 1: 1219.

14. *Selected Letters,* 148; OC 14: 214–215.

grounds for a life of serenity and contemplation. But to speak negatively in this way may leave the impression that Tocqueville was indecisive, or a victim of superior, contending forces controlling him. Such is not the case. Positively, it was his view that greatness requires attention to politics and elevation above politics. "Restiveness" (*inquiétude*) is for him the normal, and perhaps the highest, condition of the human soul. The difficulty is that greatness invites pride of soul, and pride of soul comes from one's recognition of the perfection of one's soul. But a perfect soul is not restive. Tocqueville, it seems, can neither claim satisfaction nor abandon pride for the human soul.

Tocqueville saw greatness in the politics of revolution, including the democratic revolution, and though he hated the Terror and the despotism in the French Revolution, he admired the ambitious spirit in the intent of its first makers which made them seek to constitute a new democratic nation from top to bottom. But for Tocqueville greatness is inseparable from freedom (he was never tempted to admire Napoleon). The mere desire for mastery over subjects (or slaves) debases master as well as subject, for when the master denies the humanity common to both, he loses his own and lets himself be ruled by his passions. Unlike Edmund Burke, whom he criticized, Tocqueville did not reject the French Revolution in toto. He approved it in its first phase, when it was devoted to both freedom and equality.[15] Yet the greatness of that democratic revolution has inspired the passion for equality and produced the growing equality of conditions that are hardly welcoming, even profoundly hostile, to human greatness.

Today Tocqueville seems readily accessible to us. His recognition of the democratic revolution and its problems appears right on the mark, and the success of most of his predictions seems uncanny. (He was, however, wrong about a coming war between the races; *DA* I 2.10.) In America he is, as noted above, quoted with approval by intellectuals and politicians from both the Left and the Right. On the Left he is the philosopher of community and civic engagement who warns against the appearance of an industrial aristocracy and against the bourgeois or commercial passion for material well-being: in sum, he is for democratic citizenship. On the Right he is quoted for his strictures on "Big Government" and his liking for decentralized administration, as well as for celebrating individual energy and opposing egalitarian excess: he is a balanced liberal, defending both freedom and moderation. For both parties he is welcome in an era when democracy has defeated the totalitarians and is no longer under challenge to its existence, when suspicion of the state

---

15. Alexis de Tocqueville, *The Old Regime and the Revolution*, A. Kahan trans. (Chicago, Ill.: University of Chicago Press, 1998), Preface, 85; *OC* 2.1: 72.

is widespread, and when modern progress is no longer taken for granted as good.

In France, Tocqueville came into vogue in the 1970s and is now a strong presence. He benefits from national pride, which, not only in France, has often been less than discerning. Although Democracy in America was a huge success when it first appeared, soon thereafter Tocqueville was allowed to fall into neglect. His books were not read and his style, his importance, and his insight were slighted. After World War II, Marxism, existentialism, and deconstructionism were on stage in France and liberalism was in hiding. But in the last thirty years, through the brave example and teaching of Raymond Aron, French scholars and intellectuals have awakened to their heritage of nineteenth-century liberals, and above all to the discomforting sagacity of Tocqueville, always more sensitive than reassuring. But after much false assurance from ready solutions, the wary observation and cool advice of liberalism can come as a relief.

Among French liberals of the early nineteenth century, chastened by excesses of the Revolution done in the name of freedom, the two most outstanding were Benjamin Constant (1767–1830) and François Guizot (1787–1874). Tocqueville's originality in his time can be gauged from his differences with them, his contemporary fellow liberals. Constant and Guizot took up the cause of representative government in France as the positive alternative to the despotisms of the Revolution and of Napoleon. They were impressed by the woeful contrast between the French Revolution and the Glorious Revolution of 1688 in England, and they thought it possible to recapture the moderation and open-minded modernity of the English aristocracy, and the usages of the English Parliament, for application in France. They took inspiration from Montesquieu rather than Rousseau while lacking the respect for circumstance in the former and the rhetorical force of the latter.

Constant understands representation as the modern discovery that subordinates politics to the private independence of the complex of individuals and groups in civil society. That is modern freedom, and it is to be opposed to ancient freedom, which is participation in political power. The error in the French Revolution was to confound the two, and thus to transform freedom into despotism. Modern representative government expresses a doubt that government can truly reflect popular will; even when ruling, such government is doubtful of itself. Its essence is to be found not in itself but in the parliamentary opposition to itself. For Guizot, however, a man and a thinker more given to governing, a representative government seeks and finds the dominant powers in society, which after the Revolution are no longer hereditary, and represents them. It gives them the public respect they deserve, and in return they give it the superiority it deserves. Guizot sees representative government to be rationally responsive to society and its capacities, not tyrannizing over them as happened in the Revolution.

Tocqueville does not put much stock in representative government; his theme is *democracy*. Although he surely discusses representative institutions in *Democracy in America*, he does not discourse at length, as do Constant and Guizot, on the principle of representation.[16] For him, representative institutions are democratic; they may have been designed to hold democracy at bay (as was the United States Senate), but in their actual functioning they give expression to democracy. At best they may instruct democratic citizens, but they do not serve to check democratic impulses or passions. Tocqueville says quite emphatically, in a chapter entitled "How One Can Say Strictly That in the United States the People Govern," that although the "form of government is representative," "the opinions, the prejudices, the interests, and even the passions of the people" find no lasting obstacles preventing them from taking effect in the daily direction of society (*DA* I 2.1).

Tocqueville always understands democracy in contrast to aristocracy. He constantly compares them not merely as forms of government in a narrow sense but as opposed ways of life. In this Tocqueville's political science has the look of Aristotle's, which also considers politics comprehensively in the regime (*politeia*), and presents the typical political and social alternative as between democracy and oligarchy.[17] But while Aristotle argues that these two regimes offer an open choice ever present to human beings because each is rooted in a constant and fixed human nature, all human beings always being arguably equal and arguably unequal, Tocqueville describes them as distinct historical epochs: once there was aristocracy, now we have democracy.

By turning to history and away from human nature, Tocqueville joins Constant and Guizot and other nineteenth-century liberals who also described irrevocable historical change in civil society, from ancients to moderns, or from the old regime to the new, to which governments would have to conform. They not only disagree with Aristotle's view but they also depart from the position of earlier liberals who began from an abstract, ahistorical state of nature. The state of nature was thought to reveal the nature of man as he was essentially, stripped of conventional (which means historical) advantages and disadvantages. It was the very contrary of Aristotle's picture of man as naturally political, but it did at least rely on a fixed human nature. The liberalism of James Madison (1751–1836), for example, whom American readers especially, then and now, would want to compare with Tocqueville,

---

16. See *DA* I 1.8, 2.1, 2.4, 2.5, 2.7, 2.9, 2.10; II 1.21.
17. Aristotle, *Politics*, 1278b12, 1280a7, 1290a12–29, 1293b33.

still relies on the rights of man in the state of nature. Tocqueville, however, does not build his understanding of democracy on the liberal state of nature first conceived by Thomas Hobbes, Benedict Spinoza, and John Locke. He does not refer to that concept in *Democracy in America*.[18] He also was far from developing a "philosophy of history" in the thoroughgoing manner of the German philosopher Georg W. F. Hegel (1770–1831).[19] But his liberalism, while totally lacking in Hegel's confidence that history was progress in reason, joined in his protest against abstract, state-of-nature liberalism.

From Tocqueville's viewpoint, even Madison's liberalism seemed lacking in concrete observation of America, above all of the democratic revolution there. In *Federalist* 10, Madison's most famous statement of his liberalism, he distinguishes a democracy from a republic. A democracy is popular government in which the people rule directly, as in ancient cities; and a republic is one in which the people rule indirectly through their representatives, who "refine and enlarge" their views. The system of representation was largely unknown to the ancients and was invented by modern political science, says Alexander Hamilton, helpfully, in *Federalist* 9. Representation works best, Madison continues, in large, heterogeneous countries with many conflicting interests and sects that make it difficult to form a majority faction, the bane of popular government.

Tocqueville does not share Madison's confidence that the problem can be solved. He fears majority tyranny in America and actually sees it at work there in public opinion. For him, the danger is not so much factious interest or passion as the degradation of souls in democracy, a risk to which Madison does not directly refer but which Tocqueville states prominently in his Introduction to *Democracy in America*. As a sign of his fear, he habitually calls the American government a "democratic republic," thus spanning and overriding the distinction that Madison was at pains to establish. A modern republic, Tocqueville means to say, cannot help being a democracy, and a modern democracy necessarily has a hard task in getting equal citizens to accept authority without feeling they have been subjected and degraded. Madison's reliance on the state of nature was a way of avoiding examination of the human soul, for in that early liberal concept the soul disappears as a whole

18. See *DA* II 2.1 for the closest approximation to the state of nature; in I 2.10 AT says that a republic is "the natural state of the Americans," and in that chapter and in I 1.5 he also gives an account of the origin of sovereignty without referring to the state of nature.

19. In two nearly contemporary letters on the study of the Old Regime in France that AT was planning, he spoke of "historical philosophy" and "philosophy of history" to describe his intent not merely of narrating the facts but of mixing his judgment with narration. Letter to Louis de Kergorlay of December 15, 1850, *Selected Letters*, 256; *OC* 13.2: 232; and letter to Gustave de Beaumont, December 26, 1850, *OC* 8.2: 343.

while being divided into disconnected passions such as fear, vanity, or pity. Tocqueville looks at the whole soul and at all of democracy. He considers individual, society, and government as involved with one another without the simplifying state-of-nature abstraction.

Among other liberals of Tocqueville's time we cannot omit the English philosopher John Stuart Mill (1806–1873), who wrote long reviews saluting the two volumes of *Democracy in America* as they appeared in 1835 and 1840. After the first of these Tocqueville exclaimed to Mill: "Of all the articles written on my book, yours is *the only one* in which the author mastered my thought perfectly and was able to display it to the regard of others."[20] At Mill's invitation Tocqueville wrote an essay, "Political and Social Condition of France Before and Since 1789," published in *The London and Westminster Review* in 1836, and he exchanged letters with Mill for the rest of his life. But there remain pronounced differences between Mill and Tocqueville that are evident even in the very favorable reviews Mill wrote of Tocqueville's book.

These two liberals are together, and in contrast to Constant and Guizot, in their appreciation of democracy, which both understand to be here to stay and welcome too. Yet Tocqueville's reservations, his criticisms, his forebodings are not shared by Mill, who in a letter confessed to Tocqueville with some understatement that his article is "a shade or two more favorable to democracy than your book."[21] Mill believes, for example, that the tyranny of the majority that Tocqueville warns of in the first volume of *Democracy in America* could be avoided "if the people entertained the right idea of democracy."[22] To Tocqueville's remark that the American people cheerfully exclude the ablest men from government, Mill responds that great talents are not ordinarily needed and that "in a settled state of things, the commanding intellects will always prefer to govern mankind from their closets, by means of literature and science, leaving the mechanical details of government to mechanical minds."[23] Here is wondrous confidence in the capability of intelligence to run the world, unsurprisingly combined with contempt for the actual operation of self-government, of which Tocqueville made so much. Mill's partisanship for democracy, warmer than Tocqueville's, depends on his confidence that the commanding intellects will direct it. They will do that through representative government, keeping the flow of influence moving

<hr>

20. Letter to John Stuart Mill, October 10, 1840, *OC* 6.1: 329; in reply to Mill's letter of May 11, 1840, to AT, in which he says: "You have changed the face of political philosophy ..." *OC* 6.1: 328.
21. John Stuart Mill, *Collected Works*, J. M. Robson ed., 19 vols. (Toronto: University of Toronto Press, 1965–), 12: 272.
22. Mill, *Collected Works*, 18: 71.
23. Mill, *Collected Works*, 18: 76.

from the intellects to the people and not in reverse, from the people to the intellects, as Tocqueville saw it. For Mill, in contrast to Tocqueville, representative government would not be overwhelmed by democracy, and in contrast to Constant and Guizot, it did not have to fear democracy.

Thus Mill felt free to call for more democracy and to press the case against aristocracy, for he, unlike Tocqueville, regarded aristocracy as a present menace still impeding the progress of civilization. It may be doomed, but only if it is hastened along to extinction. In Mill's view the best minds could ensure their ascendancy by demanding more democracy, for democracy aided by representation does not threaten to cause debasement of intelligence or cultural deprivation. The people, Mill believed against Tocqueville, will not insist on their sovereignty. At the same time, the commanding intellects will govern or direct but not dominate society, because their intellects keep them impartial. Representative democracy promises in sum that a free society will be without a dominant power, effectively classless. It is a pretty picture, attractive to liberals in Mill's day and ours, but it is not Tocqueville's. He did not think that society could exist without a sovereign power or that intellects would be unaffected by democracy (see *DA* II 1, as a whole). Yet he somehow gives the impression of being as impartial as Mill. He sees democracy and aristocracy as distinct and contrasting social states. Democracy is more just than aristocracy since it relies less on compulsion, but it nonetheless has its own character and its own stamp, he shows, that leave their mark effortlessly by consent and insinuation.

Constant accepted the advent of popular sovereignty in the French Revolution, but he thought it could be restrained. The error of the Revolution, again, was to impose an anachronistic, illiberal democracy, derived from the ancient polis, on modern individuals who need only to be represented, not ruled. But the unintended consequence of this thought is to absolve modern democracy for crimes committed when it forgot itself during the Revolution, and then to imply that it has no ills of its own. It is as if all it needs to resolve its problems is self-doubt supplied by liberal thinkers and expressed through parliamentary opposition. Guizot, too, underestimated the power of modern democracy. He believed (as did Tocqueville) that merit would have its way in modern democracy because individual talent and the social power to which it gives rise cannot be denied. But he failed to see that mediocrity would also have its way in modern democracy. Constant, Guizot, Madison, Mill: all were confident that liberal rationality could contain the sovereign wills that liberalism set loose when it denied any basis to traditional authority. Tocqueville stands out from other nineteenth-century liberals by refusing to accept either a safe distancing of freedom from democracy or an easy convergence of the two.

PASCAL, MONTESQUIEU, AND ROUSSEAU

From Tocqueville's fellow liberals, contemporaries with whom he shares an outlook, we turn to the philosophers—all French—whom he chose as daily companions. Writing in 1836 to his friend Louis de Kergorlay, he said: "There are three men with whom I live a little every day; they are Pascal, Montesquieu, and Rousseau."[24]

Besides being French, these are modern philosophers. Tocqueville's thinking has many points of similarity with that of the ancients; he shares their acute power of observation, their willingness to stop and reflect, their noble simplicity of judgment all the while questioning both nobility and simplicity. But although he does appreciate them as authors, and welcomes the spiritualism and moral elevation of Plato, he does not accept them as authorities or guides for modern times.[25] Above all, he does not care for the best regime as they do. He does not, like the ancients, carry every discussion of the usual and the ordinary toward the best. He "places" democracy on the scale of human imperfection without a glance, it seems, to gauge the distance from utopian perfection. He is, of course, always comparing democracy to aristocracy, and always revealingly. But his "aristocracy" is the conventional aristocracy of inherited property, not the true natural aristocracy of the wise set forth in the tradition of Socrates. Come to think of it, where is Socrates in Tocqueville? In *Democracy in America* Socrates appears as a doctrinaire believer in the immortality of the soul, in which guise he serves both the permanent need of human greatness to be attached to an immaterial principle and the historical social state of aristocracy, now obsolete (*DA* II 1.15). Perhaps the questioning Socrates is also in Tocqueville himself, an ironical friend of democracy, praising virtues of which it is unaware and condemning as faults the excesses of which it is sometimes most proud.

Thus Tocqueville has none of the enthusiasm of modernity in the heyday of its founding ambition. As he does not care for the rule of the wise, so too he does not believe in any scientific, methodological, or institutional substitute for the rule of the wise—the rule of the duly enlightened. Pascal, Montesquieu, and Rousseau are modern philosophers to some extent critical of modernity. They are not captains of the first wave of the modern revolution. Montesquieu (1689–1755) and Rousseau (1712–1778) came after, and Pascal (1623–1662) kept a certain distance. We note the absence of Descartes, the unread, unacknowledged philosopher of the Americans (*DA* II 1.1), in Tocque-

---

24. Letter to Louis de Kergorlay, November 12, 1836, *OC* 13.1: 418.
25. See *DA* I 2.9; II 1.15; letter to Louis de Kergorlay of August 8, 1838, *OC* 13.2: 40–41; letter to Gustave de Beaumont, April 22, 1838, *Selected Letters*, 130; *OC* 8.1: 292.

ville's list of daily counselors. The founder of modern rationalism, however wonderfully French, was not to his taste. Tocqueville was convinced that a great revolution in human affairs was leading all men to one regime, democracy, but he was not persuaded that this was simply the regime of reason. Democracy for him is surely not unreason; much can be said on its behalf, and he says it. But he does not claim, as did the French revolutionaries, that it is light after darkness.

Pascal was not a liberal, and it is strange to see plain marks of his influence in the thought of a liberal. Pascal tells of the vanity of human knowledge and of the misery of the human soul, conclusions in which Christianity and his philosophy converge. They are also matters that liberalism, with its faith in applied science and confidence in the self, would generally rather avoid or ignore. But Tocqueville's liberalism does not put aside yearnings of the soul and does not join in the attempt of Descartes, Hobbes, Spinoza, and Locke to contain them and to reduce the complexity of satisfying the soul to the single task of preserving the self. Tocqueville cares little for ancient metaphysics, yet he cares less for its modern substitute, epistemology, which is designed to protect liberalism from dangerous involvement in deep questions.

Thanks in good part to what he learned from Pascal, Tocqueville is a liberal with depth. This does not merely mean, as it might today, that he has picked up some psychology, and been informed of the turmoil at the bottom of the self; for that kind of depth is preparatory to a therapy that renders the soul as harmless as it was before the discovery of unreason in it. Tocqueville's depth is in his view of the soul's irremediable "restiveness" (*inquiétude*) that he shares with Pascal. "The condition of man," said Pascal, is "inconstancy, boredom, restiveness."[26]

In *Democracy in America* Tocqueville has a chapter on the restiveness of Americans in the midst of their well-being (*DA* II 2.13). Although they are the most enlightened people on earth, he says, they appear "grave and almost sad even in their pleasures." By their very enlightenment they are instructed that all goods are of this world and that many more of them are attainable than was believed in the past. So they pursue them avidly but inconstantly because they know there is always something better in the world than what they have got. Life is too short to enjoy present goods at the expense of future ones; so they keep on pursuing happiness in such manner as to assume they will never reach it. However enlightened, Americans live in a contradiction: they are attached to material goods as if they will never die, yet they are never satisfied with them because they do know they will die. Here is a reasoned

26. Pascal, *Pensées*, 127 Br.

critique, based on thoughtful observation, of the liberal doctrines of progress, property, and the right of self-preservation. One commentator has said that the "Tocquevillian description of democratic man sometimes appears as a page torn from the *Pensées* of Pascal."[27]

What Pascal calls the condition of man Tocqueville displays in democratic man—more politically and against the background of modern enlightenment. In discussing democratic theater and poetry, Tocqueville says that democratic ages are absorbed in the portrayal not of particular individuals or peoples but of the whole human race. Since poets deal with the ideal, democratic poets must perforce envisage the depths of man's "immaterial nature." In man they find infinite greatness and pettiness, for man comes from nothing and returns to God, momentarily wandering on the edge of two abysses (*DA* II 1.17). All this unmistakably Pascalian language presents a Pascalian thought adapted by Tocqueville. It invokes Pascal's picture of the nature of man in which he is not so much placed in an ordered whole as swallowed up in the infinite.[28] Men know enough of themselves, says Tocqueville, to sustain poetry but not enough to get beyond it. While speaking of democratic man he lapses as it were unconsciously into speaking of man. Democratic man is petty and weak, but he dreams of a destiny that is vast.

Yet when Tocqueville comes to consider Pascal himself by name, the context is aristocracy. Contrasting democratic eagerness to get practical applications of science to the "ardent, haughty, and disinterested love of the true" characteristic of a few, Tocqueville singles out Pascal to illustrate the latter. Pascal, he says, devoted his soul so entirely to a "pure desire to know" that he broke the bonds attaching it to his body and died of old age before he was forty (*DA* II 1.10). It is unclear whether he altogether admires this dramatic example,[29] but his words reveal that in his opinion, contrary to Pascal, the love of truth can be "haughty" as well as "disinterested." Somehow human greatness is in the individual, and in that sense proud and aristocratic, as well as in the species democratically. A man such as Pascal is less likely in democracy. Tocqueville was not, like Pascal, an enemy of pride, and so, unlike Pascal, he found human greatness in politics, and under democracy, in political freedom.[30] In a letter written in 1857 he discloses that at age sixteen he was

27. Pierre Manent, *Tocqueville and the Nature of Democracy,* J. Waggoner trans. (Lanham, Md.: Rowman and Littlefield, 1996), 60.

28. Pascal, *Pensées* 69, 72 Br. See AT, *DA* II 2.12, speaking of man's "taste for the infinite."

29. Compare Peter A. Lawler, *The Restless Mind: Alexis de Tocqueville on the Origin and Perpetuation of Human Liberty* (Lanham, Md.: Rowman and Littlefield, 1993), ch. 4, with Allan Bloom, *The Closing of the American Mind* (New York: Simon and Schuster, 1987), 251.

30. In *DA* II 3.19 AT quotes Pascal on the advantage that aristocratic rank provides to men of great ambition; see Pascal, *Pensées,* 322 Br., and see also *Trois discours sur la condition des grands.*

seized by an encompassing doubt, which he describes in Pascalian terms as an "inner malaise that I have never been able to cure myself of," producing "restiveness of mind."[31] Perhaps it was because, like Pascal, he saw Christian faith as incomprehensible and hostile to human pride, that he was unable to persuade himself to accept it. He was with Pascal except for his passion on behalf of human greatness—but what an exception!

Pierre-Paul Royer-Collard, the moderate royalist statesman under the Restoration, wrote to a friend of his concerning *Democracy in America* that "to find a work to compare it with, you have to go back to Aristotle's *Politics* and [Montesquieu's] *Spirit of the Laws*."[32] Clearly Royer-Collard (also a correspondent of Tocqueville's) had the comprehensiveness of the book in view when paying this interesting compliment. Like Aristotle and Montesquieu, Tocqueville begins from politics as it is lived and observed. No grand principle is imposed from the outside. Unlike Aristotle, who begins from actual politics but always tends toward something higher, Tocqueville does not discuss the best regime or use it to urge on his readers or, on the contrary, to set a limit on political ambition. (Occasionally he may refer to what God, as opposed to humans, is capable of; *DA* II 1.3, 4.8.) Yet, like Montesquieu, he also refrains from joining the search for a single legitimate regime that would change the political question from what is best to what is universally attainable. Neither style of abstraction, ancient or modern, appeals to him. So, like Montesquieu, his philosophy is modest and self-effacing, and his comprehensiveness counts against his reputation as a philosopher. No one would deny that title to Aristotle, who combines broad sensitivity with stern judgment, moral and metaphysical, but Montesquieu and Tocqueville hold judgment in abeyance by accepting outstanding facts as given. They have no hankering for the impossible, for the rule of the wise.[33]

Tocqueville accepts the "providential fact" of democracy and he turns to

---

31. Letter to Mme. Swetchine of February 28, 1857, *OC* 15.2: 314. See also *Selected Letters*, 348; *OC* 15.2: 309; and *Selected Letters*, 52–53; *OC* 13.1: 225–236.

32. Quoted in Jean-Claude Lamberti, *Tocqueville and the Two Democracies*, A. Goldhammer trans. (Cambridge, Mass.: Harvard University Press, 1989), 122.

33. In *DA* AT refers to Montesquieu three times directly (I 1.5, I 2.6, I 2.10) and twice indirectly (II 3.11, 3.18). Among commentators who had laid emphasis on their relationship are Raymond Aron, *Main Currents in Sociological Thought*, 2 vols. (New Brunswick, N.J.: Transaction Publishers, 1998), 1: 237–302; Melvin Richter, "The Uses of Theory: Tocqueville's Adaptation of Montesquieu," in Melvin Richter ed., *Essays in Theory and History* (Cambridge, Mass.: Harvard University Press, 1970), 74–102; Anne M. Cohler, *Montesquieu's Comparative Politics and the Spirit of American Constitutionalism* (Lawrence, Kans.: University Press of Kansas, 1988), ch. 8; Pierre Manent, *An Intellectual History of Liberalism*, Rebecca Balinski trans. (Princeton, N.J.: Princeton University Press, 1994), ch. 10, and *Tocqueville and the Nature of Democracy;* Lamberti, *Tocqueville and the Two Democracies;* James W. Ceaser, *Liberal Democracy and Political Science* (Baltimore, Md.: Johns Hopkins University Press, 1990), ch. 3.

America, thus denying himself the luxuriant cosmopolitanism in which Montesquieu indulged. He cannot adopt the "general spirit of a nation," which Montesquieu develops as a whole comprising each nation, composed of mores, manners, and laws.[34] For Tocqueville, something similar can be conceived, the social state (*état social*), but it is a whole connecting particular laws, customs, and mores that refers to the equality or inequality of conditions prevailing in democracy or aristocracy. In our time, when the democratic revolution is underway, democracy is or is becoming the only social state. That is the fact to be accepted, and it reduces both the cosmopolitan variety of regimes to be found in Montesquieu's work and Aristotle's several regimes to one possible condition, if not a single government.

What Montesquieu and Tocqueville share is a political science that centers on the facts of human existence rather than on human nature. Tocqueville relies on human nature more than Montesquieu; he invokes it to mark the limits to democracy and aristocracy. He does not refer to it as the cause of those regimes. When he says in the Introduction to *Democracy in America* that "a new political science is needed for a world altogether new," he may have in mind for replacement Montesquieu's old-world political science, not centered on democracy; but more profoundly he may also mean to supersede, with Montesquieu, Aristotle's premodern political science. Aristotle's classification of regimes presupposes that monarchy, aristocracy, and democracy are always possible because they are based on monarchical, aristocratic, and democratic inclinations of human nature, one of which may become dominant in certain circumstances. Tocqueville, following Montesquieu, particularizes those regimes, taking the circumstances rather than human nature as given, thus setting aside human nature as a permanent potentiality beyond those circumstances. The result is to create what has been called the "authority of the present moment."[35] Once human nature has been made historical and particular, it can then be made more general, or remade as general, in the "general spirit of the nation" (Montesquieu) or the "social state" (Tocqueville). In Tocqueville's case the new generality has to do with aristocratic or democratic man, and only indirectly with man simply. The democratic social state, generalized from the providential fact of democracy's advance, has its own logic and a definite coherence enabling it to regain a certain distance from the facts. Thus for Tocqueville "democracy" is something different from "America," as he frequently reminds his readers, even though it is America that reveals the fact of democracy's arrival.

34. Montesquieu, *The Spirit of the Laws*, XIX.
35. Pierre Manent, *The City of Man*, M. LePain trans. (Princeton, N.J.: Princeton University Press, 1998), 15.

The combination of particular and general, historical and theoretical, that Tocqueville learned from Montesquieu anticipates the "ideal type" invented by Max Weber which is a commonplace of social science today. Weber's name for it is misleading because the very purpose of the notion is to separate "ideal" from "type." When Tocqueville speaks of "democracy," he does so without Aristotle's calm negative judgment. Of course democracy has its disadvantages, but they do not come from its failure to achieve the best regime. They arise because "one inconvenience can never be suppressed without another's cropping up"[36]—because there is no best regime, only democracy and the misnamed "aristocracy."

The liberalism of Tocqueville and Montesquieu does not rest on law or on the sovereignty of the legislator as does that of Hobbes and Locke. The two later liberals bring in mores to soften the punitiveness of relying mainly on law to order society. To Montesquieu such reliance can be as hostile to freedom as was the devotion to virtue in ancient cities; both the fearfulness of law and self-sacrifice in virtue are too demanding on men. By asking so much, law and virtue humiliate those whom they are supposed to empower or ennoble. So Montesquieu turns to "mildness" (*douceur*) in mores, which he believes will be secured by the habits of commerce. In commercial dealings the lure of monetary gain eclipses the force of anger and the satisfaction of vengeance, and skill in calculation replaces honorable resentment. One learns not to take oneself and slights to oneself so seriously, to the end that mildness and moderation help free men to live together without offending one another.

Tocqueville departs from Montesquieu just on this point. His concern is not so much about the despotism hostile to liberalism as about *democratic* despotism, one characterized not by fear as in Montesquieu's scheme but by the very mildness Montesquieu wanted to induce in free societies. Tocqueville's "mild despotism" in democracies is indeed inoffensive, but without being overbearing the schoolmaster state he describes is nonetheless overwhelming (*DA* II 4.6). Democratic citizens are likely to feel incapable on their own and to seek the protection, while becoming the dependents, of a state that suffocates them with its mildness. In this condition one remedy is the enterprise and even the honor to be found in hardy commercial ventures (*DA* I 2.10, II 3.18), so that for Tocqueville as contrasted with Montesquieu, commerce is a source of honor, not its dissolver, and a counteraction to mildness, not its precipitating cause.

The reason for the disagreement over commerce between Tocqueville and Montesquieu is that for the former democracy has arrived, whereas for the

36. Machiavelli, *Discourses on Livy*, I 6.3.

latter aristocracy is still viable. Montesquieu wants to make use of the French nobility as an "intermediate body" capable of resisting the monarch; it must then be kept intact and excluded from commerce. But Tocqueville sees that after the French Revolution a separate nobility, nonexistent in America, is obsolete in France, and democratic means must be sought to perform the function of restraining the central government. The whole apparatus of liberalized monarchy that spreads over Montesquieu's *The Spirit of the Laws* is summarily enrolled in Tocqueville's catch-all "aristocracy," comprising all predemocratic regimes. In this aspect, Montesquieu has become obsolete.

Yet perhaps Montesquieu taught Tocqueville the notion of "obsolete." Montesquieu's presentation of ancient, republican virtue is admiring but deeply critical. Greek political philosophy is historicized as the practice of Greek cities that no longer exist. The self-sacrificing virtue of those cities, therefore, no longer exists. Tocqueville plays the same card against Montesquieu's nobility, which no longer exists except in Europe for the sake of vengeance or out of nostalgia. The best regime having been abandoned, what is left is fact, and facts become obsolete. Somehow Tocqueville will have to secure the advantages of nobility—its sense of honor and its capacity for action—from within the democratic social state. But any connection between nobility's advantages and its claim to rule has been severed by the resort to history that he shares with Montesquieu.

Of the Rousseau in Tocqueville there are also interpreters, one of whom considers him so close to Rousseau that the problem is more to distinguish them than to assimilate them.[37] Tocqueville does not direct attention to the "intimate relation" he had with Rousseau, it is suggested, because he wanted to reconcile his readers in Europe, the well-born and well-educated, to democracy; and to use Rousseau's name, which was anathema to such people, was not the way to do that. To say that Tocqueville is fundamentally Rousseauian is also to say that he is less conservative than he is often taken to be, and perhaps that Rousseau is more so. They share the general outlook that aristocracy is dead, democracy is inevitable, and the question of modern politics is between egalitarian democracy and egalitarian tyranny. Politically Tocqueville is much closer to Rousseau than to Pascal and Montesquieu, a kinship somewhat hidden by the partisan use of Rousseau's name and thought by the Jacobins in support of the Terror.

In response, one could say again that Tocqueville did not occupy himself

37. Allan Bloom, *Giants and Dwarfs* (New York: Simon and Schuster, 1990), 313; John Koritansky, *Alexis de Tocqueville and the New Science of Politics* (Durham, N.C.: Carolina Academic Press, 1986); Wilhelm Hennis, "In Search of 'the New Science of Politics,'" in Ken Masugi ed., *Interpreting Tocqueville's "Democracy in America"* (Savage, Md.: Rowman and Littlefield, 1991).

with the "principles of political right" that were Rousseau's concern in *Social Contract*. When discussing the "real advantages" of democracy (*DA* I 2.6), Tocqueville says that the majority "can be mistaken, but cannot have an interest contrary to itself." This is redolent of Rousseau, but it is not what he says, which is almost the opposite: the majority can have private interests contrary to itself, but its general will cannot be mistaken.[38] In his concern for principles, Rousseau insists on the question of legitimacy as Tocqueville does not. Rousseau states that "every legitimate government is republican,"[39] but when Tocqueville considers legitimacy in the introduction to *Democracy in America*, he ignores arguments over right and focuses on people's actual feelings. He fears that, just because legitimacy has been transformed from custom to principles, democratic peoples now regard their governments as less legitimate than peoples under aristocracies used to regard theirs. While Rousseau opposed the social contract theory of Hobbes and Locke, he did so by radicalizing their formulations so that natural rights disappeared and were replaced by conventional rights once civil society was formed. Rousseau's political philosophy therefore delights those who like to deal in radical abstractions, even though the principles he sets down are qualified and moderated by insight and observation usually associated with political conservatism. Tocqueville, however, as in the discussion just mentioned, makes repeated use of the distinction between democracy and aristocracy, two forms of government, as opposed to that between civil society in any government and the state of nature outside of government, a distinction required for a social contract theory. Aristocracy is obsolete, it is true, but just for that reason it is useful, and needs to be recalled. Aristocracy is the alternative to democracy, enlarged by Tocqueville, created as it were to serve that function. It is presented as no less legitimate than democracy, indeed in its day more legitimate, but that day is gone.

At the end of *Democracy in America* Tocqueville says that equality is more just than inequality (*DA* II 4.8), and this conclusion certainly agrees with Rousseau's statement that in the social compact unequal men "become equal through convention and by right."[40] But Tocqueville indicates that he is also concerned with the "particular prosperity" of the few and with greatness, and he says that democracy's greatness and beauty are in its justice, as if to imply that justice is less valuable than greatness and beauty. The passage repays careful examination and comparison with others, since everyone who

38. Rousseau, *Social Contract*, II 3.
39. Rousseau, *Social Contract*, II 6.
40. Rousseau, *Social Contract*, I 9.

reads *Democracy in America* wants to know how much of a democrat Tocqueville was.[41] The same is true for Rousseau, of course, but somehow his writings, which do not feature praise of aristocracy like Tocqueville's—though they do praise nobility—leave the question less doubtful. The two men are in accord over the inevitability of democracy, and on the need for salutary modifications of its extreme principles, but Rousseau gives voice to those principles and Tocqueville does not.

Other points of resemblance between Tocqueville and Rousseau, visible especially in Rousseau's less political works, deserve mention. Tocqueville put his politics and psychology together in one book, thus avoiding abstract principle. Rousseau did, however, elaborate a formal politics in the *Social Contract*, and he supplemented or counteracted it in such books as *Emile* and *La nouvelle Héloïse*, more attentive to the soul, more widely read, and perhaps more interesting to Tocqueville. Tocqueville agrees with Rousseau that compassion is a necessary corrective to self-interest. But he does not rhapsodize over sympathetic feeling for one's fellow creatures in the Rousseauian style; he is rather cool about compassion (*DA* II 3.1–4). Compassion is as much an extension of self-interest as a corrective, and as such it is limited to temporary acts of kindness. The suffering of others, in fact, can add to one's own sense of impotence, thus to the deepest ill of democratic equality, which Tocqueville calls "individualism," the self-isolation induced by the belief that an individual by himself can do nothing within a mass of people ruled by vast social forces.

Tocqueville shares Rousseau's disdain for the pettiness of the bourgeois. Particularly in his *Souvenirs*, when, recounting the faults of the regime of Louis Philippe in France (1830–1848), Tocqueville gives vent to his exasperation at a government confined to the middle class, thus timid and mediocre, and lacking in both virtue and greatness.[42] But this was his private sentiment on France, not America, for a memoir not intended to be published that did not appear until 1893. In *Democracy in America*, intended for the public and therefore a truer statement of his teaching if not his feeling, he does not condemn. He does not oppose bourgeois to citizen or set interest against virtue in the manner of Rousseau,[43] although he surely does not abandon these distinctions. He apparently welcomes the American doctrine of "self-

41. AT claims for his book "a true impartiality in its theoretical judgment of the two societies [democratic and aristocratic]"—which of course does not mean that he loves them equally; letter to Henry Reeve, September 9, 1839, *OC* 6.1: 48. See also letter to Henry Reeve, March 22, 1837, *Selected Letters*, 115–116; *OC* 6.1: 38.

42. *Recollections*, 2–3; *OC* 12: 30–31.

43. See the famous footnote in Rousseau's *Social Contract*, I 6.

interest well understood" (his expression for what we call "enlightened self-interest"), and clearly celebrates the American penchant for association, both of which cause self-interest to expand and to move in the direction of virtue. He is not enamored of sincerity and authenticity opposed to self-interest, as was Rousseau. Tocqueville, with his balanced appreciation of middle-class America, could never be put among the number of Rousseau's followers, on the Right as well as the Left, who condemn America as the quintessence of the bourgeois way of life.

Tocqueville looks at the mix of religion with democracy, and of democracy with religion, as did Rousseau; but unlike Rousseau he does not adopt a civil religion or criticize and abandon Christianity. He praises religion as much for producing healthy, capable individuals as for strengthening community.

Last, he praises Indians for their aristocratic pride, but for nothing else. In themselves they are inferior to the civilized whites and their way of life is no reproach to the sophistication of white civilization. Rather than a Rousseauian comparison of this kind, Tocqueville says quite severely that the civilized whites did not deal justly with the Indians. That treatment calls into question the superiority of civilized justice, but does not imply an endorsement of the noble savage.

THE WRITING OF DEMOCRACY IN AMERICA[44]

Before writing *Democracy in America,* Tocqueville took a trip to America of a little more than nine months in the company of his friend Gustave de Beaumont (1802–1866). Like Tocqueville, Beaumont was a magistrate; the two had studied law together and served on the same court at Versailles.[45] In 1829 they both attended Guizot's lectures on the "history of civilization in France," a statement of the historical liberalism Tocqueville himself was to maintain.[46] Then, in 1831, they came to America as collaborators in a grand project to see "what a great republic is," as Tocqueville put it in a letter to another friend.[47]

---

44. The following section is based on three classic works of Tocqueville scholarship: George W. Pierson, *Tocqueville in America* (Baltimore, Md.: Johns Hopkins University Press, 1996; orig. pub. 1938); James T. Schleifer, *The Making of Tocqueville's "Democracy in America"* (Chapel Hill: University of North Carolina Press, 1980); Jardin, *Tocqueville: A Biography.*

45. Jardin, *Tocqueville: A Biography,* 79–84.

46. For the resulting "dialogue" between Tocqueville and Guizot, see François Furet, *Interpreting the French Revolution,* Elborg Forster trans. (New York: Cambridge University Press, 1981), 135–139; Larry Siedentop, *Tocqueville* (Oxford: Oxford University Press, 1994), ch. 2.

47. Quoted in Jardin, *Tocqueville: A Biography,* 90.

Tocqueville was drawn to America to observe the future society of "almost complete equality of social conditions" toward which he believed Europe was moving inexorably. Although he said later that he did not go to America with the idea of writing a book, it seems clear that he and Beaumont went with a large joint project in mind, for both refer to it in contemporaneous letters. They also had a definite smaller project to study penal reform in America, which Tocqueville described as a "pretext" for the voyage.[48] But on returning to France he and Beaumont made good on the pretext and wrote a book, *On the Penitentiary System in the United States and Its Application to France,* which appeared soon after, in January 1833. The topic of penal reform gives evidence of the liberalism in which Tocqueville made his home, but the point made by the two authors reveals him to be characteristically at variance with the most advanced liberals. He was as much opposed to the enthusiasm of the reformers as he was in favor of reform, for which he held modest hopes. He certainly did not believe, as did the reformers, that reform could do away with crime or that it could replace punishment.

During the nine-month trip in America, Tocqueville and Beaumont followed an efficient itinerary. With time out for rest, research, and conversation with useful or important Americans, they still went almost everywhere. Starting from New York they traveled upstate to Buffalo, proceeding through the Great Lakes to the frontier, as it was then, in Michigan and Wisconsin. There followed two weeks in Canada, from which they descended to Boston and Philadelphia and Baltimore. Next they went west to Pittsburgh and Cincinnati, then south to Nashville, Memphis, and New Orleans, then north through the southeastern states to Washington and at last back to New York, from which they returned to France. Like tourists seeking characteristic experiences, they rode on steamboats (one of which sank) and stayed in a log cabin. They found it easy to gain access to prominent Americans, and met with John Quincy Adams, Andrew Jackson, Albert Gallatin, James Kent, Francis Lieber, Daniel Webster, Sam Houston, Roger Taney, Charles Carroll, and many others less well known.[49] They both kept journals, and Tocqueville's has been published under the title *Journey to America.*[50] It contains notes for the two books he was to write and was not intended for publication. Though full of interest the notes are mostly not composed or developed, and the result cannot be considered part of the abundant contemporary travel literature on America produced by English and French writers come to have

48. Letter to Louis de Kergorlay of January 1835, *Selected Letters,* 93–96; *OC* 13.1: 373–375. See Jardin, *Tocqueville: A Biography,* 93.

49. Pierson, *Tocqueville in America,* 782–786.

50. Alexis de Tocqueville, *Journey to America,* J. P. Mayer ed. (New Haven, Conn.: Yale University Press, 1959); also AT, *Oeuvres,* 1: 29–413.

a look at the new democracy. Among those diaries Tocqueville would have been especially mindful of Chateaubriand's *Voyage to America,* with its brilliant reflections on democracy, which appeared in 1827.

At a certain point during their stay the collaborative work on America planned by Tocqueville and Beaumont came apart. The "we" expressed by Beaumont in a letter of April 1831 becomes the "I" of Tocqueville's in a letter of his of January 1832.[51] Instead of the joint project, Tocqueville's friend wrote a separate work on the question of race, *Marie,* in novel form with didactic footnotes, published in 1835. The book on democracy in America was to be Tocqueville's alone, and his genius could assert itself.

The two volumes of *Democracy in America* were published five years apart, in 1835 and 1840. They had different contents and different receptions. The first volume, with its lively picturing of America, was a sensation and made Tocqueville famous; in France it was saluted by such great names as Chateaubriand, Lamartine, Guizot, Royer-Collard, and Sainte-Beuve. The second volume with its somber analysis of democracy was received without enthusiasm, an event that somewhat disconcerted its author.[52] The letter to John Stuart Mill quoted above, in which Tocqueville said that Mill was the only one to have understood him, was written in 1840 after the second volume came out. He went on to muse that there was something obscure and problematic in the second volume that "does not capture the mind of the crowd," and that he had wanted to portray the "general traits of democratic societies of which no complete model yet exists." In response, Mill assured him that the thoughts in the second volume were deeper and more recondite than those in the first.[53]

The polish, style, and insight of *Democracy in America* obscure the research that preceded it.[54] Footnotes that document his research can be found in some chapters of the first volume (*DA* I 1.1, 1.2, 1.5, 1.8, 2.5, 2.9, 2.10), and there are longer endnotes that both document and elaborate. But there are long stretches of text, especially in the second volume, that seem to flow directly from his mind unmediated by previous scholarship and unsubstantiated by reference to sources. The original working manuscript for the book tells a different story, however.[55] It shows how well he had studied, how far

51. Jardin, *Tocqueville: A Biography,* 195–196.

52. In a deleted fragment AT wrote of the two volumes: "The first book more American than democratic. This one more democratic than American"; see Schleifer, *The Making of Tocqueville's "Democracy in America,"* 29. See also Jardin, *Tocqueville: A Biography,* 271–276.

53. *OC* 6.1: 330–331.

54. Jean-Claude Lamberti, *DA, Oeuvres,* 2: 904; Jardin, *Tocqueville: A Biography,* 201.

55. The manuscript given to the printer has not survived, but AT's working manuscripts are preserved at the Beinecke Library at a university located in New Haven, Conn. See *Oeuvres,* 2: 934.

he had cast his net for fact and opinion, how ingeniously he had sought and produced the telling example, how surely he had reduced the manifold to the salient, how thoroughly he had prepared his generalizations, and how carefully he had formulated them.

Tocqueville wrote his text only on the right side of each page, leaving the left for outlines, queries of his own, critical comments of others, and textual variants. In addition to the working manuscript, there are notebooks of materials from which Tocqueville composed his text and early drafts of the second volume, called "rubish" by him in misspelled English.[56] For the first volume he used two American research assistants, Francis Lippit and Theodore Sedgwick. Once he began, he wrote rapidly; the first volume took less than a year to finish, from September 1833 to August 1834. The second volume was delayed by a number of things: by his trip to England: by his romance with Mary Mottley, the Englishwoman who became his wife; by his illness; by articles he wrote; and by his entrance into politics.

Democracy in America is the work of a genius, but it was not produced in solitary isolation. While composing, Tocqueville showed his text to his brother Edouard, his father Hervé, and his friends Beaumont and Kergorlay, all of whom responded with suggestions and criticisms that survive on the wide margin of his manuscript, in his notes, and in their letters. Nor did he ignore American authorities in writing his book. Besides the many Americans, prominent and obscure, whom he met on his trip, he acknowledged relying on "three most respected commentaries" on American democracy.[57] The first of these was of course *The Federalist,* praised and cited fourteen times in Tocqueville's text. The second was James Kent's *Commentaries on American Law* in four volumes (1826–1830), the author being a Federalist who had been Chief Justice and Chancellor of the State of New York. Third was Joseph Story's *Commentaries on the Constitution of the United States,* the notable work of a justice on the Supreme Court who served from 1811 to 1845.[58] Kent and Story, mainly men of the law, still deserve to be read even though they are not. *The Federalist* remains the leading authority for anyone who wants to understand American politics, save only for Tocqueville's book, which by relying upon it, transformed and surpassed it.

56. See Eduardo Nolla's edition of *Democracy in America,* 2 vols. (Paris: Vrin, 1990), Introduction.

57. Jardin, *Tocqueville: A Biography,* 201.

58. For Story's sour appreciation of AT's use of his work in *DA,* see Pierson, *Tocqueville in America,* 730–732.

TOCQUEVILLE'S POLITICAL SCIENCE

We may preface our brief study of Tocqueville's text with remarks on his method, his political science.[59] Hardly any statement of his is more prominent and provocative than the assertion in the Introduction to *Democracy in America* that "a new political science is needed for a world altogether new." What political science is that? we want to know. But Tocqueville does not tell us. Nowhere in the book does he elaborate this new political science; in fact, he does not refer to it again. "Political science" per se is spoken of four other times in the first volume, and not at all in the second. After raising our expectations, Tocqueville disappoints them, or perhaps returns them to us for elaboration. That he offers no methodology or compendium of axioms may be the first lesson of his new political science. It is not to consist in abstraction, nor is it to be made by or for disinterested observers. The new political science is for use in a new world.

The new world cannot be other than the world made by the democratic revolution we shall discuss next—our world, the Western world, the modern world. The four references to "political science" following in the first volume cite inventions of modern political science already known and applied, such as the advantage of bicameralism, the novelty of American federalism, the neutralizing of press bias (*DA* I 1.5; 1.8, twice; 2.3). These institutional devices, though important, are not the "new political science" that Tocqueville calls for. They are items of the kind recommended in *The Federalist*, designed as brakes on the headlong rush of democracy toward its desires. A new political science, however, would need to explain democracy before it considered how to keep it in check. Without taking credit for his discoveries Tocqueville gives political science three new features not seen before—the concept of the social state (*état social*), the notion of those like oneself (*semblables*), and the practice of making predictions.

What is the social state? The answer Tocqueville gives when introducing the concept (*DA* I 1.3) is that it is both product and cause. It is the product of a fact or of laws or of both together which then becomes the "first cause"— he calls up that heavy notion—of most of the laws, customs, and ideas that regulate nations, modifying those it does not produce. Exceptions do occur; the social state is not historically determined of necessity. With this deliberate confusion of causality Tocqueville refuses to go back to a prior event or condition that would establish the primacy of politics over society. As noted

---

59. In the following analysis, the editors do not attempt to come to terms with the vast literature on the book, though we do touch on many of its topics and themes. See the list of suggested readings.

above, there is no founding in the classical sense in Tocqueville, a planned beginning that gives a certain form and principle of rule to society. Tocqueville speaks of the American Revolution and Constitution, but not as that sort of formative event. The Constitution is rather the work of a "great people, warned by its legislators" of a problem requiring a remedy (*DA* I 1.8). To find it, the people listened to advice from the Federalists, an aristocratic party, but they were not founded as a certain people by this remedy, however impressive was the calm with which it was done. The American founding is part of the democratic revolution, the development of a social state.

More significant, apparently, than the founding was the point of departure of the American people a century and a half earlier when the Puritans arrived. The American point of departure was the seed (*germe*) of America, not its form, so to speak the baby in its cradle (*DA* I 1.2). That seed, not the later, more deliberate founding, is the key, Tocqueville says, to almost the whole of his work. Americans did not make themselves democrats but came to America as democrats. America, to which the Puritans came for a reason, is the only nation whose point of departure is clear rather than shrouded in ignorance and fable. (It is, to be sure, complicated by English influences that were not democratic [*DA* I 1.2].) But Tocqueville does not say, as might an Aristotelian, that Puritan democracy can be known to be the point of departure only retrospectively—because later the American founding established a republic which so to speak adopts the Puritan baby in the cradle. The idea of "social state" means that regimes do not have control over their pasts, although Tocqueville admits that the illiberality of Puritan democracy had to be addressed later on and was indeed reformed. In any case the Puritan point of departure seems to have an artificial clarity since Tocqueville does not go back to examine the social state that produced *it*. And he says expressly that Puritans were not the only first Americans; he has chosen them as the most significant.

If the social state precludes a classical founding, so too does it deny the liberal (or Rousseauian) distinction between state and society that derives from a prepolitical, presocial situation called the state of nature. Tocqueville indicates that one cannot understand society from a presocial standpoint as if it had been created from nothing, nor can one see it apart from politics. A democratic society will have a democratic politics, and vice versa. Thus the social state is connected to the sovereignty of the people which is somehow true of every society, even the most despotic, but out in the open in democratic society.

By avoiding the contest over causality between politics and society—one cannot say which comes first—Tocqueville enables the social state to appear and serve as a whole. It is not the product of a part, and a part does not rule the whole, as Aristotle says.[60] Tocqueville does describe the aristocratic social state, to be sure. But although an aristocracy may enjoy unquestioned legitimacy from its subjects, it rests ultimately on force, not consent, on a part, not the whole. Aristocracy is less of a society than democracy, and that is why it is less equitable (*DA* I 2.10, II 3.1). Its social state is curtailed and clouded over by lack of mutual understanding, despite the responsibility that nobles may feel for their dependents. Its social state, therefore, is less explicit than the democratic, based as it is on implication and unstated obligation. It is *less* a social state than the democratic social state. Since the social state is now revealed to be a quintessentially democratic concept, it is no surprise that it belongs to the political science of the altogether new democratic world.

If one puts together the democratic social state with the sovereignty of the people, the result is the power of public opinion in democracies, of which Tocqueville makes so much. Public opinion is milder and less explicit than political authority, yet more confining than mere social agreement. It is political and social combined, with a shift of weight from the former to the latter. "Public" opinion takes opinion out of private society and places it in broad daylight, to use one of Tocqueville's favorite phrases. Public and private are blurred together, and it becomes clear that democracy is government by public opinion. Private opinion—in the sense of what might be reserved to oneself against what most people think—tends to disappear; it proves to have required an aristocratic social state in which independent nobles had the standing to say what they pleased. We see why Tocqueville put little trust in the power of representative institutions to hold out against the people's desires: public opinion makes the people's representatives conform to their desires regardless of the apparent latitude that representative offices with constitutional terms might seem to afford. He would have seen the public opinion polls of our day as vivid confirmation, with the aid of science, of the trend he saw already in his day. Strangely enough, our political science, while claiming unlike Tocqueville's to be purely descriptive, now eagerly offers to do the work of the democratic social state, using the authority of science to extend the power of public opinion.

One might even say that the democratic social state seems to dissociate men so that they pass quickly from subjects to citizens to individuals. The social state in its completion is really an asocial state of sovereign individuals, each of them capable, according to the democratic dogma, of running his own life—while in truth, as one in a mass, powerless to do so. In this way the state of nature, expelled from Tocqueville's political science when it conceived an imaginary presocial and prepolitical condition, returns to describe

---

60. Aristotle, *Politics*, 1278b10–15, 1279a28.

the actual facts of democracy now and in the foreseeable future. We are living now in a state of nature, though not the one called the "war of all against all." It is closer to Montesquieu's picture of individuals made timid by their sense of powerlessness.[61] If this is the conclusion of Tocqueville's social state, then he seems to both deny and affirm Aristotle's dictum that man is by nature a political animal. For him, as noted above, it is not true that one part of society always rules the whole; that is the case only in an aristocratic social state. In a democratic social state, the whole seems to rule itself. The social state either masks rule or dissolves it.

Thus the phenomenon of ruling, vital to Aristotle's understanding, is relegated to past history in Tocqueville's; and he appears much more democratic than Aristotle. Yet the desire to rule others does not disappear in a democracy. Ruling remains, first, in the desire to rule oneself, which follows from rejecting others' rule over oneself. But above all it remains in the belief that others should not be treated better than oneself: whatever is good enough for you is good enough for them. But when you have said that, you have formulated a rule. Hence we have rule without, so to speak, the desire to rule. Precisely by not wanting to lord it over your fellows you justify the rule of public opinion, the nonrule that rules modern democracy. Somehow we end up as political animals without meaning to be, even when meaning *not* to be. Aristotle's dictum remains in force, but twisted to conform to new facts, to the democratic revolution.

The difficulty in going halfway with Aristotle can be seen in the title of Tocqueville's book. Despite the fact that democracy is in America, democracy and America are two distinct subjects for Tocqueville. When reading his book, one would do well to notice whether he is speaking of the nature and penchants of democracy or of the peculiarities of America, the country that had the Puritans as its point of departure and that held slaves and mistreated Indians. Democracy and America are not quite like form and matter, however, as if the one were active and the other passive. When Tocqueville speaks of the concept of the *social state*, he seems to say that democracy is produced by the social facts of a democratic society and to deny that democracy as a principle imposes itself on a society so as to make it democratic. Yet in discussing the tyranny of the majority (in volume 1) and mild despotism (in volume 2), does he not imply that democracy is imposed on society, that the democratic social state in America comes from democracy? The relationship of democracy to America, the meaning of "democracy in America," is something of a problem. Can one say which of the two comes first?

61. Montesquieu, *The Spirit of the Laws*, I 2.

The democratic social state comprises those like oneself (*semblables*).[62] Tocqueville sees in democracy not only self and other but a third thing, those like oneself.[63] This notion may be taken as a second original feature of Tocqueville's new political science. Since all individuals in a democracy regard themselves and are accepted as equal, other individuals are not really different from oneself but similar. They are not really *other* in the deep sense implied by the dichotomy of self-other to be found in Hegel's theory or its variants. Here there is no real reconciliation between self and other in which one self finds itself in the other. Rather, that reconciliation is assumed from the beginning. The democrat considers others to be like himself, and if they are truly different, he *sees* them to be like himself regardless. He ignores or flattens out any differences that might call equality into question. Humanity consists of those like oneself, and so compassion for those in distress is not demeaning, admiration for those who have done better is not humiliating. Envy is more likely, however. With the notion of *semblables,* humanity goes from biological or philosophical abstraction to political fact. For if one's countrymen are like oneself, so too are persons in all countries. Tocqueville speaks of appealing, in matters of justice, from the jury of one's fellow citizens to that of all humanity (*DA* I 2.7). It is not that democratic patriotism cannot exist; on the contrary it can be more fervent than any previous patriotism. But it has to come to terms with humanity by claiming superior progress instead of insisting on excluding others by virtue of some permanent inequality such as race or nation.

Tocqueville's new political science makes predictions. These are not mere implicit predictions that we might infer; he repeatedly mentions trends or results that he "predicts," "augurs," or "foresees." He does not try to anticipate the scientific prediction of some political science in our day by seeking to establish exact or determinate outcomes. He says that it is imprudent "to want to limit the possible and to judge the future" (*DA* I 1.8); so prediction is not the object of his political science. His most famous particular prediction occurs at the end of the first volume. American and Russia, he says, stand for the democratic future, the one with freedom, the other with servitude. Each seems to have been called "by a secret design of Providence" to hold in its hands "the destinies of half the world" (*DA* I 2.10). During the Cold War this picture seemed uncannily true to fact, but now we see that it was a representation. It represents an undetermined choice for us attributed

62. What had once been taken for mere benevolence to fellow humans—*humani generis similitudo*—now acquires an egalitarian political significance for fellow citizens; Cicero, *Laws* I 31.

63. See Manent, *Tocqueville and the Nature of Democracy,* 48.

by Tocqueville to Providence, not political science strictly. And his most general prediction, that of the democratic revolution, he calls a "providential fact" (*DA* Intro.).

Tocqueville's predictions and his mention of Providence belong together, however, because they are designed to remind us of a given fact, the democratic revolution. His political science is designed for this circumstance, and it does not attempt to rise above circumstance or to prescribe for a variety of circumstances, like Aristotle's for example. Tocqueville writes for a foreseeable epoch in history, the democratic era, and he does not try to see beyond the foreseeable as did the ancients when they wrote of a cycle of regimes or even of civilizations.[64] If he does not accept the democratic belief in indefinite progress, he does base his political science on linear history, from aristocracy to democracy, rather than on the nature of man as holding the potential for several regimes and several histories. In his prediction he ministers to our human desire, common to both science and religion, to know what will befall us in the future. At the same time, forcing us to keep in mind the outstanding fact of our time, he requires us to make our choices without indulging our wishes. He reminds opponents of democracy that they must come to terms with democracy, and he tells proponents that democracy too can lead to despotism. By opening our mind to the new world of democracy and closing it to the old aristocratic world, he sharpens our choices. His political science has the focus of a statesman.

Tocqueville was a liberal but he did not adhere to what might be called the formal liberalism of John Locke and his followers in Tocqueville's time and ours. He did not think it necessary or wise to lay down universal principles or rights to serve as the formal basis of politics, nor to leave the actual exercise of those rights unspecified, open to experience, and free to be applied as circumstances permit. His political science is concerned with the society actually inspired by liberal principles. But Tocqueville does not make the criticism Karl Marx was to set forth, that liberalism is merely formal, untrue to its universal principles because it offers rights only to the bourgeoisie. That criticism has been repeated recently by many who are not Marxists and who consider themselves liberals. For Tocqueville, liberal society is actually democracy and not a sham. In a way it is more democratic than liberal principles, because they are *designed* to be formal in order to protect and foster human inequalities. For liberalism of course asserts that all men are *created* equal, but they are equal only in the state of nature before they have consented to civil society and its inevitable inequalities.

Tocqueville shows, however, that equality in the state of nature tends to

---

64. But see AT's reference to past civilization in *DA* I 1.1.

become equality in society too. He does not speak of the state of nature, but he makes clear that the formal principle of equality has a constant democratizing effect. The fact that equality is not perfect, that all citizens are not equally secure, does not mean that equality does not exist; on the contrary, it creates pressure to perfect equality (*DA* II 4.3). It cannot be said too often that democracy, or modern democracy, is a democratic revolution. One could call it an institutionalized revolution if it were not apparent that the revolution operates against every institution so as to make it more democratic.

Tocqueville addresses a topic left undiscussed, for the most part, in formal liberalism—the actual capacity of individuals to exercise their rights and stand up in their defense. Liberalism assumes that by relying on the desire for self-preservation, supposed to be active in everyone, one need not enter into the question of capacity. Marxists, and others who demand more democracy, make the same assumption that everyone's capacity for exercising rights is or can be made adequate. But Tocqueville does not. He argues that modern democracy makes its people increasingly incapable as citizens as they become more isolated and weak.

Formal liberalism relies on institutions instead of virtue; in the manner stated most extremely by Kant, a republic can be maintained for a nation of devils if only they are intelligent (not a slight condition, by the way). Tocqueville believes that the working of institutions requires virtue, not lofty virtue but the virtue available in democracy ranging from raw intractability to active self-interest to moderate ambition. Formal liberalism does not appreciate that formal practices and institutions in a democracy have to be defended against the laziness and impatience of a democratic people. That liberalism was conceived, not for "a world altogether new" like Tocqueville's new political science (*DA* I Intro.), but to attack the privileges and prejudices of the Old Regime. It does not see that the principle used to attack the customary forms of the Old Regime will also be applied to undermine the artificially constructed forms of democracy.

THE DEMOCRATIC REVOLUTION

"A great democratic revolution is taking place among us": that is the beginning and the guiding thought of *Democracy in America*. The democratic revolution is new, and first seen to its astonishing extent in the United States. But it is also seven hundred years old, the time from which the aristocratic power of a few feudal families began to be challenged. A kind of democratic equality appeared in the clergy, which was open to all. Then it passed to lawyers, who checked the power of barons, and to merchants, whose wealth introduced a rival influence to that of arms. Competition between the king and the nobles led both, especially the former, to raise the condition of the people, and events from the Crusades to the discovery of America turned to the advantage of equality. Not least, the Enlightenment made intelligence a social force to be reckoned with.

These groups—clergy, lawyers, merchants, and experts of all kinds—might seem to have brought only rival inequalities to that of the feudal lords who ruled aristocracies. But for Tocqueville, feudal lords are the essential inequality on which inequality as a principle depends. They hold landed property and they acquire it by inheritance. They sit on their lands; the other groups rise from social conditions that invite movement and offer opportunity. Opportunity makes for equality even though it leads to new inequalities because you feel that someone risen from your status is like yourself (*semblable*). The new elites (as we would call them) bring ever-increasing equality of conditions.

Tocqueville defines the democratic revolution historically and socially rather than politically. In the Introduction to *Democracy in America* he does not speak of the French Revolution and only alludes to the conflict that the coming of democracy has brought in Europe by contrast to America. In the *Old Regime* the burden of his argument is to show that the French Revolution was a long time in coming, that it merely culminated changes toward democracy initiated under the monarchy.[65] This "gradual development" makes it possible to call democracy "a providential fact" (*DA* Intro.). Although the changes Tocqueville mentions were made politically, they were not made intentionally to bring about democracy, and if they seem to have been coordinated, this could have happened only through a higher power than political choice.

Accordingly, *Democracy in America* does not appear to be a book of political philosophy. As we have seen, it is not about the best regime in the manner of Plato and Aristotle, nor does it describe the sole legitimate regime like Rousseau's *Social Contract*. It asserts that there is no choice of regime now; the regime of the present and future is democracy. The only choice is how to control democracy. And yet Tocqueville is always reasoning his way through his book, not merely describing and predicting but also examining the virtues and defects of democracy. In his recounting, democracy's constant shadow companion is the aristocracy we have left behind. His repeated comparison between them implies a best regime mixed of the two, which he ex-

---

65. AT, *The Old Regime,* I 5, II 5, marvelously prefigured twenty years earlier in the essay AT had written for John Stuart Mill: "Social and Political Condition of France," in *OC* 2.1: 65.

pressly declares to be impossible (*DA* I 2.7) but which would comprise the full flourishing of human nature, the advantages of both democracy and aristocracy. Tocqueville does not confine himself to what is today called "democratic political theory," for which democracy is the only conceivable regime and the difference between the democratic status quo and a more democratic possible future is the only interesting comparison. But his political philosophy takes place *within* democracy, in our era, the only possible regime whether good or ill.

While Tocqueville deprecates the grander political aspect of the democratic revolution, he seems altogether to ignore the other aspect that allows for human choice, its intellectual roots or causes. He hardly mentions the great philosophers of liberalism, Hobbes, Spinoza, and Locke, and as we have seen, he is too wary to describe the influence of their great critic, Rousseau, who insisted that the only legitimate regime was a republic and with this baneful thought inspired the Jacobins. He does discuss Descartes but precisely to dismiss the influence of Descartes (*DA* II 1.1). He says that America is "the one country in the world where the precepts of Descartes are least studied and best followed." For Descartes represents the doubt and distrust of authority and the reliance on individual reason that are characteristic of the American social state. Descartes, the enemy of all authority, is himself an authority to Americans, who, however, have not read his books. It is hard to say whether the joke is more on America or on Descartes, both heedless that reason itself becomes a yoke. Descartes, it seems, was in no way a cause of the democratic revolution but only its beneficiary. The least political of all modern philosophers, he came into his own, if one can call it that, when the democratic social state made it convenient for Americans to "follow" him, or rather to create their democracy without his help.

Democracy in America contains a chapter called "Why Great Revolutions Will Become Rare" (*DA* II 3.21). The reason given is that in democracies, interests take precedence over passions and beliefs are stubbornly held. The great majority are in the middle class, neither rich nor poor, very much attached to their property and consequently desirous of order. Democracies are stable, all too stable perhaps. They may have been introduced by a great revolution such as the French Revolution, but once made, democracies last. America, the model of democracy, did not reach that state by revolution: "The great advantage of the Americans is to have arrived at democracy without having to suffer democratic revolutions, and to be born equal instead of becoming so" (*DA* II 2.3).

Thus Tocqueville's presentation of the democratic revolution differs markedly from Aristotle's—the traditional or premodern understanding.

Aristotle gave three meanings to the term "revolution": change of regime, the cycle of regimes, and an indignant uprising.[66] For Tocqueville, the democratic revolution was not so much a change of regime as a gradual change of the social state from which democracy emerged rather than being founded. It was also not in a cycle or alternation of regimes, in which the defects of partisan rule by the few lead to revolution on behalf of the many, and the defects of democracy in turn bring on oligarchy, and so forth. Although Tocqueville said great revolutions will be rare, not impossible, it does appear that democracy is here to stay for the foreseeable future. His view is historical and predictive, not cyclical and based on the nature of politics. And last, democrats are not likely to give themselves over to revolutionary indignation. They think they have too much to lose.

TYRANNY OF THE MAJORITY

Tocqueville's theme in *Democracy in America* is what is to be hoped for and what is to be feared from the democratic revolution (*DA* I Intro., II 4.1, 4.5, 4.6). The book is rich with detail, descriptive and predictive, of America in particular and democracy in general. Tocqueville depicts, especially in volume 1, America's politics and administration—from the New England town meeting to state constitutional provisions for education to Andrew Jackson's tariff policies; its economy—from southern slave-based agriculture to patterns of westward migration to the annual tonnage of its global maritime trade; its customary intellectual and moral life—from newspaper layouts to literary styles, the fine arts, and scientific research, from sexual mores to habits of conversation and political oratory to religious revivalism. He speculates, especially in volume 2, on how democracy will continue to transform men's thoughts and sentiments and mores, and thereby politics and government, not just in America, but everywhere. To summarize Tocqueville's analyses would be to try the reader's patience mercilessly, as well as to deny him the pleasure of discovering Tocqueville's numerous astute observations and felicitous turns of phrase; for example, the proclivity he remarks in democracy to a new "hypocrisy of luxury," added to the moral hypocrisy of other times (*DA* II 1.11). Instead of attempting such a summary we shall concentrate our efforts on exploring a theme of great concern to Tocqueville himself, and one that continues to engage defenders and critics of democracy alike: Will the new democracy give rise either to a majority tyranny or to a new sort of democratic despotism? If so, what might be done to mitigate each danger?

66. Aristotle, *Politics*, 1302a16–1303b18, 1316a15–22.

In the penultimate chapter of *Democracy in America,* Tocqueville remarks that his practical concern in writing has been to enable those who are "true friends of freedom and human greatness" to secure the "independence and dignity" of their fellows in the modern democratic world (*DA* II 4.7). In the book, he describes two particular threats that democracy poses to independence and dignity: "tyranny of the majority" and "mild despotism," the latter of which he also calls "democratic" or "administrative" despotism. Although Tocqueville's name is associated with both terms, "tyranny of the majority" is discussed only in the first volume and "mild despotism" is found only in the second. He explains that a more detailed examination of the subject and "five years of new meditations" changed the object of his fears (*DA* II 4.6).[67] The phenomenon long conceived of as tyranny of the majority turns out to be more complex in the modern democratic world, and Tocqueville deepened his appreciation of its new character, even if his prescribed remedies for the two ills do not differ substantially.

Tocqueville was surely not the first to recognize the phenomenon of tyranny of the majority. Aristotle observes it in ancient democracy, and all but equates democracy, which he defines as the rule of many, usually poor, for their own advantage, with tyranny.[68] At the same time, he distinguishes democracy from polity, which is also the rule of many, but for the common advantage, a mixed or "middling" sort of regime where the principles and concerns of rich as well as poor are taken into account. *The Federalist* speaks of majority tyranny as "majority faction," arising when a majority either violates the rights of a minority or acts contrary to "the permanent and aggregate interests of the community" (*Federalist* 10). Tocqueville, in contrast, gives no precise definition of either tyranny or majority tyranny, although in distinguishing tyranny from arbitrariness, he limits tyranny to the exercise of power not "in the interest of the governed" (*DA* I 2.7). At the same time, he finds the seed of tyranny in "the right and the ability to do everything" (*DA* I 2.7), presumably even in the interest of the governed. For Tocqueville, who explicitly denies the possibility of the mixed regime Aristotle favors, there is potential for tyranny wherever unmixed authority is found, which is everywhere; and tyranny becomes actual where this authority meets no formidable obstacle. Let us look more closely at Tocqueville's reason for fearing tyranny especially in the new democracies.

For Tocqueville, the *foundation* of American democracy, as distinguished

67. In the margin, AT notes: "New despotism. It is in the portrayal of this that resides all the originality and depth of my idea. What I wrote in my first work was hackneyed and superficial." Cited in Jean-Claude Lamberti, "Two Ways of Conceiving the Republic," in Masugi, *Interpreting Tocqueville's "Democracy in America,"* 18.

68. Aristotle, *Politics,* 1281a14–24; see also Plato, *Republic,* 564a.

from its point of departure, is the principle or dogma of the sovereignty of the people, first announced in the fourth chapter of the book, and reiterated near the end of the first volume (*DA* I 2.10):

> Providence has given to each individual, whoever he may be, the degree of reason necessary for him to be able to direct himself in things that interest him exclusively. Such is the great maxim on which civil and political society in the United States rests. . . . Extended to the entirety of the nation, it becomes the dogma of the sovereignty of the people.

In politics, this means that each individual is supposed to be "as enlightened, as virtuous, as strong as any other of those like him," and he obeys society not because he is less capable than another man of governing himself but because union with those like him appears useful to him (*DA* I 1.5).

While even the most ardent democrat might well doubt that each individual is really as enlightened and as virtuous as every other, Tocqueville shows how the principle of popular sovereignty can work rather well in America, particularly in the New England township of which he paints a vivid, if idealized, picture (*DA* I 1.5). Here citizens take common decisions in frequent town meetings and then execute them through the numerous, short-term elective offices that so many of them come to hold. When exercising sovereignty in this way, the people's reason is informed by firsthand knowledge and keen interest; they know how badly a road or a school is needed, and how well its costs can be borne. And because the consequences of choices are readily visible, choosing well seems worth the time and effort; good results evoke personal pride (*DA* I 1.5, 2.6). Ambition is piqued, and it gravitates toward these offices, which afford independence and power. Yet since the objects of township concern remain modest, ambition stays within manageable bounds. Moreover, what citizens decide and how they decide it may be tempered by affection for friends and neighbors. Thus the majority's will is guided by passion that is partly selfish, partly caring, and moderated by practical experience. Were tyranny to occur here, it would be petty and intrusive; but there is rarely cause or opportunity for such oppression, and occasional injustices are scarcely noticeable (*DA* I 1.5, 1.8). In the township the will of the majority may not always be prudent or just, but it is more or less well-informed, animated by pride, relatively benign, and in any case, not always very effective (*DA* I 1.5, 2.8). And it meets with obstacles; it can be checked by the higher authority of the county and the state. Here, in the township, one finds democratic self-government at its best (*DA* I 1.8).

Beyond the township, however, the majority's willfulness has potential to do great harm, not only to minorities but also to itself (*DA* I 1.8), as Tocqueville shows in the second part of volume 1.

It was the hope of America's founders that republican forms, especially representative institutions and an "enlarged orbit" for the union of states, would remedy the defects of popular government by diminishing opportunities for demagogic manipulation of factious majorities; perhaps these forms would improve the quality of public deliberations (*Federalist* 9, 10). Tocqueville gives little cause for optimism on these points (*DA* I 1.8, 2.5). His analysis, which is more orderly than it may appear, treats the *forms* of American democracy in the first part of volume 1, and then moves to the *matter* so to speak in the second part (beginning of *DA* I 2). Many of these forms are praised at length, notably the political practices of America's Puritan settlers and the New England township, already in place when the federal constitution was drafted, and the founders' specific constitutional provisions designed to curb majoritarian and legislative tyranny. Although the commendation is restated near the end of part 2 (*DA* I 2.9), the intervening lengthy discussion of how democracy tends to work in practice raises doubts about whether even these praiseworthy forms of democracy will be adequate to contain the matter of democracy—the people's actual sovereign will.

While *The Federalist* presents representation as a great improvement on simple popular government, Tocqueville doubts that it can make much difference (*DA* I 2.1, 2.5). The majority cannot be expected to discern a common good, either as individuals or as a people, even if they should sincerely desire it; much less can they see the means needed to effect it. That, of course, is one reason why Tocqueville says American moralists feel the need to teach a doctrine of self-interest *well* understood (*DA* II 2.8). Earnest and able democratic citizens will often lack the time to choose representatives wisely. Others will be given to envy of those who they suspect really are their betters. And these better men will not be inclined to stand for election, preferring to make their fortunes by relying on themselves. Moreover, even well-meaning, but untutored, unsure or merely busy, citizens can easily be led astray by political partisans; and in a democracy, they tend to be swayed by partisans who advocate the unlimited expansion of popular power (*DA* I 2.2). Democratic citizens will constantly be urged, and tempted, to press for increasing the power of the majority without being able to assure its wisdom or justice. Thus, contrary to widespread hopes, elections will not by themselves serve to bring "enlightened statesmen" to the helm.

Meanwhile, those who are elected will remain subject to envy and personal distrust. Every instance of petty corruption in which they might indulge will exacerbate ill will toward themselves and other elected officials, precisely because it is petty and therefore readily intelligible to ordinary citizens. Such distrust will, however, not prevent their being allowed considerable arbitrary authority, to be used for good or ill. For the majority prizes arbitrariness to further its ends, and it knows well the punishment it can inflict at the next election on those who violate its sometimes misplaced trust or who merely displease it now. So it will show itself quite tolerant of lawlessness when used in its name (*DA* I 2.5, 2.7).

For these reasons, the majority's government is as likely to be poorly administered as the majority is likely to be willful and undisciplined; it will often be lacking in apparent purpose and sustained effort, inexpert, wasteful (*DA* I 2.5). One may suppose that democratic government will rarely be effective, efficient or economical, even if it does not always produce tyranny. The majority itself will want to ignore its own laws and policies when inconvenienced by them, or to change them hurriedly to suit its convenience and change them again according to newer convenience. This means that democracy's elected representatives, however feckless, will always find much to do. Democratic government will have an appearance of restive, almost anarchic, activity; one will easily remark a superficial legislative and administrative instability (*DA* I 1.8, 2.5, 2.7, 2.9, 2.10), which is especially worrisome because it reflects and aggravates democracy's tendency to regard the formalities of government as mere inconveniences (*DA* I 2.8, II 4.7). Beneath appearances, however, Tocqueville perceives a deeper and no less worrisome stability, or even immobility.

As Tocqueville describes the workings of America's majoritarian government and anticipates the future, he emphasizes not so much its incompetence as its omnipotence and its potential for tyranny or despotism.[69] In the modern world, the will of the majority comes to exercise a kind of "moral empire" previously unknown (*DA* I 2.7), a new authority that has two sources. Never before had the principle that everyone is as enlightened, as virtuous, and as strong as anyone else been accepted (*DA* II 1.3). Nor does Tocqueville himself accept it! (*DA* I 1.3, II 2.13). In the ancient world, the special claims of the rich and well-born, as well as those reputed for virtue or wisdom, were considered legitimate both in theory and fact. But once the dogma of equality is established, it becomes difficult to see why a greater number of supposedly equally enlightened and virtuous voters is not always more right than a lesser number. It becomes all but impossible to see how wrong opinions could ever arise except from malicious intent. For on what basis could some few correctly discern legitimate interests that differ from those of the majority?

The majority's moral authority will be further enhanced where no viable aristocracy has ever existed, as in the United States, by the notion that the

---

69. The term "tyranny of the majority" is used in I 2.4, 2.7 (4 times), 2.8. "Despotism of the majority" is used in I 1.8, 2.7, 2.9. The "omnipotence" of the people or the majority is mentioned in I 1.8, 2 (beginning), 2.4, 2.7 (8 times).

interests, not just the opinions, of the many should always prevail over those of the few. Where there is no aristocratic few long acknowledged to be distinctive, all are presumed to have the same interests, and all are therefore potential members of the majority. Though this situation might seem harmonious and beneficial, it worries Tocqueville. He sees that in the politics of democracy, no minority whose opinions or interests are held to merit respect will stand ready to offer an obstacle to the majority's will. Should someone nonetheless doubt the majority's wisdom or justice, and still feel the need to hear concerns that might once have been voiced by an aristocracy, these doubts can be expressed effectively only by objecting that a particular pronouncement of the majority has not been sufficiently inclusive (*DA* I 2.7). While such objections may suffice to improve the majority's judgment in any given instance, they may also serve to strengthen its authority in the long term.

In a footnote to his discussion of majority tyranny Tocqueville gives two examples of it: In Baltimore, two journalists who opposed the War of 1812 were killed by a mob of supporters of the war, and in Philadelphia, black freedmen were invariably too intimidated to exercise their right to vote (*DA* I 2.7). The majority's patriotism—and as Tocqueville later shows, its religiosity as well—might be valuable supports for democratic republicanism; or one could also say, the majority's tyranny sometimes appears to be exercised in the interest of the governed. But America also prides itself on the right of free speech, and here we see the majority chilling freedom of speech to an unprecedented degree. "I do not know any country where, in general, less independence of mind and genuine freedom of discussion reign than in America," Tocqueville observes (*DA* I 2.7). If democracy's problem at first seems to be merely that too much is said and not enough is listened to, in the end the result is that unpopular truths will no longer be spoken at all, and popular untruths, especially those that flatter the majority, will be reiterated incessantly. One might lament this situation because it can deprive the majority of information and ideas useful to good governance, but Tocqueville remarks its effect especially on the few who might proffer unpopular thoughts. Men of independent mind will become utterly dispirited. "The theory of equality applied to intellects," he remarks, "attacks the pride of man in its last asylum" (*DA* I 2.7). One might add that egalitarian theory will be verified when none but mediocre or pusillanimous intellects remain.

PRIDE AND RACE IN AMERICA

Tocqueville's second example of majority tyranny, racial discrimination, is one he returns to at length. Volume 1 of *Democracy in America* ends with a very long chapter ostensibly treating subjects that are American in particular rather than democratic in general. More precisely, its theme is the races or peoples that inhabit the New World, or one might say, the modern world; thus its theme is broader as well as narrower than democracy. In the narrower sense, Tocqueville looks at what the unfettered will of the American people— in effect, the white or "Anglo-American" majority—had thus far wrought, for good and ill, including the most egregious examples of its tyranny: virtual extermination of the Indians and enslavement of blacks. Tocqueville calls this tyranny, and he shows its effects on the tyrant as well as on its victims. In the broader sense, one can see more clearly how the seed of tyranny, "the right and the ability to do everything," germinates especially in modern peoples, becoming the use of power—even by a majority—that is not "in the interest of the governed." Modern philosophy posits that there are in principle no limits on human will—for that is one meaning of the sovereignty of the people (*DA* I 1.4)—and the political forms of modern democracy are inadequate to contain a people's willfulness. Tocqueville nonetheless suggests how even in the unlimited exercise of that will, an inherent limit on its exercise still remains.

In this chapter, Tocqueville takes up five topics, prefacing them with an introductory section in which the chapter's unstated theme of pride emerges. Later, he will worry explicitly that pride is too easily dismissed as a vice by modern moralists (*DA* II 3.19); and he has already observed that the intellect is the last asylum of human pride. He begins by noting that the New World's white or Anglo-American appears as "man par excellence"; he acts toward other races as does man to the beasts. If he is truly superior, Tocqueville suggests, it is with respect to his pride. The Indian, like the European aristocrat, is proud of his origins; in this, his pride is not only excessive, but arrested. The black, having been deprived of the attributes in which humans can take pride and denied any opportunity to reclaim them, has virtually no pride and is therefore all but incapable of self-improvement. Neither will survive and prosper. Should the white in the New World fail to take pride in the right qualities, to the proper extent, he will fare no better than his victims. Here, then, is the natural limit to the will of the majority. Tocqueville shows that when the majority's will is asserted so as to disregard, deny, or destroy human pride in man's capacity for rational self-determination, then that will meets its limit in its own destruction.

Tocqueville's account of the plight of the Indians chillingly brings to light the ease and hypocrisy with which majority tyranny comes to be exercised in the New World. Anglo-Americans, motivated not by ill will, much less by racial hatred or prejudice, but merely by greed and contempt, not only denied native Americans their rights, but were well on their way to exterminating them "with marvelous facility—tranquilly, legally, philanthropically, without spilling blood, without violating a single one of the great principles of morality in the eyes of the world" (*DA* I 2.10).

How could this have happened? The Anglo-Americans, superior in modern learning and soon in strength as well, destroyed the wild game on which the Indians lived, thereby driving them from their traditional hunting grounds and leaving them to face death at nature's hand. They contemptuously dismissed the Indians' appeals to justice and common humanity. In so doing, they were, in effect, armed with the newly respected natural law teaching of John Locke: labor alone gives a title to property, and infringements of right are punished by men so far as they are capable. The Indian, for his part, was easily enough corrupted by modern man's luxuries; but at the same time, he was too proud of his traditional ways, too trusting in nature's goodness, to learn new arts to satisfy new desires or new arguments to counter new sophistries.

For his extermination of the Indian the Anglo-American would pay little or no price. But in his enslavement of the black, Tocqueville saw the greatest threat to the United States. Here tyranny comes to follow a logic of its own when human will no longer sees any prohibitions arising from "nature and humanity." What Tocqueville saw occurring in the American South was, he says, "the most horrible and the most natural consequence of slavery" (*DA* I 2.10).

In *Democracy in America* Tocqueville does not address the question of the natural inferiority of blacks; he attributes the character of the American black to the effects of tyranny.[70] The slave as Tocqueville found him had neither the pride befitting a human being nor cause for such pride, having been deprived of almost all the "privileges of humanity"—family, homeland, language, religion, mores, even ownership of his person (*DA* I 2.10). Having lost virtually all pride in himself, he had lost the ambition to acquire the skills and habits that would enable him to set and accomplish goals and exhibit virtues in which he might reasonably take pride. Accustomed to acting only at the command of others, "the very use of thought seem[ed] to him a useless gift of Providence" (*DA* I 2.10). His only experience of uncoerced behavior was servile imitation of his master, which was an expression of his shame, the last remnant of his human pride. Unaccustomed to hearing reason's voice, he would, if freed, likely give himself over entirely to his own needs or desires as to a new master. Thus tyranny had denied the black not only responsibility

70. In a letter to his friend Arthur de Gobineau, November 17, 1853 (*Selected Letters*, 297–301; *OC* 9: 201–204), AT criticizes the racialist theories of Gobineau's *Essai sur l'inégalité des races humaines* (1853) as "very probably false and very certainly pernicious."

for his actions, but a suitable model of responsible behavior; he effectively lacked the moral and intellectual faculties that justify human pride.

Once slavery had been reintroduced into the modern world and now limited to blacks, it became all but impossible to dissociate the master's prejudice against his legal inferior from racial prejudice. The master deemed his black slave his moral and intellectual inferior, and the racial stigma could not then be overlooked. Moreover, these two prejudices were to be reinforced by what Tocqueville curiously refers to as "the prejudice of the white."

Abolition of slavery should have been dictated by the principles of the new science of economics; and to do so would surely have been consistent both with Christian morality and with the modern political principles of democracy and enlightenment (*DA* I 2.10). Abolition would not, however, have permitted the white southerner to maintain his way of life; and even the northerner abolished slavery only on the assumption that he would not have to live amid black freedmen. In his way of life the Anglo-American took great pride. This pride would prove strong enough to overcome rational economic interest, moral and political principle, and even sexual passion and its natural consequence (*DA* I 2.10). Yet to maintain slavery against all these forces, it would become ever more necessary to justify it by keeping the black man as close to the brute as possible.

Tocqueville's Anglo-Americans had "spiritualized" despotism and violence (*DA* I 2.10). Convinced that they would never live with their former slaves as equals and fearful of living with them as an inferior class whose presence would either bring society down to its level or breed revolutionaries, they did not hold their slaves in chains. Instead, they determined to keep them capable of nothing better than servitude by denying them the hope of freedom in the future, of the aspirations such hope gives rise to, and of any opportunity to educate themselves in preparation for freedom. How could someone who exhibited virtually none of the moral or intellectual qualities of a human being justly complain of being denied the rights to which human beings are equally entitled?

Altering the status of blacks in the New World, Tocqueville said, would be peculiarly difficult because of the prejudice of the white. What does he mean by this? He remarks that democratic freedom gives rise to a certain individual haughtiness; "the white man in the United States is proud of his race and proud of himself" (*DA* I 2.10). The rest of the chapter on the New World treats the survival of the Union and of republican institutions, and the spirit of its commerce—all matters that concern the pride of white Americans. Above all, Tocqueville's Anglo-Americans are united among themselves and separated from all other peoples by a sentiment of pride in the success of their democracy, a success which they attribute to reason. They take pride in placing "moral authority in universal reason, as they do political power in the universality of citizens" (*DA* I 2.10).

From Tocqueville's contrast of the white man to the black and the Indian we can infer that the distinctiveness of the white lies in the superiority not only of his way of life, but of the kind of pride he takes in it. His pride in reason, he believes, enables him to sustain his way of life. Yet in the account of the vitality of the American Union and republic, Tocqueville also suggests that in fact the (white) American *necessarily* misconceives both the source and extent of his pride. He puts his faith in universal reason, which in practice is the majority's reason. According to Tocqueville, this is at least in part a mistake. He is impressed with how well American democracy has prospered, but the reason he gives is that in America, willfulness has been kept vigorous and informed by salutary mores and political institutions, not that the majority has always acted reasonably. But the majority believes it has acted reasonably, and there is some value in that misconception. Things are much worse when a majority loses sight of that desideratum and severs the connection between its will and reason.

Consider Tocqueville's analysis of the future prospects for the Union: He expected the Union to remain weaker than the states for as long as citizens continued to be moved less by shared reasoning or common need and more by habit or passion. The Union was constituted so as to respond effectively to a few great general needs (*DA* I 1.8), while the states had long attached men's hearts through custom and unreflective patriotism. Stated less kindly, local and regional attachments were sustained by "a blind democratic instinct" in the face of the national government's "salutary control" (*DA* I 2.10). For both good and ill, a willfulness or restiveness appeared to have animated Americans, and Tocqueville predicted that it would continue to do so barring "a change of opinion, an internal crisis, [or] a war" (*DA* I 2.10)—that is, unless citizens should come to be preoccupied with providing efficiently for a few great general needs. Then the national government would prevail.

The American majority exhibited "*decentralizing* passions" (*DA* I 2.10). Their lives were shaped not simply by needs, but by a willfulness informed by mores. Mores, one might say, "habits of the heart" (*DA* I 2.9),[71] consist of certain distinct forms peculiar to a people of which they are proud: they are forms of pride. They are at a distance from and sometimes at odds with needs, which as such are nothing to be proud of. Adhering to mores enables men to meet their needs as they wish, thus to some extent dissociating them-

---

71. Robert Bellah has made Tocqueville's phrase current; see Robert N. Bellah, Richard Madsen, William M. Sullivan, Ann Swidler, and Steven M. Tipton, *Habits of the Heart: Individualism and Commitment in American Life* (Berkeley, Calif.: University of California Press, 1985).

selves from their needs, having an opportunity to take a critical look at them, and forming an opinion about them. The diversity of mores in America suggests a degree of freedom from needs, which are universal. The states and regions to which the hearts of Tocqueville's Americans were attached had served to preserve their distinctive forms of pride.

Tocqueville says, indeed, that all bodies, whatever they may be, have a "secret instinct that carries them toward independence" (*DA* I 2.10). It is not just a few great general needs that are universal to human beings; so too is willful pride. Of course, willfulness in itself is, again, not much to be proud of. But the (white) American's conceit is that his secret instinct is guided by reason and directed toward human perfection. That pretension must be maintained—dogmatically if necessary, as in the dogma of the sovereignty of the people—to serve as the basis of democratic freedom. Hence comes the Americans' determination to locate universal reason in the universality of citizens. It is especially when men will without respect for distinctively human pride, when they ignore the human striving for rational self-determination, that their will becomes self-destructive. That is what we see when the Indian fails to abandon his old ways for the white man's new arts, and when the white majority acquiesces in the brutalization of the black slave. As if to reinforce this suggestion, Tocqueville predicts that the problem of racial injustice in the New World will be solved only by wars in which sheer numbers, of white or black bodies, prevail.

Might one undertake to ensure that the willful pride of a democratic majority is expressed in better ways than the tyrannical extermination of the Indian and enslavement of the black? Not solely by democratic means, it appears. Tocqueville remarks that the American people, in submitting to the federal constitution, "put itself in a way above itself" (*DA* I 2.10). For him, what was remarkable about the American Revolution was not the victory over the British in war, but the patient deliberation that went into the drafting and ratification of the new Constitution (*DA* I 1.8). (This may be why he dates the Constitution not from 1787 when the work began, as do most historians, but from 1789, when the Constitution was finally ratified and put into effect.) In ratifying the Constitution, the majority proudly joined reason to will. But that was for the people willingly to put the reasoning of the founders above its own will.

Thus Tocqueville lacks the confidence of his American democrats in the infallibility of majority reason. He nonetheless shares their determination to ground politics on the principle that most human beings are capable of acting reasonably enough. At the same time, he distinguishes himself, here and even more explicitly in his *Old Regime,* from those who would attempt to establish a rule of a reason not dependent on the active will of the majority.[72] Such attempts will prove at best futile, hence unreasonable, or worse, dehumanizing to all. Rather, the task is to facilitate a majority's acting as reasonably as it can.

FROM THE PROUD MAJORITY TO A HERD

Tocqueville begins his second volume (*DA* II 1.1) by drawing a distinction between modern politics, which is suffused with, if not actually derived from philosophic doctrine, and premodern politics, which was not. Americans practice the new politics, which takes as its foundation the principle that one should rely only on the effort of one's own reason, not on the opinions of others—whether fellow citizens or forebears. At the same time, Americans are unaware of this dependence on philosophic doctrine. Tocqueville now looks at this principle, the sovereignty of the people, under a different name—individualism—and comes to a very different conclusion (*DA* II 2.2). He shows how the very principle that seems to support majority rule, and even majority tyranny, threatens eventually to transform a willful or restive and proud democratic majority into a "herd of timid and industrious animals" living under a new sort of despotism (*DA* II 4.6). The second volume is a study of the likely *practical* consequences of modern political theory, of its effects on the human soul, on reason and sentiment, and consequently on habits or mores, and thereby on politics.

In speaking of the modern principle as individualism, Tocqueville attributes it to an erroneous judgment (*DA* II 2.2). Although similar to the sentiment of self-love or self-preference, it is not so much a sentiment as a conviction that one should live one's life without paying serious attention to anyone but oneself, or at most to one's family and friends. How can this peculiarly modern sensibility sustain society and political life?

Modern political theory begins by positing autonomous individuals living in a state of nature. Its purpose is to show us that it is reasonable even for those who most pride themselves on their power and capability to leave this natural state once and for all, to agree to live as members of some polity with laws, moral rules, customs, and authorities of various sorts, accepting these as legitimate and authoritative. But in the democratic practice Tocqueville describes, each individual insists, in effect, that his consent to depart from the state of nature be obtained in each instance and in each aspect of life. Forget the sovereign! Every act tends to be referred to the pretension of each

72. *DA* I 2.10, II 4.4, 4.6; *The Old Regime* III 1, 8.

to be capable of a rational determination of his own interests. Far from convincing the individual to leave the state of nature, modern political theory induces him to hold on to it.

What consequences might follow from this frame of mind? To say it more harshly than Tocqueville ever would have said it: the fundamental principle of modern democratic life is untenable; it is not true that each and every human being can judge everything for himself. Then what can individuals do? Since they are supposedly equal and equally capable of figuring out how to live their lives, they cannot look elsewhere for help; they cannot consult any of their contemporaries for advice or adopt some tradition as embodying a collective wisdom. To do so would be to bow to an authority, to admit that they are not all equal and equally capable on their own. Modern man probably has more choices than anyone in history has ever had, yet he has fewer guidelines for making choices. With no help—but with full responsibility—judgment becomes a burden too heavy to bear. Tocqueville shows in the first part of volume 2 how democratic thought is affected by this burden.

First, the weight is eased somewhat by simplification. By making broad generalizations, relying on "general ideas" (DA II 1.3), one can bring oneself to believe that *similar* facts and beings are actually identical or equal. This makes thinking a bit easier. Since this manner of thinking permits the organization of a large number of facts, it may also facilitate the scientific progress on which the modern world prides itself. But excessive use of general ideas may also stem from haste or laziness, and so lead to intellectual sloppiness (see also DA II 3.15). And of course, generalizations, particularly about people, can sometimes be inaccurate.

Effective relief can also be found by seeking refuge in public opinion (DA II 1.2). An individual looks around and sees many other people holding more or less similar opinions, and their similarity makes them more credible. What everyone thinks must be so! At the same time, no particular person claims responsibility for these common opinions; so no one's pride is at risk in adopting them. Modern democracy, Tocqueville predicts, will be characterized by an unprecedented respect for public opinion. Already in the first volume, Tocqueville claimed to find less real freedom of thought in America than in any other time or place.

Yet the most problematic movements of the democratic intellect will start in philosophy and then eventually proceed to politics (DA II 1.7, 1.17, 1.20). The Cartesian notion of reason modern democrats knowingly or unwittingly apply, having liberated all men from existing authorities by exposing these as unreasonable, eventually comes to endanger the very democratic individuality it was used to justify. We are told that democrats increasingly depend on an anonymous public opinion, that they rely excessively on general ideas;

and then that they may succumb to a tendency Tocqueville calls "pantheism," in which the distinctiveness not merely of individual men, but of man, is lost to sight.

> As conditions become more equal and each man in particular becomes more like all the others, weaker and smaller, one gets used to no longer viewing citizens so as to consider only the people; one forgets individuals so as to think only of the species.
>
> In these times the human mind loves to embrace a host of diverse objects at once; . . . it willingly seeks to enlarge and simplify its thought by enclosing God and the universe within a single whole. . . . [S]uch a system, although it destroys human individuality, or rather *because* it destroys it, will have secret charms for men who live in democracy; all their intellectual habits prepare them to conceive it and set them on the way to adopting it. (*DA* II 1.7, emphasis added)

One must not be confused by the fact that Tocqueville's notion of "individualism" accuses democrats of living only for themselves and a close circle around them, while that of "pantheism" accuses them of forgetting the individual. The individual described under "individualism" has, in his weakness and vulnerability, lost his individuality. He seeks his identity in the very universal, mass forces to which he regards himself as subject. Democracy creates individuals, then leaves them unprotected so that, abetted by pantheism and "democratic historians," they easily fall into individualism.

Near the end of part 1 (*DA* II 1.20), Tocqueville makes clear the threat that pantheistic opinions pose to democratic politics. This he does in an uncharacteristically vigorous attack on "democratic historians"—who seem to include social and political scientists, as well as those influenced by them.[73] Democratic historians trace all events to a few general causes or to historical systems, rather than to influential individuals. By denying power to some individuals, they bring people to believe that no one acts voluntarily, that whole peoples, even the whole human race, are moved as if in obedience to a power above or below them. Worse, one attributes to that power an inexorable necessity that forecloses human choice. In this view, politics is meaningless and human freedom is impossible. It is a view of history that Tocqueville deems both inaccurate and harmful. But it could also be self-fulfilling, because people under its influence who *could* act decisively might abandon their attempts as futile.

Tocqueville suggests that many democratic intellects will resist the fatal-

---

73. For a similar attack on historians of the French Revolution of 1848, see *Recollections of Alexis de Tocqueville*, 67–75; *OC* 12: 83–89.

ism of the truth supposed by the democratic historians, seeking refuge along the way in democratic "poetry," a new sort of idealism and inspiration to action (*DA* II 1.17). Democracy displaces the traditional sources of poetry in the heroic and the supernatural. Its poets turned first to nature, with Romanticism. But America's romance was with the frontier, with the notion of progress; Americans believe ardently in "the indefinite perfectibility of man" (*DA* II 1.8). When democrats idealize "man" they imagine not the weak, indistinguishable individuals they are taught to see, but the general idea of man, and thus a nation or the human race as a whole.

In democratic poetry, as distinguished from democratic history, the progress of the human race brings to light God's plan for mankind "without showing the hand of the sovereign master." It points to the truth of democratic history, but stops short of articulating its system of general causes which leaves no place for human responsibility. At the same time, democratic poetry brings to light another problematic truth. Its ultimate source will still be the soul of the democratic individual, and Tocqueville asserts that human destinies will become the principal and almost unique object of poetry for democratic peoples. As the democratic poet explores the human soul he does not reveal the strengths enabling human beings to take responsibility for their own freedom and progress, but rather the "doubts," "unheard-of prosperity," and "incomprehensible miseries" that burden it.

Shortly after Tocqueville wrote, Karl Marx came along to promise an escape from our present miserable individualism with a reassurance that we are meant to be species beings. Yet, as Tocqueville allows us to see (*DA* II 1.18), the present, with its alienated individuals, provides no basis for articulating the shape of an ideal future. It can lead as easily to the creation of monsters as to perfected men: The works of democratic poets, he fears, will often reveal fantastic beings that will make one regret the real world.

SELF-INTEREST WELL UNDERSTOOD

Since Tocqueville does not suppose that human beings always reason or act directly on reason, he shows how modern philosophy shapes democratic life, in parts 2 and 3 of volume 2, by discussing its influence on sentiments and then on mores.

At the core of democratic sentiments are love of equality and individualism, which is a natural love of self greatly enhanced by the erroneous judgment that one *should* care only about oneself. With these comes a tendency to materialism. Equality is a presupposition of individualism, because everyone, regardless of social status or group identity, is held to reason well enough about his own affairs. And besides serving as a theoretical basis, equality becomes a practical goal, sought for its own sake. After all, if individuals are equal in the most important respect, why should they not be regarded as equals and also have equal results to show for equal exertions or even from the mere fact of equal existence? The kind of equal result that most recommends itself to most democrats is in material well-being or comfort. Enjoyment of material well-being is individual, and all are more or less equally capable of it. So an "honest materialism" becomes the content of equality and the end of democratic life. In America, Tocqueville observes, "the care of satisfying the least needs of the body and of providing the smallest comforts of life preoccupies minds universally" (*DA* II 2.10).

Beneath the dull, but respectable, surface of a society committed to equality and material well-being, in which all live in relative ease, Tocqueville finds a surprising malaise. Because Americans come to think that the happiness they seek consists in experiencing pleasures of the mortal body, they fret under the awareness that they have a limited time for such experiences.

Even worse, Tocqueville shows, the goals of equality and material well-being are contradictory as well as infinite and therefore unattainable. The most efficient production of consumer goods requires both concentration of capital—large corporations—and specialization of labor—small, repetitive tasks. This kind of production gives rise to inequalities not just in the incomes but eventually in the very abilities of workers and managers. Repetition of small tasks narrows one's mental faculties, whereas the challenge of managing a large corporation may enhance them. Tocqueville foresees the possibility of an industrial aristocracy based almost exclusively on intellectual ability, the new sort of aristocracy we now call meritocracy. He worries about the likely harshness of this new aristocracy, for its members may lack the sense of moral responsibility to others that characterized feudal aristocracy. He also indicates that democrats might be hard-pressed to gainsay the justice of a meritocratic aristocracy constituted of individuals who hold their places by ability, not birth or wealth (*DA* II 1.9, 2.20). Democracies will either have to swallow the new kind of inequality for the sake of maximizing material prosperity, or else accept diminished economic productivity for the sake of equality. No wonder the Americans Tocqueville portrays are anxious and frustrated!

Individualistic Americans bring themselves to cooperate with one another by means of a doctrine, made famous by this book, that Tocqueville calls "self-interest well understood." Tocqueville endorses the doctrine, but we should note first that it may easily worsen the evil he has termed "individualism." The purpose of the doctrine is to persuade democrats to sacrifice some of their private interests for the sake of preserving the rest of them, and in this it succeeds. Thus it is an improvement on self-interest poorly under-

stood, a strict utilitarianism which declares that "the useful is never dishonest." Self-interest well understood is "of all philosophic theories the most appropriate to the *needs* of men in our time," in part because it "marvelously
accommodat[es] to the *weaknesses* of men" (*DA* II 2.8, emphasis added). Yet
for this very reason, the theory risks making men even more aware of their
needs and weaknesses and may appear to legitimate all means of alleviating
them.

Mores, the habits of the heart of a people, the unreflective ways in which
its citizens relate to one another, reveal the thoughts and sentiments of democratic individuals. Some of these manifestations are at first surprising. For, if
in part 2 Tocqueville points out the dangers of excessive or wrong-headed
democratic passions, in part 3 he shows how the excesses of individualism,
egalitarianism, and materialism culminate, paradoxically, in democratic
apathy.

Compassion, for example, forges a new sort of moral bond among democratic citizens, mitigating their individualism. But it does so in a way that is
inseparable from egalitarianism and perfectly compatible, despite what one
might think, with individualism. Compassion is literally an ability to feel
what another human being is feeling, and requires an act of imagination
to put oneself in the place of another. This act is made possible, indeed
effortless, by the equality and similarity that democracy brings, or more precisely by the dogmatic belief in equality on which it rests and by the customs
and conventions of equality that it produces and maintains. For the same
reasons, the fellow feeling it evokes is undiscriminating and shallow. Of
Americans, Tocqueville says that "each of them can judge the sensations of
all the others in a moment: he casts a rapid glance at himself; that is enough
for him" (*DA* II 3.1).

As with individualism, democracy's facile compassion reveals the difference between the political principle of equality—which is strength—and the
actual sense of weakness men feel when they are equal. In principle, the
equality that Tocqueville's Americans recognize is an equal ability to reason
about their own affairs. In fact, they are in the habit of acting on the needi-
ness they feel. Since each person is all too aware of his own misery—that is,
his needs and unsatisfied desires—he makes a "tacit and *almost involuntary*
accord" with others to lend a support now that he hopes later to claim for
himself in turn (*DA* II 3.4, emphasis added). Democracy's sense of justice
and the explicit and intentional agreements that articulate it tend to be constituted with a view to "permanent and general needs" of the human race
(*DA* II 3.18). However much claims of compassion and justice derive from
needs, the surest bonds between democratic citizens apart from family rela-

tions are not these, but fragile and narrow ones established by contracts (*DA* II 3.5) and cemented by money (*DA* II 3.7).

In public, each citizen comes to identify himself with others through the generally experienced miseries of isolation, indecision, restiveness, and impotence. Only in private are human particularities and excellences likely to show themselves: in families, where the courage and intelligence of women shine and can be respected by men (*DA* II 3.9–12), and sometimes in the small private groups that democrats will form on the basis of whatever distinctions they pride themselves on (*DA* II 3.13). In public, there will be few, if any, opportunities for these to show and be acknowledged. Eventually, democrats, having spent so much of their lives in "compel[ling] the soul to employ all its strength in doing mediocre things," will become all but unable even to conceive, much less realize, a "moderate yet vast" ambition (*DA* II 3.19). Public life will acquire an appearance of respectability and regularity, an appealing mildness and informality; but the appearance will mask and even foster an ever increasing mediocrity, softness, and pusillanimity.

Thus the daily life of a democratic society is, paradoxically, antithetical to the capability and strength of individuals that it presupposes. Tocqueville laments that moralists of our time constantly complain of pride. It is true enough that there is "no one who does not believe himself to be worth more than his neighbor," but this same man nonetheless diminishes both himself and his neighbor, by "settl[ing] into mediocre desires." What democratic men most lack is pride. "I would willingly trade several of our small virtues for this vice" (*DA* II 3.19). What does remain of pride, having few reasonable expectations in politics, is mostly turned to business, where it may still be honored (*DA* II 3.18–20); or in rare cases, pride becomes dangerously unruly, militaristic, and revolutionary (*DA* II 3.21, 3.26; AT's note XXIII, p. 702).

Each of the first three parts of volume 2 of *Democracy in America* suggests the theme that Tocqueville makes explicit in the fourth. Although the *principle* of the sovereignty of the people is intended to establish and justify self-government by individuals who "associate" for common purposes, in *practice*, it makes a new mild despotism seem desirable. Democratic individuals who begin with an exaggerated self-confidence and self-importance may in the end be overwhelmed by their sense of weakness and insignificance. With unlimited choices, unsure of everything and passionate about little else but securing their comfort, they will be tempted to surrender responsibility for making their own decisions, and simply follow public opinion. Their self-government will amount to little more than disciplined, if restive, striving to this end. Preoccupied with the well-being of themselves and their family, never as successful as they might hope in securing either the material goods they desire or the equality they crave, keenly aware of the needs all men share and forgetful of the strengths that some, or even each of them, can muster, they will find it quite reasonable to trade much, if not all, of their independence to a government that can meet these needs for them.

Although the doctrine of self-interest well understood and the habit of compassion ought to encourage democratic citizens to aid one another, thereby overcoming their individual weakness, these may also have the contrary consequence of undermining the will to associate. Individuals need to associate for common ends because they are weak, and they may perhaps do so if they can anticipate that it will be in their self-interest to have assisted each other. But can the calculation be relied on? How can a collection of self-consciously weak individuals be supposed to gather their strength together rather than merely reflect their weakness? Consequently, the citizen of democracies has contrary instincts, his sense of independence contending with his weakness. "In this extremity, he naturally turns his regard to the immense being that rises alone in the midst of universal debasement" (*DA* II 4.3). The immense being—replacing God—is the state.[74]

The new mild despotism, as Tocqueville refers to it, will not be oppressive. It will care for citizens, ever attentive to the obvious needs of all and responsive to various pressures to satisfy unfulfilled desires. But by relieving individuals of the necessity of thinking and acting on their own, it gradually "rob[s] each of them of several of the principal attributes of humanity" and finally "reduces each nation to being nothing more than a herd of timid and industrious animals of which the government is the shepherd" (*DA* II 4.7).

REMEDIES FOR MAJORITY TYRANNY AND MILD DESPOTISM

Majoritarian tyranny is the rule of a restive, prideful, often unreasonable people; mild despotism is efficient ministration by the "immense being" to the not unreasonable, though ultimately short-sighted, needs and desires of a tamed, nay, humbled mass. Neither is to be desired. Yet if Tocqueville cannot approve of majoritarian tyranny, he surely prefers the instinct animating it, "intractability" (*DA* II 4.1), to the apathy that sustains democratic despotism.

If the two volumes of *Democracy in America* address distinctly formulated

---

74. Rousseau's Savoyard Vicar refers to God as the *Etre immense; Emile*, in Jean-Jacques Rousseau, *Oeuvres complètes*, 5 vols. (Paris: Gallimard, Pléiade ed., 1959–1995), 4: 592. See also Descartes' description of God as "Immense, incomprehensible and infinite" in *Meditations* IV. Our thanks to Terence Marshall for these references. Tocqueville himself also uses the term in describing the pantheistic conception of the whole, which incorporates all of creation and the Creator himself (*DA* II 1.7).

fears, they are nonetheless a unity insofar as the dual excesses are mitigated by the same measures. Tocqueville claims to have learned in America not only what is to be feared from democracy, but what is to be hoped for from it— or what can be done within democracy to give one cause for hope. At their best, Tocqueville's Americans give cause for hope by showing how the experience of political freedom can curb democracy's self-destructive excesses (*DA* I 2.9, II 1.4). American practice, as opposed to democratic theory, reveals the mores, institutions, and ideas necessary to sustain democratic politics.

In the first volume, Tocqueville elaborates several of the institutional means Americans employ to temper majority tyranny: what he calls "decentralized administration" in federalism, local self-government, judges and juries. He also speaks at length of the benefits of their mores, especially their religion, and of their habits of political activity. Near the end of the second volume he specifies the means necessary to avert mild despotism: associations—among which he includes local government, a free press, an independent judiciary, respect for forms and formalities generally and for individual rights in particular. Because most of the remedies are recommended for each ill, we shall consider them together.

When, at the end of *Democracy in America*, Tocqueville outlines the specific elements of his plan to forestall mild despotism, he does so in the context of a repeated observation that "secondary powers" are natural to aristocracy, but foreign to democracy (*DA* II 4.2, 4.4, 4.5, 4.6; see also I 1.5). Aristocracy as Europeans knew it had been hierarchical, but neither monolithic nor highly centralized. The powerful clergy, though tied to politics by legal privilege and by the Church's property, nonetheless had had their own domain of authority. And both the nobility and the local and provincial administrators who stood between king and people had had enough independence to resist the throne, if not in the people's interests, at least in their own. Thus the premodern aristocratic monarchy, whatever its ambitions, would have found its tyrannical right and ability to do everything checked by these secondary powers. Tocqueville urges the artificial creation of such powers within democracy so as to infuse new democratic *forms* with something of the *spirit* of aristocracy: "It is necessary to give rights to these peoples and a political spirit that suggests to *each* citizen some of the interests that make nobles in aristocracies act" (*DA* II 3.26, emphasis added).

In the end, Tocqueville can praise the intractability to which democracy gives rise and on which it thrives, the same intractability that can animate majority tyranny, because he sees in it an untaught instinct for political freedom (*DA* II 4.1). He can, and does, praise American democracy for educating that instinct. Mild despotism is a "schoolmaster" (*DA* II 4.4, 4.6; see also AT's note X, p. 692) that all but suppresses political freedom; but townships, the judiciary, and associations are also said to be schools—schools of freedom (*DA* I 1.2, 1.5, 2.8; II 2.5). Moreover, the Americans have teachings, notably the idea of rights and the doctrine of self-interest well understood, that are put to work in these schools (*DA* I 2.6, II 2.8).

We have already considered Tocqueville's analysis of the New England township. When he treats free political institutions generally, he does so in conjunction with political and civil associations and with the doctrine of self-interest well understood, all in the section on the influence of democracy on the sentiments (*DA* II 2). Hearts as well as heads are schooled by ideas and political institutions, even though "legislators" and "moralists," that is, politicians and public intellectuals, cannot create sentiments or shape mores directly.

Tocqueville seems to exaggerate greatly the importance of "associations"; he even claims that association is an art, or better a science and the *mother* of all sciences! (*DA* II 2.5, 2.7). Perhaps he does this to counter the exaggerated individualism arising from the theory of modern democracy. At the same time, he claims to have been astonished by the ease with which Americans he saw associate (*DA* II 2.5; see also I 2.6). They formed economic and social, moral and intellectual associations, and most important, political associations. How does this come about?

For Tocqueville, what we now refer to as "voluntary associations" are an indispensable supplement to government in a democracy, though not a substitute for it. On the contrary, he contends that "civil" associations could not easily be maintained without institutions of self-government (*DA* II 2.7). Tocqueville is a critic of big government, not of all government; he even grants that "the sovereign must be more uniform, more centralized, more extended, more penetrating, and more powerful" in democracies (*DA* II 4.7). What matters is how the sovereign's power is structured, how it is divided among secondary powers, to preserve some degree of individual independence. A democratic sovereign can enable and encourage citizens to do more for themselves, while for that reason doing what it must do more effectively.

The belief that perfect independence is feasible is, for Tocqueville, the characteristic American error. But there are various ways to depend on others. Tocqueville's mentor Rousseau had argued that dependence could be made compatible with freedom and dignity only by making it perfectly impartial: each citizen was to be made wholly dependent on the whole society of which he was a part, not partly dependent on any particular, identifiable persons. He had rejected the latter form of dependence because it gives opportunities to self-interest, hence to injustice, and because it challenges human dignity by requiring people to recognize the inequalities inevitably found in their lives. But in Tocqueville's judgment, dependence on a "general will" effectively vitiates each person's awareness of his or her particular interests and abilities, and thus increases the extent of everyone's dependence and degradation. He proposes instead mutual but partial dependence, in the form of participation in associations of all sorts, from private contractual agreements to interest groups to political institutions and organizations.

Private contracts allow us to confront our necessary dependence with a semblance of dignity because they maintain both real and illusory freedom and equality. For example, American women in Tocqueville's day more or less had to marry, but with whom they contracted to marry was, to an unprecedented degree, a matter of informed choice. Women would have to make the best of the situation; by choosing well, they could make it better. American men, he observed, were all expected to work, however fortunate their economic and social position might be. So even the greatest entrepreneur would be in need of hiring workers, *almost* as the lowest laborer was in need of a daily wage to survive. Maintaining the pretense that an employment contract is *as* necessary to the first party as to the other might in fact embolden workers to demand more equal terms and more freedom of contract (*DA* II 3.7). Democratic contracts do not create partners who care about each other, as aristocratic lords and vassals might have done, and as democracy's despotic shepherd may claim to do, but they can require partners to respect each other as beings equally capable of exercising will and reason.

In a democracy, associations for economic and social purposes should be generated easily enough by democratic materialism and compassion; and they help citizens to meet the daily needs they could never meet as individuals. But associations will depend on spontaneous efforts for their creation and maintenance, and so can be haphazard and temporary. Even when successful, they involve risks and often bring only modest benefits. And on the whole, they neither enlarge self-interest nor set anyone's sights beyond provision for relatively short-term needs. Yet they are useful because they do serve real needs, and because they enable associates to perfect techniques they can then use to associate for other purposes. But with their limited gains and substantial risks, they may fail to inspire individuals to make the efforts required to maintain them—especially when it appears that needs might be met in some other way, for example, by government.

Less obvious, but more instructive and potentially more valuable, are the associations Tocqueville's Americans form for moral and intellectual ends. In bringing to the public eye new, uncommon sentiments and ideas, individuals influence one another, persuade others, perhaps even change mores and ultimately laws; thus "the heart is enlarged, and the human mind is developed" (*DA* II 2.5). Tocqueville's example is the temperance societies that at first so amused him. By their means ordinary democratic citizens try to educate their equals by making a public example of themselves, as an aristocratic lord once did for those who looked up to him. Here is a less authoritarian method than Puritan legislation or bureaucratic regulation (*DA* I 1.2, 2.4, 2.5, 2.6; II 2.5). Moreover, in uniting over a moral issue, they help to temper democracy's greater intoxications, individualism and materialism (see *DA* II 2.3, 2.10).

Associations would be difficult to maintain without a readily available means to air the unpopular sentiments and ideas they often stand for, and in Tocqueville's day, this was a newspaper (*DA* II 2.6). Here one person articulates a sentiment or thought shared by other readers, giving encouragement to each, and providing a forum in which to debate and persuade. The felt need for many forums and for the vitality of a free press, Tocqueville contends, depends in turn on political associations, especially local governments (*DA* II 2.6). Among citizens who take a hand in local government, one can expect to find some who have an interest in public affairs as well as in their own private concerns, perhaps even a certain earnestness about doing their duty as citizens. They feel the need to keep up with the little matters of the day and to have a quick and easy means of exposing and being exposed to a range of opinions about them. If Tocqueville found the American newspapers he read to be of rather low quality and still lower repute—too much commercial advertising, too few talented journalists (*DA* I 2.3)—he nonetheless seemed to anticipate the evolution of the modern Op-Ed page.

Once citizens have the habit of associating, political associations should be relatively easy to sustain. The greatness of what is at stake—the government of society—and the impossibility that one individual can accomplish it alone, are readily visible to all. Nor are governments, unlike economic associations, either haphazard or short term. Political associations like New England townships are "permanent associations created by law" (*DA* I 2.4, II 2.6). At the same time, the township is the only association "so much in nature that . . . [it] forms by itself" (*DA* I 1.5). Nevertheless, township freedom "is a rare and fragile thing" because it must be sustained by a "spirit of freedom" (*DA* I 1.5). That spirit must exist independent not only of momentary passions, of interests and circumstances, but also of *rational* calculations about how interests are served most efficiently. Tocqueville commends America's numerous local governments and nongovernmental associations not for their efficiency or even their justice, but because they develop citizens' attachments to political freedom.

Although the township is but a primary school in freedom, citizens who attend it acquire the taste for freedom and its exercise (*DA* I 1.5). They come to appreciate how their choices might affect the world. The township is individual choice and responsibility, shared and writ large: A school, once built, stands.

Similarly, the jury is a free school, "the most energetic means of making the people reign, [and] the most efficacious means of teaching them to reign" (*DA* I 2.8). An independent judiciary gives even the weakest citizen an established weapon with which to fight the tyranny of either government or society. But the weapon will be powerful only as long as judicial niceties, formal rights and procedures, are respected. Fortunately, the American democracy Tocqueville saw had a distinct, and large, class of lawyers and judges, who by professional training and personal interest were encouraged to maintain this respect in society. It could also avail itself of county administrators called justices of the peace, who combine a respect for formalities, which poses an obstacle to despotism, with worldly common sense (*DA* I 1.5).

Tocqueville has specific hopes for the institution of the jury. Characteristically, he looks at the jury not from the point of view of how well it dispenses justice, for which there may be better ways, but as a "political" institution (*DA* I 2.8), for how it teaches jurors about justice and sovereignty in practice. Jurors are randomly selected members of the majority, and Tocqueville's admiring description of the jury is in the context of how to temper majoritarian tyranny, or, one could say, how to make democratic majorities more just. When serving on a jury at least some citizens come to look closely at a general idea like justice, and to see that its precise meaning in a given instance can be of great importance to ordinary people like themselves. It forces them to think about matters beyond the self-centered concerns that usually preoccupy them, but now narrowly and concretely, without generalizing. It teaches responsibility; in having to form a judgment and then defend it, jurors are forced not only to think but also to act like sovereigns. But since this can be hard to do, they may want to listen to the arguments of lawyers and to the views of other jurors, as well as to the judge's instructions. Because the final say will still be their own, they can accept without resentment the guidance of others, some of whom may be wiser than they are.

If townships and juries are schools of freedom, political associations like interest groups and parties, too, are "great schools, free of charge, where all citizens come to learn the general theory of association" (*DA* II 2.7). Political associations bring citizens together in a way that neither democratic compassion nor mild despotism's schoolmaster can do: "A political association draws a multitude of individuals outside themselves at the same time; however separated they are naturally by age, mind, fortune, it brings them together and puts them in contact. They meet each other once and learn to find each other always." Political associations energize citizens and then force them to reason about what is required to organize common efforts. This organization of efforts does not require a sacrifice of self-interest, nor is it begun by a facile identification of one's own interests with the interests of everyone. Otherwise different but similarly interested selves unite to advance one shared goal that is nonetheless recognized as partisan, or partial. Thus deliberation on how to link partial interests to what really might be general interests in a democracy is promoted over the unreflective and abstract identification of needs characteristic of democratic compassion. Political associations are free schools: they are free because they are inexpensive and relatively painless ways of exercising the habits of freedom; they are schools because they employ and instill reasonable expectations about what makes freedom possible for individuals and political communities.

Among political associations are parties, great and small. Great parties, Tocqueville explains, are those that are visible at times of great political conflict—revolution or civil war. They divide over matters of principle. Small parties emerge when there seem to be no matters of principle but only personal ambition at stake. Tocqueville qualifies this distinction by observing that there is one substantive dispute that lies at the base of all political partisanship, based on opinions: "One opinion want[s] to restrict popular power, the other to extend it indefinitely" (*DA* I 2.2). The first opinion, he says, is aristocratic; the second, democratic. Thus Tocqueville revises the traditional formulation of the distinction between aristocracy, the rule of the few best, often though not necessarily wealthy, and democracy, the rule of many, usually poor. For Tocqueville, the crucial distinction between aristocratic and democratic opinions is a disagreement over the proper extent of popular or, in an alternate formulation, public, power. He uses both terms because, in a democracy, *popular* power is almost inevitably *public* power, because many individuals who are weak can easily become dependent on big government, and also because of the power of public opinion, which makes the few all but voiceless. In America, it is true, the popular party started out opposed to big government, but in the twentieth century it reverted to Tocqueville's expectation and discovered the affinity between an insecure people and a caring government.

Tocqueville notes that at the time of Jefferson's election in 1800, proponents of the aristocratic opinion lost their authority in American politics to partisans of the democratic opinion. This means that what is now seen as partisan politics takes place within a fundamentally democratic political horizon, below which the greater political dispute can be aired only indirectly. What form does the greater dispute then take in American political life? The aristocratic principle of limiting popular or public power was in part established by the federal constitution; in part it continued to be held only by people who avoided politics altogether; and in part it was "introduced under the creed of their adversaries" (*DA* I 2.2). One such creed Tocqueville may have in mind is the idea of rights, which we shall consider below.

Tocqueville is celebrated as the great advocate of civil associations and political participation, especially at the local level. But to cast him as a decentralizer and privatizer and nothing more is not enough. Even as he fears and denounces big government, Tocqueville insists on the value of great nations. This does not necessarily mean militarism, but it does mean "think[ing] a little more of making great men" (*DA* II 4.7). In France's case and, we can suppose, in America's as well, he understands that national greatness requires a vigorous defense of the principles of the Revolution in the world, for the sake of the nation's soul.[75] Sustaining the independence and dignity of individuals must always be a matter for national attention, even when best accomplished by decentralized means.

THE VIRTUE OF WOMEN

No survey of the schooling done by American associations would be complete without a peek inside the "conjugal association," for, Tocqueville says, all that influences the condition of women has "great political interest in my eyes" (*DA* II 3.9, 3.12).

Tocqueville's American democratic family is almost a mirror image of the formal, hierarchical, patriarchal aristocratic family; and it looks comely indeed. In the absence of the formal, conventional bonds of aristocracy, natural familial bonds should become stronger. Relations between parents and children will be markedly milder and more intimate. But a lifelong tie to a spouse is, of course, not simply natural. What principle will then govern these bonds?

Tocqueville not only compares American attitudes about marriage and relations between men and women in society favorably with aristocratic patriarchalism, but he also presents a picture quite unlike the democratic egalitarianism of the late twentieth century. Within marriage as he portrays it, spouses are faithful to one another, with little or no public tolerance for infidelity. This he attributes partly to America's being religious, partly to its being commercial, but mostly to the fact that democrats marry by choice, not by parental arrangement, and that they choose with few if any arbitrary barriers, for example, between social or economic classes. American mar-

---

75. While arguing in the Chamber of Deputies for the abolition of slavery in the French colonies, AT reminded his colleagues that the idea of freedom and therefore the "great idea [of abolition] is not only your property, it is not only among the mother ideas of your Revolution, but it lives or it dies in your hearts, depending on whether one sees living or reborn there all the elevated sentiments, all the noble instincts that your Revolution developed, those noble instincts by which you have done everything great that you have accomplished in the world and without which, I do not fear to say, you will do nothing and you will be nothing." "Intervention dans la discussion de la loi sur le régime des esclaves dans les colonies," in *OC* 3.1: 125–126.

riages join hearts, not pedigrees or bank accounts. And since the parties contract freely, it does not seem unreasonable for public opinion to hold them to their choices by frowning on adultery and divorce. There are no respectable excuses for such lapses. Moreover, Americans tend to hold on to their marriages because they are not great romantics; instead, they value "the sort of profound, regular, and peaceful affection that makes up the charm and security of life" (*DA* II 3.11).

In societal relations between men and women, Americans earn Tocqueville's praise for thinking that "the true notion of democratic progress" means treating men and women equally, but *differently*, and concerning themselves with elevating women intellectually and morally, while leaving them socially inferior and dependent. He goes so far as to assert: "If one asked me to what do I think one must principally attribute the singular prosperity and growing force of this people, I would answer that it is to the superiority of its women" (*DA* II 3.12).

Americans hold that nature has made men and women so physically and morally different that one ought to put their different natural abilities to different uses. What are these natural physical and moral differences? Strikingly, Tocqueville says nothing of the most obvious physical difference, that women bear children; he merely suggests that women might be less suited for hard physical labor. And he is so far from finding moral differences that he speaks at length of women's courage and strength of will, of their *virile* habits and energy, of their *manly* reason; they show themselves to be *like*, not unlike, men in heart and mind (*DA* II 3.9–12). American men are nonetheless said to recognize their wives' intelligence and resolve, to esteem them, as well as to respect their freedom. Perhaps, then, they can seek from such women in private the kind of advice that democratic individualism and egalitarianism deny them in public.

Women, for their part, make an informed choice to marry and voluntarily accept the social constraints marriage brings. As young women and then matrons, they learn many of the same habits one would learn from participating in more public associations—to see the world and their own possibilities in it for what they are, to reason about how best to secure the good of present and future members of *their* association, then to subordinate their own will to common purposes. Within marriage they come to understand the marital contract and their husbands' authority as the social contract of liberal political theory was meant to be understood—as the surest way to "regulate and legitimate necessary powers" (*DA* II 3.12).

Contrary to what his Americans claim, Tocqueville shows that American women are intellectually and morally *similar* to men, and arguably superior. He himself never says that it is natural for women as distinguished from men to live a private and subordinate life in the sense that their natures (as mothers) suit them to it. So, insofar as Tocqueville approves of American attitudes toward women, he seems to approve of the assignment of "gender roles," as we would now say. What he shows is that in America, public policy first mistakes or at least greatly exaggerates the significance of natural differences, then goes on to make them the basis of a great conventional inequality. "The true notion of democratic progress" requiring different treatment for the sexes obviously violates the democratic dogma of the natural similarity of all human beings. At the same time, it inverts the notion of natural aristocracy, where the naturally, not conventionally, best rule. For the intellectual and moral superiority of women is, by convention, denied a title to political authority. Democratic progress seems to require that natural superiorities be fostered, yet in the case of women, be obscured from public view. How can this be justified?

Tocqueville's America appears as a whole that is greater than the sum of its parts. At several points in the book, Tocqueville cannot help but express his admiration for the Americans' conduct of business: the way they do battle with nature astonishes him; what they endure in the service of the bottom line is almost heroic. Hard-working, determined businessmen are essential to America's national greatness. Another part of America's greatness is, of course, an unprecedented amount of political activity. Political participation teaches the habits of freedom and nourishes a love of it. Why would America not be all the greater for having its superior women join men in economic and political life?

Tocqueville's characterization of American men, especially in the chapters on women, is hardly flattering. These men exhaust themselves and their wives in a relentless, ever restive, unsatisfying, and ultimately petty pursuit of material well-being. They are decent, to be sure, if for no other reason than that they are too prosaic to imagine any really interesting indecencies in which to indulge; but they do not seem to be especially admirable or even happy human beings. Women, for their part, seem to spend their youths happily flirting and their married lives resolutely, even proudly, but sadly, packing and unpacking family copies of the Bible and Shakespeare as their husbands move on to the next business venture. What Tocqueville refers to as women's making "a sort of glory for themselves out of the voluntary abandonment of their wills" (*DA* II 3.12) we might call inordinate passivity. It is difficult to imagine a vigorous society composed entirely of individuals resembling either American men or women as described.

For Tocqueville, democratic society is characterized by excessive individualism, egalitarianism, and materialism, and by an ever greater centralization of power. Each in its way contributes to the destruction of democratic freedom. If democratic society is to check its own excesses, it will do so in part by diffusing, or decentralizing, public power by employing associations, and in part by appreciating the limits on it that lie so to speak behind and above public life.

In the America Tocqueville describes, democracy limits itself chiefly in two ways: first and most obviously, by religion. Even in democracy, human beings may experience a dissatisfaction with existence that serves to remind them that there are yearnings that go beyond material well-being and even justice. To fulfill such yearnings the indefinite extension of public power would be useless. And where political power should not venture, religion is there to provide individuals with what guidance they might need.

Another keenly felt limit on the desire to extend public power is, perhaps still today, the family. Here, to repeat, one can hope to experience not an abstract compassion, but "the sort of profound, regular, and peaceful affection that makes up the charm and security of life." Here passions that find no rest in economic and political life can be calmed and ordered. Both religion and family serve to restrain the frenetic activity of men, ultimately for the sake of allowing them to focus and deploy their energies more effectively in places where social and political power can reach the goals set. This distinction between domains is necessary, even though a line drawn along gender seems arbitrary. Insofar as there is a natural basis for this arguably arbitrary convention, it lies in sexual attraction, which brings the two distinct domains together.

The nineteenth-century American marriage Tocqueville describes is one important aspect of modern democratic life that had not yet been thoroughly politicized. Could it have been expected to last? Marriage begins with a contract, with a choice, and therefore with self-interest, well or poorly understood. Whatever the charm and security of family life, democracy encourages immediate gratification of desires. So, why keep a marriage contract when something more desirable comes along? Democracy also promises equality; so, why stop short of public recognition of women's equal abilities? In short, why should one not expect democratic theory to overwhelm the mores that sustain the family? Tocqueville says that what happens in the family is more important in shaping life as a whole than what happens in politics (*DA* I 2.9, II 3.8). But that judgment applies to aristocracy. In democracy, the contrary is more likely to occur (*DA* I 2.6, 2.9).

THE SUPERIORITY OF PRACTICE

Democracy in America shows the superiority of American practice to democratic theory, partly because some aspects of American practice had not yet been transformed by democratic theory, partly because practice tends to correct theory (*DA* II 1.4, 2.4). Nonetheless, America's vocational schools of freedom do teach two doctrines: "self-interest well understood" and the idea of rights.

How can the doctrine of self-interest well understood be helpful? Tocqueville presents self-interest well understood as a moral doctrine universally accepted in America. It is meant to replace older moral teachings that urged almost divine selflessness or praised the beauty of virtue and the glory of sacrifice. The new moralists defend virtue as useful, and one learns to think that one always prefers oneself, but also that it is part of one's interest to see that one's "particular interest is to do good" (*DA* II 2.8). Americans take to explaining everything they do by means of self-interest, even denying that they are ever given to the "disinterested and unreflective sparks that are natural to man." In so doing, "they would rather do honor to their philosophy than to themselves." This, Tocqueville says, is to do themselves an injustice. It is also to contradict their doctrine by honoring it above their interests, or to demonstrate that honoring something above oneself and one's interests is in one's interest.

Tocqueville contends that self-interest well understood is the moral doctrine best suited to modern democratic times, even though it is neither complete nor altogether self-evident. But it is "clear and sure"; and since it "marvelously accommodat[es] to the weaknesses of men, it obtains a great empire with ease" (*DA* II 2.8). It is unlikely to produce either true or lofty virtue, but it is nonetheless well suited to democracy because it is accessible to everyone and shows all how to behave well enough: "Consider some individuals, they are lowered. View the species, it is elevated" (*DA* II 2.8).

The doctrine of self-interest runs a risk in making citizens well aware of their needs and in appealing to them; but it also urges on citizens the importance of attending to their needs in a responsible way. No less than older moral doctrines or democratic compassion, it is meant to prompt democrats to come to one another's aid. And it is more compatible than the alternatives with democratic self-government. Free political institutions and the habit of participating in them are still necessary to show democratic citizens what useful things they can do for themselves by combining their efforts. Self-interest *well understood* would keep citizens from being overwhelmed by their needs and succumbing to dependence on a schoolmaster government that might otherwise be understood as serving them.

How does the idea of rights support association and self-government? Near the end of *Democracy in America,* Tocqueville makes a remark that might strike Americans today as strange: "Another instinct very natural to democratic peoples and very dangerous is the one that brings them to scorn individual rights and hold them of little account. . . . [T]he very idea of these sorts of rights constantly tends to be distorted and lost among us" (*DA* II 4.7). Tocqueville insists that democracy is naturally hostile to individual rights, that rights are aristocratic in origin and character (*DA* II 4.4). Yet the great theorists of rights—Hobbes, Locke, Kant—were all profoundly and emphatically antiaristocratic. How might one account for Tocqueville's apparent error?

Tocqueville's remarks on the subject of rights are scattered throughout his book, the most extended discussion being in the chapter on the "real advantages of democratic government." Here he links or equates rights not to interest but to virtue: "After the general idea of virtue I know of none more beautiful than that of rights, or rather these two ideas are confounded. The idea of rights is nothing other than the idea of virtue introduced into the political world. . . . Enlightened by it, each could show himself independent without arrogance and submissive without baseness" (*DA* I 2.6). Citizens who show themselves independent without arrogance and submissive without baseness exhibit the political virtues of courage and moderation, virtues essential to self-government. When exercised in political activity they inspire a rational, if interested, patriotism, a concern for and pride in public outcomes—as one's own achievement, in which one takes pride.

For Tocqueville, rights are essentially political, not social or economic, in content and in consequence. They make possible self-government and political responsibility, giving citizens more self-confidence and making them less cynical or resentful toward government. The newer, more cherished rights of late twentieth-century America—reproductive rights, the rights of various sorts of minorities, and increasingly, environmental and health-related rights—have, on the whole, the object of security, freedom from risk. Some are understood to be entitlements, rights whose existence depends on a governmental program and often a governmental expenditure. To rights of this sort American democracy seems far from hostile. The fact that Tocqueville seems to have been so wrong about how rights would come to be viewed suggests either that his predictions have gone awry or that they were all too accurate.

When Tocqueville speaks at length at the end of his book on the means of forestalling the new despotism (*DA* II 4.7), he refers to his project as a "holy enterprise"; yet he makes no mention of the American religious mores to which he seems to attach so much importance in volume 1. How might this be understood?

Insofar as Tocqueville has hopes for religion, they are of two sorts. Religion may diminish the threat of mild despotism by reminding citizens of the seriousness of life outside the busy search for material well-being in democracies. Belief in the soul and its afterlife may moderate materialism; and the sure answers any religion offers to the hardest questions can strengthen individual judgment in both private and public life (*DA* II 1.5). In these ways religion may forestall democrats' psychological and intellectual susceptibility to mild despotism. But once again, Tocqueville's objective in strengthening the personal or nonpublic as against the public can only be one aspect of religion's potential benefit, since he also contemns those who neglect public concerns.[76] His second hope for religion is that it may serve as a reminder of what transcends the mediocrity of democratic public life, and thus of a greatness not usually within its scope.

When Tocqueville discusses the Puritans (*DA* I 1.2), he shows that while they combined the spirits of religion and freedom, they did so by putting politics in the service of their religion. The context of that discussion is the point of departure that American democracy began with, then moved away from. In describing the Americans of his day (*DA* I 2.9), Tocqueville says they are still religious, but shows them now putting their religion in the service of their politics. While Tocqueville was traveling in America, he received a letter from his friend Kergorlay, who asked him about the state of beliefs in America. In his reply, Tocqueville speaks not at all of religious beliefs, but of America's republicanism and of its doctrine of human perfectibility.[77] The true beginning of American democracy is the dogma of the sovereignty of the people, a dogma logically incompatible with the acceptance of *any* authority, including traditional religion. But people rarely live by logic alone (*DA* II 1.6), and Americans in particular had thus far been spared the most dire consequences of individualism because they had never turned Descartes's radical doubt on their religious beliefs. Tocqueville observes that "in the United States . . . the sovereign is religious, and consequently hypocrisy ought to be common" (*DA* I 2.9). This makes it difficult to say whether in Tocqueville's mind Americans were then or still could be true believers. Do they, as sovereigns, appreciate that religion is politically useful, lending support to political virtues, especially moderation? Or do they convince themselves that they are believers because they, as individuals, cannot live without any beliefs at all (*DA* II 1.2)?

In the second volume of *Democracy in America* Tocqueville refers to religion as "the most precious inheritance from aristocratic centuries" (*DA* II 2.15), as if it were foreign to democratic eras. And the Introduction to the book makes it a question whether religion can be relied on to play an important role elsewhere in the modern world. Tocqueville claims to have learned from American democracy that religion can remain vital in the new world if

---

76. For an emphatic restatement of this point, see *The Old Regime*, Preface, 86–89; *OC* 2.1: 73–76.

77. Letter to Louis de Kergorlay, June 29, 1831, *Selected Letters*, 47; *OC* 13.1: 225–238.

it is kept separate from politics. In America, clergy were precluded by custom, if not law, from holding political office; they entered into partisan political controversies no further than to support the general view that republicanism is a good thing. Later (*DA* II 1.2), Tocqueville clarifies his characterization of the separation of church and state, showing that it cannot be complete because at the base of politics and religion is one public opinion that sustains them both. He expects democracy to transform religion to make its form and content more consistent with democracy; and by 1830, American religion had made that accommodation.

To appreciate the political significance of Tocqueville's understanding of the role of religion in American public life, one might first connect it to his remarks on political parties and on the importance of women to America's prosperity, and then to his brief discussion of the goals of democratic governments. At one point, he says that religion remains powerful in America because women remain pious, and they are the ones who shape mores (*DA* I 2.9). Yet in discussing the education of women, he insists that Americans have not relied on religion alone to defend the virtue of woman—"they have sought to arm her reason"—and American girls, we are assured in passing, are not reared in cloisters (*DA* II 3.9). Perhaps what Tocqueville's American women and clergy share most is not piety so much as a dignified acceptance of their exclusion from political life, as if they sensed that democracy's excesses cannot be effectively moderated by a democratic politics that lacks "great parties." Without a great party, the best way to defend the principle of restricting public power might be by an exemplary abstinence from attempts to capture political power to further any end whatever. If so, this point might best be brought home, so to speak, by showing that the nonpolitical remains a vital supplement to political life. Religion and family may be separate from government, but both are parts of *self*-government; so the separation must itself be understood politically. This is how Tocqueville can say that religion ought to be considered as "the first of [America's] political institutions" (*DA* I 2.9).

When Tocqueville calls the reader's attention to Americans' insistence on separating church and state, he makes it clear that he thinks that the human power released by modern philosophy needs to impose some sense of limitation on itself. Yet the purpose of his recommendation of self-limitation is to keep democratic political power vigorous within its proper sphere (*DA* I 2.9).

In Tocqueville's view (*DA* II 2.17), democratic eras as well as ages of religious skepticism suffer from an instability both of desire and of condition, which tends to confine those who live in them to immediate goals requiring only brief exertions. Although modern political theory was meant to increase human power and give men better control of events, in practice, the instability of democracy may give greater scope to chance than was seen in political life when people did not believe everything was in their control, but was instead at the mercy of higher powers. From democratic instability arises the possibility of a majoritarian politics characterized by a continuous, meaningless flux. The flux may seem to justify an apathy that leaves the field to passionate, if fleetingly aroused, majorities; then, in the end, it subsides into mild despotism.

What is necessary, Tocqueville insists, is for democratic governments to set distant goals, goals to be achieved by moderate, yet steadfast, efforts. Surprisingly, however, Tocqueville specifies no great project. Instead he suggests the seemingly limited, not to say modest, task of seeing to it that political office come only as a reward for skill and effort, for moderate ambition—and not for pleasing the people. But this modest goal is in truth an infinite one that calls forth continuous diligence. There will always be elections that can be won by pleasing the people; and winning the favor of the people, especially of a democratic people with unstable desires, will depend in large part on chance. It is beyond the capacity of a democracy to reward virtue regularly. Partial success is within reach to the extent that political institutions and mores can be well shaped; but without the support of a greater power, the goal will always remain elusive. Insofar as men do act confidently in the hope that virtue will be rewarded—accomplishing much along the way—they will, in effect, have returned to a kind of religious faith from which politics may benefit politically.

In the new democratic world, the willfulness or intractability with which a majority can act contrary to its own interest, let alone that of minorities, is less cause for concern than the frightening political apathy in the majority, which permits the emergence of a mild despotism that degrades all. To appreciate these dangers is not to surrender to despair, but rather to arm oneself with an attentive "salutary fear" (*DA* II 4.7). Tocqueville's journey to America and his further reflections on what he had observed there taught him to hope that, educated by political institutions and sustained in the better habits of their hearts, citizens of the new democratic world could secure their independence and dignity.

Tocqueville learned to admire democracy, sincerely, if not wholeheartedly: it would be different from aristocracy, with its own virtues and vices, its own good and bad penchants, its own ideas, its own sort of greatness and beauty, neither incontrovertibly superior nor inferior to what had preceded it (*DA* II 4.8). The fact that he criticizes democracy does not mean that he does not also speak ill of aristocracy or that he could not speak better of democracy, had he not deliberately left that to others (*DA* II Notice). In the end, Tocqueville was a democrat, and more of a democrat than many of his contemporaries. Because he insisted that only political freedom could remedy the ills to which equality of conditions gives rise (*DA* II 2.4), he hopefully accepted that equality and, despite his fears, embraced the political freedom that democracy promised.

SUGGESTED READINGS

Aron, Raymond. *Main Currents in Sociological Thought.* Vol 1. New Brunswick, N.J.: Transaction Publishers, 1998–1999.

Beaumont, Gustave de. *Marie; or, Slavery in the United States: A Novel of Jacksonian America.* Translated by Barbara Chapman. Baltimore, Md.: Johns Hopkins University Press, 1999.

Bellah, Robert N., Richard Madsen, William M. Sullivan, Ann Swidler, and Steven M. Tipton. *Habits of the Heart: Individualism and Commitment in American Life.* Berkeley, Calif.: University of California Press, 1985.

Boesche, Roger. *The Strange Liberalism of Alexis de Tocqueville.* Ithaca, N.Y.: Cornell University Press, 1987.

Ceaser, James. *Liberal Democracy and Political Science.* Baltimore, Md.: Johns Hopkins University Press, 1990.

Drescher, Seymour. *Dilemmas of Democracy: Tocqueville and Modernization.* Pittsburgh, Penn.: University of Pittsburgh Press, 1968.

Eden, Robert. "Tocqueville and the Problem of Natural Right." *Interpretation* 17 (1990): 379–388.

Eisenstadt, Abraham S., ed. *Reconsidering Tocqueville's "Democracy in America."* New Brunswick, N.J.: Rutgers University Press, 1988.

Frohnen, Bruce. *Virtue and the Promise of Conservatism: The Legacy of Burke and Tocqueville.* Lawrence, Kans.: University Press of Kansas, 1993.

Furet, François. *In the Workshop of History.* Chicago, Ill.: University of Chicago Press, 1984.

———. *Interpreting the French Revolution.* Translated by Elborg Forster. New York: Cambridge University Press, 1981.

Goldstein, Doris S. *Trial of Faith: Religion and Politics in Tocqueville's Thought.* New York: Elsevier, 1975.

Hadari, Saguiv. *Theory in Practice: Tocqueville's New Science of Politics.* Stanford, Calif.: Stanford University Press, 1989.

Hereth, Michael. *Alexis de Tocqueville: Threats to Freedom in Democracy.* Translated by George Bogardus. Durham, N.C.: Duke University Press, 1986.

Jardin, André. *Tocqueville: A Biography.* Translated by L. Davis. New York: Farrar Straus Giroux, 1988.

Kessler, Sanford. *Tocqueville's Civil Religion.* Albany, N.Y.: State University of New York Press, 1994.

Koritansky, John. *Alexis de Tocqueville and the New Science of Politics.* Durham, N.C.: Carolina Academic Press, 1986.

Lakoff, Sanford. *Democracy: History, Theory, Practice.* Boulder, Colo.: Westview Press, 1996.

Lamberti, Jean-Claude. *Tocqueville and the Two Democracies.* Translated by Arthur Goldhammer. Cambridge, Mass.: Harvard University Press, 1989.

Lawler, Peter Augustine. *The Restless Mind.* Lanham, Md.: Rowman and Littlefield, 1993.

———. "Tocqueville on the Doctrine of Interest." *Government and Opposition* 30 (spring 1995).

———, ed. *Tocqueville's Political Science: Classic Essays.* New York: Garland, 1992.

———, and Joseph Alulis, eds. *Tocqueville's Defense of Human Liberty.* New York: Garland, 1993.

Lefort, Claude. *Democracy and Political Theory.* Minneapolis: University of Minnesota Press, 1988.

Lerner, Max. *Tocqueville and American Civilization.* New York: Harper and Row, 1969.

Lively, Jack. *The Social and Political Thought of Alexis de Tocqueville.* Oxford: Clarendon Press, 1962.

Manent, Pierre. *An Intellectual History of Liberalism.* Translated by Rebecca Balinski. Princeton, N.J.: Princeton University Press, 1994.

———. *Tocqueville and the Nature of Democracy.* Translated by John Waggoner. Lanham, Md.: Rowman and Littlefield, 1996.

Masugi, Ken, ed. *Interpreting Tocqueville's "Democracy in America."* Savage, Md.: Rowman and Littlefield, 1991.

Mayer, J. P. *Alexis de Tocqueville.* New York: Viking Press, 1966.

Mélonio, Françoise. *Tocqueville et les Français.* Paris: Aubier, 1993.

Mill, John Stuart. *Collected Works.* Toronto: University of Toronto Press, 1965– .

———. "M. de Tocqueville on Democracy in America," pp. 119–184 in *The Philosophy of John Stuart Mill,* Marshall Cohen, ed. New York: Modern Library (Random House), 1961.

Mitchell, Harvey. *Individual Choice and the Structures of History: Alexis de Tocqueville as Historian Reappraised.* Cambridge, U.K.: Cambridge University Press, 1996.

Mitchell, Joshua. *The Fragility of Freedom: Tocqueville on Religion, Democracy, and the American Future.* Chicago: University of Chicago Press, 1995.

Pierson, George Wilson. *Tocqueville in America.* New York: Oxford University Press, 1938.

Raynaud, Philippe. "Tocqueville," in *Dictionnaire de philosophie politique.* Philippe Raynaud and Stéphanie Rials, eds. Paris: Presses Universitaires de France, 1997.

Reinhardt, Mark. *The Art of Being Free: Taking Liberties with Tocqueville, Marx, and Arendt.* Ithaca, N.Y.: Cornell University Press, 1997.

Richter, Melvin, ed. *Essays in Theory and History: An Approach to the Social Sciences.* Cambridge, Mass.: Harvard University Press, 1970.

———. "Tocqueville's Contributions to the Theory of Revolution," pp. 73–121 in *Revolution,* Carl J. Friedrich, ed. New York: Atherton Press, 1966.

Salomon, Albert. "Tocqueville, Moralist and Sociologist," *Social Research* 2 (1935).

Schleifer, James T. *The Making of Tocqueville's "Democracy in America."* Chapel Hill: University of North Carolina Press, 1980.

Siedentop, Larry. *Tocqueville.* Oxford: Oxford University Press, 1994.

Tesini, Mario. *Tocqueville tra destra e sinistra.* Rome: Edizioni Lavoro, 1997.

Tocqueville, Alexis de. *De la démocratie en Amérique.* Eduardo Nolla, ed. 2 vols. Paris: Vrin, 1990.

———. *Journey to America.* Edited by J. P. Mayer. Translated by George Lawrence. New Haven, Conn.: Yale University Press, 1959.

———. *Journeys to England and Ireland.* Edited by J. P. Mayer. Translated by George Lawrence and J. P. Mayer. Garden City, N.Y.: Anchor Books (Doubleday), 1968.

———. *Oeuvres.* 2 vols. Edited by A. Jardin. Paris: Gallimard, Edition Pléiade, 1991–1992.

———. *Oeuvres, papiers et correspondances.* J. P. Mayer, ed. 18 vols. Paris: Gallimard, 1951–1989.

———. *The Old Regime and the Revolution.* Edited by François Furet and Françoise Mélonio. Translated by Alan S. Kahan. Chicago: University of Chicago Press, 1998.

———. *Recollections.* Edited by J. P. Mayer and A. P. Kerr. Translated by George Lawrence. Garden City, N.Y.: Anchor Books (Doubleday), 1971.

———. *Selected Letters on Politics and Society.* Translated by James Toupin and Roger Boesche. Berkeley: University of California Press, 1985.

Volkmann-Schluck, Karl-Heinz. *Politische Philosophie: Thukydides, Kant, Tocqueville.* Frankfurt: Klostermann, 1974.

Winthrop, Delba. "Tocqueville's American Woman and 'The True Conception of Democratic Progress.'" *Political Theory* 14 (1986): 239–261.

Wolin, Sheldon. *The Presence of the Past.* Baltimore, Md.: Johns Hopkins University Press, 1989.

Zetterbaum, Marvin. *Tocqueville and the Problem of Democracy.* Stanford, Calif.: Stanford University Press, 1967.

A NOTE ON
THE TRANSLATION

Our intent has been to make our translation of Tocqueville's text as literal and consistent as we can, while still readable. By "readable" we mean what can easily be read now, not what we might normally say. Of the two extremes in translating, staying as close as possible to the original and bringing it as close as possible to us, we are closer to the former. A book as great as Tocqueville's should inspire a certain reverence in translators, not only because it is so intelligent or because its style is so perfect but also because the intelligence and the style go together and need as much as possible to be conveyed together in English. Precisely to bring Tocqueville to us requires an effort, both in translating and in reading, to get close to him, and to become familiar with his terms, his rhetorical flights, his favorite expressions.

Recognizing that translation is always imperfect, we have sought all the more to be modest, cautious, and faithful. Every translator must make many choices, but in making ours we have been guided by the principle, admittedly an ideal, that our business is to convey Tocqueville's thought as he held it rather than to restate it in comparable terms of today. By refraining as much as possible from interpretation, we try to make it possible for readers to do their own thinking and figure out for themselves what Tocqueville means. As translators we respect the diversity of interpretation best when we do not offer one ourselves. Tocqueville wrote the following reproach to Henry Reeve, his friend and author of the first English translation of *Democracy in America:* "Without wishing to do so and by following the instinct of your opinions, you have quite vividly colored what was contrary to Democracy and almost erased what could do harm to Aristocracy."[1] We are not likely to

1. Letter to Henry Reeve, October 15, 1839; *OC* 6.1: 48.

receive such an authoritative message, but we hope very much that we do not deserve one.

Henry Reeve was trying to be helpful to Tocqueville's readers by preventing them from thinking too well of democracy, but he was being too kind to them. It is better to let them, or force them, to make their own discoveries. We would rather attract readers to Tocqueville than bring him to them, and make him too cheaply available for our purposes today (which are not those of Henry Reeve). We do not want people to stop quoting Tocqueville— God forbid! But perhaps they should quote more faithfully, and work a little harder when they read him. Yet, having spoken up for fidelity, we have to confess immediately that the very title of Tocqueville's work would be translated more accurately as *On Democracy in America.* The book is not known in America under that title, and in translating, even the most stringent rule has its exceptions.

We do provide notes meant to be helpful, identifying events and allusions no longer familiar in our day. We also specify Tocqueville's references to other places in his own text. Because the book is long and Tocqueville has so many notes of his own, we have not attempted to reproduce the many marginal notations and rejected drafts that can be found in the two French editions of the work, one by Jean-Claude Lamberti and James T. Schleifer (published by Pléiade) and the other by Eduardo Nolla (published by Vrin). We were also somewhat averse to implicating ourselves in the risky business of interpreting what Tocqueville meant from what he decided not to say. Tocqueville's text and notes frequently quote passages into French from English, for example from Thomas Jefferson's *Notes on the State of Virginia* and *The Federalist.* Instead of retranslating such quotations we have merely used the original English, while remarking any changes Tocqueville may have made in his translation or citation (for he sometimes exercised a right to be unfaithful that we as his inferiors do not claim). Tocqueville's own footnotes are numbered in our translation, editorial notes are marked with symbols. His longer endnotes, which should not be overlooked, are given roman numerals. His references in both footnotes and endnotes have been checked and corrected. All editorial insertions in Tocqueville's text are enclosed in brackets.

We also offer an extensive subject index to *Democracy in America.* We do this somewhat against our inclination, as such an index may give a sense of false security to those users who are pressed for time. But the book is large and various, and the author frequently reverts to a subject taken up earlier in a different context. It may be useful to have these instances collected even if many relevant passages not expressly raising a particular subject are necessarily omitted from its entry in the index. The reader should treat the index as the beginning of his search and not the end. We also supply a corrected list of the sources Tocqueville cites in the book.

We have kept Tocqueville's long sentences and short paragraphs. Among problems we encountered in translating particular words or phrases was *semblables*, "those like oneself," which Tocqueville uses frequently when one might expect "equals." *Intelligence* is sometimes "intelligence," sometimes "intellect"; and on the contrary, *pouvoir* and *puissance* have both to be translated "power," thus losing the subtle distinction in French, which derives from the Latin *potestas* and *potentia*. *Chaque jour* is rendered "every day," sometimes "each day," depending on whether the point seems to be repetition or separateness. We also sometimes say "daily." For the important word *inquiet* we settled on "restive," with its connotation of rebelliousness and intent, better, it seems to us, than the more random "restless." Occasionally we had to translate *inquiet* as anxious, and the reflexive *s'inquiéter* is milder still, "worry." *Esprit* is either "spirit" or "mind." *Moeurs* are "mores," on some occasions "morals" or "morality"; the term is not ethically neutral for Tocqueville, as it is today. We give *liberté* as "freedom" to preserve the connection with *libre*, "free," even though this choice would have produced "freedom, equality, and fraternity" if Tocqueville had cited the revolutionary formula. We would have loved to translate *sein* as "bosom," to preserve the reputation of the French, and sometimes we do; but usually, it is "heart," a nearby organ, and sometimes merely "within." We render *particuliers* as "particular persons," saving the word "individuals" for *individus*.

We have used the French text printed in the Pléiade edition, essentially the same as the one in the Gallimard edition, which is based on the last editions of the two volumes that Tocqueville saw himself. Following the Pléiade edition we have omitted two texts of speeches that Tocqueville added himself to the 1848 edition. They are readily available and they are not part of the book.

We wish to acknowledge the indispensable help of Bryan Garsten and Kathryn Shea, who researched Tocqueville's notes, worked the computer and gave us an abundance of intelligent suggestions. We are grateful, too, for the extraordinary editing of Russell Harper at the University of Chicago Press, and we thank our longtime friend there, John Tryneski.

For financial support we are grateful to the Lynde and Harry Bradley Foundation; to the John M. Olin Foundation; to Robert S. Krupp of San Francisco, California, through the American Council of Trustees and Alumni; and to our generous employer, Harvard University.

DEMOCRACY IN AMERICA

Volume

A mong the new objects that attracted my attention during my stay in the United States, none struck my eye more vividly than the equality of conditions. I discovered without difficulty the enormous influence that this primary fact exerts on the course of society; it gives a certain direction to public spirit, a certain turn to the laws, new maxims to those who govern, and particular habits to the governed.

Soon I recognized that this same fact extends its influence well beyond political mores and laws, and that it gains no less dominion over civil society than over government: it creates opinions, gives birth to sentiments, suggests usages, and modifies everything it does not produce.

So, therefore, as I studied American society, more and more I saw in equality of conditions the generative fact from which each particular fact seemed to issue, and I found it before me constantly as a central point at which all my observations came to an end.

Then I brought my thinking back to our hemisphere, and it seemed to me I distinguished something in it analogous to the spectacle the New World offered me. I saw the equality of conditions that, without having reached its extreme limits as it had in the United States, was approaching them more each day; and the same democracy reigning in American societies appeared to me to be advancing rapidly toward power in Europe.

At that moment I conceived the idea of the book you are going to read.

A great democratic revolution is taking place among us: all see it, but all do not judge it in the same manner. Some consider it a new thing, and taking it for an accident, they still hope to be able to stop it; whereas others judge it irresistible because to them it seems the most continuous, the oldest, and the most permanent fact known in history.

For a moment I take myself back to what France was seven hundred years ago: I find it divided among a few families who possess the land and govern the inhabitants; at that time right of command passes from generation to generation by inheritance; men have only one means of acting upon one another—by force; only one origin of power is to be discovered—landed property.

But then the political power of the clergy comes to be founded and soon spreads. The clergy opens its ranks to all, to the poor and to the rich, to the commoner and to the lord; equality begins to penetrate through the church to the heart of government, and he who would have vegetated as a serf in eternal slavery takes his place as a priest in the midst of nobles, and will often take a seat above kings.

As society becomes in time more civilized and stable, the different relations among men become more complicated and numerous. The need for civil laws makes itself keenly felt. Then jurists are born; they leave the dark precincts of the courts and the dusty recesses of the registries and go to sit at the court of the prince beside the feudal barons covered with ermine and mail.

The kings ruin themselves in great undertakings; the nobles exhaust themselves in private wars; the commoners enrich themselves in commerce. The influence of money begins to make itself felt in the affairs of the state. Trade becomes a new source opening the way to power, and financiers become a political power that is scorned and flattered.*

Little by little enlightenment spreads; one sees the taste for literature and the arts awaken; then the mind becomes an element in success; science is a means of government, intelligence a social force; the lettered take a place in affairs.

Meanwhile, as new routes for coming to power are discovered, the value of birth is seen to decline. In the eleventh century, nobility had an inestimable price; in the thirteenth it is bought; the first ennobling takes place in 1270,† and equality is finally introduced into government by the aristocracy itself.

During the seven hundred years that have since elapsed, it sometimes happened that the nobles, in order to struggle against royal authority or to take power from their rivals, gave political power to the people.

Even more often one saw the kings have the lower classes of the state participate in the government in order to bring down the aristocracy.

In France, the kings showed themselves to be the most active and constant

---

*In this sentence, AT uses two different words for "power," *pouvoir* and *puissance*. *Puissance*, used in the first instance, has a connotation of physical strength; *pouvoir*, of formal authority as well as capacity.

†Louis IX (d. 1270) first asserted the exclusive right of the king to confer knighthood; Philip IV issued the first "letter of ennoblement" in about 1290.

levelers. When they were ambitious and strong, they worked to elevate the people to the level of the nobles; and when they were moderate and weak, they permitted the people to be placed above themselves. Some aided democracy by their talents, others by their vices. Louis XI* and Louis XIV† took care to equalize everything beneath the throne, and finally Louis XV‡ himself descended with his court into the dust.

As soon as citizens began to own land other than by feudal tenure, and transferable wealth was recognized, and could in its turn create influence and give power, discoveries in the arts could not be made, nor improvements in commerce and industry be introduced, without creating almost as many new elements of equality among men. From that moment on, all processes discovered, all needs that arise, all desires that demand satisfaction bring progress toward universal leveling. The taste for luxury, the love of war, the empire of fashion, the most superficial passions of the human heart as well as the most profound, seem to work in concert to impoverish the rich and enrich the poor.

Once works of the intellect had become sources of force and wealth, each development of science, each new piece of knowledge, each new idea had to be considered as a seed of power put within reach of the people. Poetry, eloquence, memory, the graces of the mind, the fires of the imagination, depth of thought, all the gifts that Heaven distributed haphazardly, profited democracy, and even if they were found in the possession of its adversaries, they still served its cause by putting into relief the natural greatness of man; its conquests therefore spread with those of civilization and enlightenment, and literature was an arsenal open to all, from which the weak and the poor came each day to seek arms.

When one runs through the pages of our history, one finds so to speak no great events in seven hundred years that have not turned to the profit of equality.

The Crusades§ and the wars with the English‖ decimate the nobles and divide their lands; the institution of townships introduces democratic freedom into the heart of the feudal monarchy; the discovery of firearms# equalizes the villein and the noble on the battlefield; printing** offers equal resources to their intelligence; the mail comes to deposit enlightenment on the

---

*King of France, 1461–1483.
†King of France, 1643–1715.
‡King of France, 1715–1774.
§1095–1291.
‖The Hundred Years' War, 1337–1453.
#Firearms were developed in the fourteenth century.
**The printing press was invented around 1450.

doorstep of the poor man's hut as at the portal of the palace; Protestantism asserts that all men are equally in a state to find the path to Heaven.* America, once discovered, presents a thousand new routes to fortune and delivers wealth and power to the obscure adventurer.

If you examine what is happening in France every fifty years from the eleventh century on, at the end of each of these periods you cannot fail to perceive that a double revolution has operated on the state of society. The noble has fallen on the social ladder, and the commoner has risen; the one descends, the other climbs. Each half century brings them nearer, and soon they are going to touch.

And this is not peculiar to France. In whichever direction we cast a glance, we perceive the same revolution continuing in all the Christian universe.

Everywhere the various incidents in the lives of peoples are seen to turn to the profit of democracy; all men have aided it by their efforts: those who had in view cooperating for its success and those who did not dream of serving it; those who fought for it and even those who declared themselves its enemies; all have been driven pell-mell on the same track, and all have worked in common, some despite themselves, others without knowing it, as blind instruments in the hands of God.

The gradual development of equality of conditions is therefore a providential fact, and it has the principal characteristics of one: it is universal, it is enduring, each day it escapes human power; all events, like all men, serve its development.

Would it be wise to believe that a social movement coming from so far can be suspended by the efforts of one generation? Does one think that after having destroyed feudalism and vanquished kings, democracy will recoil before the bourgeoisie and the rich? Will it be stopped now that it has become so strong and its adversaries so weak?

Where then are we going? No one can say; for we already lack terms for comparison: conditions are more equal among Christians in our day than they have ever been in any time or any country in the world; thus the greatness of what has already been done prevents us from foreseeing what can still be done.

The entire book that you are going to read was written under the pressure of a sort of religious terror in the author's soul, produced by the sight of this irresistible revolution that for so many centuries has marched over all obstacles, and that one sees still advancing today amid the ruins it has made.

It is not necessary that God himself speak in order for us to discover sure signs of his will; it suffices to examine the usual course of nature and the

*Martin Luther published his 95 Theses in 1517.

continuous tendency of events; I know without the Creator's raising his voice that the stars follow the arcs in space that his finger has traced.

If long observation and sincere meditation led men in our day to recognize that the gradual and progressive development of equality is at the same time the past and the future of their history, this discovery alone would give that development the sacred character of the sovereign master's will. To wish to stop democracy would then appear to be to struggle against God himself, and it would only remain for nations to accommodate themselves to the social state that Providence imposes on them.

Christian peoples in our day appear to me to offer a frightening spectacle; the movement that carries them along is already strong enough that it cannot be suspended, and it is not yet rapid enough to despair of directing it: their fate is in their hands, but soon it will escape them.

To instruct democracy, if possible to reanimate its beliefs, to purify its mores, to regulate its movements, to substitute little by little the science of affairs for its inexperience, and knowledge of its true interests for its blind instincts; to adapt its government to time and place; to modify it according to circumstances and men: such is the first duty imposed on those who direct society in our day.

A new political science is needed for a world altogether new.

But that is what we hardly dream of: placed in the middle of a rapid river, we obstinately fix our eyes on some debris that we still perceive on the bank, while the current carries us away and takes us backward toward the abyss.

Among no people of Europe has the great social revolution I have just described made more rapid progress than among us; but here it has always proceeded haphazardly.

Never have heads of state thought at all to prepare for it in advance; it is made despite them or without their knowing it. The most powerful, most intelligent, and most moral classes of the nation have not sought to take hold of it so as to direct it. Democracy has therefore been abandoned to its savage instincts; it has grown up like those children who, deprived of paternal care, rear themselves in the streets of our towns and know only society's vices and miseries. One still seemed ignorant of its existence when it unexpectedly took power. Each then submitted with servility to its least desires; it was adored as the image of force; when afterwards it was weakened by its own excesses, legislators conceived the imprudent project of destroying it instead of seeking to instruct and correct it; and since they did not want to teach it to govern, they thought only of driving it from government.

As a result, the democratic revolution has taken place in the material of society without making the change in laws, ideas, habits, and mores that would have been necessary to make this revolution useful. Thus we have democracy without anything to attenuate its vices and make its natural advantages emerge; and while we already see the evils it brings, we are still ignorant of the goods it can bestow.

When royal power, leaning on the aristocracy, peacefully governed the peoples of Europe, society, amid its miseries, enjoyed several kinds of happiness one can conceive and appreciate only with difficulty in our day.

The power of some subjects raised insurmountable barriers against the tyranny of the prince; moreover, the kings, feeling themselves vested in the eyes of the crowd with an almost divine character, drew from the very respect they generated the will not to abuse their power.

The nobles, placed at an immense distance from the people, nevertheless took the sort of benevolent and tranquil interest in the lot of the people that the shepherd accords to his flock; and without seeing in the poor man their equal, they watched over his destiny as a trust placed by Providence in their hands.

The people, not having conceived the idea of a social state other than their own nor imagining that they could ever be equal to their chiefs, received their benefits and did not discuss their rights. They loved their chiefs when the chiefs were lenient and just, and they submitted to their rigors without trouble and without baseness, as they would to inevitable evils sent by the arm of God. Moreover, usage and mores had established boundaries for tyranny and had founded a sort of right in the very midst of force.

As the noble had no thought that anyone wanted to wrest from him privileges that he believed legitimate, and the serf regarded his inferiority as an effect of the immutable order of nature, one conceives a sort of reciprocal benevolence that could have been established between two classes sharing such different fates. One would see inequality and misery in society at that time, but souls were not degraded.

It is not the use of power or the habit of obedience that depraves men, but the use of power that they consider illegitimate, and obedience to a power they regard as usurped and oppressive.

On one side were [material] goods, force, leisure, and with these, pursuits of luxury, refinements of taste, pleasures of the mind, and cultivation of the arts; on the other side, work, coarseness, and ignorance.

But in the hearts of this ignorant and coarse crowd were energetic passions, generous sentiments, profound beliefs, and savage virtues.

Thus organized, the social body could have stability, power, and above all, glory.

But now ranks are confused; the barriers raised among men are lowered; estates are divided, power is partitioned, enlightenment spreads, intelligence is equalized; the social state becomes democratic, and finally the empire of democracy is peacefully established over institutions and mores.

I conceive a society, then, which all, regarding the law as their work, would love and submit to without trouble; in which the authority of government is respected as necessary, not divine, and the love one would bear for a head of state would not be a passion, but a reasoned and tranquil sentiment. Each having rights and being assured of preserving his rights, a manly confidence and a sort of reciprocal condescension between the classes would be established, as far from haughtiness as from baseness.

The people, instructed in their true interests, would understand that to profit from society's benefits, one must submit to its burdens. The free association of citizens could then replace the individual power of nobles, and the state would be sheltered from both tyranny and license.

I understand that in a democratic state constituted in this manner, society will not be immobile; but the movements of the social body can be regular and progressive; if one encounters less brilliance than within an aristocracy, one will find less misery; enjoyments will be less extreme and well-being more general; sciences less great and ignorance rarer; sentiments less energetic and habits milder; one will note more vices and fewer crimes.

In the absence of enthusiasm and ardent beliefs, enlightenment and experience will sometimes obtain great sacrifices from citizens; each man, equally weak, will feel an equal need of those like him; and knowing that he can obtain their support only on condition of his lending them his cooperation, he will discover without difficulty that his particular interest merges with the general interest.

The nation, taken as a body, will be less brilliant, less glorious, less strong, perhaps; but the majority of its citizens will enjoy a more prosperous lot, and the people will show themselves to be peaceful, not because they despair of being better-off, but because they know how to be well-off.

If everything were not good and useful in an order of things like this, society would at least have appropriated all the useful and good that it can present; and men, abandoning forever the social advantages that aristocracy can furnish, would have taken from democracy all the goods it can offer them.

But we, leaving the social state of our forebears, throwing their institutions, their ideas, and their mores pell-mell behind us—what have we gained in its place?

The prestige of royal power has vanished without being replaced by the majesty of the laws; in our day the people scorn authority, but they fear it, and fear extracts more from them than was formerly given out of respect and love.

I perceive that we have destroyed the individual entities that were able to struggle separately against tyranny; but I see that it is government alone that inherits all the prerogatives extracted from families, from corporations, or from men: the force of a small number of citizens, sometimes oppressive, but often protective, has therefore been succeeded by the weakness of all.

The division of fortunes has diminished the distance separating the poor from the rich; but in coming closer they seem to have found new reasons for hating each other, and casting glances full of terror and envy, they mutually repel each other from power; for the one as for the other, the idea of rights does not exist, and force appears to both as the sole argument in the present and the only guarantee of the future.

The poor man has kept most of the prejudices of his fathers without their beliefs; their ignorance without their virtues; he has taken the doctrine of interest as the rule of his actions without knowing the science of it, and his selfishness is as lacking in enlightenment as was formerly his devotion.

Society is tranquil not because it is conscious of its force and well-being, but on the contrary, because it believes itself weak and infirm; it fears it will die if it makes an effort: each feels the ill, but no one has the courage and energy needed to seek something better; like the passions of old men that end only in impotence, desires, regrets, sorrows, and joys produce nothing visible or lasting.

Thus we have abandoned what goods our former state could present without acquiring what useful things the current state could offer; we have destroyed an aristocratic society, and having stopped complacently amid the debris of the former edifice, we seem to want to settle there forever.

What is happening in the intellectual world is no less deplorable.

Hindered in its advance or abandoned without any support against its disordered passions, French democracy has overturned all that it has encountered in its way, shaking whatever it has not destroyed. We did not see it as it took hold of society little by little so as to establish its empire peacefully; it has not ceased its advance in the midst of the disorders and agitation of combat. Animated by the heat of the struggle, pushed beyond the natural limits of his opinion by the opinions and excesses of his adversaries, each loses sight of the very object of his pursuits and takes up a language that corresponds poorly to his true sentiments and secret instincts.

Hence the strange confusion we are forced to witness.

I search my memories in vain, and I find nothing that should evoke more sadness and more pity than what is passing before our eyes; it seems that in our day the natural bond that unites opinions to tastes and actions to beliefs has been broken; the sympathy that has been noticeable in all times between the sentiments and ideas of men appears destroyed; one would say that all the laws of moral analogy have been abolished.

One still encounters Christians among us, full of zeal, whose religious souls love to nourish themselves from the truths of the other life; doubtless they are going to be moved to favor human freedom, the source of all moral greatness. Christianity, which has rendered all men equal before God, will not be loath to see all citizens equal before the law. But by a strange concurrence of events, religion finds itself enlisted for the moment among the powers democracy is overturning, and it is often brought to reject the equality it loves and to curse freedom as an adversary, whereas by taking it by the hand, it could sanctify its efforts.

Alongside these men of religion I discover others whose regard is turned toward earth rather than Heaven; partisans of freedom not only because they see in it the origin of the noblest virtues, but above all because they consider it the source of the greatest goods, they sincerely desire to assure its empire and to have men taste its benefits: I understand that they are going to hasten to call religion to their aid, for they must know that the reign of freedom cannot be established without that of mores, nor mores founded without beliefs; but they have perceived religion in the ranks of their adversaries, and this is enough for them: some attack it, and others do not dare to defend it.

Past centuries have seen base and venal souls extol slavery, while independent minds and generous hearts were struggling without hope to save human freedom. But in our day one often encounters naturally noble and proud men whose opinions are in direct opposition to their tastes, and who vaunt the servility and baseness they have never known for themselves. There are others, on the contrary, who speak of freedom as if they could feel what is holy and great in it, and who noisily claim for humanity the rights they have always misunderstood.

I perceive virtuous and peaceful men whose pure mores, tranquil habits, ease, and enlightenment naturally place them at the head of the populations that surround them. Full of a sincere love of their native country, they are ready to make great sacrifices for it: nevertheless they are often found to be adversaries of civilization; they confuse its abuses with its benefits, and in their minds the idea of evil is indissolubly united with the idea of the new.

Nearby I see others who, in the name of progress, striving to make man into matter, want to find the useful without occupying themselves with the just, to find science far from beliefs, and well-being separated from virtue: these persons are said to be the champions of modern civilization, and they insolently put themselves at its head, usurping a place that has been abandoned to them, but from which they are held off by their unworthiness.

Where are we then?

Men of religion combat freedom, and the friends of freedom attack religions; noble and generous spirits vaunt slavery, and base and servile souls extol independence; honest and enlightened citizens are enemies of all progress, while men without patriotism and morality make themselves apostles of civilization and enlightenment!

Have all centuries, then, resembled ours? Has man, as in our day, always had before his eyes a world where nothing is linked, where virtue is without genius and genius without honor; where love of order is confused with a taste for tyrants and the holy cult of freedom with contempt for laws; where conscience casts only a dubious light on human actions; where nothing seems any longer to be forbidden or permitted, or honest or shameful, or true or false?

Shall I think that the Creator has made man so as to leave him to debate endlessly in the midst of the intellectual miseries that surround us? I cannot believe this: God prepares a firmer and calmer future for European societies; I am ignorant of his designs, but I will not cease to believe in them [merely] because I cannot penetrate them, and I would rather doubt my enlightenment than his justice.

There is one country in the world where the great social revolution I am speaking of seems nearly to have attained its natural limits; there it has operated in a simple and easy manner, or rather one can say that this country sees the results of the democratic revolution operating among us without having had the revolution itself.

The emigrants who came to settle in America at the beginning of the seventeenth century in some fashion disengaged the democratic principle from all those against which it struggled within the old societies of Europe, and they transplanted it alone on the shores of the New World. There it could grow in freedom, and advancing along with mores, develop peacefully in laws.

It appears to me beyond doubt that sooner or later we shall arrive, like the Americans, at an almost complete equality of conditions. I do not conclude from this that we are destined one day necessarily to draw the political consequences the Americans have drawn from a similar social state. I am very far from believing that they have found the only form of government that democracy can give itself; but it is enough that in the two countries the generative cause of laws and mores be the same, for us to have an immense interest in knowing what it has produced in each of them.

Therefore it is not only to satisfy a curiosity, otherwise legitimate, that I have examined America; I wanted to find lessons there from which we could profit. One would be strangely mistaken to think that I wanted to make a panegyric; whoever reads this book will be well convinced that such was not my design; nor was my goal to advocate such a form of government in general; for I number among those who believe that there is almost never any absolute good in the laws; I have not even claimed to judge whether the social revolution, whose advance seems to me irresistible, was advantageous or fatal to humanity; I have accepted this revolution as an accomplished fact or one about to be accomplished; and among the peoples who have seen it operating in their midst, I have sought the one in whom it has attained the most complete and peaceful development, in order to discern clearly its natural consequences, and to perceive, if possible, the means of rendering it profitable to men. I confess that in America I saw more than America; I sought there an image of democracy itself, of its penchants, its character, its prejudices, its passions; I wanted to become acquainted with it if only to know at least what we ought to hope or fear from it.

In the first part of this work I have therefore tried to show the direction that democracy, left in America to its penchants and abandoned almost without restraint to its instincts, has naturally given to the laws, the course it has imposed on the government, and in general, the power it has obtained over affairs. I wanted to know what have been the goods and ills produced by it. I searched for the precautions the Americans had made use of to direct it, and others they had omitted, and I undertook to distinguish the causes that permit it to govern society.

My goal was, in a second part, to paint the influence that equality of conditions and government by democracy in America exert on civil society, on habits, ideas, and mores; but I am beginning to feel less ardent to achieve this design. Before I could provide for the task I had proposed for myself, my work will have become almost useless. Another will soon show readers the principal features of the American character, and hiding the gravity of the portraits under a light veil, lend to truth charms with which I would not be able to adorn it.[1]

I do not know if I have succeeded in making known what I saw in America, but I am sure of sincerely having had the desire to do so and of

1. At the time I published the first edition of this work, M. Gustave de Beaumont [1802–1866], my traveling companion in America, was still working on his book, entitled *Marie: or, Slavery in the United States,* which has since appeared [published in 1835 as *Marie; ou, L'esclavage aux Etats-Unis: Tableau de moeurs américaines,* in the form of a novel with extensive notes and appendices]. Beaumont's principal goal was to put into relief and make known the situation of Negroes in the midst of Anglo-American society. His work will throw a vivid new light on the question of slavery, a vital question for the united republics. I do not know if I am mistaken, but it seems to me that Beaumont's book, after having keenly interested those who want to draw on its emotion and to find portraits there, will attain a still more solid and lasting success among readers who first of all desire real insights and profound truths.

never having knowingly succumbed to the need to adapt facts to ideas instead of submitting ideas to the facts.

When a point could be established with the aid of written documents, I took care to recur to original texts and to the most authentic and esteemed works.[2] I have indicated my sources in notes, and everyone can verify them. When it was a question of opinions, political usages, or observations of mores I sought the most enlightened men to consult. If it happened that the thing was important or dubious, I did not content myself with one witness, but made my determination only on the basis of all the testimonies together.

Here the reader must necessarily take me at my word. Often I could have cited as support for what I advance the authority of names known to him, or at least worthy of being known; but I have kept myself from doing so. The stranger often learns important truths in the home of his host that the latter would perhaps conceal from a friend; with a stranger one is relieved of obligatory silence; one does not fear his indiscretion because he is passing through. I recorded each of these confidences as soon as I received it, but they will never leave my portfolio;* I would rather diminish the success of my account than add my name to the list of those travelers who send back sorrows and embarrassments in return for the generous hospitality they have received.

I know that, despite my care, nothing will be easier than to criticize this book if anyone ever thinks of criticizing it.

I think those who want to regard it closely will find, in the entire work, a mother thought that so to speak links all its parts. But the diversity of the objects I had to treat is very great, and whoever undertakes to oppose an isolated fact to the sum of facts I cite or a detached idea to the sum of ideas will succeed without difficulty. I should therefore wish that one do me the favor of reading me in the same spirit that presided over my work, and that

---

*Some of these confidences did leave AT's portfolio after his death. His travel notebooks have been published under the title *Journey to America*.

2. Legislative and administrative documents were furnished to me with a kindness whose memory still prompts my gratitude. Among the American officials who thus favored my researches I shall cite above all Mr. Edward Livingston [1764–1836], then Secretary of State [under Andrew Jackson, 1831–1833] (now Minister Plenipotentiary at Paris [1833–1835]). During my visit to Congress, Mr. Livingston was very willing to hand over to me most of the documents I possess relative to the federal government. Mr. Livingston is one of those rare men whom one likes from having read their writings, whom one admires and honors even before having met them, and to whom one is happy to owe gratitude. [As a member of the state legislature of Louisiana, Livingston wrote his *Civil Code of the State of Louisiana* (1825); although not adopted by the legislature, it gained wide influence in Europe and the United States.]

one judge this book by the general impression it leaves, just as I myself decided, not by such and such a reason, but by the mass of reasons.

Nor must it be forgotten that the author who wants to make himself understood is obliged to push each of his ideas to all its theoretical consequences and often to the limits of the false and impractical; for if it is sometimes necessary to deviate from the rules of logic in actions, one cannot do so in discourse, and a man finds it almost as difficult to be inconsistent in his words as he does ordinarily to be consistent in his actions.

I end by pointing out myself what a great number of readers will consider the capital defect in the work. This book is not precisely in anyone's camp; in writing it I did not mean either to serve or to contest any party; I undertook to see, not differently, but further than the parties; and while they are occupied with the next day, I wanted to ponder the future.

PART ONE

Chapter 1 EXTERNAL CONFIGURATION OF NORTH AMERICA

North America divided into two vast regions, one sloping toward the pole, the other toward the equator.—Mississippi Valley.—Traces one encounters there of the revolutions of the earth.—Shore of the Atlantic Ocean on which the English colonies were founded.—Different aspects that South America and North America presented at the period of discovery.—Forests of North America.—Prairies.—Wandering tribes of natives.—Their external [appearance], their mores, their languages.—Traces of an unknown people.

North America, in its external configuration, presents general features that are easy to discern at first glance.

A sort of methodical order presided over the separation of land and water, of mountains and valleys. A simple and majestic arrangement reveals itself in the very midst of a confusion of objects and amongst the extreme variety of tableaux.

Two vast regions divide it in an almost equal manner.

One has its limit to the north at the Arctic pole; to the east, to the west, are the two great oceans. It then moves toward the south and forms a triangle whose irregularly drawn sides finally meet below the Great Lakes of Canada.

The second begins where the first ends and extends over all the rest of the continent.

One is slightly inclined toward the pole, the other toward the equator.

The lands comprised by the first region slope toward the north on an incline so insensible that one could almost say they form a plateau. In the interior of this immense platform one encounters neither high mountains nor deep valleys.

The waters there wind almost randomly; rivers intermingle, join, part, find each other again, are lost in a thousand marshes, wander at each instant in the midst of a damp labyrinth they have created, and finally reach the polar seas only after innumerable circuits. The Great Lakes that end this first region are not encased, like most of those of the Old World, in hills or rocks; their banks are flat and rise only a few feet above the level of the water. Each of them therefore forms something like a vast bowl filled to the brim: the slightest changes in the global structure would propel their waves to the pole or toward the tropical sea.

The second region is more uneven and better prepared to become the permanent dwelling of man; two long chains of mountains divide it down all its length: one, under the name Alleghenies, follows the coast of the Atlantic Ocean; the other* runs parallel to the South Sea.†

The space enclosed between the two chains of mountains comprises 228,843 square leagues.[1] Its area is therefore around six times greater than that of France.[2]

This vast territory nevertheless forms only one valley, which, descending from the rounded summit of the Alleghenies, rises again, without meeting any obstacle, to the peaks of the Rocky Mountains.

At the bottom of the valley flows an immense river. One sees waters rushing toward it, descending from the mountains from all directions.

Formerly the French had called the river St. Louis, in memory of their absent native country; and the Indians, in their pompous language, named it the Father of Waters, or the Mississippi.

The Mississippi has its source at the boundary of the two great regions that I spoke of above, toward the summit of the plateau that separates them.

Near it another river[3] rises that discharges in the polar seas. The Mississippi itself sometimes seems uncertain of the path that it will take: several times it retraces its steps, and it is only after having slowed its course in the midst of lakes and marshes that it finally makes up its mind and slowly traces its route toward the south.

Sometimes tranquil at the bottom of the clay bed that nature has dug for it, sometimes swollen by storms, the Mississippi waters more than a thousand leagues in its course.[4]

Six hundred leagues[5] above its mouth, the river still has a mean depth of 15 feet, and ships of 300 tons go up it for a distance of nearly two hundred leagues.

Fifty-seven great navigable rivers bring their waters to it. Among the tributaries of the Mississippi may be counted a river of 1,300 leagues long,[6] one

---

*The Rocky Mountains.
†The Pacific Ocean.

1. 1,341,649 [square] miles. See *Darby's View of the United States* [William Darby, *View of the United States: Historical, Geographical, and Statistical* (Philadelphia: H. S. Tanner, 1828)], 469. I have reduced the miles to leagues of 2,000 toises [a toise is a unit of measure of 6½ feet].

2. France has 35,181 square leagues.

3. The Red River.

4. 2,500 miles, 1,032 leagues. See *Description of the United States*, by Warden, vol. 1, 166. [David Bailie Warden, *Description statistique, historique et politique des Etats-Unis de l'Amérique septentrionale, depuis l'époque des premiers établissemens jusqu'à nos jours* (Paris: Rey et Gravier, 1820). Warden (1772–1845), a naturalized American citizen, moved to Paris in 1814, where he served as a valuable resource for AT during the writing of *Democracy in America*.]

5. 1,364 miles, 563 leagues. See Warden, vol. 1, 169.

6. The Missouri. See Warden, vol. 1, 132 (1,278 leagues) [3,096 miles].

of 900,[7] one of 600,[8] one of 500,[9] four of 200,[10] without speaking of an innumerable multitude of streams rushing from all directions only to lose themselves within it.

The valley watered by the Mississippi seems to have been created for it alone; it dispenses good and evil at will, and in that it is like the god. Along the river, nature shows an inexhaustible fertility; as one moves away from its shores, the vigor of plants is exhausted, the soil grows thin, everything languishes or dies. Nowhere have the great convulsions of the earth left more evident traces than in the Mississippi Valley. The whole aspect of the country attests to the work of the waters. Its sterility as well as its abundance is their work. The flow of the primitive ocean has accumulated enormous layers of arable land at the bottom of the valley, which it has had time to level out. On the right bank of the river one encounters immense plains, smoothed like the surface of a field over which a laborer has passed his roller. By contrast, as one approaches the mountains, the terrain becomes more and more uneven and sterile; the soil there is so to speak broken in a thousand places, and primitive rocks appear here and there like the bones of a skeleton after time has consumed the muscles and flesh around them. A granite sand and irregularly cut stones cover the surface of the land; with great difficulty a few plants push their shoots through these obstacles; one would say it is a fertile field covered with the debris of a vast edifice. In analyzing these stones and sand it is easy, in fact, to remark a perfect analogy between their substances and those that compose the arid and broken peaks of the Rocky Mountains. After having hurled the earth to the bottom of the valley, the waters doubtless in the end carried away with them part of the rocks themselves; they rolled them over the nearest slopes; and after having dashed one against another, they left the base of the mountains strewn with debris torn from their summits.*

The Mississippi Valley is, all in all, the most magnificent dwelling that God has ever prepared for the habitation of man, and nonetheless one can say that it still forms only a vast wilderness.

On the eastern slope of the Alleghenies, between the foot of those mountains and the Atlantic Ocean, extends a long band of rocks and sand that the sea, in retreating, seems to have forgotten. That territory is on average only

---

*See AT's note I, page 677.

7. The Arkansas. See Warden, vol. 1, 188 (877 leagues) [2,173 miles].

8. The Red River. See Warden, vol. 1, 190 (598 leagues) [1,450 miles].

9. The Ohio. See Warden, vol. 1, 192 (490 leagues) [1,188 miles].

10. The Illinois, the St. Pierre, the St. Francis, the Des Moines. In the above measures, I have taken for a base the legal mile (*statute mile*) and the post league of 2,000 toises [about 2.4 miles].

48 leagues in width,[11] but it measures 390 leagues in length.[12] The soil on this part of the American continent lends itself only with difficulty to the labors of the farmer. The vegetation on it is meager and uniform.

It was on that inhospitable coast that the first efforts of human industry were concentrated. On that tongue of arid land were born and grew the English colonies that were one day to become the United States of America. There one still finds the home of power today, while behind it are assembling, almost in secret, the true elements of the great people to whom the future of the continent doubtless belongs.

When the Europeans landed on the shores of the West Indies and later on the coasts of South America, they believed themselves transported to the fabulous regions that poets had celebrated. The sea sparkled with the fires of the tropics; for the first time the extraordinary transparency of its waters uncovered to the eyes of the navigator the depth of its chasms.[13] Here and there perfumed little islands were revealed that seemed to float like baskets of flowers on the tranquil surface of the ocean. All that was offered to view in those enchanted places seemed prepared for the needs of men or calculated for his pleasures. Most of the trees were laden with nourishing fruits, and those least useful to man charmed his regard with the dazzle and variety of their colors. In a forest of fragrant lemon trees, wild figs, round-leafed myrtle, acacias and oleander, all interlaced by flowering vines, a multitude of birds unknown in Europe displayed their wings, sparkling with purple and azure, and mixed the concert of their voices with the harmonies of a nature full of movement and life.*

Death was hidden beneath that brilliant cloak; but they did not then perceive it, and besides, in the air of those climates reigned a certain enervating influence that attached man to the present and rendered him careless of the future.

North America presented a different aspect: everything there was grave, serious, solemn; one would have said that it had been created to become the domain of the intellect, as the other was to be the dwelling of the senses.

*See AT's note II, page 678.

11. 100 miles.

12. Around 900 miles.

13. The waters are so transparent in the sea of the West Indies, says Malte-Brun, vol. 5, p. 726, that one distinguishes coral and fish 60 fathoms deep. A vessel seems to glide on air; a sort of vertigo seizes the traveler whose eye stares through the crystalline fluid into the midst of submarine gardens in which shellfish and gilded fish shine among the clumps of fucus and thickets of marine algae. [Conrad Malte-Brun, *Précis de la géographie universelle; ou, Description de toutes les parties du monde, sur un plan nouveau*, 8 vols. (Paris, 1810–1829). English edition: *Universal Geography; or, A Description of All Parts of the World, on a New Plan*, 8 vols. (Boston, 1824–).]

A turbulent, foggy ocean enveloped its shores; granite rocks or sandy shores served to ring it; the woods that covered its banks spread a somber and melancholy foliage; one saw hardly anything but pine, larch, live oak, wild olive, and laurel growing in them.

After having penetrated this first enclosure, one entered the shade of the central forest; there, a mix of the largest trees that grow in the two hemispheres was found. Plantain, catalpa, sugar maple, and Virginia poplar interlaced their branches with those of oak, beech, and linden.

As in forests subject to man's domain, death struck here relentlessly; but no one took charge of taking away the debris left behind. It therefore accumulated: time could not suffice to reduce it quickly enough to powder and to prepare new space. But in the very midst of this debris, the work of reproduction was constantly being pursued. Climbers and plants of every species came to light through the obstacles; they crept along fallen trees, insinuated themselves into their dust, lifted and broke the shriveled bark that still covered them, and cleared the way for their young shoots. Thus death came in a way to the aid of life. The one attended the other; they seemed to have wished to mix and confuse their works.

These forests concealed a profound darkness; a thousand streams, whose course human industry had not yet come to direct, maintained an eternal dampness. One barely saw a few flowers, a few wild fruits, a few birds.

The fall of a tree overturned by age, the cataract of a river, the bellowing of buffalo, and the whistling of the winds alone troubled the silence of nature.

To the east of the great river the woods partly disappeared; in their place boundless prairies spread out. Had nature in its infinite variety refused the seeding of trees in that fertile country, or had the forest that once covered them instead been destroyed by the hand of man? This is what neither tradition nor the research of science has been able to discover.

That immense wilderness was, however, not entirely deprived of the presence of man; for centuries, a few small tribes wandered under the shade of the forest or in the pastures of the prairie. From the mouth of the St. Lawrence to the delta of the Mississippi, from the Atlantic Ocean to the South Sea, these savages had points of resemblance among them that attested to their common origin. Yet they differed from all known races:[14] they were

---

14. One has since discovered some resemblance between the physical formation, language, and habits of the Indians of North America and those of the Tungus, Manchus, Mongols, Tartars, and other nomadic tribes of Asia. These are located near the Bering Strait, which permits one to suppose that in an ancient period they were able to come to people the wilderness continent of America. But science has not yet succeeded in clarifying this point. See on this question Malte-Brun, vol. 5; the works of Mr. [Alexander von] Humboldt [*Vues des Cordillères, et monumens des peuples indigènes de l'Amérique* (Paris: Chez F. Schoell, 1810)]; Fischer, *Conjectures on*

neither white like Europeans nor yellow like most Asians nor black like Negroes; their skin was reddish, their hair long and shiny, their lips thin, and the bones of their cheeks very prominent. The tongues spoken by the small savage tribes of America differed in their words, but all were subject to the same grammatical rules. These rules diverged at several points from those that had appeared until then to direct the formation of language among men.

The idiom of the Americans seemed the product of new combinations; it announced an effort of intelligence on the part of its inventors of which the Indians of our day appear hardly capable.*

The social state of those peoples also differed in several respects from what one saw in the Old World: one would have said that they had multiplied freely in the heart of their wilderness, having no contact with races more civilized than theirs. One therefore did not encounter among them those dubious and incoherent notions of good and evil, that profound corruption that is ordinarily mixed with ignorance and rudeness of mores in orderly nations that have reverted to barbarism. The Indian owed nothing except to himself; his virtues, his vices, his prejudices were his own work; he had grown up in the savage independence of his nature.

The coarseness of men of the people in orderly countries comes not only from the fact that they are ignorant and poor, but from the fact that while being so, they find themselves in daily contact with enlightened and wealthy men.

The sight of their misfortune and weakness, which contrasts every day with the happiness and power of some of those like them, excites anger and fear at the same time in their hearts; the sense of their inferiority and dependence irritates and humiliates them. That internal state of soul is reproduced in their mores as well as in their language; they are at once insolent and base.

The truth of this is easily proved by observation. The people are coarser in aristocratic countries than everywhere else, in opulent cities than in the countryside.

In places where one encounters men so strong and so wealthy, the weak

---

*See AT's note III, page 678.

---

the Origin of the Americans [Jean-Eberhard Fischer, De l'origine des Américains (Saint Petersburg, 1771)]; Adair, History of the American Indians [James Adair, The History of the American Indians: Particularly Those Nations Adjoining to the Mississippi, East and West Florida, Georgia, South and North Carolina, and Virginia; Containing an Account of Their Origin, Language, Manners, Religious and Civil Customs, Laws, Form of Government, Punishments, Conduct in War and Domestic Life; Their Habits, Diet, Agriculture, Manufactures, Disease and Methods of Cure . . . (London, 1775)].

and poor feel overwhelmed by their own baseness; not discovering any point by which they could regain equality, they wholly despair for themselves and allow themselves to fall below human dignity.

This distressing effect of the contrast of conditions is not found in savage life: the Indians, at the same time that they are all ignorant and poor, are all equal and free.

At the arrival of the Europeans, the native of North America was still ignorant of the value of wealth and showed himself indifferent to the well-being that civilized man acquires with it. Nevertheless, there was nothing coarse to be perceived in him; on the contrary, in his modes of acting there reigned an habitual reserve and a sort of aristocratic politeness.

Mild and hospitable in peace, pitiless in war, even beyond the known boundaries of human ferocity, the Indian would expose himself to die of hunger in order to assist the stranger who knocked at the door of his hut in the night, and with his own hands he would tear off the palpitating limbs of his prisoner. The most famous ancient republics had never admired a firmer courage, prouder souls, a more intractable love of independence than was then hiding in the wild woods of the New World.[15] The Europeans made only a small impression in landing on the shores of North America; their presence gave rise neither to envy nor to fear. What hold could they have had on such men? The Indian knew how to live without needs, to suffer without complaining, to die singing.[16] Furthermore, like all other members of the great

15. "One has seen among the Iroquois attacked by superior forces," says President Jefferson (*Notes on Virginia*, 148), "old men disdain to recur to flight or to survive the destruction of their country, and brave death like the ancient Romans in the sack of Rome by the Gauls."

Further on, p. 150: "There never was an instance known of an Indian begging his life when in the power of his enemies: on the contrary, he courts death by every possible insult and provocation." [AT has used a French edition of the *Notes on the State of Virginia: Observations sur la Virginie* (Paris, 1786). Jefferson's friend Charles Thomson, Secretary of Congress, wrote a commentary on the *Notes*, which Jefferson included as an appendix to his work. The edition used by AT quietly incorporates both Thomson's comments and Jefferson's own notes directly into the text of *Notes on the State of Virginia*. Thus the sentence AT quotes from p. 148 is in fact from Thomson's commentary; the words from p. 150 are from Jefferson's notes to the work.]

16. See *History of Louisiana*, by Lepage-Dupratz [Le Page du Pratz, *Histoire de la Louisiane, contenant la découverte de ce vaste pays; sa description géographique; un voyage dans les terres; l'histoire naturelle, les moeurs, coutumes and religion des naturels, avec leurs origines; deux voyages dans le nord du nouveau Mexique, dont un jusqu'à la Mer du Sud*, 3 vols. (Paris, 1758). English edition: *The History of Louisiana, or of the Western Parts of Virginia and Carolina . . .* , 2 vols. (London, 1763)]; Charlevoix, *History of New France* [Pierre-François-Xavier de Charlevoix, *Histoire et description générale de la Nouvelle France*, 6 vols. (Paris, 1744)]; Letters of R. Hecwelder, *Transactions of the American Philosophical Society*, vol. 1 [Rev. John Heckewelder, "Correspondence between Mr. Heckewelder and Mr. Duponceau, On the Languages of the American Indians," in *Transactions of the Historical and Literary Committee of the American Philosophical Society*

human family, these savages believed in the existence of a better world, and under different names they adored God, the creator of the universe. Their notions on great intellectual truths were generally simple and philosophical.*

However primitive appears the people whose character we are tracing here, nonetheless, one cannot doubt that another people more civilized, more advanced than it in all things, preceded it in these same regions.

An obscure but widespread tradition among most of the Indian tribes on the shores of the Atlantic teaches us that formerly the dwelling of the same peoples had been located to the west of the Mississippi. Along the banks of the Ohio and in all of the central valley, every day one still finds mounds raised by the hand of man. When one digs to the center of these monuments, they say, one can scarcely fail to encounter human remains, strange instruments, arms, utensils of all kinds—made of metal, or recalling usages unknown to current races.

The Indians of our day cannot give any information about the history of that unknown people. Nor did those who lived three hundred years ago, at the discovery of America, say anything from which one can even infer an hypothesis. Traditions, those perishable and constantly re-emergent monuments of a primitive world, furnish no light. There, however, lived thousands of those like us; one cannot doubt it. When did they come, what was their origin, their destiny, their history? When and how did they perish? No one could say.

A strange thing! There are peoples who have so completely disappeared from the earth that the very memory of the name has been effaced; their languages are lost, their glory has vanished like a sound without an echo; but I do not know if there is a single one of them that has not at least left a tomb in memory of its passing. Thus, of all the works of man, the most lasting is still the one that best recounts his nothingness and his miseries!

Although the vast country that I have just described was inhabited by numerous tribes of natives, one can justly say that at the period of discovery it still formed only a wilderness. The Indians occupied it, but they did not possess it. It is by agriculture that man appropriates the soil, and the first

---

*See AT's note IV, page 679.

(Philadelphia, 1819): vol. 1, 351–450.]; Jefferson, *Notes on Virginia*, 135–190. [AT's edition rearranges Jefferson's work; the pages cited are from Query VI and Query XI, and also from the notes of Jefferson and the comments of Charles Thomson on the text (see note 15 above). Cf. *Notes on the State of Virginia* (Chapel Hill, N.C., 1955), 58–65, 100–102, 199–202, 207, 273–277, 282.] What Jefferson says is above all of great weight because of the personal merit of the writer, his particular position, and the positive and exact century in which he wrote.

inhabitants of North America lived from products of the hunt. Their implacable prejudices, their indomitable passions, their vices, and perhaps still more their savage virtues, delivered them to an inevitable destruction. The ruin of these peoples began on the day when the Europeans landed on their shores; it has continued ever since; in our day it is finishing its work. Providence, in placing them in the midst of the wealth of the New World, seemed to have given them only a short lease on it; they were there, in a way, only *in the meantime.* Those coasts, so well prepared for commerce and industry, those rivers so deep, that inexhaustible Mississippi Valley, that continent as a whole, then appeared as the still-empty cradle of a great nation.

It was there that civilized men were to try to build a society on new foundations, and applying for the first time theories until then unknown or reputed inapplicable, they were going to give the world a spectacle for which the history of the past had not prepared it.

෴ ෴ ෴ ෴ ෴ ෴ ෴ ෴ ෴ ෴ ෴ ෴ ෴ ෴ ෴ ෴ ෴ ෴ ෴ ෴

Chapter 2 ON THE POINT OF DEPARTURE AND ITS IMPORTANCE FOR THE FUTURE OF THE ANGLO-AMERICANS

Utility of knowing the point of departure of peoples in order to understand their social state and their laws.—America is the only country where one has been able to perceive clearly the point of departure of a great people.—How all the men who came to people English America resembled each other.—How they differed.—Remark applicable to all the Europeans who came to settle on the shores of the New World.—Colonization of Virginia.—Same of New England.—Original character of the first inhabitants of New England.—Their arrival.—Their first laws.—Social contract.—Penal code borrowed from the legislation of Moses.—Religious ardor.—Republican spirit.—Intimate union of the spirit of religion and the spirit of freedom.

A man comes to be born; his first years are passed obscurely among the pleasures or travails of infancy. He grows up; manhood begins; the doors of the world finally open to receive him; he enters into contact with those like him. Then one studies him for the first time, and one believes one sees the seed of the vices and virtues of his mature age forming in him.

That, if I am not mistaken, is a great error.

Go back; examine the infant even in the arms of his mother; see the exter-

nal world reflected for the first time in the still-obscure mirror of his intelligence; contemplate the first examples that strike his eye; listen to the first
words that awaken the sleeping powers of his thought; finally, attend the first
struggles that he has to sustain; and only then will you understand where the
prejudices, habits, and passions that are going to dominate his life come
from. The man is so to speak a whole in the swaddling clothes of his cradle.

Something analogous takes place in nations. Peoples always feel [the
effects of] their origins. The circumstances that accompanied their birth and
served to develop them influence the entire course of the rest of their lives.

If it were possible for us to go back to the elements of societies and to
examine the first monuments of their history, I do not doubt that we could
discover in them the first cause of prejudices, habits, dominant passions, of
all that finally composes what is called national character; we would come to
encounter the explanation of usages that today appear contrary to the reigning mores; of laws that seem in opposition to recognized principles; of incoherent opinions that are encountered here and there in society like those
fragments of broken chains that one sometimes sees still dangling from the
vaults of an old building, no longer supporting anything. Thus would be
explained the destiny of certain peoples that an unknown force seems to
carry along toward a goal of which they themselves are ignorant. But until
now the facts have been lacking for such a study; the spirit of analysis has
come to nations only as they aged, and when at last they thought of contemplating their cradle, time had already enveloped it in a cloud, ignorance and
pride had surrounded it with fables behind which the truth lies hidden.

America is the only country where one has been able to witness the natural and tranquil developments of a society, and where it has been possible to
specify the influence exerted by the point of departure on the future of states.

At the period when European peoples descended on the shores of the New
World, the features of their national character had already been well fixed;
each of them had a distinct physiognomy; and as they had already reached
that degree of civilization that brings men to the study of themselves, they
have transmitted to us a faithful picture of their opinions, mores, and laws.
Men of the fifteenth century are almost as well known to us as those of ours.
America therefore shows us in broad daylight what the ignorance or barbarism of the first ages hid from our regard.

Near enough to the period when the American societies were founded to
know their elements in detail, already far enough from that time to be able
to judge what those seeds have produced, men of our day seem to be destined
to see much further into human events than their predecessors. Providence
has put a torch within our reach that our fathers lacked and has permitted

us to discern in the destiny of nations first causes that the obscurity of the past concealed from them.

When, after having attentively studied the history of America, one carefully examines its political and social state, one feels profoundly convinced of this truth: there is not one opinion, one habit, one law, I could say one event, that the point of departure does not explain without difficulty. Those who read this book will therefore find in the present chapter the seed of what is to follow and the key to almost the whole work.

The emigrants who came at different periods to occupy the territory that today covers the American Union differed from one another in many points; their goal was not the same, and they governed themselves according to diverse principles.

Nevertheless, these men had some common features among themselves, and they all found themselves in an analogous situation.

The bond of language is perhaps the strongest and most lasting that can unite men. All the emigrants spoke the same tongue; they were all children of one and the same people. Born in a country that the struggle of parties had agitated for centuries, and where factions had been obliged in their turn to place themselves under the protection of the laws, their political education had taken place in that rough school, and one saw more notions of rights, more principles of true freedom spread among them than in most of the peoples of Europe. In the period of the first emigrations, township government, that fertile seed of free institutions, had already entered profoundly into English habits, and with it the dogma of the sovereignty of the people was introduced into the very heart of the Tudor monarchy.

They were then in the midst of the religious quarrels that agitated the Christian world. England had thrown itself with a sort of fury onto this new course. The character of the inhabitants, which had always been grave and reflective, had become austere and argumentative. Education had been much increased in these intellectual struggles; the mind had received a more profound cultivation. While they had been absorbed in speaking of religion, mores had become purer. All these general features of the nation were found more or less in the physiognomy of those of its sons who had come to seek a new future on the opposite shores of the ocean.

One remark, moreover, which we shall have occasion to come back to later,* is applicable not only to the English, but also to the French, the Spanish, and all the Europeans who came successively to settle on the shores of the New World. All the new European colonies contained, if not the develop-

*DA I 2.9.

ment, at least the seed of a complete democracy. Two causes led to this result: one can say that in general, on their departure from the mother country, the emigrants had no idea of any superiority whatsoever of some over others. It is hardly the happy and the powerful who go into exile, and poverty as well as misfortune are the best guarantees of equality known among men. It nevertheless happened that on several occasions great lords came to America as a consequence of political or religious quarrels. Laws were made to establish a hierarchy of ranks, but they soon perceived that the American soil absolutely repelled territorial aristocracy. They saw that to clear that rebellious land, nothing less than the constant and interested efforts of the property owner himself were necessary. When the ground was prepared, it was found that its profits were not great enough to enrich a master and a tenant farmer at once. The territory was therefore naturally cut up into small estates that the property owner alone cultivated. Now, aristocracy takes to the land; it attaches to the soil and leans on it; it is not established by privileges alone, nor constituted by birth; it is landed property transmitted by heredity. A nation can offer immense fortunes and great miseries; but if these fortunes are not territorial, one sees poor and rich within it; there is, to tell the truth, no aristocracy.

All the English colonies therefore had among them, at the period of their birth, a great family resemblance. All, from their beginning,* seemed destined to offer the development of freedom, not the aristocratic freedom of their mother country, but the bourgeois and democratic freedom of which the history of the world had still not offered a complete model.

In this general complexion, however, were very strong nuances that are necessary to show.

In the great Anglo-American family one can distinguish two principal offshoots that, up to the present, have grown without being entirely confused, one in the South, the other in the North.

Virginia received the first English colony. The emigrants arrived there in 1607. Europe at that period was still singularly preoccupied with the idea that gold and silver mines made the wealth of peoples: a fatal idea that has more impoverished the European nations that gave themselves to it, and destroyed more men in America, than have war and all bad laws together. It was thus gold seekers who were sent to Virginia,[1] people without resources or without

---

*Or, "from their principle."

1. The charter granted by the English Crown in 1609 had among other clauses that the colonists should pay the Crown a fifth of the profit of gold and silver mines. See *Life of Washington*, by Marshall, vol. 1, 18–66. [John Marshall, *Vie de George Washington*, 5 vols. (Paris: Dentu, 1807). English edition: *The Life of George Washington* (London, 1804). John Marshall (1755–1835) was Chief Justice of the United States Supreme Court from 1801 until his death.]

[good] conduct, whose restive and turbulent spirits troubled the infancy of the colony[2] and rendered its progress uncertain. Afterwards, the industrialists and farmers arrived, a more moral and tranquil race, but one that was elevated in almost no points above the level of the lower classes of England.[3] No noble thought, no immaterial scheme presided at the foundation of the new settlements. Hardly had the colony been created when they introduced slavery;[4] that was the capital fact that was bound to exert an immense influence on the character, the laws, and the whole future of the South.

Slavery, as we shall explain later,* dishonors work; it introduces idleness into society, and with it, ignorance and haughtiness, poverty and luxury. It enervates the forces of the intellect and puts human activity to sleep. The influence of slavery, combined with the English character, explains the mores and social state of the South.

In the North, altogether contrary nuances were woven into this same English background. Here I shall be permitted some details.

In the English colonies of the North, better known under the name of the New England states,[5] the two or three principal ideas that today form the bases of the social theory of the United States were combined.

New England's principles spread at first to the neighboring states; later, they gradually won out in the most distant, and in the end, if I can express

---

* DA I 2.10.

2. A great part of the new colonists, says [William] Stith (*History of Virginia*), were young people of disordered families whose parents had sent them to spare them from an ignominious fate; former domestics, fraudulent bankrupts, debauched persons and other people of this kind, more suited to pillage and destroy than to consolidate the settlement, formed the rest. Seditious heads easily carried this troop along into all sorts of extravagances and excesses. See, relative to the history of Virginia, the following works:

   History of Virginia from the First Settlements to the Year 1624, by Smith [John Smith, *The Generall Historie of Virginia, New England, and the Summer Isles: With the Names of the Adventurers, Planters, and Governours from Their First Beginning, Ano. 1584, to This Present 1624* (London: Michael Sparkes, 1624)].

   History of Virginia, by William Stith [William Stith, *The History of the First Discovery and Settlement of Virginia: Being an Essay towards a General History of This Colony*, 8 vols. (Williamsburg, Va.: William Parks, 1747)].

   History of Virginia from the Earliest Period, by Beverley, translated into French in 1807 [Robert Beverley, *The History and Present State of Virginia* (London: R. Parker, 1705). French edition: *Histoire de la Virginie* (Amsterdam: T. Lombrail, 1707)].

3. Only later did a certain number of rich English property owners come to settle in the colony.

4. Slavery was introduced around the year 1620 by a Dutch vessel that unloaded twenty Negroes on the shores of the James River. See Chalmer [George Chalmers, *An Introduction to the History of the Revolt of the American Colonies*, vol. 1, 13 (London, 1782)].

5. The states of New England are those situated to the east of the Hudson: today they are six in number: (1) Connecticut; (2) Rhode Island; (3) Massachusetts; (4) Vermont; (5) New Hampshire; (6) Maine.

myself so, they *penetrated* the entire confederation. They now exert their influence beyond its limits, over the whole American world. The civilization of
New England has been like those fires lit in the hills that, after having spread
heat around them, still tinge the furthest reaches of the horizon with their
light.

The founding of New England offered a new spectacle; everything there
was singular and original.

Almost all colonies have had for their first inhabitants men without education and without resources, whom misery and misconduct drove out of
the country that gave birth to them, or greedy speculators and industrial
entrepreneurs. There are colonies that cannot even claim this origin: Santo
Domingo was founded by pirates, and in our day the English courts of justice
have taken charge of peopling Australia.

The emigrants who came to settle on the shores of New England all belonged to the well-to-do classes of the mother country. Their gathering on
American soil presented, from the origin, the singular phenomenon of a society in which there were neither great lords nor a people, and, so to speak,
neither poor nor rich. Proportionately, there was a greater mass of enlightenment spread among those men than within any European nation of our day.
All, perhaps without a single exception, had received a quite advanced education, and several among them had made themselves known in Europe by
their talents and their science. The other colonies had been founded by adventurers without family; the emigrants of New England brought with them
admirable elements of order and morality; they went to the wilderness accompanied by their wives and children. But what distinguished them above
all from all the others was the very goal of their undertaking. It was not
necessity that forced them to abandon their country; they left a social position they might regret and secure means of living; nor did they come to the
New World in order to improve their situation or to increase their wealth;
they tore themselves away from the sweetness of their native country to obey
a purely intellectual need; in exposing themselves to the inevitable miseries
of exile, they wanted to make *an idea* triumph.

The emigrants or, as they so well called themselves, the *pilgrims*, belonged
to that sect in England whose austere principles had brought the name Puritan to be given to it. Puritanism was not only a religious doctrine; it also
blended at several points with the most absolute democratic and republican
theories. Hence came its most dangerous adversaries. Persecuted by the government of the mother country, the rigor of their principles offended by the
daily workings of the society in which they lived, the Puritans sought a land
so barbarous and so abandoned by the world that they might yet be permitted to live there in their manner and pray to God in freedom.

A few quotations will make the spirit of these pious adventurers better known than anything we ourselves could add.

Nathaniel Morton, historian of the first years of New England, enters into the matter this way: "I have for some length of time," he says, "looked upon it as a duty incumbent, especially on the immediate successors of those that have had so large experience of those many memorable and signal demonstrations of God's goodness, viz. the first beginners of this plantation in New England, to commit to writing his gracious dispensations on that behalf; [...] that so, what we have seen, and what our fathers have told us, we may not hide from our children, showing to the generations to come the praises of the Lord. Psal. 78.3, 4. That especially the seed of Abraham his servant, and the children of Jacob his chosen, may remember his marvelous works (Psal. 105.5, 6.) [...] how that God brought a vine into this wilderness; that he cast out the heathen and planted it; and he also made room for it, and he caused it to take deep root, and it filled the land; so that it hath sent forth its boughs to the sea, and its branches to the river. Psal. 80.13, 15 [8, 9]. And not only so, but also that He hath guided his people by his strength to his holy habitation, and planted them in the mountain of his inheritance; (Exod. 15.13) [...] that as especially God may have the glory of all, unto whom it is most due; so also some rays of glory may reach the names of those blessed saints that were the main instruments [...]."[6]

It is impossible to read this beginning without receiving, despite oneself, a religious and solemn impression; one seems to breathe an air of antiquity and a sort of biblical perfume.

The conviction that animates the writer elevates his language. In your eyes, as in his, it is no longer a small troop of adventurers going to seek fortune beyond the seas; it is the seed of a great people that God comes to deposit from his hands onto a predestined land.

The author continues and paints the departure of the first emigrants in this manner:[7]

"So they left that goodly and pleasant city (Delft Haven), which had been their resting place [...]; but they knew that they were pilgrims and strangers here below, and looked not much upon these things, but lifted up their eyes

---

6. *New England's Memorial*, [13–]14: Boston, 1826. [The quote continues, "... of the beginning of this happy enterprise." Nathaniel Morton, *New-England's Memorial; or, A Brief Relation of the Most Memorable and Signal Passages of the Providence of God, Manifested to the Planters of New-England in America: With Special Reference to the First Colony Thereof, Called New-Plimouth* (Boston, 1826).] See as well Hutchinson's *History*, vol. 2, 440 [Thomas Hutchinson, *The History of the Colony of Massachusets-Bay: From the First Settlement Thereof in 1628 until Its Incorporation with the Colony of Plimouth, Province of Main, &c. by the Charter of King William and Queen Mary, in 1691*, 2d ed. (London, 1765)].

7. Morton, *New England's Memorial*, 22 [23–24].

to heaven, their dearest country, where God hath prepared for them a city
[...]. When they came to the place, they found the ship and all things ready;
and such of their friends as could not come with them, followed after them
[...]. One night was spent with little sleep with the most, but with friendly
entertainment, and Christian discourse, and other real expressions of true
Christian love. The next day [...] they went on board, and their friends with
them, where truly doleful was the sight of that sad and mournful parting, to
hear what sighs and sobs, and prayers did sound amongst them; what tears
did gush from every eye, [...] that sundry of the [...] strangers [...] could
not refrain from tears [...]. But the tide [...] calling them away, [...] their
reverend pastor falling down on his knees, and they all with him, with watery
cheeks commended them with most fervent prayers unto the Lord [...] and
then [...] they took leave one of another, which proved to be the last leave
to many of them."

The emigrants numbered nearly one hundred fifty men, women, and children. Their goal was to found a colony on the banks of the Hudson; but,
after having wandered on the ocean for a long time, they were finally forced
to land on the arid coasts of New England, at the place where the town of
Plymouth stands today. The rock on which the pilgrims descended is still
shown.[8]

"But before we pass on," says the historian that I have already cited, "let
the reader, with me, make a pause, and seriously consider this poor people's
present condition, the more to be raised up to the admiration of God's goodness towards them in their preservation:[9]

"For being now passed the vast ocean, and a sea of troubles before in their
preparation, they had now no friends to welcome them [...] no houses [...]
to repair unto to seek for succour: [...] for the season it was winter, and they
that know the winters of the country, know them to be sharp and violent,
subject to cruel and fierce storms, dangerous to travel to known places, much
more to search unknown coasts.—Besides, what could they see but a hideous
and desolate wilderness, full of wild beasts and wild men? And what multitudes of them there were, they then knew not; [...] all things stand in appearance with a weather-beaten face, and the whole country full of woods

8. This rock has become an object of veneration in the United States. I have seen fragments
of it carefully preserved in several towns of the Union. Does this not show very clearly that the
power and greatness of man is wholly in his soul? Here is a stone that the feet of some miserable
persons touched for an instant, and this stone becomes celebrated; it attracts the regard of a great
people; they venerate its remnants, they parcel out its dust in the distance. What has become of
the thresholds of so many palaces? Who cares about them?

9. [Morton,] *New England's Memorial*, 35[–36]. [AT omits some clauses in his quotation
from Morton, and AT's last clause is taken from the middle of Morton's passage. These changes
may perhaps alter Morton's meaning; see his full text.]

and thickets, represented a wild and savage hue; if they looked behind them, there was the mighty ocean which they had passed, and was now as a main bar and gulf to separate them from all the civil parts of the world.—[. . .] which way soever they turned their eyes (save upward to heaven) they could have little solace or content."

One must not believe that the piety of the Puritans was only speculative or that it showed itself foreign to the course of human things. Puritanism, as I said above, was almost as much a political theory as a religious doctrine. As soon as they disembarked on the inhospitable shore that Nathaniel Morton has just described, the first care of the emigrants was therefore to organize themselves in a society. They immediately passed an act stating:[10]

"We whose names are under written [. . .] having undertaken for the glory of God, and advancement of the Christian faith, and the honour of our King and country, a voyage to plant the first colony in the northern parts of Virginia; do by these presents solemnly and mutually, in the presence of God and one another, covenant and combine ourselves together into a civil body politick, for our better ordering and preservation, and furtherance of the ends aforesaid: And by virtue hereof, do enact, constitute and frame such just and equal laws, ordinances, acts, constitutions and officers, from time to time, as shall be thought most meet and convenient for the general good of the colony; unto which we promise all due submission and obedience."*

This took place in 1620. From that period onward, emigration never ceased. Each year, the religious and political passions that rent the British Empire during all the reign of Charles I drove a new swarm of sectarians to the coasts of the Atlantic. In England, the home of Puritanism continued to have its place in the middle classes; it was from the heart of the middle classes that most of the emigrants came. The population of New England grew rapidly, and while the hierarchy of ranks still classed men despotically in the mother country, the colony more and more offered the new spectacle of a society homogeneous in all its parts. Democracy such as antiquity had not dared to dream of sprang full-grown and fully armed from the midst of the old feudal society.

---

* [Morton,] *New England's Memorial,* 37–38.

10. The immigrants who created the state of Rhode Island in 1638, those who settled at New Haven in 1637, the first inhabitants of Connecticut in 1639, and the founders of Providence in 1640 also began by drafting a social contract that was submitted to the approval of all interested persons. Pitkin's *History,* 42, 47 [Timothy Pitkin, *A Political and Civil History of the United States of America: From the Year 1763 to the Close of the Administration of President Washington, in March, 1797: Including a Summary View of the Political and Civil State of the North American Colonies Prior to That Period,* 2 vols. (New Haven, 1828)].

Content to keep the seeds of trouble and the elements of new revolutions at a distance, the English government looked unworried on this numerous emigration. It even favored it with all its power and seemed hardly occupied with the destiny of those who came to American soil to seek refuge from the harshness of its laws. One would have said that it regarded New England as a region left to the dreams of the imagination, which one ought to abandon to the free trials of innovators.

The English colonies, and this was one of the principal causes of their prosperity, always enjoyed more internal freedom and more political independence than the colonies of other peoples; but nowhere was this principle of freedom more completely applied than in the New England states.

It was then generally accepted that the lands of the New World belonged to the European nation that had first discovered them.

In this manner, almost the whole coastal region of North America became an English possession toward the end of the sixteenth century. The means employed by the British government to people these new domains were of different natures: in certain cases, the king subjected a portion of the New World to a governor of his choice, charged with administering the country in his name and under his immediate orders;[11] this was the colonial system adopted in the rest of Europe. At other times, he conceded ownership of certain portions of a country to one man or to one company.[12] All civil and political powers were then concentrated in the hands of one or several individuals who, under the inspection and control of the Crown, sold the land and governed the inhabitants. Finally, a third system consisted in giving to a certain number of emigrants the right to form themselves into a political society under the patronage of the mother country, and to govern themselves in everything that was not contrary to its laws.

This mode of colonization, so favorable to freedom, was put into practice only in New England.[13]

---

11. That was the case of the state of New York.

12. Maryland, the Carolinas, Pennsylvania, and New Jersey were under this case. See Pitkin's *History*, vol. 1, 11–31 [13–30].

13. See in the work entitled *Historical Collection[s, Consisting] of State Papers and Other Authentic Documents Intended as Materials for an History of the United States of America*, by Ebenezer Hazard, printed at Philadelphia, MDCCXCII, a very great number of documents precious for their content and their authenticity, relative to the first age of the colonies, among others the different charters that were granted to them by the Crown of England as well as the first acts of their governments.

See also the analysis that Mr. Story, judge of the Supreme Court of the United States, makes of all these charters in the introduction of his *Commentary on the Constitution of the United States* [8–83 in the abridged edition used by AT (Boston, 1833)].

In 1628,[14] a charter of this nature was granted by Charles I to some emigrants who came to found the colony of Massachusetts.

But, in general, charters were granted to the colonies of New England only long after their existence had become an accomplished fact. Plymouth, Providence, New Haven, the states of Connecticut and Rhode Island[15] were founded without the concurrence and in a way without the knowledge of the mother country. The new inhabitants, without denying the supremacy of the metropolis, were not going to draw the source of their powers from its heart; they constituted themselves, and it was only thirty or forty years after, under Charles II, that a royal charter came to legalize their existence.

Thus it is often difficult, in running through the first historical and legislative memorials of New England, to perceive the bond that attaches the emigrants to the country of their ancestors. One sees them at each instant performing an act of sovereignty; they name their magistrates, make peace and war, establish police regulations, give themselves laws, as if they came under God alone.[16]

Nothing is both more singular and more instructive than the legislation of this period; there above all one finds the password to the great social enigma that the United States presents to the world in our day.

Among these memorials, we particularly distinguish, as one of the most characteristic, the code of laws that the little state of Connecticut passed in 1650.[17]

The legislators of Connecticut[18] occupied themselves first with penal laws;

It results from all these documents that the principles of representative government and the external forms of political freedom were introduced into all the colonies almost at their birth. These principles had received greater development in the North than in the South, but they existed everywhere.

14. See Pitkin's *History*, vol. 1, 35 [36]. See *The History of the Colony of Massachusetts*, by Hutchinson, vol. 1, 9.

15. See Pitkin, 42–47.

16. The inhabitants of Massachusetts deviated from usages followed in England in establishing criminal laws and civil procedures and courts of justice; in 1650, the name of the king no longer appeared at the head of judicial mandates. See Hutchinson, vol. 1, 452.

17. *Code of 1650*, 28[f.] (Hartford, 1830) [*The Code of 1650: Being a Compilation of the Earliest Laws and Orders of the General Court of Connecticut: Also, the Constitution, or Civil Compact, Entered Into and Adopted by the Towns of Windsor, Hartford, and Wethersfield in 1638–39: To Which Is Added Some Extracts from the Laws and Judicial Proceedings of New-Haven Colony, Commonly Called Blue Laws*].

18. See also in Hutchinson's *History*, vol. 1, 435–456, the analysis of the penal code adopted in 1648 by the colony of Massachusetts; that code was drafted on principles analogous to Connecticut's.

and, to compose them, they conceived the strange idea of drawing from sacred texts:

"If any man [after legal conviction], shall have or worship any other God but the Lord God," they say to begin with, "he shall be put to death."*

There follow ten or twelve provisions of the same nature, borrowed from the texts of Deuteronomy, Exodus, and Leviticus.

Blasphemy, sorcery, adultery,[19] and rape are punished by death; insult done by a son to his parents is struck with the same penalty. In this way they carried the legislation of a rude and half-civilized people into the heart of a society whose spirit was enlightened and mores mild; so one never saw the death penalty laid down more profusely in the laws, or applied to fewer of the guilty.

In this body of penal laws, the legislators are above all preoccupied with the care of maintaining moral order and good mores in society; so they constantly penetrate into the domain of conscience, and there is almost no sin that does not fall subject to the censure of the magistrate. The reader has been able to remark how severely these laws struck at adultery and rape. Simple keeping company among unmarried people is severely repressed. They allow the judge the right to inflict on the guilty one of three penalties: a fine, the whip, or marriage;[20] and, if one must believe the registers of the old tribunals of New Haven, prosecutions of this nature were not rare; one finds, on the date of May 1, 1660, a judgment bearing a fine and reprimand against a young woman who was accused of having pronounced some indiscreet words and of having allowed herself to be given a kiss.[21] The Code of 1650 abounds with preventive measures. Laziness and drunkenness are severely punished.[22] Innkeepers cannot furnish more than a certain quantity of wine to each consumer: a fine or the whip repress a simple lie when it can

---

* Code of 1650, 28.

19. Adultery was likewise punished by death by the law of Massachusetts, and Hutchinson, vol. 1, 441, says that several people in fact suffered death for that crime; he cites in this connection a curious anecdote that relates to the year 1663. A married woman had had amorous relations with a young man; she became a widow, she married him; several years passed; the public finally having come to suspect the intimacy that had reigned in the past between the two spouses, they were criminally prosecuted; they were put in prison, and both were very nearly condemned to death.

20. Code of 1650, 48. Apparently it sometimes happened that judges pronounced these various penalties cumulatively, as one sees in the decree rendered in 1643 (p. 114, New Haven Antiquities [appendix to the Code of 1650], holding that Marguerite Bedfort, convicted of engaging in reprehensible acts, shall submit to the penalty of the whip and that she shall be enjoined to marry Nicolas Jemmings, her accomplice).

21. New Haven Antiquities [Code of 1650], 104[–106]. See also in Hutchinson's History, vol. 1, 436, several judgments as extraordinary as that one.

22. [Code of 1650], 50, 57[–58].

do harm.[23] In other places, the legislator, forgetting completely the great principles of religious liberty he himself demanded in Europe, forces attendance at divine service by fear of fines,[24] and he goes as far as to strike with severe penalties,[25] and often death, Christians who wish to worship God according to a form other than his.[26] Sometimes, finally, the ardor for regulation that possesses him brings him to become occupied with cares most unworthy of him. So it is that one finds in the same code a law that prohibits the use of tobacco.[27] Furthermore, one must not lose sight of the fact that these bizarre or tyrannical laws were not imposed; that they were voted by the free concurrence of all the interested persons themselves; and that mores were still more austere and more puritanical than the laws. At the date of 1649, one sees a solemn association being formed in Boston having for its purpose to prevent the worldly luxury of long hair.[28]*

Such lapses doubtless bring shame to the human mind; they attest to the inferiority of our nature, which, incapable of firmly grasping the true and the just, is most often reduced to choosing between two excesses.

Beside this penal legislation, so strongly imprinted with the narrow spirit of sect and all the religious passions that persecution had exalted and that still fermented in the depth of souls, was placed and in a way connected to them a body of political laws which, drafted two hundred years ago, still seems to anticipate from very far the spirit of freedom in our age.

The general principles on which modern constitutions rest, the principles that most Europeans of the seventeenth century hardly understood and whose triumph in Great Britain was then incomplete, were all recognized and fixed by the laws of New England: intervention of the people in public affairs, free voting of taxes, responsibility of the agents of power, individual freedom and judgment by jury were established there without discussion and in fact.

*See AT's note V, page 680.

23. [Code of 1650], 64[–65].

24. [Code of 1650], 44.

25. This was not particular to Connecticut. See among others the law made on September 13, 1644, in Massachusetts that sentences the Anabaptists to banishment. Historical Collection of State Papers [by Hazard], vol. 1, 538. See also the law published on October 14, 1656, against the Quakers: "Whereas," says the law, "there is a cursed sect of heretics lately risen up [. . .] which are commonly called Quakers . . ." Provisions follow that sentence captains of vessels that bring Quakers into the country to a very great fine. Quakers who succeed in getting in are to be whipped and confined to prison to work. Those who defend their opinions are first to be given a fine, then sentenced to prison and expelled from the province. Same collection, vol. 1, 630.

26. In the penal law of Massachusetts, the Catholic priest who sets foot in the colony after having been expelled from it is punished by death.

27. Code of 1650, 96[–97].

28. [Morton,] New England's Memorial, 316.

These generative principles were applied and developed as no nation of Europe has yet dared to do.

In Connecticut the electoral body was composed, from the origin, of the universality of citizens, and that may be conceived without difficulty.[29] Among this nascent people there reigned then an almost perfect equality in fortunes and still more in intelligence.[30]

In Connecticut at that period all the agents of the executive power were elected, even the governor of the state.[31]

Citizens above sixteen years were obliged to bear arms; they formed a national militia that named its officers and had to be ready at all times to march for the defense of the country.[32]

In the laws of Connecticut, as in all those of New England, one sees arise and develop the township independence that in our day still forms the principle and the life of American freedom.

In most European nations, political existence began in the higher regions of society and was communicated little by little and always in an incomplete manner to the various parts of the social body.

In America, on the contrary, one can say that the township had been organized before the county, the county before the state, the state before the Union.

In New England, the township was completely and definitively constituted from 1650 on. Interests, passions, duties, and rights came to be grouped around the township's individuality and strongly attached to it. In the heart of the township one sees a real, active, altogether democratic and republican political life reigning. The colonies still recognize the supremacy of the metropolis; monarchy is the law of the state, but a republic is already very much alive in the township.

The township names its magistrates* of every kind; it taxes itself; it apportions and levies the impost on itself.[33] In the New England township the law of representation is not followed. Affairs that touch the interest of all are treated in the public square and within the general assembly of citizens, as in Athens.

---

*As AT will make clear in *DA* I 2.5, he uses the term "magistrate" to mean "all those who are charged with having the laws executed."

29. Constitution of 1638 [*Code of 1650*], 17.

30. In 1641, the General Assembly of Rhode Island declared unanimously that the government of the state consisted in a democracy and that power resided in the body of the free men, who alone had the right to make laws and to oversee the execution of them. *Code of 1650*, 70 [the correct reference is Pitkin's *History*, 47].

31. Pitkin's *History*, 47 [the correct reference is Constitution of 1638, 12].

32. Constitution of 1638, 12 [the correct reference is *Code of 1650*, 70].

33. *Code of 1650*, 80[f.].

When one studies attentively the laws that were promulgated during this first age of the American republics, one is struck by the intelligence about government and advanced theories of the legislator.

It is evident that he has a more elevated and more complete idea of the duties of society toward its members than European legislators at that time, and that he imposes on it obligations that it still avoided elsewhere. In the New England states, from the origin, the lot of the poor was made secure;[34] severe measures were taken for the upkeep of highways, they named officials to oversee them;[35] townships had public registers in which the result of general deliberations, deaths, marriages, the birth of citizens were inscribed;[36] court clerks were assigned for the keeping of these registers;[37] some officers were charged with administering vacant estates, others with overseeing the boundaries of inheritances; several had as their principal function to maintain public tranquillity in the township.[38]

The law enters into a thousand diverse details to anticipate and satisfy a host of social needs, about which in our day there are still only confused sentiments in France.

But it is by the prescriptions relative to public education that, from the beginning,* one sees revealed in the full light of day the original character of American civilization.

"It being one chief project," says the law, "of that old deluder, Satan, to keep men from the knowledge of the scriptures, as in former times, keeping them in an unknown tongue, so in these latter times, by persuading them from the use of tongues, so that at least, the true sense and meaning of the original might be clouded with false glosses of saint seeming deceivers; and that learning may not be buried in the grave of our forefathers, in church and commonwealth, the Lord assisting our endeavors . . ."[39] There follow the provisions that create schools in all townships and oblige the inhabitants, under penalty of heavy fines, to tax themselves to support them. In the most populous districts, high schools are founded in the same manner. Municipal magistrates must see to it that parents send their children to schools; they

---

*Or, "from principle."

34. *Code of 1650*, 78.

35. *Code of 1650*, 49[-50].

36. See the Hutchinson's *History*, vol. 1, 455.

37. *Code of 1650*, 86[f.].

38. *Code of 1650*, 40[-41].

39. *Code of 1650*, 90[-91]. [AT's version of the quotation is: "Whereas," says the law, "Satan, enemy of the human race, finds in the ignorance of men his most powerful arms, and whereas it is important that the enlightenment our fathers brought not remain buried in their tombs;—whereas the education of children is one of the first interests of the state, with the assistance of the Lord . . ."]

have the right to levy fines on those who refuse to; and if the resistance continues, society, then putting itself in place of the family, takes possession of the child and takes away from the parents the rights that nature gave them, but which they so poorly knew how to use.[40] The reader will doubtless have remarked the preamble of these ordinances: in America, it is religion that leads to enlightenment; it is the observance of divine laws that guides man to freedom.

When, after casting a rapid glance at American society in 1650, one examines the state of Europe, and particularly the continent, around that same period, one feels suffused with profound astonishment: everywhere on the continent of Europe at the beginning of the seventeenth century, absolute royalty was triumphing over the debris of the oligarchic and feudal freedom of the Middle Ages. In the heart of that brilliant and literary Europe the idea of rights had perhaps never been more completely misunderstood; never had peoples less lived a political life; never had notions of true freedom less preoccupied minds; and it was then that these same principles, unknown in European nations or scorned by them, were being proclaimed in the wilderness of the New World and were becoming the future creed of a great people. In that society, so humble in appearance, the boldest theories of the human mind, with which undoubtedly no statesman then had deigned to be occupied, were brought into practice; left to the originality of its nature, the imagination of man improvised there an unprecedented legislation. In the bosom of that obscure democracy, which still had not sired generals, or philosophers, or great writers, a man could rise in the presence of a free people and give, to the acclamation of all, this beautiful definition of freedom:

"[N]or would I have you to mistake in the point of your own *liberty*. There is a *liberty* of corrupt nature, which is affected both by *men* and *beasts*, to do what they list; and this *liberty* is inconsistent with *authority*, impatient of all restraint; by this *liberty*, *Sumus Omnes Deteriores* [we are all inferior]; 'tis the grand enemy of *truth* and *peace*, and all the *ordinances* of God are bent against it. But there is a civil, a moral, a federal *liberty*, which is the proper end and object of *authority*; it is a *liberty* for that only which is *just* and *good*; for this *liberty* you are to stand with the hazard of your very *lives*."[41]

40. *Code of 1650*, 83 [38–39, 91].

41. Mather's *Magnalia Christi Americana*, vol. 2, 13. [Cotton Mather, *Magnalia Christi Americana; or, The Ecclesiastical History of New-England* (Hartford, 1820). The correct reference is vol. 1, 116–117.]

This discourse was held by Winthrop; they accused him of having committed, as a magistrate, arbitrary acts; after having pronounced the discourse of which I have just recalled a fragment, he was acquitted with applause, and from then on he was always reelected governor of the state. See Marshall, vol. 1, 166. [AT cites the French edition. Cf. the English edition: *Life of George Washington*, 173f.]

I have already said enough to put the character of Anglo-American civilization in its true light. It is the product (and this point of departure ought constantly to be present in one's thinking) of two perfectly distinct elements that elsewhere have often made war with each other, but which, in America, they have succeeded in incorporating somehow into one another and combining marvelously. I mean to speak of the *spirit of religion* and the *spirit of freedom*.

The founders of New England were at once ardent sectarians and exalted innovators. While held within the tightest bonds of certain religious beliefs, they were free of all political prejudices.

Hence there are two tendencies, diverse but not contrary, traces of which it is easy to find everywhere in mores as in laws.

Men sacrifice their friends, their family, and their native country to a religious opinion; one can believe them to be absorbed in the pursuit of the intellectual good that they have come to buy at such a high price. One nevertheless sees them seeking with an almost equal ardor material wealth and moral satisfactions, Heaven in the other world and well-being and freedom in this one.

In their hands, political principles, laws, and human institutions seem malleable things that can be turned and combined at will.

Before them fall the barriers that imprisoned the society in whose bosom they were born; old opinions that have been directing the world for centuries vanish; an almost boundless course, a field without a horizon, are discovered: the human mind rushes toward them; it traverses them in all directions; but, when it arrives at the limits of the political world, it halts; trembling, it leaves off the use of its most formidable faculties; it abjures doubt; it renounces the need to innovate; it even abstains from sweeping away the veil of the sanctuary; it bows with respect before truths that it accepts without discussion.

Thus in the moral world, everything is classified, coordinated, foreseen, decided in advance. In the political world, everything is agitated, contested, uncertain; in the one, there is passive though voluntary obedience; in the other, there are independence, contempt for experience, and jealousy of every authority.

Far from harming each other, these two tendencies, apparently so opposed, advance in accord and seem to lend each other a mutual support.

Religion sees in civil freedom a noble exercise of the faculties of man; in the political world, a field left by the Creator to the efforts of intelligence. Free and powerful in its sphere, satisfied with the place that is reserved for it, it knows that its empire is all the better established when it reigns by its own strength alone and dominates over hearts without support.

Freedom sees in religion the companion of its struggles and its triumphs, the cradle of its infancy, the divine source of its rights. It considers religion as the safeguard of mores; and mores as the guarantee of laws and the pledge of its own duration.*

REASONS FOR SOME SINGULARITIES THAT THE LAWS AND CUSTOMS OF THE ANGLO-AMERICANS PRESENT

Some remains of aristocratic institutions in the heart of the most complete democracy.— Why?—One must distinguish carefully what is of Puritan origin and of English origin.

The reader must not draw consequences too general and too absolute from what precedes. The social condition, religion, and mores of the first emigrants doubtless exerted an immense influence on the destiny of their new country. Still, it was not for them to found a society whose point of departure was placed only in themselves; no one can disengage himself entirely from the past; they came, either voluntarily or without knowing it, to mix, with ideas and usages that were their own, other usages and other ideas that they got from their education or from the national traditions of their country.

When one wants to know and judge the Anglo-Americans of our day, one ought therefore to distinguish carefully what is of Puritan origin or of English origin.

In the United States, one often encounters laws or customs that contrast with all that surrounds them. These laws appear drafted in a spirit opposed to the dominant spirit of American legislation; these mores seem contrary to the sum of the social state. If the English colonies had been founded in a century of darkness, or if their origin were already lost in the night of time, the problem would be insoluble.

I shall cite a single example to make my thought understood.

The civil and criminal legislation of the Americans recognizes only two means of action: *prison* or *bail*. The first act of a proceeding consists in obtaining bail from the defendant, or if he refuses, in incarcerating him; afterwards, one discusses the validity of the title or the gravity of the charges.

It is evident that such legislation is directed against the poor and favors only the rich.

The poor man does not always find bail, even in civil matters, and if he is constrained to go await justice in prison, his forced inaction soon reduces him to misery.

The rich man, on the contrary, always succeeds in escaping imprisonment

*See AT's note VI, page 683.

in civil matters; even more, should he have committed a punishable offense, he easily escapes the punishment that ought to reach him: after having furnished bail, he disappears. One can therefore say that for him, all penalties that the law inflicts are reduced to fines.[42] What is more aristocratic than legislation like this?

In America, however, it is the poor who make the law, and they habitually reserve for themselves the greatest advantages of society.

It is in England that one must seek the explanation of this phenomenon: the laws I speak of are English.[43] The Americans have not changed them even though they are repugnant to the sum of their legislation and to the mass of their ideas.

The thing that a people changes least, after its usages, is its civil legislation. Civil laws are familiar only to jurists, that is to say, to those who have a direct interest in maintaining them as they are, good or bad, for the reason that they know them. The bulk of the nation hardly knows them; it sees them act only in particular cases, grasps their tendency only with difficulty, and submits to them without thinking about it.

I have cited one example, I could have pointed out many others.

The picture that American society presents is, if I can express myself so, covered with a democratic finish, beneath which from time to time one sees the old colors of aristocracy showing through.

෨෩ ෨෩

Chapter 3   SOCIAL STATE OF THE ANGLO-AMERICANS

The social state is ordinarily the product of a fact, sometimes of laws, most often of these two causes united; but once it exists, one can consider it as the first cause of most of the laws, customs, and ideas that regulate the conduct of nations; what it does not produce, it modifies.

In order to know the legislation and mores of a people, one must therefore begin by studying its social state.

---

42. There are doubtless crimes for which one does not receive bail, but they are very few in number.

43. See Blackstone [William Blackstone, *Commentaries on the Laws of England* (London, 1809)] and Delolme [Jean Louis de Lolme, *The Constitution of England* (London, 1826)], bk. 1, chap. 10.

THAT THE SALIENT POINT OF THE SOCIAL STATE OF THE ANGLO-AMERICANS IS ITS BEING ESSENTIALLY DEMOCRATIC

First emigrants of New England.—Equal among themselves.—Aristocratic laws intro-duced in the South. Period of the Revolution.—Change in estate laws.*—Effects pro-duced by this change.—Equality pushed to its furthest limits in the new states of the West.—Equality in intelligence.

One could make several important remarks about the social state of the Anglo-Americans, but there is one that dominates all others.

The social state of the Americans is eminently democratic. It has had this character since the birth of the colonies; it has it even more in our day.

I said in the preceding chapter that a very great equality reigned among the emigrants who came to settle on the shores of New England. Not even the seed of aristocracy was ever deposited in this part of the Union. One could never found any but intellectual influences here. The people were in the habit of revering certain names as emblems of enlightenment and of vir-tues. The voices of some citizens obtained a power over them that one per-haps rightly would have called aristocratic if it could have been regularly transmitted from father to son.

This took place east of the Hudson; to the southwest of this river and downward to Florida it was otherwise.

In most of the states situated to the southwest of the Hudson, great En-glish property owners had come to settle. Aristocratic principles, and with them English estate laws, had been imported. I have made known the reasons that prevented anyone from ever being able to establish a powerful aristoc-racy in America. These reasons, while holding southwest of the Hudson, nev-ertheless had less power there than east of that river. To the south one man alone, with the aid of slaves, could cultivate a great extent of land. One there-fore saw wealthy landed property owners in this part of the continent; but their influence was not precisely aristocratic as it is understood in Europe since they possessed no privileges, and since cultivation by slaves gave them no tenant farmers and consequently no patronage. Still, the great proprietors to the south of the Hudson formed a superior class, having ideas and tastes of its own and generally concentrating political action within itself. It was a sort of aristocracy little different from the mass of the people, whose passions and interests it easily embraced, exciting neither love nor hate; in sum, weak and not lively. It was this class that, in the South, put itself at the head of the insurrection: to it the American Revolution owes its greatest men.

*Lit.: "laws of succession."

In this period the whole of society was shaken: the people in whose name they had fought—the people, become a power, conceived the desire to act by themselves; democratic instincts were awakened; in breaking the yoke of the mother country, they got a taste for every kind of independence: little by little individual influences ceased to make themselves felt; habits as well as laws began to march in accord toward the same goal.

But it was estate law that made equality take its last step.

I am astonished that ancient and modern political writers have not attributed to estate laws[1] a greater influence on the course of human affairs. These laws belong, it is true, to the civil order; but they ought to be placed at the head of all political institutions, for they have an incredible influence on the social state of peoples, of which political laws are only the expression. They have, in addition, a sure and uniform manner of operating on society; in a way, they take hold of generations before their birth. Man is armed by them with an almost divine power over the future of those like him. The legislator regulates the estates of citizens once and he rests for centuries: motion having been given to his work, he can withdraw his hand from it; the machine acts by its own force and is directed as if by itself toward a goal indicated in advance. Constituted in a certain manner, it gathers, it concentrates, and it groups around some head property and soon after power; in a way, it makes aristocracy shoot up from the soil. Guided by other principles and launched on another track, its action is more rapid still; it divides, it partitions, it disperses goods and power; sometimes then it happens that one is frightened by the rapidity of its advance; despairing of stopping its movement, one seeks at least to create difficulties and obstacles before it; one wants to counterbalance its action by contrary efforts: useless cares! It crushes or shatters all that comes across its path, it rises up and falls back incessantly on the earth until all that can be seen is a shifting and impalpable dust on which democracy sits.

When estate law permits, and even more so when it orders equal partition of the father's goods among all the children, its effects are of two sorts; it is important to distinguish them carefully, although they tend to the same goal.

By virtue of estate law, the death of each property owner brings a revolution in property; not only do goods change masters, but they change, so to speak, nature; they are constantly fragmented into smaller portions.

1. I understand by estate laws all laws whose principal goal is to regulate the fate of goods after the death of the property owner.

The law of entail [lit.: "law on substitutions"] is among this number; it also has the result, it is true, of preventing the property owner from disposing of his goods before his death; but it imposes on him the obligation to preserve them only with a view to having them reach his inheritor intact. The principal goal of the law of entail is therefore to regulate the fate of goods after the death of the property owner. The rest is the means it employs.

That is the direct and in a way material effect of the law. In countries where legislation establishes equality of partition, goods and particularly territorial fortunes will therefore have a permanent tendency to diminish. Still, the effects of this legislation would make themselves felt only in the long term if the law were abandoned to its own forces; for if ever the family is not composed of more than two children (and the average of families in a country populated like France, it is said, is only three), these children, in partitioning the fortune of their father and mother, will not be poorer than each of the latter individually.

But the law of equal partition does not exert its influence only on the fate of goods; it acts on the very souls of property owners and calls their passions to its aid. It is its indirect effects that rapidly destroy great fortunes and above all great domains.

In peoples where estate law is founded on the right of primogeniture, territorial domains pass most often from generation to generation without being divided. The result is that family spirit is in a way materialized in the land. The family represents the land, the land represents the family; it perpetuates its name, its origin, its glory, its power, its virtues. It is an imperishable witness to the past and a precious pledge of existence to come.

When estate law establishes equal partition, it destroys the intimate connection that exists between the spirit of the family and preservation of the land; the land ceases to represent the family, for, since it cannot fail to be partitioned at the end of one or two generations, it is evident that it must constantly be diminished and in the end disappear entirely. The sons of a great landed property owner, if they are few in number, or if fortune is favorable to them, can indeed preserve the hope of being no less wealthy than their author, but not of possessing the same goods as he; their wealth will necessarily be composed of other elements than his.

Now, from the moment when you take away from landed property owners a great interest of sentiment, memories, pride, and ambition in preserving the land, you can be assured that sooner or later they will sell it, for they have a great pecuniary interest in selling it, since transferable assets produce more interest than others and lend themselves much more easily to satisfying passions of the moment.

Once divided, great landed properties are no longer remade; for the small property owner draws more revenue from his field[2] proportionately than the great property owner from his; he therefore sells it much more dearly than

---

2. I do not want to say that the small property owner cultivates better, but he cultivates with more ardor and care and regains by work what he lacks on the side of art.

the latter. Thus the economic calculations that brought the rich man to sell vast properties will with greater reason prevent him from buying small ones to reconstitute the great ones.

What is called family spirit is often founded on an illusion of individual selfishness. One seeks to perpetuate and in a way to immortalize oneself in one's remote posterity. Whenever the spirit of family ends, individual self-ishness reenters into the reality of its penchants. As the family no longer pre-sents itself to the mind as anything but vague, indeterminate, and uncertain, each concentrates on the comfort of the present; he dreams of the establish-ment of the generation that is going to follow, and nothing more.

One therefore does not seek to perpetuate one's family, or at least one seeks to perpetuate it by other means than landed property.

Thus not only does estate law make it difficult for families to preserve the same domains intact, but it takes away from them the desire to make the attempt, and it brings them in a way to cooperate with it in their own ruin.

The law of equal partition proceeds on two tracks: in acting on the thing, it acts on the man; in acting on the man, it arrives at the thing.

By these two manners it succeeds in profoundly attacking landed property and in making families as well as fortunes disappear with rapidity.[3]

It is doubtless not for us, the French of the nineteenth century, daily wit-nesses to the political and social changes to which estate law gives birth, to put its power in doubt. Every day we see it pass and repass constantly over our soil, overturning the walls of our dwellings in its path and destroying the enclosures of our fields. But if estate law has already done so much among us, much still remains for it to do. Our memories, our opinions, and our habits pose powerful obstacles to it.

In the United States, its work of destruction is nearly ended. It is there that one can study its principal results.

English legislation on the transmission of goods was abolished in almost all the states in the period of the Revolution.

---

3. Land being the most solid property, from time to time one encounters rich men who are disposed to make great sacrifices to acquire it and who willingly lose a considerable portion of their revenue to secure the rest. But those are accidents. The love of landed property is no longer habitually found except among the poor. The small landed property owner, who has less enlightenment, less imagination, and fewer passions than the great, is generally preoccupied only with the desire to increase his domain, and it often happens that inheritances, marriages, or the opportunities of commerce furnish him, little by little, the means for it.

Beside the tendency that brings men to divide land, therefore, there exists another that brings them to aggregate it. This tendency, which suffices to prevent properties from being divided infinitely, is not strong enough to create great territorial fortunes, nor above all to maintain them in the same families.

The law of entail was modified in such a manner as to hinder the free circulation of goods only in an imperceptible manner.*

The first generation passed; lands began to be divided. The movement became more and more rapid as time advanced. Today, when hardly sixty years have elapsed, the aspect of society is already unrecognizable; the families of the great landed property owners have almost all been swallowed up within the common mass. In the state of New York, where one used to count a very great number of them, hardly two† float above the chasm ready to seize them. Today the sons of these opulent citizens are men of commerce, attorneys, doctors. Most have fallen into the most profound obscurity. The least trace of ranks and hereditary distinctions is destroyed; estate law has done its leveling everywhere.

It is not that there are no rich in the United States as elsewhere; indeed, I do not know a country where the love of money holds a larger place in the heart of man and where they profess a more profound scorn for the theory of the permanent equality of goods.‡ But fortune turns there with incredible rapidity and experience teaches that it is rare to see two generations collect its favors.

However colored one supposes this picture, it still gives only an incomplete idea of what is taking place in the new states of the West and Southwest.

At the end of the last century hardy adventurers began to penetrate the valleys of the Mississippi. That was almost a new discovery of America: soon the bulk of the emigration came there; then one saw unknown societies issue all at once from the wilderness. States whose very names did not exist a few years before took their place within the American Union. In the West one can observe democracy reaching its furthest limit. In those states, improvised in a way by fortune, the inhabitants arrived only yesterday on the soil they occupy. They hardly know one another, and each is ignorant of the past of his closest neighbor. In that part of the American continent, the population therefore escapes not only the influence of great names and great wealth, but of that natural aristocracy that flows from enlightenment and virtue. No one there exercises the respectable power that men accord to the memory of an entire life occupied in doing good before one's eyes. The new states of the West already have inhabitants; society does not yet exist there.

But it is not only fortunes that are equal in America; up to a certain point equality extends to intelligence itself.

*See AT's note VII, page 689.

†In a marginal note, crossed out, AT specified the Livingstons and the Van Rensselaers.

‡Apparently a reference to the theories of the "Equalitarians" (as they were called in France in the 1830s), later called communists or socialists, and in France associated with the followers of François Babeuf (1760–1797).

I do not think that there is a country in the world where, in proportion to population, so few ignorant and fewer learned men are found than in America.

Primary instruction there is within reach of each; higher instruction is within reach of almost no one.

One understands this without difficulty, and it is so to speak the necessary result of what we advanced above.

Almost all Americans are comfortable; they can therefore readily procure for themselves the first elements of human knowledge.

In America there are few rich; almost all Americans therefore need to practice a profession. Now, every profession requires an apprenticeship. Americans, therefore, can only give the first years of life to the general cultivation of intelligence: at fifteen they enter into a career; thus their education most often ends in the period when ours begins. If it is pursued beyond this, it is then directed only toward a special and lucrative matter; one studies a science as one takes up a trade; and one takes from it only the applications whose present utility is recognized.

In America most of the rich have begun by being poor; almost all the idle were, in their youth, employed; the result is that when one could have the taste for study, one does not have the time to engage in it; and when one has acquired the time to engage in it, one no longer has the taste for it.

There does not exist in America, therefore, any class in which the penchant for intellectual pleasures is transmitted with comfort and inherited leisure, and which holds the works of the intellect in honor.

Thus the will to engage in these works is lacking as much as is the power.

In America a certain common level in human knowledge has been established. All minds have approached it; some by being raised to it, others by being lowered to it.

One therefore encounters an immense multitude of individuals who have nearly the same number of notions in matters of religion, of history, of science, of political economy, of legislation, of government.

Intellectual inequality comes directly from God, and man cannot prevent it from existing always.

But it happens, at least from what we have just said, that intelligence, while remaining unequal as the Creator wished, finds equal means at its disposition.

So, therefore, in our day in America the aristocratic element, always weak since its birth, is, if not destroyed, at least weakened, so that it is difficult to assign it any influence whatsoever in the course of affairs.

Time, events, and the laws have, on the contrary, rendered the democratic element not only preponderant there, but so to speak unique. No influence of family or corporation is allowed to be perceived; often one cannot even discover any individual influence however little lasting.

America therefore presents the strangest phenomenon in its social state. Men show themselves to be more equal in their fortunes and in their intelligence or, in other terms, more equally strong than they are in any country in the world and than they have been in any century of which history keeps a memory.

POLITICAL CONSEQUENCES OF THE SOCIAL STATE OF THE ANGLO-AMERICANS

The political consequences of such a social state are easy to deduce.

It is impossible to understand how equality will not in the end penetrate the political world as elsewhere. One cannot conceive of men eternally unequal among themselves on one point alone, equal on all others; they will therefore arrive in a given time at being equal on all.

Now I know only two manners of making equality reign in the political world: rights must be given to each citizen or to no one.

For peoples who have reached the same social state as the Anglo-Americans it is therefore very difficult to perceive a middle term between the sovereignty of all and the absolute power of one alone.

One must not dissimulate the fact that the social state I have just described lends itself almost as readily to the one as to the other of its two consequences.

There is in fact a manly and legitimate passion for equality that incites men to want all to be strong and esteemed. This passion tends to elevate the small to the rank of the great; but one also encounters a depraved taste for equality in the human heart that brings the weak to want to draw the strong to their level and that reduces men to preferring equality in servitude to inequality in freedom. It is not that peoples whose social state is democratic naturally scorn freedom; on the contrary, they have an instinctive taste for it. But freedom is not the principal and continuous object of their desire; what they love with an eternal love is equality; they dash toward freedom with a rapid impulse and sudden efforts, and if they miss the goal they resign themselves; but nothing can satisfy them without equality, and they would sooner consent to perish than to lose it.

On the other hand, when citizens are all nearly equal, it becomes difficult for them to defend their independence against the aggressions of power. Since no one among them is strong enough then to struggle alone to advantage, it is only the combination of the forces of all that can guarantee freedom. Now, such a combination is not always met with.

Peoples can therefore draw two great political consequences from the same social state: these consequences differ prodigiously between themselves, but they both issue from the same fact.

The first to be submitted to the formidable alternative that I have just described, the Anglo-Americans have been happy enough to escape absolute power. Circumstances, origin, enlightenment, and above all mores have permitted them to found and maintain the sovereignty of the people.

꒜ ꒜

Chapter 4 ON THE PRINCIPLE OF THE SOVEREIGNTY OF THE PEOPLE IN AMERICA

It dominates all of American society.—Application that the Americans already made of this principle before their revolution.—Development that their revolution gave to it.— Gradual and irresistible lowering of the property qualification.

When one wants to speak of the political laws of the United States, it is always with the dogma of the sovereignty of the people that one must begin.

The principle of the sovereignty of the people, which is always more or less at the foundation of almost all human institutions, ordinarily dwells there almost buried. One obeys it without recognizing it, or if sometimes it happens to be brought out in broad daylight for a moment, one soon hastens to plunge it back into the darkness of the sanctuary.

National will is one of the terms that intriguers in all times and despots in all ages have most largely abused. Some have seen its expression in the bought suffrage of a few agents of power; others in the votes of an interested or fearful minority; there are even some who have discovered it fully expressed in the silence of peoples, and who have thought that from the *fact* of obedience arises the *right* for them to command.

In America, the principle of the sovereignty of the people is not hidden or sterile as in certain nations; it is recognized by mores, proclaimed by the laws; it spreads with freedom and reaches its final consequences without obstacle.

If there is a single country in the world where one can hope to appreciate the dogma of the sovereignty of the people at its just value, to study it in its application to the affairs of society, and to judge its advantages and its dangers, that country is surely America.

I said previously that from the origin, the principle of the sovereignty of the people was the generative principle of most of the English colonies of America.*

It was nevertheless very far from dominating the government of society then as it does in our day.

Two obstacles, one external, the other internal, slowed its pervasive advance.

It could not come to light outwardly within the laws since the colonies were still constrained to obey the mother country; it was therefore reduced to hiding itself in provincial assemblies and above all in the township. There it spread in secret.

American society then was not yet prepared to adopt it in all its consequences. As I brought out in the preceding chapter, enlightenment in New England and wealth to the south of the Hudson long exerted a sort of aristocratic influence that tended to narrow into few hands the exercise of social powers. They were still very far from having all public officials elected and all citizens electors. Everywhere electoral rights were confined within certain limits and subordinated to the existence of a property qualification. That property qualification was very low in the North, more considerable in the South.

The American Revolution broke out. The dogma of the sovereignty of the people came out from the township and took hold of the government; all classes committed themselves to its cause; they did combat and they triumphed in its name; it became the law of laws.

A change almost as rapid was effected in the interior of society. Estate law served to break down local influences.

At the moment when this effect of the laws and of the Revolution began to reveal itself to all eyes, victory had already been irrevocably pronounced in favor of democracy. Power was, in fact, in its hands. It was no longer permissible even to struggle against it. The upper classes therefore submitted without a murmur and without combat to an evil henceforth inevitable. What happens ordinarily to powers that fall happened to them: individual selfishness took hold in their members; as they could no longer tear force from the hands of the people and as they did not detest the multitude enough to take pleasure in defying it, they no longer dreamed of anything except gaining its good will at any price. The most democratic laws were therefore voted in a rivalry among the men whose interests they bruised the most. In this manner the upper classes did not excite popular passions against them; but they themselves hastened the triumph of the new order. Thus, a singular

*DA I 1.2.

thing! One saw the democratic impulse more irresistible in states where aristocracy had the deepest roots.

The state of Maryland, which had been founded by great lords, proclaimed universal suffrage[1] first and introduced into its entire government the most democratic forms.

When a people begins to touch the electoral qualification, one can foresee that it will sooner or later make it disappear completely. That is one of the most invariable rules that govern societies. As one moves the limit of electoral rights back, one feels the need to move it back more; for after each new concession, the forces of democracy increase and its demands grow with its new power. The ambition of those who are left below the property qualification becomes irritated in proportion to the great number of those who are found above. The exception finally becomes the rule; concessions succeed each other relentlessly and there is no stopping until they have arrived at universal suffrage.

In our day the principle of the sovereignty of the people has tried out all practical developments in the United States that the imagination can conceive. It has been disengaged from all the fictions with which one has taken care to surround it elsewhere; one sees it reclothed successively in all forms, according to the necessity of the case. Sometimes the people in a body makes the laws as at Athens; sometimes deputies whom universal suffrage has created represent it and act in its name under its almost immediate surveillance.

There are countries where a power in a way external to the social body acts on it and forces it to march on a certain track.

There are others where force is divided, placed at once in society and outside it. Nothing like this is seen in the United States; there society acts by itself and on itself. Power exists only within its bosom; almost no one is encountered who dares to conceive and above all to express the idea of seeking it elsewhere. The people participate in the drafting of laws by the choice of the legislators, in their application, by the election of the agents of the executive power; one can say that they govern themselves, so weak and restricted is the part left to the administration, so much does the latter feel its popular origin and obey the power from which it emanates. The people reign over the American political world as does God over the universe. They are the cause and the end of all things; everything comes out of them and everything is absorbed into them.*

---

*See AT's note VIII, page 691.

1. Amendments made to the constitution of Maryland in 1801 and 1809 [articles 12 and 14, ratified in 1810].

ᘓᘓᘓᘓᘓᘓᘓᘓᘓᘓᘓᘓᘓᘓᘓᘓᘓᘓᘓᘓᘓ

Chapter 5 NECESSITY OF STUDYING WHAT TAKES PLACE IN THE PARTICULAR STATES BEFORE SPEAKING OF THE GOVERNMENT OF THE UNION

I propose to examine in the following chapter what, in America, is the form of government founded on the principle of the sovereignty of the people; what are its means of action, its encumbrances, its advantages, and its dangers.

A first difficulty presents itself: the United States has a complex constitution; one notes in it two distinct societies enmeshed and, if I can explain it so, fitted into one another; one sees two governments completely separated and almost independent: one, habitual and undefined, that responds to the daily needs of society, the other, exceptional and circumscribed, that applies only to certain general interests. They are, in a word, twenty-four little sovereign nations, the sum of which forms the great body of the Union.

To examine the Union before studying the state is to embark on a route strewn with obstacles. The form of the federal government of the United States appeared last; it was only a modification of the republic, a summary of the political principles spread through the entire society before it and subsisting independent of it. Moreover, the federal government, as I have just said, is only an exception; the government of the states is the common rule. The writer who would make known the sum of such a picture before having shown its details would necessarily fall into obscurities or repetitions.

The great political principles that govern American society today were born and developed in the *state;* one cannot doubt it. It is therefore the state that one must know to have the key to all the rest.

As for the external aspect of institutions, the states that compose the American Union in our day all present the same spectacle. Political or administrative life is found concentrated around three sources of action that could be compared to the various nervous centers that make the human body move.

At the first stage is the *township,** higher the *county,* finally the *state.*

---

*Lit.: "commune." In contrast to the American township described by AT, the French commune is governed by a municipal council and a mayor, who is an agent of the central government.

ON THE TOWNSHIP SYSTEM IN AMERICA

Why the author begins the examination of political institutions with the township.—The township is found among all peoples.—Difficulty of establishing and preserving township freedom.—Its importance.—Why the author has chosen the township organization of New England for the principal object of his examination.

It is not by chance that I examine the township first.

The township is the sole association that is so much in nature that everywhere men are gathered, a township forms by itself.

Township society therefore exists among all peoples, whatever their usages and their laws may be; it is man who makes kingdoms and creates republics; the township appears to issue directly from the hands of God. But if the township has existed since there have been men, the freedom of a township is a rare and fragile thing. A people can always establish great political assemblies; for it habitually finds within it a certain number of men in whom, up to a certain point, enlightenment replaces experience in affairs. The township is composed of coarser elements that often resist the action of the legislator. The difficulty of founding the independence of townships, instead of diminishing as nations become enlightened, increases with their enlightenment. A very civilized society tolerates only with difficulty the trials of freedom in a township; it is revolted at the sight of its numerous lapses and despairs of success before having attained the final result of experience.

Among all freedoms, that of townships, which is established with such difficulty, is also the most exposed to the invasions of power. Left to themselves, the institutions of a township can scarcely struggle against an enterprising and strong government; in order to defend themselves successfully they must have completed all their developments and have been mixed with national ideas and habits. Thus as long as township freedom has not entered into mores, it is easy to destroy it, and it can enter into mores only after having subsisted for a long time in the laws.

Township freedom therefore eludes, so to speak, the effort of man. Thus it rarely happens that it is created; it is in a way born of itself. It develops almost secretly in the bosom of a half-barbaric society. It is the continuous action of laws and mores, of circumstances and above all time that comes to consolidate it. Of all the nations of the continent of Europe, one can say that not a single one knows it.

It is nonetheless in the township that the force of free peoples resides. The institutions of a township are to freedom what primary schools are to science; they put it within reach of the people; they make them taste its peaceful employ and habituate them to making use of it. Without the institutions of a township a nation can give itself a free government, but it does not have the spirit of freedom. Fleeting passions, the interests of a moment, the chance of circumstances can give it the external forms of independence; but despotism suppressed in the interior of the social body reappears sooner or later on the surface.

To make the reader understand well the general principles on which the political organization of the township and the county in the United States rests, I believed it useful to take for a model one state in particular, to examine in detail what takes place in it, and afterwards to cast a rapid glance at the rest of the country.

I have chosen one of the states of New England.

The township and the county are not organized in the same manner in all parts of the Union; it is easy to recognize, however, that in all the Union nearly the same principles have presided at the formation of both.

Now, it appeared to me that these principles had received more considerable development and reached more extensive consequences in New England than anywhere else. There they show themselves so to speak in higher relief and are thus more easily open to the observation of a foreigner.

The institutions of the township in New England form a complete and regular ensemble; they are old; they are strong by law, stronger still by mores; they exert an enormous influence on the entire society.

Under all these heads, they deserve to attract our attention.

SIZE OF THE TOWNSHIP

The township of New England is midway between the district [*canton*] and the township [*commune*] of France.* It generally numbers two to three thousand inhabitants;[1] it is therefore not so extensive that all its inhabitants do not have nearly the same interests and, on the other hand, it is sufficiently populated so that one is always sure of finding within it the elements of a good administration.

POWERS OF THE TOWNSHIP IN NEW ENGLAND

The people, origin of all powers in the township as elsewhere.—They treat its principal affairs by themselves.—No municipal council.—The greatest part of the authority of the

---

*AT uses the French word *commune* for the American township, but here he states that the American township is actually larger, and is between the French *canton* ("district") and *commune* in size.

1. The number of townships in the state of Massachusetts in 1830 was 305; the number of inhabitants 610,014; this gives an average of nearly 2,000 inhabitants per township.

township concentrated in the hands of the selectmen.—*How the* selectmen *act.*—*General assembly of the inhabitants of the township* (town meeting).—*Listing of all township officials.*—*Obligatory and compensated offices.*

In the township as everywhere, the people are the source of social powers, but nowhere do they exercise their power more immediately. The people in America are a master who has to be pleased up to the furthest limits of the possible.

In New England, the majority acts through representatives when it must treat general affairs of the state. It was necessary that it be so; but in the township, where legislative and governmental action is brought closer to the governed, the law of representation is not accepted. There is no municipal council; the body of electors, after having named its magistrates, directs them itself in everything that is not pure and simple execution of the laws of the state.[2]

This order of things is so contrary to our ideas and so much opposed to our habits that it is necessary to furnish a few examples here to make it possible to understand it well.

Public offices are extremely numerous and very divided in the township, as we shall see below; nevertheless, the greatest part of administrative powers is concentrated in the hands of a small number of individuals elected each year whom they name selectmen.[3]

The general laws of the state have imposed a certain number of obligations on the selectmen. They do not need the authorization of their constituents to fulfill them, and they cannot shirk them without taking personal responsibility. State law charges them, for example, with forming electoral lists in their township; if they omit doing it they commit a punishable offense. But in all things that are left to the direction of the township's power, the select-

2. The same rules are not applicable to large townships. These generally have a mayor and a municipal body divided into two branches; but that is an exception that needs to be authorized by law. See the law of February 22, 1822, regulating the powers of the city of Boston. *Laws of Massachusetts*, vol. 2, 588 [*The General Laws of Massachusetts* (Boston, 1823), vol. 2, 588–599; law of February 23, 1822]. This applies to large cities. It also frequently happens that small cities are submitted to a particular administration. In 1832 there were 104 townships administered in this manner in the state of New York. (*Williams' Register*) [Edwin Williams, *The New York Annual Register* (New York, 1832)].

3. They elect three of them in the smallest townships, nine in the largest. See *The Town Officer*, 186 [Isaac Goodwin, *Town Officer; or, Laws of Massachusetts Relative to the Duties of Municipal Officers* (Worcester, 1829)]. See also the principal laws of Massachusetts relative to selectmen:

Law of February 20, 1786, vol. 1, 219; of February 24, 1796, vol. 1, 488; March 7, 1801, vol. 2, 45; June 16, 1795 [June 12, 1795], vol. 1, 475; March 12, 1808, vol. 2, 186; February 28, 1787, vol. 1, 302; June 22, 1797, vol. 1, 539.

men are executors of popular will as among us the mayor is the executor of the deliberations of the municipal council. Most often they act on their private responsibility and in practice do nothing but follow the consequences of principles that the majority has previously laid down. But should they wish to introduce any change whatsoever in the established order, should they desire to engage in a new undertaking, they must go back to the source of their power. If I suppose that it is a question of establishing a school: the selectmen convoke the sum of electors on a certain day in a place indicated in advance; there they set out the need that is felt; they make known the means of satisfying it, the money that must be spent, the place that is suitable to choose. The assembly, consulted on all these points, adopts the principle, fixes the place, votes the tax, and puts the execution of its will in the hands of the selectmen.

The selectmen alone have the right to convoke the town meeting, but one can induce them to do it. If ten property owners conceive a new project and want to submit it to the consent of the township, they call for a general convocation of the inhabitants; the selectmen are obliged to endorse it, and they retain only the right to preside over the assembly.[4]

These political mores, these social usages are doubtless very far from us. At this moment I do not wish to judge them or to make known the hidden causes that produce them and bring them to life; I limit myself to setting them forth.

The selectmen are elected every year in the month of April or May. At the same time the assembly of the township chooses a host of other municipal magistrates,[5] assigned to certain important administrative details. Some, under the name of assessors, must establish the tax; others, under that of collectors, must levy it. An officer, called a *constable,* is charged with doing the policing, watching over public places, and taking in hand the material execution of the laws. Another, named the clerk of the township, records all deliberations; he takes note of birth, marriage, and death certificates.* A cashier keeps the township's funds. Add to these officials an overseer of the poor, whose duty, very difficult to fulfill, is to have legislation relative to indigents executed; school commissioners, who direct public instruction; highway inspectors, who are charged with all the details of the network of large and small highways—and you will have the list of the principal agents of a township's administration. But the division of offices does not stop there: one also

*Lit.: "acts of the civil state."

4. See *Laws of Massachusetts,* vol. 1, 150 [vol. 1, 252–253]; law of March 25, 1786 [March 23, 1786].

5. Ibid.

finds among municipal officers[6] parish commissioners, who must regulate expenditures for worship; inspectors of several kinds, some charged with directing the efforts of citizens in case of fire; others with overseeing harvests; others with provisionally removing the difficulties that can arise relative to enclosures; others with overseeing the measuring of woods or of inspecting weights and measures.

In all, the principal offices in the township number nineteen. Each inhabitant is constrained, under penalty of fine, to accept these different offices; but also most of them are compensated so that poor citizens can devote their time to them without suffering disadvantage from it. Yet the American system is not to give a fixed salary to officials. Generally each act of their ministry has a price, and they are paid only in proportion to what they have done.

ON TOWNSHIP EXISTENCE

Each is the best judge of what concerns himself alone.—Corollary to the principle of the sovereignty of the people.—Application that American townships make of these doctrines.—The New England township, sovereign over all that relates only to it, subject in all the rest.—Obligation of the township to the state.—In France, the government lends its agents to the township.—In America, the township lends its to the government.

I said previously that the principle of the sovereignty of the people hovers over the whole political system of the Anglo-Americans.* Each page of this book will make known some new applications of this doctrine.

In nations where the dogma of the sovereignty of the people reigns, each individual forms an equal portion of the sovereign and participates equally in the government of the state.

Each individual is therefore supposed to be as enlightened, as virtuous, as strong as any other of those like him.

Why therefore does he obey society, and what are the natural limits of this obedience?

He obeys society not because he is inferior to those who direct it or less capable than another man of governing himself; he obeys society because union with those like him appears useful to him and because he knows that this union cannot exist without a regulating power.

---

*DA I 1.4.

6. All these magistrates really exist in practice.

To learn the details of the offices of all these magistrates of a township, see the book entitled *Town Officer* by Isaac Goodwin (Worcester, 1827 [1829]); and the collection of the general laws of Massachusetts in 3 vols. (Boston, 1823).

In all that concerns the duties of citizens among themselves, he has therefore become a subject. In all that regards only himself he has remained master: he is free and owes an account of his actions only to God. Hence this maxim: that the individual is the best as well as the only judge of his particular interest, and that society has the right to direct his actions only when it feels itself injured by his deed or when it needs to demand his cooperation.

This doctrine is universally accepted in the United States. Elsewhere I shall examine what general influence it exerts even on the ordinary actions of life;* but I speak at this moment of townships.

The township, taken *en masse* and in relation to the central government, is only one individual like another, to which the theory that I have just pointed out applies.

The freedom of a township in the United States therefore flows from the very dogma of the sovereignty of the people; all American republics have more or less recognized this independence; but among the peoples of New England, circumstances have particularly favored its development.

In this part of the Union, political life was born in the very bosom of the townships; one could almost say that each of them at its origin was an independent nation. When afterwards the kings of England reclaimed their part of sovereignty, they were limited to taking the central power. They left the township in the state they found it in; now the townships of New England are subjects; but in the beginning† they were not or were scarcely so. They therefore did not receive their powers; on the contrary, it was they that seemed to relinquish a portion of their independence in favor of the state— an important distinction that ought to be present in the mind of the reader.

The townships generally submit to the state only when it is a question of an interest that I shall call *social,* that is to say, which they share with others.

For all that relates to themselves alone, the townships have remained independent bodies; and one encounters no one among the inhabitants of New England, I think, who recognizes in the government of the state the right to intervene in the direction of interests that are purely the township's.

One therefore sees the townships of New England sell and buy, attack and defend themselves before the courts, burden their budget or relieve it, without having any administrative authority whatsoever think of opposing it.[7]

As for social duties, they are held [responsible] for satisfying them. Thus, should the state need money, the township is not free to grant or to refuse its cooperation.[8] Should the state want to open a route, the township is not

---

DA I 2.6.

†Or, "in principle."

7. See *Laws of Massachusetts,* law of March 23, 1786, vol. 1, [249–]250.

8. *Laws of Massachusetts,* law of February 20, 1786, vol. 1, 217[–225].

a master who might close its territory to it. Should it make a police regulation, the township must execute it. Should it want to organize instruction on a uniform plan over the whole extent of the country, the township is held [responsible] for creating the schools the law wants.[9] We shall see when we speak of the administration of the United States how and by whom the townships in all these different cases are constrained to obedience.* Here I only want to establish the existence of the obligation. The obligation is strict, but the state government, in imposing it, does nothing but decree a principle; for its execution the township generally recovers all its rights of individuality. Thus it is true that the tax is voted by the legislature, but it is the township that apportions and collects it; the existence of a school is imposed, but the township builds it, pays for it, and directs it.

In France, the tax collector of the state levies the taxes of the commune; in America, the tax collector of the township levies the tax of the state.

Thus, among us, the central government lends its agents to the township; in America, the township lends its officials to the government. That alone makes understandable the degree to which the two societies differ.

ON THE SPIRIT OF THE TOWNSHIP IN NEW ENGLAND

Why the New England township attracts the affections of those who inhabit it.—Difficulty that is encountered in Europe in creating the spirit of the township.—Rights and duties of the township cooperating in America to form this spirit.—The native country has more of a physiognomy in the United States than elsewhere.—How the spirit of the township manifests itself in New England.—What happy effects it produces.

In America not only do the institutions of a township exist, but also a spirit of the township that sustains them and brings them to life.

The New England township unites two advantages that, everywhere they are found, keenly excite men's interest; that is to say: independence and power. It acts, it is true, in a circle that it cannot leave, but its movements within that are free. That independence alone would already give it a real importance if its population and its extent did not assure it.

One must indeed be persuaded that men's affections are generally brought only to where there is force. One does not see love of the native country reign for long in a conquered country. The inhabitant of New England is attached to his township not so much because he was born there as because he sees in

---

*See in this chapter the section "On Administration in New England."

9. See the same collection, laws of June 25, 1789, and March 8, 1827, vol. 1, 367[–371], and vol. 3, 179[–192].

that township a free and strong corporation that he is a part of and that is worth his trouble to seek to direct.

It often happens in Europe that those who govern regret themselves the absence of the spirit of a township; for everyone agrees that the spirit of a township is a great element of order and of public tranquillity; but they do not know how to produce it. In rendering the township strong and independent, they fear partitioning social power and exposing the state to anarchy. Now, remove force and independence from the township, and you will always find only those under its administration and no citizens.

Remark an important fact, moreover: the New England township is so constituted that it can serve as the home of lively affections, and at the same time nothing is next to it that strongly attracts the ambitious passions of the human heart.

County officials are not elected and their authority is restricted. The state itself has only a secondary importance; its existence is obscure and tranquil. There are few men who, to obtain the right to administer it, consent to depart from the center of their interests and to trouble their lives.

The federal government confers power and glory on those who direct it, but the men to whom it is given to influence its destinies are very few in number. The presidency is a high magistracy that one can scarcely reach except at an advanced age; and when one arrives at other federal offices of an elevated rank, it is in a way haphazardly and after one has already become celebrated by following another career. Ambition cannot make them the permanent goal of its efforts. It is in the township, at the center of the ordinary relations of life, that desire for esteem, the need of real interests, the taste for power and for attention, come to be concentrated; these passions, which so often trouble society, change character when they can be expressed so near the domestic hearth and in a way in the bosom of the family.

See with what art they have taken care in the American township, if I can express myself so, to *scatter* power in order to interest more people in public things. Independently of electors called from time to time to perform the acts of government, how many diverse offices, how many different magistrates, who all, within the sphere of their prerogatives, represent the powerful corporation in whose name they act! How many men thus exploit the power of the township for their profit and take interest in it for themselves!

The American system, at the same time that it partitions municipal power among a great number of citizens, does not fear to multiply the duties of the township either. In the United States they rightly think that love of one's native country is a kind of worship to which men are attached by its observances.

In this manner life in a township makes itself felt in a way at each instant;

it manifests itself each day by the accomplishment of a duty or by the exercise of a right. This political existence impresses on society a continual, but at the same time peaceful, movement that agitates it without troubling it.

The Americans are attached to the city by a reason analogous to the one that makes inhabitants of the mountains love their country. Among them, the native country has marked and characteristic features; it has more of a physiognomy than elsewhere.

New England townships generally have a happy existence. Their government is to their taste as well as of their choice. In the bosom of the profound peace and material prosperity that reign in America, the storms of municipal life are few. The direction of interests in a township is easy. In addition, the political education of the people has long been done, or rather they arrived wholly instructed on the soil they occupy. In New England, division of ranks does not even exist in memory; there is, therefore, no portion of the township that is tempted to oppress the other, and injustices, which strike only isolated individuals, are lost in the general contentment. Should the government show defects, and certainly it is easy to point them out, they do not strike the eye, because the government really does emanate from the governed and because it is enough for it to work, even with great difficulty, for a sort of paternal pride to protect it. Besides, they have nothing to compare it to. England formerly reigned over the entirety of the colonies, but the people always directed affairs in townships. The sovereignty of the people in the township is therefore not only an old state, but a primitive state.

The inhabitant of New England is attached to his township because it is strong and independent; he is interested in it because he cooperates in directing it; he loves it because he has nothing to complain of in his lot; he places his ambition and his future in it; he mingles in each of the incidents of township life: in this restricted sphere that is within his reach he tries to govern society; he habituates himself to the forms without which freedom proceeds only through revolutions, permeates himself with their spirit, gets a taste for order, understands the harmony of powers, and finally assembles clear and practical ideas on the nature of his duties as well as the extent of his rights.

ON THE COUNTY IN NEW ENGLAND

The New England county, analogue of the arrondissement in France.—Created in a purely administrative interest.—Has no representation.—Is administered by unelected officials.

The American county is very analogous to the *arrondissement* in France. As with the latter, an arbitrary district has been drawn for it; it forms a body of which the different parts have no necessary ties between them and to which are attached neither affection nor memory nor community of existence. It is created only for a purely administrative interest.

The extent of the township was too restricted to be able to include the administration of justice. The county therefore forms the first judicial center. Each county has a court of justice,[10] a sheriff to execute the decrees of tribunals, a prison to hold criminals.

There are needs that are felt in a nearly equal manner by all the townships of the county; it was natural that a central authority be charged with providing for them. In Massachusetts this authority resides in the hands of a certain number of magistrates whom the governor of the state designates with the advice[11] of his council.[12]

The administrators of the county have only a limited and exceptional power that applies only to a very few cases that are foreseen in advance. The state and the township suffice in the ordinary course of things. These administrators do nothing but prepare the budget of the county; the legislature votes it.[13] There is no assembly that directly or indirectly represents the county.

The county therefore has, to tell the truth, no political existence.

In most of the American constitutions one remarks a double tendency that brings legislators to divide executive power and concentrate legislative power. The New England township by itself has a principle of existence that they do not strip from it; but one would have to create that life fictitiously in the county, and the utility of doing so has not been felt: all the townships united have only one single representation, the state, center of all national* powers; outside township and national action one can say that there are only individual forces.

ON ADMINISTRATION IN NEW ENGLAND

In America one does not perceive administration.—Why.—Europeans believe they found freedom by taking away some of the rights of social power; Americans, by dividing its exercise.—Almost all administration properly speaking contained in the township and divided among the township's officials.—One perceives no trace of administrative hierarchy either in the township or above it.—Why it is so.—How it nevertheless happens that the state is administered in a uniform manner.—Who is charged with making

---

*Here "national" refers to the states.

10. See the law of February 14, 1821, *Laws of Massachusetts*, vol. 1 , 551 [vol. 2, 551–556].

11. See the law of February 20, 1819, *Laws of Massachusetts*, vol. 2, 494.

12. The governor's council is an elected body.

13. See the law of November 2, 1791 [November 2, 1781]. *Laws of Massachusetts*, vol. 1, 61.

township and county administrations obey the law.—On the introduction of judicial power into administration.—Consequence of the principle of election extended to all officials.—The justice of the peace in New England.—Named by whom.—Administers the county.—Assures the administration of townships.—Court of sessions.—Manner in which it acts.—Who brings matters before it.—The rights of inspection and of complaint, scattered like all administrative functions.—Informers encouraged by the sharing of fines.

What most strikes the European who travels through the United States is the absence of what is called among us government or administration. In America you see written laws; you perceive their daily execution; everything moves around you and nowhere do you discover the motor. The hand that directs the social machine vanishes at each instant.

Nevertheless, just as all peoples, to express their thoughts, are obliged to have recourse to certain grammatical forms constitutive of human languages, so all societies, to subsist, are constrained to submit to a certain amount of authority without which they fall into anarchy. That authority can be distributed in different manners; but it must always be found somewhere.

There are two means of diminishing the force of authority in a nation.

The first is to weaken power in its very principle by removing from society the right or the ability to defend itself in certain cases: to weaken authority in this manner is in general what in Europe is called founding freedom.

There is a second means of diminishing the action of authority: this does not consist of stripping society of some of its rights, or paralyzing its efforts, but of dividing the use of its forces among several hands; of multiplying officials while allocating to each of them all the power he needs to do what he is destined to execute. One encounters peoples whom this division of social powers can also bring to anarchy; by itself, however, it is not anarchic. In partitioning authority in this way, it is true, one renders its action less irresistible and less dangerous, but one does not destroy it.

The revolution in the United States was produced by a mature and reflective taste for freedom, and not by a vague and indefinite instinct of independence. It was not supported by passions of disorder; but, on the contrary, it advanced with a love of order and of legality.

In the United States, therefore, they did not claim that a man in a free country has the right to do everything; on the contrary, they imposed on him more varied social obligations than elsewhere; they did not have the idea of attacking the power of society in its principle and of contesting its rights; they limited themselves to dividing it in its exercise. They wanted in this manner to arrive at the point where authority is great and the official is small, so that society would continue to be well regulated and remain free.

There is no country in the world where the law speaks a language as absolute as in America, and neither does one exist where the right to apply it is divided among so many hands.

The administrative power of the United States offers in its constitution nothing central or hierarchical; that is what causes one not to perceive it. Power exists, but one does not know where to find its representative.

We saw above that the New England townships were not under supervision. They themselves took care of their particular interests.

It is also municipal magistrates who, most often, are charged with taking in hand the execution of the general laws of the state or with executing them themselves.[14]

Independently of general laws, the state makes some general police regulations; but ordinarily it is the townships and officers of townships who, conjointly with justices of the peace and according to the needs of the localities, regulate the details of social existence and promulgate prescriptions relative to public health, good order, and the morality of citizens.[15]

Finally, it is municipal magistrates who, by themselves and without needing to receive an impulse from outside, provide for those unforeseen needs that societies often feel.[16]

It results from what we have just said that in Massachusetts administrative power is almost entirely confined within the township;[17] but it is divided there among many hands.

In the commune in France, there is, to tell the truth, only a single administrative official, the mayor.

We have seen that they number at least nineteen in the New England township.

Those nineteen officials do not in general depend on one another. The law has carefully drawn a circle of action around each of those magistrates.

---

14. See [Goodwin's] *Town Officer,* particularly on the words *selectmen, assessors, collectors, schools, surveyors of highways* ... One example among a thousand: the state forbids traveling without good reason on Sundays. It is the *tything men,* officers of the township, who are specially charged with taking in hand the execution of this law.

See the law of March 8, 1792, *Laws of Massachusetts,* vol. 1, [407–]410.

The selectmen draw up the electoral lists for the election of the governor and transmit the result of the ballot to the secretary of the republic. Law of February 24, 1796, vol. 1, 488[–491].

15. Example: the selectmen authorize the construction of sewers, and designate the places where one can have slaughterhouses and where one can establish certain kinds of commerce harmful to the vicinity. See the law of June 7, 1785, vol. 1, 193[–194].

16. Example: the selectmen oversee public health in case of contagious diseases and take necessary measures conjointly with justices of the peace. Law of June 22, 1797, vol. 1, 539[–545].

17. I say *almost,* for there are several incidents of township life that are regulated either by justices of the peace in their individual capacity or by justices of the peace gathered in a body at the administrative center of the county. Example: it is justices of the peace who grant licenses. See the law of February 28, 1787, vol. 1, 297[–304].

Within that circle, they are all-powerful to fulfill the duties of their position and do not come under any authority of the township.

If one turns one's regard to above the township, one hardly perceives a trace of an administrative hierarchy. It sometimes happens that county officials reformulate a decision taken by townships or by magistrates of the townships,[18] but in general one can say that county administrators do not have the right to direct the conduct of township administrators.[19] They command them only in things relating to the county.

The township's magistrates and those of the county are held [responsible], in a very few cases foreseen in advance, for communicating the result of their operations to officers of the central government.[20] But the central government is not represented by a man charged with making general police regulations or ordinances for the execution of laws, with communicating habitually with county and township administrators, with inspecting their conduct, with directing their actions and punishing their faults.

Thus nowhere does there exist a center at which the spokes of administrative power converge.

How, therefore, does one succeed in conducting society on a nearly uniform plan? How can one make counties and their administrators, townships and their officials obey?

In the New England states, the legislative power extends to more objects than among us. The legislator penetrates in a way into the very heart of administration; the law descends to minute details; it prescribes at the same time the principles and the means of applying them; it thus encloses secondary bodies and their administrators in a multitude of strict and rigorously defined obligations.

Hence it results that if all secondary bodies and all officials conform to the law, society proceeds in a uniform manner in all its parts; but it still remains to know how one can force the secondary bodies and their officials to conform to the law.

18. Example: one grants a license only to those who present a certificate of good conduct given by the selectmen. If the selectmen refuse to give that certificate, the person can complain to the justices of the peace gathered in a court of sessions, and the latter can grant the license. See the law of March 12, 1808, vol. 2, 186. The townships have the right to make regulations (*by-laws*) and to oblige those regulations to be observed through fines whose rate is fixed; but those regulations need to be approved by the court of sessions. See the law of March 23, 1786, vol. 1, 254.

19. In Massachusetts, county administrators are often called on to evaluate the actions of a township's administrators; but further on it will be seen that they engage in this examination as a judicial power, and not as an administrative authority.

20. Example: township school committees are held [responsible] for making a report annually on the state of a school to the secretary of the republic. See the law of March 10, 1827, vol. 3, 183[–184].

One can say in a general manner that society finds at its disposition only two means to oblige officials to obey the laws:

It can confide a discretionary power in one of them to direct all the others and to discharge them in case of disobedience;

Or instead it can charge the courts to inflict judicial penalties on offenders.

One is not always free to take one or the other of these means.

The right to direct the official presumes the right to discharge him if he does not follow the orders that one transmits to him, or to raise him in grade if he zealously fulfills all his duties. Now, one can neither discharge an elected magistrate nor raise him in grade. It is of the nature of elective offices to be irrevocable until the end of the mandate. In reality, the elected magistrate has nothing to expect or to fear except from the electors when all public offices are the product of election. A genuine hierarchy among officials therefore cannot exist, since one cannot unite in the same man the right to order and the right to suppress disobedience efficaciously, and since one cannot join to the power of commanding that of rewarding and punishing.

Peoples who introduce election into the secondary workings of their government are therefore forcibly led to make great use of judicial penalties as a means of administration.

This is not discovered at first glance. Those who govern regard it as a first concession to make offices elective and as a second concession to submit the elected magistrate to the decrees of judges. They are equally afraid of these two innovations; and as they are called upon to do the first more than the second, they grant election to the official and leave him independent of the judge. Nevertheless, the one of these two measures is the sole counterweight that can be given to the other. One should indeed be careful, for an elective power that is not subject to a judicial power sooner or later escapes from all control or is destroyed. Between the central power and elected administrative bodies only tribunals can serve as an intermediary. They alone can force the elected official to obedience without violating the right of the elector.

The extension of the judicial power into the political world ought therefore to be correlative to the extension of the elective power. If these two things do not go together, in the end the state falls into anarchy or into servitude.

At all times it has been remarked that judicial habits prepare men quite badly for the exercise of administrative power.

The Americans have taken from their fathers, the English, the idea of an institution that has no analogy with what we know on the continent of Europe, which is justices of the peace.

The justice of the peace is midway between man of the world and magistrate, [between] administrator and judge. The justice of the peace is an enlightened citizen, but who is not necessarily versed in knowledge of the law. So they charge him only with keeping the order of society, a thing that demands more good sense and rectitude than science. The justice of the peace brings to administration, when he takes part in it, a certain taste for forms and for publicity that makes him a very troublesome instrument for despotism; but he does not show himself a slave to those legal superstitions that render magistrates hardly capable of governing.

Americans have appropriated the institution of justices of the peace, while removing from it the aristocratic character that distinguishes it in the mother country.

The governor of Massachusetts[21] names a certain number of justices of the peace in all counties, whose offices are to last for seven years.[22]

In addition, among these justices of the peace he designates three in each county who form what is called the *court of sessions.*

Justices of the peace take part individually in public administration. Sometimes they are charged, concurrently with the elected officials, with certain administrative acts;[23] sometimes they form a tribunal before which magistrates summarily accuse the citizen who refuses to obey, or the citizen denounces punishable offenses of the magistrates. But it is in the court of sessions that the justices of the peace exercise the most important of their administrative functions.

The court of sessions meets twice a year at the county seat. In Massachusetts it is charged with maintaining the greatest number[24] of public officials in obedience.[25]

21. We shall see further on [in the section of this chapter "On the Executive Power of the State"] what a governor is; I should say at present that the governor represents the executive power of the whole state.

22. See the constitution of Massachusetts, chap. 2, section 1, paragraph 9; chap. 3, paragraph 3.

23. One example among many others: a foreigner arrives in a township, coming from a country ravaged by a contagious disease. He falls ill. Two justices of the peace can, with the advice of the selectmen, give the county sheriff an order to transport him elsewhere and to watch over him. Law of June 22, 1797, vol. 1, 540 [539–541].

In general, justices of the peace intervene in all the important acts of administrative life and give them a semijudicial character.

24. I say *the greatest number* because in fact certain administrative offenses are referred to ordinary tribunals. Example: when a township refuses to pass the necessary funds for its schools or to name the school committee, it is given a very considerable fine. It is the court called *supreme judicial court,* or the court of *common pleas,* that pronounces this fine. See the law of March 10, 1827, vol. 3, 190. Similarly, when a township omits making provision for munitions of war. Law of February 21, 1822, vol. 2, 570 [573–574].

25. Justices of the peace take part in their individual capacities in the government of townships and counties. The most important acts of the life of a township are generally done only with the concurrence of one of them.

We have said that the county[26] has only an administrative existence. It is the court of sessions that by itself directs the few interests that relate to several townships at the same time or to all the townships of the county at once, and that are consequently interests with which one cannot charge any of them in particular.

When it is a question of the county, the duties of the court of sessions are therefore purely administrative, and if it often introduces judicial forms into its manner of proceeding, it is only a means of making itself clear[27] and a guarantee that it gives to those under its administration. But when it must assure the administration of the townships, it almost always acts as a judicial body and only in a few rare cases as an administrative body.

The first difficulty that presents itself is to get the township, an almost independent power, to obey the general laws of the state.

We have seen that each year townships must name a certain number of magistrates who, under the name of assessors, apportion the tax. A township attempts to escape the obligation of paying the tax by not naming assessors. The court of sessions fines it heavily.[28] The fine is levied on all the inhabitants as a body. The county sheriff, an officer of justice, executes the decree. Thus it is that in the United States power seems carefully jealous to evade regard. Administrative commands are almost always veiled by judicial mandates, for which they are only the more powerful, having then on their behalf the almost irresistible force that men accord to legal form.

This course is easy to follow and is understood without trouble. What one requires of the township is generally clear and defined; it consists in a simple, not a complex, fact, in a principle, not an application of detail.[29] But the difficulty begins when it is no longer a question of making the township, but the township's officials, obey.

---

26. The objects that relate to the county, with which the court of sessions is occupied, can be reduced to these: (1) erecting prisons and courts of justice; (2) projecting the county budget (it is the state legislature that votes it); (3) apportioning the taxes thus voted; (4) distributing certain patents; (5) establishing and repairing county highways.

27. Thus it is that when it is a question of a highway, the court of sessions decides almost all the difficulties of execution with the aid of a jury.

28. See the law of February 20, 1786, vol. 1, 217[–224].

29. There is an indirect way of making the township obey. Townships are obliged by law to keep their highways in good condition. Should they neglect to vote the funds that their upkeep requires, the township's magistrate charged with highways is then authorized to levy the necessary money without consultation. As he himself is responsible to particular persons for the bad condition of the roads, and as he can be sued by them before the court of sessions, one is assured that he will use the extraordinary right that the law gives him against the township. Thus, by threatening the official, the court of sessions forces the township into obedience. See the law of March 5, 1787, vol. 1, 305[–311].

All the reprehensible actions that a public official can commit fit, after all is said and done, into one of these categories:

He can do, without ardor and without zeal, what the law commands him.

He can not do what the law commands him.

Finally, he can do what the law forbids him.

A tribunal can only reach the conduct of an official in the latter two cases. One must have a positive and appreciable fact to serve as the basis of a judicial action.

Thus, [say] the selectmen omit fulfilling the formalities demanded by the law in the case of a township election; they can be fined.[30]

But when the public official fulfills his duty without intelligence; when he obeys the prescriptions of the law without ardor and without zeal, he finds himself entirely outside the reach of a judicial body.

The court of sessions, even if it is vested with administrative prerogatives, is powerless to force him in this case to fulfill his obligations fully. Only the fear of dismissal can prevent these quasi-offenses, and the court of sessions does not have the original powers of the township; it cannot dismiss officials that it does not name.

Besides, to be sure that there has been negligence and lack of zeal, one would have to exercise a continual surveillance over the lower official. Now, the court of sessions sits only twice a year; it does not inspect, it judges reprehensible facts that are alleged to it.

The arbitrary power to discharge public officials can alone guarantee that sort of enlightened and active obedience on their part that judicial interdiction cannot impose on them.

In France, we seek that final guarantee in *administrative hierarchy*; in America, they seek it in *election*.

Thus, to sum up in a few words what I have just set forth:

Should the public official of New England commit a *crime* in the exercise of his functions, the ordinary tribunals are *always* called in to do justice upon him.

Should he commit an *administrative fault*, a purely administrative tribunal is charged with punishing him, and when the thing is grave or pressing, the judge does what the official should have done.[31]

Finally, should the same official be guilty of one of these elusive offenses that human justice can neither define nor appraise, he appears annually be-

30. *Laws of Massachusetts*, [law of March 11, 1801,] vol. 2, 45.

31. Example: if a township is obstinate in not naming assessors, the court of sessions names them, and the magistrates thus chosen are vested with the same powers as elected magistrates. See the previously cited law of February 20, 1787 [February 20, 1786 (vol. 1, 217–224)].

fore a tribunal without appeal that can reduce him suddenly to impotence; his power departs from him with his mandate.

This system surely contains great advantages, but in its execution it encounters a practical difficulty that it is necessary to point out.

I have already remarked that the administrative tribunal named the court of sessions does not have the right to inspect the magistrates of a township; it can, in legal terms, act only when it is *seised* of a matter. Now, there is the delicate point of the system.

Americans of New England have not instituted a public minister at the court of sessions,[32] and it will be conceived that it was difficult for them to establish one. If they had limited themselves to putting a prosecuting magistrate at each county seat and had not given him agents in the townships, why would this magistrate have been better instructed in what happened in the county than the members of the court of sessions themselves? If they had given him agents in each township, they would have centralized the most formidable of powers in his hands, that of administering judicially. Besides, laws are children of habits, and nothing like this existed in English legislation.

Americans have therefore divided the rights of inspection and complaint like all other administrative functions.

Members of the grand jury must, in terms of law, notify the court at which they act of every kind of punishable offense that might be committed in their county.[33] There are certain great administrative offenses that the public minister ordinarily must prosecute without consultation;[34] most often the obligation to punish delinquents is imposed on the fiscal officer, charged with collecting the income from the fine; thus the treasurer of the township is charged with prosecuting most of the administrative offenses that are committed before his eyes.

But it is above all to particular interest that American legislation appeals;[35] that is the great principle one constantly finds when studying the laws of the United States.

32. I say *at the court of sessions.* There is a magistrate at the ordinary courts who fulfills some of the functions of a public minister.

33. Grand juries are obliged, for example, to notify the courts of the bad state of highways. *Laws of Massachusetts,* [law of March 5, 1787,] vol. 1, 308.

34. If, for example, the county treasurer does not furnish his accounts. *Laws of Massachusetts,* [law of March 8, 1792,] vol. 1, [405–]406.

35. One example among a thousand: a particular person damages his vehicle or is injured on a badly maintained highway; he has the right to demand damages before the court of sessions from the township or the county in charge of the highway. *Laws of Massachusetts,* [law of March 5, 1787,] vol. 1, 309.

American legislators show but little confidence in human honesty; but they always suppose man to be intelligent. They therefore rely most often on personal interest for the execution of the laws.

When an individual is positively and currently wronged by an administrative offense, they understand, in effect, that personal interest guarantees a complaint.

But it is easy to foresee that if it is a question of a legal prescription, which while being useful to society does not have a utility currently felt by an individual, everyone will hesitate to bring himself forward as an accuser. In this manner, and by a sort of tacit accord, the laws could well fall into disuse.

In the extremity into which their system casts them, Americans are obliged to interest denouncers by calling on them in certain cases to share in fines.[36]

This is a dangerous means that assures the execution of the laws while degrading mores.

Above the county magistrates there is, to tell the truth, no longer administrative power but only a governmental power.

GENERAL IDEAS ABOUT ADMINISTRATION IN THE UNITED STATES

How the states of the Union differ among themselves by their systems of administration.—Life of the township less active and less complete as one descends toward the south.—The power of the magistrate then becomes greater, that of the elector, smaller.— Administration passes from the township to the county.—States of New York, Ohio, Pennsylvania.—Administrative principles applicable to all the Union.—Election of public officials or irremovability from their offices.—Absence of hierarchy.—Introduction of judicial means into administration.

36. In case of invasion or insurrection, when the officers of a township neglect to furnish necessary objects and munitions to the militia, the township can be fined 200 to 500 dollars (1,000 to 2,500 francs).

One conceives very well that in such a case, it can happen that no one has either the interest or the desire to take the role of accuser. So the law adds [that the fine is] "to be sued for and recovered by any person, who may prosecute for the same, [. . .] one moiety to the prosecutor." See the law of March 6, 1810, vol. 2, 236.

One very frequently finds the same arrangement reproduced in the laws of Massachusetts.

Sometimes it is not a particular person whom the law excites in this manner to prosecute public officials; it is the official whom it thus encourages to have the disobedience of particular persons punished. Example: an inhabitant refuses to take part in the work that was assigned to him on a large highway. The overseer of highways must prosecute him; and if he gets him fined, half the fine comes back to him. See the previously cited laws, [law of March 5, 1787,] vol. 1, 308.

I announced previously that after having examined in detail the constitutions of the township and the county in New England, I would cast a general glance at the rest of the Union.*

There are townships and township life in each state; but in none of the confederated states does one encounter a township identical to that of New England.

As one descends toward the south, one perceives that township life becomes less active; the township has fewer magistrates, rights, and duties; the population does not exert so direct an influence on its affairs; the assemblies of the townships are less frequent and cover fewer objects. The power of the elected magistrate is therefore comparatively greater and that of the elector, smaller; the spirit of the township is less awake and less powerful.[37]

One begins to perceive these differences in the state of New York; they are already very palpable in Pennsylvania; but they become less striking when one moves toward the northwest. Most of the emigrants who go to found the states of the Northwest come from New England, and they carry the administrative habits of the mother country to their adopted country. The township of Ohio is very analogous to the township of Massachusetts.

We have seen that in Massachusetts the principle of public administration is found in the township. The township is the hearth around which the interests and affections of men come to gather. But it ceases to be so as one descends toward the states in which enlightenment is not so universally widespread and in which, consequently, the township offers fewer guarantees of wisdom and fewer elements of administration. Therefore as one moves away from New England, the life of the township passes in a way to the county. The county becomes the great administrative center and forms the intermediate power between the government and plain citizens.

I have said that in Massachusetts the affairs of the county are directed by the court of sessions. The court of sessions is composed of a certain number

*In this chapter, in "On the Township System in America."

37. See, for the details, *The Revised Statutes* of the state of New York [*The Revised Statutes of the State of New York*, 3 vols. (Albany, 1829)], at part 1, chap. 11, entitled "Of the Powers, Duties and Privileges of Towns." On the rights, obligations, and privileges of townships, vol. 1, 336–364 [336–363].

See in the collection entitled *Digest of the Laws of Pennsylvania* [by John Purdon (Philadelphia, 1831)], the words *assessors, collectors, constables, overseers of the poor, supervisor of highways.* And in the collection entitled *Acts of a General Nature of the State of Ohio* [Columbus, 1831], the law of February 25, 1834 [1824], relative to townships, p. 412. And then the particular arrangements relative to the various officers of townships, as: *township's clerk, trustees, overseers of the poor, fence viewers, appraisers of property, township's treasurer, constables, supervisors of highways.*

of magistrates named by the governor and his council. The county has no representation and its budget is voted by the national* legislature.

In the great state of New York, on the contrary, in the state of Ohio and in Pennsylvania, the inhabitants of each county elect a certain number of deputies; the meeting of these deputies forms a representative assembly of the county.[38]

The county assembly possesses, within certain limits, the right to tax the inhabitants; it constitutes, in this relation, a genuine legislature; at the same time, it administers the county, directs in several cases the administration of the townships, and compresses their powers within much narrower limits than in Massachusetts.

These are the principal differences in the constitutions of township and county in the various confederated states. If I wanted to descend to the details of the means of execution, I would have many other dissimilarities to point out. But my goal is not to give a course on American administrative law.

I have already said enough, I think, to make understood the general principles on which the administration of the United States rests. These principles are applied diversely; they furnish more or less numerous consequences according to the place; but at bottom they are everywhere the same. The laws vary, their physiognomy changes; one same spirit animates them.

The township and the county are not constituted in the same manner everywhere; but one can say that the organization of the township and the county in the United States rests on this same idea everywhere: that each is the best judge of whatever relates only to himself, and is in the best position to provide for his particular needs. The township and the county are therefore charged with looking after their special interests. The state governs and does not administer. One encounters exceptions to this principle, but not a contrary principle.

The first consequence of this doctrine has been to have all the administrators of the township and the county chosen by the inhabitants themselves, or at least to have those magistrates chosen exclusively from among them.

As administrators are everywhere elected, or at least irrevocable, the result is that no one has been able to introduce rules of hierarchy anywhere. There

---

*Here "national" means statewide.

38. See *Revised Statutes of the State of New York,* part 1, chap. 11, vol. 1, 340; chap 12, 366. *Acts of the State of Ohio.* Law of February 25, 1824, relative to *county commissioners,* 263.

See *Digest of the Laws of Pennsylvania,* on the words *county-rates and levies,* 170.

In the state of New York, each township elects a deputy, and this same deputy participates at the same time in the administration of the county and that of the township.

have been almost as many independent officials as offices. Administrative power is found diffused in a multitude of hands.

Since administrative hierarchy exists nowhere, since administrators are elected and irrevocable until the end of the mandate, there has followed the obligation to introduce courts, more or less, into administration. Hence the system of fines, by means of which secondary bodies and their representatives are constrained to obey the laws. One finds this system from one end of the Union to the other.

Yet the power to repress administrative offenses or to take administrative action as needed has not been accorded in all states to the same judges.

The Anglo-Americans have drawn the institution of justices of the peace from a common source; one finds it in all states. But they have not always taken the same advantage of it.

Everywhere justices of the peace cooperate in the administration of townships and counties,[39] either by administering them themselves or by repressing certain administrative offenses; but in most of the states, the most serious of these offenses are subject to the ordinary courts.

So, therefore, election of administrative officials or irremovability from their offices, absence of administrative hierarchy, introduction of judicial means into the secondary government of society—such are the principal characteristics by which one recognizes American administration from Maine to Florida.

There are several states in which one begins to perceive traces of administrative centralization. The state of New York is the most advanced along this track.

In the state of New York, officials of the central government exercise, in certain cases, a sort of surveillance and control over the conduct of secondary bodies.[40] In certain others they form a kind of court of appeal for deciding

39. There are even states in the South where the magistrates of the county courts are charged with every detail of administration. See *The Statutes of the State of Tennessee* [*The Statute Laws of the State of Tennessee* (Knoxville, 1831)], at the article "Judiciary, Taxes . . ."

40. Example: the direction of public instruction is centralized in the hands of the government. The legislature names the members of the university, called regents; the governor and the lieutenant-governor of the state are necessarily part of it (*Revised Statutes*, vol. 1, 456). The regents of the university visit colleges and academies every year and make an annual report to the legislature; their supervision is no illusion, for these particular reasons: colleges, in order to become constituted bodies (corporations) that can buy, sell, and own, need a charter; now, this charter is only granted by the legislature on advice of the regents. Each year the state distributes to colleges and academies the interest from a special fund created for the encouragement of studies. It is the regents who are the distributors of this money. See chap. 15, "Public Instruction," *Revised Statutes*, vol. 1, 455.

Each year, commissioners of public schools are held [responsible] for sending a report on the situation to the superintendent of the republic. *Revised Statutes*, 488.

affairs.[41] In the state of New York, judicial penalties are employed less than elsewhere as an administrative means. The right to prosecute administrative offenses is also placed in fewer hands.[42]

The same tendency may be remarked slightly in several other states.[43] But, generally, one can say that the salient characteristic of public administration in the United States is to be enormously decentralized.

ON THE STATE

I have spoken of the townships and of administration; it remains for me to speak of the state and the government.

Here I can make haste without fear of not being understood; what I have to say is found drawn up in the written constitutions that anyone can easily procure for himself.[44] These constitutions themselves rest on a simple and rational theory.

Most of the forms that they evidence have been adopted by all constitutional peoples; so they have become familiar to us.

I therefore have to give only a short exposition here. Later I shall try to judge what I am going to describe.

A report like this must be made to him annually on the number and state of the poor. *Revised Statutes,* 631.

41. When someone believes himself injured by certain actions emanating from the school commissioners (these are officials of the township), he can appeal to the superintendent of primary schools, whose decision is final. *Revised Statutes,* vol. 1, 487.

From time to time one finds in the laws of the state of New York arrangements analogous to those I have just cited as examples. But generally these attempts at centralization are feeble and unproductive. In giving high officials of the state the right to oversee and direct lower agents, they do not give the right to reward or punish them. The same man is almost never charged with giving an order and repressing disobedience; he therefore has the right to command, but not the ability to make himself obeyed.

In 1830, the superintendent of schools, in his annual report to the legislature, complained that despite his warning, several school commissioners had not transmitted to him the accounts they owed him. "If this omission is repeated," he added, "I shall be reduced to prosecuting them, under the terms of the law, before the competent tribunals."

42. Example: the officer of the public ministry in each county (district attorney) is charged with prosecuting for the recovery of all fines above 50 dollars, unless that right has been expressly given by the law to another magistrate. *Revised Statutes,* part. 1, ch. 10 [12], vol. 1, 383.

43. There are several traces of administrative centralization in Massachusetts. Example: school committees of a township are charged with making a report to the Secretary of State each year. *Laws of Massachusetts,* [law of June 25, 1789,] vol. 1, 367[–371].

44. See the text of the constitution of New York.

LEGISLATIVE POWER OF THE STATE

Division of the legislative body into two houses.—Senate.—House of Representatives.—
Different prerogatives of these two bodies.

The legislative power of the state is entrusted to two assemblies; the first generally bears the name of Senate.

The Senate is usually a legislative body; but sometimes it becomes an administrative and judicial body.

It takes part in administration in several ways according to the different constitutions;[45] but it is by concurring in the choice of officials that it ordinarily enters the sphere of executive power.

It participates in judicial power by pronouncing on certain political offenses, and sometimes also in ruling on certain civil cases.[46]

Its members are always few in number.

The other branch of the legislature, ordinarily called the House of Representatives, participates in no administrative power and takes part in judicial power only by accusing public officials before the Senate.

Members of the two houses almost everywhere are subject to the same conditions of eligibility. Both are elected in the same manner and by the same citizens.

The only difference that exists between them stems from the fact that the term of senators is generally longer than that of representatives. The latter rarely remain in office more than a year; the former ordinarily sit for two or three years.

In granting senators the privilege of being named for several years, and in renewing them consecutively, the law has taken care to maintain among the legislators a core of men already habituated to the business, who can exert a useful influence over new arrivals.

By dividing the legislative body into two branches, Americans did not therefore want to create one hereditary assembly and another elective; they did not intend to make one an aristocratic body and the other a representative of democracy; nor was their goal to give in the first a support to power, while leaving to the second the interests and the passions of the people.

To divide legislative strength, thus to slow the movement of political assemblies, and to create a court of appeal for the revision of laws—such are the sole advantages that result from the current constitutions of the two houses in the United States.

Time and experience have brought Americans to know that, when re-

---

45. In Massachusetts, the Senate is not vested with any administrative function.
46. As in the state of New York.

duced to these advantages, the division of legislative powers is still a necessity of the first order. Alone among all the united republics, Pennsylvania had at first tried to establish a single assembly. Franklin* himself, carried away by the logical consequences of the dogma of the sovereignty of the people, had concurred in this measure. They were soon obliged to change the law and to constitute two houses. The principle of the division of legislative power thus received its last consecration; from now on one can therefore consider as a demonstrated truth the necessity of partitioning legislative action among several bodies. This theory, nearly ignored in ancient republics, introduced into the world almost haphazardly like most great truths, unknown to several modern peoples, has at length passed into the political science of our day as an axiom.

ON THE EXECUTIVE POWER OF THE STATE

What the governor is in an American state.—What position he occupies in regard to the legislature.—What his rights and his duties are.—His dependence on the people.

The executive power of the state has the governor for representative.

It is not by chance that I have picked this word, representative. The governor of the state in fact represents the executive power; but he exercises only some of its rights.

The supreme magistrate, whom they name the governor, is placed next to the legislature as a moderator and counsel. He is armed with a suspensive veto that permits him to stop or at least to slow movement at his will. He sets out the needs of the country to the legislative body and makes it known what means he judges useful to employ in order to provide for them; he is the natural executor of its wishes for all undertakings that interest the entire nation.[47] In the absence of the legislature he must take all appropriate measures to guarantee the state against violent shocks and unforeseen dangers.

The governor gathers in his hands all the military power of the state. He is commander of the militia and chief of the armed forces.

When the power of opinion that men have agreed to grant to the law is

---

*Benjamin Franklin (1706–1790). According to James Madison's notes on the Constitutional Convention in Philadelphia, "the 3d resolution 'that the national Legislature ought to consist of two branches' was agreed to without debate or dissent, except that of Pennsylvania, given probably from complaisance to Doc. Franklin who was understood to be partial to a single House of Legislation." *Notes of Debates in the Federal Convention of 1787 Reported by James Madison* (New York: Norton, 1987), 38–39.

47. In practice, it is not always the governor who executes undertakings that the legislature has conceived; it often happens that the latter, at the same time that it votes a principle, names special agents to oversee its execution.

flouted, the governor advances at the head of the material force of the state; he breaks the resistance and reestablishes the accustomed order.

Yet the governor does not enter into the administration of townships and counties, or at least he takes part in it only very indirectly by the nomination of justices of the peace which he cannot afterwards revoke.[48]

The governor is an elective magistrate. They generally even take care to elect him for only one or two years, so that he always remains in a strict dependence on the majority that created him.

ON THE POLITICAL EFFECTS OF ADMINISTRATIVE DECENTRALIZATION IN THE UNITED STATES

Distinction to establish between governmental centralization and administrative central-ization.—In the United States, no administrative centralization, but very great govern-mental centralization.—Some distressing effects that result from extreme administrative decentralization in the United States.—Administrative advantages of this order of things.—The force that administers society, less regulated, less enlightened, less learned, much greater than in Europe.—Political advantages of the same order of things.—In the United States the native country makes itself felt everywhere.—Support that the governed lend to the government.—Provincial institutions more necessary as the social state be-comes more democratic.—Why.

Centralization is a word that is constantly repeated in our day and whose sense no one, in general, seeks to clarify.

Nevertheless, two very distinct kinds of centralization exist, which it is important to know well.

Certain interests are common to all parts of the nation, such as the forma-tion of general laws and the relations of the people with foreigners.

Other interests are special to certain parts of the nation, such as, for ex-ample, the undertakings of the township.

To concentrate the power to direct the first in the same place or in the same hand is to found what I shall call governmental centralization.

To concentrate the power to direct the second in the same manner is to found what I shall name administrative centralization.

There are some points at which these two kinds of centralization come to be confused. But in taking as a sum the objects that fall more particularly in the domain of each of them, one easily succeeds in distinguishing them.

It is understood that governmental centralization acquires an immense force when it is joined to administrative centralization. In this manner it

---

48. In several states, justices of the peace are not named by the governor.

habituates men to make a complete and continual abstraction from their wills; to obey not once and on one point, but in everything and every day. It then not only subdues them by force, but it also captures them through their habits; it isolates them and afterwards fastens them one by one onto the common mass.

These two kinds of centralization lend each other a mutual assistance, drawing on one another; but I cannot believe that they are inseparable.

Under Louis XIV, France saw the greatest governmental centralization that one could conceive of, since the same man made general laws and had the power to interpret them, represented France to the outside [world] and acted in its name. "L'Etat, c'est moi,"* he said; and he was right.

Nevertheless, under Louis XIV there was much less administrative centralization than in our day.

In our time we see one power, England, in which governmental centralization is brought to a very high degree: there the state seems to move like a single man; it stirs up immense masses at its will, gathers and brings the effort of its whole power everywhere that it wishes.

England, which has done such great things for fifty years, has no administrative centralization.

For my part, I cannot conceive that a nation can live or above all prosper without strong governmental centralization.

But I think that administrative centralization is fit only to enervate the peoples who submit to it, because it constantly tends to diminish the spirit of the city in them. Administrative centralization, it is true, succeeds in uniting at a given period and in a certain place all the disposable strength of the nation, but it is harmful to the reproduction of strength. It makes [the nation] triumph on the day of combat and diminishes its power in the long term. It can therefore contribute admirably to the passing greatness of one man, not to the lasting prosperity of a people.

One should be careful indeed to say that a state cannot act because it has no centralization; one almost always speaks without knowing it of governmental centralization. The German empire, one repeats, could never take the fullest possible advantage of its strength. Agreed. But why?—because national force was never centralized there; because the state was never able to make its general laws obeyed; because the separate parts of that great body always had the right or the opportunity to refuse to the agents of common authority their cooperation in the very things that interested all citizens; in other words, because there was no governmental centralization. The same remark is applicable to the Middle Ages: what produced all the miseries of

* "The state, it is I."

feudal society is that the power not only to administer, but to govern, was partitioned among a thousand hands and fragmented in a thousand ways; the absence of all governmental centralization at that time prevented the nations of Europe from advancing with energy toward any goal.

We have seen that in the United States administrative centralization does not exist. One hardly finds a trace of hierarchy there. Decentralization has been carried to a degree that no European nation can tolerate, I think, without profound unrest, and which even produces distressing effects in America. But in the United States, governmental centralization exists to the highest point. It would be easy to prove that national power is more concentrated there than it was in any of the old monarchies of Europe. Not only is there only a single body in each state that makes the laws; not only does there exist only a single power that can create political life around it; but in general they have avoided gathering numerous district or county assemblies for fear that these assemblies be tempted to go outside their administrative prerogatives and impede the working of the government. In America, the legislature of each state has before it no power capable of resisting it. Nothing can stop it on its way, neither privileges, nor local immunity, nor personal influence, not even the authority of reason, for it represents the majority that claims to be the unique organ of reason. It therefore has no other limits in its action than its own will. Next to it, and under its hand, is placed the representative of the executive power who, with the aid of material force, will compel malcontents to obedience.

Weakness is encountered only in certain details of governmental action.

American republics do not have a permanent armed force to put down minorities, but up to the present, minorities there have never been reduced to making war, and the necessity of an army has still not been felt. The state most often makes use of the township's or the county's officials to act on citizens. So, for example, in New England it is the township's assessor who apportions the tax, the township's tax collector levies it; the township's cashier has the income from it come to the public treasury, and the claims that arise are submitted to the ordinary courts. Such a manner of collecting the tax is slow, encumbered; it would impede at each moment the workings of a government that had great pecuniary needs. Generally, one should desire, for all that is essential to its life, that the government have its own officials, chosen by it, revocable by it, and rapid forms of proceeding; but it will always be easy for the central power, organized as it is in America, to introduce more energetic and more efficacious means of action according to its needs.

Therefore it is not, as is often repeated, because there is no centralization in the United States that the republics of the New World will perish; far indeed from not being centralized enough, one can affirm that the American governments are too much so; I shall prove it later.* Every day legislative assemblies swallow up the dregs of governmental powers; they tend to gather them all to themselves, just as the Convention had done.† The social power, thus centralized, constantly changes hands because it is subordinated to popular power. Often it comes to lack wisdom and foresight because it can do everything. That is the danger for it. It is therefore because of its very force, and not as a consequence of its weakness, that it is threatened with extinction one day.

Administrative decentralization produces several diverse effects in America.

We have seen that Americans have almost entirely isolated administration from government; in that they seem to me to have overstepped the limits of sound reason; for order, even in secondary things, is still a national interest.[49]

As the state has no administrative officials of its own, placed at fixed posts at different points in the territory, on whom it can impress a common impulse, the result is that it rarely attempts to establish general rules of order. Now, the need for these rules makes itself keenly felt. A European often notices their absence. The appearance of disorder reigning on the surface at first persuades him that there is complete anarchy in society; it is only when examining the bottom of things that he is undeceived.

Certain undertakings interest the entire state and nevertheless cannot be executed because there is no national administration to direct them. Abandoned to the care of townships and counties, left to elected and temporary agents, they lead to no result or produce nothing lasting.

Partisans of centralization in Europe assert that governmental power administers localities better than they could administer themselves: that can be true when the central power is enlightened and localities are without enlightenment, when it is active and they are inert, when it is in the habit of acting and they are in the habit of obeying. One even understands that the more centralization there is, the more this double tendency increases and the more the capacity of one part and the incapacity of the other become prominent.

DA I 2.7.

†The National Convention during the French Revolution (1792–1795).

49. The authority that represents the state, even if it does not administer itself, ought not, I think, to relinquish the right to inspect local administration. I suppose, for example, that an agent of the government, placed at a fixed post in each county, could refer the punishable offenses that are committed in the townships and the county to the judicial power; would order not be more uniformly followed without compromising the independence of localities? Now, nothing like this exists in America. Above the county courts there is nothing; and those courts are made cognizant in a way only haphazardly of the administrative offenses that they must repress.

But I deny that it is so when the people are enlightened, awakened to their interests, and habituated to thinking about them as they are in America.

I am persuaded, on the contrary, that in this case the collective force of citizens will always be more powerful to produce social well-being than the authority of government.

I avow that it is difficult to point out in a sure manner the means of awakening a people that sleeps, so as to give it passions and enlightenment that it does not have; I am not ignorant that to persuade men that they ought to occupy themselves with their affairs is an arduous undertaking. It would often be less toilsome to interest them in the details of court etiquette than in the repair of their town hall.

But I also think that when the central administration claims to replace completely the free cooperation of those primarily interested, it deceives itself or wants to deceive you.

A central power, however enlightened, however learned one imagines it, cannot gather to itself alone all the details of the life of a great people. It cannot do it because such a work exceeds human strength. When it wants by its care alone to create so many diverse springs and make them function, it contents itself with a very incomplete result or exhausts itself in useless efforts.

Centralization, it is true, easily succeeds in subjecting the external actions of man to a certain uniformity that in the end one loves for itself, independent of the things to which it applies, like those devotees who adore the statue forgetting the divinity that it represents. Centralization succeeds without difficulty in impressing a regular style on current affairs; in skillfully regimenting the details of social orderliness; in repressing slight disorders and small offenses; in maintaining society in a status quo that is properly neither decadence nor progress; in keeping in the social body a sort of administrative somnolence that administrators are accustomed to calling good order and public tranquillity.[50] It excels, in a word, at preventing, not at doing. When it is a question of moving society profoundly or pressing it to a rapid advance, its force abandons it. If its measures need the concurrence of individuals, one is then wholly surprised at the weakness of that immense machine; it finds itself suddenly reduced to impotence.

Then sometimes it happens that centralization tries, in desperation, to

50. China appears to me to offer the most perfect emblem of the kind of social well-being that a very centralized administration can furnish to peoples who submit to it. Travelers tell us that the Chinese have tranquillity without happiness, industry without progress, stability without force, and material order without public morality. Among them society always runs well enough, never very well. I imagine that when China is open to the Europeans, the latter will find the most beautiful model of administrative centralization that exists in the universe.

call citizens to its aid; but it says to them: "You shall act as I wish, as long as I wish, and precisely in the direction that I wish. You shall take charge of these details without aspiring to direct the sum; you shall work in the darkness, and later you shall judge my work by its results." It is not under such conditions that one obtains the concurrence of the human will. It must have freedom in its style, responsibility in its actions. Man is so made that he prefers standing still to marching without independence toward a goal of which he is ignorant.

I shall not deny that in the United States one often regrets not finding those uniform rules that seem constantly to be watching over each of us.

From time to time one encounters great examples there of insouciance and social negligence. Here and there gross stains appear that seem in complete discord with the surrounding civilization.

Some useful undertakings that demand a continual care and a rigorous exactitude to succeed are often abandoned in the end; for, in America as elsewhere, the people proceed by momentary efforts and sudden impulses.

The European, accustomed to finding an official constantly at hand who mixes in nearly everything, gets used to these different workings of a township's administration only with difficulty. In general, one can say that the little details of social orderliness that render life sweet and comfortable are neglected in America; but the essential guarantees to man in society exist there as much as everywhere else. Among the Americans, the force that administers the state is less well regulated, less enlightened, less skillful, but a hundred times greater than in Europe. There is no country in the world where, after all is said and done, men make as many efforts to create social well-being. I do not know a people who has succeeded in establishing schools as numerous and as efficacious; churches more in touch with the religious needs of the inhabitants; common highways better maintained. One must therefore not seek in the United States uniformity and permanence of views, minute care of details, perfection of administrative procedures;[51] what one

51. A writer of talent [Sébastien L. Saulnier] who, in a comparison between the finances of the United States and those of France, has proven that spirit cannot always substitute for knowledge of facts, rightly reproaches the Americans for the kind of confusion that reigns in the budgets of their townships, and after having given the model of a departmental budget in France, he adds: "Thanks to centralization, admirable creation of a great man, the municipal budgets from one end of the kingdom to the other, those of the great cities like those of the most humble communes, present no less order and method." [Saulnier, "Nouvelles observations sur les finances des Etats-Unis, en réponse à une brochure publiée par le Général La Fayette," *Revue Britannique*, October 8, 1831: 195–260 at 239.] There, certainly, is a result that I admire; but I see most of those French communes, whose accountancy is so perfect, plunged in a profound ignorance of their true interests and left in such an invincible apathy that society seems rather to vegetate than to live in them; on the other hand, I perceive in those same American townships,

finds there is the image of force, a little wild it is true, but full of power; [the image] of life accompanied by accidents, but also by movement and efforts.

Furthermore, I shall admit, if one wishes, that the villages and counties of the United States would be more usefully administered by a central authority located far away from them, and that would remain foreign to them, than by officials taken from within them. I shall recognize, if one requires it, that more security would reign in America, that they would make a wiser and more judicious use of social resources, if the administration of the whole country were concentrated in a single hand. The *political* advantages that Americans derive from the system of decentralization would still make me prefer it to the contrary system.

What does it matter to me, after all, that there should be an authority always on its feet, keeping watch that my pleasures are tranquil, flying ahead of my steps to turn away every danger without my even needing to think about it, if this authority, at the same that it removes the least thorns on my path, is absolute master of my freedom and my life, if it monopolizes movement and existence to such a point that everything around it must languish when it languishes, that everything must sleep when it sleeps, that everything must perish if it dies?

There are nations of Europe where an inhabitant considers himself a kind of colonist, indifferent to the destiny of the place that he inhabits. The greatest changes come about in his country without his concurrence; he does not even know precisely what has taken place; he suspects; he has heard the event recounted by chance. Even more, the fortune of his village, the policing of his street, the fate of his church and of his presbytery do not touch him; he thinks that all these things do not concern him in any fashion and that they belong to a powerful foreigner called the government. For himself, he enjoys these goods as a tenant, without a spirit of ownership and without ideas of any improvement whatsoever. This disinterest in himself goes so far that if his own security or that of his children is finally compromised, instead of occupying himself with removing the danger, he crosses his arms to wait for the nation as a whole to come to his aid. Yet this man, although he has made such a complete sacrifice of his free will, likes obedience no more than any

---

whose budgets are not drawn up on methodical and above all uniform plans, an enlightened, active, enterprising population; I contemplate a society always at work there. That spectacle astonishes me; for in my eyes, the principal goal of a good government is to produce the well-being of peoples and not to establish a strict order in the midst of their misery. I therefore wonder if it would not be possible to attribute to the same cause the prosperity of the American township and the apparent disorder of its finances, the distress of the commune in France and the perfection of its budget. In any case I distrust a good that I find mixed with so many evils, and I easily console myself for an evil that is compensated by so much good.

other. He submits, it is true, at the pleasure of a clerk; but it pleases him to defy the law like a defeated enemy, as soon as force is withdrawn. Thus one sees him swinging constantly between servitude and license.

When nations have arrived at this point, they must modify their laws and their mores or they perish, for the source of public virtues is almost dried up; one still finds subjects in them, but one no longer sees citizens.

I say that such nations have been prepared for conquest. If they do not disappear from the world stage, it is because they are surrounded by nations like them or inferior to them; it is because there still remains in their bosom a sort of indefinable instinct of the native country, some unreflective pride in the name that it bears, some vague memory of their past glory, which, without being linked precisely to anything, is enough to impress on them a conservative impulse as needed.

One would be wrong to reassure oneself by thinking that certain peoples have made prodigious efforts to defend a native country in which they have been living so to speak as foreigners. One should be careful indeed here, and one will see that religion was then almost always their principal motive.

The duration, glory, or prosperity of the nation had become sacred dogmas for them, and in defending their native country, they were also defending that holy city in which they were all citizens.

Turkish populations never took any part in the direction of the affairs of society; they nevertheless accomplished immense undertakings as long as they saw the triumph of the religion of Mohammed in the conquests of the sultans. Today religion is passing away; despotism alone remains to them: they fall.

Montesquieu, in giving despotism a force of its own, has, I think, done it an honor that it does not merit.* Despotism all alone by itself can maintain nothing lasting. When one looks at it from close up, one perceives that what has long made absolute governments prosper is religion and not fear.

One will never encounter, whatever one does, genuine power among men except in the free concurrence of wills. Now, there is nothing in the world but patriotism or religion that can make the universality of citizens advance for long toward the same goal.

One does not depend on laws to reanimate beliefs that are extinguished; but one does depend on laws to interest men in the destiny of their country. One depends on laws to awaken and direct that vague instinct of the native country that never abandons the heart of man, and in binding it to daily thoughts, passions, and habits, to make of it a reflective and lasting sentiment. And let it not be said that it is too late to attempt it; nations do not

* *The Spirit of the Laws,* III 9–10.

grow old in the same manner as men. Each generation born within them is like a new people that comes to offer itself to the hand of the legislator.

What I admire most in America are not the *administrative* effects of decentralization, but its *political* effects. In the United States the native country makes itself felt everywhere. It is an object of solicitude from the village to the entire Union. The inhabitant applies himself to each of the interests of his country as to his very own. He is glorified in the glory of the nation; in the success that it obtains he believes he recognizes his own work, and he is uplifted by it; he rejoices in the general prosperity from which he profits. He has for his native country a sentiment analogous to the one that he feels for his family, and it is still by a sort of selfishness that he takes an interest in the state.

Often the European sees in the public official only force; the American sees in him right. One can therefore say that in America man never obeys man, but justice or law.

Thus he has conceived an often exaggerated but almost always salutary opinion of himself. He trusts fearlessly in his own forces, which appear to him to suffice for everything. A particular person conceives the thought of some undertaking; should this undertaking have a direct relation to the well-being of society, the idea of addressing himself to the public authority to obtain its concurrence does not occur to him. He makes known his plan, offers to execute it, calls individual forces to the assistance of his, and struggles hand to hand against all obstacles. Often, doubtless, he succeeds less well than if the state were in his place; but in the long term the general result of all the individual undertakings far exceeds what the government could do.

As administrative authority is placed at the side of those whom it administers, and in some way represents them, it excites neither jealousy nor hatred. As its means of action are limited, each feels that he cannot rely solely on it.

Therefore when the administrative power intervenes within the circle of its prerogatives, it does not find itself abandoned to itself as in Europe. One does not believe that the duties of particular persons have ceased because the representative of the public comes to act. On the contrary, each person guides, supports, and sustains it.

Since the action of individual forces is joined to the action of social forces, they often succeed in doing what the most concentrated and most energetic administration would be in no condition to execute.*

I could cite many facts in support of what I advance; but I would rather take a single one and choose the one that I know best.

*See AT's note IX, page 691.

In America, the means that are put at the disposal of authority to uncover crimes and prosecute criminals are few.

An administrative order does not exist; passports are unknown. The judicial order in the United States cannot be compared with ours; police detectives are few; they do not always have the initiative in prosecutions; training is rapid and oral. I nevertheless doubt that crime in any country so rarely escapes punishment.

The reason for this is that everyone believes himself interested in providing proof of the offense and catching the offender.

During my stay in the United States, I saw the inhabitants of a county where a great crime had been committed spontaneously form committees for the purpose of pursuing the guilty one and delivering him to the courts.

In Europe, the criminal is an unfortunate who fights to hide his head from the agents of power; the population in some way assists in the struggle. In America, he is an enemy of the human race, and he has humanity as a whole against him.

I believe provincial institutions useful to all peoples; but none seems to me to have a more real need of these institutions than one whose social state is democratic.

In an aristocracy, one is always sure of maintaining a certain order in the bosom of freedom.

Since those who govern have much to lose, order is a great interest for them.

One can also say that in an aristocracy the people are sheltered from the excesses of despotism, because organized forces are always to be found ready to resist the despot.

A democracy without provincial institutions possesses no guarantee against such evils.

How make a multitude support freedom in great things when it has not learned to make use of it in small ones?

How resist tyranny in a country in which each individual is weak and in which individuals are not united by any common interest?

Those who fear license and those who dread absolute power should therefore equally desire the gradual development of provincial freedoms.

I am convinced, furthermore, that no nations are more at risk of falling under the yoke of administrative centralization than those whose social state is democratic.

Several causes concur in this result, but among others these:

The permanent tendency of these nations is to concentrate all governmental power in the hands of the sole power that directly represents the people, because beyond the people one perceives no more than equal individuals confused in a common mass.

Now, when the same power is already vested with all the attributes of government, it is very difficult for it not to seek to enter into the details of administration, and it hardly ever fails to find the occasion to do it in the long term. We have been witnesses to this among ourselves.

In the French Revolution there were two movements in contrary directions that must not be confused: one favorable to freedom, the other favorable to despotism.

In the old monarchy, the king alone made the law. Below the sovereign power some half-destroyed remains of provincial institutions were placed. Those provincial institutions were incoherent, badly ordered, often absurd. In the hands of the aristocracy, they had sometimes been instruments of oppression.

The Revolution pronounced itself at the same time against royalty and against provincial institutions. It confused in one and the same hatred all that had preceded it, absolute power and whatever had been able to temper its rigors; it was at once both republican and centralizing.

This double character of the French Revolution is a fact that the friends of absolute power have very carefully laid hold of. When you see them defending administrative centralization, do you believe they are working in favor of despotism? Not at all, they are defending one of the great conquests of the Revolution.* In this manner, one can remain popular and be an enemy of the rights of the people; a hidden servant of tyranny and an avowed lover of freedom.

I have visited the two nations that have developed the system of provincial freedoms to the highest degree and I have listened to the voices of the parties that divide these nations.

In America, I found men who aspired in secret to destroy the democratic institutions of their country. In England, I found others who openly attacked aristocracy; I did not encounter a single one who did not regard provincial freedom as a great good.

In those two countries I saw the evils of the state imputed to an infinite variety of causes, but never to freedom of the township.

I heard citizens attribute the greatness or the prosperity of their native country to a multitude of reasons; but I heard all of them put provincial freedom first in line and class it at the head of all other advantages.

Shall I believe that men naturally so divided, who agree neither on religious doctrines nor on political theories, fall into accord on one sole fact that

*See AT's note X, page 692.

they can best judge since it passes before their eyes daily—and that this fact is erroneous?

It is only peoples who have few or no provincial institutions who deny their utility; that is to say, only those who do not know the thing speak ill of it.

෪ ෪

Chapter 6 ON JUDICIAL POWER IN THE UNITED STATES AND ITS ACTION ON POLITICAL SOCIETY

The Anglo-Americans have preserved in the judicial power all the characteristics that distinguish it among other peoples.—Nevertheless, they have made of it a great political power.—How.—How the judicial system of the Anglo-Americans differs from all others.—Why American judges have the right to declare laws unconstitutional.—How American judges use that right.—Precautions taken by the legislator to prevent the abuse of that right.

I believed I ought to devote a separate chapter to judicial power. Its political importance is so great that it appeared to me that to speak of it in passing would diminish it in the eyes of readers.

There have been confederations elsewhere than in America; republics have been seen in places other than on the shores of the New World; the representative system has been adopted in several European states; but I do not think that, until now, any nation in the world has constituted judicial power in the same manner as the Americans.

What a foreigner understands only with the greatest difficulty in the United States is the judicial organization. There is so to speak no political event in which he does not hear the authority of the judge invoked; and he naturally concludes that in the United States the judge is one of the prime political powers. When, next, he comes to examine the constitution of the courts, he discovers at first only judicial prerogatives and habits in them. In his eyes the magistrate never seems to be introduced into public affairs except by chance, but this same chance recurs every day.

When the Parlement of Paris* made remonstrances and refused to register an edict, when it had a corrupt official cited at its bar, one openly perceived

---

*The French Parlements were not legislatures, but courts.

the political action of judicial power. But nothing similar is seen in the United States.

Americans have preserved in the judicial power all the characteristics by which one is accustomed to recognize it. They have enclosed it exactly in the circle in which it is in the habit of moving.

The first characteristic of judicial power among all peoples is to serve as an arbiter. In order that action on the part of the courts take place, there must be a dispute. In order that there be a judge, there must be a case. As long as a law does not give rise to a dispute, therefore, the judicial power has no occasion to occupy itself with it. The law exists, but the judicial power does not see it. When a judge, in connection with a case, attacks a law relative to that case, he extends the circle of his prerogatives, but he does not go outside it, since it was necessary in some way for him to judge the law in order to come to judge the case. When he pronounces on a law without starting from a case, he goes outside his sphere completely and enters that of the legislative power.

The second characteristic of judicial power is to pronounce on particular cases and not on general principles. Should a judge, in deciding a particular question, destroy a general principle by the certitude people have that, each of the consequences of this same principle being struck down in the same manner, the principle becomes sterile, he remains in the natural circle of his action; but should the judge attack the general principle directly and destroy it without having a particular case in view, he goes outside the circle in which all peoples have agreed to enclose him: he becomes something more important, more useful perhaps than a magistrate, but he ceases to represent judicial power.

The third characteristic of judicial power is to be able to act only when it is appealed to, or, following the legal expression, when it is *seised* [of a matter]. This characteristic is not encountered as generally as the other two. I believe nevertheless that despite exceptions, one can consider it essential. In its nature judicial power is without action; for it to move one must put it in motion. One denounces a crime to it, and it punishes the guilty; one appeals to it to redress an injustice, and it redresses it; one submits an act to it, and it interprets it; but it does not go by itself to prosecute criminals, search for injustice, and examine facts. The judicial power would in a way do violence to this passive nature if it took the initiative by itself and established itself as censor of the laws.

Americans have preserved these three distinctive characteristics in the judicial power. The American judge can only pronounce when there is litigation. He is never occupied except with a particular case; and in order to act he must always wait until he has been seised [of a matter].

The American judge therefore resembles perfectly the magistrates of other nations. Nevertheless, he is vested with an immense political power.

How did that come about? He moves in the same circle and makes use of the same means as other judges; why does he possess a power that the latter do not have?

The cause of it is in this sole fact: Americans have recognized in judges the right to found their rulings on the *Constitution* rather than on the *laws.* In other words, they have permitted them not to apply laws that might appear to them unconstitutional.

I know that a right like this has sometimes been claimed by courts of other countries; but it has never been conceded to them. In America, it is recognized by all powers; one encounters no party nor even a man who disputes it.

The explanation for this will be found in the very principle of American constitutions.

In France, the constitution is an immutable work, or supposed to be so. No power can change anything in it: such is the received theory.*

In England, they recognize in Parliament the right to modify the constitution. In England, the constitution can therefore change constantly, or rather it does not exist. Parliament is at the same time the legislative body and the constituting body.†

In America, political theories are simpler and more rational.

An American constitution is not supposed to be immutable as in France; it cannot be modified by the ordinary powers of society as in England. It forms a separate work that, representing the will of all the people, obliges legislators as well as plain citizens, but that can be changed by the will of the people following forms that have been established and in cases that have been foreseen.

In America, the Constitution can therefore vary; but as long as it exists, it is the origin of all powers. The predominant force is in it alone.

It is easy to see how these differences must influence the position and rights of a judicial body in the three countries that I have cited.

If, in France, the courts could disobey the laws on the ground that they find them unconstitutional, the constituting power would really be in their hands, since they alone would have the right to interpret a constitution whose terms no one could change. They would therefore put themselves in the place of the nation and would dominate society, at least as much as the inherent weakness in the judicial power permitted them to do so.

I know that in refusing judges the right to declare the laws unconstitu-

---

*See AT's note XI, page 693.
†See AT's note XII, page 694.

tional we indirectly give the legislative body the power to change the constitution, since it no longer encounters a legal barrier that stops it. But it is still better to grant the power to change the people's constitution to men who imperfectly represent the will of the people than to others who represent only themselves.

It would be much more unreasonable yet to give English judges the right to resist the will of the legislative body, since Parliament, which makes the law, also makes the constitution, and since, consequently, one cannot in any case call a law unconstitutional when it emanates from the three powers.

Neither of these two reasonings is applicable to America.

In the United States, the Constitution dominates legislators as it does plain citizens. It is therefore the first of laws, and it cannot be modified by a law. It is therefore just that the courts obey the Constitution in preference to all laws. This is due to the very essence of judicial power: to choose among legal arrangements the ones that fetter him most tightly is in a way the natural right of the magistrate.

In France, the constitution is equally the first of laws, and judges have an equal right to take it for the basis of their rulings; but in exercising this right, they could not fail to encroach on another still more sacred than theirs: that of the society in whose name they act. Here ordinary reason must yield before reason of state.

In America, where the nation, by changing its constitution, can always reduce magistrates to obedience, a danger like this is not to be feared. On this point politics and logic are therefore in accord, and there the people as well as the judge equally preserve their privileges.

When one invokes a law before the courts of the United States that the judge deems contrary to the Constitution, he can therefore refuse to apply it. This power is the only one that is particular to the American magistrate, but a great political influence flows from it.

There are in fact very few laws of a nature to escape judicial analysis for long, for there are very few that do not hurt an individual interest and that litigants cannot or will not invoke before the courts.

Now, on the day when the judge refuses to apply a law in a case, at that instant it loses a part of its moral force. Those whom it has wronged are then notified that a means exists of escaping the obligation of obeying it: cases multiply, and it falls into impotence. One of two things then happens: the people change their constitution or the legislature rescinds its law.

Americans have therefore entrusted an immense political power to their courts; but in obliging them to attack the laws only by judicial means, they have much diminished the dangers of this power.

If the judge had been able to attack laws in a theoretical and general manner, if he had been able to take the initiative and censure the legislator, he would have entered onto the political stage with a bang; having become the champion or adversary of one party, he would have appealed to all the passions that divide the country to take part in the conflict. But when the judge attacks a law in an obscure debate and over a particular application, he in part hides the importance of the attack from the regard of the public. His ruling has the goal only of striking an individual interest; the law is injured only by chance.

Besides, the law thus censured is not destroyed: its moral force is diminished, but its material effect is not suspended. It is only little by little and under the repeated blows of jurisprudence that it finally succumbs.

Furthermore, one understands without difficulty that in charging a particular interest with provoking the censure of laws, in intimately binding the case made against the law with the case made against one man, one is assured that legislation will not be attacked lightly. In this system, it is no longer exposed to the daily aggression of the parties. In pointing out the faults of the legislator, one obeys a real need: one starts from a positive and appreciable fact, since it must serve as the basis for a case.

I do not know if this manner of action by American courts is not, at the same time that it is most favorable to public order, also most favorable to liberty.

If the judge could only attack legislators head on, there are some times when he would fear to do it; there are others when the spirit of party would push him every day to dare it. Thus it would happen that the laws would be attacked when the power from which they emanate was weak, and that one would submit to them without murmuring when it was strong; that is to say, one would often attack the laws when it was most useful to respect them and one would respect them when it became easy to oppress in their name.

But the American judge is led despite himself onto the terrain of politics. He judges the law only because he has to judge a case, and he cannot prevent himself from judging the case. The political question that he must resolve is linked to the interest of the litigants, and he cannot refuse to decide it without making a denial of justice. It is in fulfilling the narrow duties imposed on the profession of the magistrate that he performs the act of the citizen. It is true that in this manner judicial censure, exercised by the courts on legislation, cannot extend without distinction to all laws, for there are some of them that can never give rise to the sort of clearly formulated dispute that one calls a case. And when such a dispute is possible, one can still conceive that no one will be encountered who wishes the courts to assume jurisdiction.

Americans have often felt this inconvenience, but they have left the remedy incomplete for fear of giving it a dangerous efficacy in all cases.

Confined within its limits, the power granted to American courts to pronounce on the unconstitutionality of laws still forms one of the most powerful barriers that has ever been raised against the tyranny of political assemblies.

OTHER POWERS GRANTED TO AMERICAN JUDGES

In the United States all citizens have the right to accuse public officials before the ordinary courts.—How they use this right.—Article 75 of the French constitution of the year VIII.—The Americans and the English cannot understand the sense of this article.

I do not know if I need to say that, among a free people like the Americans, all citizens have the right to accuse public officials before ordinary judges and all judges have the right to sentence public officials, so natural is the thing.

It is not to grant a particular privilege to the courts to permit them to punish agents of the executive when they violate the law. To forbid them to do so would be to deny them a natural right.

It did not appear to me that by rendering all officials responsible to the courts in the United States they had weakened the springs of government.

It seemed to me, on the contrary, that Americans in so acting had increased the respect that is owed to those who govern, as the latter take much more care to escape criticism.

Nor did I observe that in the United States they brought many political cases, and I explain this to myself without trouble. A case, whatever its nature may be, is always a difficult and costly enterprise. It is easy to accuse a public man in the newspapers, but it is not without serious grounds that one decides to summon him before justice. To prosecute an official judicially one must therefore have a just ground for complaint; and officials scarcely ever furnish a ground like this when they fear being prosecuted.

This is not due to the republican form that the Americans have adopted, for the same experience can be had every day in England.

These two peoples did not believe that they had secured their independence by permitting the principal agents of power to be brought to judgment. They thought that it was by little cases, brought within reach of the least citizens daily, that one succeeds in guaranteeing freedom, rather than by great proceedings to which one never has recourse or that one employs too late.

In the Middle Ages, when it was very difficult to reach criminals, when judges assumed jurisdiction over some of them, it often happened that they inflicted frightful tortures on these unfortunate ones—which did not diminish the number of the guilty. One has since discovered that in rendering justice at once surer and milder, one renders it at the same time more efficacious.

The Americans and the English think that one must treat arbitrary power and tyranny like theft: make prosecution easy and make the penalty milder.

In year VIII of the French Republic, a constitution appeared in which article 75 was conceived thus: "Agents of the government, other than ministers, can only be prosecuted for deeds relative to their offices by virtue of a decision of the Council of State; and in this case, the prosecution takes place before the ordinary courts."*

The constitution of the year VIII passed on, but not this article, which remained after it; and it is still opposed daily to the just claims of citizens.

I have often tried to make the sense of this article 75 understood by Americans or English, and it has always been very difficult for me to succeed.

What they perceived at first is that the Council of State in France was a great court fixed at the center of the kingdom; there was a sort of tyranny in sending as a preliminary all complainants before it.

But when I sought to make them understand that the Council of State was not a judicial body in the ordinary sense of the word, but an administrative body whose members depended on the king, in such a way that the king, after having sovereignly commanded one of his servants, called a prefect, to commit an iniquity, could sovereignly command another of his servants, called a counselor of state, to prevent the first from being punished; when I showed them the citizen, injured by the order of the prince, reduced to demanding from the prince himself authorization to obtain justice, they refused to believe in enormities like this and accused me of lying or ignorance.

It often happened in the former monarchy that the Parlement decreed the arrest of the public official who committed a punishable offense. Sometimes royal authority intervened to have the proceeding annulled. Then despotism showed itself openly, and in obeying, one submitted only to force.

We have therefore moved far back from the point at which our fathers had arrived; for we allow to be done under color of justice and consecrate in the name of law what violence alone imposed on them.

---

*The Council of State was the chief agency of government under Napoleon Bonaparte's constitution of the year VIII (1799 of the Christian calendar).

☁ ☁

Chapter 7 ON POLITICAL JUDGMENT IN THE UNITED STATES

What the author means by political judgment.—How political judgment is understood in France, England, the United States.—In America, the political judge is occupied only with public officials.—He pronounces removals rather than penalties.—Political judgment, habitual means of government.—Political judgment, as it is intended in the United States, is, despite its mildness and perhaps because of its mildness, a very powerful arm in the hands of the majority.

By political judgment I mean the decree that a political body, temporarily vested with the right to judge, pronounces.

In absolute governments, it is useless to give judgments extraordinary forms; the prince in whose name the accused is prosecuted, being master of tribunals as of everything else, has no need to seek a guarantee elsewhere than in the idea people have of his power. The sole fear he can conceive is that even the external appearances of justice will not be kept and that in wishing to affirm his authority, it will be dishonored.

But in most free countries, where the majority can never act on tribunals as an absolute prince would do, it has sometimes happened that judicial power is temporarily placed in the hands of the representatives of society themselves. They would rather temporarily confuse the powers in this way than violate the necessary principle of unity of government. England, France, and the United States have introduced political judgment into their laws: it is curious to examine the advantage that these three great peoples have gotten from it.

In England and France, the House of Lords forms the high criminal court of the nation.[1] It does not judge all political offenses, but it can judge them all.

Beside the House of Lords is another political power, vested with the right to accuse. The sole difference that exists on this point between the two countries is this: in England deputies can accuse whomsoever it well pleases them before the Lords, while in France they can prosecute only ministers of the king in this manner.

Furthermore, in both countries the House of Lords has at its disposition all penal laws with which to strike offenders.

---

1. In addition, the House of Lords in England forms the last stage of appeal in certain civil affairs. See Blackstone, bk. 3, chap. 4 [*Commentaries*, vol. 3, 57].

In the United States as in Europe, one of the two branches of the legislature is vested with the right to accuse, and the other with the right to judge. The [House of] Representatives denounces the guilty one, the Senate punishes him.

But the Senate can be *seised* only by the *representatives*, and the representatives can accuse only *public officials* before it. Thus the Senate has a more restricted competence than the court of lords in France, and the representatives have a more extensive right of accusation than our deputies.

But here is the greatest difference that exists between America and Europe: in Europe, political tribunals can apply all the provisions of the penal code; in America, when they have taken away from a guilty person the public character with which he had been vested and have declared him unworthy of occupying any political office in the future, their right is exhausted and the task of ordinary tribunals begins.

I suppose that the president of the United States has committed a crime of high treason.

The House of Representatives accuses him, the senators pronounce his deposition. Afterwards, he appears before a jury, which alone can take away his freedom or life.

This serves to cast a bright light on the subject that occupies us.

In introducing political judgment into their laws, the Europeans wanted to reach great criminals, whatever was their birth, their rank, or their power in the state. To succeed at it, they have temporarily gathered all the prerogatives of tribunals within one great political body.

The legislator has then been transformed into a magistrate; he can establish the crime, classify it, and punish it. In giving him the rights of a judge, the law has imposed on him all its obligations, and it has bound him to observe all the forms of justice.

When a political tribunal, French or English, has a public official answerable to it, and it pronounces a conviction against him, by that fact it takes his office away from him and can declare him unworthy of occupying any in the future: but here the political removal and interdiction are a consequence of the decree and not the decree itself.

In Europe, political judgment is therefore a judicial act rather than an administrative measure.

The contrary is seen in the United States, and it is easy to be convinced that political judgment there is indeed an administrative measure rather than a judicial act.

It is true that the decree of the Senate is judicial in form; to render it, senators are obliged to conform to the solemnity and usages of the proceeding. It is also judicial in the grounds on which it is founded; the Senate is generally obliged to take for the basis of its decision an offense of the common law. But it is administrative in its object.

If the principal goal of the American legislator had really been to arm a political body with great judicial power, it would not have confined its action within the circle of public officials, for the most dangerous enemies of the state may not be vested with any office; this is above all true in republics, where the favor of parties is the primary power and where one is often all the stronger for not legally exercising any power.

If the American legislator had wanted to give to society itself the right to prevent great crimes in the manner of the judge, by fear of punishment, he would have put at the disposition of political tribunals all the resources of the penal code; but he furnished them only an incomplete arm that cannot reach the most dangerous of criminals. For a judgment of political interdiction matters little to one who wants to overturn the laws themselves.

The principal goal of political judgment in the United States is therefore to withdraw power from someone who makes a bad use of it and to prevent this same citizen from being vested with it in the future. It is, as one sees, an administrative action to which they have given the solemnity of a [judicial] decree.

In this matter, therefore, the Americans have created something mixed. They have given to administrative removal all the guarantees of political judgment, and they have removed from political judgment its greatest rigors.

This point fixed, everything follows; one then discovers why American constitutions submit all civil officials to the jurisdiction of the Senate and exempt the military from it, whose crimes are nevertheless more to be dreaded. In the civil order, the Americans have so to speak no dismissible officials: some are irremovable, others have their rights by a mandate that cannot be abrogated. In order to take power away from them, it is therefore necessary to judge them all. But the military depend on the head of state, who is himself a civil official. In reaching the head of state, one strikes them all with the same blow.[2]

Now if one comes to compare the European system and the American system in the effects that each produces or can produce, one discovers differences no less tangible.

In France and England political judgment is considered as an extraordinary arm that society ought not to make use of except to save itself in moments of great peril.

One cannot deny that political judgment, as intended in Europe, violates

2. It is not that one can remove an officer's rank, but one can take his command away from him.

the conservative principle of the division of powers and that it constantly threatens the freedom and the lives of men.

Political judgment in the United States makes only an indirect attack on the principle of the division of powers; it does not threaten the existence of citizens; it does not hang over all heads, as in Europe, since it strikes only those who, by accepting public offices, have submitted in advance to its rigors.

It is all at once less dreadful and less efficacious.

Thus the legislators of the United States did not consider it as an extreme remedy for the great ills of society, but as an habitual means of government.

From this point of view, it perhaps exerts more real influence on the social body in America than in Europe. One must not, in fact, allow oneself to be taken in by the apparent mildness of American legislation in what relates to political judgments. One should remark in the first place that in the United States the tribunal that pronounces these judgments is composed of the same elements and is subject to the same influences as the body charged with accusing, which gives an almost irresistible impetus to the vindictive passions of the parties. If political judges in the United States cannot pronounce penalties as severe as political judges in Europe, there are therefore fewer chances of being acquitted by them. Conviction is less dreadful and more certain.

Europeans, in establishing political tribunals, had for their principal object to *punish* the guilty; Americans, to *take power away* from them. Political judgment in the United States is in some fashion a preventive measure. One therefore ought not to fetter the judge with very exact criminal definitions.

Nothing is more frightening than the vagueness of American laws when they define political crimes properly speaking. "The President [. . .] shall be removed from Office on Impeachment for, and Conviction of" (says the Constitution of the United States, art. 1, sec. 4) "Treason, Bribery or other high Crimes and Misdemeanors."* Most of the state constitutions are still more obscure.

"The senate shall [. . .] hear and determine all impeachments made [. . .] against any officer or officers of the commonwealth," says the constitution of Massachusetts, "for misconduct and maladministration in their offices."[3] "All [. . .] offending against the State, either by maladministration, corruption, neglect of duty, or any other high crime or misdemeanor," says the constitution of Virginia, "shall be impeachable by the house of delegates."† There

*The provisions for impeachment are found in art. 2, sec. 4.
†Virginia constitution of 1830, art. 3, sec. 13.
3. Chap. 1, sec. 2, no. 8.

are some constitutions that, in order to allow an unlimited responsibility to weigh on public officials, do not specify any crime.[4]

But what renders the American laws so dreadful in this matter arises, I will dare to say, from their mildness itself.

We have seen that in Europe, the removal of an official and his political interdiction is one consequence of the penalty and that in America, it is the penalty itself. This is the result: in Europe, political tribunals are vested with terrible rights that they sometimes do not know how to use; and it happens that they do not punish for fear of punishing too much. But in America, they do not recoil before a penalty that does not make humanity tremble: to condemn a political enemy to death in order to take away his power is a horrible assassination in the eyes of all; to declare one's adversary unworthy of possessing that same power and to remove it from him, leaving him his freedom and his life, can appear the honest result of a conflict.

Now, this judgment, so easy to pronounce, is not less the height of misfortune for the common sort among those to whom it applies. Great criminals will doubtless brave its futile rigors; ordinary men will see in it a decree that destroys their position, stains their honor, and condemns them to a shameful idleness worse than death.

Political judgment in the United States therefore exerts an influence on the working of society so much the greater as it seems less dreadful. It does not act directly on the governed, but it renders a majority the entire master of those who govern; it does not give to the legislature an immense power that it could exercise only on the day of a crisis; it allows it to have a moderated, regular power that it can use every day. If the force is less great, on the other hand, the use is more convenient and the abuse easier.

In preventing political tribunals from pronouncing judicial penalties, the Americans therefore seem to me to have prevented the most terrible consequences of legislative tyranny rather than the tyranny itself. And I do not know if, all in all, political judgment, as it is intended in the United States, is not the most formidable arm that has ever been put in the hands of the majority.

When the American republics begin to degenerate, I believe that one will be able to recognize it easily: it will be enough to see if the number of political judgments rises.*

*See AT's note XIII, page 694.
4. See the constitutions of Illinois, Maine, Connecticut, and Georgia.

Chapter 8 ON THE FEDERAL CONSTITUTION

Up to now I have considered each state as forming a complete whole, and I have shown the different springs that the people have to move it, as well as the means of action they make use of. But all the states that I have viewed as independent are, however, forced in certain cases to obey a superior authority, that of the Union. The time has come to examine the portion of sovereignty that has been conceded to the Union and to cast a rapid glance at the federal constitution.[1]

HISTORY OF THE FEDERAL CONSTITUTION

Origin of the first Union.—Its weakness.—Congress appeals to its constituent power.— Interval of two years that elapses between that moment and the one when the new constitution is promulgated.

The thirteen colonies that simultaneously shook off the yoke of England at the end of the last century had, as I have already said,* the same religion, the same language, the same mores, almost the same laws; they struggled against a common enemy; they should therefore have had strong reasons to unite intimately with one another and to be absorbed into one and the same nation.

But each of them, having always had a separate existence and a government within its scope, had created interests as well as particular usages for itself and repudiated a solid and complete union that might have made its individual importance disappear into a common importance. Hence, two opposed tendencies: one that brought the Anglo-Americans to unite, the other that brought them to divide.

As long as the war with the mother country lasted, necessity made the principle of union prevail. And although the laws that constituted this union were defective, the common bond subsisted despite them.[2]

---

* *DA* I 1.2.

1. See the text of the federal constitution.

2. See the articles of the first confederation, formed in 1778. That federal constitution was adopted by all the states only in 1781.

See also the analysis of that constitution given by *The Federalist,* from No. 15 up to and including No. 22, and Mr. Story in his *Commentaries on the Constitution of the United States,* 85–115. [AT refers to an abridged edition of Story's *Commentaries* (Boston, 1833), 84–104. Joseph

But as soon as peace was concluded, the vices of the legislation showed themselves openly: the state appeared to dissolve all at once. Each colony, having become an independent republic, took possession of its entire sovereignty. The federal government, condemned by its very constitution to weakness and no longer sustained by the sentiment of public danger, saw its flag abandoned to outrages by the great peoples of Europe, while it could not find enough resources to stand up to the Indian nations and to pay the interest on debts contracted during the War of Independence. Close to perishing, it officially declared its impotence and appealed to the constituent power.[3]

If ever America was able to elevate itself for a few instants to that height of glory to which the proud imagination of its inhabitants would constantly like to show us, it was in that supreme moment when the national power came, in a way, to abdicate its empire.

The spectacle of a people's struggling energetically to win its independence is one that every century has been able to furnish. Moreover, the efforts the Americans made to escape from the yoke of the English have been much exaggerated. Separated by 1,300 leagues of sea from their enemies, aided by a powerful ally, the United States owed victory much more to its position than to the valor of its armies or to the patriotism of its citizens. Who would dare to compare the American war to the wars of the French Revolution, and the Americans' efforts to ours, when France was up against attacks from all Europe, without money, without credit, without allies, casting a twentieth of its population before its enemies, one hand smothering the fire that was devouring its entrails and the other parading the torch around with it? But what is new in the history of societies is to see a great people, warned by its legislators that the wheels of the government are stopping, turn its regard on itself without haste and without fear, sound the depth of the ill, contain itself for two entire years in order to discover the remedy at leisure, and when the remedy is pointed out, submit voluntarily to it without its costing humanity one tear or drop of blood.

Story (1779–1845) was a Supreme Court justice and author of two works that AT consulted in writing *Democracy in America*: the *Commentaries* and *Public and General Statutes Passed by the Congress of the United States, 1789–1823*. In a letter to Francis Lieber, Story wrote: "The work of De Tocqueville has a great reputation abroad, partly founded on their ignorance that he has borrowed the greater part of his reflections from American works, and little from his own observations. The main body of his materials will be found in the Federalist, and in Story's Commentaries on the Constitution [. . .]. You know ten times as much as he does of the actual workings of our system and of its true theory." Letter of May 9, 1840; cited by G. W. Pierson, *Tocqueville in America*, 731.]

3. It was on February 21, 1787, that Congress made this declaration.

When the insufficiency of the first federal constitution was felt, the exuberance of the political passions to which the revolution had given rise was calmed in part, and all the great men that it had created were still alive. This was a double blessing for America. The assembly, few in number,[4] that was charged with drafting the second constitution included the finest minds and noblest characters that had ever appeared in the New World. George Washington presided over it.

That national commission, after long and mature deliberations, finally offered for adoption by the people the body of organic laws that still regulates the Union in our day. All the states successively adopted it.[5] The new federal government took up its office in 1789, after a two-year interregnum. So the American Revolution ended precisely at the moment when ours began.

SUMMARY PICTURE OF THE FEDERAL CONSTITUTION

Division of powers between federal sovereignty and that of the states.—State governments remain the common rule;—the federal government, the exception.

An initial difficulty must have presented itself to the minds of the Americans. It was the question of apportioning sovereignty in such a way that the different states that formed the Union might continue to govern themselves in all that concerned only their internal prosperity, without having the entire nation, represented by the Union, cease to make up a body and to provide for all its general needs. A complex question, difficult to resolve.

It was impossible to fix beforehand, in an exact and complete manner, the portion of power that would fall to each of the two governments between which sovereignty was going to be apportioned.

Who could foresee in advance all the details of the life of a people?

The duties and the rights of the federal government were simple and easy enough to define, because the Union had been formed with the goal of responding to a few great general needs. The duties and rights of the state governments were, on the contrary, multiple and complicated, because these governments entered into all the details of social life.

The prerogatives of the federal government were therefore carefully defined, and it was declared that everything that was not comprised in that

---

4. It was composed of only fifty-five members. Washington, Madison, Hamilton, the two Morrises [Gouverneur Morris and Robert Morris] were part of it.

5. It was not the legislators who adopted it. The people named deputies for this sole object. In each of these assemblies the new constitution was the object of profound discussions.

definition returned to the prerogatives of the state governments. Thus the state governments remained the common rule; the federal government was the exception.[6]

But as it was foreseen that, in practice, questions could arise relative to the exact limits of this exceptional government, and that it would be dangerous to abandon the solution of these questions to ordinary tribunals instituted in the different states by the states themselves, they created a high federal court,[7] a unique tribunal, one attribute of which was to maintain the division of power between the two rival governments as the Constitution had established it.[8]

PREROGATIVES OF THE FEDERAL GOVERNMENT

Power granted to the federal government to make peace, war, to establish general taxes.—Objects of internal politics with which it can occupy itself.—The government of the Union, more centralized on some points than was the royal government under the former French monarchy.

Among themselves peoples are only individuals. It is above all to appear with advantage towards foreigners that a nation has need of a unitary government.

---

6. See amendments to the federal constitution [particularly the tenth]. *Federalist* 32. Story, *Commentaries*, 711[–714]. *Kent's Commentaries*, vol. 1, 364.

Remark even that every time the Constitution has not reserved for Congress the *exclusive* right to regulate certain matters, the states can do it while awaiting that Congress be pleased to occupy itself with them. Example: the Congress has the right to make a general bankruptcy law, it does not do it: each state could make one in its manner. Besides, this point was established only after discussion before the courts. It exists only in jurisprudence.

7. The action of this court is indirect, as we shall see below.

8. Thus *Federalist* 45 explains the apportionment of sovereignty between the Union and the particular states: "The powers delegated by the proposed Constitution to the federal government," it says, "are few and defined. Those which are to remain in the state governments are numerous and indefinite. The former will be exercised principally on external objects, as war, peace, negotiation, and foreign commerce[; . . .] The powers reserved to the several States will extend to all the objects which, in the ordinary course of affairs, concern the lives, liberties [. . .] and prosperity of the State."

I shall often have occasion to cite the *Federalist* in this work. When the project of law that has since become the Constitution of the United States was still before the people and submitted for their adoption, three men, already celebrated, and who have since become even more so, John Jay, Hamilton, and Madison, associated for the purpose of making stand out in the eyes of the nation the advantages of the project that had been submitted to it. With this design, they published in newspaper form a series of articles the sum of which forms a complete treatise. They had given to their newspaper [series] the name *Federalist*, which was kept for the work.

The *Federalist* is a fine book that, though special to America, ought to be familiar to statesmen of every country.

The Union, therefore, was granted the exclusive right to make peace and war; to conclude commercial treaties; to raise armies, to equip fleets.[9]

The necessity of a national government does not make itself felt as imperiously in directing the internal affairs of society.

Still, there are certain general interests for which only a general authority can usefully provide.

To the Union was given over the right to regulate all that relates to the value of money; it was charged with the postal service; it was given the right to open the great [lines of] communication that would unite the various parts of the territory.[10]

In general, the governments of the different states were considered free in their sphere; they could, however, abuse that independence and by imprudent measures compromise the security of the entire Union; in those rare cases, defined in advance, the federal government is permitted to intervene in the internal affairs of the states.[11] Thus while in each of the confederated republics the power to modify and change its legislation is recognized, they are nevertheless forbidden to make retroactive laws and to create a body of nobles within themselves.[12]

Finally, as it was necessary that the federal government be able to fulfill the obligations that were imposed on it, it was given the unlimited right to levy taxes.[13]

When one pays attention to the apportionment of powers as the federal constitution established it; when one examines, on the one hand, the share of sovereignty that was reserved to the particular states, and on the other hand, the portion of power that the Union has taken, one readily discovers that the federal legislators had formed very clear and very just ideas of what I have previously named governmental centralization.*

Not only does the United States form a republic, but also a confederation. Nevertheless, its national authority was in some regards more centralized than it was in the same period in several of the absolute monarchies of Europe. I shall cite only two examples.

---

*DA I 1.5.

9. See Constitution, [art. 1,] sec. 8, *Federalist* 41 and 42. *Kent's Commentaries*, vol. 1, 207ff. Story, *Commentaries*, 358–382, 409–426.

10. There are still several other rights of this kind, such as that of making a general law about bankruptcies, and of granting patents of invention . . . One senses well enough what made the intervention of the entire Union necessary in these matters.

11. Even in that case its intervention is indirect. The Union intervenes through its courts, as we shall see further on.

12. Federal constitution, art. 1, sec. 10.

13. Constitution, [art. 1,] secs. 8, 9, and 10. *Federalist* 30–36, 41, 42, 43, 44. *Kent's Commentaries*, vol. 1, 207 [222] and 381. Story, *Commentaries*, 329[–357], 514.

France had thirteen sovereign courts that, most often, had the right to interpret the law without appeal. It possessed, in addition, certain provinces called *pays d'état*,* which, after the sovereign authority charged with representing the nation had ordered the levying of a tax, could refuse their cooperation.

The Union has only a single court to interpret the law, like the single legislature that makes it; the tax voted by the representatives of the nation obliges all citizens. The Union is therefore more centralized on these two essential points than was the French monarchy; nevertheless, the Union is only an assemblage of confederated republics.

In Spain, certain provinces had the power to establish a system of customs that was their own, a power that is joined, by its very essence, to national sovereignty.

In America, Congress alone has the right to regulate the commercial relations of the states among themselves. The government of the confederation is therefore more centralized on this point than that of the kingdom of Spain.

It is true that in France and in Spain, the royal power always being in a position to execute, by force if need be, what the constitution of the kingdom refused it the right to do, one arrived after all is said and done at the same point. But I am speaking here of the theory.

FEDERAL POWERS

After having enclosed the federal government within its clearly drawn circle of action, it was a question of knowing how to make it move within that.

LEGISLATIVE POWERS

Division of the legislative body into two branches.—Differences in the manner of forming the two houses.—The principle of the independence of the states triumphs in the formation of the Senate.—The dogma of national sovereignty in the composition of the House of Representatives.—Singular effects that result from the fact that constitutions are logical only when peoples are young.

In the organization of the powers of the Union, on many points they followed plans that had been drawn before by the particular constitutions of each of the states.

The federal legislative body of the Union was composed of a Senate and a House of Representatives.

---

* *Pays d'état* were French provinces that had traditional assemblies known as provincial estates, some of them with considerable rights and privileges.

In forming each of these assemblies the spirit of conciliation brought diverse rules to be followed.

Above I gave the sense that when they wanted to establish the federal constitution, two opposed interests were presented to each other. Those two interests had given birth to two opinions.

Some wanted to make the Union a league of independent states, a kind of congress, where the representatives of distinct peoples would come to discuss certain points of common interest.

Others wanted to unite all the inhabitants of the former colonies into one and the same people, and to give them a government that, although its sphere was limited, could nevertheless act in this sphere as the sole, unique representative of the nation. The practical consequences of these two theories were very different.

Thus, if it was a question of organizing a league and not a national government, it was for the majority of the states to make the law, and not the majority of the inhabitants of the Union. For each state, great or small, would then preserve its character as an independent power and would enter the Union on a footing of perfect equality.

In contrast, from the moment that the inhabitants of the United States were considered to form one and the same people, it would be natural that the majority of citizens of the Union alone make the law.

One understands that the small states could not consent to the application of this doctrine without completely abdicating their existence in whatever concerned federal sovereignty; for from having the power of a co-ruler they would become an insignificant fraction of a great people. The first system would have granted them unreasonable power; the second annulled them.

In this state of things, what happened was what almost always happens when interests are opposed to reasonings: they bent the rules of logic. The legislators adopted a middle term that reconciled by force two theoretically irreconcilable systems.

The principle of the independence of the states triumphed in the formation of the Senate; the dogma of national sovereignty, in the composition of the House of Representatives.

Each state would send two senators to Congress and a certain number of representatives in proportion to its population.[14]

---

14. Every ten years Congress fixes anew the number of deputies that each state will send to the House of Representatives. The total number was 69 in 1789; in 1833 it was 240 (*American Almanac:* 1834, 194). [*The American Almanac and Repository of Useful Knowledge* (Boston: Gray and Bowen, 1834). The correct reference is p. 124.]

The Constitution said that there would not be more than one representative for 30,000 persons; but it did not fix a limit for fewer. Congress has not believed it should increase the number

As a result of this arrangement, in our day the state of New York has forty representatives in Congress and only two senators; the state of Delaware, two senators and only one representative. The state of Delaware is, therefore, the equal of the state of New York in the Senate, whereas in the House of Representatives the latter has forty times more influence than the former. Thus it can happen that a minority of the nation, dominating the Senate, entirely paralyzes the will of the majority represented by the other house, which is contrary to the spirit of constitutional governments.

All this shows well to what degree it is rare and difficult to bind all the parts of legislation in a logical and rational manner.

In the long term, time always gives birth to different interests in the same people and consecrates diverse rights. When it is then a question of establishing a general constitution, each of those interests and rights forms just as many natural obstacles that oppose any political principle in following out all its consequences. It is therefore only at the birth of societies that one can be completely logical in the laws. When you see a people enjoying this advantage, do not hasten to conclude that it is wise; think rather that it is young.

In the period when the federal constitution was formed, there still existed among the Anglo-Americans only two interests positively opposed one to another: the interest of individuality for the particular states, the interest of union for the entire people; and it was necessary to come to a compromise between them.

Still, one ought to recognize that this part of the Constitution has, up to the present, not produced the evils that one could have feared.

All the states are young; they are close to one another; they have homogeneous mores, ideas, and needs; the difference that results from their greater or lesser size is not enough to give them very opposed interests. Therefore the small states have never been seen to join forces in the Senate against the designs of the great. Besides, there is such an irresistible force in the legal expression of the will of a whole people that when the majority comes to express itself through the organ of the House of Representatives, the Senate finds itself very weak in its presence.

In addition, one must not forget that it was not the responsibility of the American legislators to make one and the same nation of the people to whom

---

of representatives in proportion to the increase of the population. By the first law passed on this subject, April 14, 1792 (see *Laws of the United States* by Story, vol. 1, 235) [Joseph Story, *Public and General Statutes Passed by the Congress of the United States, 1789–1827* (Boston, 1828)], it was decided that there would be one representative for 33,000 inhabitants. The latest law, which was passed in 1832, fixed the number at one representative for 48,000 inhabitants. The population represented is composed of all free men and three-fifths of the number of slaves.

they wished to give laws. The goal of the federal constitution was not to destroy the existence of the states, but only to restrict it. Therefore from the moment when these secondary bodies were allowed real power (and it could not be taken away from them), one renounced in advance the habitual use of constraint to bend them to the will of the majority. This postulated, the introduction of their individual strength into the wheels of the federal government was nothing extraordinary. It only certified an existing fact, that of a recognized power that had to be managed and not assaulted.

ANOTHER DIFFERENCE BETWEEN THE SENATE AND THE HOUSE OF REPRESENTATIVES

The Senate named by provincial legislators.—The [House of] Representatives, by the people.—Two stages of election for the first.—A single one for the second.—Duration of the different mandates.—Prerogatives.

The Senate differs from the other house not only by the principle of representation itself, but also by the mode of election, by the duration of the mandate, and by the diversity of prerogatives.

The House of Representatives is named by the people; the Senate, by the legislators of each state.

The one is the product of direct election, the other, of election in two stages.

The mandate of the representatives lasts only two years; that of the senators, six.

The House of Representatives has only legislative functions; it participates in judicial power only in accusing public officials; the Senate concurs in the formation of laws; it judges political offenses that are referred to it by the House of Representatives; it is, in addition, the great executive council of the nation. Treaties concluded by the president must be validated by the Senate; his choices, to be definitive, need to receive the approbation of that same body.[15]

ON THE EXECUTIVE POWER[16]

Dependence of the president.—Elective and responsible.—Free in his sphere, the Senate oversees him and does not direct him.—The salary of the president fixed when he takes his office.—Suspensive veto.

---

15. See *Federalist* 52–66. Story, [*Commentaries,*] 199–314. Constitution, [art. 1,] secs. 2 and 3.

16. *Federalist* 67–77. Constitution, art. 2. Story, [*Commentaries,*] 315, 515–780 [317–325, 515–580]. *Kent's Commentaries,* [vol. 1,] 255 [253–271].

The American legislators had a difficult task to fulfill: they wanted to create an executive power that depended on the majority and that was nonetheless strong enough by itself to act freely in its sphere.

Maintenance of the republican form required that the representative of executive power be subject to the national will.

The president is an elective magistrate. His honor, his goods, his freedom, his life answer constantly to the people for the good use he makes of his power. In exercising that power, moreover, he is not completely independent: the Senate oversees his relations with foreign powers as well as the distribution of posts, so that he can neither be corrupted nor corrupt.

The legislators of the Union recognized that the executive power could not fulfill its task with dignity and utility if they did not succeed in giving it more stability and more force than it had been granted in the particular states.

The president was named for four years and could be reelected. With a future, he would have the courage to work for the public good and the means of effecting it.

They made the president the sole, unique representative of the executive power of the Union. They even guarded against subordinating his will to that of a council: a dangerous means that, while weakening the action of the government, diminishes the responsibility of those who govern. The Senate has the right to make some of the acts of the president fruitless; but it can neither force him to act nor share the executive power with him.

The action of the legislature on the executive power can be direct; we have just seen that Americans took care that it not be. It can also be indirect.

In depriving a public official of his salary, the houses remove a part of his independence; one must fear that they, as masters of lawmaking, will, little by little, take away from him the share of power that the Constitution wanted to preserve for him.

This dependence of the executive power is one of the vices inherent in republican constitutions. The Americans were not able to destroy the inclination that brings legislative assemblies to take hold of the government, but they rendered this inclination less irresistible.

The salary of the president is fixed, at his entry into office, for the time that his magistracy will last. In addition, the president is armed with a suspensive veto that permits him to stop laws from being passed that could destroy the share of independence that the Constitution has left him. Nonetheless, the struggle between the president and the legislature can only be unequal, since the latter, if it perseveres in its designs, can always master the resistance opposed to it; but the suspensive veto at least forces it to retrace its steps; it obliges it to consider the question anew, and this time, it can no longer decide it except with a majority of two-thirds in agreement. The veto, moreover, is a sort of appeal to the people. The executive power, which could have been oppressed in secret without this guarantee, then pleads its cause and makes its reasons heard. But if the legislature perseveres in its designs, can it not always defeat the resistance opposed to it? To that I shall respond that in the constitution of all peoples, whatever the rest of its nature may be, there is a point at which the legislator is obliged to rely on the good sense and virtue of citizens. That point is closer and more visible in republics, more distant and more carefully hidden in monarchies; but it is always to be found somewhere. There is no country where the law can foresee everything and where institutions will take the place of reason and mores.

HOW THE POSITION OF THE PRESIDENT OF THE UNITED STATES DIFFERS FROM THAT OF A CONSTITUTIONAL KING IN FRANCE

The executive power in the United States, limited and exceptional like the sovereignty in whose name it acts.—The executive power in France extends to everything, like the sovereignty.—The king is one of the authors of the law.—The president is only the executor of the law.—Other differences that arise from the duration of the two powers.—The president hindered in the sphere of the executive power.—The king is free in it.—France, despite these differences, resembles a republic more than the Union resembles a monarchy.—Comparison of the number of officials in the two countries who depend on the executive power.

The executive power plays such a great role in the destiny of nations that I want to stop here for a moment to make the place it occupies among the Americans better understood.

In order to conceive a clear and precise idea of the position of the president of the United States, it is useful to compare it to that of a king in one of the constitutional monarchies of Europe.

In this comparison I shall not be much attached to external signs of power; they deceive the eye of the observer more than guide it.

When a monarchy is transformed little by little into a republic, the executive power in it preserves titles, honors, respect, and even money, for a long time after it has lost the reality of its power. The English, after having cut off the head of one their kings and having chased another of them from the throne,* still get on their knees to speak to the successors of those princes.

---

*Charles I was beheaded in 1649; James II was chased from the throne in 1688. The French, it may be noted, had likewise beheaded a king (Louis XVI in 1793) and chased one from the throne (Charles X in 1830).

On the other hand, when republics fall under the yoke of one alone, power continues to show itself simple, even, and modest in its manners, as if it were not already elevated above everyone. When the emperors disposed despotically of the fortunes and lives of their fellow citizens, in speaking to them one still called them Caesar, and they went to sup familiarly at their friends' homes.

One must therefore leave the surface and penetrate further.

Sovereignty in the United States is divided between the Union and the states, whereas among us it is one and compact; hence arises the first and the greatest difference that I perceive between the president of the United States and the king of France.

In the United States the executive power is limited and exceptional, like the very sovereignty in whose name it acts; in France it extends to everything, just like the sovereignty.

The Americans have a federal government; we have a national government.

That is a first cause of inferiority, resulting from the very nature of things; but it is not the only one. The second in importance is this: one can, properly speaking, define sovereignty as the right to make laws.

The king in France really constitutes a part of the sovereign, since laws do not exist if he refuses to sanction them; he is, in addition, the executor of the laws.

The president is equally the executor of the law, but he does not really concur in making it since, in refusing his assent, he cannot prevent it from existing. He therefore makes up no part of the sovereign; he is only its agent.

Not only does the king in France constitute one share of the sovereign, but he also participates in the formation of the legislature, which is the other share of it. He participates in it by naming the members of one house and by putting an end to the duration of the mandate of the other at his will. The president of the United States does not concur at all in the composition of the legislative body and cannot dissolve it.

The king shares with the houses the right to propose a law.

The president has no such initiative.

The king is represented, within the houses, by a certain number of agents who set forth his views, support his opinions, and make his maxims of government prevail.

The president has no entry into Congress; his ministers are excluded from it as is he, and it is only by indirect channels that he can make his influence and opinions penetrate this great body.

The king of France therefore walks as an equal with the legislature, which cannot act without him as he cannot act without it.

The president is placed beside the legislature as an inferior and dependent power.

In the exercise of the executive power properly speaking, the point at which his position seems to come closest to that of the king of France, the president still has several very great causes of inferiority.

The power of the king in France has, first, the advantage of longevity over that of the president. For longevity is one of the first elements of force. One loves and fears only what will exist for a long time.

The president of the United States is a magistrate elected for four years. The king in France is a hereditary head.

In the exercise of executive power, the president of the United States is continually subject to jealous supervision. He prepares treaties, but he does not make them; he designates [candidates] for posts, but he does not name them.[17]

The king of France is absolute master in the sphere of executive power.

The president of the United States is responsible for his actions. French law says that the person of the king of France is inviolable.

Nevertheless, above the one as above the other stands a directing power, that of public opinion. This power is less defined in France than in the United States; less recognized, less formulated in the laws; but it does in fact exist there. In America, it proceeds by elections and decrees; in France, by revolutions. France and the United States, despite the diversity of their constitutions, thus have this point in common, that public opinion is, as a result, the dominant power. The generative principle of the laws is therefore, to tell the truth, the same in the two peoples, although its development is more or less free and the consequences one draws from it are often different. This principle, in its nature, is essentially republican. Thus I think that France, with its king, resembles a republic more than the Union, with its president, resembles a monarchy.

In all that precedes, I have taken care to point out only the chief points of difference. If I had wanted to enter into details, the picture would have been still more striking. But I have too much to say not to wish to be brief.

I have remarked that the power of the president of the United States is exercised only in the sphere of a restricted sovereignty, whereas that of the king in France acts within the circle of a complete sovereignty.

I could have shown the governmental power of the king in France ex-

17. The Constitution had left doubtful the point of knowing whether the president had to take the advice of the Senate in the case of discharging as in the case of nominating a federal official. *Federalist 77* seemed to establish the affirmative; but in 1789 Congress decided with all reason that, since the president was responsible, he could not be forced to make use of agents who did not have his confidence. See *Kent's Commentaries*, vol. 1, 289.

ceeding even its natural limits, however extended those might be, and penetrating in a thousand ways into the administration of individual interests.

To that cause of influence, I could add the one that results from the great number of public officials, who almost all owe their mandate to the executive power. Among us this number has surpassed all known bounds; it comes to 138,000.[18] Each of these 138,000 ought to be considered as an element of force. The president does not have the absolute right to name [officials] to public posts, and those posts scarcely exceed 12,000.[19]

ACCIDENTAL CAUSES THAT CAN INCREASE THE INFLUENCE OF THE EXECUTIVE POWER

External security the Union enjoys.—A waiting policy.—Army of 6,000 soldiers.—Only a few warships.—The president possesses great prerogatives that he has no occasion to make use of.—In what he does have occasion to execute, he is weak.

If the executive power is less strong in America than in France, one must attribute the cause of it perhaps more to circumstances than laws.

It is principally in relations with foreigners that the executive power of a nation finds occasion to deploy its skill and force.

If the life of the Union were constantly threatened, if its great interests were mixed every day with those of other powerful peoples, one would see the executive power grow larger in opinion, through what one would expect from it and what it would execute.

The president of the United States is, it is true, the chief of the army, but that army is composed of six thousand soldiers; he commands the fleet, but the fleet counts only a few warships; he directs the affairs of the Union towards foreign peoples, but the United States has no neighbors. Separated from the rest of the world by the ocean, still too weak to wish to dominate the sea, it has no enemies, and its interests are only rarely in contact with those of other nations of the globe.

This makes one see well that the practice of government must not be judged by the theory.

18. The sums paid by the state to these various officials amount each year to 200,000,000 francs.

19. Each year they publish an almanac in the United States called *National Calendar* [Peter Force, *The National Calendar and Annals of the United States* (Washington, 1833)]; one finds in it the names of all federal officials. It is the *National Calendar* of 1833 that furnished me the figure that I give here.

It would result from what precedes that the king of France has eleven times more places at his disposal than the president of the United States, although the population of France is only one and a half times more considerable than that of the Union.

The president of the United States possesses almost royal prerogatives, which he has no occasion to make use of, and the rights which, up to now, he can use are very circumscribed: the laws permit him to be strong, circumstances keep him weak.

It is, on the contrary, circumstances more than laws that give to the royal authority of France its greater force.

In France, the executive power struggles constantly against immense obstacles and disposes of immense resources to defeat them. It is increased by the greatness of the things that it executes and by the importance of the events that it directs, without modifying its constitution because of them.

Had the laws created it as weak and as circumscribed as that of the Union, its influence would soon become much greater.

WHY THE PRESIDENT OF THE UNITED STATES DOES NOT NEED TO HAVE A MAJORITY IN THE HOUSES IN ORDER TO DIRECT AFFAIRS

It is an established axiom in Europe that a constitutional king cannot govern when the opinion of the legislative chambers does not accord with his.

Several presidents of the United States have been seen to lose the support of the majority in the legislative body without being obliged to abandon power and without its resulting in any great evil for society.

I have heard this fact cited to prove the independence and force of the executive power in America. It suffices to reflect a few moments to see, on the contrary, the proof of his powerlessness in it.

A king in Europe needs to obtain the support of the legislative body to fulfill the task that the constitution imposes on him, because that task is immense. A constitutional king in Europe is not only the executor of the law: care for its execution has so completely devolved to him that if the law were against him, he could paralyze its force. He has need of the chambers to make the law, the chambers have need of him to execute it: these are two powers that cannot live without each other; the wheels of government stop the moment there is discord between them.

In America, the president cannot prevent the forming of laws; he cannot escape the obligation to execute them. His zealous and sincere cooperation is doubtless useful, but it is not necessary to the working of the government. In everything essential that he does, he is directly or indirectly subject to the legislature; where he is entirely independent of it, he can do almost nothing. It is therefore his weakness, and not his force, that permits him to live in opposition to the legislative power.

In Europe, there must be an accord between the king and the chambers because there can be a serious struggle between them. In America, the accord is not obligatory because struggle is impossible.

ON THE ELECTION OF THE PRESIDENT

The danger of the system of elections increases in proportion to the extent of the preroga-tives of the executive power.—Americans can adopt this system because they can do with-out a strong executive power.—How circumstances favor the establishment of the elective system.—Why the election of the president does not make the principles of government vary.—Influence that the election of the president exerts on the fate of secondary officials.

The system of elections, applied to the head of the executive power among a great people, presents dangers that experience and historians have sufficiently pointed out.*

Thus I want to speak of it only in relation to America.

The dangers that one fears in the system of elections are more or less great according to the place that the executive power occupies and its importance in the state, and according to the mode of election and the circumstances in which the people that elects finds itself.

What one reproaches, not without reason, in the elective system applied to the head of state is that it offers such a great lure to particular ambitions, and inflames them so much in the pursuit of power, that often, legal means no longer sufficing for them, they appeal to force when right happens to fail them.

It is clear that the more prerogatives the executive power has, the greater the lure is; the more the ambition of the pretenders is excited, the more also it finds support in a crowd of [those with] secondary ambitions who hope to share in power after their candidate has triumphed.

The dangers of the elective system therefore grow in direct proportion to the influence exerted by the executive power on affairs of state.

The revolutions of Poland ought not to be attributed solely to the elective system in general, but to the fact that the elective magistrate was the head of a great monarchy.†

Before discussing the absolute good of the elective system, there is there-fore always an intervening question to decide, which is knowing whether the

---

*Among possible "historians" are Hume, "Essay IX: Of the Protestant Succession," in *Essays, Moral, Political, and Literary* (1777); Montesquieu, *The Spirit of the Laws*, II 2; Rousseau, *Consid-erations on the Government of Poland* (1772), chaps. 8, 14; *Federalist* 71. As to "experience," the question of electing the executive was debated in France in 1789 and 1830.

†See Rousseau, *Considerations on the Government of Poland* (1772), chaps. 8, 14.

geographic position, the laws, the habits, the mores, and the opinions of the people among whom one wishes to introduce it permit one to establish a weak and dependent executive power; for to wish all at once that the representative of the state remain armed with a vast power and be elected is to express, according to me, two contradictory wills. For my part, I know only a sole means of making hereditary royalty pass to the status of an elective power: one must first narrow its sphere of action, gradually diminish its prerogatives, and habituate the people little by little to living without its aid. But with that, European republicans scarcely concern themselves. Since many of them hate tyranny only because they come up against its rigors, the extent of the executive power does not offend them; they attack only its origin without perceiving the close bond that binds these two things.

No one has yet been encountered who cares to risk his honor and life to become president of the United States, because the president has only a temporary, limited, and dependent power. Fortune has to put an immense prize in play for desperate players to present themselves in the lists. No candidate up to now has been able to arouse ardent sympathies and dangerous popular passions in his favor. The reason for this is simple: having come to the head of the government, he can distribute to his friends neither much power nor much wealth nor much glory, and his influence in the state is too feeble for the factions to see their success or their ruin in his elevation to power.

Hereditary monarchies have a great advantage: as the particular interest of a family is continually bound in a strict manner to the interest of the state, not a single moment ever passes in which the latter is left abandoned to itself. I do not know if affairs are better directed in these monarchies than elsewhere; but at least there is always someone who, well or ill according to his capacity, is occupied with them.

In elective states, on the contrary, at the approach of the election and long before it arrives, the wheels of government in a way no longer function except of themselves. One can doubtless combine laws in such a manner that the election works in a single stroke and with rapidity, and the seat of executive power so to speak never remains vacant; but whatever one does, the void exists in minds despite the efforts of the legislator.

At the approach of an election, the head of the executive power thinks only of the conflict being prepared; he no longer has a future; he can undertake nothing and pursues only feebly what another is perhaps going to complete. "I am so near the moment of retiring," wrote President Jefferson on January 21, 1809 (six weeks before the election), "that I take no part in affairs beyond the expression of an opinion. I think it fair that my successor should now originate those measures of which he will be charged with the execution and responsibility, . . .".*

For its part, the nation has its eyes turned towards but a single point: it is occupied only in watching over the work of giving birth that is being prepared.

The vaster the place that executive power occupies in the direction of affairs, the greater and more necessary its habitual action is, and the more dangerous such a state of things is. Among a people that has contracted the habit of being governed by the executive power and, even more so, of being administered by it, election could not fail to produce a profound disturbance.

In the United States the action of the executive power can be slowed with impunity because that action is weak and circumscribed.

When the head of the government is elected, a lack of stability in the internal and external politics of the state almost always results. That is one of the principal vices of the system.

But that vice is more or less felt according to the portion of power granted to the elected magistrate. In Rome, although the consuls were changed every year, the principles of government did not vary, because the Senate was the directing power, and the Senate was an hereditary body. In most of the monarchies of Europe, if one elected the king, the kingdom would change face with each new choice.

In America the president exerts a very great influence on affairs of state, but he does not conduct them; the preponderant power resides in the national representation as a whole. It is therefore the mass of people that must change, and not only the president, in order that the maxims of politics vary. So in America, the system of election applied to the head of the executive power does not impair the fixity of government in a very perceptible manner.

Yet, the lack of fixity is an evil so inherent in the elective system that it is still keenly felt in the president's sphere of action, however circumscribed it may be.

The Americans rightly thought that the head of the executive power, to fulfill his mission and to bear the weight of responsibility as a whole, ought to remain, as much as possible, free to choose his agents by himself and to dismiss them at will; the legislative body watches over the president rather than directing him. Hence it follows that at each new election, it is as if the fate of all federal employees is in doubt.

*Jefferson to James Monroe, actually on January 28, 1809, and not "before the election" but before leaving office. The letter continues: ". . . and that it is my duty to clothe them with forms of authority. Five more weeks will relieve me of a drudgery to which I am no longer equal, and restore me to a scene of tranquillity, amidst my family and friends, more congenial to my age and natural inclinations."

In the constitutional monarchies of Europe the complaint is that the destiny of obscure agents of the administration often depends on the fate of the ministers. It is much worse in states where the head of the government is elected. The reason for this is simple: in constitutional monarchies, ministers succeed each other rapidly; but the principal representative of the executive power never changes, which confines the spirit of innovation within certain limits. Their administrative systems therefore vary in details rather than in principles; they cannot substitute one for another abruptly without causing a sort of revolution. In America, that revolution is made every four years in the name of the law.

As for the individual miseries that are the natural consequence of such a law, one must avow that the lack of fixity in the fate of officials does not produce the evils in America that one could expect from it elsewhere. In the United States it is so easy to create an independent existence for oneself that to take from an official the place that he occupies is sometimes to remove the ease from his life, but never the means of sustaining it.

I said at the beginning of this chapter that the dangers of the mode of election applied to the head of the executive power were more or less great according to the circumstances in which the people that elects finds itself.

One strives in vain to lessen the role of the executive power; there is one thing on which this power exerts a great influence, whatever place the laws have made for it—that is external politics: a negotiation can scarcely be opened and followed fruitfully except by a single man.

The more a people finds itself in a precarious and perilous position, and the more the need for continuity and fixity is felt in the direction of external affairs, the more also the application of the system of election to the head of state becomes dangerous.

The policy of the Americans toward the entire world is simple; one could almost say that no one has need of them and that they have need of no one. Their independence is never threatened.

Among them the role of the executive power is therefore as restricted by circumstances as by laws. The president can change his views frequently without the state's suffering or perishing.

Whatever may be the prerogatives with which the executive power is vested, one ought always to consider the time immediately preceding the election and during it as a period of national crisis.

The more troubled the internal situation of a country and the greater its external perils, the more dangerous is this moment of crisis for it. Among the peoples of Europe, there are few indeed who would not have to fear conquest or anarchy every time they gave themselves a new head.

In America, society is so constituted that it can sustain itself without aid;

external dangers are never pressing there. The election of the president is a cause of agitation, not of ruin.

MODE OF ELECTION

Skill that the American legislators have shown in the choice of the mode of election.— Creation of a special electoral body.—Separate vote of the special electors.—In what case the House of Representatives is called on to choose the president.—What has happened in the twelve elections that have taken place since the Constitution has been in force.

Independent of the dangers inherent in the principle, there are many others that arise from the forms of election themselves and that can be avoided by the care of the legislator.

When a people gathers in arms on the public square to choose its head, it is exposed not only to the dangers that the elective system presents in itself, but also to all those of civil war arising from a mode of election like this.

When Polish laws made the choice of the king depend on the veto of a single man, they invited the murder of that man or constituted anarchy in advance.

As one studies the institutions of the United States and casts a more attentive regard on the political and social situation of that country, one notices a marvelous accord between the fortune and the efforts of man. America was a new land; nevertheless, the people who inhabited it had already made a long use of freedom elsewhere: two great causes of internal order. In addition, America did not fear conquest. American legislators, taking up these favorable circumstances, had no trouble establishing a weak and dependent executive power; having created it so, they could render it elective without danger.

Nothing more remained for them except to choose, among the different systems of election, the least dangerous; the rules that they drew up in this regard admirably completed the guarantees that the physical and political constitution of the country already furnished.

The problem to solve was to find the mode of election that, while expressing the real will of the people, hardly excited their passions and held them in the least possible suspense. First they accepted that a *simple* majority would make the law. But it was still a very difficult thing to get this majority without having to fear the delays that they wanted before all else to avoid.

It is rare, in fact, to see a man gather a majority of votes in a great people at the first stroke. The difficulty increases in a republic of confederated states, where local influences are much more developed and more powerful.

To get around this second obstacle, the means presented itself of delegating the electoral powers of the nation to a body that represented it.

This mode of election rendered a majority more probable; for the fewer the electors, the easier it is for them to agree. It also presented more guarantee of the goodness of the choice.

But ought one to have entrusted the right to elect to the legislative body itself, usual representative of the nation, or, on the contrary, should an electoral college have been formed whose sole object was to proceed to the nomination of the president?

The Americans preferred this latter option. They thought that the men they sent to make ordinary laws would only incompletely represent the voice of the people in regard to the election of its first magistrate. Besides, being elected for more than one year, they could have represented a will that had already changed. They judged that if they charged the legislature with electing the head of the executive power, its members would become, long before the election, objects of corrupting maneuvers and playthings of intrigue, whereas special electors, like jurors, would remain unknown in the crowd until the day when they would have to act, and would appear only for an instant to pronounce their decree.

They therefore established that each state would name a certain number of electors,[20] who in their turn would elect the president. And as they had remarked that assemblies charged with choosing heads of government in elective countries inevitably became hotbeds of passion and cabal, that they sometimes took up powers that did not belong to them, and that their operations and the consequent incertitude were often prolonged long enough to put the state in peril, they ruled that the electors would all vote on one fixed day, but without being gathered together.[21]

The mode of election in two stages rendered a majority probable, but did not assure it, for it was possible that the electors would differ among themselves as those who commissioned them could have done.

This case presenting itself, they were necessarily brought to take one of these three measures: either they had to have new electors named, consult again those already named, or, finally, defer the choice to a new authority.

The first two methods, independent of the fact that they were hardly reliable, brought delays and perpetuated an always dangerous agitation.

They therefore settled on the third, and they agreed that the votes of electors would be transmitted sealed to the president of the Senate; that on a fixed day and in the presence of the two houses he would do the counting of them. If none of the candidates had gathered a majority, the House of Representatives would proceed immediately by itself to the election; but they

20. As many as they sent members to Congress. The number of electors in the election of 1833 was 288 ([Force,] *The National Calendar*).

21. Electors of the same state gathered together; but they transmitted to the seat of the central government the list of individual votes, not the product of the vote of the majority.

took care to limit its right. The representatives could only elect one of the three candidates who had obtained the most votes.[22]

As we see, it is only in a rare case, difficult to foresee in advance, that the election is entrusted to the ordinary representatives of the nation, and still they can only choose a citizen already designated by a strong minority of special electors; a happy combination that reconciles the respect that is owed to the will of the people with the rapidity of execution and the guarantees of order that the interest of the state requires. Yet by having the question decided by the House of Representatives in the case of a split, they still did not arrive at a complete solution of all difficulties; for the majority in the House of Representatives could in its turn be doubtful, and this time the Constitution offered no remedy. But in establishing obligatory candidacies, in restricting their number to three, in relying on the choice of a few enlightened men, they had ironed out all the obstacles[23] over which they could have some power; the others were inherent in the elective system itself.

During the forty-four years that the federal constitution has existed, the United States has elected its president twelve times.

Ten elections were made in a moment, by the simultaneous vote of special electors placed at different points of the land.

As yet, the House of Representatives has only twice used the exceptional right with which it is vested in case of a split. The first time was in 1801 during the election of Mr. Jefferson; and the second, in 1825, when Mr. Quincy Adams was named.

CRISIS OF THE ELECTION

One can consider the moment of the election of the president as a moment of national crisis.—Why.—Passions of the people.—Preoccupation of the president.—Calm that succeeds the agitation of the election.

I have said in what favorable circumstances the United States found itself for the adoption of its elective system, and I have made known the precautions that the legislators took to diminish its dangers. Americans are habituated to

---

22. In this circumstance it is the majority of states, and not the majority of members, that decides the question. In this way, New York has no more influence over the deliberation than Rhode Island. Thus one first consults the citizens of the Union as forming but one and the same people; and when they cannot agree, one revives the division by states and gives each of these a separate and independent vote.

That again is one of the peculiarities that the federal constitution presents and that only the clash of contrary interests can explain.

23. Jefferson, in 1801, was nevertheless named only on the thirty-sixth ballot.

carrying out all kinds of elections. Experience has taught them what degree of agitation they can reach and ought to stop at. The vast extent of their territory and the dispersal of inhabitants make a collision between the different parties less probable and less perilous there than anywhere else. The political circumstances in which the nation finds itself during elections have, up to now, presented no real danger.

Nevertheless, one can still consider the moment of the election of the president of the United States as a period of national crisis.

The influence that the president exerts on the course of affairs is doubtless weak and indirect, but it extends to the entire nation; the choice of the president matters only moderately to each citizen, but it matters to all citizens. Now, an interest, however small it may be, takes on great importance from the moment that it becomes a general interest.

Compared to a king in Europe, the president doubtless has few means of creating partisans for himself; still, the places at his disposal are great enough in number so that several thousand electors are directly or indirectly interested in his cause.

In addition, parties in the United States as elsewhere feel the need to group themselves around one man in order more easily to reach the intelligence of the crowd. They therefore generally make use of the name of the presidential candidate as a symbol; they personify their theories in him. So the parties have a great interest in determining the election in their favor, not so much to make their doctrines triumph with the aid of the president-elect as to show by his election that those doctrines have acquired a majority.

Long before the appointed moment arrives, the election becomes the greatest and so to speak sole business preoccupying minds. The factions at that time redouble their ardor; in that moment all the factitious passions that the imagination can create in a happy and tranquil country become agitated in broad daylight.

For his part, the president is absorbed by the care of defending himself. He no longer governs in the interest of the state, but in that of his reelection; he prostrates himself before the majority and often, instead of resisting its passions, as his duty obliges him to do, he runs to meet its caprices.

As the election approaches, intrigues become more active, agitation more lively and more widespread. Citizens divide into several camps, each of which takes the name of its candidate. The entire nation falls into a feverish state; the election is then the daily text of public papers, the subject of particular conversations, the goal of all reasoning, the object of all thoughts, the sole interest of the present.

As soon as fortune has pronounced, it is true, this ardor is dissipated, everything becomes calm, and the river, one moment overflowed, returns peacefully to its bed. But should one not be astonished that the storm could have arisen?

ON THE REELECTION OF THE PRESIDENT

When the head of the executive power is reeligible, it is the state itself that intrigues and corrupts.—Desire to be reelected, which dominates all the thoughts of the president of the United States.—Inconvenience of reelection, special to America.—The natural vice of democracies is the gradual enslavement of all powers to the least desires of the majority.— The reelection of the president favors this vice.

Were the legislators of the United States wrong or right to permit the reelection of the president?

To prevent the head of the executive power from being able to be reelected appeared, at first, contrary to reason. We know what influence the talents or the character of a single man exerts on the destiny of a whole people, above all in difficult circumstances and in times of crisis. Laws that forbid citizens to reelect their first magistrate would take away from them the best means of making the state prosper or of saving it. One would, moreover, arrive in this way at the peculiar result that a man would be excluded from the government at the very moment when he had succeeded in proving that he was capable of governing well.

These reasons are doubtless powerful; can one nevertheless not oppose to them still stronger ones?

Intrigue and corruption are vices natural to elective governments. But when the head of state can be reelected, the vices spread indefinitely and compromise the very existence of the country. When a plain candidate can succeed by intrigue, his maneuvers can only be exercised in a limited space. When, on the contrary, the head of state puts himself in the running, he borrows the force of the government for his own use.

In the first case, it is one man, with his feeble means; in the second, it is the state itself, with its immense resources, that intrigues and corrupts.

The plain citizen who uses reprehensible maneuvers to attain power can only harm public prosperity in an indirect manner; but if the representative of the executive power descends into the lists, the care of the government becomes a secondary interest to him; his principal interest is his election. Negotiations, like laws, are no longer anything but electoral schemes for him; places become the recompense for services rendered, not to the nation, but to its head. Even though the action of the government might not always be contrary to the interest of the country, it would, in any case, no longer serve [the country]. It is, however, for his use alone that it is taken.

It is impossible to consider the ordinary course of affairs in the United States without noticing that the desire to be reelected dominates the thoughts of the president; that the whole policy of his administration tends toward that point; that his least steps are subordinated to that object; that above all as the moment of the crisis approaches, individual interest is substituted in his mind for the general interest.

The principle of reelection therefore renders the corrupting influence of elective governments more extensive and more dangerous. It tends to degrade the political morality of the people and to replace patriotism with cleverness.

In America it attacks even more closely the sources of national existence.

Each government brings with it a natural vice that seems attached to the very principle of its life; the genius of the legislator consists in discerning it well. A state can triumph over many bad laws, and often one exaggerates the evil they cause. But every law whose effect is to develop this seed of death cannot fail in the long term to become fatal, although its bad effects may not be immediately perceived.

The principle of ruin in absolute monarchies is the unlimited and unreasonable extension of royal power. A measure that took away the counterweights to that power allowed by the constitution would therefore be radically bad, even if its effects appeared insensible for a long time.

Likewise, in countries where democracy governs and where the people constantly attract everything to themselves, laws that render their action more and more prompt and irresistible attack the existence of the government in a direct manner.

The greatest merit of the American legislators is to have clearly perceived this truth and to have had the courage to put it into practice.

They conceived that outside of the people there must be a certain number of powers that, without being completely independent of it, nonetheless enjoyed a rather large degree of freedom in their own sphere; so that, when forced to obey the permanent direction of the majority, they could nevertheless struggle against its caprices and refuse its dangerous demands.

To this effect, they concentrated all the executive power of the nation in a single hand; they gave the president extensive prerogatives and armed him with the veto in order to resist the encroachments of the legislature.

But in introducing the principle of reelection, they destroyed their work in part. They granted a great power to the president and took away from him the will to make use of it.

Not reeligible, the president would not be independent of the people, for he would not cease to be responsible to them; but the favor of the people would not be so necessary to him that he had to bend to their will in everything.

Reeligible (and this is true above all in our day, when political morality is relaxed and when great characters are disappearing), the president of the United States is only a docile instrument in the hands of the majority. He loves what it loves, hates what it hates; he flies to meet its will, anticipates its complaints, bends to its least desires: the legislators wanted him to guide it, and he follows it.

Thus, in order not to deprive the state of the talents of one man, they have rendered those talents almost useless; and in order to provide a resource for extraordinary circumstances, they have exposed the country to dangers every day.

ON THE FEDERAL COURTS [24]

Political importance of the judicial power in the United States.—Difficulty of treating this subject.—Utility of justice in confederations.—Which tribunals could the Union make use of?—Necessity of establishing courts of federal justice.—Organization of federal justice.—The Supreme Court.—How it differs from all courts of justice that we are familiar with.

I have examined the legislative power and the executive power of the Union. It still remains for me to consider the judicial power.

Here I must set forth my fears to readers.

Judicial institutions exert a great influence on the destiny of the Anglo-Americans; they hold a very important place among political institutions properly so-called. From this point of view, they particularly deserve to attract our regard.

But how make the political action of American courts understood without entering into some technical details about their constitution and their forms; and how descend to the details without having the natural dryness of such a

24. See chapter 6 [*DA* I 1.6], entitled "On the Judicial Power of the United States." That chapter makes known the general principles of the Americans in the matter of justice. See also the federal constitution, art. 3.

See the work that has for a title *The Federalist* 78–83; *Constitutional Law, being a View of the Practice and Juridiction* [sic] *of the Courts of the United States,* by Thomas Sargeant [Philadelphia, 1830].

See Story, [*Commentaries,*] 134–162, 489–511, 581, 668 [581–668]. See the organic law of September 24, 1789, in the collection entitled *Laws of the United States* [*Public and General Statutes Passed by the Congress of the United States*], by Story, vol. 1, 53[f].

subject put off the curiosity of the reader? How remain clear without ceasing to be short?

I do not flatter myself that I have escaped these different perils. Men of the world will still find that I am too long; jurists will think that I am too brief. But that is an inconvenience attached to my subject generally and to the special matter that I am treating at this moment.

The greatest difficulty was not to know how one would constitute a federal government, but how one would make its laws obeyed.

Governments generally have only two means of defeating the resistance that the governed oppose to them: the material force that they find in themselves; the moral force that the decrees of courts lend to them.

A government that had only warfare to make its laws obeyed would be very near its ruin. One of two things would probably happen to it: if it were weak and moderate, it would employ force only at the last extremity and would allow a host of [acts of] partial disobedience to pass unnoticed; then the state would fall little by little into anarchy.

If it were audacious and powerful, it would have daily recourse to the use of violence, and soon one would see it degenerate into a pure military despotism. Its inaction and its activity would be equally fatal to the governed.

The great object of justice is to substitute the idea of right for that of violence; to place intermediaries between the government and the use of material force.

The power of opinion generally accorded by men to the intervention of courts is a surprising thing. This power is so great that it still attaches to the judicial form when the substance no longer exists; it gives a body to the shadow.

The moral force with which courts are vested renders the use of material force infinitely rarer by substituting for it in most cases; and when the latter must finally act, it [material force] doubles its power by being joined to it [moral force].

A federal government ought more than any other to desire to obtain the support of justice, because in its nature it is weaker, and one can more easily organize resistance against it.[25] If it had to come always and at first to the use of force, it would not suffice for its task.

Thus the Union, to make the citizens obey its laws or to repel aggression that had the laws for its object, had particular need of courts.

But which courts ought it to have made use of? Each state already had a

25. Federal laws have most need of courts, and yet they have least allowed for them. The cause of this is that most confederations have been formed by independent states that did not have a real intention to obey the central government and that, while giving it the right to command, carefully reserved for themselves the ability to disobey it.

judicial power organized within it. Did one have to recur to its courts? [or] did one have to create federal justice? It is easy to prove that the Union could not adapt for its use the judicial power established in the states.

Without doubt, it is important for the security of each and for the freedom of all that the judicial power be separated from all others; but it is no less necessary to national existence that the different powers of the state have the same origin, follow the same principles, and act in the same sphere, in a word, that they be *correlative* and *homogeneous*. No one, I imagine, has ever thought to have offenses committed in France judged by foreign tribunals so as to be more sure of the impartiality of the magistrates.

Americans form a single people in relation to their federal government; but in the midst of this people, they have allowed political bodies to subsist that are dependent on the national government in some points, independent in all the others; that have their particular origin, their own doctrines, and their special means of acting. To entrust the execution of the laws of the Union to courts instituted by these political bodies was to deliver the nation to foreign judges.

Even more, each state is not only a foreigner in relation to the Union, it is also an everyday adversary, since the sovereignty of the Union can only lose out to the profit of that of the states.

In having the laws of the Union applied by courts of the particular states, one therefore delivered the nation not only to foreign judges, but also to partial judges.

Besides, it was not their character alone that rendered the courts of the states incapable of serving one national purpose; it was above all their number.

At the moment when the federal constitution was formed, there were already thirteen courts of justice in the United States judging without appeal. Twenty-four may be counted today. How suppose that a state can subsist when its fundamental laws can be interpreted and applied in twenty-four different manners at once! Such a system is as contrary to reason as to the lessons of experience.

The American legislators therefore agreed to create a federal judicial power to apply the laws of the Union and to decide certain questions of general interest that were carefully defined in advance.

All the judicial power of the Union was concentrated in a single tribunal, called the Supreme Court of the United States. But to expedite business they assigned inferior tribunals to it, charged with judging cases of little importance without appeal or with giving a ruling in the first instance in more serious disputes. Members of the Supreme Court were not elected by the people or the legislature; the president of the United States was to choose them after having taken the advice of the Senate.

In order to make them independent of the other powers, they made them irremovable, and they decided that their salary, once fixed, would be outside the control of the legislature.[26]

It was very easy to proclaim the establishment of a federal justice in principle, but a host of difficulties arose when it became a question of fixing its prerogatives.

MANNER OF SETTLING THE COMPETENCE OF THE FEDERAL COURTS

Difficulty of settling the competence of the various courts in confederations.—The courts of the Union obtained the right to settle their own competence.—Why this rule attacks the share of sovereignty the particular states had reserved for themselves.—The sovereignty of those states restricted by the laws and by the interpretation of the laws.—The particular states thus risk a danger more apparent than real.

A first question presented itself: with the Constitution of the United States setting up two distinct, opposing sovereignties, represented in regard to justice by two different orders of courts, whatever care one took to establish the jurisdiction of each of these two orders of courts, one could not prevent frequent collisions between them. Now, in that case, to whom ought the right to establish competence belong?

26. They divided the Union into districts; in each of these districts they placed a federal judge in residence. The court that this judge presided over was named the district court.

In addition, each of the judges composing the Supreme Court had every year to travel a certain portion of the territory of the republic to decide certain more important cases in the places themselves: the court presided over by this magistrate was designated by the name circuit court.

Finally, the most serious affairs had to come either directly or by appeal before the Supreme Court, at whose seat all the circuit judges gathered once a year to hold a solemn session.

The jury system was introduced in the federal courts in the same manner as in the state courts and for like cases.

There is almost no analogy, as one sees, between the Supreme Court of the United States and our Court of Cassation [the highest court of appeal in the French judicial system]. The Supreme Court can be referred to in the first instance and the Court of Cassation can only be referred to second or third in order. In truth, the Supreme Court forms, as does the Court of Cassation, a unique tribunal charged with establishing a uniform jurisprudence; but the Supreme Court judges fact as well as law and pronounces *by itself* without sending [the case] back to another tribunal, two things that the Court of Cassation cannot do.

See the organic law of September 24, 1789, *Laws of the United States* [*Public and General Statutes Passed by the Congress of the United States*], by Story, vol. 1, 53[f].

In peoples who form one and the same political society, when a question of competence arises between two courts, it is generally brought before a third that serves as arbiter.

This is done without difficulty because among these peoples questions of judicial competence have no relation to questions of national sovereignty.

But above the highest court of a particular state and the highest court of the United States it was impossible to establish any tribunal whatsoever that was neither one nor the other.

They therefore had to give one of the courts the right to judge in its own cause and to take or to retain cognizance of the business that was contested in it. They could not grant this privilege to the various courts of the states; that would have been to destroy the sovereignty of the Union in fact after having established it in right; for the interpretation of the Constitution would soon have returned to the particular states the share of independence that the terms of the Constitution had taken away from them.

In creating a federal tribunal, they had wanted to withdraw from the state courts the right to decide, each in its own manner, questions of national interest, and so to form successfully a body of uniform jurisprudence for the interpretation of the laws of the Union. The goal would not have been attained if the courts of the particular states, while abstaining from judging cases as federal, had been able to judge them by claiming that they were not federal.

The Supreme Court of the United States was therefore vested with the right to decide all questions of competence.[27]

That was the most dangerous blow delivered to the sovereignty of the states. In this way it was restricted not only by the laws, but also by the interpretation of laws; by a known boundary and by another that was not known; by a settled rule and by an arbitrary rule. The Constitution, it is true, had set precise limits for federal sovereignty; but each time that sovereignty is in competition with that of the states, a federal court will pronounce.

Yet the dangers with which this manner of proceeding seemed to threaten the sovereignty of the states were not as great in reality as they appeared to be.

We shall see further on that in America real force resides more in the

---

27. Furthermore, to make these cases about competence less frequent, they decided that in a very great number of federal cases the courts of the particular states would have the right to pronounce concurrently with the tribunals of the Union; but then the condemned party always had the ability to form an appeal before the Supreme Court of the United States. The Supreme Court of Virginia disputed the right of the Supreme Court of the United States to judge the appeal of its judgments, but in vain. See *Kent's Commentaries,* vol. 1, 300, 370f. See *Story's Comm.,* 646, and the organic law of [September 24,] 1789; *Laws of United States* [Story, *Public and General Statutes*], vol. 1, 53[f].

provincial governments than in the federal government. Federal judges feel the relative weakness of the power in the name of which they act, and they are closer to abandoning a right of jurisdiction in cases where the law gives it to them than being inclined to claim it illegally.

DIFFERENT CASES* OF JURISDICTION

The matter and the person, bases of federal jurisdiction.—Cases having to do with ambassadors,—with the Union,—with a particular state.—Judged by whom.—Cases that arise from the laws of the Union.—Why judged by federal courts.—Cases relating to the nonperformance of contracts judged by federal justice.—Consequence of this.

After having recognized the means of fixing federal competence, the legislators of the Union determined the cases of jurisdiction in which it would be exercised.

They accepted that there were certain litigants who could only be judged by the federal courts, whatever the object of the case might be.

Next they established that there were certain cases that could only be decided by these same courts, whatever the character of the litigants might be.

The person and the matter therefore became the two bases of federal competence.

Ambassadors represent nations friendly to the Union; everything that interests ambassadors interests the entire Union in some way. When an ambassador is a party in a case, the case becomes an affair that touches the well-being of the nation; it is natural that a federal court pronounce.

The Union itself can have cases: in this instance it would be contrary to reason as well as to the usage of nations to appeal to the judgment of tribunals representing another sovereignty than its own. It is for the federal courts alone to pronounce.

When two individuals belonging to two different states have a case, one cannot without inconvenience have them judged by the courts of one of the two states. It is surer to choose a court that can excite the suspicions of none of the parties, and the court that most naturally presents itself is the Union's.

When two litigants are no longer isolated individuals, but states, a political reason of the first order is joined to the same reason of equity. Here the character of the litigants gives a national importance to all cases; the least contentious question between two states interests the peace of the Union as a whole.[28]

*In this section "case" translates both *cas* (general) and *procès* (specific).

28. The Constitution also says that cases that can arise between a state and the citizens of another state shall be within the province of the federal courts. The question was soon raised of determining whether the Constitution meant all cases that can arise between a state and the

Often the very nature of the cases was to serve to regulate competence. Thus it is that all questions connected to maritime commerce were to be decided by federal courts.[29]

The reason is easy to point out: almost all these questions fit into an assessment of the law of nations. In this relation they essentially interest the entire Union in regard to foreigners. Moreover, since the sea is not included in one judicial district rather than another, only national justice can have title to jurisdiction over cases that have a maritime origin.

The Constitution has included in a single category almost all cases that by their nature will belong under the federal courts.

The rule that it draws in this regard is simple, but it comprehends in itself a vast system of ideas and a multitude of facts.

Federal courts, it says, shall judge all cases that *arise under the laws of the United States.* *

Two examples will make the thought of the legislator perfectly understood.

The Constitution forbids the states the right to make laws regarding the circulation of money; despite this prohibition, a state makes such a law. The interested parties refuse to obey it, given that it is contrary to the Constitution. [The case] must go before a federal court because the means of attack is taken from the laws of the United States.

Congress establishes an import duty. Difficulties are raised about the collection of this duty. Again, it must be presented before the federal courts because the cause of the case is the interpretation of a law of the United States.

This rule is perfectly in accord with the bases adopted for the federal constitution.

The Union, as it was constituted in 1789, has, it is true, only a restricted sovereignty, but within this sphere they wanted it to form one and the same people.[30] In this sphere, it is sovereign. When this point is set down and

---

* Article 3, section 2.

---

citizens of another state, either one or the other being the *plaintiff.* The Supreme Court pronounced for the affirmative; but that decision alarmed the particular states, who feared being brought despite themselves before federal justice at every turn. An amendment was therefore introduced into the Constitution [eleventh amendment], by virtue of which the judicial power of the Union could not be extended to judge cases that had been *brought* against one of the United States by citizens of another.

See *Story's Commentaries,* 624[–625].

29. Example: all acts of piracy.

30. Some restrictions have indeed been placed on this principle in introducing the particular states as independent powers in the Senate and in having them vote separately in the House of

accepted, all the rest becomes easy; for if you recognize that the United States, within the limits set down by its Constitution, forms only one people, it must indeed be granted rights that belong to all peoples.

Now, since the origin of societies, this point has been agreed to: each people has the right to have all questions that relate to the execution of its own laws judged by its courts. But one responds: the Union is in the singular position of forming one people only relative to certain objects; for all others it is nothing. What results from this? It is that at least for all laws that relate to those objects, it has the rights that one would grant to a complete sovereignty. The real point of the difficulty is to know which those objects are. This point decided (and we saw above, in treating competence, how it was done), there is, to tell the truth, no longer a question; for once they established that a case was federal, that is to say, came under the part of sovereignty reserved to the Union by the Constitution, it followed naturally that a federal court alone ought to pronounce.

Therefore every time one wants to attack the laws of the United States or to invoke them to defend oneself, it is the federal courts that must be addressed.

Thus the jurisdiction of the courts of the Union extends or contracts as the sovereignty of the Union itself contracts or extends.

We have seen that the principal goal of the legislators of 1789 was to divide sovereignty into two distinct parts. In one, they placed the direction of all general interests of the Union; in the other, the direction of all the interests special to some of its parts.

Their principal care was to arm the federal government with enough powers so that, in its sphere, it could defend itself against encroachments of the particular states.

As for these, they adopted as a general principle to leave them free in their sphere. The central government can neither direct them nor even inspect their conduct within it.

I pointed out in the chapter on the division of powers* that this last principle has not always been respected. There are certain laws that a particular state cannot make, however much they appear to interest it alone.

When one state of the Union makes a law of this nature, citizens who are wronged by the execution of that law can appeal to the federal courts.

So the jurisdiction of the federal courts extends not only to all cases that have their source in the laws of the Union, but also to all those that arise

* *DA* I 1.8 above, "Prerogatives of the Federal Government."

Representatives in the case of electing the president; but these are exceptions. The contrary principle is dominant.

from the laws that particular states have made contrary to the Constitution.

The states are forbidden to promulgate retroactive laws in criminal matters; a man who is condemned by virtue of a law of this kind can appeal to federal justice.

The Constitution has equally forbidden states to make laws that can destroy or alter rights acquired by virtue of a contract (*impairing the obligations of contracts*).[31]

From the moment that a particular person believes he sees that a law of his state infringes a right of this kind, he can refuse to obey it and appeal to federal justice.[32]

This arrangement appears to me to attack the sovereignty of the states more profoundly than anything else.

The rights granted to the federal government in its evidently national goals are defined and easy to understand. Those conceded to it indirectly by the article I have just cited do not fall easily under its meaning, and their limits are not clearly drawn. There is, in fact, a multitude of political laws that have an effect on the existence of contracts and that could thus furnish material for encroachment by the central power.

---

31. It is perfectly clear, says Mr. Story, [*Commentaries,*] 503, that every law that extends, narrows, or changes in any manner the intention of the parties, such as it results from stipulations contained in a contract, alters (*impairs*) the contract. In the same place, the same author carefully defines what federal jurisprudence means by a contract. The definition is very large. A concession made by the state to a particular person and accepted by him is a contract, and cannot be taken away by the effect of a new law. A charter granted by the state to a company is a contract, and is law for the state as well as for the concessionaire. The article of the Constitution we are speaking of therefore protects the existence of a great part of *acquired rights*, but not of all. I can very legitimately possess a property without its having passed into my hands as a consequence of a contract. Its possession is an acquired right for me, and that right is not guaranteed by the federal constitution.

32. Here is a remarkable example cited by Mr. Story, [*Commentaries,*] 508[–509]. Dartmouth College, in New Hampshire, had been founded by virtue of a charter granted to certain individuals before the American Revolution. Its administrators formed, by virtue of this charter, a constituted body, or, following the American expression, a *corporation.* The legislature of New Hampshire believed it should change the terms of this original charter and gave over to new administrators all the rights, privileges, and franchises resulting from that charter. The former administrators resisted and appealed to the federal court, which gave them a victory in the case; considering that the original charter was a genuine contract between the state and the concessionaires, the new law could not change the clauses of this charter without violating rights acquired by virtue of a contract, consequently without violating article 1, section 10, of the Constitution of the United States.

MANNER OF PROCEEDING OF FEDERAL COURTS

Natural weakness of justice in confederations.—Efforts that legislators should make to place, as much as possible, only isolated individuals, and not states, before federal courts.—How Americans have succeeded at this.—Direct action of federal courts on plain persons.—Indirect attack on states that violate the laws of the Union.—A decree of federal justice does not destroy provincial law, it enervates it.

I have made known what the rights of the federal courts are; it matters no less to know how they exercise them.

The irresistible force of justice in countries where sovereignty is not partitioned comes from the fact that the courts in these countries represent the nation as a whole in a conflict with the lone individual that the decree strikes. To the idea of right is added the idea of the force that supports right.

But in countries where sovereignty is divided it is not always so. There, justice most often finds before it not an isolated individual, but a fraction of the nation. Its moral power and its material force become less great.

In federal states, justice is therefore naturally weaker and the justiciable [party] stronger.

The legislator in confederations must work constantly to give the courts a place analogous to the one they hold among peoples who have not partitioned sovereignty; in other words, his most constant efforts must tend to make federal justice represent the nation and the justiciable [party] represent a particular interest.

A government, whatever its nature is, needs to act on the governed to force them to render to it what is due to it; it needs to act against them to defend itself from their attacks.

As for the direct action of the government on the governed, to force them to obey the laws, the Constitution of the United States made it (and there was its masterpiece) so that the federal courts act in the name of those laws, and never have any business except with individuals. In fact, as they declared that the confederation forms one and the same people in the sphere drawn by the Constitution, the result is that the government created by this constitution and acting within its limits was vested with all the rights of a national government, of which the principal one is to make its injunctions reach the plain citizen without an intermediary. Therefore when the Union orders the levying of a tax, for example, it does not have to address itself to the states to collect it, but to each American citizen, according to his quota. Federal justice, in its turn, charged with assuring the execution of this law of the Union, has to convict not the recalcitrant state, but the taxpayer. Like the justice of other peoples, it finds itself facing only an individual.

Remark that here the Union itself has chosen its adversary. It has chosen a weak one; it is altogether natural that he will succumb.

But when the Union, instead of attacking, is reduced to defending itself, the difficulty increases. The Constitution recognizes the power of making laws in the states. These laws can violate the rights of the Union. Here, necessarily, it is found in conflict with the sovereignty of the state that has made the law. It only remains for it to choose, among modes of action, the least dangerous. The mode was indicated in advance by the general principles that I have previously enunciated.[33]

One conceives that in the case that I have just supposed, the Union could have cited the state before a federal court that would have declared the law null; that would be to follow the most natural course of ideas. But in that manner federal justice would have found itself directly opposed to a state, which it wanted as much as possible to avoid.

The Americans thought it was almost impossible that a new law not prejudice some particular interest in its execution.

It is on that particular interest that the authors of the federal constitution rely to attack the legislative measure about which the Union can have something to complain. To it they offer a shelter.

A state sells lands to a company; one year after, a new law disposes of the same lands in another way and thus violates that part of the Constitution that prohibits changing rights acquired by a contract. When the buyer by virtue of the new law presents himself to enter into possession, the possessor who holds his rights from the former law sues him before the courts of the Union and has [the latter's] title declared null.[34] So, in reality, federal justice finds itself doing battle with the sovereignty of the state; but it attacks it only indirectly and over an application of detail. It thus strikes the law in its consequences, not in its principle; it does not destroy it, it enervates it.

Finally, a last hypothetical situation remained.

Each state formed a corporation that had an existence and civil rights separately; consequently, it could sue or be sued before the courts. A state could, for example, seek justice against another state.

In that case, it was no longer a question of the Union's attacking a provincial law, but of judging a case to which a state was a party. It was a case like any other; the character of the litigants alone was different. Here the danger indicated at the beginning of this chapter still exists, but this time one cannot avoid it; it is inherent in the very essence of federal constitutions, the result

33. See the chapter entitled "On Judicial Power in America" [DA I 1.6].
34. See *Kent's Commentaries*, vol. 1, 387[–396].

of which will always be to create within a nation particular [bodies] powerful enough so that justice is exercised against them only with difficulty.

ELEVATED RANK HELD BY THE SUPREME COURT AMONG THE GREAT POWERS OF THE STATE

No people has constituted as great a judicial power as the Americans.—Extent of its prerogatives.—Its political influence.—The peace and the very existence of the Union depend on the wisdom of seven federal judges.

When, after having examined in detail the organization of the Supreme Court, one comes to consider in sum the prerogatives that have been given it, one discovers without difficulty that a more immense judicial power has never been constituted in any people.

The Supreme Court is placed higher than any known tribunal both by the *nature* of its rights and by the *species* of those under its jurisdiction.

In all the ordered nations of Europe, the government has always shown a great repugnance to allow ordinary justice to decide questions that interested itself. This repugnance is naturally greater when the government is more absolute. On the contrary, as freedom increases, the sphere of prerogatives of the courts is always going to enlarge; but none of the European nations has yet thought that every judicial question, whatever its origin might be, could be left to judges of the common law.

In America, they have put this theory into practice. The Supreme Court of the United States is the sole, unique tribunal of the nation.

It is charged with the interpretation of laws and treaties; questions relative to maritime commerce and all those in general that are connected to the law of nations are within its exclusive competence. One can even say that its prerogatives are almost entirely political although its constitution is entirely judicial. Its unique purpose is to have the laws of the Union executed, and the Union regulates only the relations of the government with the governed and of the nation with foreigners; the relations of citizens among themselves are almost all ruled by the sovereignty of the states.

To this first cause of importance must be added another greater still. In the nations of Europe, tribunals have only particular persons under their jurisdiction; but one can say that the Supreme Court of the United States makes sovereigns appear before its bar. When the bailiff, advancing on the steps of the tribunal, comes to pronounce these few words, "The state of New York against the state of Ohio," one feels that there, one is not within the precincts of an ordinary court of justice. And when one considers that one of those litigants represents a million men and the other two million, one is astonished at the responsibility that weighs on the seven judges whose decree is going to delight or sadden such a great number of their fellow citizens.

In the hands of seven federal judges rest ceaselessly the peace, the prosperity, the very existence of the Union. Without them, the Constitution is a dead letter; to them, the executive power appeals to resist the encroachments of the legislative body; the legislature, to defend itself against the undertakings of the executive power; the Union, to have itself obeyed by the states; the states, to repel the exaggerated pretensions of the Union; the public interest against private interest; the spirit of conservation against democratic instability. Their power is immense; but it is a power of opinion. They are omnipotent as long as the people consent to obey the law; they can do nothing when they scorn it. Now, the power of opinion is that which is most difficult to make use of, because it is impossible to say exactly where its limits are. It is often as dangerous to fall short of them as to exceed them.

Federal judges, therefore, must not only be good citizens, educated and upright men—qualities necessary to all magistrates—one must also find statesmen in them; they must know how to discern the spirit of their times, to confront the obstacles they can defeat, and to turn away from the current when the flood threatens to carry away with them the sovereignty of the Union and the obedience due to its laws.

The president can fail without the state's suffering because the president has only a limited duty. Congress can err without the Union's perishing because above Congress resides the electoral body that can change its mind by changing its members.

But if the Supreme Court ever came to be composed of imprudent or corrupt men, the confederation would have to fear anarchy or civil war.

Furthermore, so that one not be mistaken about it, the original cause of the danger is not in the constitution of the tribunal, but in the very nature of federal governments. We have seen that nowhere is it more necessary to constitute the judicial power strongly than in confederated peoples, because nowhere are the individual existences that can struggle against the social body greater and in a better state to resist the use of the material force of the government.

Now, the more necessary it is that a power be strong, the more one must give it [greater] extent and independence. The more extended and independent a power is, the more dangerous is the abuse that can be done by it. The origin of the evil is therefore not in the constitution of this power, but in the very constitution of the state that necessitates the existence of such a power.

HOW THE FEDERAL CONSTITUTION IS SUPERIOR TO THE CONSTITUTIONS OF THE STATES

How one can compare the constitution of the Union to those of the particular states.—In particular, one should attribute the superiority of the constitution of the Union to the wisdom of federal legislators.—The legislature of the Union less dependent on the people than those of the states.—The executive power freer in its sphere.—The judicial power less subject to the will of the majority.—Practical consequences of this.—Federal legislators have attenuated the dangers inherent in government by democracy; state legislators have increased these dangers.

The federal constitution differs essentially from the constitutions of the states by the goal that it proposes, but as to the means of attaining this goal it closely approaches them. The object of government is different, but the forms of government are the same. From this special point of view one can usefully compare them.

I think that the federal constitution is superior to all the state constitutions. This superiority is due to several causes.

The current constitution of the Union was formed only subsequent to those of most of the states; one could therefore profit from the experience acquired.

Still, one will be convinced that this cause is only secondary if one considers that, since the establishment of the federal constitution, the American confederation has increased by eleven new states and that these have almost always exaggerated rather than attenuated the faults existing in the constitutions of their precursors.

The great cause of the superiority of the federal constitution is in the very character of the legislators.

In the period when it was formed, the ruin of the confederation appeared imminent; it was so to speak present to all eyes. In that extremity the people chose not perhaps the men they liked best, but those they esteemed the most.

I have already observed above* that the legislators of the Union were almost all remarkable for their enlightenment, more remarkable still for their patriotism.

They were all reared in the midst of a social crisis, during which the spirit of freedom had to struggle continuously against a strong and dominant authority. After the struggle ended, and while the excited passions of the crowd were, according to its habit, still engaged in combating dangers that had long

*Above, *DA* I 1.8.

since ceased to exist, they stopped; they cast a more tranquil and more penetrating regard on their native country; they saw that a definitive revolution
had been accomplished and that from then on the dangers that threatened
the people could only arise from abuses of freedom. What they thought, they
had the courage to say, because they felt at the bottom of their hearts a sincere
and ardent love for that same freedom; they dared to speak of restricting it
because they were sure that they did not wish to destroy it.[35]

Most of the constitutions of the states give a mandate to the House of
Representatives of only one year in duration, and two for the Senate. In this
way the members of the legislative body are bound constantly and in the
narrowest manner to the least desires of their constituents.

The legislators of the Union thought that this extreme dependence of the
legislature denatured the principal effects of the representative system by
placing in the people themselves not only the origin of powers, but also the
government.

They lengthened the time of the electoral mandate to allow to the deputy
a greater use of his free will.

---

35. In this period the celebrated Alexander Hamilton, one of the most influential authors of
the Constitution, did not fear to publish what follows in *The Federalist* 71:

There are some who would be inclined to regard the servile pliancy of the executive to a
prevailing current, either in the community or in the legislature, as its best recommendation. But such men entertain very crude notions, as well of the purposes for which government was instituted as of the true means by which the public happiness may be promoted.

The republican principle demands that the deliberate sense of the community should
govern the conduct of those to whom they entrust the management of their affairs; but
it does not require an unqualified complaisance to every sudden breeze of passion, or to
every transient impulse which the people may receive from the arts of men, who flatter
their prejudices to betray their interests.

It is a just observation that the people commonly *intend* the PUBLIC GOOD. This
often applies to their very errors. But their good sense would despise the adulator who
should pretend that they [always] *reason right* about the *means* of promoting it. They
know from experience that they sometimes err; and the wonder is that they so seldom
err as they do, beset as they continually are by the wiles of parasites and sycophants; by
the snares of the ambitious, the avaricious, the desperate, by the artifices of men who
possess their confidence more than they deserve it, and of those who seek to possess
rather than to deserve it.

When occasions present themselves in which the interests of the people are at variance with their inclinations, it is the duty of the persons whom they have appointed to
be the guardians of those interests to withstand the temporary delusion in order to give
them time and opportunity for more cool and sedate reflection. Instances might be cited
in which a conduct of this kind has saved the people from very fatal consequences of
their own mistakes, and has procured lasting monuments of their gratitude to the men
who [had] courage and magnanimity enough to serve them at the peril of their displeasure.

The federal constitution, like the different state constitutions, divided the legislative body into two branches.

But in the states these two parts of the legislature were composed of the same elements, according to the same mode of election. The result was that the passions and the will of the majority came to light with the same ease and found an organ and an instrument as quickly in one chamber as in the other. This gave a violent and hasty character to the formation of the laws.

The federal constitution made the two chambers come from the votes of the people as well; but it varied the conditions of eligibility and the mode of election, so that if one of the two branches of the legislature did not represent different interests from the other, as in certain nations, it at least represented a superior wisdom.

One must have attained a mature age to be a senator, and it was an assembly itself already chosen and few in number that was charged with electing.

Democracies are naturally brought to concentrate the whole social force in the hands of the legislative body. The latter being the power that emanates most directly from the people, it is also the one that participates the most in its omnipotence.

One therefore remarks a habitual tendency in it that brings it to unite every kind of authority within it.

This concentration of powers, at the same time that it singularly hinders the good conduct of affairs, founds the despotism of the majority.

The state legislators frequently abandoned themselves to these instincts of democracy; those of the Union always struggled courageously against them.

In the states, the executive power was put into the hands of a magistrate apparently placed beside the legislature, but who in reality was only a blind agent and passive instrument of its will. Where would he draw his force? From the longevity of his functions? He is generally named only for a year. From his prerogatives? He has so to speak none. The legislature can reduce him to impotence by charging with the execution of its laws special committees taken from within itself. If it wished to, it could in a way annul him by cutting his salary.

The federal constitution concentrated all the rights of the executive power, like all its responsibility, in one man alone. It gave four years of existence to the president; it assured him the enjoyment of his salary for the duration of his magistracy; it composed a constituency for him and armed him with a suspensive veto. In a word, after having carefully traced the sphere of executive power, it sought to give it as much as possible a strong and free position within that sphere.

The judicial power is, of all the powers, the one that, in the state constitutions, has remained the least dependent on the legislative power.

Still, in all the states the legislature continued to be master in fixing the emoluments of judges, which necessarily subjects them to its immediate influence.

In certain states, judges are named only for a time, which again takes away from them a great part of their force and their freedom.

In others, one sees the legislative and judicial powers entirely confused. The senate of New York, for example, forms the highest court of the state for certain cases.

The federal constitution took care, on the contrary, to separate the judicial power from all the others. In addition, it rendered judges independent by declaring their salary fixed and their offices irrevocable.

The practical consequences of these differences are easy to perceive. It is evident to every attentive observer that the affairs of the Union are infinitely better conducted than the particular affairs of any state.

The federal government follows a more just and moderate course than the states. There is more wisdom in its views, more durability and clever combination in its projects, more skill, coherence, and firmness in the execution of its measures.

A few words suffice to summarize this chapter.

Two principal dangers threaten democracies:

Complete enslavement of the legislative power to the will of the electoral body.

Concentration in the legislative power of all the other powers of government.

The legislators of the states have favored the development of these dangers. The legislators of the Union did what they could to render them less formidable.

WHAT DISTINGUISHES THE FEDERAL CONSTITUTION OF THE UNITED STATES OF AMERICA FROM ALL OTHER FEDERAL CONSTITUTIONS

The American confederation resembles all other confederations in appearance.—Nevertheless, its effects are different.—How does this come about?—How this confederation differs from all others.—The American government is not a federal government, but an incomplete national government.

The United States of America has not provided the first and only example of a confederation. Without speaking of antiquity, modern Europe has furnished several. Switzerland, the German Empire, the Republic of the Netherlands were or still are confederations.

When one studies the constitutions of these different countries, one remarks with surprise that the powers conferred by them on the federal government are nearly the same as those granted by the American constitution to the government of the United States. Like the latter, they give the central power the right to make peace and war, the right to raise men and money, to provide for general needs and to regulate the common interests of the nation.

Nevertheless, the federal government in these different peoples has almost always remained feeble and powerless, whereas that of the Union conducts affairs with vigor and ease.

There is more: the first American Union could not subsist because of the excessive weakness of its government, and nonetheless this government, so weak, had received rights as extensive as the federal government of our day. One can even say that in certain respects its privileges were greater.

In the current constitution of the United States, therefore, are some new principles that do not strike one at first, but whose influence is felt profoundly.

This constitution, which at first sight one is tempted to confuse with the federal constitutions that preceded it, in fact rests on an entirely new theory that will be marked as a great discovery in the political science of our day.

In all confederations preceding the American confederation of 1789, peoples who were allied in a common goal consented to obey the injunctions of a federal government; but they kept the right to ordain and to oversee for themselves the execution of the laws of the union.

The American states that united in 1789 not only consented that the federal government dictate their laws, but also that it execute its laws by itself.

In the two cases the right is the same; only the exercise of the right is different. But this sole difference produces immense results.

In all the confederations that had preceded the American Union of our day, the federal government, to provide for its needs, addressed itself to the particular governments. In a case where the prescribed measure displeased one of them, the latter could always evade the necessity of obeying. If it was strong, it appealed to arms; if it was weak, it tolerated resistance to the laws of the Union that had become its own, used impotence as an excuse, and had recourse to the force of inertia.

So one constantly saw one of two things happen: the most powerful of the united peoples, taking the rights of the federal authority in hand, dominated all the others in its name;[36] or the federal government was abandoned to its own forces, and then anarchy was established among the confederated, and the union became powerless to act.[37]

In America the Union has, not states, but plain citizens, for those governed. When it wants to levy a tax, it does not address itself to the government of Massachusetts, but to each inhabitant of Massachusetts. Past federal governments were faced with peoples, that of the Union has individuals. It does not borrow its force, but draws it from itself. It has its own administrators, its own courts, its own judicial officers, and its own army.

No doubt the national* spirit, the collective passions, the provincial prejudices of each state still singularly tend to diminish the extent of a federal power so constituted and to create centers of resistance to its will; restricted in its sovereignty, it cannot be as strong as one that possesses it wholly; but that is an evil inherent in the federal system.

In America, each state has many fewer occasions and temptations to resist; and if the thought comes to it, it can only put it into execution by openly violating the laws of the Union, interrupting the ordinary course of justice, raising the standard of revolt; it must, in a word, suddenly take an extreme position, which men hesitate for a long time to do.

In past confederations, the rights granted to the union were causes of war and not of power, since these rights multiplied its demands without increasing its means of making itself obeyed. So one almost always saw the real weakness of federal governments grow in direct proportion to their nominal power.

It is not this way in the American Union; like most ordinary governments, the federal government can do everything it has been given the right to execute.

The human mind invents things more easily than words: hence comes the use of so many improper terms and incomplete expressions.

[Suppose that] several nations form a permanent league and establish a

---

*Here "national" means statewide.

36. This is what one saw among the Greeks under Philip [II of Macedonia (382–336 B.C.)] when this prince was charged with executing the decree of the Amphictyons. [The Amphictyons were a league of ancient Greek tribes that could declare a "sacred war" against violators of its laws.] This was what has happened to the Republic of the Netherlands, where the province of Holland has always made the law [the United Provinces of the Netherlands, 1579–1795]. The same thing is still taking place in our day in the Germanic body. Austria and Prussia make themselves agents of the Diet and dominate the whole confederation in its name. [The Confederation of 1815 joined the thirty-nine states of Germany, of which Austria and Prussia were the largest.]

37. It has always been so for the Swiss confederation.—For centuries Switzerland would not have existed without the jealousies of their neighbors.

supreme authority that, without taking action on plain citizens as a national government could do, nevertheless takes action on each of the confederated peoples taken as a body.

That government, so different from all the others, receives the name federal.

Next, one discovers a form of society in which several peoples really meld into one only with regard to certain common interests, and remain separated and only confederated for all others.

Here the central power acts without an intermediary on the governed, administers them and judges them by itself, as national governments do, but it acts this way only in a restricted sphere. Evidently that is no longer a federal government; it is an incomplete national government. So one has found a form of government that is neither precisely national nor federal; but one stops there, and the new word that ought to express the new thing still does not exist.

It is because of not having known this new kind of confederation that all unions have come to civil war, to enslavement, or to inertia. The peoples who composed them all lacked the enlightenment to see the remedy to their ills or the courage to apply it.

The first American Union had also fallen into the same defects.

But in America, the confederated states, having arrived at independence, had long been part of the same empire; therefore they had not yet contracted the habit of governing themselves completely, and national* prejudices had not been able to sink deep roots; more enlightened than the rest of the world, they were equal in enlightenment among themselves; they felt only weakly the passions in peoples that ordinarily oppose the extension of federal power, and these passions were combated by the greatest citizens. Americans, at the same time that they felt the ill, firmly saw the remedy. They corrected their laws and saved the country.

ON THE ADVANTAGES OF THE FEDERAL SYSTEM GENERALLY, AND ITS SPECIAL UTILITY FOR AMERICA

Happiness and freedom that small nations enjoy.—Power of great nations.—Great empires favor the development of civilization.—That force is often the first element of prosperity for nations.—The federal system has for its goal to unite the advantages that peoples draw from the greatness and the smallness of their territory.—Advantages that the United States derives from this system.—Law bows to the needs of populations, and

---

*Here "national" refers to the states.

populations do not bow to the necessities of law.—Activity, prosperity, taste for and habit of freedom among the American peoples.—Public spirit in the Union is only the summa-tion *of provincial patriotism.—Things and ideas circulate freely in the territory of the United States.—The Union is free and happy like a small nation, respected like a great one.*

In small nations, the eye of society penetrates everywhere; the spirit of improvement descends to the least details: the ambition of the people being much tempered by weakness, its efforts and its resources turn almost entirely toward its internal well-being and are not subject to being dissipated in the vain smoke of glory. Moreover, as the abilities of each person generally are limited, desires are equally so. The mediocrity of fortunes renders conditions nearly equal; mores have a simple and peaceful style. So, all in all, and taking account of varying degrees of morality and enlightenment, one ordinarily encounters more ease, population, and tranquillity in small nations than in great ones.

When tyranny comes to be established in the heart of a small nation, it is more inconvenient there than anywhere else because, acting in a more restricted circle, it extends to everything in that circle. Unable to take on some great object, it occupies itself with a multitude of small ones; it shows itself at once violent and troublesome. From the political world that is, properly speaking, its domain, it penetrates private life. After actions, it aspires to dictate tastes; after the state, it wants to govern families. But that happens rarely; freedom forms, to tell the truth, the natural condition of small societies. In them the government offers too little of a lure to ambition, the resources of particular persons are too limited for the sovereign power easily to become concentrated in the hands of one alone. Should the case occur, it is not difficult for the governed to unite and, by a common effort, overturn tyrant and tyranny at the same time.

In all times, therefore, small nations have been cradles of political freedom. It has happened that most of them have lost that freedom by becoming larger, which makes it very visible that [freedom] was due to the smallness of the people and not to the people itself.

The history of the world does not furnish an example of a great nation that has long remained a republic,[38] which has caused it to be said that the thing is impracticable. As for me, I think that it is imprudent indeed for man to want to limit the possible and to judge the future—he whom the real and the present elude every day and who constantly finds himself unexpectedly surprised in the things that he knows best. What one can say with certitude

---

38. I do not speak here of a confederation of small republics, but of a great consolidated republic.

is that the existence of a great republic will always be infinitely more exposed [to peril] than that of a small one.

All the passions fatal to republics grow with the extent of the territory, whereas the virtues that serve as their support do not increase in the same measure.

The ambition of particular persons increases with the power of the state; the force of parties, with the importance of the goal they propose; but the love of the native country that must struggle against these destructive passions is not stronger in a vast republic than in a small one. It would even be easy to prove that it is less developed and less powerful. Great wealth and profound miseries, metropolises, depravity of mores, individual selfishness, complication of interests are so many perils that almost always arise from the greatness of the state. Several of these things do not harm the existence of a monarchy, some can even contribute to its duration. Besides, in monarchies the government has a force that is its own; it makes use of the people and does not depend on them; the greater the people is, the stronger the prince is; but republican government can only oppose to these dangers the support of the majority. Now, this element of force is no more powerful, relatively speaking, in a vast republic than in a small one. So whereas the means of attack constantly increase in number and power, the force of resistance remains the same. One can even say that it diminishes, for the more numerous the people are and the more diversified the natures of minds and interests, the more difficult it is to form a compact majority as a consequence.

One could remark, moreover, that human passions acquire intensity not only through the greatness of the goal they want to attain, but also through the multitude of individuals who feel them at the same time. There is no one who has not found himself more moved in the midst of an agitated crowd that shared his emotion than if he had been alone in experiencing it. In a great republic, political passions become irresistible not only because the object that they pursue is immense, but also because millions of men feel them in the same manner and at the same moment.

It is therefore permissible to say in a general manner that nothing is so contrary to the well-being and freedom of men as great empires.

Great states nevertheless have advantages that are particular to them and that must be recognized.

Just as the desire for power among vulgar men is more ardent there than elsewhere, the love of glory is also more developed in certain souls who find in the applause of a great people an object worthy of their efforts and appropriate to elevate them in a way above themselves. Thought receives a more rapid and powerful impetus in everything, ideas circulate more freely, metropolises are like vast intellectual centers where all the rays of the human mind come to shine and to combine: this fact explains to us why great nations make more rapid progress in enlightenment and in the general cause of civilization than small ones. One must add that important discoveries often require a development of national force of which the government of a small people is incapable; in great nations, the government has more general ideas, it is more completely disengaged from the routine of predecessors and the selfishness of localities. There is more genius in its conceptions, more boldness in its style.

Internal well-being is more complete and more widespread in small nations as long as they keep themselves at peace; but the state of war is more harmful to them than to great ones. In the latter, the remoteness of the frontiers sometimes permits the mass of people to remain remote from danger for centuries. For them, war is a cause of uneasiness rather than ruin.

Besides, a consideration that dominates all the rest presents itself in this matter as in many others: that of necessity.

If there were only small nations and no great ones, humanity would surely be freer and happier; but one cannot make it so that there are no great nations.

This introduces a new element of national prosperity into the world, which is force. What does it matter that a people presents the image of ease and freedom if it sees itself at risk daily of being ravaged or conquered? What does it matter that it is manufacturing and commercial if another dominates the seas and makes the law for all markets? Small nations are often miserable not because they are small, but because they are weak; great ones prosper not because they are great but because they are strong. Force is therefore often one of the first conditions of happiness and even of existence for nations. Hence it is that, except in particular circumstances, small peoples are always in the end violently unified with great ones or are unified with each other. I do not know of a condition more deplorable than that of a people that cannot defend itself or be self-sufficient.

It is to unite the diverse advantages resulting from the greatness and the smallness of nations that the federal system was created.

It is enough to cast a glance at the United States of America to perceive all the goods flowing to them from the adoption of this system.

In great centralized nations, the legislator is obliged to give a uniform character to the laws that does not comport with the diversity of places and of mores; never being instructed in particular cases, he can only proceed by general rules; men are then obliged to bow to the necessities of legislation, for legislation does not know how to accommodate itself to the needs and mores of men, which is a great cause of troubles and miseries.

This inconvenience does not exist in confederations: Congress regulates the principal actions of social existence; every detail of it is abandoned to provincial legislation.

One cannot imagine to what extent this division of sovereignty serves the well-being of each of the states of which the Union is composed. In these little societies that are not preoccupied with the care of defending themselves or enlarging themselves, all public power and all individual energy turn in the direction of internal improvements. The central government of each state, placed right beside the governed, is alerted daily to the needs that are felt: so one sees new plans presented each year which, discussed in township assemblies or before the state legislature and reproduced afterwards by the press, excite the universal interest and zeal of citizens. This need to improve constantly agitates the American republics and does not trouble them; ambition for power makes way for love of well-being, a more vulgar but less dangerous passion. It is an opinion generally widespread in America that the existence and the duration of republican forms in the New World depend on the existence and the duration of the federal system. They attribute a great part of the miseries into which the new states of South America are plunged to the fact that they wished to establish great republics there instead of fragmenting sovereignty.

It is in fact incontestable that in the United States the taste for and usage of republican government are born in the townships and within the provincial assemblies. In a small nation like Connecticut, for example, where the opening of a canal and the laying out of a road are great political affairs, where the state has no army to pay or war to sustain and cannot give those who direct it either much wealth or much glory, one can imagine nothing more natural and more appropriate to the nature of things than a republic. Now, it is this same republican spirit, these mores and habits of a free people, which, after having been born and developed in the various states, are afterwards applied without difficulty to the sum of the country. The public spirit of the Union itself is in a way only a summation of provincial patriotism. Each citizen of the United States so to speak carries over the interest that his little republic inspires in him into love of the common native country. In defending the Union, he defends the growing prosperity of his district, his right to direct affairs within it, and the hope of making plans of improvement prevail that will enrich him: all things that ordinarily touch men more than the general interests of the country and the glory of the nation.

On the other hand, if the spirit and mores of the inhabitants render them more suited than others to make a great republic prosper, the federal system has rendered the task much less difficult. The confederation of all the American states does not present the ordinary inconveniences of large aggregations of men. The Union is a great republic in extent; but one could in a way liken it to a small republic because the objects with which its government is occupied are few. Its actions are important, but they are rare. As the sovereignty of the Union is hindered and incomplete, the use of that sovereignty is not dangerous for freedom. Neither does it excite those immoderate desires for power and attention that are so fatal to great republics. As everything does not necessarily converge at a common center, neither does one see vast metropolises, or immense wealth, or great misery, or sudden revolutions there. Political passions, instead of spreading in an instant over the whole area of the country like a sheet of flames, break against the individual interests and passions of each state.

In the Union, however, as in one and the same people, things and ideas circulate freely. Nothing there stops the surge of the spirit of enterprise. Its government calls talents and enlightenment to it. Within the frontiers of the Union a profound peace reigns, as in the interior of a country subject to the same empire; outside, it takes its rank among the most powerful nations on earth; it offers to foreign commerce more than eight hundred leagues of coast; and holding in its hands the keys to a whole world, it makes its flag respected to the ends of the seas.

The Union is free and happy like a small nation, glorious and strong like a great one.

WHAT KEEPS THE FEDERAL SYSTEM FROM BEING WITHIN REACH OF ALL PEOPLES, AND WHAT HAS PERMITTED THE ANGLO-AMERICANS TO ADOPT IT

There are vices inherent in every federal system that the legislator cannot combat.—Complication of every federal system.—It requires of the governed a daily use of their intelligence.—Practical science of the Americans in matters of government.—Relative weakness of the government of the Union, another vice inherent in the federal system.—The Americans have rendered it less serious, but they have not been able to destroy it.—The sovereignty of the particular states weaker in appearance, stronger in reality than that of the Union.—Why.—There must therefore exist, independent of the laws, natural causes for union in confederated peoples.—What these causes are among the Anglo-Americans.—Maine and Georgia, four hundred leagues distant from one another, more naturally united than Normandy and Brittany.—That war is the principal shoal of confederations.—This proved by the example of the United States itself.—The Union has no great wars to fear.—Why.—Dangers that the peoples of Europe risk in adopting the federal system of the Americans.

Sometimes, after a thousand efforts, the legislator succeeds in exerting an indirect influence on the destiny of nations, and then one celebrates his genius—whereas often the geographical position of the country, about which he can do nothing, a social state that was created without his concurrence, mores and ideas of whose origin he is ignorant, a point of departure unknown to him, impart irresistible movements to society against which he struggles in vain and which carry him along in his turn.

The legislator resembles a man who plots his course in the middle of the sea. Thus he can direct the vessel that carries him, but he cannot change its structure, create winds, or prevent the ocean from rising under his feet.

I have shown what advantages the Americans derive from the federal system. It remains for me to make it understood what permitted them to adopt this system; for it is not given to all peoples to enjoy its benefits.

One finds in the federal system accidental vices born of laws; those can be corrected by legislators. One encounters others which, being inherent in the system, cannot be destroyed by peoples who adopt it. These peoples must therefore find in themselves the necessary force to tolerate the natural imperfections of their government.

Among the vices inherent in every federal system the most visible of all is the complication of the means that it employs. This system necessarily brings two sovereignties face to face. The legislator succeeds in rendering the movements of these two sovereignties as simple and as equal as possible and can confine both in cleanly drawn spheres of action; but he cannot make it so that there is only one, or prevent them from touching each other someplace.

The federal system therefore rests, whatever one does, on a complicated theory whose application requires of the governed a daily use of the enlightenment of their reason.

In general, only simple conceptions take hold of the minds of the people. A false idea, but one clear and precise, will always have more power in the world than a true, but complex, idea. Hence it is that parties, which are like small nations in a great one, always hasten to adopt for a symbol a name or a principle that often represents only very incompletely the goal that they propose and the means they employ, but without which they could neither subsist nor move ahead. Governments that rest only on a single idea or on a single, easy-to-define sentiment are perhaps not the best, but they are surely the strongest and the most lasting.

When one examines the Constitution of the United States, the most perfect of all known federal constitutions, one is frightened, on the contrary, by the quantity of diverse knowledge and by the discernment that it supposes in those whom it must rule. The government of the Union rests almost wholly on legal fictions. The Union is an ideal nation that exists so to speak only in minds, and whose extent and bounds intelligence alone discovers.

The general theory being well understood, the difficulties of application remain; they are innumerable, for the sovereignty of the Union is so enmeshed in that of the states that it is impossible at first glance to perceive their limits. Everything is conventional and artificial in such a government, and it can be suitable only for a people long habituated to directing its affairs by itself, and in which political science has descended to the last ranks of society. I never admired the good sense and the practical intelligence of the Americans more than in the manner by which they escape the innumerable difficulties to which their federal constitution gives rise. I almost never encountered a man of the people in America who did not discern with a surprising facility the obligations arising from laws of Congress and those whose origin is in the laws of his state, and who, after distinguishing the objects placed within the general prerogatives of the Union from those that the local legislature ought to regulate, could not indicate the point at which the competence of the federal courts begins and the limit at which that of the state tribunals stops.

The Constitution of the United States resembles those beautiful creations of human industry that lavish glory and goods on those who invent them, but that remain sterile in other hands.

This is what Mexico has made visible in our day.

The inhabitants of Mexico, wishing to establish a federal system, took as a model and copied almost entirely the federal constitution of the Anglo-Americans, their neighbors.[39] But in transporting the letter of the law to themselves, they could not at the same time transport the spirit that enlivened it. One therefore sees them constantly embarrassed amid the wheels of their double government. The sovereignty of the states and that of the union, leaving the circles that the constitution had drawn, penetrate one another daily. Mexico is still now incessantly carried along from anarchy to military despotism, and from military despotism to anarchy.

The second and most fatal of all the vices that I regard as inherent in the federal system itself is the relative weakness of the government of the Union.

The principle on which all confederations rest is the fragmentation of sovereignty. The legislators make this fragmentation little felt; they even keep it out of sight for a time, but they cannot make it not exist. And a fragmented sovereignty will always be weaker than a complete sovereignty.

We have seen in the account of the Constitution of the United States with what art the Americans, while confining the power of the Union within the restricted sphere of federal governments, nevertheless succeeded in giving it the appearance and, up to a certain point, the force of a national government.

In acting thus, the legislators of the Union diminished the natural danger of confederations; but they could not make it disappear entirely.

39. See the Mexican constitution of 1824.

The American government, one may say, does not address the states: it brings its injunctions to reach citizens immediately and bends them in isolation under the effort of the common will.

But if the federal law violently collided with the interests and prejudices of a state, should one not fear that each of the citizens of that state would believe himself interested in the cause of the man who refused to obey? All the citizens of the state thus finding themselves wronged at the same time in the same manner by the authority of the Union, the federal government would seek in vain to isolate them so as to combat them: they would feel instinctively that they ought to unite to defend themselves, and they would find in the share of sovereignty their state had been allowed to enjoy a wholly prepared organization. Then fiction would disappear to make way for reality, and one could see the organized power of a part of the territory in conflict with the central authority.

I shall say as much of federal justice. If, in a particular case, the courts of the Union violated an important law of a state, the conflict, if not apparently, at least in reality, would be between the wronged state, represented by a citizen, and the Union, represented by its courts.[40]

One must have very little experience of things of this world to imagine that after leaving to the passions of men a means of getting satisfaction, one will always prevent them with the aid of legal fictions from perceiving and making use of it.

The American legislators, while rendering conflict between the two sovereignties less probable, did not thereby destroy the causes of it.

One can go even further and say that they were unable, in case of a conflict, to assure that federal power would be preponderant.

They gave money and soldiers to the Union, but the states kept the love and prejudices of the peoples.

The sovereignty of the Union is an abstract being that is attached to only a few external objects. The sovereignty of the states comes before all the senses; one comprehends it without difficulty; one sees it act at each instant. One is new, the other was born with the people itself.

The sovereignty of the Union is the work of art. The sovereignty of the

40. Example: the Constitution has given the Union the right to have unoccupied lands sold for its account. I suppose that Ohio might claim this same right for those that are contained within its borders under the pretext that the Constitution meant only territory that was not yet subject to any state jurisdiction, and consequently it wants to sell them itself. The judicial question would be posed, it is true, between the buyers who hold their title from the Union and the buyers who hold their title from the state, and not between the Union and Ohio. But if the Court of the United States ordered the federal buyer to be put in possession, and the courts of Ohio sustained his competitor in his goods, then what would become of the legal fiction?

states is natural; it exists by itself without effort, like the authority of the father of a family.

The sovereignty of the Union only touches men through a few great interests; it represents an immense, distant native country, a vague and indefinite sentiment. The sovereignty of the states in a way envelops each citizen, and takes him over daily in detail. It takes charge of guaranteeing his property, his freedom, his life; at every moment it influences his well-being or his misery. The sovereignty of the states depends on memories, on habits, on local prejudices, on the selfishness of province and family; in a word, on all the things that render the instinct for one's native country so powerful in the heart of man. How could one doubt its advantages?

Since legislators cannot prevent dangerous collisions from cropping up between the two sovereignties that the federal system puts face to face, particular provisions that lead them to peace must be joined to their efforts to turn confederated peoples away from war.

Hence it results that the federal pact cannot have a long existence if, in the peoples to whom it applies, a certain number of conditions of union do not obtain that render this common life easy for them and facilitate the task of government.

Thus, to succeed, the federal system not only needs good laws, but circumstances must also favor it.

All peoples who have been seen to confederate had a certain number of common interests that formed the intellectual bonds of the association.

But beyond material interests man also has ideas and sentiments. In order that a confederation subsist for a long time, it is no less necessary that there be homogeneity in the civilization than in the needs of the various peoples that compose it. The difference between the civilization of the canton of Vaud and that of the canton of Uri is almost from the nineteenth century to the fifteenth: so Switzerland has never had, to tell the truth, a federal government. The union between its different cantons exists only on the map; and one would see it well if a central authority wanted to apply the same laws to the whole territory.

There is one fact that admirably facilitates federal government in the United States. The different states have not only nearly the same interests, the same origin, and the same language, but even the same degree of civilization, which almost always renders agreement between them an easy thing. I do not know if there is a small European nation that does not present an aspect less homogeneous in its different parts than the American people, whose territory is as great as half of Europe.

From the state of Maine to the state of Georgia one counts around four hundred leagues. Nevertheless, less difference exists between the civilization of Maine and that of Georgia than between the civilization of Normandy and that of Brittany. Maine and Georgia, placed at two ends of a vast empire, therefore naturally find more real opportunities to form a confederation than Normandy and Brittany, which are separated only by a stream.

To these opportunities, which the mores and the habits of the people offered to the American legislators, were added others arising from the geographic position of the country. To the latter the adoption and maintenance of the federal system must principally be attributed.

The most important of all the actions that can inform the life of a people is war. In war, a people acts like a single individual vis-à-vis foreign peoples: it struggles for its very existence.

As long as it is only a question of maintaining the peace in the interior of a country and of favoring its prosperity, skill in the government, reason in the governed, and a certain natural attachment that men almost always have for their native country can easily suffice; but for a nation to be in a position to make a great war, citizens must impose numerous and painful sacrifices on themselves. To believe that a great number of men will be capable of submitting to such social exigencies is to know humanity very poorly.

Hence it is that all peoples who have had to make great wars have been led almost despite themselves to increase the strength of the government. Those who have not been able to succeed at this have been conquered. A long war almost always places nations in this sad alternative: that their defeat delivers them to destruction and their triumph to despotism.

It is therefore generally in war that the weakness of a government is revealed in a more visible and more dangerous manner; and I have shown that the vice inherent in federal governments is to be very weak.

In the federal system not only is there no administrative centralization or anything that approaches it, but governmental centralization itself exists only incompletely, which is always a great cause of weakness when one must defend oneself against peoples in which it is complete.

In the federal constitution of the United States, that one of all others in which the central government is vested with more real strength, this evil is still keenly felt.

A single example will permit the reader to judge.

The constitution gives to Congress the right to call the militias of the different states to active service when it is a question of stifling an insurrection or of repelling an invasion; another article says that in this case the president of the United States is the commander in chief of the militias.

At the time of the War of 1812, the president ordered the militias of the North to go to the frontiers; Connecticut and Massachusetts, whose interests the war prejudiced, refused to send their contingents.

The Constitution, they said, authorizes the federal government to make use of the militias in case of *insurrection* and *invasion;* but as for the present, there is neither insurrection nor invasion. They added that the same constitution that gives the Union the right to call the militias to active service leaves to the states the right to name the officers; it follows, according to them, that even in war no officer of the Union has the right to command the militias except the president in person. Now it was a question of serving in an army commanded by someone other than him.

These absurd and destructive doctrines received not only the sanction of the governors and of the legislatures, but even that of the courts of justice of these two states; and the federal government was constrained to seek elsewhere the troops it lacked.[41]

How, therefore, is it that the American Union, protected as it is by the relative perfection of its laws, does not dissolve in the middle of a great war? It is that it has no great wars to fear.

Placed at the center of an immense continent, where human industry can spread without bounds, the Union is almost as isolated in the world as if it found itself confined on all sides by the ocean.

Canada numbers only a million inhabitants; its population is divided into two enemy nations. The rigors of the climate limit the extent of its territory and close its ports for six months.

From Canada to the Gulf of Mexico one still finds some half-destroyed savage tribes that six thousand soldiers push before them.

To the south, the Union touches at one point on the empire of Mexico; it is from there probably that great wars will come one day. But for a long time still, the barely advanced state of civilization, the corruption of mores, and misery will prevent Mexico from taking an elevated rank among nations. As for the powers of Europe, their distance renders them not very formidable.*

The great happiness of the United States is therefore not to have found a federal constitution that permits it to sustain great wars, but to be so situated that there are none for it to fear.

No one can appreciate more than I the advantages of a federal system. I

---

*See AT's note XIV, page 695.

41. *Kent's Commentaries,* vol. 1, 244[f]. Remark that I have chosen the example cited above from a time subsequent to the establishment of the current constitution. If I had wanted to go back to the period of the first confederation I would have pointed out still more conclusive facts. Then a genuine enthusiasm reigned in the nation; the revolution was represented by an eminently popular man and nonetheless in this period Congress disposed, properly speaking, of nothing. It lacked men and money at every moment; the plans it best conceived failed in execution, and the Union, always at the point of perishing, was saved much more by the weakness of its enemies than by its own force.

see in it one of the most powerful combinations in favor of human prosperity and freedom. I envy the lot of the nations who have been permitted to adopt it. But I nonetheless refuse to believe that confederated peoples could struggle for long, with equal force, against a nation in which governmental power were centralized.

The people that, face to face with the great military monarchies of Europe, would fragment its sovereignty, would seem to me to abdicate by that fact alone its power and perhaps its existence and its name.

Admirable position of the New World that enables man to have no enemies but himself! To be happy and free, it is enough for him to wish it.

PART TWO

Until now I have examined the institutions, I have gone over the written laws, I have depicted the current forms of political society in the United States.

But above all the institutions and outside all the forms resides a sovereign power, that of the people, which destroys them or modifies them at its will.

It remains for me to make known the ways by which this power, dominant over the laws, proceeds; what are its instincts, its passions; what secret springs drive it, slow it down, or direct it in its irresistible advance; what effects its omnipotence produces, and what future is in store for it.

ᑭᕦ ᑭᕦ

Chapter 1 HOW ONE CAN SAY STRICTLY THAT IN THE UNITED STATES THE PEOPLE GOVERN

In America the people name those who make the law and those who execute it; they themselves form the jury that punishes infractions of the law. Not only are institutions democratic in their principle, but also in all their developments; thus the people name their representatives *directly* and generally choose them *every year* in order to keep them more completely under their dependence. It is therefore really the people who direct, and although the form of government is representative, it is evident that the opinions, the prejudices, the interests, and even the passions of the people can find no lasting obstacles that prevent them from taking effect in the daily direction of society.

In the United States, as in all countries where the people reign, it is the majority that governs in the name of the people.

This majority is composed principally of peaceful citizens who, either by taste or by interest, sincerely desire the good of the country. Around them parties constantly agitate, seeking to draw them to their bosom and to get support from them.

Chapter 2 ON PARTIES IN THE UNITED STATES

One must make a great division among parties.—Parties that are like rival nations among themselves.—Parties properly speaking.—Difference between great and small parties.—In what times they arise.—Their various characteristics.—America had great parties.—It no longer has them.—Federalists.—Republicans.—Defeat of the Federalists.—Difficulty of creating parties in the United States.—What one does to succeed at it.—Aristocratic or democratic characteristics that are found in all parties.—Struggle of General Jackson* against the bank.

I should first establish a great division among parties.

There are countries so vast that the different populations that inhabit them, although united under the same sovereignty, have contradictory interests from which a permanent opposition arises between them. The various fractions of the same people do not then form parties properly speaking, but distinct nations; and if a civil war arises, it is a conflict between rival peoples rather than a struggle between factions.

But when citizens differ among themselves on points that interest all portions of the country equally, such as, for example, the general principles of government, then one sees arise what I shall truly call parties.

Parties are an evil inherent in free governments; but they do not have the same characteristics and the same instincts at all times.

There come periods in which nations feel tormented by such great evils that the idea of a total change in their political constitution presents itself to their thinking. There are others in which the malaise is still more profound and the social state itself is compromised. That is the time of great revolutions and great parties.

Between those centuries of disorders and miseries one encounters others when societies rest and when the human race seems to catch its breath. That is still, to tell the truth, only an appearance; time no more suspends its course for peoples than for men; both advance daily toward a future of which they are unaware; and when we believe them stationary, it is because their movements escape us. These are people who walk; they appear immobile to those who are running.

Be this as it may, there come periods when the changes that are at work

---

*Andrew Jackson, seventh president of the United States, 1829–1837.

in the political constitution and social state of peoples are so slow and so imperceptible that men think they have arrived at a final state; the human mind then believes itself firmly seated on certain bases and does not lift its regard beyond a certain horizon.

That is the time of intrigues and small parties.

What I call great political parties are those that are attached more to principles than to their consequences; to generalities and not to particular cases; to ideas and not to men. These parties generally have nobler features, more generous passions, more real convictions, a franker and bolder aspect than the others. Particular interest, which always plays the greatest role in political passions, hides more skillfully here under the veil of the public interest; it sometimes even succeeds in evading the regard of those whom it animates and brings to act.

Small parties, on the contrary, are generally without political faith. As they do not feel themselves elevated and sustained by great objects, their character is stamped with a selfishness that shows openly in each of their acts. They always become heated in a cool way; their language is violent but their course is timid and uncertain. The means that they employ are miserable, as is the very goal they propose for themselves. Hence it is that when a time of calm follows a violent revolution, great men seem to disappear all at once and souls withdraw into themselves.

Great parties overturn society, small ones agitate it; the former tear it apart and the latter deprave it; the first sometimes save it by shaking it up, the second always trouble it without profit.

America has had great parties; today they no longer exist: it has gained much in happiness, but not in morality.

When the War of Independence came to an end and it was a question of establishing the bases of the new government, the nation found itself divided between two opinions. These opinions were as old as the world, and one finds them over and over in different forms and reclothed with diverse names in all free societies. One opinion wanted to restrict popular power, the other to extend it indefinitely.

The struggle between these two opinions among the Americans never took on the violent character that has often marked it elsewhere. In America, the two parties were in agreement on the most essential points. To win, neither of the two had to destroy an old order or overturn a whole social state. Consequently, neither of the two linked a great number of individual lives to the triumph of its principles. But they touched immaterial interests of the first order, such as love of equality and of independence. This was enough to stir up violent passions.

The party that wanted to restrict popular power sought above all to make its doctrines apply to the Constitution of the Union, by which it earned the name *federal*.

The other, which claimed to be the exclusive lover of freedom, took the title *republican*.

America is the land of democracy. The Federalists were therefore always in a minority; but they counted in their ranks almost all the great men the War of Independence had given birth to, and their moral power was very extensive. Moreover, circumstances were favorable to them. The ruin of the first confederation made the people fear they would fall into anarchy, and the Federalists profited from this passing disposition. For ten or twelve years they directed affairs and were able to apply, not all their principles, but some of them; for day by day the opposing current was becoming too violent for them to dare to struggle against it.

In 1801, the Republicans finally took possession of the government. Thomas Jefferson was named president; he brought them the support of a celebrated name, a great talent, and an immense popularity.

The Federalists had never maintained themselves except by artificial means and with the aid of temporary resources; it was the virtue or talents of their chiefs as well as fortunate circumstances that had carried them to power. When the Republicans arrived in their turn, the opposing party was as if enveloped in the midst of a sudden flood. An immense majority declared itself against it, and right away it saw itself in so small a minority that it immediately despaired of itself. Since that moment, the Republican or Democratic Party* has advanced from conquest to conquest, and has taken possession of society as a whole.

The Federalists, feeling themselves defeated, without resources, and seeing themselves isolated in the midst of the nation, became divided; some joined the victors, others laid down their banner and changed their name. It has already been a fairly large number of years since they ceased entirely to exist as a party.†

The coming of the Federalists to power is, in my opinion, one of the most fortunate events that accompanied the birth of the great American Union. The Federalists struggled against the irresistible inclination of their century and of their country. Whatever their goodness or vice, their theories were wrong in being inapplicable in their entirety to the society they wanted to rule; what happened under Jefferson would therefore have happened sooner

*The original Republican Party of the 1790s, also known as the Democratic-Republican Party, had by 1832 become the Democratic Party.

†By the election of 1816 the Federalists had become a small regional party and had ceased to offer presidential candidates.

or later. But their government at least left the new republic time to settle in and afterwards permitted it to bear without inconvenience the rapid development of the doctrines they had combated. Moreover, a large number of their principles were in the end introduced under the creed of their adversaries; and the federal constitution, which still subsists in our time, is a lasting monument to their patriotism and their wisdom.

So in our day, one does not perceive great political parties in the United States. One does indeed encounter parties that threaten the future of the Union; but none appear to attack the current form of government and the general course of society. The parties that threaten the Union rest not on principles, but on material interests. These interests in the different provinces of such a vast empire constitute rival nations rather than parties. Thus it is that one recently saw the North support the system of commercial prohibitions and the South take up arms in favor of freedom of commerce, for the sole reason that the North is in manufacturing and the South in farming, and the restrictive system acts to the profit of the one and the detriment of the other.*

For want of great parties, the United States swarms with small ones, and public opinion becomes infinitely fragmented over questions of detail. One cannot imagine the trouble they take there to create parties; it is not an easy thing in our time. In the United States there is no religious hatred because religion is universally respected and no sect is dominant; there is no class hatred because the people are everything and no one yet dares to struggle with them; finally, there are no public miseries to exploit because the material state of the country offers such an immense scope for industry that it is enough to leave man to himself for him to do prodigies. Nonetheless, ambition must succeed in creating parties, for it is difficult to overthrow the one who holds power for the sole reason that someone wants to take his place. All the skill of politicians therefore consists in composing parties: a politician in the United States at first seeks to discern his interest and to see what the analogous interests are that could be grouped around his; afterwards, he busies himself with discovering whether there might not by chance exist in the world a doctrine or principle that could suitably be placed at the head of the new association to give it the right to introduce itself and circulate freely. It

---

* AT is referring to the debate over the Tariff Act of 1828, the "Tariff of Abominations," which raised duties on imported raw materials such as iron and hemp. Northern states favored protective tariffs because manufacturers sought protection from British competition. Southern farmers opposed tariffs because they needed inexpensive manufactured goods, and because they feared that other countries would retaliate by raising duties on American agricultural goods. In 1832 South Carolina went so far as to nullify the tariff law, creating a constitutional crisis that was resolved by Representative Henry Clay's famous legislative compromise the following year.

is like the privilege of the king that our fathers formerly printed on the first page of their works and that they incorporated in the book although it was no part of it.

This done, they introduce the new power into the political world.

To a stranger, almost all the domestic quarrels of Americans at first appear incomprehensible or puerile, and one does not know if one ought to take pity on a people that is seriously occupied with miseries like these or envy it the good fortune of being able to be occupied with them.

But when one comes to study carefully the secret instincts that govern factions in America, one readily discovers that most of them are more or less linked to one or the other of the two great parties that have divided men since there have been free societies. As one penetrates the innermost thoughts of these parties more deeply, one perceives that some of them work to narrow the use of public power, the others to extend it.

I do not say that American parties always have for an ostensible goal or even a hidden goal to make aristocracy or democracy prevail in the country; I say that aristocratic or democratic passions are readily found at the foundation of all parties; and that although they may escape one's glance, they form as it were the sensitive spot and the soul of them.

I shall cite a recent example: the president attacks the Bank of the United States; the country is aroused and divided; the enlightened classes are generally ranged on the side of the Bank, the people in favor of the president.* Do you think that the people could discern the reasons for his opinion amid the twists and turns of such a difficult question when experienced men hesitate? Not at all. But the Bank is a great establishment that has an independent existence; the people, who destroy or raise all powers, can do nothing about it, which astonishes them. In the midst of the universal movement of society, the sight of this unmovable point shocks them, and they want to see if they cannot get it going like the rest.

ON THE REMAINS OF THE ARISTOCRATIC PARTY IN THE UNITED STATES

Secret opposition of the rich to democracy.—They retire to private life.—Taste they show inside their dwellings for exclusive pleasures and luxury.—Their simplicity outside.— Their affected condescension toward the people.

---

* Jackson questioned the constitutionality of the Bank of the United States in his first annual message in 1829. On July 10, 1832, he vetoed a bill to extend the Bank's charter (which was due to expire in 1836). In doing so he antagonized conservative interests but gained popularity among the many people who associated the Bank with monopolies and special privileges of the wealthy.

It sometimes happens in a people divided in opinions that when the equilibrium between the parties comes to be upset, one of them acquires an irresistible preponderance. It crushes all obstacles, overwhelms its adversary, and exploits the entire society to its profit. The defeated, despairing then of success, hide or keep silent. A universal immobility and silence come about. The nation seems reunited in one same thought. The winning party rises up and says, "I have restored peace to the country, it owes me thanks."

But under this apparent unanimity, profound divisions and a real opposition are still hidden.

This is what happened in America: when the democratic party had obtained a preponderance, one saw it take possession of the exclusive direction of affairs. Since then it has not ceased to model mores and laws to its desires.

In our day one can say that in the United States the wealthy classes of society are almost entirely out of political affairs and that wealth, far from being a right [to power], is a real cause of disfavor and an obstacle to coming to power.

The rich, therefore, would rather abandon the lists than sustain an often unequal struggle against the poorest of their fellow citizens. Not being able to take up a rank in public life analogous to the one they occupy in private life, they abandon the first to concentrate on the second. In the midst of the state they form as it were a particular society that has separate tastes and enjoyments.

The rich man submits to this state of things as to an irremediable evil; he even very carefully avoids showing that it wounds him; one therefore hears him publicly extol the mildness of republican government and the advantages of democratic forms. For after the fact of hating their enemies, what is more natural to men than flattering them?

Do you see this opulent citizen? Would one not think of a Jew in the Middle Ages who fears to allow his wealth to be suspected? His dress is simple, his walk is modest; within the four walls of his dwelling luxury is adored; he allows only some chosen guests whom he insolently calls his equals to penetrate this sanctuary. One finds no noble in Europe who shows himself to be more exclusive than he in his pleasures or more jealous of the least advantages that a privileged position assures. But here he is leaving his home to go to work in a dusty den that he occupies in the center of town and of business, where each is free to come approach him. In the middle of the road his shoemaker comes to pass by, and they stop: both then set to discussing. What can they be saying? These two citizens are occupied with affairs of state, and they do not leave each other without having shaken hands.

At the bottom of this enthusiasm for convention and in the midst of these forms, obsequious toward the dominant power, it is easy to perceive in the rich a great disgust for the democratic institutions of their country. The people are a power that they fear and scorn. If the bad government of democracy led to a political crisis one day; if monarchy were ever presented as something practical in the United States, one would soon discover the truth of what I am advancing.

The two great weapons that the parties employ in order to succeed are *newspapers* and *associations*.

ᏜᏜᏜᏜᏜᏜᏜᏜᏜᏜᏜᏜᏜᏜᏜᏜᏜᏜᏜᏜᏜ

Chapter 3 ON FREEDOM OF THE PRESS IN THE UNITED STATES

Difficulty of restricting the freedom of the press.—Particular reasons certain peoples have for holding on to this freedom.—Freedom of the press is a necessary consequence of the sovereignty of the people as it is understood in America.—Violence of the language of the periodical press in the United States.—The periodical press has instincts that are its own; the example of the United States proves it.—Opinion of the Americans about judicial repression of the offenses of the press.—Why the press is less powerful in the United States than in France.

Freedom of the press makes its power felt not only over political opinions, but also over all opinions of men. It modifies not only laws, but mores. In another part of this work I shall seek to determine the degree of influence that freedom of the press has exerted on civil society in the United States;* I shall try to discern the direction it has given to ideas, and the habits it has brought to the minds and sentiments of Americans. For the moment I want to examine only the effects produced by freedom of the press in the political world.

I avow that I do not hold that complete and instantaneous love for the freedom of the press that one accords to things whose nature is unqualifiedly good. I love it out of consideration for the evils it prevents much more than for the good it does.

If someone were to show me, between complete independence and entire enslavement of thought, an intermediate position that I could hope to hold to, I would perhaps establish myself there; but who will discover that inter-

*DA II 2.6.

mediate position? You depart from the license of the press and you go further toward order: What do you do? At first you submit writers to juries; but the juries acquit, and what was only the opinion of an isolated man becomes the opinion of the country. You have therefore done too much and too little; you must go further still. You deliver the authors to permanent magistrates; but the judges are obliged to hear before condemning; what they had feared to avow in the book they proclaim with impunity in the plea; what they said obscurely in one telling is thus found repeated in a thousand others. Expression is the exterior form and, if I can express myself so, the body of thought, but it is not thought itself. Your courts arrest the body, but the soul escapes them and slips subtly between their hands. You have therefore done too much and too little; you must continue to go further. You finally abandon the writers to censors; fine! now we are getting close. But is the political forum not free? You have therefore still done nothing; I am mistaken, you have increased the evil. Would you by chance take thought as one of those material powers that are increased by the number of their agents? Will you count writers like soldiers in an army? Contrary to all material powers, the power of thought is often even augmented by the small number of those who express it. The word of one powerful man that penetrates alone into the midst of the passions of a mute assembly has more power than the confused cries of a thousand orators; and if ever one can speak freely in a single public place, it is as if one were speaking publicly in each village. You must therefore destroy freedom of speech like that of writing; this time, you reach harbor: each is silent. But where have you arrived? You had departed from the abuses of freedom and I find you at the feet of a despot.

You have gone from extreme independence to extreme servitude without encountering in so long a space a single place where you can perch.

There are peoples who have particular reasons, independent of the general ones I have just enunciated, that ought to attach them to freedom of the press.

In certain nations that claim to be free, each agent of power can violate the law with impunity without the country's constitution giving the oppressed the right to complain before justice. In these peoples one must no longer consider the independence of the press as one of the guarantees but as the sole remaining guarantee of the freedom and security of citizens.

Therefore if the men who govern these nations spoke of taking independence away from the press, the whole people could respond to them: let us prosecute your crimes before ordinary judges, and perhaps then we shall consent not to appeal to the court of opinion.

In a country where the dogma of the sovereignty of the people reigns openly, censorship is not only a danger but also a great absurdity.

When one accords to each a right to govern society, one must surely recognize his capacity to choose among the different opinions that agitate his contemporaries and to appreciate different facts, the knowledge of which can guide him.

The sovereignty of the people and freedom of the press are therefore two entirely correlative things: censorship and universal suffrage are, on the contrary, two things that contradict each other and cannot be found in the political institutions of the same people for long. Among the twelve million men who live in the territory of the United States, there is not *a single one* who has yet dared to propose restricting the freedom of the press.

The first newspaper that fell before my eyes on arriving in America contained the following article, which I translate faithfully:

> In all this affair the language held to by Jackson (the President) has been that of a heartless despot occupied solely with preserving his power. Ambition is his crime, and he will find his penalty in it. He has intrigue for a vocation, and intrigue will confound his designs and wrest his power from him. He governs by corruption, and his guilty maneuvers will turn to his confusion and shame. He has shown himself in the political arena as a player without modesty and without a bridle. He has succeeded; but the hour of justice approaches; soon he will have to give back what he has won, throw his crooked dice far from himself, and end in some retirement where he can blaspheme in freedom against his folly; for to repent is not a virtue that has ever been given to his heart to know. (*Vincennes Gazette*)*

Many people in France imagine that the violence of the press among us is due to the instability of the social state, to our political passions, and to the general malaise that is their sequel. So they constantly await a period when, after society has again taken a quiet seat, the press in its turn will become calm. As for me, I would gladly attribute the extreme ascendancy it has over us to the causes indicated above; but I do not think that these causes influence its language much. The periodical press appears to me to have its own instincts and passions independent of the circumstances amidst which it acts. What is taking place in America serves to prove it to me.

America is perhaps at this moment, of the world's countries, the one that contains within it the fewest seeds of revolution. Nevertheless, in America the press has the same destructive tastes as in France and the same violence without the same causes for anger. In America as in France, this is an extraordinary power, so strangely mixed of goods and evils, without which freedom cannot live and with which order can hardly be maintained.

*Citation not found.

What one must say is that the press has much less power in the United States than among us. Yet nothing is rarer in that country than to see a judicial prosecution directed against it. The reason for this is simple: the Americans, in accepting among themselves the dogma of the sovereignty of the people, have made its application sincere. They did not have any idea of founding constitutions whose duration is eternal with elements that change every day. To attack existing laws is therefore not criminal, provided that one does not want to escape them by violence.

Moreover, they believe that courts are powerless to moderate the press and that since the suppleness of human language constantly escapes judicial analysis, offenses of this nature somehow elude the hand that is extended to seize them. They think that in order to be able to act effectively on the press, one would have to find a court that was not only devoted to the existing order but that could also place itself above the public opinion that agitates around it; a court that judged without allowing publicity, pronounced without giving the reasons for its decrees, and punished intention even more than words. Whoever had the power to create and maintain a court like this would waste his time in prosecuting freedom of the press; for then he would be absolute master of society itself and could get rid of the writers at the same time as their writings. In the matter of the press there is therefore really no middle between servitude and license. To get the inestimable good that freedom of the press assures one must know how to submit to the inevitable evil it gives rise to. To want to have the one while avoiding the other is to indulge in one of those illusions with which sick nations ordinarily lull themselves when, tired out by struggles and exhausted by efforts, they seek the means of making opposing opinions and contrary principles coexist at once on the same ground.

The lack of power of newspapers in America is due to several causes, of which these are the principal ones.

The freedom to write, like all others, is the more formidable the newer it is; a people that has never heard affairs of state treated in front of it believes the first tribune who presents himself. Among the Anglo-Americans this freedom is as old as the founding of the colonies; besides, the press, which knows so well how to inflame human passions, nevertheless cannot create them by itself alone. Now in America, political life is active, varied, even agitated, but it is rarely troubled by profound passions; it is rare that the latter are stirred up when material interests are not compromised, and in the United States these interests prosper. To judge the difference that exists on this point between the Anglo-Americans and us, I have only to cast a glance at the newspapers of the two peoples. In France, commercial advertisements take up only a very restricted space and even news items are not very numerous; the vital part of a newspaper is the one where political discussions are found. In America three-quarters of the immense newspaper that is placed before your eyes is filled with advertisements, the rest is most often occupied by political news or simple anecdotes; only from time to time does one perceive in an overlooked corner one of the burning discussions that are the daily fodder of readers among us.

Every power increases the action of its forces as it centralizes their direction; that is a general law of nature that examination demonstrates to the observer and that an even surer instinct has always made known to the least of despots.

In France, the press unites two distinct kinds of centralization.

Almost all its power is concentrated in the same place and so to speak in the same hands, for its organs are very few in number.

So constituted in the midst of a skeptical nation, the power of the press will be almost without bounds. It is an enemy with which a government can make more or less lengthy truces, but in the face of which it is difficult to live for a long time.

Neither of the two kinds of centralization I have just spoken of exists in America.

The United States has no capital: enlightenment like power is disseminated in all parts of this vast region; the rays of human intelligence, instead of starting from a common center, therefore cross each other going in all directions; the Americans have placed the general direction of thought nowhere, no more than that of affairs.

This is due to local circumstances that do not depend on men; but here is what comes from the laws:

In the United States there are no licenses for printers, no stamp or registration for newspapers; finally the rule of sureties is unknown.*

The result is that the creation of a newspaper is a simple and easy undertaking; a few subscribers are enough for the journalist to be able to cover his costs: so the number of periodical or semi-periodical writings in the United States passes beyond all belief. The most enlightened Americans attribute the lack of power of the press to this incredible scattering of its strength: it is an axiom of political science in the United States that the sole means of neutralizing the effects of newspapers is to multiply their number. I cannot fancy that a truth so evident still has not become more common[†] among us. That those who want to make revolutions with the aid of the press seek to supply it with only a few powerful organs I understand without difficulty; but that

*A surety is a legal guarantee.
†Lit.: "vulgar."

the official partisans of the established order and the natural supporters of the existing laws believe that they attenuate the action of the press in concentrating it—that I absolutely cannot conceive. The governments of Europe seem to me to act toward the press in the same fashion as knights formerly acted toward their adversaries: they noted from their own usage that centralization was a powerful weapon, and they want to provide it to their enemy doubtless so as to get more glory in resisting him.

In the United States there is almost no small town that does not have its newspaper. One conceives without difficulty that among so many combatants neither discipline nor unity of action can be established: hence we see each one raising its banner. It is not that all the political newspapers in the Union are ranged for or against the administration; but they attack it and defend it by a hundred diverse means. Newspapers in the United States, therefore, cannot establish great currents of opinion that sweep away or overflow the most powerful dikes. This dividing of the strength of the press produces still other, no less remarkable effects: the creation of a newspaper being an easy thing, everyone can take it on; on the other hand, competition makes a newspaper unable to hope for very great profits, which prevents those with great industrial capabilities from meddling in these sorts of undertakings. Besides, were newspapers a source of wealth, since they are exceedingly numerous, there could not be enough writers of talent to direct them. Journalists in the United States, therefore, in general hardly have an elevated position; their education is only sketchy, and the turn of their ideas is often vulgar. Now, in all things the majority makes the law; it establishes certain styles to which each then conforms; the sum of these common habits is called a spirit: there is the spirit of the bar, the spirit of the court. The spirit of the journalist in France is to discuss in a violent but elevated and often eloquent manner the great interests of the state; if it is not always so, that is because every rule has its exceptions. The spirit of the journalist in America is to attack coarsely, without preparation and without art, the passions of those whom it addresses, to set aside principles in order to grab men; to follow them into their private lives, and to lay bare their weaknesses and their vices.

One must deplore such an abuse of thought; later I shall have occasion to inquire about the influence newspapers exert on the taste and morality of the American people;* but, I repeat, at this moment I am concerned only with the political world. One cannot conceal the fact that the political effects of this license of the press contribute indirectly to the maintenance of public

*The role journalists play in American literature is treated briefly in *DA* II 1.16; the way in which newspapers facilitate association, in *DA* II 2.6.

tranquillity. Its result is that men who already have an elevated position in the opinion of their fellow citizens do not dare to write in the newspapers and so lose the most formidable weapon they could make use of to stir up popular passions to their profit.[1] Above all the result is that the personal views expressed by journalists have so to speak no weight in the eyes of readers. What they seek in a newspaper is knowledge of the facts; it is only in altering or in denaturing the facts that the journalist can acquire some influence for his opinion.

Reduced to these resources alone, the press still exercises an immense power in America. It makes political life circulate in all sections of this vast territory. Its eye, always open, constantly lays bare the secret springs of politics and forces public men to come in turn to appear before the court of opinion. It rallies interests around certain doctrines and formulates the creeds of the parties; through it they speak to each other without seeing each other and understand each other without being put in contact. When a large number of organs of the press come to advance along the same track, their influence becomes almost irresistible in the long term, and public opinion, struck always from the same side, ends by yielding under their blows.

In the United States each newspaper has little power individually; but the periodical press is still, after the people, the first of powers.*

That opinions established under the dominion of the freedom of the press in the United States are often more tenacious than those formed elsewhere under the dominion of censorship.

In the United States, democracy constantly brings new men to the direction of affairs; the government therefore has little sequence and order in its measures. But the general principles of government are more stable there than in many other countries, and the principal opinions that rule society are shown to be more lasting. When an idea has taken possession of the mind of the American people, whether it is just or unreasonable, nothing is more difficult than to root it out.

The same fact has been observed in England, the country of Europe where for a century one has seen the greatest freedom of thought and the most invincible prejudices.

I attribute this effect to the very cause that at first, it would seem, ought

---

*See AT's note XV, page 696.

1. They write in newspapers only in the rare cases when they want to address the people and speak in their own name: when, for example, calumnious imputations have been spread regarding them and they desire to establish the truth of the facts.

to prevent it from occurring—freedom of the press. Peoples in whom this freedom exists are attached to their opinions by pride as much as by conviction. They love them because they seem just to them, and also because they are their choice, and they hold to them not only as something true, but also as something that is their own.

There are several more reasons.

A great man has said that *ignorance is at both ends of science.** Perhaps it would have been truer to say that profound convictions are found only at both ends and that in the middle is doubt. One can in fact consider human intelligence in three distinct and often successive states.

Man believes firmly because he adopts without going deeply. He doubts when objections are presented. Often he comes to resolve all his doubts, and then he begins to believe again. This time he no longer seizes the truth haphazardly and in the shadows, but he sees it face to face and advances directly into its light.[2]

When freedom of press finds men in the first state, for a long time it still leaves them in the habit of believing firmly without reflecting; it only changes the object of their unreflective beliefs daily. Over the whole intellectual horizon the mind of man continues, therefore, to see only one point at a time; but the point varies constantly. This is the time of sudden revolutions. Woe to generations that are the first all at once to accept freedom of the press!

Soon, however, the circle of new ideas is almost run through. Experience arrives, and man is plunged into doubt and universal distrust.

One can reckon that the majority of men will always stop in one of these two states: they will believe without knowing why, or not know precisely what one must believe.

As for the other species of conviction, reflective and master of itself, which is born of science and raised in the very midst of agitations of doubt, it will ever be given only to the efforts of a very few men to attain it.

Now, it has been remarked that in centuries of religious fervor, men sometimes change belief, whereas in centuries of doubt each obstinately guards his own. It happens so in politics under the reign of freedom of the press. All social theories having been contested and combated in their turn, those who have settled on one of them guard it not so much because they are sure that it is good as because they are not sure that there is a better one.

In these centuries, one is not made to die so easily for one's opinions; but

---

*Blaise Pascal, *Pensées,* 327 Br.

2. Still I do not know if this conviction, reflective and master of itself, ever raises man to the degree of ardor and devotion that dogmatic beliefs inspire.

one does not change them, and one encounters at once fewer martyrs and fewer apostates.

Add to this reason another more powerful still: in their doubt of opinions, men in the end attach themselves solely to instincts and material interests, which are much more visible, more tangible, and more permanent in their nature than opinions.

To know which governs best, democracy or aristocracy, is a very difficult question to decide. But it is clear that democracy hinders some and aristocracy oppresses others.

There is a truth that establishes itself, and that one has no need to discuss: you are rich and I am poor.

Chapter 4 ON POLITICAL ASSOCIATION IN THE UNITED STATES

Daily use the Anglo-Americans make of the right of association.—Three kinds of political associations.—How the Americans apply the representative system to associations.—Dangers that result from this for the state.—Great convention of 1831 concerning the tariff.—Legislative character of that convention.—Why the unlimited exercise of the right of association is not as dangerous in the United States as elsewhere.—Why one can consider it necessary there.—Utility of associations in democratic peoples.

America is, among the countries of the world, the one where they have taken most advantage of association and where they have applied that powerful mode of action to a greater diversity of objects.

Independent of the permanent associations created by law under the names of townships, cities, and counties, there is a multitude of others that owe their birth and development only to individual will.

The inhabitant of the United States learns from birth that he must rely on himself to struggle against the evils and obstacles of life; he has only a defiant and restive regard for social authority and he appeals to its power only when he cannot do without it. This begins to be perceived from school onward, where children submit even in their games to rules they have established and punish among themselves offenses defined by themselves. The same spirit is found in all the acts of social life. An obstacle comes up on the public highway, passage is interrupted, traffic stops; neighbors immediately establish themselves in a deliberating body; from this improvised assembly will issue an executive power that will remedy the ill—before the idea of an authority preexisting that of those interested has presented itself to anyone's imagination. Should it be a question of pleasure, they will associate to give more splendor and regularity to the fête. Finally, they will unite to resist wholly intellectual enemies: they fight intemperance in common. In the United States, they associate for the goals of public security, of commerce and industry, of morality and religion. There is nothing the human will despairs of attaining by the free action of the collective power of individuals.

I shall have occasion later to speak of the effects that association produces in civil life.* I must confine myself at this moment to the political world.

The right of association being recognized, citizens can use it in different manners.

An association consists solely in the public adherence that a certain number of individuals give to such and such a doctrine, and in the engagement in which they contract to cooperate in a certain fashion to make it prevail. Thus the right to associate is almost confused with the freedom to write; already, however, an association possesses more power than the press. When an opinion is represented by an association, it is obliged to take a clearer and more precise form. It counts its partisans and implicates them in its cause. The latter teach themselves to know one another, and their ardor is increased by their number. The association gathers the efforts of divergent minds in a cluster and drives them vigorously toward a single goal clearly indicated by it.

The second degree in the exercise of the right of association is the power to assemble. When one allows a political association to place centers of action at certain important points of the country, its activity becomes greater and its influence more extended. There men see each other; means of execution are combined and opinions are deployed with the force and heat that written thought can never attain.

Finally, there is a last degree in the exercise of the right of association in political matters: partisans of the same opinion can gather in electoral colleges and name agents to go to represent them in a central assembly. It is properly speaking the system of representation applied to a party.

Thus, in the first case, men who profess the same opinion establish a purely intellectual bond among themselves; in the second, they gather in small assemblies that represent only a fraction of the party; finally, in the third, they form almost a separate nation inside the nation, a government inside the government. Their agents, like the agents of the majority, represent in themselves alone all the collective force of their partisans; like the latter, they arrive with an appearance of nationality and all the moral power that

*DA II 2.5. See also DA I 2.6.

results from it. It is true that they do not have, like them, the right to make law; but they have the power to attack the one that exists and to formulate in advance the one that should exist.

Let me suppose a people who are not perfectly habituated to the use of freedom or in whom profound political passions are in ferment. Beside the majority that makes the laws, I place a minority that is charged solely with *considering* and stops before the *pronouncement*, and I cannot help believing that public order is exposed to great hazards.

Between proving that one law is better in itself than another, and proving that one ought to substitute it for the other, it is undoubtedly far. But where the minds of enlightened men still see a great distance, the imagination of the crowd no longer perceives it. Moreover, times come when the nation is partitioned almost equally between two parties, each of which claims to represent the majority. If, near to the directing power, a power comes to be established whose moral authority is almost as great, can one believe that it will long limit itself to speaking without acting?

Will it always stop before the metaphysical consideration that the goal of associations is to direct opinions and not to constrain them, to counsel the law, not to make it?

The more I view the independence of the press in its principal effects, the more I convince myself that among the moderns the independence of the press is the capital and so to speak constitutive element of freedom. A people that wants to remain free, therefore, has the right to require that one respect it at all costs. But *unlimited* freedom of association in political matters cannot be entirely confused with the freedom to write. The former is at once less necessary and more dangerous. A nation can set bounds for it without ceasing to be master of itself; it sometimes must do that to continue to be such.

In America, the freedom to associate for political goals is unlimited.

One example will make the degree to which it is tolerated known better than all I could add.

One recalls how the question of the tariff or of freedom of commerce agitated minds in America. The tariff favored or attacked not only opinions, but very powerful material interests. The North attributed a part of its prosperity to it, the South almost all its miseries. One can say that for a long time the tariff gave birth to the only political passions that agitated the Union.

In 1831, when the quarrel was the most envenomed, an obscure citizen of Massachusetts thought to propose to all the enemies of the tariff, by way of newspapers, that they send deputies to Philadelphia in order to take joint counsel as to the means of restoring freedom of commerce. By the power of printing, this proposition circulated in a few days from Maine to New Orleans. The enemies of the tariff adopted it eagerly. They gathered from all parts and named deputies. The largest number of the latter were well-known men, and some of them had become celebrated. South Carolina, which has since been seen to take up arms in the same cause, for its part sent sixty-three delegates. On October 1, 1831, the assembly, which according to the American habit had taken the name of convention, was constituted at Philadelphia; it counted more than two hundred members. The discussions were public and from the first day took on a wholly legislative character; they discussed the extent of the powers of Congress, theories of freedom of commerce, and finally the various provisions of the tariff. At the end of ten days, the assembly separated after drafting an address to the American people. In this address it was set out: first, that Congress does not have the right to make a tariff, and that the existing tariff is unconstitutional; second, that it is not in the interest of any people, and in particular of the American people, that commerce not be free.

One must recognize that unlimited freedom of association in political matters has up to the present not produced the dire results in the United States that one could perhaps expect elsewhere. The right of association there is an English import, and it has existed in all times in America. Today, the use of this right has passed into habits and mores.

In our time, freedom of association has become a necessary guarantee against the tyranny of the majority. In the United States, once a party has become dominant, all public power passes into its hands; its particular friends occupy all the posts and all organized forces are at its disposal. As the most distinguished men of the opposing party are unable to get over the barrier that separates them from power, they must surely be able to establish themselves outside it; the minority must oppose its moral force as a whole to the material power that oppresses it. It is, therefore, one danger that is opposed to another danger more to be feared.

The omnipotence of the majority appears to me such a great peril for the American republics that the dangerous means used to limit it seem to me even a good.

Here I shall express a thought that will recall what I said elsewhere on the occasion of township freedoms:* there are no countries where associations are more necessary to prevent the despotism of parties or the arbitrariness of the prince than those in which the social state is democratic. In aristocratic nations, secondary bodies form natural associations that halt abuses of power. In countries where such associations do not exist, if particular persons

*DA I 1.5.

cannot create artificially and temporarily something that resembles them, I no longer perceive a dike of any sort against tyranny, and a great people can be oppressed with impunity by a handful of factious persons or by one man.

The gathering of a great political convention (for there are all kinds of them), which can often become a necessary measure, is always, even in America, a grave event that friends of their country view only with fear.

This was seen very clearly in the convention of 1831, when all the efforts of the distinguished men who took part in the assembly strained to modify its language and to restrict its object. It is probable that the convention of 1831 in fact exerted a great influence on the spirit of the malcontents and prepared them for the open revolt against the commercial laws of the Union that took place in 1832.

One cannot conceal from oneself that unlimited freedom of association in political matters is, of all freedoms, the last that a people can tolerate. If it does not make it fall into anarchy, it makes it so to speak touch it at each instant. This freedom, dangerous as it is, nevertheless offers guarantees on one point: in the country where associations are free, secret societies are unknown. In America there are factious persons, but no conspirators.

The different manner in which the right of association is understood in Europe and in the United States, and the different use made of it.

After the freedom to act alone, the most natural to man is that of combining his efforts with the efforts of those like him and acting in common. The right of association therefore appears to me to be almost as inalienable in its nature as individual freedom. The legislator cannot wish to destroy it without attacking society itself. Nevertheless if there are peoples in whom the freedom to unite is only beneficent and productive of prosperity, there are also others who denature it by their excesses and make a cause of destruction out of an element of life. It seemed to me that a comparison of the diverse paths that associations follow, in countries where freedom is understood and in those where that freedom changes to license, would be useful at once to governments and to parties.

Most Europeans still see in association a weapon of war that one forms in haste to go try it out immediately on a field of battle.

One does indeed associate with the purpose of speaking, but the thought of acting next preoccupies all minds. An association is an army; one speaks in it so as to be counted and to be inspired, and then one marches toward the enemy. In the eyes of those who compose it, legal resources can appear to be means, but they are never the sole means of succeeding.

This is not the manner in which the right of association is understood in the United States. In America, citizens who form the minority associate at first to establish their number and thus to weaken the moral empire of the majority; the second object of those associating is to set up a competition and in this manner to discover the most appropriate arguments with which to make an impression on the majority; for they always have the hope of attracting the latter to them and afterwards of disposing of power in its name.

Political associations in the United States are therefore peaceful in their objects and legal in their means; and when they claim to wish to triumph only through laws they are generally telling the truth.

The difference to be remarked on this point between the Americans and us is due to several causes.

In Europe, there exist parties that differ from the majority so much that they cannot ever hope to get it to support them, and those same parties believe they are strong enough on their own to struggle against it. When a party of this kind forms an association, it does not want to convince, but to do combat. In America, men who are placed very far from the majority by their opinion can do nothing against its power: all others hope to gain it.

The exercise of the right of association, therefore, becomes dangerous to the degree to which it is impossible for great parties to become the majority. In a country like the United States, in which opinions differ only by nuances, the right of association can remain so to speak without limits.

What still brings us to see in freedom of association only the right to make war on those who govern is our inexperience as regards freedom. The first idea that presents itself to the mind of a party, as to that of a man when strength comes to him, is the idea of violence: the idea of persuasion arrives only later; it is born of experience.

The English, who are divided among themselves in such a profound manner, rarely abuse the right of association because they have had a longer use of it.

Among us, furthermore, there is such a passionate taste for war that there is no undertaking so insane, even if it should overturn the state, in which one would not be esteemed glorious for dying with arms in hand.

But of all the causes that cooperate in the United States to moderate the violence of political association, perhaps the most powerful is universal suffrage. In countries where universal suffrage is accepted, the majority is never doubtful because no party can reasonably establish itself as the representative of those who have not voted. Associations know, therefore, and everyone knows, that they do not represent the majority. This results from the very fact of their existence; for if they represented it, they themselves would change the law instead of demanding its reform.

The moral force of the government that they attack is much increased by this; theirs, much weakened.

In Europe, there are almost no associations that do not claim or do not believe that they represent the will of the majority. That claim or belief tremendously increases their strength and serves marvelously to legitimate their actions. For what is more excusable than violence to bring triumph for the cause of right when it is oppressed?

Thus it sometimes happens in the immense complication of human laws that extreme freedom corrects the abuses of freedom and that extreme democracy prevents the dangers of democracy.

In Europe, associations consider themselves in a way as the legislative and executive council of the nation, which itself cannot raise its voice; starting from this idea, they act and command. In America, where in the eyes of all they represent only a minority in the nation, they speak and petition.

The means that associations in Europe make use of are in accord with the goal they propose for themselves.

The principal goal of those associations being to act and not to speak, to do combat and not to convince, they are naturally brought to give themselves an organization that is in no way civil and to introduce military habits and maxims within them: thus does one see them centralize the direction of their strength as much as they can and put the power of all in the hands of a very few.

The members of these associations respond to the words of an order like soldiers on a campaign; they profess the dogma of passive obedience, or rather, in uniting, they have made the entire sacrifice of their judgment and their free will in a single stroke: thus there often reigns within these associations a tyranny more insupportable than that exercised in society in the name of the government that is attacked.

That very much diminishes their moral force. Thus they lose the sacred character that attaches to the struggle of the oppressed against oppressors. For one who consents in certain cases to obey with servility some of those like him, who delivers his will to them, and submits even his thought to them—how can that one claim that he wants to be free?

Americans have also established a government within associations; but it is, if I can express myself so, a civil government. Individual independence finds its part there: as in society, all men in it march at the same time toward the same goal; but each one is not required to march to it exactly on the same path. They make no sacrifice of their will and reason to it; but will and reason are applied in making a common undertaking succeed.

✤ ✤

Chapter 5 ON THE GOVERNMENT OF DEMOCRACY IN AMERICA

I know that here I am walking on ground that is afire. Each word of this chapter must offend on some points the different parties that divide my country. I shall not speak less than all my thought.

In Europe, we have trouble judging the genuine character and permanent instincts of democracy because in Europe there is a struggle between two contrary principles, and one does not know precisely what part one must attribute to the principles themselves or to the passions to which the combat has given birth.

It is not the same in America. There the people dominate without obstacles; there are no perils to fear or injuries to avenge.

In America, therefore, democracy is given over to its own inclinations. Its style is natural and all its movements are free. It is there that one must judge it. And for whom would this study be interesting and profitable if not for us, whom an irresistible movement carries along daily and who advance as blind men, perhaps toward despotism, perhaps toward a republic, but surely toward a democratic social state?

ON UNIVERSAL SUFFRAGE

I said previously that all the states of the Union had accepted universal suffrage.* It is found among populations placed on different rungs of the social ladder. I have had occasion to see its effects in diverse places and among races of men whom language, religion, or mores render almost strangers to one another; in Louisiana as in New England, in Georgia as in Canada. I remarked that in America universal suffrage was far from producing all the good and all the evils that people in Europe expect from it, and that its effects were generally other than one supposes them to be.

ON THE CHOICES OF THE PEOPLE AND THE INSTINCTS OF AMERICAN DEMOCRACY IN ITS CHOICES

In the United States the most remarkable men are rarely called to the direction of public affairs.—Causes of this phenomenon.—The envy that animates the lower classes of

*DA I 1.4.

France against the upper is not a French sentiment, but democratic.—Why in America distinguished men often turn away on their own from a public career.

Many people in Europe believe without saying, or say without believing, that one of the great advantages of universal suffrage is to call to the direction of affairs men worthy of public confidence. The people cannot govern themselves, it is said, but they always sincerely want the good of the state, and their instinct scarcely ever fails to designate for them those animated by the same desire who are the most capable of holding power in their hands.

As for me, I must say, what I have seen in America does not authorize me to think that this is so. On my arrival in the United States, I was struck with surprise to discover the extent to which merit was common among those who were governed and how little there was among those who governed. It is a constant fact that in our day, in the United States, the most remarkable men are rarely called to public offices, and one is obliged to recognize that it has been so to the degree that democracy has passed beyond all its former limits. It is evident that the race of American statesmen has shrunk singularly in a half century.

One can indicate several causes of this phenomenon.

It is impossible, whatever one does, to raise the enlightenment of the people above a certain level. It will do no good to facilitate approaches to human knowledge, to improve the methods of teaching and to make science cheap; one will never make it so that men are instructed and develop their intelligence without devoting time to it.

The greater or lesser the facility that the people encounter in living without working, therefore, forms the necessary limit of their intellectual progress. This limit is placed further in certain countries, less far in certain others; but for it not to exist, it would be necessary that the people not have to occupy themselves with the material cares of life, that is to say, that they no longer be the people. It is, therefore, as difficult to conceive of a society in which all men are very enlightened as of a state in which all citizens are rich; those are two correlative difficulties. I shall have no trouble admitting that the mass of citizens very sincerely wants the good of the country; I even go further and say that the lower classes of society seem to me generally to mix fewer combinations of personal interest with this desire than do the elevated classes; but what they always lack, more or less, is the art of judging the means, even while sincerely wishing the end. What long study, what diverse notions are necessary in order to get for oneself an exact idea of the character of a single man! The greatest geniuses lose their way, and the multitude would succeed at it! The people never find the time and means to engage in this work. They must always judge in haste and attach themselves to the most salient objects. Hence charlatans of all kinds know so well the secret of pleasing them, whereas most often their genuine friends fail at it.

Furthermore, it is not always the capacity that democracy lacks for choosing men of merit, but the desire and the taste.

One must not conceal from oneself that democratic institutions develop the sentiment of envy in the human heart to a very high degree. It is not so much because they offer to each the means of becoming equal to others, but because these means constantly fail those who employ them. Democratic institutions awaken and flatter the passion for equality without ever being able to satisfy it entirely. Every day this complete equality eludes the hands of the people at the moment when they believe they have seized it, and it flees, as Pascal said, in an eternal flight;* the people become heated in the search for this good, all the more precious as it is near enough to be known, far enough not to be tasted. The chance of succeeding stirs them, the uncertainty of success irritates them; they are agitated, they are wearied, they are embittered. All that surpasses them, in whatever place, then appears to them as an obstacle to their desires, and there is no superiority so legitimate that the sight of it does not tire their eyes.

Many people imagine that the secret instinct that brings the lower classes among us to keep the upper away from the direction of affairs as much as they can is found only in France; that is an error: the instinct I speak of is not French, it is democratic; political circumstances could have given it a particular character of bitterness, but they did not give rise to it.

In the United States, the people have no hatred for the elevated classes of society; but they feel little good will for them and carefully keep them out of power; they do not fear great talents, but they have little taste for them. In general, one remarks that everything that rises without their support obtains their favor only with difficulty.

While the natural instincts of democracy bring the people to keep distinguished men away from power, an instinct no less strong brings the latter to distance themselves from a political career, in which it is so difficult for them to remain completely themselves and to advance without debasing themselves. This thought is very naively expressed by Chancellor Kent. The celebrated author I speak of, after having given great eulogies to the portion of the Constitution that accords the nomination of judges to the executive power, adds: "It is probable, in fact, that the most appropriate men to fill

---

*Pascal, *Pensées*, 72 Br.

these places would have too much reserve in their manners and too much severity in their principles ever to be able to gather the majority of votes at an election that rested on universal suffrage." (Kent's *Commentaries*, vol. 1, 272.)* That was printed in America in the year 1830 without contradiction.

It has demonstrated to me that those who regard universal suffrage as a guarantee of the goodness of choices make a complete illusion for themselves. Universal suffrage has other advantages, but not that one.

ON THE CAUSES THAT CAN IN PART CORRECT THESE INSTINCTS OF DEMOCRACY

Contrary effects produced on peoples as on men by great perils.—Why America saw so many remarkable men at the head of its affairs fifty years ago.—Influence that enlightenment and mores exert on the choices of the people.—Example of New England.—States of the Southwest.—How certain laws influence the choices of the people.—Election in two stages.—Its effects on the composition of the Senate.

When great perils threaten the state, one often sees the people fortunately choose the most appropriate citizens to save it.

It has been remarked that when a danger presses, man rarely remains at his habitual level; he elevates himself well above or falls below. So does it happen to peoples themselves. Instead of elevating a nation, extreme perils sometimes succeed in pulling it down; they stir up its passions without guiding them, and far from enlightening its intelligence, cloud it. The Jews still cut each other's throats in the midst of the smoking debris of the Temple. But it is more common to see, among nations as among men, extraordinary virtue born of the very imminence of danger. Then great characters appear in relief, like monuments hidden by the obscurity of night that one sees suddenly outlined by the light of a fire. Genius no longer disdains to reproduce itself on its own and the people, struck by their own perils, forget their envious passions for a time. At that time it is not rare to see celebrated names come out of the ballot box. I said above that in America statesmen of our day seem very inferior to those who appeared at the head of affairs fifty years ago.† This is due not only to the laws, but to circumstances. When America struggled for the most just of causes, that of a people escaping from the yoke of another people; when it was a question of introducing a new nation into the world, all souls rose to reach to the height of the goal of their efforts. In that general excitement, superior men ran to meet the people, and the

---

*Kent, *Commentaries on American Law*, 2: 14.1.
†*DA* I 1.8.

people, taking them in their arms, placed them at their head. But such events are rare; it is by the ordinary pace of things that one must judge.

If passing events sometimes succeed in combating the passions of democracy, enlightenment, and above all mores, exert a no less powerful, and more lasting, influence on its penchants. This is well perceived in the United States.

In New England, where education and freedom are the children of morality and religion; where society, already old and long established, has been able to form maxims and habits, the people, at the same time that they escape all the superiorities that wealth and birth have ever created among men, have been habituated to respect intellectual and moral superiorities and to submit to them without displeasure: thus one sees that democracy in New England makes better choices than everywhere else.

On the contrary, as one descends toward the south into states where the social bond is less old and less strong, where instruction is less widespread, and where the principles of morality, religion, and freedom are combined in a less fortunate manner, one perceives that talents and virtues become ever rarer among those who govern.

When one finally penetrates into the new states of the Southwest, where the social body, formed yesterday, still presents nothing but an agglomeration of adventurers or speculators, one is confounded to see into whose hands public power is placed, and one wonders by what force, independent of legislation and of men, the state can grow and society prosper there.

There are certain laws whose nature is democratic and which nonetheless succeed in part in correcting these dangerous instincts of democracy.

When you enter the House of Representatives in Washington, you feel yourself struck by the vulgar aspect of this great assembly. Often the eye seeks in vain for a celebrated man within it. Almost all its members are obscure persons, whose name furnishes no image to one's thought. They are, for the most part, village attorneys, those in trade, or even men belonging to the lowest classes. In a country where instruction is almost universally widespread, it is said that the people's representatives do not always know how to write correctly.

Two steps away is the chamber of the Senate, whose narrow precincts enclose a large portion of the celebrities of America. One perceives hardly a single man there who does not recall the idea of a recent illustrious [deed]. They are eloquent attorneys, distinguished generals, skillful magistrates, or well-known statesmen. All the words that issue from this assembly would do honor to the greatest parliamentary debates of Europe.

Whence this peculiar contrast? Why is the elite of the nation found in this chamber rather than in the other? Why are so many vulgar elements gathered in the first assembly when the second seems to have the monopoly on talents and enlightenment? Both nevertheless emanate from the people, both are the product of universal suffrage, and up to now no voice has been raised in America to assert that the Senate is the enemy of popular interests. Where, therefore, does such an enormous difference come from? I see only a single fact that explains it: the election that produces the House of Representatives is direct; that from which the Senate emanates is subject to two stages. The universality of citizens names the legislature of each state, and the federal constitution, transforming each of these legislatures in their turn into an electoral body, draws the members of the Senate from them. Therefore the senators express, however indirectly, the result of universal suffrage; for the legislature that names the senators is not an aristocratic or privileged body that draws its electoral right from itself; it depends essentially on the universality of citizens; it is generally elected by them every year, and they can always direct its choices by filling it with new members. But it suffices that the popular will pass through this chosen assembly for it to be worked over in some way, and it comes out reclothed in more noble and more beautiful forms. The men so elected, therefore, always represent exactly the majority of the nation that governs; but they represent only the elevated thoughts that are current in the midst of it, the generous instincts that animate it, and not the small passions that often agitate it and the vices that dishonor it.

It is easy to perceive a moment in the future when the American republics will be forced to multiply [the use of] two stages in their electoral system under penalty of being miserably lost on the shoals of democracy.

I shall not have difficulty avowing it; I see in the electoral double stage the sole means of putting the use of political freedom within the reach of all classes of the people. Those who hope to make of this means the exclusive weapon of one party, and those who fear it, appear to me to fall into an equal error.

INFLUENCE THAT AMERICAN DEMOCRACY EXERTS ON ELECTORAL LAWS

Rarity of elections exposes the state to great crises.—Their frequency keeps it in a feverish agitation.—Americans have chosen the second of these two evils.—Volatility of the law.—Opinions of Hamilton, Madison, and Jefferson on this subject.

When election comes only at long intervals, the state runs a risk of being overturned in each election.

At that time, the parties make prodigious efforts to seize for themselves a fortune that comes so rarely within their reach; and the evil being almost without remedy for candidates who fail, one must fear everything from their ambition, pushed to despair. If, on the contrary, an equal struggle will soon be renewed, the defeated are patient.

When elections succeed each other rapidly, their frequency keeps a feverish movement going in society and maintains public affairs in a state of continuous volatility.

Thus, on one side, there is a chance of unrest for the state; on the other, a chance of revolution; the first system harms the goodness of government, the second threatens its existence.

Americans would rather expose themselves to the first evil than to the second. In that, they are directed by instinct much more than by reasoning, as democracy drives the taste for variety to a passion. A singular mutability in legislation results from this.

Many Americans consider the instability of their laws as a necessary consequence of a system whose general effects are useful. But there is no one in the United States, I believe, who pretends to deny that this instability exists or who does not regard it as a great evil.

Hamilton, after having demonstrated the utility of a power that could prevent or at least retard the promulgation of bad laws, adds: "It may perhaps be said that the power of preventing bad laws includes that of preventing good ones; and may be used to the one purpose as well as to the other. But this objection will have little weight with those who can properly estimate the mischiefs of that inconstancy and mutability in the laws which *forms the greatest blemish in the character and genius of the government*" (*Federalist* 73).*

"The facility," says Madison, "and excess of law-making seem to be the diseases to which our governments are most liable" (*Federalist* 62).

Jefferson himself, the greatest democrat who has yet issued from within American democracy, has pointed out the same perils.

"The instability of our laws is really a very grave inconvenience," he says. "I think that we ought to have provided for it by deciding that there would always be an interval of a year between the presentation of a law and the definitive vote. It would then be discussed and voted on without anyone's being able to change a word, and if circumstances seemed to require a more prompt resolution, the proposition could be adopted not by a simple majority, but a majority of two thirds of both houses."[1]

---

*AT renders the quotation in French, but repeats the italicized phrase—in English—after his translation.

1. Jefferson to Madison, December 20, 1787. [Conseil, *Mélanges politiques et philosophiques*. See also *Writings of Thomas Jefferson*, vol. 6 (Washington, 1903), 393.]

ON PUBLIC OFFICIALS UNDER THE EMPIRE
OF AMERICAN DEMOCRACY

Simplicity of American officials.—Absence of uniforms.*—All officials are paid.—Political consequences of this fact.—In America there is no public career.—What results from this.

Public officials in the United States remain intermingled with the crowd of citizens; they have neither palaces, nor guards, nor ceremonial uniforms. The simplicity of those who govern is due not only to a particular turn of the American spirit, but to the fundamental principles of the society.

In the eyes of democracy, government is not a good; it is a necessary evil. Officials must be accorded a certain power; for without this power, what use would they serve? But the external appearances of power are not indispensable to the operation of affairs; they needlessly offend the public's sight.

Officials themselves sense perfectly well that they have only obtained the right to be placed above others by their power on the condition that they descend to the level of all by their manners.

I can imagine no one more plain in his way of acting, more accessible to all, more attentive to requests, and more civil in his responses than a public man in the United States.

I like this natural style of the government of democracy; in the internal force that is attached more to the office than to the official, more to the man than to the external signs of power, I perceive something of virility that I admire.

As for the influence that uniforms can exert, I believe that one exaggerates much the importance that they are likely to have in a century like ours. I did not remark in America that the official, in the exercise of his power, was welcomed with less regard and respect because he was reduced to his merit alone.

On the other hand, I strongly doubt that a particular clothing brings public men to respect themselves when they are not naturally disposed to do it; for I cannot believe that they have more regard for their dress than for their person.

When I see certain magistrates among us being brusque with parties or addressing them with witticisms, shrugging their shoulders at the means of the defense and smiling complacently at the enumeration of charges, I would like to have someone try to remove their robes in order to discover if, being now clothed as simple citizens, that would not recall them to the natural dignity of the human species.

*Lit.: "costume."

None of the public officials in the United States has a uniform, but all receive a wage.

This flows from democratic principles still more naturally than the preceding. A democracy can surround its magistrates with pomp and cover them with silk and gold without directly attacking the principle of its existence. Such privileges are passing; they depend on the place and not the man. But to establish unpaid offices is to create a class of wealthy and independent officials, to form the core of an aristocracy. If the people still preserve the right of choice, the exercise of that right then has necessary bounds.

When one sees a democratic republic make remunerated offices unpaid, I believe one can conclude that it is going toward monarchy. And when a monarchy begins to remunerate unpaid offices, it is a sure mark that one is going toward a despotic state or toward a republican state.

The substitution of salaried offices for unpaid offices therefore seems to me to constitute all by itself a genuine revolution.

I regard the complete absence of unpaid offices as one of the most visible signs of the absolute empire that democracy exercises in America. Services rendered to the public, whatever they are, are paid: thus, each has not only the right, but the possibility, of rendering them.

If in democratic states all citizens can obtain posts, all are not tempted to solicit them. Not the conditions of candidacy, but the number and the capacity of the candidates, often limits the choice of electors.

Among peoples where the principle of election extends to all, there is no public career, properly speaking. Men come to offices in a way only haphazardly, and they have no assurance of being kept in them. That is above all true when elections are annual. It results from this that in times of calm, public offices offer little lure for ambition. In the United States, it is people moderate in their desires who involve themselves in the twists and turns of politics. Great talents and great passions generally turn away from power in order to pursue wealth; and it often happens that one takes charge of directing the fortune of the state only when one feels oneself barely capable of conducting one's own affairs.

It is to these causes as much as to the bad choices of democracy that one must attribute the great number of vulgar men who occupy public offices. In the United States, I do not know if the people would choose superior men who might solicit their votes, but it is certain that such men do not solicit them.

ON THE ARBITRARINESS OF MAGISTRATES[2]
UNDER THE EMPIRE OF AMERICAN DEMOCRACY

Why the arbitrariness of magistrates is greater under absolute monarchies and in democratic republics than in temperate monarchies.—Arbitrariness of magistrates in New England.

There are two kinds of governments under which there is much arbitrariness mixed with the action of magistrates; it is so under the absolute government of one alone and under the government of democracy.

This same effect comes from nearly analogous causes.

In despotic states, the lot of no one is assured, no more that of public officials than of mere particular persons. Since the sovereign always holds in his hands the lives, the fortunes, and sometimes the honor of the men he employs, he thinks he has nothing to fear from them, and he allows them great freedom of action because he believes he is assured that they will never abuse it against him.

In despotic states, the sovereign is so in love with his power that he fears the inconvenience of his own rules; and he likes to see his agents go about almost haphazardly, so as to be sure of never encountering in them a tendency contrary to his desires.

In democracies, the majority, being able to take power each year out of the hands in which it had entrusted it, also does not fear that it may be abused against itself. A master at making its will known at each instant to those who govern, it would rather abandon them to their own efforts than chain them to an invariable rule that, by limiting them, would in a way limit itself.

Looking closely, one even discovers that under the empire of democracy the arbitrariness of the magistrate will be much greater than in despotic states.

In those states, the sovereign can punish in a moment all the faults that he perceives; but he cannot flatter himself that he perceives all the faults that he ought to punish. In democracies, on the contrary, at the same time that the sovereign is all-powerful, it is everywhere at once; thus one sees that American officials are much freer in the scope of action that the law traces for them than any official in Europe. Often one is limited to showing them the goal toward which they ought to strive, leaving them masters of choosing the means.

In New England, for example, the *selectmen* of each township are relied

---

2. Here I understand the word *magistrate* in its most extended sense: I apply it to all those who are charged with having the laws executed.

on for the care of forming the jury list; the sole rule drawn up for them is this: they must choose the jurors from among citizens who enjoy electoral rights and who have a good reputation.[3]

In France we would believe the lives and freedom of men to be in danger if we entrusted to an official, whoever he might be, the exercise of so formidable a right.

In New England these same magistrates can post the names of drunkards in taverns and prevent inhabitants from furnishing them with wine under penalty of fine.[4]

Such power of censoring would appall the people in the most absolute monarchy; here, however, they submit to it without trouble.

Nowhere has the law left a greater part to arbitrariness than in democratic republics, because in them, what is arbitrary does not appear fearful. One can even say that the magistrate becomes freer as the right of electing descends further and as the time of the magistracy is more limited.

Hence it is that to make a democratic republic change into a state of monarchy is so difficult. In ceasing to be elective, the magistrate ordinarily keeps the rights and preserves the usages of the elected magistrate. One then arrives at despotism.

It is only in temperate monarchies that the law, at the same time that it defines the scope of action for public officials, still takes care to guide them at each step. The cause of this fact is easy to say.

In temperate monarchies, power is divided between the people and the prince. Both have an interest in the magistrate's position being stable.

The prince does not want to put the fate of officials in the hands of the people for fear that they will betray his authority; on their side, the people fear that the magistrates, placed in absolute dependence on the prince, will serve only to oppress freedom; one therefore makes them depend in a way on no one.

---

3. See the law of February 27, 1813. *General Collection of the Laws of Massachusetts,* vol. 2, 331. One ought to say that after that, jurors are drawn by lot from the lists.

4. Law of February 28, 1787. See *General Collection of the Laws of Massachusetts,* vol. 1, 302 [Isaac Goodwin, *Town Officer; or, Laws of Massachusetts Relative to the Duties of Municipal Officers* (Worcester, 1829), 180].

Here is the text:

"The Selectmen in each town shall cause to be posted up in the houses and shops of all taverners, innholders and retailers, within such towns, a list of the names of all persons reputed common drunkards, common tipplers, or common gamesters, mispending their time and estate in such houses. And every keeper of such house or shop, after notice given him, that shall be convicted before one or more Justices of the Peace, of entertaining or suffering any of the persons in such list, to drink or tipple, or game, in his or her house, or any of the dependencies thereof, or of selling them spiritous liquor, shall forfeit and pay the sum of thirty shillings."

The same cause that brings the prince and the people to render the official independent brings them to seek guarantees against the abuse of his independence, so that he does not turn it against the authority of the one or the freedom of the other. Both therefore agree on the necessity of tracing out a line of conduct in advance for the official, and see their interest in imposing rules on him from which it is impossible for him to deviate.

ADMINISTRATIVE INSTABILITY IN THE UNITED STATES

In America the acts of society often leave fewer traces than the actions of a family.— Newspapers, the only historical monuments.—How extreme administrative instability harms the art of governing.

Since men come to power only for an instant, afterwards to be lost in a crowd that itself changes face daily, the result is that the acts of society in America often leave less trace than the actions of a simple family. Public administration there is in a way oral and traditional. It is not written, or what is written flies off at the least wind, like the leaves of Sibyl,* and disappears without returning.

The only historical monuments of the United States are newspapers. If a number comes to be missing, the chain of time is almost broken: present and past are no longer joined. I do not doubt that in fifty years it will be more difficult to gather authentic documents on the details of the social existence of Americans of our day than on the administration of the French in the Middle Ages; and if an invasion of barbarians came to surprise the United States, it would be necessary to recur to the history of other nations in order to know something of the people who inhabit it.

Administrative instability began by penetrating into habits; I could almost say that today each person has in the end contracted the taste for it. No one worries about what has been done before him. No method is adopted; no collection is composed; no documents are gathered, even if it would be easy to do it. When by chance one possesses them, one scarcely holds onto them. I have in my papers original pieces that were given to me by public administrators to respond to some of my questions. In America, society seems to live from day to day, like an army on a campaign. Nevertheless, the art of administering is surely a science; and all sciences, in order to make progress, need to bind together the discoveries of different generations as they succeed each other. One man, in the short space of his life, notices a fact, another

---

*See Virgil, *Aeneid*, 3: 441–452.

conceives an idea; this one invents a means, that one finds a formula; humanity, in passing, harvests the diverse fruits of individual experience and forms sciences. It is very difficult for American administrators to learn anything from one another. Thus they bring to the conducting of society the enlightenment that they find widespread within it, and not knowledge that is proper to them. Therefore democracy, pushed to its final limits, harms progress in the art of governing. In this regard it suits a people whose administrative education is already accomplished better than a people new to the experience of affairs.

Moreover, this relates not only to administrative science. Democratic government, which is founded on an idea so simple and natural, nevertheless always supposes the existence of a very civilized and very learned society.[5] At first one would believe it to be contemporaneous with the first ages of the world; looking at it closely, one easily discovers that it could only have come last.

ON PUBLIC COSTS UNDER THE EMPIRE OF AMERICAN DEMOCRACY

In all societies, citizens are divided into a certain number of classes.—Instinct that each of these classes brings to the direction of the finances of the state.—Why public expenditures must tend to grow when the people govern.—What makes the profuse spending* of democracy less to be feared in America.—Use of public funds under democracy.

Is the government of a democracy economical? One must first know what we intend to compare it to.

The question would be easy to resolve if one wanted to establish a parallel between a democratic republic and an absolute monarchy. One would find that public expenditures in the first are more considerable than in the second. But that is so for all free states compared to those that are not. It is certain that despotism ruins men more by preventing them from producing than by taking the fruits of production away from them; it dries up the source of wealth and often respects acquired wealth. Freedom, on the contrary, begets a thousand times more goods than it destroys, and in the nations that know it, the resources of the people always grow more quickly than do taxes.

What is important to me at the moment is to compare free peoples among themselves, and to ascertain what influence democracy exerts on the finances of the state.

---

*Lit.: "profusions."

5. It is needless to say that I am speaking here of democratic government applied to a people and not to a small tribe.

Societies, like organized bodies, follow certain fixed rules in their formation from which they cannot deviate. They are composed of certain elements
that one finds everywhere and at all times.

Ideally, it will always be easy to divide each people into three classes.

The first class will be composed of the rich. The second will comprise
those who, without being rich, live amidst ease in all things. In the third
will be contained those who have only a little or no property and who live
particularly by the work that the first two furnish them.

The individuals contained in these different categories can be more or less
numerous, according to the social state; but you cannot fix it so that these
categories do not exist.

It is evident that each of these classes will bring to the handling of the
finances of the state certain instincts that are their own.

Suppose that the first alone makes the laws: probably it will be little
enough concerned about economizing on public funds, because a tax that
strikes a considerable fortune takes away only from the surplus and produces
little sensible effect.

Accept, on the contrary, that it is the middle classes who alone make the
law. One can reckon that they will not be prodigal with taxes because there
is nothing so disastrous as a large tax striking a small fortune.

It seems to me that among free governments, government of the middle
classes will be, I shall not say the most enlightened, nor above all the most
generous, but the most economical.

Let me suppose now that the final class is exclusively charged with making
the law; I see every chance that public costs will increase instead of decrease,
and this for two reasons:

The greatest part of those who then vote the law having no taxable property, all the money that is expended in the interest of society seems able only
to profit them without ever harming them; and those who do have a little
property readily find the means of assessing the tax in a manner that strikes
only the rich and profits only the poor, something that the rich cannot do
for their part when they are masters of the government.

Countries where the poor[6] were charged exclusively with making the law
therefore could not hope for great economy in public expenditures; those
expenditures will always be considerable, either because taxes cannot reach
those who vote them or because they are assessed in a manner so as not to

6. One understands well that the word *poor* here, as in the rest of the chapter, has a relative
sense and not an absolute meaning. The poor of America, compared to those of Europe, could
often appear to be the wealthy: one is right, however, to name them the poor when one opposes
them to those of their fellow citizens who are wealthier than they.

reach them. In other words, the government of democracy is the only one in which he who votes the tax can escape the obligation to pay it.

In vain will one object that the self-interest well understood of the people is to spare the fortunes of the rich because [the people] will not be slow to feel [the effects of] the trouble to which [the people] would give rise. But is it not in the interest of kings as well to make their subjects happy, and that of nobles to know just the moment to open up their ranks? If long-term interest could prevail over the passions and needs of the moment, there would never be tyrannical sovereigns or an exclusive aristocracy.

One may stop me again to say: Who has ever imagined entrusting the poor alone with making the law? Who? Those who established universal suffrage. Is it the majority or the minority that makes the law? Without doubt, the majority; and if I prove that the poor always compose the majority, shall I not be right to add that in countries where they are called on to vote, the poor alone make the law?

Now, it is certain that so far, in all the nations of the world, the greatest number has always been composed of those who did not have property, or of those whose property was too restricted for them to be able to live in ease without working. Therefore universal suffrage really gives the government of society to the poor.

The distressing influence that popular power can sometimes exert on the finances of the state was well displayed in certain democratic republics of antiquity, where the public treasury was exhausted in assisting indigent citizens, or in giving games and spectacles to the people.

It is true to say that the representative system was nearly unknown in antiquity. In our day, it is more difficult for popular passions to produce themselves in public affairs; one can nevertheless reckon that in the long term, he who has the mandate will in the end always conform to the spirit of his constituents, making their penchants as well as their interests prevail.

The profuse spending of democracy is, furthermore, less to be feared as the people become property owners, because then, on the one hand, the people have less need of the money of the rich, and on the other, they encounter more difficulties in not striking themselves with the tax they establish. In this respect, universal suffrage would be less dangerous in France than in England, where almost all the taxable property is gathered in a few hands. America, where the great majority of citizens are possessors, is in a situation more favorable than France.

There are still other causes that can raise the sum of public expenditures in democracies.

When aristocracy governs, the men who conduct affairs of state escape all needs by their very position; content with their lot, they demand of society above all power and glory; and placed above an obscure crowd of citizens, they do not always perceive clearly how the general well-being will work toward their own greatness. It is not that they see the sufferings of the poor man without pity; but they cannot feel his miseries as if they themselves shared them; provided that the people seem to accommodate themselves to their fortune, they therefore take them to be satisfied and expect nothing more from the government. Aristocracy considers maintaining more than perfecting.

When, on the contrary, public power is in the hands of the people, the sovereign seeks everywhere for what is better because it feels bad itself.

The spirit of improvement then spreads to a thousand diverse objects; it descends to infinite details, and above all it is applied to the kinds of improvement that can only be obtained by paying; for it is a question of bettering the condition of the poor man who cannot aid himself.

There exists in addition in democratic societies agitation without a precise goal; there reigns a sort of permanent fever that is turned to innovation of all kinds, and innovations are almost always costly.

In monarchies and aristocracies, the ambitious flatter the natural taste that carries the sovereign toward renown and power and thus often drives it to great expenditures.

In democracies, where the sovereign is necessitous, one can scarcely acquire its good will except by increasing its well-being, which can almost never be done except with money.

In addition, when the people themselves begin to reflect on their position, a host of needs arises in them that they had not felt at first, and which one can satisfy only by having recourse to the resources of the state. Hence it is that public costs generally seem to increase with civilization, and that one sees taxes rise as enlightenment spreads.

There is one last cause that often renders democratic government dearer than another. Sometimes democracy wants to put economy into its expenditures, but it cannot achieve it, because it does not have the art of being economical.

As it frequently changes its views and more frequently still its agents, it will happen that its undertakings may be badly conducted or remain unfinished: in the first case, the state makes expenditures disproportionate to the greatness of the goal that it wants to attain; in the second, it makes unproductive expenditures.

ON THE INSTINCTS OF AMERICAN DEMOCRACY IN FIXING THE SALARIES OF OFFICIALS

In democracies those who institute large salaries do not have a chance to profit from them.—Tendency of American democracy to raise the salary of secondary officials and to lower that of the principal ones.—Why that is so.—Comparative table of salaries of public officials in the United States and in France.

There is one great reason that in general brings democracy to economize on the salaries of public officials.

In democracies those who institute salaries, being very many, have very little chance of ever getting to draw them.

In aristocracies, on the contrary, those who institute large salaries almost always have the vague hope of profiting from them. These are capital that they create for themselves or at least resources that they prepare for their children.

It must be avowed, however, that democracy shows itself to be very parsimonious only toward its principal agents.

In America, officials of secondary rank are paid more than elsewhere, but high officials much less.

These contrary effects are produced by the same cause; the people in these two cases fix the wage of public officials; they think of their own needs, and this comparison enlightens them. As they live in great ease themselves, it seems natural that those they make use of should share it.[7] But when they come to fix the lot of the great officers of the state, their rule escapes them, and they no longer proceed except haphazardly.

The poor man does not have a distinct idea of the needs that the upper classes of society can feel. What would appear a modest sum to a wealthy man appears a prodigious sum to him, as one who contents himself with the necessary; and he estimates that the governor of a state, provided with two thousand *écus*, still ought to be found happy and to excite envy.[8]

If you should undertake to make him understand that the representative of a great nation ought to appear with a certain splendor in the eyes of foreigners, he will comprehend you at first; but when, coming to think of his simple dwelling and of the modest fruits of his hard labor, he thinks of all

---

7. The ease in which secondary officials live in the United States is due to still another cause; and this is foreign to the general instincts of democracy: every kind of private career is very productive; the state would not find secondary officials if it did not consent to pay them well. It is therefore in the position of a commercial enterprise, obliged, whatever its economical tastes may be, to keep up a burdensome competition.

8. The state of Ohio, which counts a million inhabitants, gives the governor a wage of only 1,200 dollars, or 6,504 francs.

that he himself could do with this same wage that you judge insufficient, he will be surprised and almost frightened at the sight of so much wealth.

Add to this that the secondary official is almost at the level of the people, whereas the other dominates them. The first can therefore still excite their interest, but the other begins to make them envious.

This is seen very clearly in the United States, where wages seem in a way to decrease as the power of officials is greater.[9]

Under the empire of aristocracy, on the contrary, it happens that high officials receive very great emoluments, whereas the small ones often have scarcely enough to live on. It is easy to find the reason for this fact in causes analogous to those we have indicated above.

If democracy does not conceive of the pleasures of the wealthy man or envies him, for its part aristocracy does not understand the miseries of the poor man, or rather it is ignorant of him. The poor man is not, properly speaking, the like of the wealthy man; he is a being of another species. Aristocracy, therefore, worries rather little about the lot of its inferior agents. It raises their salaries only when they refuse to serve it at too low a price.

It is the parsimonious tendency of democracy toward principal officials

---

9. To render this truth visible to the eye, it is enough to examine the salaries of some of the agents of the federal government. I believed I ought to place in view the wage attached to analogous offices in France so that the comparison serves to enlighten the reader.

UNITED STATES
　　Ministry of Finances (*Treasury Department*)

Bailiff (messenger)	3,734 fr.
Lowest paid clerk	5,420
Highest paid clerk	8,672
Secretary general (*chief clerk*)	10,840
Minister (*secretary of state*)	32,520
Head of the government (president)	135,000

FRANCE
　　Ministry of Finances

Bailiff of the minister	1,500 fr.
Lowest paid clerk	1,000 to 1,800
Highest paid clerk	3,200 to 3,600
Secretary general	20,000
Minister	80,000
Head of the government (king)	12,000,000

Perhaps I was wrong to take France for the point of comparison. In France, where democratic instincts pervade the government more every day, one already perceives a strong tendency that brings the chambers to raise small salaries and above all to lower great ones. Thus the minister of finances who, in 1834, receives 80,000 francs, received 160,000 under the Empire; the general directors of finances, who receive 20,000, then received 50,000.

that has made one attribute to it great penchants toward economy that it does not have.

It is true that democracy gives those who govern it hardly enough to live on honestly, but it expends enormous sums to succor the needs or facilitate the enjoyments of the people.[10] That is a better use of the product of taxes, not an economy.

Democracy generally gives little to those who govern and much to the governed. The contrary is seen in aristocracies, where the money of the state profits above all the class at the head of affairs.

DIFFICULTY OF DISCERNING THE CAUSES THAT INCLINE THE AMERICAN GOVERNMENT TO ECONOMY

Whoever searches the facts for the real influence that laws exert on the lot of humanity is exposed to great mistakes, for there is nothing so difficult to appreciate as a fact.

One people is naturally light and enthusiastic; another, reflective and calculating. This is due to its physical constitution or to distant causes of which I am ignorant.

One sees peoples who like shows, noise and joy, and who do not regret a million spent going up in smoke. One sees others who prize only solitary pleasures and who seem ashamed to appear contented.

In certain countries, they attach a great price to the beauty of buildings. In certain others, they put no value on art objects, and they scorn that which brings in nothing. Finally, there are some in which they love renown, and others in which they put money ahead of everything.

All these causes, independent of laws, influence the conducting of the finances of the state in a very powerful manner.

If Americans have never spent the people's money on public festivals, it is not only because the people vote taxes there, it is because the people do not like to enjoy themselves.

---

10. See among others, in American budgets, what it costs for the upkeep of indigents and for free instruction.

In 1831 the sum of 1,290,000 francs was expended in the state of New York for the support of indigents. And the sum devoted to public instruction is estimated to rise to at least 5,420,000 francs. (*Williams' New York Annual Register*, 1832, pp. 205 and 243.)

The state of New York had only 1,900,000 inhabitants in 1830, which forms less than twice the population of the Département du Nord [one of 83 administrative units in France, dating from the Revolution].

If they reject ornaments in their architecture and prize only material and positive advantages, it is not only because they form a democratic nation, it is also because they are a commercial people.

Habits of private life are continued into public life; and one must distinguish well between economies that depend on institutions and those that flow from habits and mores.

CAN THE PUBLIC EXPENDITURES OF THE UNITED STATES BE COMPARED TO THOSE OF FRANCE?

Two points to be established in order to appreciate the extent of public costs: the national wealth and taxation.—The fortune of and costs to France are not known exactly.—Why one cannot hope to know the fortune of and costs to the Union.—Researches of the author to learn the amount of taxes in Pennsylvania.—General signs by which one can recognize the extent of the costs to a people.—Result of this examination for the Union.

People have been much occupied in recent times with comparing the public expenditures of the United States to ours. All this work has been without result, and a few words will be enough, I believe, to prove that it had to be so.

In order to be able to appreciate the extent of public costs for a people, two operations are necessary: one must first learn what the wealth of that people is, and afterwards what portion of that wealth it devotes to the expenditures of the state. He who would research the amount of taxes without showing the extent of the resources that must provide them engages in unproductive work; for, it is not the expenditure, but the relation of the expenditure to revenue that it is interesting to know.

The same tax that a wealthy contributor easily tolerates will serve to reduce a poor man to misery.

The wealth of peoples is composed of several elements: immovable funds form the first, movable goods constitute the second.

It is difficult to know the extent of cultivable lands that a nation possesses and their natural or acquired worth. It is more difficult still to estimate all the movable goods a people disposes of. By their diversity and number, they elude almost all efforts at analysis.

Also we see that the oldest civilized nations of Europe, the very ones in which administration is centralized, have up to the present not established the state of their fortune in a precise manner.

In America, the idea of attempting it has not even been conceived. And how could one flatter oneself to have succeeded at it in this new country, when society has still not settled into a tranquil and definitive seat, where the national government does not have at its disposition, as does ours, a multitude of agents whose efforts it can command and direct simultaneously; where finally statistics are not cultivated because no one may be found there who has the ability to gather documents or the time to go through them?

So, therefore, the constitutive elements of our calculations cannot be obtained. We are ignorant of the comparative fortunes of France and the Union. The wealth of one is still not known, and the means of establishing that of the other do not exist.

But I am quite willing to agree for a moment to put aside this necessary term of comparison; I renounce learning what is the relation of taxation to revenue, and I limit myself to the wish to establish what the tax is.

The reader is going to recognize that in narrowing the scope of my research, I have not made my task easier.

I do not doubt that the central administration of France, aided by all the officials it disposes of, would succeed in discovering exactly the amount of direct or indirect taxes that weigh on its citizens. But this work, which one particular person cannot undertake, the French government itself has still not achieved; or at least it has not made their results known. We know what the costs to the state are; the total of departmental expenditures is known to us; we are ignorant of what takes place in the communes: therefore no one can say, for the present, what is the sum of public expenditures in France.

If I now return to America, I perceive difficulties that become more numerous and more insurmountable. The Union makes known to me exactly what the amount of its costs is; I can procure the particular budgets of the twenty-four states of which it is composed; but who will teach me what citizens spend for the administration of the county and the township?[11]

11. The Americans, as one sees, have four kinds of budgets: the Union has its own; the states, counties, and townships have theirs as well. During my stay in America I did much research to learn the amount of public expenditures in the townships and counties of the principal states of the Union. I could easily obtain the budgets of the largest townships, but it was impossible for me to procure those of the small ones. I can therefore form no exact idea of township expenditures. For what concerns the expenditures of counties, I possess some documents which, although incomplete, are perhaps of a nature to merit the curiosity of the reader. I owe to the kindness of Mr. Richards [Benjamin Richards (1797–1851)], former mayor of Philadelphia, the budgets of thirteen counties of Pennsylvania for the year 1830, which are those of Lebanon, Center, Franklin, Lafayette, Montgomery, Luzerne, Dauphin, Butler, Allegheny, Columbia, Northumberland, Northampton, Philadelphia. In 1830 there were 495,207 inhabitants. If one casts a glance at a map of Pennsylvania, one will see that these thirteen counties are dispersed in every direction and subject to all the general causes that can influence the state of the country, so that it would be impossible to say why they should not furnish an exact idea of the financial state of the counties of Pennsylvania. Now, in the year 1830 these same counties expended 1,800,221 francs, which gives 3 francs 64 centimes per inhabitant. I have calculated that during the year 1830 each of these same inhabitants devoted 12 francs 70 centimes to the needs of the federal Union and 3 francs 80 centimes to those of Pennsylvania; from this it results that in the year 1830 these same citizens gave the sum of 20 francs 14 centimes to society to meet all public

Federal authority cannot be extended to oblige the state governments to enlighten us on this point; and had these governments themselves simultaneously wanted to lend us their cooperation, I doubt that they were in a position to satisfy us. Independent of the natural difficulty of the undertaking, the political organization of the country would still be opposed to the success of their efforts. The magistrates of the township and the county are not named by the administrators of the state and do not depend on them. It is therefore permitted to believe that if the state wanted to obtain the information that is necessary to us, it would encounter great obstacles in the negligence of the lower officials they would be obliged to make use of.[12]

Besides, it is useless to inquire what the Americans could do in such a matter, since it is certain that, up to now, they have done nothing.

Therefore, not a single man exists today in America or in Europe who can teach us what each citizen of the Union pays annually to meet the costs of society.[13]

---

expenditures (except township expenditures). This result is doubly incomplete, as one sees, since it only applies to a single year and to a portion of public costs, but it has the merit of being certain.

12. Those who wanted to establish a parallel between the Americans' expenditures and ours have indeed felt that it would be impossible to compare the total public expenditures of France to the total public expenditures of the Union; but they have sought to compare detached portions of these expenditures. It is easy to prove that this second manner of operating is no less defective than the first.

To what, for example, shall I compare our national budget? To the budget of the Union? But the Union is occupied with many fewer objects than our central government, and its costs will naturally be much less. Shall I oppose our departmental budgets to the budgets of the particular states the Union is composed of? But in general the particular states watch over more important and more numerous interests than the administrations of our departments; their expenditures are therefore naturally more considerable. As for the budgets of the counties, one encounters nothing in our system of finances that resembles them. Shall we enter the expenditures that are carried in them in the budget of the state or in that of the townships? Township expenditures exist in the two countries, but they are not always analogous. In America, the township takes charge of several cares that are left to the department or the state in France. Besides, what must be understood by township expenditures in America? The organization of the township differs according to state. Shall we take for a rule what takes place in New England or in Georgia, in Pennsylvania or in the state of Illinois?

It is easy to perceive, between some of the budgets of the two countries, a sort of analogy; but between the elements that compose them, always differing more or less, one cannot establish a serious comparison.

13. Should one come to know the precise sum that each French or American citizen renders to the public treasury, one would still have only a part of the truth.

Governments demand not only money of taxpayers, but also personal efforts that are calculable in money. The state raises an army; independent of the pay that the entire nation is charged with furnishing, the soldier must also give his time, which has a value more or less great according to the use that he could make of it if he remained free. I shall say as much of militia service. The man who takes part in the militia temporarily devotes precious time to the public

Let us conclude that it is as difficult to compare fruitfully the social expenditures of the Americans to ours as the wealth of the Union to that of France. I add that it would even be dangerous to attempt it. When statistics are not founded on rigorously true calculations, they lead astray instead of directing. The mind easily lets itself be taken in by false airs of exactitude that statistics retain even in their lapses, and it rests without trouble on errors that in its eyes are clothed with mathematical forms of truth.

Let us therefore abandon figures and try to find our proofs elsewhere.

Does a country present the aspect of material prosperity? After having paid the state, does the poor man have some resources and the wealthy man superfluity? Do they both appear satisfied with their lot, and seek daily to improve it still more, so that industry is never lacking in capital, capital in its turn never lacking industry? Such are the signs to which, for want of positive documents, it is possible to resort to learn if the public costs that weigh on a people are proportionate to its wealth.

The observer who depended on this testimony would judge without doubt that the American of the United States gives a lesser part of his revenue to the state than the Frenchman.

But how could one conceive that it should be otherwise?

A part of the French debt is the result of two invasions; the Union has none to fear. Our position obliges us habitually to keep a numerous army in arms; the isolation of the Union permits it to have only 6,000 soldiers. We maintain nearly 300 vessels; the Americans have only 52 of them.[14] How could the inhabitant of the Union pay as much to the state as the inhabitant of France?

---

safety and gives really to the state what he fails to acquire himself. I have cited these examples; I could have cited many others. The governments of France and America collect taxes of this nature: these taxes weigh on citizens: but who can evaluate with exactitude the amount in the two countries?

That is not the final difficulty that stops you when you want to compare the public expenditures of the Union to ours. The state in France sets itself certain obligations that it does not impose on itself in America, and vice versa. The French government pays the clergy; the American government leaves this care to the faithful. In America, the state takes charge of the poor; in France, it delivers them to the charity of the public. We set a fixed salary for all our officials, the Americans permit them to collect certain fees. In France, benefits in kind have a place only on a few routes; in the United States, on almost all roads. Our ways are open to travelers, who can go on them without paying anything; in the United States, one encounters many toll roads. All these differences in the manner by which the taxpayer comes to repay the costs of society render comparison between the two countries very difficult; for there are certain expenditures that citizens would not make or that would be less if the state did not take charge of acting in their name.

14. See the detailed budgets of the Ministry of the Navy in France, and for America, the *National Calendar* of 1833, p. 228. [Force, *National Calendar*, vol. 11, 221.]

There is therefore no parallel to establish between the finances of countries situated so differently.

It is by examining what takes place in the Union, and not in comparing the Union to France, that we can judge whether American democracy is genuinely economical.

I cast my glance on each of the various republics of which the confederation is formed, and I discover that their government often lacks perseverance in its designs and that it does not exercise a continued surveillance on the men that it employs. I naturally draw the consequence that it must often spend the money of taxpayers uselessly or devote more than is necessary to its undertakings.

I see that, faithful to its popular origin, it makes prodigious efforts to satisfy the needs of the lower classes of society, to open paths to power for them, and to spread well-being and enlightenment among them. It maintains the poor, distributes millions to schools each year, pays for all services, and remunerates its least agents generously. If such a manner of governing seems useful and reasonable to me, I am obliged to recognize that it is extravagant.

I see the poor man who directs public affairs and disposes of national resources, and I cannot believe that, profiting from the expenditures of the state, he does not often carry the state along into new expenditures.

I therefore conclude, without having recourse to incomplete figures and without wanting to establish risky comparisons, that the democratic government of the Americans is not, as people sometimes claim, a cheap government; and I do not fear to predict that if great troubles came one day to assail the peoples of the United States, one would see taxes raised as high among them as in most of the aristocracies or monarchies of Europe.

ON THE CORRUPTION AND VICES OF THOSE WHO GOVERN IN DEMOCRACY; ON THE EFFECTS ON PUBLIC MORALITY THAT RESULT

In aristocracies, those who govern sometimes seek to corrupt.—In democracies, they often show themselves to be corrupt.—In the first, their vices attack the morality of the people directly.—In the second, they exert an indirect influence on them that is more formidable still.

Aristocracy and democracy mutually cast at each other the reproach of facilitating corruption; but one must distinguish:

In aristocratic governments, men who arrive at [the head of] affairs are rich people who only desire power. In democracies, statesmen are poor and have their fortunes to make.

It follows that in aristocratic states, those who govern are hardly accessible to corruption and have only a very moderate taste for money, whereas the contrary happens in democratic peoples.

But in aristocracies, as those who want to arrive at the head of affairs have great wealth at their disposal, and as the number of those who can enable them to reach it is often circumscribed within certain limits, the government finds itself in a way up for auction. In democracies, on the contrary, those who crave power are almost never wealthy, and the number of those who concur in giving it is very great. Perhaps in democracies there are no fewer men for sale, but one finds almost no buyers there; and besides, one would have to buy too many people at once to attain the goal.

Among the men who have held power in France for forty years, several have been accused of having made a fortune at the expense of the state and its allies, a reproach that was rarely addressed to public men in the former monarchy. But in France there is almost no example of buying the vote of an elector for money, whereas the thing is done notoriously and publicly in England.

I have never heard it said that in the United States one employs one's wealth to win over the governed, but I have often seen the probity of public officials put in doubt. Still more often I have heard their success attributed to low intrigues or to guilty maneuvers.

If, therefore, men who direct aristocracies sometimes seek to corrupt, chiefs of democracies show themselves to be corrupt. In the former, they attack the morality of the people directly; in the latter, they exert an indirect action on the public conscience that must be dreaded still more.

As those who are at the head of the state among democratic peoples are almost always the butt of distressing suspicions, they in a way give the support of the government to the crimes of which they are accused. Thus they offer dangerous examples for still-struggling virtue and furnish glorious comparisons for hidden vice.

In vain might one say that dishonest passions are encountered in all ranks; that they often mount to the throne by right of birth; that one can thus encounter very contemptible men at the head of aristocratic nations as within democracies.

That response does not satisfy me: in the corruption of those who arrive at power haphazardly something coarse and vulgar is uncovered that renders it contagious to the crowd; on the contrary, even in the depravity of great lords there reigns a certain aristocratic refinement, an air of greatness that often prevents its being communicated.

The people will never penetrate into the obscure labyrinth of the spirit of the court; they will always discover only with difficulty the baseness that is hidden under an elegance of manners, a refinement of tastes, and grace of language. But robbing the public treasury or selling the favors of the state for money, the first miserable person understands that and can flatter himself with doing as much in his turn.

What one must fear, moreover, is not so much the sight of the immorality of the great as that of immorality leading to greatness. In democracy, plain citizens see a man who issues from their ranks, and who in a few years achieves wealth and power; the spectacle excites their surprise and their envy; they inquire how he who was their equal yesterday is vested today with the right to direct them. To attribute his elevation to his talents or his virtues is inconvenient, for it is to avow that they are less virtuous and less skillful than he. They therefore place the principal cause of it in some of his vices, and often they are right in doing so. Thus there is at work some sort of odious mixing of ideas of baseness and power, of unworthiness and success, of utility and dishonor.

OF WHAT EFFORTS DEMOCRACY IS CAPABLE

The Union has struggled only once for its existence.—Enthusiasm at the beginning of the war.—Cooling down at the end.—Difficulty of establishing conscription or maritime conscription in America.—Why a democratic people is less capable than any other of continuous great efforts.

I warn the reader that I am speaking here of a government that follows the real will of the people, and not of a government that limits itself to commanding in the name of the people.

There is nothing so irresistible as a tyrannical power that commands in the name of the people, because, being vested with the moral power that belongs to the will of the greatest number, it acts at the same time with the decision, the promptness, and the tenacity that a single man would have.

It is quite difficult to say what degree of effort a democratic government is capable of in times of national crisis.

Until now, a great democratic republic has never been seen. It would do injury to republics to call the oligarchy that reigned over France in 1793 by this name. The United States alone presents this new spectacle.

Now, in the half-century since the Union was formed, its existence has been put into question only one time, during the War of Independence. At the beginning of that long war, there was an extraordinary show of enthusiasm for the country's* service.[15] But as the struggle was prolonged, one saw

---

* *Patrie*, elsewhere "native country."

15. One of the most singular, in my opinion, was the resolution by which the Americans temporarily renounced the use of tea. Those who know that men generally hold more to their

individual selfishness reappear: money no longer came to the public treasury; men no longer presented themselves for the army; the people still wanted independence, but they recoiled before the means of obtaining it. "Tax laws have in vain been multiplied—new methods to enforce the collection have in vain been tried," says Hamilton in *Federalist* 12; "the public expectation has been uniformly disappointed, and the treasuries of the States have remained empty. The popular system of administration inherent in the nature of popular government, coinciding with the real scarcity of money, incident to a languid and mutilated state of trade, has hitherto defeated every experiment for extensive collections, and has at length taught the different legislatures the folly of attempting them."

Since that period, the United States has not had a single serious war to sustain.

To judge what sacrifices democracies know how to impose on themselves, one must therefore await the time when the American nation is obliged to put half of the revenue from goods into the hands of its government, like England, or must throw a twentieth of its population on the fields of battle at once, as France has done.

In America conscription is unknown; they enroll men there for money. Forced recruitment is so contrary to the ideas and so foreign to the habits of the people of the United States that I doubt that one would ever dare to introduce it into the laws. What is called conscription in France surely forms the heaviest of our taxes; but without conscription, how could we support a great continental war?

The Americans themselves have not adopted the impressment of the English. They have nothing that resembles our maritime conscription. The navy of the state, like the merchant marine, is recruited with the aid of voluntary enlistment.

Now, it is not easy to conceive that a people can sustain a great maritime war without resorting to one of the two methods indicated above: thus the Union, which has already fought at sea with glory, has nonetheless never had many ships, and the armament of the small number of its vessels has always cost it very dearly.

I have heard American statesmen avow that the Union will have trouble maintaining its rank on the seas if it does not resort to impressment or to maritime conscription; but the difficulty is to oblige the people, who govern, to suffer impressment or maritime conscription.

It is incontestable that free peoples, in danger, generally display an energy

---

habits than to their lives will doubtless be astonished at this great and obscure sacrifice obtained from a whole people.

infinitely greater than those who are not, but I am inclined to believe that this is above all true of free peoples in which the aristocratic element dominates. Democracy appears to me to be much more appropriate to directing a peaceful society, or to making a sudden and vigorous effort as needed, than to braving great storms in the political life of a people for a long time. The reason for this is simple: men expose themselves to dangers and privations out of enthusiasm, but they remain exposed to them for a long time only out of reflection. In what is called instinctive courage itself, there is more calculation than people think; and although passions alone generally bring one to make the first efforts, it is with a view to the result that one continues them. One risks a part of what is dear in order to save the rest.

Now, it is this clear perception of the future, founded on enlightenment and experience, that democracy will often lack. The people feel much more than they reason; and if the present evils are great, it is to be feared that they will forget the greater evils that perhaps await them in case of defeat.

There is still another cause that ought to render the efforts of a democratic government less lasting than the efforts of an aristocracy.

The people not only see less clearly than the upper classes what they can hope or fear from the future, but they also suffer quite differently from the evils of the present. The noble, in exposing his person, has as many chances of glory as of peril. In delivering the greatest part of his revenue to the state, he temporarily deprives himself of some of the pleasures of wealth; but for the poor man, death is without prestige, and the tax that bothers the rich man often attacks the sources of life for him.

The relative weakness of democratic republics in times of crisis is perhaps the greatest obstacle posed to the founding of such a republic in Europe. In order that a democratic republic subsist without trouble in one European people it would be necessary for it to be established at the same time in all the others.

I believe that the government of democracy will in the long term augment the real strength of society; but it cannot gather at once, on one point, and at a given time as much strength as an aristocratic government or an absolute monarchy. If a democratic country remained subject to a republican government for a century, one can believe that at the end of the century it would be wealthier, more populous, and more prosperous than the neighboring despotic states; but during this century it would have run the risk several times of being conquered by them.

ON THE POWER THAT AMERICAN DEMOCRACY GENERALLY EXERCISES OVER ITSELF

That the American people lend themselves only at length, and sometimes refuse, to do what is useful to their well-being.—Capacity Americans have to make repairable mistakes.

The difficulty that democracy finds in defeating the passions and silencing the needs of the moment in view of the future is noticed in the United States in the least things.

The people, surrounded by flatterers, come to triumph over themselves only with difficulty. Each time that one wants to get them to impose deprivation or bother on themselves, even in a goal that their reason approves, they almost always begin by refusing it. The obedience that the Americans accord to the laws is rightly praised. It must be added that in America legislation is made by the people and for the people. In the United States, therefore, the law shows itself favorable to those who, everywhere else, have the most interest in violating it. Thus it is permitted to believe that a bothersome law, whose present utility the majority might not feel, would not be carried or would not be obeyed.

In the United States, no legislation exists relative to fraudulent bankruptcies. Would this be because there are no bankruptcies? No, on the contrary, it is because there are many of them. The fear of being prosecuted as a bankrupt surpasses the fear of being ruined by bankrupts in the mind of the majority; and a sort of guilty tolerance is produced in the public conscience for the offense that each one individually condemns.

In the new states of the Southwest, citizens almost always take the law into their own hands, and there murders are constantly recurring. That comes about because the habits of the people are too rude and enlightenment too little widespread in the wilderness for them to feel the utility of giving force to the law: they still prefer duels to lawsuits.

Someone said to me one day in Philadelphia that almost all crimes in America are caused by the abuse of strong liquor, which baser people could use at will because it was sold to them at a low price. "How is it," I asked, "that you do not put a fee on spirits?" "Our legislators have indeed often thought of it," he replied, "but the undertaking is difficult. A revolt is feared; and besides, the members who voted such a law would be very sure of not being reelected." "So therefore," I responded, "among you, drinkers are in the majority, and temperance is unpopular."

When one gets statesmen to notice these things, they limit themselves to answering you: Let time do it; a sense of the evil will enlighten the people and show them their needs. That is often true: if democracy has more chance of being mistaken than a king or a body of nobles, it also has more chance of coming back to the truth, once enlightenment comes to it, because generally there are within it no interests contrary to that of the greatest number, and which struggle against reason. But democracy can only obtain truth from experience, and many peoples cannot await the results of their errors without perishing.

The great privilege of the Americans is therefore not only to be more enlightened than others, but to have the ability to make repairable mistakes.

Add that in order to put the experience of the past to profit easily, it is necessary that democracy already have achieved a certain degree of civilization and enlightenment.

One sees peoples whose first education has been so vicious, and whose character presents such a strange mixture of passions, ignorance, and erroneous notions of all things, that by themselves they cannot discern the cause of their miseries; they succumb under evils of which they are ignorant.

I passed through vast regions formerly inhabited by powerful Indian nations that no longer exist today; I lived among already mutilated tribes that saw their number decrease daily and the dazzle of their savage glory disappear; I heard these Indians themselves foresee the final destiny reserved to their race. There is, however, no European who does not perceive what must be done to preserve these unfortunate peoples from an inevitable destruction. But the Indians do not see it; they feel the evils that accumulate on their heads each year, and they will perish to the last one, rejecting the remedy. One would have to use force to constrain them to live.

One is surprised to perceive the new nations of South America agitated for a quarter of a century in the midst of constantly reviving revolutions, and each day one waits to see them reenter what is called their *natural state*. But who can affirm that the revolutions are not, in our time, the most natural state of the Spanish of South America? In that region, society struggles at the bottom of an abyss from which its own efforts cannot make it rise.

The people who inhabit this beautiful half of a hemisphere seem obstinately attached to tearing out each other's entrails; nothing can turn them from it. Exhaustion makes them fall into repose for an instant, and repose soon brings them back to new furies. When I come to consider them in this alternating state of misery and of crime, I am tempted to believe that for them despotism would be a benefit.

But these two words could never be found united in my thought.

THE MANNER IN WHICH AMERICAN DEMOCRACY CONDUCTS EXTERNAL AFFAIRS OF STATE

Direction given to the external policy of the United States by Washington and Jefferson.—Almost all the natural defects of democracy are felt in the direction of external affairs, and its [good] qualities are hardly felt there.

We have seen that the federal constitution puts the permanent direction of the external interests of the nation in the hands of the president and the Senate,[16] which, up to a certain point, places the general policy of the Union outside the direct and daily influence of the people. Therefore one cannot say in an absolute manner that the democracy in America conducts the external affairs of state.

Two men have impressed a direction on the policy of the Americans that is still followed in our day; the first is Washington, and Jefferson is the second.

Washington, in that admirable letter addressed to his fellow citizens, which forms the political testament of that great man, said:

The Great rule of conduct for us, in regard to foreign Nations is in extending our commercial relations to have with them as little political connection as possible. So far as we have already formed engagements let them be fulfilled, with perfect good faith. Here let us stop.

Europe has a set of primary interests, which to us have none, or a very remote relation. Hence she must be engaged in frequent controversies, the causes of which are essentially foreign to our concerns. Hence therefore it must be unwise in us to implicate ourselves, by artificial ties, in the ordinary vicissitudes of her politics, or the ordinary combinations and collisions of her friendships, or enmities:

Our detached and distant situation invites and enables us to pursue a different course. If we remain one People, under an efficient government, the period is not far off, when we may defy material injury from external annoyance; when we may take such an attitude as will cause the neutrality we may at any time resolve upon to be scrupulously respected; when belligerent nations, under the impossibility of making acquisitions upon us, will not lightly hazard the giving us provocation; when we may choose peace or war, as our interest guided by our justice shall Counsel.

Why forego the advantages of so peculiar a situation? Why quit our

---

16. "The President," says the Constitution, art. 2, sec. 2, no. 2, "shall have power, by and with the advice and consent of the Senate, to make treaties." The reader ought not to lose sight of the fact that the mandate of senators lasts six years, and that in being chosen by the legislators of each state, they are the product of an election in two stages.

own to stand upon foreign ground? Why, by interweaving our destiny with that of any part of Europe, entangle our peace and prosperity in the toils of European ambition, rivalship, interest, humor or caprice?

'Tis our true policy to steer clear of permanent alliances, with any portion of the foreign world. So far, I mean, as we are now at liberty to do it, for let me not be understood as capable of patronising infidelity to existing engagements (I hold the maxim no less applicable to public than to private affairs, that honesty is always the best policy). I repeat it therefore, let those engagements be observed in their genuine sense. But in my opinion, it is unnecessary and would be unwise to extend them.

Taking care always to keep ourselves, by suitable establishments, on a respectably defensive posture, we may safely trust to temporary alliances for extraordinary emergencies.[*]

Previously Washington had announced this beautiful and just idea: "The nation that delivers itself to habitual sentiments of love or of hatred toward another becomes a sort of slave to them. It is a slave to its hatred or to its love."[†]

The political conduct of Washington was always directed according to these maxims. He succeeded in keeping his country at peace when all the rest of the universe was at war, and he established as a point of doctrine that the self-interest well understood of Americans was never to take part in the internal quarrels of Europe.

Jefferson went still further, and he introduced this other maxim into the policy of the Union: "That Americans ought never to demand privileges from foreign nations in order not to be obliged to accord them themselves."[‡]

These two principles, whose evident justice easily puts them within reach of the crowd, have simplified the external politics of the United States extremely.

The Union, not meddling in the affairs of Europe, has so to speak no external interests to discuss, for it still has no powerful neighbors in America. Placed by its situation as much as by its will outside the passions of the Old World, it has neither to guarantee itself against them nor to espouse them. As for those of the New World, the future hides them still.

The Union is free of previous engagements; it therefore profits from the experience of the old peoples of Europe without being obliged, like them, to take part in the past and to accommodate it to the present; it is not, like

---

[*]See John Marshall, *Life of Washington*, vol. 5 (Philadelphia, 1807), 705.

[†]See John Marshall, *Life of Washington*, vol. 5, 702.

[‡]Source not found.

them, forced to accept an immense inheritance that its fathers have willed to it, a mixture of glory and misery, of friendships and national hatred. The external politics of the United States is eminently expectant; it consists much more in abstaining than in doing.

It is therefore very difficult to know, for the present, what skill American democracy will develop in the conduct of the external affairs of state. On this point, its adversaries, like its friends, must suspend their judgment.

As for me, I shall have no difficulty in saying that it is in the direction of the external interests of society that democratic governments appear to me decidedly inferior to others. In a democracy, experience, mores, and instruction in the end almost always create the sort of everyday practical wisdom and science of small events in life that one names good sense. Good sense suffices in the ordinary course of society; and in a people whose education is completed, democratic freedom applied to internal affairs of state produces more good than the errors of the government of democracy can lead to evils. But it is not always so in the relations of a people to a people.

External policy requires the use of almost none of the qualities that are proper to democracy, and demands, on the contrary, the development of almost all those it lacks. Democracy favors the increase of the internal resources of the state; it spreads ease, develops public spirit; fortifies respect for law in the different classes of society—all things that have only an indirect influence on the position of one people vis-à-vis another. But only with difficulty can democracy coordinate the details of a great undertaking, fix on a design, and afterwards follow it with determination through obstacles. It is hardly capable of combining measures in secret and of patiently awaiting their result. Those are the qualities that belong more particularly to one man or to an aristocracy. Now, it is precisely those qualities that in the long term make a people, like an individual, in the end dominate.

If, on the contrary, you turn your attention to the natural defects of aristocracy, you will find that the effect they can produce is almost never noticeable in the direction of the external affairs of the state. The capital vice for which aristocracy is reproached is that of working only for itself, and not for the mass. In external policy, it is very rare that aristocracy has an interest distinct from that of the people.

The inclination that brings democracy to obey sentiment rather than reasoning in politics, and to abandon a long matured design to satisfy a momentary passion, was very well brought out in America when the French Revolution broke out. The simplest light of reason was enough then, as today, to make Americans conceive that their interest was not to engage in the struggle that was going to cover Europe with blood, and from which the United States could suffer no damage.

The sympathies of the people in favor of France were however declared with so much violence that nothing less than the inflexible character of Washington and the immense popularity that he enjoyed were needed to prevent war from being declared on England. And, still, the efforts that the austere reason of this great man made to struggle against the generous but unreflective passions of his fellow citizens almost took from him the sole recompense that he had ever reserved for himself, the love of his country. The majority pronounced against his policy; now the entire people approves it.[17]

If the Constitution and public favor had not given the direction of the external affairs of the state to Washington, it is certain that the nation would have done then precisely what it condemns today.

Almost all the peoples that have acted strongly on the world, those who have conceived, followed, and executed great designs, from the Romans to the English, were directed by an aristocracy, and how can one be astonished by that?

That which is most fixed in the world in its views is an aristocracy. The mass of the people can be seduced by their ignorance or their passions; one can surprise the mind of a king and make him vacillate in his projects; and besides, a king is not immortal. But an aristocratic body is too numerous to be captured, too small in number to yield readily to the intoxication of unreflective passions. An aristocratic body is a firm and enlightened man who does not die.

🐦 🐦

Chapter 6 WHAT ARE THE REAL ADVANTAGES THAT AMERICAN SOCIETY DERIVES FROM THE GOVERNMENT OF DEMOCRACY

Before beginning the present chapter I feel the need to recall to the reader what I have already indicated several times in the course of this book.

The political constitution of the United States appears to me to be one of the forms that democracy can give to its government; but I do not consider

---

17. See the fifth volume of the *Life of Washington,* by Marshall [Marshall, *Vie de George Washington*]. "In a government constituted like that of the United States," he says, page 314, "the first magistrate, cannot, whatever his firmness may be, long hold a dike against the torrent of popular opinion; and the one that prevailed then seemed to lead to war." In fact, in the session of Con-

American institutions the only ones or the best that a democratic people should adopt.

In making known what goods the Americans derive from the government of democracy I am therefore far from claiming or thinking that such advantages can be obtained only with the aid of the same laws.*

ON THE GENERAL TENDENCY OF THE LAWS UNDER THE EMPIRE OF AMERICAN DEMOCRACY, AND ON THE INSTINCT OF THOSE WHO APPLY THEM

The vices of democracy are seen all at once.—Its advantages are perceived only at length.—American democracy is often unskillful, but the general tendency of its laws is profitable.—Public officials under American democracy do not have permanent interests that differ from those of the greatest number. What results from this.

The vices and weaknesses of the government of democracy are seen without trouble; they are demonstrated by patent facts, whereas its salutary influence is exerted in an insensible and, so to speak, occult manner. Its faults strike one at first approach, but its [good] qualities are discovered only at length.

The laws of American democracy are often defective or incomplete; they may happen to violate acquired rights or to sanction dangerous ones: were they good, their frequency would still be a great evil. All this is perceived at first glance.

How is it therefore that the American republics maintain themselves and prosper?

In laws, one ought to distinguish carefully the goal they pursue from the manner in which they advance toward this goal; their absolute goodness, from that which is only relative.

Let me suppose that the object of the legislator is to favor the interests of the few at the expense of the many; his provisions are combined in such a fashion as to obtain the result that is proposed in the least time and with the

---

*See also *DA* I Intro., 2.9.

---

gress held in that period, it was very frequently perceived that Washington had lost the majority in the House of Representatives. Outside, the violence of language used against him was extreme: in a political gathering they did not fear to compare him indirectly to the traitor Arnold (page 265). "Those who held to the party of the opposition," Marshall also says (page 335) [355], "claimed that the partisans of the administration composed an aristocratic faction that had submitted to England and that, wanting to establish a monarchy, was consequently the enemy of France; a faction whose members constituted a sort of nobility that had the stock of the Bank as securities and that so feared every measure that could influence its funds that it was insensitive to the affronts that the honor and the interest of the nation commanded it equally to repel."

least possible effort. The law will be well made, its goal bad; it will be dangerous in proportion to its very efficacy.

The laws of democracy generally tend to the good of the greatest number,
for they emanate from the majority of all citizens, which can be mistaken,
but cannot have an interest contrary to itself.*

Those of aristocracy tend, on the contrary, to monopolize wealth and
power in the hands of the few because aristocracy by its nature always forms
a minority.

One can therefore say in a general manner that the object of democracy
in its legislation is more useful to humanity than is the object of aristocracy
in its.

But there its advantages end.

Aristocracy is infinitely more skillful in the science of the legislator than
democracy can be. Master of itself, it is not subject to getting carried away in
passing distractions; it has long designs that it knows how to ripen until a
favorable occasion presents itself. Aristocracy proceeds wisely; it knows the
art of making the collective force of all its laws converge at the same time
toward the same point.

It is not so in democracy: its laws are almost always defective or unsea-
sonable.

The means of democracy are therefore more imperfect than those of aristocracy: often it works against itself, without wanting to; but its goal is
more useful.

Imagine a society that nature or its constitution has organized in such a
manner as to bear the transient operation of bad laws, and that can await the
result of the *general tendency* of the laws without perishing, and you will
conceive that the government of democracy, despite its faults, is still the most
appropriate of all to make this society prosper.

That is precisely what happens in the United States; I repeat here what I
have already expressed elsewhere: the great privilege of the Americans is to
be able to have repairable mistakes.†

I shall say something analogous about public officials.

It is easy to see that American democracy is often mistaken in the choice
of the men in whom it entrusts power; but it is not so easy to say why the
state prospers in their hands.

Remark first that if those who govern in a democratic state are less honest
or less capable, the governed are more enlightened and more attentive.

*Cf. Rousseau, *Social Contract,* II 3.
†*DA* I 2.5.

The people in democracies, constantly occupied as they are with their affairs, and jealous of their rights, prevent their representatives from deviating from a certain general line that their interest traces for them.

Remark again that if the democratic magistrate uses power worse than someone else, he generally possesses it for less time.

But there is a more general reason than that one, and more satisfying.

It is doubtless important to the good of nations that those who govern have virtues or talents; but what is perhaps still more important to them is that those who govern do not have interests contrary to the mass of the governed; for in that case the virtues could become almost useless and the talents fatal.

I said that it is important that those who govern not have interests contrary to or different from the mass of the governed; I did not say that it is important that they have interests like those of *all* the governed, because I do not know that the thing has ever been encountered.

A political form that equally favors the development and prosperity of all the classes of which society is composed has not been discovered up to now. These classes have continued to form almost so many distinct nations in the same nation, and experience has proven that it is nearly as dangerous to rely completely on any of them for the fate of the others, as to make one people the arbiter of the destinies of another people. When the rich govern alone, the interest of the poor is always in peril; and when the poor make the law, that of the rich runs great risks. What therefore is the advantage of democracy? The real advantage of democracy is not, as has been said, to favor the prosperity of all, but only to serve the well-being of the greatest number.

Those charged with directing the affairs of the public in the United States are often inferior in capacity and morality to the men that aristocracy would bring to power; but their interest intermingles and is identified with that of the majority of their fellow citizens. They can therefore commit frequent infidelities and grave errors, but they will never systematically follow a tendency hostile to that majority; and they cannot succeed in impressing an exclusive and dangerous style on the government.

Moreover, the bad administration of one magistrate under democracy is an isolated fact that has influence only for the short duration of that administration. Corruption and incapacity are not common interests that can bind men among themselves in a permanent manner.

A corrupt or incapable magistrate will not combine his efforts with another magistrate for the sole reason that the latter is incapable and corrupt like him, and these two men will never work in concert to make corruption and incapacity flourish in their posterity. On the contrary, the ambition and maneuvers of the one will serve to unmask the other. In democracies, the vices of the magistrate are in general wholly personal to him.

But public men under the government of aristocracy have a class interest which, if it is sometimes intermingled with that of the majority, often remains distinct from it. That interest forms a common and lasting bond among them; it invites them to unite and to combine their efforts toward a goal that is not always the happiness of the greatest number: it not only binds those who govern with one another; it also unites them to a considerable portion of the governed; for many citizens, without being vested with any post, make up a part of the aristocracy.

The aristocratic magistrate therefore encounters constant support in society at the same time that he finds it in the government.

The common object that unites the magistrates in aristocracies to the interest of a part of their contemporaries also identifies them and subjects them, so to speak, to that of future races. They work for the future as well as for the present. The aristocratic magistrate is therefore pushed toward the same point all at once by the passions of the governed, by his own, and I could almost say by the passions of his posterity.

How be surprised if he does not resist? One often also sees the spirit of class in aristocracies carry along even those it does not corrupt and, little by little without their knowing it, make them accommodate the society to their use and prepare it for their descendants.

I do not know if an aristocracy as liberal as that of England has ever existed, which without interruption has furnished men as worthy and enlightened to the government of the country.

It is, however, easy to recognize that in English legislation the good of the poor has in the end often been sacrificed to that of the rich, and the rights of the greatest number to the privileges of some: thus England in our day unites within itself all the most extreme fortunes, and one meets with miseries there that almost equal its power and glory.

In the United States, where public officials have no class interest to make prevail, the general and continuous course of government is beneficent although those who govern are often unskillful and sometimes contemptible.

There is, therefore, at the base of democratic institutions, a hidden tendency that often makes men cooperate for the general prosperity despite their vices or errors, whereas in aristocratic institutions a secret inclination is sometimes discovered that, despite talents and virtues, brings them to contribute to the miseries of those like them. Thus it can happen that in aristocratic governments public men do evil without wanting to, and in democracies they produce good without having any thought of doing so.

ON PUBLIC SPIRIT IN THE UNITED STATES

Instinctive love of native country.—Reflective patriotism.—Their different characteristics.—That people ought to strive with all their strength toward the second when the first disappears.—Efforts the Americans have made to achieve this.—The interest of the individual intimately bound to that of the country.

There exists a love of native country that has its source principally in the unreflective, disinterested, and indefinable sentiment that binds the heart of the man to the place where the man was born. This instinctive love intermingles with the taste for old customs, with respect for ancestors and memory of the past; those who feel it cherish their country as one loves a paternal home. They love the tranquillity they enjoy; they hold to the peaceful habits they have contracted there; they are attached to the memories it presents to them, and even find some sweetness in living there obediently. Often that love of native country is further exalted by religious zeal, and then one sees prodigies done. It is a sort of religion itself; it does not reason, it believes, it feels, it acts. Peoples have been encountered who have, in some fashion, personified the native country and have caught a glimpse of it in the prince. They have therefore carried over to him a part of the sentiment of which patriotism is composed; they have become haughty with his triumphs and have taken pride in his power. There was a time, under the former monarchy, when the French experienced a sort of joy in feeling themselves delivered without recourse to the arbitrariness of the monarch, and they used to say haughtily: "We live under the most powerful king in the world."

Like all unreflective passions, this love of country pushes one to great, fleeting efforts rather than to continuity of efforts. After having saved the state in a time of crisis, it often allows it to decline in the midst of peace.

When peoples are still simple in their mores and firm in their beliefs; when society rests gently on an old order of things whose legitimacy is not contested, one sees this instinctive love of native country reign.

There is another more rational than that one; less generous, less ardent perhaps, but more fruitful and more lasting; this one is born of enlightenment; it develops with the aid of laws, it grows with the exercise of rights, and in the end it intermingles in a way with personal interest. A man understands the influence that the well-being of the country has on his own; he knows that the law permits him to contribute to producing this well-being, and he interests himself in the prosperity of his country at first as a thing that is useful to him, and afterwards as his own work.

But sometimes a moment arrives in the lives of peoples when old customs are changed, mores destroyed, beliefs shaken, the prestige of memories faded away, and when, however, enlightenment remains incomplete and political rights are badly secured or restricted. Then men no longer perceive the native country except in a weak and doubtful light; they no longer place it in the soil, which has become a lifeless land in their eyes, nor in the usages of their ancestors, which they have been taught to regard as a yoke; nor in the religion which they doubt; nor in the laws they do not make, nor in the legislator whom they fear and scorn. They therefore see it nowhere, no more with its own features than with any other, and they withdraw into a narrow and unenlightened selfishness. These men escape prejudices without recognizing the empire of reason; they have neither the instinctive patriotism of the monarchy nor the reflective patriotism of the republic; but they have come to a stop between the two, in the midst of confusion and miseries.

What is one to do in such a state? Retreat. But peoples no more come back to the sentiments of their youth than do men to the innocent tastes of their first years; they can regret them, but not make them revive. One must therefore go further ahead and hasten to unite in the eyes of the people individual interest to the interest of the country, for disinterested love of one's native country is fleeing away without return.

I am surely far from claiming that, to arrive at this result, one ought to accord the exercise of political rights to all men all at once; but I say that the most powerful means, and perhaps the only one that remains to us, of interesting men in the fate of their native country is to make them participate in its government. In our day, the spirit of the city seems to me inseparable from the exercise of political rights; and I think that from now on one will see the number of citizens in Europe increase or diminish in proportion to the extension of these rights.

How is it that in the United States, where the inhabitants arrived yesterday on the soil they occupy, where they have brought neither usages nor memories; where they meet for the first time without knowing each other; where, to say it in a word, the instinct of the native country can scarcely exist; how is it that each is interested in the affairs of his township, of his district, and of the state as a whole as in his own? It is that each, in his sphere, takes an active part in the government of society.

In the United States, the man of the people understands the influence that general prosperity exerts on his happiness—an idea so simple and yet so little known by the people. Furthermore, he is accustomed to regarding this prosperity as his own work. He therefore sees in the public fortune his own, and he works for the good of the state not only out of duty or out of pride, but I would almost dare say out of cupidity.

One does not need to study the institutions and history of Americans to know the truth of what precedes; mores advertise it enough to you. The

American, taking part in all that is done in this country, believes himself interested in defending all that is criticized there; for not only is his country then attacked, he himself is: thus one sees his national pride have recourse to all the artifices and descend to all the puerilities of individual vanity.

There is nothing more annoying in the habits of life than this irritable patriotism of the Americans. A foreigner would indeed consent to praise much in their country; but he would want to be permitted to blame something, and this he is absolutely refused.

America is therefore a country of freedom where, in order not to wound anyone, the foreigner must not speak freely either of particular persons, or of the state, or of the governed, or of those who govern, or of public undertakings, or of private undertakings; or, finally, of anything one encounters except perhaps the climate and the soil; and still, one finds Americans ready to defend both as if they had helped to form them.

In our day one must know how to resign oneself and dare to choose between the patriotism of all and the government of the few, for one cannot at once unite the social force and activity given by the first with the guarantees of tranquillity sometimes furnished by the second.

ON THE IDEA OF RIGHTS IN THE UNITED STATES

There are no great peoples without an idea of rights.—What is the means of giving the idea of rights to the people.—Respect for rights in the United States.—How it arises.

After the general idea of virtue I know of none more beautiful than that of rights, or rather these two ideas are intermingled. The idea of rights is nothing other than the idea of virtue introduced into the political world.

It is with the idea of rights that men have defined what license and tyranny are. Enlightened by it, each could show himself independent without arrogance and submissive without baseness. The man who obeys violence bows and demeans himself; but when he submits to the right to command that he recognizes in someone like him, he raises himself in a way above the very one who commands him. There are no great men without virtue; without respect for rights, there is no great people: one can almost say that there is no society; for, what is a union of rational and intelligent beings among whom force is the sole bond?

I wonder what, in our day, is the means of inculcating in men the idea of rights and of making it, so to speak, fall upon their senses; and I see only one, which is to give the peaceful exercise of certain rights to all of them: one sees that well among children, who are men except for force and experience. When the child begins to move in the midst of external objects, instinct brings him to put to his use all that he encounters in his hands; he has no idea of the property of others, not even of its existence; but as he is made aware of the price of things and he discovers that he can be stripped of his in his turn, he becomes more circumspect and ends by respecting in those like him what he wants to be respected in himself.

What happens to the infant with his playthings happens later to the man with all the objects that belong to him. Why in America, country of democracy par excellence, does no one make heard those complaints against property in general that often ring out in Europe? Is there need to say it?—it is that in America there are no proletarians. Each one, having a particular good to defend, recognizes the right of property in principle.

In the political world it is the same. In America, the man of the people has conceived a lofty idea of political rights because he has political rights; so that his own are not violated, he does not attack those of others. And whereas in Europe this same man does not recognize sovereign authority, the American submits without murmur to the power of the least of its magistrates.

This truth appears even in the smallest details of the existence of peoples. In France there are few pleasures reserved exclusively for the upper classes of society; the poor man is admitted almost everywhere the wealthy man can enter: so he is seen to conduct himself with decency, and to respect everything that serves enjoyments he shares. In England, where wealth has the privilege of pleasure like the monopoly of power, they complain that when the poor man comes to introduce himself furtively into the place destined for the pleasures of the rich he likes to cause useless damage: how can one be surprised at this?—they have taken care that he has nothing to lose.

The government of democracy makes the idea of political rights descend to the least of citizens, as the division of goods puts the idea of the right of property in general within reach of all men. There is one of its greatest merits in my eyes.

I do not say that it is an easy thing to teach all men to make use of political rights; I say only that when that can be done, the resulting effects are great.

And I add that if there is a century in which such an undertaking ought to be attempted, that century is ours.

Do you not see that religions are weakening and that the divine notion of rights is disappearing? Do you not find that mores are being altered, and that with them the moral notion of rights is being effaced?

Do you not perceive on all sides beliefs that give way to reasoning, and sentiments that give way to calculations? If in the midst of that universal disturbance you do not come to bind the idea of rights to the personal interest that offers itself as the only immobile point in the human heart, what will then remain to you to govern the world, except fear?

Therefore when I am told that the laws are weak and the governed turbulent; that passions are lively and virtue without power, and that in this situation one must not think of augmenting the rights of democracy, I respond that it is because of these very things that I believe one must think of it; and in truth I think that governments have still more interest in it than society, for governments perish, and society cannot die. Furthermore, I do not want to abuse the example of America.

In America, the people were vested with political rights at a period when it was difficult for them to make bad use of them, because the citizens were few and simple in mores. In becoming larger, Americans did not so to speak increase the powers of democracy; rather, they extended its domain.

One cannot doubt that the moment when one accords political rights to a people who have been deprived of them until then is a moment of crisis, a crisis often necessary, but always dangerous.

The child puts to death when he is ignorant of the price of life; he takes away the property of others before knowing that one can rob him of his. The man of the people, at the instant when he is accorded political rights, finds himself, in relation to his rights, in the same position as the child vis-à-vis all nature, and that is the case in which to apply to him these celebrated words: *Homo puer robustus.**

This truth is exposed in America itself. The states where citizens have enjoyed their rights longest are those where they know best how to make use of them.

One cannot say it too often: There is nothing more prolific in marvels than the art of being free; but there is nothing harder than the apprenticeship of freedom. It is not the same with despotism. Despotism often presents itself as the mender of all ills suffered; it is the support of good law, the sustainer of the oppressed, and the founder of order. Peoples fall asleep in the bosom of the temporary prosperity to which it gives birth; and when they awaken, they are miserable. Freedom, in contrast, is ordinarily born in the midst of storms, it is established painfully among civil discords, and only when it is old can one know its benefits.

ON RESPECT FOR THE LAW IN
THE UNITED STATES

Respect of Americans for the law.—Paternal love that they feel for it.—Personal interest that each finds in increasing the power of the law.

---

*"Man is a robust boy." AT wrote "famous from Hobbes" in a draft note. See Thomas Hobbes, *De Cive*, Preface, though Hobbes says *vir malus* (a wicked man) instead of *homo*. Cf. Jean-Jacques Rousseau, *Discourse on the Origin of Inequality*, part 1.

It is not always permissible to call the entire people, either directly or indirectly, to the making of the law; but one cannot deny that when that is practicable, the law acquires great authority from it. That popular origin, which often harms the goodness and wisdom of legislation, contributes singularly to its power.

There is a prodigious force in the expression of the will of a whole people. When it is uncovered in broad daylight, the very imagination of those who would wish to struggle against it is overwhelmed.

The truth of this is well known to parties.

And so one sees them contest for a majority everywhere they can. When they lack it among those who have voted, they place it among those who have abstained from voting, and when it still happens to escape them there, they find it among those who did not have the right to vote.

In the United States, excepting slaves, domestics, and indigents nourished by the townships, there is no one who is not an elector, and whoever has this title concurs indirectly in the law. Those who want to attack the laws are therefore reduced to doing openly one of these two things: they must either change the opinion of the nation or ride roughshod over its will.

Add to this first reason, another more direct and more powerful, that in the United States each finds a sort of personal interest in everyone's obeying the laws; for whoever does not make up a part of the majority today will perhaps be in its ranks tomorrow; and the respect that he professes now for the will of the legislator he will soon have occasion to require for his. However distressing the law may be, the inhabitant of the United States submits to it without trouble, therefore, not only as the work of the greatest number, but also as his own; he considers it from the point of view of a contract to which he would have been a party.

One therefore does not see in the United States a numerous and always turbulent crowd, which, regarding the law as a natural enemy, casts only glances of fear and suspicion on it. On the contrary, it is impossible not to perceive that all classes show great confidence in the legislation that rules the country and feel a sort of paternal love for it.

I am mistaken in saying all classes. In America, the European ladder of powers being reversed, the rich are found in a position analogous to that of the poor in Europe; it is they who often mistrust the law. I have said it elsewhere: the real advantage of democratic government is not to guarantee the interests of all, as it has sometimes been claimed, but only to protect those of the greatest number.* In the United States, where the poor man governs, the rich always have to fear lest he abuse his power against them.

*DA I 2.6.

REAL ADVANTAGES THAT AMERICA DERIVES FROM DEMOCRACY

This disposition of the mind of the rich can produce a muted discontent; but society is not violently troubled by it; because the same reason that prevents the rich man from granting his confidence to the legislator prevents him from defying his commandments. He does not make the law because he is rich, and he does not dare to violate it because of his wealth. In civilized nations it is generally only those who have nothing to lose who revolt. So, therefore, if the laws of democracy are not always respectable, they are almost always respected; for those who generally violate the laws cannot fail to obey those that they have made and from which they profit, and citizens who could have an interest in breaking them are brought by character and by position to submit to the will of the legislator, whatever it may be. Furthermore, the people in America obey the law not only because it is their work, but also because they can change it when by chance it hurts them; they submit to it in the first place as an evil that is imposed by themselves and after that as a passing evil.

ACTIVITY REIGNING IN ALL PARTS OF THE BODY POLITIC OF THE UNITED STATES; INFLUENCE THAT IT EXERTS ON SOCIETY

It is more difficult to conceive of the political activity reigning in the United States than of the freedom or equality encountered there.—The great movement that constantly agitates legislatures is only an episode, a prolongation of this universal movement.—Difficulty that the American finds in occupying himself only with his own affairs.—Political agitation spreads into civil society.—Industrial activity of the Americans coming in part from this cause.—Indirect advantages that society derives from the government of democracy.

When one passes from a free country into another that is not, one is struck by a very extraordinary spectacle: there, all is activity and movement; here, all seems calm and immobile. In the one, it is only a question of betterment and progress; one would say that society in the other, after having acquired all goods, aspires only to rest in order to enjoy them. Nevertheless, the country that gives itself so much agitation so as to be happy is generally richer and more prosperous than the one that appears so satisfied with its lot. And in considering them both, one has trouble conceiving how so many new needs make themselves felt daily in the first, whereas one seems to feel so few in the second.

If this remark is applicable to free countries that have preserved the monarchical form and to those where aristocracy dominates, it is still more so in democratic republics. There, it is no longer one portion of the people that undertakes to better the state of society; the entire people takes charge of this care. It is not only a question of providing for the needs and the conveniences of one class, but of all classes at the same time.

It is not impossible to conceive the immense freedom that Americans enjoy; one can get an idea of their extreme equality as well; but what one cannot comprehend without having already been witness to it is the political activity that reigns in the United States.

Scarcely have you descended on the soil of America when you find yourself in the midst of a sort of tumult; a confused clamor is raised on all sides; a thousand voices come to your ear at the same time, each of them expressing some social needs. Around you everything moves: here, the people of one neighborhood have gathered to learn if a church ought to be built; there, they are working on the choice of a representative; farther on, the deputies of a district are going to town in all haste in order to decide about some local improvements; in another place, the farmers of a village abandon their furrows to go discuss the plan of a road or a school. Citizens assemble with the sole goal of declaring that they disapprove of the course of government, whereas others gather to proclaim that the men in place are the fathers of their country.* Here are others still who, regarding drunkenness as the principal source of the evils of the state, come solemnly to pledge themselves to give an example of temperance.[1]

The great political movement that constantly agitates American legislatures, the only one that is perceived from the outside, is only one episode and a sort of prolongation of the universal movement that begins in the lowest ranks of the people and afterwards spreads gradually to all classes of citizens. One cannot work more laboriously at being happy.

It is difficult to say what place the cares of politics occupy in the life of a man in the United States. To meddle in the government of society and to speak about it is the greatest business and, so to speak, the only pleasure that an American knows. This is perceived even in the least habits of life: women themselves often go to political assemblies and, by listening to political discourses, take a rest from household tedium.† For them, clubs replace theatergoing to a certain point. An American does not know how to converse, but he discusses; he does not discourse, but he holds forth. He always speaks to you as to an assembly; and if he happens by chance to become heated, he will say "sirs" in addressing his interlocutor.

---

* *Patrie,* elsewhere "native country."

† Or "annoyances": *ennuis.*

1. Temperance societies are associations whose members pledge to abstain from strong liquors. On my visit to the United States, temperance societies already counted more than 270,000 members, and their effect had been to diminish consumption of strong liquors in the state of Pennsylvania alone by 500,000 gallons a year.

In certain countries, the inhabitant only accepts with a sort of repugnance the political rights that the law accords him; it seems that to occupy him with common interests is to steal his time, and he likes to enclose himself in a narrow selfishness of which four ditches topped by a hedge form the exact limits.

On the contrary, from the moment when an American were reduced to occupying himself only with his own affairs, he would have been robbed of half of his existence; he would feel an immense void in his days, and he would become incredibly unhappy.[2]

I am persuaded that if despotism ever comes to be established in America, it will find more difficulties in defeating the habits to which freedom has given birth than in surmounting the love of freedom itself.

This agitation, constantly reborn, that the government of democracy has introduced into the political world, passes afterwards into civil society. I do not know if, all in all, that is not the greatest advantage of democratic government, and I praise it much more because of what it causes to be done than for what it does.

It is incontestable that the people often direct public affairs very badly; but the people cannot meddle in public affairs without having the scope of their ideas extended and without having their minds be seen to go outside their ordinary routine. The man of the people who is called to the government of society conceives a certain self-esteem. As he is then a power, very enlightened intellects put themselves at the service of his. People constantly address themselves to him to get his support, and in seeking to deceive him in a thousand different manners, they enlighten him. In politics, he participates in undertakings that he has not conceived, but that give him a general taste for undertakings. Every day people indicate to him new improvements to make to the common property; and he feels the desire being born to improve what is personal to him. He is perhaps neither more virtuous nor happier, but he is more enlightened and more active than his precursors. I do not doubt that democratic institutions, joined to the physical nature of the country, are not the direct cause, as so many people say, but the indirect cause of the prodigious motion of industry to be remarked in the United States. Laws do not give birth to it, but the people learn to produce it by making the law.

When the enemies of democracy claim that one alone does better what he takes charge of than the government of all, it seems to me that they are right.

2. The same fact was already observed in Rome under the Caesars.

Montesquieu remarks somewhere [*On the Greatness of the Romans and Their Decadence,* XIV 12] that nothing equaled the despair of certain Roman citizens who, after the agitations of a political existence, suddenly reentered the calm of private life.

The government of one alone, supposing equality of enlightenment on both sides, puts more coherence into its undertakings than the multitude; it shows more perseverance, more of an idea of an ensemble, more perfection of detail, a more just discernment in the choice of men. Those who deny these things have never seen a democratic republic or have judged by only a few examples. Democracy, even if local circumstances and the dispositions of the people permit it to be maintained, does not present to the eye administrative regularity and methodical order in government; that is true. Democratic freedom does not execute each of its undertakings with the same perfection as intelligent despotism; often it abandons them before having received their fruit, or it risks dangerous ones: but in the long term democracy produces more than despotism; it does each thing less well, but it does more things. Under its empire, what is great is above all not what public administration executes but what is executed without it and outside it. Democracy does not give the most skillful government to the people, but it does what the most skillful government is often powerless to create; it spreads a restive activity through the whole social body, a superabundant force, an energy that never exists without it, and which, however little circumstances may be favorable, can bring forth marvels. Those are its true advantages.

In this century, when the destinies of the Christian world appear to be unresolved, some hasten to attack democracy as an enemy power while it is still getting larger; others already adore it as a new god that issues from nothingness; but both know the object of their hatred or their desire only imperfectly; they do combat in the shadows and strike only haphazardly.

What do you ask of society and its government? We must understand each other.

Do you want to give a certain loftiness to the human spirit, a generous way of viewing the things of this world? Do you want to inspire in men a sort of contempt for material goods? Do you desire to give birth to or to maintain profound convictions and to prepare for great devotions?

Is it a question for you of polishing mores, of elevating manners, of making the arts shine? Do you want poetry, renown, glory?

Do you intend to organize a people in such a manner as to act strongly on all others? Do you destine it to attempt great undertakings and, whatever may be the result of its efforts, to leave an immense mark on history?

If this is, according to you, the principal object that men ought to propose for themselves in society, do not take the government of democracy; it would surely not lead you to the goal.

But if it seems to you useful to turn the intellectual and moral activity of man to the necessities of material life and to employ it in producing well-being; if reason appears to you to be more profitable to men than genius; if your object is not to create heroic virtues but peaceful habits; if you would rather see vices than crimes, and if you prefer to find fewer great actions on condition that you will encounter fewer enormities; if instead of acting within a brilliant society it is enough for you to live in the midst of a prosperous society; if, finally, the principal object of a government, according to you, is not to give the most force or the most glory possible to the entire body of the nation, but to procure the most well-being for each of the individuals who compose it and to have each avoid the most misery, then equalize conditions and constitute the government of a democracy.

If there is no longer time to make a choice and if a force superior to man already carries you along toward one of the two governments without consulting your desires, seek at least to derive from it all the good that it can do; and knowing its good instincts as well as its evil penchants, strive to restrict the effects of the latter and develop the former.

𝒸𝒶 𝒸𝒶

Chapter 7 ON THE OMNIPOTENCE OF THE MAJORITY IN THE UNITED STATES AND ITS EFFECTS

Natural force of the majority in democracies.—Most of the American constitutions have artificially increased this natural force.—How.—Imperative mandates.—Moral empire of the majority.—Opinion of its infallibility.—Respect for its rights. What augments it in the United States.

It is of the very essence of democratic governments that the empire of the majority is absolute; for in democracies, outside the majority there is nothing that resists it.

Most of the American constitutions have also sought to augment this natural force of the majority artificially.[1]

1. We have seen, during the examination of the federal constitution [*DA* I 1.8], that the legislators of the Union made contrary efforts. The result of these efforts was to render the federal government more independent in its sphere than that of the states. But the federal government is scarcely occupied with any but external affairs; it is the state governments that really direct American society.

Of all political powers, the legislature is the one that obeys the majority most willingly. Americans wanted the members of the legislature to be named *directly* by the people, and for a *very short* term, in order to oblige them to submit not only to the general views, but even to the daily passions of their constituents.

They have taken the members of the two houses from the same classes and named them in the same manner, so that the motions of the legislative body are almost as rapid and no less irresistible than those of a single assembly.

The legislature thus constituted, they have united almost all the government in it.

At the same time that the law increased the force of powers that were naturally strong, it enervated more and more those that were naturally weak. It accorded neither stability nor independence to the representatives of the executive power; and, in submitting them completely to the caprices of the legislature, it took away from them the little influence that the nature of democratic government would have permitted them to exert.

In several states it left the judicial power to the election of the majority, and in all, it made its existence depend in a way on the legislative power by leaving to the representatives the right to fix the salary of the judges each year.

Usages have gone still further than the laws.

A custom that in the end will make the guarantees of representative government vain is spreading more and more in the United States: it very frequently happens that electors, in naming a deputy, lay out a plan of conduct for him and impose a certain number of positive obligations on him from which he can in no way deviate. It is as if, except for the tumult, the majority itself were deliberating in the public square.

Several particular circumstances also tend to render the power of the majority in America not only predominant, but irresistible.

The moral empire of the majority is founded in part on the idea that there is more enlightenment and wisdom in many men united than in one alone, in the number of legislators than in their choice. It is the theory of equality applied to intellects. This doctrine attacks the pride of man in its last asylum: so the minority accepts it only with difficulty; it habituates itself to it only in the long term. Like all powers, and perhaps more than any of them, therefore, the power of the majority needs to be lasting in order to appear legitimate. When it begins to establish itself, it makes itself obeyed by constraint; it is only after having lived for a long time under its laws that one begins to respect it.

The idea of the right to govern society that the majority possesses by its enlightenment was brought to the soil of the United States by its first inhabitants. This idea, which alone would suffice to create a free people, has passed into mores today, and one finds it in even the least habits of life.

The French under the former monarchy held as a constant that the king could never fail; and when he happened to do evil, they thought that the fault was in his counselors. That marvelously facilitated obedience. One could murmur against the law without ceasing to love and respect the legislator. The Americans have the same opinion of the majority.

The moral empire of the majority is also founded on the principle that the interests of the greatest number ought to be preferred to those of the few. Now, one understands without difficulty that the respect that is professed for the right of the greatest number naturally increases or diminishes according to the state of the parties. When a nation is partitioned among several great irreconcilable interests, the privilege of the majority is often unrecognized because it becomes too painful to submit to it.

If there existed in America a class of citizens whom the legislator was trying to strip of certain exclusive advantages possessed for centuries, and wanted to make them descend from an elevated situation so as to reduce them to the ranks of the multitude, it is probable that the minority would not easily submit to his laws.

But the United States having been peopled by men equal among themselves, there is not as yet a natural and permanent dissidence among the interests of its different inhabitants.

There is a certain social state in which the members of the minority cannot hope to attract the majority to them, because for that it would be necessary to abandon the very object of the struggle that they sustain against it. An aristocracy, for example, cannot become a majority while preserving its exclusive privileges, and it cannot let its privileges escape without ceasing to be an aristocracy.

In the United States, political questions cannot be posed in a manner so general and so absolute, and all the parties are ready to recognize the rights of the majority because they all hope to be able to exercise them to their profit one day.

The majority in the United States therefore has an immense power in fact, and a power in opinion almost as great; and once it has formed on a question, there are so to speak no obstacles that can, I shall not say stop, but even delay its advance, and allow it the time to hear the complaints of those it crushes as it passes.

The consequences of this state of things are dire and dangerous for the future.

HOW THE OMNIPOTENCE OF THE MAJORITY IN AMERICA INCREASES THE LEGISLATIVE AND ADMINISTRATIVE INSTABILITY THAT IS NATURAL TO DEMOCRACIES

How Americans increase the legislative instability that is natural to democracy by changing the legislator each year and arming him with a power almost without limits.—The same effect produced on administration.—In America the force brought to social improvements is infinitely greater, but less continuous than in Europe.

I have spoken previously of the vices that are natural to the government of democracy;* there is not one of them that does not grow at the same time as the power of the majority.

And, to begin with, the most apparent of all:

Legislative instability is an evil inherent in democratic government because it is of the nature of democracies to bring new men to power. But this evil is more or less great according to the power and the means of action granted to the legislator.

In America they hand over sovereign power to the authority that makes the laws. It can indulge each of its desires rapidly and irresistibly, and every year it is given other representatives. That is to say, they have adopted precisely the combination that most favors democratic instability and that permits democracy to apply its changing will to the most important objects.

Thus in our day, of the world's countries, America is the one in which the laws have the least duration. Almost all the American constitutions have been amended within thirty years. There is therefore no American state that has not modified the principle of its laws during this period.

As for the laws themselves, it is enough to cast a glance at the archives of the different states of the Union to be convinced that in America the action of the legislator never slows. It is not that American democracy is more unstable than any other by its nature, but it has been given the means to follow the natural instability of its penchants in the forming of laws.[2]

The omnipotence of the majority and the rapid and absolute manner in which its will is executed in the United States not only renders the law un-

---

*DA I 2.5.

2. The legislative acts promulgated in the state of Massachusetts alone, from 1780 to our day, already fill three large volumes. Moreover, it must be remarked that the collection I am speaking of had been revised in 1823, and it removed many of the laws that were old or had become purposeless. Now, the state of Massachusetts, which is no more populous than one of our departments, can pass for the most stable in all the Union and the one that puts the most coherence and wisdom in its undertakings.

stable, it also exerts the same influence on the execution of the law and on the action of public administration.

The majority being the sole power that is important to please, the works that it undertakes are eagerly agreed to; but from the moment that its attention goes elsewhere, all efforts cease; whereas in the free states of Europe, where the administrative power has an independent existence and a secure position, the will of the legislator continues to be executed even when it is occupied with other objects.

In America, much more zeal and activity is brought to certain improvements than is done elsewhere.

In Europe, a social force infinitely less great, but more continuous, is employed in these same things.

Several years ago, some religious men undertook to improve the state of the prisons.* The public was moved by their voices, and the rehabilitation of criminals became a popular work.

New prisons were then built. For the first time, the idea of reforming the guilty penetrated the dungeon at the same time as the idea of punishment. But the happy revolution with which the public had associated itself so eagerly, and which the simultaneous efforts of citizens rendered irresistible, could not work in a moment.

Alongside the new penitentiaries, whose development was hastened by the wish of the majority, the old prisons still remained and continued to confine a great number of the guilty. The latter seemed to become more unhealthful and more corrupting as the new ones turned more to reform and became more healthful. This double effect is easily understood: the majority, preoccupied with the idea of founding the new establishment, had forgotten the one that already existed. Everyone then having turned his eyes from the object that no longer held the regard of the master, oversight had ceased. One first saw the salutary bonds of discipline slacken, and then, soon after, break. And alongside the prison, lasting monument to the mildness and the enlightenment of our time, was a dungeon that recalled the barbarism of the Middle Ages.

TYRANNY OF THE MAJORITY

How one must understand the principle of the sovereignty of the people.—Impossibility of conceiving a mixed government.—The sovereign power must be somewhere.—Precau-

---

* AT probably has in mind the Quakers in Pennsylvania, who had long opposed the harshness of the Anglican penal code and who in the 1780s effected reforms in the penal code and organized the Philadelphia Society for the Alleviation of the Miseries of the Public Prisons.

tions that ought to be taken to moderate its action.—These precautions have not been
taken in the United States.—What results from this.

I regard as impious and detestable the maxim that in matters of government the majority of a people has the right to do everything, and nonetheless I place the origin of all powers in the will of the majority. Am I in contradiction with myself?

A general law exists that has been made or at least adopted not only by the majority of this or that people, but by the majority of all men. This law is justice.

Justice therefore forms the boundary of each people's right.

A nation is like a jury charged with representing the universal society and with applying the justice that is its law. Ought the jury that represents society have more power than the society itself for which it applies the laws?

Therefore, when I refuse to obey an unjust law, I do not deny to the majority the right to command; I only appeal from the sovereignty of the people to the sovereignty of the human race.

There are people who have not feared to say that a people, in the objects that interested only itself, could not go entirely outside the limits of justice and reason, and thus one must not fear giving all power to the majority that represents it. But that is the language of a slave.

What therefore is a majority taken collectively, if not an individual who has opinions and most often interests contrary to another individual that one names the minority? Now, if you accept that one man vested with omnipotence can abuse it against his adversaries, why not accept the same thing for a majority? Have men changed in character by being united? Have they become more patient before obstacles by becoming stronger?[3] As for me, I cannot believe it; and I shall never grant to several the power of doing everything that I refuse to a single one of those like me.

It is not that I believe that in order to preserve freedom one can mix several principles in the same government in a manner that really opposes them to one another.

The government called mixed has always seemed to me to be a chimera. There is, to tell the truth, no mixed government (in the sense that one gives to this word), because in each society one discovers in the end one principle of action that dominates all the others.

England in the last century, which has been cited particularly as an ex-

---

3. No one would want to maintain that a people cannot abuse its strength vis-à-vis another people. Now, parties form almost so many little nations in a great one; they are in the relation of foreigners among themselves. If it is agreed that one nation can be tyrannical toward another nation, how can it be denied that one party can be so toward another party?

ample of these sorts of governments, was an essentially aristocratic state, although large elements of democracy were found within it; for laws and mores there had been established so that aristocracy always had to predominate in the long term and direct public affairs at its will.

The error has come from the fact that, seeing constantly the interests of the great doing battle with those of the people, one thought only of the struggle instead of paying attention to the result of that struggle, which was the important point. When a society really comes to have a mixed government, that is to say equally divided between contrary principles, it enters into revolution or it is dissolved.

I think, therefore, that one must always place somewhere one social power superior to all the others, but I believe freedom to be in peril when that power finds no obstacle before it that can restrain its advance and give it time to moderate itself.

Omnipotence seems to me to be an evil and dangerous thing in itself. Its exercise appears to me above the strength of man, whoever he may be, and I see only God who can be omnipotent without danger, because his wisdom and justice are always equal to his power. There is therefore no authority on earth so respectable in itself or vested with a right so sacred that I should wish to allow to act without control and to dominate without obstacles. Therefore, when I see the right and the ability to do everything granted to any power whatsoever, whether it is called people or king, democracy or aristocracy, whether it is exercised in a monarchy or in a republic, I say: there is the seed of tyranny, and I seek to go live under other laws.

What I most reproach in democratic government, as it has been organized in the United States, is not, as many people in Europe claim, its weakness, but on the contrary, its irresistible force. And what is most repugnant to me in America is not the extreme freedom that reigns there, it is the lack of a guarantee against tyranny.

When a man or a party suffers from an injustice in the United States, whom do you want him to address? Public opinion? that is what forms the majority; the legislative body? it represents the majority and obeys it blindly; the executive power? it is named by the majority and serves as its passive instrument; the public forces? the public forces are nothing other than the majority in arms; the jury? the jury is the majority vested with the right to pronounce decrees: in certain states, the judges themselves are elected by the majority. Therefore, however iniquitous or unreasonable is the measure that strikes you, you must submit to it.[4]

---

4. During the War of 1812, one saw a striking example in Baltimore of the excesses that the despotism of the majority can lead to. In this period the war was very popular in Baltimore. A

Suppose on the contrary a legislative body composed in such a manner that it represents the majority without necessarily being the slave of its passions; an executive power with a force that is its own and a judicial power independent of the other two powers; you will still have democratic government, but there will be almost no more chance of tyranny.

I do not say that at the present time frequent use is made of tyranny in America, I say that no guarantee against it may be discovered, and that one must seek the causes of the mildness of government in circumstances and mores rather than in the laws.

EFFECTS OF THE OMNIPOTENCE OF THE MAJORITY ON THE ARBITRARINESS OF AMERICAN OFFICIALS

Freedom that American law leaves to officials within the circle that it has drawn.— Their power.

One must distinguish well arbitrariness from tyranny. Tyranny can be exercised by means of law itself, and then it is not arbitrariness; arbitrariness can be exercised in the interest of the governed, and then it is not tyrannical.

Tyranny ordinarily makes use of arbitrariness, but in case of need it knows how to do without it.

In the United States, at the same time that the omnipotence of the major-

---

newspaper that showed itself strongly opposed excited the indignation of the inhabitants by this conduct. The people assembled, broke the presses, and attacked the homes of the journalists. They wanted to call up the militia, but it did not respond to the appeal. In order to save the unfortunate ones whom the public furor threatened, they opted for conducting them to prison like criminals. This precaution was useless: during the night, the people assembled again; the magistrates having failed to call up the militia, the prison was forced, one of the journalists was killed on the spot, the others left for dead: the guilty referred to the jury were acquitted.

I said one day to an inhabitant of Pennsylvania: "Explain to me, I pray you, how in a state founded by Quakers and renowned for its tolerance, freed Negroes are not allowed to exercise the rights of citizens. They pay tax, is it not just that they vote?"—"Do not do us the injury," he responded to me, "of believing that our legislators have committed so gross an act of injustice and intolerance."—"So, among you, blacks have the right to vote?"—"Without any doubt."— "Then how is it that in the electoral college this morning I did not perceive a single one of them in the assembly?"—"This is not the fault of the law," the American said to me; "It is true, Negroes have the right to be present at elections, but they abstain voluntarily from appearing there."—"That indeed is modesty on their part."—"Oh! It is not that they refuse to go there, but they fear that they will be mistreated there. It sometimes happens that the law lacks force among us when the majority does not support it. Now, the majority is imbued with the greatest prejudices against Negroes, and the magistrates do not feel they have the force to guarantee to them the rights that the legislator has conferred on them."—"What! The majority that has the privilege of making the law still wants to have that of disobeying the law?"

ity favors the legal despotism of the legislator, it favors the arbitrariness of the magistrate as well. The majority, being an absolute master in making the law and in overseeing its execution, having equal control over those who govern and over those who are governed, regards public officials as its passive agents and willingly deposits in them the care of serving its designs. It therefore does not enter in advance into the details of their duties and hardly takes the trouble to define their rights. It treats them as a master could do to his servants if, always seeing them act under his eye, he could direct or correct their conduct at each instant.

In general, the law leaves American officials much freer than ours within the circle that it draws around them. It sometimes even happens that the majority permits them to leave it. Guaranteed by the opinion of the greatest number and made strong by its concurrence, they then dare things that a European, habituated to the sight of arbitrariness, is still astonished at. Thus are formed, in the bosom of freedom, habits that can one day become fatal to it.

ON THE POWER THAT THE MAJORITY IN AMERICA EXERCISES OVER THOUGHT

In the United States, when the majority has irrevocably settled on a question, there is no more discussion.—Why.—Moral power that the majority exercises over thought.— Democratic republics make despotism immaterial.

When one comes to examine what the exercise of thought is in the United States, then one perceives very clearly to what point the power of the majority surpasses all the powers that we know in Europe.

Thought is an invisible and almost intangible power that makes sport of all tyrannies. In our day the most absolute sovereigns of Europe cannot prevent certain thoughts hostile to their authority from mutely circulating in their states and even in the heart of their courts. It is not the same in America: as long as the majority is doubtful, one speaks; but when it has irrevocably pronounced, everyone becomes silent and friends and enemies alike then seem to hitch themselves together to its wagon. The reason for this is simple: there is no monarch so absolute that he can gather in his hands all the strength of society and defeat resistance, as can a majority vested with the right to make the laws and execute them.

A king, moreover, has only a material power that acts on actions and cannot reach wills; but the majority is vested with a force, at once material and moral, that acts on the will as much as on actions, and which at the same time prevents the deed and the desire to do it.

I do not know any country where, in general, less independence of mind and genuine freedom of discussion reign than in America.

There is no religious or political theory that cannot be preached freely in the constitutional states of Europe and that does not penetrate the others; for there is no country in Europe so subject to one single power that he who wants to speak the truth does not find support capable of assuring him against the consequences of his independence. If he has the misfortune to live under an absolute government, he often has the people for him; if he inhabits a free country, he can take shelter behind royal authority if need be. The aristocratic fraction of the society sustains him in democratic regions, and the democracy in the others. But in the heart of a democracy organized as that of the United States, one encounters only a single power, a single element of force and success, and nothing outside it.

In America the majority draws a formidable circle around thought. Inside those limits, the writer is free; but unhappiness awaits him if he dares to leave them. It is not that he has to fear an auto-da-fé, but he is the butt of mortifications of all kinds and of persecutions every day. A political career is closed to him: he has offended the only power that has the capacity to open it up. Everything is refused him, even glory. Before publishing his opinions, he believed he had partisans; it seems to him that he no longer has any now that he has uncovered himself to all; for those who blame him express themselves openly, and those who think like him, without having his courage, keep silent and move away. He yields, he finally bends under the effort of each day and returns to silence as if he felt remorse for having spoken the truth.

Chains and executioners are the coarse instruments that tyranny formerly employed; but in our day civilization has perfected even despotism itself, which seemed, indeed, to have nothing more to learn.

Princes had so to speak made violence material; democratic republics in our day have rendered it just as intellectual as the human will that it wants to constrain. Under the absolute government of one alone, despotism struck the body crudely, so as to reach the soul; and the soul, escaping from those blows, rose gloriously above it; but in democratic republics, tyranny does not proceed in this way; it leaves the body and goes straight for the soul. The master no longer says to it: You shall think as I do or you shall die; he says: You are free not to think as I do; your life, your goods, everything remains to you; but from this day on, you are a stranger among us. You shall keep your privileges in the city, but they will become useless to you; for if you crave the vote* of your fellow citizens, they will not grant it to you, and if you demand

*Lit.: "choice."

only their esteem, they will still pretend to refuse it to you. You shall remain among men, but you shall lose your rights of humanity. When you approach those like you, they shall flee you as being impure; and those who believe in your innocence, even they shall abandon you, for one would flee them in their turn. Go in peace, I leave you your life, but I leave it to you worse than death.

Absolute monarchies had dishonored despotism; let us be on guard that democratic republics do not rehabilitate it, and that in rendering it heavier for some, they do not remove its odious aspect and its demeaning character in the eyes of the greatest number.

In the proudest nations of the Old World, works destined to paint faithfully the vices and ridiculousness of contemporaries were published; La Bruyère lived at the palace of Louis XIV when he composed his chapter on the great, and Molière criticized the Court in plays that he had performed before courtiers.* But the power that dominates in the United States does not intend to be made sport of like this. The slightest reproach wounds it, the least prickly truth alarms it; and one must praise it from the forms of its language to its most solid virtues. No writer, whatever his renown may be, can escape the obligation of singing the praises of his fellow citizens. The majority, therefore, lives in perpetual adoration of itself; only foreigners or experience can make certain truths reach the ears of the Americans.

If America has not yet had great writers, we ought not to seek the reasons for this elsewhere: no literary genius exists without freedom of mind, and there is no freedom of mind in America.

The Inquisition could never prevent books contrary to the religion of the greatest number from circulating in Spain. The empire of the majority does better in the United States: it has taken away even the thought of publishing them. One encounters nonbelievers in America, but disbelief finds so to speak no organ.

One sees governments that strive to protect mores by condemning the authors of licentious books. In the United States no one is condemned for these sorts of works; but no one is tempted to write them. It is not, however, that all the citizens have pure mores, but the majority is regular in its.

Here the use of power is doubtless good: so I speak only of the power in itself. This irresistible power is a continuous fact, and its good use is only an accident.

---

*Jean de la Bruyère (1645–1696) was a French satirist, whose "chapter on the great" is to be found in his book *Characters* (1688); Molière (Jean Baptiste Poquelin, 1622–1673) was a French comic playwright.

EFFECTS OF THE TYRANNY OF THE MAJORITY ON THE NATIONAL CHARACTER OF THE AMERICANS; ON THE SPIRIT OF A COURT IN THE UNITED STATES

Up to the present, the effects of the tyranny of the majority have made themselves felt more on mores than on the conduct of society.—They arrest the development of great characters.—Democratic republics organized like those of the United States put the spirit of a court within reach of the many.—Proofs of this spirit in the United States.—Why there is more patriotism in the people than in those who govern in its name.

The influence of the preceding still makes itself felt only feebly in political society; but one already remarks its distressing effects on the national character of the Americans. I think that the small number of remarkable men who show themselves on the political scene today must above all be attributed to the always growing activity of the despotism of the majority in the United States.

When the American Revolution broke out, a crowd of them appeared; public opinion then directed wills and did not tyrannize over them. The celebrated men of this period, associating freely in the movement of minds, had a greatness that was proper to them; they spread their brilliance over the nation and did not borrow [their brilliance] from it.

In absolute governments, the great who are near the throne flatter the passions of the master and voluntarily bend to his caprices. But the mass of the nation does not lend itself to servitude; it often submits to it out of weakness, out of habit, or out of ignorance; sometimes out of love of royalty or of the king. One has seen peoples take a kind of pleasure and pride in sacrificing their will to that of the prince, and so place a sort of independence of soul even in the midst of obedience. In these peoples one encounters much less degradation than misery. Besides, there is a great difference between doing what one does not approve of and feigning approval of what one does: the one is the part of a weak man, but the other belongs only to the habits of a valet.

In free countries, where each is more or less called to give his opinion about affairs of state; in democratic republics, where public life is incessantly mixed with private life, where the sovereign is approachable from all sides and where it is only a question of raising one's voice to reach its ear, one encounters many more people who seek to speculate about its weakness and to live at the expense of its passions than in absolute monarchies. It is not that men are naturally worse there than elsewhere, but the temptation there is very strong and is offered to more people at the same time. A much more general abasement of souls results from it.

Democratic republics put the spirit of a court within reach of the many and let it penetrate all classes at once. That is one of the principal reproaches that can be made against them.

That is above all true in democratic states organized like the American republics, where the majority possesses an empire so absolute and so irresistible that one must in a way renounce one's rights as a citizen and so to speak one's quality as a man when one wants to deviate from the path it has traced.

Among the immense crowd that flocks to a political career in the United States, I have seen few men indeed who show that virile candor, that manly independence of thought, that often distinguished Americans in previous times and that, everywhere it is found, forms the salient feature of great characters. One would say at first approach that in America, spirits have all been formed on the same model, so much do they follow exactly the same ways. The foreigner, it is true, sometimes encounters Americans who deviate from the rigor of formulas; they come to deplore the defectiveness of the laws, the volatility of democracy, and its lack of enlightenment; they often even go so far as to note the faults that alter the national character, and they point out the means that could be taken to correct them; but no one except you listens to them; and you, to whom they confide these secret thoughts, you are only a foreigner, and you pass on. They willingly deliver to you truths that are useless to you, and when they descend to the public square, they hold to another language.

If these lines ever come to America, I am sure of two things: first, that readers will all raise their voices to condemn me; second, that many among them will absolve me at the bottom of their consciences.

I have heard the native country spoken of in the United States. I have encountered genuine patriotism in the people; I have often sought it in vain in those who direct it. This is easily understood by analogy: despotism depraves the one who submits to it much more than the one who imposes it. In absolute monarchies, the king often has great virtues, but the courtiers are always base.

It is true that courtiers in America do not say "Sire" and "Your Majesty"— a great and capital difference; but they speak constantly of the natural enlightenment of their master; they do not hold a competition on the question of knowing which one of the virtues of the prince most merits being admired; for they are sure that he possesses all the virtues, without having acquired them and so to speak without wanting to do so; they do not give him their wives and their daughters so that he may deign to elevate them to the rank of his mistresses; but in sacrificing their opinions to him, they prostitute themselves.

Moralists and philosophers in America are not obliged to wrap their opinions in veils of allegory; but before hazarding a distressing truth they say: We know that we are speaking to a people too much above human weaknesses not to remain always master of itself. We would not use language like this if we did not address men whose virtues and enlightenment rendered them alone among all others worthy of remaining free.

How could the flatterers of Louis XIV do better?

As for me, I believe that in all governments, whatever they may be, baseness will attach itself to force and flattery to power. And I know only one means of preventing men from being degraded: it is to grant to no one, along with omnipotence, the sovereign power to demean them.

THAT THE GREATEST DANGER OF THE AMERICAN REPUBLICS COMES FROM THE OMNIPOTENCE OF THE MAJORITY

It is by the bad use of their power, and not by powerlessness, that democratic republics are liable to perish.—The government of the American republics more centralized and more energetic than that of the monarchies of Europe.—Danger that results from this.— Opinions of Madison and Jefferson on this subject.

Governments ordinarily perish by powerlessness or by tyranny. In the first case power escapes them; in the other, it is torn from them.

Many people, on seeing democratic states fall into anarchy, have thought that government in these states was naturally weak and powerless. The truth is that when war among their parties has once been set aflame, government loses its action on society. But I do not think that the nature of democratic power is to lack force and resources; I believe, on the contrary, that almost always the abuse of its strength and the bad use of its resources bring it to perish. Anarchy is almost always born of its tyranny or its lack of skillfulness, but not of its powerlessness.

One must not confuse stability with force, the greatness of the thing and its duration. In democratic republics, the power that directs society is not stable, for it often changes hands and purpose.[5] But everywhere it is brought, its force is almost irresistible.

The government of the American republics appears to me to be as centralized and more energetic than that of absolute monarchies of Europe. I therefore do not think that it will perish from weakness.[6]

---

5. Power can be centralized in an assembly; then it is strong, but not stable; it can be centralized in a man: then it is less strong, but it is more stable.

6. It is needless, I think, to alert the reader that here, as in all the rest of the chapter, I am speaking not of the federal government, but of the particular governments of each state, which the majority directs despotically.

If ever freedom is lost in America, one will have to blame the omnipotence of the majority that will have brought minorities to despair and have forced them to make an appeal to material force. One will then see anarchy, but it will have come as a consequence of despotism.

President James Madison expressed the same thoughts. (See *Federalist* 51.)

"It is of great importance in a republic," he says, "not only to guard the society against the oppression of its rulers, but to guard one part of the society against the injustice of the other part. [. . .]* Justice is the end of government. It is the end of civil society. It ever has been and ever will be pursued until it be obtained or until liberty be lost in the pursuit. In a society under the forms of which the stronger faction can readily unite and oppress the weaker, anarchy may as truly be said to reign as in the state of nature, where the weaker individual is not secured against the violence of the stronger; and as, in the latter state, even the stronger individuals are prompted, by the uncertainty of their condition, to submit to a government which may protect the weak as well as themselves; so, in the former state, will the more powerful factions or parties be gradually induced, by a like motive, to wish for a government which will protect all parties, the weaker as well as the more powerful. It can be little doubted that if the State of Rhode Island was separated from the confederacy and left to itself, the insecurity of rights under the popular form of government† within such narrow limits would be displayed by such reiterated oppressions of factious majorities that some power altogether independent of the people would soon be called for by the voice of the very factions whose misrule had proved the necessity of it."

Jefferson as well said: "The executive in our governments is not the sole, it is scarcely the principal object of my jealousy. The tyranny of the legislatures is the most formidable dread at present, and will be for long years. That of the executive will come in its turn, but it will be at a remote period."[7]

I like to cite Jefferson in preference to everyone else on this matter because I consider him to be the most powerful apostle that democracy has ever had.

---

*AT omits the following passage here: "Different interests necessarily exist in different classes of citizens. If a majority be united in a common interest, the rights of the minority will be insecure. There are but two methods of providing against this evil: the one by creating a will in the community independent of the majority—that is of the society itself; the other by comprehending in the society so many separate descriptions of citizens as will render an unjust combination of a majority very improbable, if not impracticable."

†AT substitutes "tyranny of the majority" for "popular form of government."

7. Jefferson to Madison, March 15, 1789. [Conseil, *Mélanges politiques et philosophiques*. Cf. *Writings of Thomas Jefferson*, 7: 312.]

༄ ༄ ༄ ༄ ༄ ༄ ༄ ༄ ༄ ༄ ༄ ༄ ༄ ༄ ༄ ༄ ༄ ༄ ༄

Chapter 8 ON WHAT TEMPERS THE TYRANNY OF THE MAJORITY IN THE UNITED STATES

ABSENCE OF ADMINISTRATIVE CENTRALIZATION

The national majority does not have any idea of doing everything.—It is obliged to make use of the magistrates of the township and the counties to execute its sovereign will.

Previously I distinguished two kinds of centralization; I called one governmental and the other administrative.* The first alone exists in America; the second is nearly unknown there.

If the power that directs American societies found these two means of government at its disposal, and added the capacity and the habit of executing everything by itself to the right of commanding everything; if, after having established the general principles of government, it entered into the details of application, and after having regulated the great interests of the country it could descend to the limit of individual interests, freedom would soon be banished from the New World.

But in the United States, the majority, which often has the tastes and instincts of a despot, still lacks the most perfected instruments of tyranny.

In none of the American republics has the central government ever been occupied but with a few objects, whose importance attracted its regard. It has not undertaken to regulate secondary things in society. Nothing indicates that it has even conceived the desire for it. The majority, in becoming more and more absolute, has not increased the prerogatives of the central power; it has only rendered itself all-powerful in its sphere. Thus despotism can be very heavy on one point, but it cannot extend to all.

Moreover, however carried away the national majority can be by its passions, however ardent it may be in its projects, it cannot make all citizens in all places, in the same manner, at the same moment, bend to its desires. When the central government that represents it has sovereignly ordained, it must rely for the execution of its commandment on agents who often do not depend on it, and whom it cannot direct at each instant. Municipal bodies and the administrations of counties therefore form so many hidden shoals that delay or divide the flood of the popular will. Were the law oppressive,

*DA I 1.5.

freedom would still find shelter in the manner in which the law was executed; and the majority could not descend into the details and, if I dare say it, into the puerilities of administrative tyranny. It does not even imagine that it can do it, for it does not have entire consciousness of its power. It still knows only its natural strength, and it is ignorant of where art could extend its bounds.

This deserves to be thought about. If a democratic republic like that of the United States ever came to be founded in a country where the power of one alone would already have established administrative centralization and made it pass into habits as into laws, I do not fear to say, in a republic like this, despotism would become more intolerable than in any of the absolute monarchies of Europe. One would have to cross over to Asia to find something to compare to it.

ON THE SPIRIT OF THE LAWYER IN THE UNITED STATES AND HOW IT SERVES AS A COUNTERWEIGHT TO DEMOCRACY

Utility of inquiring what are the natural instincts of the spirit of the lawyer.—Lawyers called to play a great role in the society seeking to be born.—How the kind of work lawyers engage in gives an aristocratic turn to their ideas.—Accidental causes that can oppose the development of these ideas.—Facility that an aristocracy has in uniting with lawyers.— How a despot could turn lawyers to account.—How lawyers form the sole aristocratic element that is of a nature to be combined with the natural elements of democracy.— Particular causes that tend to give an aristocratic turn to the spirit of the English and American lawyer.—The American aristocracy is at the attorneys' bar and on the judges' bench.—Influence exerted by lawyers on American society.—How their spirit penetrates to the heart of legislatures, into administration, and in the end gives to the people themselves something of the instincts of magistrates.

When one visits Americans and when one studies their laws, one sees that the authority they have given to lawyers and the influence that they have allowed them to have in the government form the most powerful barrier today against the lapses of democracy. This effect seems to me to have a general cause that is useful to inquire about, for it can be reproduced elsewhere.

Lawyers have been involved in all the movements of political society in Europe for five hundred years. Sometimes they have served as instruments of political power, sometimes they have taken political power as an instrument. In the Middle Ages, lawyers cooperated marvelously in extending the domination of the kings; since that time, they have worked powerfully to restrict this same power. In England, they have been seen to unite intimately with the aristocracy; in France, they have shown themselves to be its most dangerous enemies. Do lawyers therefore only yield to sudden, momentary impulses, or do they more or less obey, according to circumstances, instincts that are natural to them and that are reproduced always? I would like to clarify this point; for perhaps lawyers are called on to play the primary role in the political society that is seeking to be born.

Men who have made the laws their special study have drawn from their work the habits of order, a certain taste for forms, a sort of instinctive love for the regular sequence of ideas, which naturally render them strongly opposed to the revolutionary spirit and unreflective passions of democracy.

The special knowledge that lawyers acquire in studying the law assures them a separate rank in society; they form a sort of privileged class among [persons of] intelligence. Each day they find the idea of this superiority in the exercise of their profession; they are masters of a necessary science, knowledge of which is not widespread; they serve as arbiters between citizens, and the habit of directing the blind passions of the litigants toward a goal gives them a certain scorn for the judgment of the crowd. Add to this that they naturally form *a body*. It is not that they agree among themselves and direct themselves in concert toward the same point; but community of studies and unity of methods bind their minds to one another as interest could unite their wills.

Hidden at the bottom of the souls of lawyers one therefore finds a part of the tastes and habits of aristocracy. They have its instinctive penchant for order, its natural love of forms; they conceive its great disgust for the actions of the multitude and secretly scorn the government of the people.

I do not want to say that these natural penchants of lawyers are strong enough to link them in an irresistible fashion. What dominates among lawyers, as among all men, is particular interest, and above all the interest of the moment.

There is a certain society where men of law cannot take a rank in the political world analogous to the one that they occupy in private life; one can be assured that in a society organized in this manner, lawyers will be very active agents of revolution. But one must inquire whether the cause that then brings them to destroy or to change arises in them from a permanent disposition or an accident. It is true that lawyers contributed singularly to overturning the French monarchy in 1789. It remains to be known if they acted this way because they had studied the laws or because they could not share in making them.

Five hundred years ago, the English aristocracy put itself at the head of the people and spoke in their name; today it supports the throne and makes itself the champion of royal authority. The aristocracy, however, has instincts and penchants that are its own.

One must also guard against taking isolated members of the body for the body itself.

In all free governments, whatever their form may be, lawyers will be found in the first ranks of all parties. This same remark is also applicable to aristocracy. Almost all the democratic movements that have agitated the world have been directed by nobles.

An elite body can never be enough for all the ambitions that it contains; it always has more talents and passions than posts, and one does not fail to encounter many men in it who, being unable to become great quickly enough by using the privileges of the body, seek to do so by attacking these privileges.

I therefore do not claim that a period is coming in which *all* lawyers, or most of them in *all* times, will show themselves to be friends of order and enemies of change.

I say that in a society in which lawyers occupy without dispute the elevated position that naturally belongs to them, their spirit will be eminently conservative and will show itself as antidemocratic.

When the aristocracy closes its ranks to lawyers, it makes them enemies all the more dangerous because although below it in wealth and power, they are independent of it by their work and feel themselves to be at its level by their enlightenment.

But every time that the nobles wanted to make lawyers share some of their privileges, these two classes have had great ease in uniting and have so to speak found themselves to be from the same family.

I am equally brought to believe that it will always be easy for a king to make lawyers the most useful instruments of his power.

There is infinitely more natural affinity between men of law and the executive power than between them and the people, although lawyers often have to overturn the first; likewise, there is more natural affinity between the nobles and the king than between the nobles and the people, although the upper classes of society have often been seen to unite with the others to struggle against royal power.

What lawyers love above all things is a life of order, and the greatest guarantee of order is authority. One must not forget, moreover, that if they prize freedom, they generally place legality well above it; they fear tyranny less than arbitrariness, and provided that the legislator takes charge of taking away men's independence, they are nearly content.

I think therefore that a prince who, in the presence of an encroaching democracy, sought to bring down the judicial power in his states and to diminish the political influence of lawyers in them, would commit a great error. He would let go the substance of authority in order to seize its shadow.

I do not doubt that it would be more profitable for him to introduce lawyers into the government. After having entrusted despotism to them in the form of violence, perhaps he would take it back from their hands [now provided] with the features of justice and law.

The government of democracy is favorable to the political power of lawyers. When the rich man, the noble, and the prince are excluded from the government, the lawyers arrive there so to speak in full right; for they then form the only enlightened and skilled men whom the people can choose outside themselves.

If lawyers are naturally brought by their tastes toward the aristocracy and the prince, they are therefore naturally brought toward the people by their interest.

Thus lawyers like the government of democracy without sharing its penchants and without imitating its weaknesses—a double cause for being powerful through it and over it.

The people in democracy do not distrust lawyers, because they know that their interest is to serve the people's cause; they listen to them without anger, because they do not suppose them to have ulterior motives. In fact, lawyers do not wish to overturn the government that democracy has given itself, but they strive constantly to direct it according to a tendency that is not its own and by means that are foreign to it. The lawyer belongs to the people by his interest and by his birth, and to the aristocracy by his habits and his tastes; he is like a natural liaison between the two things, like the link that unites them.

The body of lawyers forms the sole aristocratic element that can be mixed without effort into the natural elements of democracy and be combined in a happy and lasting manner with them. I am not ignorant of the inherent defects of the spirit of the lawyer; without this mixture of the spirit of the lawyer with the democratic spirit, however, I doubt that democracy could long govern society, and I cannot believe that in our day a republic could hope to preserve its existence if the influence of lawyers in its affairs did not grow in proportion with the power of the people.

The aristocratic character that I perceive in the spirit of the lawyer is much more pronounced in the United States and England than in any other country. That is due not only to the study that English and American lawyers make of the laws, but to the very nature of the legislation and to the position that these interpreters occupy in these two peoples.

The English and the Americans have preserved the legislation of precedents; that is to say, they continue to draw from the opinions and legal decisions of their fathers the opinions that they will hold in matters of law and the decisions that they will take.

In an English or an American lawyer, taste and respect for what is old is therefore almost always joined with love of what is regular and legal.

This has still another influence on the turn of mind of lawyers, and consequently on the course of society.

The English or the American lawyer inquires into what has been done, the French lawyer into what one ought to wish to do; the one wants rulings, the other reasons.

When you listen to an English or an American lawyer, you are surprised to see him cite the opinion of others so often and to hear him speak so little on his own, whereas the contrary happens among us.

There is no affair so small that a French attorney consents to treat without introducing a system of ideas belonging to him, and he will discuss even the constitutive principles of the laws, to the end that it please the court, to move the boundary of a contested inheritance back by a toise.*

The sort of abnegation that the English and American lawyer makes of his own sense in order to rely on the sense of his fathers, the kind of servitude in which he is obliged to maintain his thought, will give the lawyer's mind more timid habits and make him contract more static penchants in England and America than in France.

Our written laws are often difficult to understand, but each man can read them; there is nothing, on the contrary, more obscure for the vulgar and less within his reach than legislation founded on precedents. The need one has of a lawyer in England and the United States, the lofty idea that one forms of his enlightenment, separate him more and more from the people and serve to put him in a class apart. The French lawyer is only a learned man; but the English or American man of law resembles in a way the priests of Egypt; like them, he is the lone interpreter of an occult science.

The position that men of law occupy in England and America exerts an influence no less great on their habits and their opinions. The aristocracy of England, which has taken care to attract into it all who have had some natural analogy with it, has made a very great place for lawyers in consideration and power. In English society, lawyers are not of the first rank, but they consider themselves content with the rank that they occupy. They form as it were the younger branch of the English aristocracy, and they love and respect their elders without sharing all their privileges. English lawyers therefore mix with the aristocratic interests of their profession the aristocratic ideas and tastes of the society in the midst of which they live.

Thus in England above all one can see in relief the type of lawyer that I

---

*A toise is six and a half feet.

am seeking to portray: the English lawyer esteems the laws, not so much because they are good as because they are old; and if he sees that he is reduced to modifying them in some point so as to adapt to changes that time makes societies undergo, he resorts to the most incredible subtleties in order to persuade himself that in adding something to the work of his fathers, he is only developing their thought and completing their work. Do not hope to make him recognize that he is an innovator; he will consent to go to absurd lengths before admitting that he is guilty of a crime so great. It is in England that this legal mind was born, which seems indifferent to the foundation of things so as to pay attention only to the letter, and which would rather depart from reason and humanity than from the law.

English legislation is like an ancient tree on which the lawyers have constantly grafted the most foreign branches in the hope that, while yielding different fruits, they will at least intermingle their foliage with the venerable trunk that supports them.

In America there are neither nobles nor men of letters, and the people distrust the rich. Lawyers therefore form the superior political class and the most intellectual portion of society. Thus, they could only lose by innovating: this adds a conservative interest to the natural taste that they have for order.

If one asked me where I place the American aristocracy, I would respond without hesitation that it is not among the rich, who have no common bond that brings them together. The American aristocracy is at the attorneys' bar and on the judges' bench.

The more one reflects on what takes place in the United States, the more one feels convinced that the body of lawyers forms the most powerful and so to speak the lone counterweight to democracy in this country.

In the United States one discovers without difficulty how much the spirit of the lawyer, by its qualities and, I shall say, even by its defects, is appropriate for neutralizing the vices inherent in popular government.

When the American people let themselves be intoxicated by their passions or become so self-indulgent as to be carried away by their ideas, the lawyers make them feel an almost invisible brake that moderates and arrests them. To their democratic instincts they secretly oppose their aristocratic penchants; to their love of novelty, their superstitious respect for what is old; to the immensity of their designs, their narrow views; to their scorn for rules, their taste for forms; and to their enthusiasm, their habit of proceeding slowly.

The courts are the most visible organs used by the body of lawyers to act on democracy.

The judge is a lawyer who, independently of the taste for order and for rules that he has contracted in the study of the laws, also derives a love of stability from the irremovability of his office. His legal knowledge had already assured him an elevated position among his like; his political power serves to place him in a rank apart and to give him the instincts of the privileged classes.

Armed with the right to declare laws unconstitutional, the American magistrate constantly enters into political affairs.[1] He cannot force the people to make laws, but at least he constrains them not to be unfaithful to their own laws and to remain in accord with themselves.

I am not ignorant that in the United States a secret tendency exists that brings the people to reduce the judicial power; in most of the particular state constitutions, the government, at the demand of two houses, can remove judges from the bench. Certain constitutions make the members of courts *elected* and submit them to frequent reelections. I dare to predict that sooner or later these innovations will have dire results and that one day it will be perceived that by so diminishing the independence of the magistrates, not only has the judicial power been attacked, but the democratic republic itself.

One must not believe, furthermore, that in the United States the spirit of the lawyer is uniquely confined within the precincts of the courts; it extends well beyond.

Lawyers, forming the sole enlightened class that the people do not distrust, are naturally called on to occupy most public offices. They fill the legislatures and are at the head of administrations; they therefore exert a great influence on the formation of the law and on its execution. Lawyers are, however, obliged to yield to the current of public opinion that carries them along; but it is easy to find some indications of what they would do if they were free. Americans, who have innovated so much in their political laws, have introduced only slight changes, and with great difficulty, in their civil laws, although several of these laws are deeply repugnant to their social state. That comes from the fact that in the matter of civil law, the majority is always obliged to rely on lawyers; and American lawyers, left to their own will, do not innovate.

It is a very singular thing for a Frenchman to hear the complaints that are raised in the United States against the static mind and prejudices of lawyers in favor of what is established.

The influence of the spirit of the lawyer extends still further than the precise limits I have just traced.

There is almost no political question in the United States that is not resolved sooner or later into a judicial question. Hence the obligation under which the parties find themselves in their daily polemics to borrow from the

---

1. See in the first volume what I say of the judicial power [*DA* I 1.6].

ideas and language of justice. As most public men are or have formerly been lawyers, they bring the usages and the turn of ideas that are their own into the handling of affairs. The jury serves to familiarize all classes with them. Judicial language thus becomes in a way the vulgar language; the spirit of the lawyer, born inside the schools and the courts, therefore spreads little by little beyond their precincts; it so to speak infiltrates all society, it descends into the lowest ranks, and the people as a whole in the end contract a part of the habits and the tastes of the magistrate.

Lawyers in the United States form a power that is hardly feared, scarcely perceived, that has no banner of its own, that bows with flexibility to the exigencies of the times, and lets itself go without resistance to all movements of the social body; but it envelops society as a whole, penetrates into each of the classes that compose it, works in secret, acts constantly on it without its knowing, and in the end models it to its desires.

ON THE JURY IN THE UNITED STATES CONSIDERED AS A POLITICAL INSTITUTION

The jury, which is one of the modes of the sovereignty of the people, ought to be placed in relation to the other laws that establish this sovereignty.—Composition of the jury in the United States.—Effects produced by the jury on national character.—Education that it gives to the people.—How it tends to establish the influence of the magistrates and to spread the spirit of the lawyer.

Since my subject has naturally led me to speak of justice in the United States, I shall not leave this matter without concerning myself with the jury.

One must distinguish two things in the jury: a judicial institution and a political institution.

If it were a question of knowing up to what point the jury, and above all the jury in a civil matter, serves the good administration of justice, I would admit that its utility could be contested.

The institution of the jury had its birth in a society barely advanced, in which one scarcely submitted any but simple questions of fact to the courts; and it is not an easy task to adapt it to the needs of a very civilized people, when the relations of men among themselves have singularly multiplied and have taken on a learned and intellectual character.[2]

2. It would be a useful and curious thing to consider the jury as a judicial institution, to appreciate the effects that it produces in the United States, and to inquire about the manner in which the Americans have taken advantage of it. One could find the subject of an entire book in the examination of this single question, and of an interesting book for France. One would inquire, for example, as to what portion of American institutions relative to the jury could be introduced among us, and by what stages. The American state that would furnish the most light on this subject would be the state of Louisiana. Louisiana contains a mixed population of French

My principal goal at this moment is to view the political side of the jury: another path would turn me aside from my subject. As for the jury considered as a judicial means, I shall say only two words about it. When the English adopted the institution of the jury, they formed a half-barbarous people; they have since become one of most enlightened nations on the globe, and their attachment to the jury has appeared to grow with their enlightenment. They have left their territory and one has seen them spread through all the universe: some have formed colonies, others, independent states; the body of the nation has kept a king, several of the emigrants have founded powerful republics; but everywhere the English have also extolled the institution of the jury.[3] They have established it everywhere, or have hastened to reestablish it. A judicial institution that thus obtains the vote of a great people during a long sequence of centuries, that has been reproduced with zeal in all periods of civilization, in all climates and under all forms of government, cannot be contrary to the spirit of justice.[4]

---

and English. The two legislations are present like the two peoples and are being amalgamated little by little with one another. The most useful books to consider would be the collection of the laws of Louisiana in two volumes entitled *Digest of the Laws of Louisiana* [L. Moreau Lislet, *A General Digest of the Acts of the Legislature of Louisiana Passed from the Year 1804, to 1827, Inclusive*, 2 vols. (New Orleans, 1828)]; and still more perhaps a course of civil procedure written in the two languages and entitled *Treatise on the Rules of Civil Actions*, published in 1830 in New Orleans by Buisson [possibly *Code of Practice in Civil Cases, for the State of Louisiana*, in French and English (New Orleans, 1825), in *Louisiana Legal Archives*, vol. 2, 1937]. This work presents a special advantage; it furnishes the French a certain and authentic explanation of English legal terms. The language of the laws forms almost a language apart with all peoples, and with the English more than with any other.

3. All English and American lawyers are unanimous on this point. Mr. Story, a judge of the Supreme Court of the United States, in his *Treatise on the Federal Constitution*, again comes back to the excellence of the jury in civil matters. "The inestimable privilege of a trial by Jury in civil cases," he says, "a privilege scarcely inferior to that in criminal cases, which is conceded by all persons to be essential to political and civil liberty." (Story, bk. 3, chap. 38.) [Story, *Commentary*, 633; AT quotes in English.]

4. If one wanted to establish what the utility of the jury is as a judicial institution, one would have many other arguments to give, and among them these:

As you introduce jurors into affairs, you can diminish the number of judges without inconvenience, which is a great advantage. When judges are very numerous, each day death makes a gap in the judicial hierarchy and opens new places in it for those who survive. The ambition of magistrates is therefore continually panting, and it naturally makes them depend on the majority or on the man who names them to vacant posts: one then advances in the courts as one gains ranks in an army. This state of things is entirely contrary to the good administration of justice and to the intention of the legislator. One wants judges to be irremovable in order that they remain free; but what does it matter that no one can rob them of their independence if they themselves voluntarily make the sacrifice of it?

When judges are very numerous, it is impossible not to encounter many incapable ones among them: for a great magistrate is not an ordinary man. Now, I do not know whether a half-

But let us quit this subject. It would narrow one's thought singularly to limit oneself to viewing the jury as a judicial institution; for, if it exerts a great influence on the fate of cases, it exerts a much greater one still on the very destinies of society. The jury is, therefore, before everything a political institution. This is the point of view where one must always place oneself to judge it.

I understand by a jury a certain number of citizens taken at random and temporarily vested with the right to judge.

To apply the jury to the suppression of crimes appears to me to introduce into the government an eminently republican institution. Let me explain myself.

The institution of the jury can be aristocratic or democratic, according to the class from which jurors are taken; but it always preserves a republican character, in that it places the real direction of society in the hands of the governed or in a portion of them, and not in those who govern.

Force is never anything but a transient element in success: immediately after it comes the idea of right. A government reduced to being able to reach its enemies only on the battlefield would soon be destroyed. The genuine sanction of political laws is therefore found in the penal laws, and if the sanction is lacking, the law sooner or later loses its force. Therefore, the man who judges the *criminal* is really the master of society. Now, the institution of the jury places the people themselves, or at least one class of citizens, on the judge's bench. The institution of the jury, therefore, really puts the direction of society into the hands of the people or of this class.[5]

In England, the jury is recruited from the aristocratic portion of the nation. The aristocracy makes the laws, applies the laws, and judges infractions of the laws.* All is in accord: so England forms, to tell the truth, an aristocratic republic. In the United States, the same system is applied to the entire

*See AT's note XVI, page 696.

---

enlightened court is not the worst of all combinations for arriving at the ends that are proposed in establishing courts of justice.

As for me, I would rather abandon the decision of a lawsuit to ignorant jurors directed by a skillful magistrate than to deliver it to judges the majority of whom would have only an incomplete knowledge of jurisprudence and of the laws.

5. One must nonetheless make an important remark:

The institution of the jury, it is true, gives a general right of control over the actions of citizens to the people, but it does not furnish them the means of exercising this control in all cases, nor in an always tyrannical manner.

When an absolute prince has the ability to have crimes judged by his delegates, the fate of the accused is, so to speak, fixed in advance. But should the people be resolved to condemn, the composition of the jury and its nonaccountability would still offer favorable chances to innocence.

people. Each American citizen is elector, eligible [for office], and juror.* The system of the jury, as it is understood in America, appears to me as direct and as extreme a consequence of the dogma of the sovereignty of the people as universal suffrage. These are two equally powerful means of making the majority reign.

All sovereigns who have wanted to draw the sources of their power from themselves, and to direct society instead of allowing themselves to be directed by it, have destroyed the institution of the jury or have enervated it. The Tudors sent jurors who did not want to condemn to prison, and Napoleon had them chosen by his agents.

However evident are most of the preceding truths, they do not strike all minds, and often among us, one still seems to have only a confused idea of the institution of the jury. Should one want to know the elements from which the list of jurors ought to be composed, one is limited to discussing what are the enlightenment and the capacity of those called upon to take part in it, as if it were only a question of a judicial institution. In truth, it seems to me that this is the least portion of the subject to be preoccupied with; the jury is before everything a political institution; one ought to consider it as a mode of the sovereignty of the people; one must reject it entirely when one resists the sovereignty of the people, or place it in relation to the other laws that establish this sovereignty. The jury forms the part of the nation charged with assuring the execution of the laws, as the houses [of the legislature] are the part of the nation charged with making the laws; and in order that society be governed in a fixed and uniform manner, it is necessary that the list of jurors extend or contract with that of electors. It is this point of view that, according to me, ought always to attract the principal attention of the legislator. The rest is so to speak incidental.

I am so convinced that the jury is a political institution before everything that I still consider it in that manner when it is applied in a civil matter.

Laws are always unstable as long as they do not lean on mores; mores form the sole resistant and lasting power in a people.

When the jury is reserved for criminal affairs, the people see it act only from time to time and in particular cases; they are habituated to doing without it in the ordinary course of life, and they consider it as one means and not as the sole means of obtaining justice.[6]

When, on the contrary, the jury is extended to civil affairs, its application falls before one's eyes at each instant; then it touches all interests; each comes to cooperate in its action; it thus penetrates into the usages of life; it bends

*See AT's note XVII, page 697.
6. This is true with greater reason when the jury is only applied to certain criminal affairs.

the human mind to its forms, and is so to speak intermingled with the very idea of justice.

The institution of the jury, limited to criminal affairs, is therefore always in peril; once introduced into civil matters, it defies time and the efforts of men. If one had been able to take away the jury from the mores of the English as easily as from their laws, it would have succumbed entirely under the Tudors. It is therefore the civil jury that really saved the freedoms of England.

In whatever manner the jury is applied, it cannot fail to exert a great influence on the national character; but that influence is infinitely increased the more it is introduced in civil matters.

The jury, and above all the civil jury, serves to give to the minds of all citizens a part of the habits of mind of the judge; and these habits are precisely those that best prepare the people to be free.

It spreads to all classes respect for the thing judged and the idea of right. Remove these two things, and love of independence will be no more than a destructive passion.

It teaches men the practice of equity. Each, in judging his neighbor, thinks that he could be judged in his turn. That is above all true of the jury in a civil matter; there is almost no one who fears being the object of a criminal prosecution one day; but everyone can have a lawsuit.

The jury teaches each man not to recoil before responsibility for his own acts—a virile disposition without which there is no political virtue.

It vests each citizen with a sort of magistracy; it makes all feel that they have duties toward society to fulfill and that they enter into its government. In forcing men to occupy themselves with something other than their own affairs, it combats individual selfishness, which is like the blight of societies.

The jury serves incredibly to form the judgment and to augment the natural enlightenment of the people. There, in my opinion, is its greatest advantage. One ought to consider it as a school, free of charge and always open, where each juror comes to be instructed in his rights, where he enters into daily communication with the most instructed and most enlightened members of the elevated classes, where the laws are taught to him in a practical manner and are put within reach of his intelligence by the efforts of the attorneys, the advice of the judge, and the very passions of the parties. I think that the practical intelligence and good political sense of the Americans must principally be attributed to the long use that they have made of the jury in civil matters.

I do not know if the jury is useful to those who have lawsuits, but I am sure that it is very useful to those who judge them. I regard it as one of the most efficacious means society can make use of for the education of the people.

What precedes applies to all nations; but here follows what is special to Americans and to democratic peoples generally.

I said above that in democracies lawyers, and among them magistrates, form the sole aristocratic body that can moderate the movements of the people. This aristocracy is vested with no material power; it exerts its conservative influence only on minds. Now, it is in the institution of the civil jury that it finds the principal sources of its power.

In criminal cases, when society struggles against one man, the jury is brought to see in the judge the passive instrument of the social power, and it distrusts his advice. In addition, criminal cases rest entirely on simple facts that good sense easily comes to appreciate. On this terrain, judge and juror are equal.

It is not the same in civil cases; then the judge appears as a disinterested arbiter between the passions of the parties. The jurors view him with confidence, and they listen to him with respect; for here his intelligence entirely dominates theirs. It is he who unfolds before them the various arguments with which their memories have been tired, and he who takes them by the hand to direct them through the turns of the proceeding; it is he who circumscribes them to the point of fact and teaches them the response that they ought to make to the question of law. His influence over them is almost boundless.

Finally, must I say why I feel myself so little moved by arguments drawn from the incapacity of jurors in civil matters?

In civil cases, at least every time that it is not an issue of questions of fact, the jury has only the appearance of a judicial body.

The jurors pronounce the ruling that the judge has rendered. To this ruling, they lend the authority of the society that they represent, and he, that of reason and of the law.*

In England and America, judges exert an influence on the fate of criminal cases that the French judge has never known. It is easy to understand the reason for this difference: the English or American magistrate has established his power in civil matters; he only exercises it later in another theater; he does not acquire it there.

There are cases, and these are often the most important, where the American judge has the right to pronounce alone.[7] Then he finds himself, by the occasion, in the position in which the French judge habitually finds himself; but his moral power is much greater indeed: the memories of the jury follow

---

*See AT's note XVIII, page 698.

7. Federal judges almost always settle alone questions that touch the government of the country more nearly.

him still, and his voice has almost as much power as that of the society of which the jurors were the organ.

His influence extends well beyond the precincts of the courts: in the relaxations of private life as in the work of political life, in the public square as in the heart of legislatures, the American judge constantly finds men around him who are habituated to seeing in his intelligence something superior to theirs; and after being exercised in trials, his power makes itself felt on all habits of mind and even on the very souls of those who have taken part with him in judging them.

The jury, which seems to diminish the rights of the magistracy, therefore really founds its empire, and there is no country where judges are as powerful as those where the people comes into a share of their privileges.

It is above all with the aid of the jury in civil matters that the American magistracy makes what I have called the spirit of the lawyer penetrate down to the lowest ranks of society.

Thus the jury, which is the most energetic means of making the people reign, is also the most efficacious means of teaching them to reign.

Chapter 9 ON THE PRINCIPAL CAUSES
TENDING TO MAINTAIN A DEMOCRATIC
REPUBLIC IN THE UNITED STATES

A democratic republic subsists in the United States. The principal goal of this book has been to make the causes of this phenomenon understood.

Among these causes are several that the flow of my subject has carried me away from despite myself, and that I have only indicated from afar in passing. There are others with which I could not be occupied; and those I have been permitted to dwell on have remained behind me almost buried under the details.

I thought, therefore, that before going further and speaking of the future, I ought to gather in a narrow frame all the reasons that explain the present.

In this kind of résumé I shall be brief, for I shall take care to make the reader recall only very summarily what he already knows, and I shall choose only the principal facts among those I have not yet had occasion to set forth.

I have thought that all the causes tending to the maintenance of a democratic republic in the United States can be reduced to three:

The particular and accidental situation in which Providence has placed the Americans forms the first;

The second comes from the laws;

The third flows from habits and mores.

ON THE ACCIDENTAL OR PROVIDENTIAL CAUSES CONTRIBUTING TO THE MAINTENANCE OF A DEMOCRATIC REPUBLIC IN THE UNITED STATES

The Union has no neighbors.—No great capital.—The Americans had the chance of birth working for them.—America is an empty country.—How this circumstance powerfully serves the maintenance of the democratic republic.—Manner in which the wilderness of America is peopled.—Avidity with which the Anglo-Americans take possession of the solitudes of the New World.—Influence of material well-being on the political opinions of the Americans.

There are a thousand circumstances independent of men's will that facilitate the democratic republic in the United States. Some are known, others are easy to make known: I shall limit myself to setting forth the principal ones.

The Americans have no neighbors and consequently no great wars, financial crisis, ravages, or conquest to fear; they need neither large taxes, nor a numerous army, nor great generals; they have almost nothing to dread from a scourge more terrible for republics than all those things put together—military glory.

How can one deny the incredible influence that military glory exerts on the spirit of a people? General Jackson,* whom the Americans have twice chosen to place at their head, is a man of violent character and middling capacity; nothing in all the course of his career had ever proved that he had the requisite qualities to govern a free people: so the majority of the enlightened classes of the Union had always been opposed to him. What therefore placed him in the seat of the president and still keeps him there? The memory of a victory carried off by him before the walls of New Orleans twenty years ago;† now, this victory of New Orleans is a very ordinary feat of arms with which one could long be occupied only in a country not given to battles; and the people that thus allows itself to be carried away by the prestige of glory is surely the coldest, the most calculating, the least military, and if I can express myself so, the most prosaic of all the peoples in the world.

*See *DA* I 2.2.
†The Battle of New Orleans, won over the British in 1815.

America does not have a great capital[1] whose direct or indirect influence makes itself felt over the whole extent of its territory, which I consider to be one of the first causes of the maintenance of republican institutions in the United States. In towns, men can scarcely be prevented from concerting with each other, from getting heated up in common, from taking sudden and passionate resolves. Towns form as it were great assemblies of which all inhabitants are members. There the people exert a prodigious influence on their magistrates, and often they execute their will without an intermediary.

To submit the provinces to the capital is therefore to put the destiny of the whole empire not only in the hands of a portion of the people, which is unjust, but also in the hands of the people acting by itself, which is very dangerous. The preponderance of capitals therefore makes a serious breach in the representative system. It makes modern republics fall into the defect of the republics of antiquity, which all perished for not having known this system.

It would be easy for me to enumerate a large number of other secondary causes here that have favored the establishment and assured the maintenance of the democratic republic in the United States. But in the midst of this host of happy circumstances, I perceive two principal ones, and I hasten to point them out.

I already said before that I saw in the origin of the Americans, in what I called their point of departure, the first and the most efficacious of all the causes to which the current prosperity of the United States can be attributed.* Americans had the chance of birth working for them: their fathers had

---

*DA I 1.2.

1. America does not yet have a great capital, but it already has very great towns. In 1830 Philadelphia counted 161,000 inhabitants, and New York, 202,000. The low people who inhabit these vast cities form a populace more dangerous than that even of Europe. It is composed first of freed Negroes, whom law and opinion condemn to a state of hereditary degradation and misery. One also encounters within it a multitude of Europeans whom misfortune and misconduct drive toward the shores of the New World each day; these men bring our greatest vices to the United States, and they have none of the interests that could combat their influence. Inhabiting the country without being citizens of it, they are ready to take part in all the passions that agitate it; so for some time we have seen serious riots break out in Philadelphia and New York. Such disorders are unknown in the rest of the country, which is not anxious about them, because up to the present, the population of the towns has not exercised any power or influence on the countryside.

I nevertheless regard the greatness of certain American cities and, above all, the nature of their inhabitants, as a genuine danger that threatens the future of the democratic republics of the New World, and I do not fear to predict that it is through this that they will perish, unless their government comes to create an armed force that, while remaining submissive to the wills of the national majority, is still independent of the people of the towns and can reduce their excesses.

long since brought equality of conditions and of intelligence onto the soil they inhabited, from which the democratic republic would one day issue as from its natural source. This is still not all; with a republican social state, they willed to their descendants the most appropriate habits, ideas, and mores to make a republic flourish. When I think about what this original fact produced, it seems to me that I see the whole destiny of America contained in the first Puritan who landed on its shores, like the whole human race in the first man.

Among the fortunate circumstances that also favored the establishment and assured the maintenance of a democratic republic in the United States, the first in importance is the choice itself of the country that the Americans inhabit. Their fathers gave them the love of equality and of freedom, but it was God himself who, in leaving them a boundless continent, accorded them the means to remain equal and free for a long time.

General well-being favors the stability of all governments, but particularly of democratic government, which rests on the disposition of the greatest number, and principally on the disposition of those who are the most exposed to needs. When the people govern, it is necessary that they be happy in order for them not to overturn the state. Misery produces in them what ambition does in kings. Now, the material causes, independent of laws, that can lead to well-being are more numerous in America than they have been in any country in the world at any period in history.

In the United States, it is not only legislation that is democratic; nature itself works for the people.

Where does one find, among the memories of man, anything like what is taking place before our eyes in North America?

The celebrated societies of antiquity were all founded in the midst of enemy peoples whom one had to defeat so as to settle in their place. The moderns themselves found vast regions in some parts of South America inhabited by peoples less enlightened than they, but who had already appropriated the soil by cultivating it. To found their new states they had to destroy or enslave many populations, and they have made civilization blush from its triumphs.

But North America was inhabited only by wandering tribes who did not think of using the natural riches of the soil. North America was still, properly speaking, an empty continent, a wilderness land, that awaited inhabitants.

Everything about the Americans is extraordinary, their social state as well as their laws; but what is more extraordinary still is the soil that supports them.

When the land was delivered to men by the Creator, it was young and inexhaustible, but they were weak and ignorant; and when they had learned to take advantage of the treasures contained within it, they already covered its face, and soon they had to fight to acquire the right to possess a refuge and to repose there in freedom.

It is then that North America is discovered, as if God had held it in reserve and it had only just emerged from beneath the waters of the flood.

It presents, as in the first days of the creation, rivers whose source does not dry up, green and moist solitudes, boundless fields that the plowshare of the laborer has not yet turned. In this state, it is offered no longer to the isolated, ignorant, and barbaric man of the first ages, but to man already master of the most important secrets of nature, united with those like him, and instructed by an experience of fifty centuries.

At the moment I am speaking, thirteen million civilized Europeans are quietly spreading into the fertile wilderness whose resources and extent they themselves still do not know exactly. Three or four thousand soldiers push the wandering race of natives before them; behind the armed men advance woodcutters who pierce through the forests, ward off ferocious beasts, explore the course of rivers, and prepare the triumphant march of civilization across the wilderness.

Often in the course of this work I have alluded to the material well-being that the Americans enjoy; I have pointed to it as one of the great causes of the success of their laws. This reason had already been given by a thousand others before me: falling in a way before the senses of Europeans, it is the only one that has become popular among us. I shall therefore not dwell on a subject so often treated and so well understood; I shall only add a few new facts.

It is generally imagined that the wilderness of America is being peopled with the aid of the European emigrants who descend on the shores of the New World each year, while the American population grows and multiplies on the soil that its fathers occupied: that is a great error. The European who lands in the United States arrives there without friends and often without resources; he is obliged to hire out his services in order to live, and it is rare to see him go beyond the great industrial zone that extends the length of the ocean. One cannot open up the wilderness without capital or credit; before risking oneself in the midst of the forests, one's body must be habituated to the rigors of a new climate. It is therefore Americans who, abandoning the place of their birth daily, go to create vast domains in the distance. Thus the European quits his cottage to go to inhabit transatlantic shores, and the American who is born on this same coast plunges in turn into the solitudes of the center of America. This double movement of emigration never stops: it begins deep in Europe, it continues over the great ocean, it follows across the solitudes of the New World. Millions of men advance at once toward the same point on the horizon: their language, their religion, their mores differ, their goal is common. They were told that fortune is to be found somewhere toward the west, and they go off in haste to meet it.

Nothing can be compared to this continuous displacement of the human species, unless perhaps what happened at the fall of the Roman Empire. Then, as today, one saw men run all in a crowd toward the same point and meet each other tumultuously in the same places; but the designs of Providence were different. Each newcomer brought destruction and death in his wake; today each of them brings with him a seed of prosperity and life.

The long-term consequences of this migration of Americans toward the west are still hidden from us by the future, but the immediate results are easy to recognize: as a portion of the former inhabitants moves away each year from the states where they were born, it happens that these states, though they are getting older, are being populated very slowly; thus in Connecticut, which still has only fifty-nine inhabitants per square mile, the population has only grown by a quarter in forty years, whereas in England it has increased by a third during the same period. The emigrant from Europe therefore always lands in a half-full country, where industry lacks arms; he becomes well-off as a worker; his son goes to seek a fortune in an empty country, and he becomes a rich property owner. The first amasses the capital that the second turns to good account, and there is misery neither for the foreigner nor for the native.

Legislation in the United States favors the division of property as much as possible; but a cause more powerful than legislation prevents property from being divided beyond due measure.[2] They perceive it well in the states that are finally beginning to be filled. Massachusetts is the most densely populated region in the Union; they have eighty inhabitants per square mile there, which is infinitely less than in France, where one hundred sixty-two are gathered in the same space.

In Massachusetts, nevertheless, it is already rare that small estates are divided: the eldest generally takes the land; the younger ones go to seek a fortune in the wilderness.

The law has abolished the right of primogeniture; but one can say that Providence has reestablished it without anyone's having any complaint, and this time at least it does not offend justice.

By a single fact one will judge the enormous number of individuals who quit New England in this way to go move their homes into the wilderness. We have been assured that in 1830, there were thirty-six among the members

2. In New England the soil is partitioned into very small estates, but it is not further divided.

of Congress who were born in the little state of Connecticut. The population of Connecticut, which forms only a forty-third part of that of the United States, therefore furnished an eighth of its representatives.

The state of Connecticut itself, however, sends only five deputies to Congress: the thirty-one others appear there as representatives of the new states of the West. If these thirty-one individuals had resided in Connecticut, it is probable that instead of being wealthy property owners they would have remained small laborers, that they would have lived in obscurity without being able to open up a political career for themselves, and that, far from becoming useful legislators, they would have been dangerous citizens.

These considerations escape the minds of Americans no more than ours.

"It would be very unfounded to suppose," says Chancellor Kent in his *Treatise on American Law* (vol. 4, p. 380),* "that the evils of the equal partition of estates have been seriously felt in the United States, or that they have borne any proportion to the advantages of the policy, or that such evils are to be anticipated for generations to come. The extraordinary extent of our unsettled territories, the abundance of uncultivated land in the market, and the constant stream of emigration from the Atlantic to the interior states, operates sufficiently to keep paternal inheritances unbroken."

It would be difficult to depict the avidity with which the American throws himself on the immense prey that fortune offers him. To pursue it he braves without fear the arrow of the Indian and the maladies of the wilderness; the silence of the woods has nothing to astonish him, the approach of ferocious beasts does not move him: a passion stronger than love of life spurs him constantly. Before him lies an almost boundless continent, and one would say that, already afraid of losing his place in it, he hastens for fear of arriving too late. I have spoken of emigration from older states; but what shall I say of that from new ones? It is only fifty years since Ohio was founded; the greatest number of its inhabitants did not come into the world there; its capital has not been in existence for thirty years, and an immense extent of wild lands still covers its territory; yet already the population of Ohio has gone on the move again toward the West: most of those who descend onto the fertile prairies of Illinois are inhabitants of Ohio. These men have left their first native country to be well-off; they leave their second to be still better-off: almost everywhere they encounter fortune, but not happiness. Among them the desire for well-being has become a restive and ardent passion that increases while it is being satisfied. They have long since broken the bonds that attached them to native soil; they have not formed others since

*Kent, *Commentaries,* vol. 4, 385.

then. For them, emigration began by being a need; today, it has become in their eyes a sort of game of chance, in which they love the sensation as much as the gain.

Sometimes man advances so quickly that the wilderness reappears behind him. The forest has only bent underneath his feet; as soon as he has passed, it recovers. It is not rare, when passing through the new states of the West, to encounter abandoned dwellings in the middle of the woods; often one discovers the debris of a hut in the deepest solitude, and one is astonished to come across partial clearings which attest at once to human power and human inconstancy. The ancient forest is not slow to push up new shoots among the abandoned fields, over the day-old ruins; animals retake possession of their empire: laughing, nature comes to cover over the vestiges of man with green branches and flowers, and hastens to make his ephemeral traces disappear.

I remember that in crossing one of the wilderness districts that still cover the state of New York, I reached the shore of a lake surrounded with forest, as if at the beginning of the world. A small island rose amid the waters. The woods that covered it, extending their foliage around it, hid its shore entirely. On the banks of the lake nothing told of the presence of man; only on the horizon did one perceive a column of smoke, going perpendicularly from the treetops to the clouds, which seemed to hang from the height of the heavens rather than to mount to them.

An Indian canoe was drawn up on the sand; I used it to go visit the island that had at first attracted my regard, and soon after I reached its shore. The entire island formed one of those delightful solitudes of the New World that almost make civilized man regret savage life. By its marvels, a vigorous vegetation told of the incomparable wealth of the soil. A profound silence reigned, as in all the wilderness of North America, interrupted only by the monotonous cooing of the wood pigeons or by the tapping of the green woodpeckers on the bark of trees. I was far indeed from believing that this place had once been inhabited, so much did nature still seem abandoned to itself; but when I reached the center of the island, I suddenly believed I had encountered the vestiges of man. Then I carefully examined all the surrounding objects, and soon I no longer doubted that a European had come to seek refuge in this place. But how his work had changed face! The wood that he had formerly cut in haste to make a shelter had since pushed up shoots; its fences had become live hedges, and his hut had been transformed into a grove. In the midst of these shrubs, one still perceived some stones blackened by fire around a small heap of cinders; doubtless this place was the hearth: the chimney, in crumbling, had covered it with debris. For some time I admired in silence the resources of nature and the weakness of man; and when finally I had to leave these enchanted places, I kept repeating sadly: What! already in ruins!

In Europe we habitually regard restiveness of mind, immoderate desire for wealth, extreme love of independence as great social dangers. It is precisely all these things that guarantee a long and peaceful future to the American republics. Without these restive passions, the population would be concentrated around certain places and would, as among us, soon feel needs difficult to satisfy. What a happy country is the New World, where man's vices are almost as useful to society as his virtues!

This exerts a great influence on the manner in which human actions are judged in the two hemispheres. Often the Americans call a praiseworthy industry what we name love of gain, and they see a certain cowardly heart in what we consider moderation of desires.

In France, one regards simplicity of taste, tranquillity of mores, the spirit of family, and love of one's birthplace as great guarantees of tranquillity and happiness for the state; but in America, nothing appears more prejudicial to society than virtues like these. The French of Canada, who have faithfully preserved the traditions of old mores, already have difficulty in living on their territory, and this small people, which has just been born, will soon be prey to the miseries of old nations. In Canada, the men who have the most enlightenment, patriotism, and humanity make extraordinary efforts to disgust the people with the simple happiness that still suffices for them. They celebrate the advantages of wealth, just as among us they would perhaps vaunt the charms of an honest mediocrity, and they put more care into spurring the human passions than elsewhere one makes efforts to calm them. To exchange the pure and tranquil pleasures that the native country offers even to the poor for the sterile enjoyments that well-being provides under a foreign sky; to flee the paternal hearth and the fields where one's ancestors rest; to abandon the living and the dead to run after fortune—there is nothing that merits more praise in their eyes.

In our time, America delivers to men a fund [of capital] always vaster than industry can put to work.

In America, therefore, one cannot give out enough enlightenment; for all the enlightenment, at the same time that it can be useful to whoever possesses it, also turns to the profit of those who do not have it. New needs are not to be feared there, since all needs are satisfied without trouble: one must not be afraid of giving rise to too many passions, since all passions find an easy and salutary nourishment; one cannot make men too free there, because they are almost never tempted to make a bad use of freedom.

The American republics in our day are like companies of merchants, formed to exploit in common the wilderness lands of the New World, and busy in a commerce that is prospering.

The passions that agitate the Americans most profoundly are commercial passions and not political passions, or rather, they carry the habits of trade into politics. They love order, without which affairs cannot prosper, and they particularly prize regularity of mores, on which good houses [of business] are founded; they prefer the good sense that creates great fortunes to the genius that often dissipates them; general ideas frighten their minds, accustomed to positive calculations, and among them, practice is more in honor than theory.

One must go to America to understand what power material well-being exerts on political actions and even on opinions themselves, which ought to be subject only to reason. It is among foreigners that one principally discovers the truth of this. Most of the emigrants from Europe bring into the New World that savage love of independence and change that so often arises in the midst of our miseries. I sometimes encountered in the United States Europeans who had once been obliged to flee their country because of their political opinions. All astonished me by their discourse; but one of them struck me more than any other. As I crossed one of the most remote districts of Pennsylvania, the night took me by surprise, and I went to ask refuge at the door of a wealthy planter: he was a Frenchman. He had me sit beside his hearth, and we set to discoursing freely, as befits people who find themselves in the depths of the woods two thousand leagues from the country that had seen them born. I was not ignorant that forty years before my host had been a great leveler and an ardent demagogue. His name had remained in history.*

I was therefore strangely surprised to hear him discuss the right of property as an economist, I was almost going to say a property owner, would have been able to do; he spoke of the necessary hierarchy that fortune establishes among men, of obedience to established law, of the influence of good mores in republics, and of the assistance that religious ideas lend to order and to freedom: he even came, as if inadvertently, to cite the authority of Jesus Christ in support of one of his political opinions.

In listening to him I wondered at the imbecility of human reason. That is true or false: how does one discover which amid the uncertainties of science and the diverse lessons of experience? A new fact comes up that dispels all my doubts. I was poor, here I am rich: if only well-being, in acting on my conduct, left my judgment in freedom! But no, my opinions are in fact changed with my fortune, and in the happy event from which I profit, I have really discovered the determining reason that I had lacked until then.

*The man's identity is unknown.

The influence of well-being is exerted still more freely on Americans than on foreigners. The American has always seen before his eyes order and public prosperity linked to one another and marching in the same step; he does not imagine that they can live separately: he therefore has nothing to forget and will not lose, like so many Europeans, what he owes to his early education.

ON THE INFLUENCE OF THE LAWS ON THE MAINTENANCE OF A DEMOCRATIC REPUBLIC IN THE UNITED STATES

Three principal causes of the maintenance of the democratic republic.—Federal form.—Township institutions.—Judicial power.

The principal goal of this book was to make the laws of the United States known; if this goal has been attained, the reader has already been able to judge for himself which among these laws really tend to maintain a democratic republic and which put it in danger. If I have not succeeded in the whole course of the book, I would succeed still less in one chapter.

I therefore do not wish to return to the course that I have already run through, and a few lines ought to suffice for me to summarize.

Three things seem to concur more than all others to maintain a democratic republic in the New World:

The first is the federal form that the Americans have adopted, which permits the Union to enjoy the power of a great republic and the security of a small one.

I find the second in the township institutions that, moderating the despotism of the majority, at the same time give the people the taste for freedom and the art of being free.

The third is encountered in the constitution of the judicial power. I have shown how the courts serve to correct the aberrations of democracy, and how, without ever being able to stop the movements of the majority, they succeed in slowing and directing them.

ON THE INFLUENCE OF MORES ON THE MAINTENANCE OF A DEMOCRATIC REPUBLIC IN THE UNITED STATES

I said above that I consider mores to be one of the great general causes to which the maintenance of a democratic republic in the United States can be attributed.*

---

* DA I 2.9, beginning.

I understand here the expression *mœurs* in the sense the ancients attached to the word *mores;* not only do I apply it to mores properly so-called, which one could call habits of the heart, but to the different notions that men possess, to the various opinions that are current in their midst, and to the sum of ideas of which the habits of the mind are formed.

I therefore comprehend under this word the whole moral and intellectual state of a people. My goal is not to make a picture of American mores; I limit myself at this moment to searching among them for what is favorable to the maintenance of political institutions.

ON RELIGION CONSIDERED AS A POLITICAL INSTITUTION; HOW IT SERVES POWERFULLY THE MAINTENANCE OF A DEMOCRATIC REPUBLIC AMONG THE AMERICANS

North America peopled by men who professed a democratic, republican Christianity.— Arrival of the Catholics.—Why in our day Catholics form the most democratic and the most republican class.

Next to each religion is a political opinion that is joined to it by affinity.

Allow the human mind to follow its tendency and it will regulate political society and the divine city in a uniform manner; it will seek, if I dare say it, to *harmonize* the earth with Heaven.

The greatest part of English America has been peopled by men who, after having escaped the authority of the pope, did not submit to any religious supremacy; they therefore brought to the New World a Christianity that I cannot depict better than to call it democratic and republican: this singularly favors the establishment of a republic and of democracy in affairs. From the beginning,* politics and religion were in accord, and they have not ceased to be so since.

Around fifty years ago, Ireland began to pour a Catholic population into the United States. For its part, American Catholicism made proselytes: today one encounters more than a million Christians in the Union who profess the truths of the Roman Church.

These Catholics show great fidelity in the practices of their worship and are full of ardor and zeal for their beliefs; nevertheless they form the most republican and democratic class there is in the United States. This fact surprises one at first approach, but reflection easily uncovers its hidden causes.

I think that it is wrong to regard the Catholic religion as a natural enemy

*Lit.: "principle."

of democracy. Among the different Christian doctrines, Catholicism appears to me, on the contrary, one of the most favorable to equality of conditions. Among Catholics, religious society is composed of only two elements: the priest and the people. The priest alone is raised above the faithful: everything is equal below him.

In the matter of dogmas, Catholicism places the same standard on all intellects; it forces the details of the same beliefs on the learned as well as the ignorant, the man of genius as well as the vulgar; it imposes the same practices on the rich as on the poor, inflicts the same austerities on the powerful as the weak; it compromises with no mortal, and applying the same measure to each human, it likes to intermingle all classes of society at the foot of the same altar, as they are intermingled in the eyes of God.

If Catholicism disposes the faithful to obedience, it does not therefore prepare them for inequality. I shall say the contrary of Protestantism, which generally brings men much less to equality than to independence.

Catholicism is like an absolute monarchy. Remove the prince and conditions are more equal in it than in republics.

It often happened that the Catholic priest left the sanctuary to enter society as a power, and that he came to seat himself there amid the social hierarchy; then sometimes he used his religious influence to assure the longevity of a political order of which he was a part: then also one could see Catholics become partisans of aristocracy by the spirit of religion.

But once the priests are turned away or turn themselves away from government as they do in the United States, there are no men more disposed by their beliefs than Catholics to carry the idea of equality of conditions into the political world.

If, therefore, Catholics in the United States are not carried violently by the nature of their beliefs toward democratic and republican opinions, at least they are not naturally opposed to them, and their social position as well as their small number bring them, as by a law, to embrace them.

Most Catholics are poor, and they need all citizens to govern in order to come to government themselves. Catholics are in the minority, and they need all rights to be respected to be assured of the free exercise of theirs. These two causes drive them even without their knowing it toward political doctrines that they would perhaps adopt with less eagerness if they were wealthy and predominant.

The Catholic clergy of the United States has not tried to struggle against this political tendency; rather, it seeks to justify it. Catholic priests in America have divided the intellectual world into two parts: in one, they have left revealed dogmas, and they submit to them without discussing them; in the other, they have placed political truth, and they think that God has abandoned it to the free inquiries of men. Thus Catholics in the United States are at once the most submissive of the faithful and the most independent of citizens.

One can say, therefore, that in the United States there is no single religious doctrine that shows itself hostile to democratic and republican institutions. All the clergy there hold to the same language; opinions are in accord with the laws, and there reigns so to speak only a single current in the human mind.

I was temporarily inhabiting one of the largest towns of the Union when I was invited to attend a political gathering whose purpose was to come to the assistance of the Poles and to get arms and money to them.

So I found two or three thousand persons gathered in a vast hall that had been prepared to receive them. Soon after, a priest clothed in his ecclesiastical habit advanced to the edge of the platform meant for orators. Those attending, after removing their hats, remained standing in silence, and he spoke in these words:

God Almighty! God of hosts! thou who did maintain the hearts and guide the arms of our fathers when they sustained the sacred rights of their national independence; thou who made them triumph over an odious oppression and granted our people the benefits of peace and freedom, O Lord! turn a favorable eye toward the other hemisphere; regard with pity an heroic people who today struggles as we did formerly for the defense of the same rights! Lord, who have created all men on the same model, do not permit despotism to come to deform thy work and to maintain inequality on earth. God Almighty! watch over the destiny of the Poles, render them worthy of being free; that thy wisdom reign in their counsels, that thy strength be in their arms; spread terror over their enemies, divide the powers that hatch their ruin, and do not permit the injustice to which the world has been witness for fifty years to be consummated today. Lord, who hold in thy powerful hand the hearts of peoples, like those of men, arouse allies to the sacred cause of right; make the French nation finally rise, and, leaving the repose in which its heads keep it, come to fight once again for the freedom of the world.

O Lord! never turn thy face away from us; permit us always to be the most religious people as well as the most free.

God Almighty, answer our prayer today; save the Poles. We ask this of thee in the name of thy much loved son, our Lord Jesus Christ, who died on the cross for the salvation of all men. Amen.

The whole assembly repeated *Amen* with reverence.

INDIRECT INFLUENCE THAT RELIGIOUS BELIEFS EXERT ON POLITICAL SOCIETY IN THE UNITED STATES

Christian morality found in all sects.—Influence of religion on the mores of Americans.—Respect for the marriage bond.—How religion confines the imagination of Americans within certain limits and moderates their passion for innovation.—Opinion of Americans about the political utility of religion.—Their efforts to extend and secure its empire.

I have just shown what the direct action of religion on politics is in the United States. Its indirect action seems to me more powerful still, and it is when it does not speak of freedom that it best teaches Americans the art of being free.

There is an innumerable multitude of sects in the United States. All differ in the worship one must render to the Creator, but all agree on the duties of men toward one another. Each sect therefore adores God in its manner, but all sects preach the same morality in the name of God. If it serves man very much as an individual that his religion be true, this is not so for society. Society has nothing to fear nor to hope from the other life; and what is most important to it is not so much that all citizens profess the true religion but that they profess a religion. Besides, all the sects in the United States are within the great Christian unity, and the morality of Christianity is everywhere the same.

It is permissible to think that a certain number of Americans follow their habits more than their convictions in the worship they render to God. In the United States, moreover, the sovereign is religious, and consequently hypocrisy ought to be common; America is, however, still the place in the world where the Christian religion has most preserved genuine powers over souls; and nothing shows better how useful and natural to man it is in our day, since the country in which it exercises the greatest empire is at the same time the most enlightened and most free.

I have said that American priests pronounce themselves in a general manner to be in favor of civil freedom without excepting even those who do not accept religious freedom; however, one does not see them lend their support to any political system in particular. They take care to keep themselves outside affairs and do not mix in the schemes of the parties. Therefore one cannot say that in the United States religion exerts an influence on the laws or on the details of political opinions, but it directs mores, and it is in regulating the family that it works to regulate the state.

I do not doubt for an instant that the great severity of mores that one remarks in the United States has its primary source in beliefs. Religion there is often powerless to restrain man in the midst of the innumerable temptations that fortune presents to him. It cannot moderate the ardor in him for enriching himself, which everything comes to excite, but it reigns as a sovereign over the soul of woman, and it is woman who makes mores. Of the world's countries, America is surely the one where the bond of marriage is most respected and where they have conceived the highest and most just idea of conjugal happiness.

In Europe, almost all the disorders of society are born around the domestic hearth, not far from the nuptial bed. It is there that men conceive their scorn for natural bonds and permitted pleasures, their taste for disorder, their restiveness of heart, their instability of desires. Agitated by the tumultuous passions that have often troubled his own dwelling, the European submits only with difficulty to the legislative powers of the state. When, on leaving the agitations of the political world, the American returns to the bosom of his family, he immediately meets the image of order and peace. There, all his pleasures are simple and natural, his joys innocent and tranquil; and as he arrives at happiness through regularity of life, he becomes habituated to regulating his opinions as well as his tastes without difficulty.

While the European seeks to escape his domestic sorrows by troubling society, the American draws from his home the love of order, which he afterwards brings into affairs of state.

In the United States religion not only regulates mores, but extends its empire over intelligence.

Among the Anglo-Americans, some profess Christian dogmas because they believe them, others because they are afraid of not looking like they believe them. Christianity therefore reigns without obstacles, on the admission of all; the result, as I have already said elsewhere,* is that everything is certain and fixed in the moral world, although the political world seems to be abandoned to the discussion and attempts of men. So the human spirit never perceives an unlimited field before itself: however bold it may be, from time to time it feels that it ought to halt before insurmountable barriers. Before innovating, it is forced to accept certain primary givens and to submit its boldest conceptions to certain forms that delay and halt it.

The imagination of Americans in its greatest leaps has therefore only a circumspect and uncertain step; its pace is hindered and its works are incomplete. These habits of restraint are to be found in political society and singularly favor the tranquillity of the people as well as the longevity of the institutions it has given itself. Nature and circumstances have made the inhabitant of the United States an audacious man; it is easy to judge of this when one sees the manner in which he pursues his fortune. If the spirit of the Ameri-

*DA I 1.2.

cans were free of all impediments, one would soon encounter among them the boldest innovators and the most implacable logicians in the world. But revolutionaries in America are obliged to profess openly a certain respect for the morality and equity of Christianity, which does not permit them to violate its laws easily when they are opposed to the execution of their designs; and if they could raise themselves above their own scruples, they would still feel they were stopped by those of their partisans. Up to now, no one has been encountered in the United States who dared to advance the maxim that everything is permitted in the interest of society. An impious maxim—one that seems to have been invented in a century of freedom to legitimate all the tyrants to come.

So, therefore, at the same time that the law permits the American people to do everything, religion prevents them from conceiving everything and forbids them to dare everything.

Religion, which, among Americans, never mixes directly in the government of society, should therefore be considered as the first of their political institutions; for if it does not give them the taste for freedom, it singularly facilitates their use of it.

It is also from this point of view that the inhabitants of the United States themselves consider religious beliefs. I do not know if all Americans have faith in their religion—for who can read to the bottom of hearts?—but I am sure that they believe it necessary to the maintenance of republican institutions. This opinion does not belong only to one class of citizens or to one party, but to the entire nation; one finds it in all ranks.

In the United States, when a political man attacks a sect, it is not a reason for the partisans even of that sect not to support him; but if he attacks all sects together, each flees him and he remains alone.

While I was in America, a witness presented himself to the assizes of the county of Chester (state of New York) and declared that he did not believe in the existence of God and the immortality of the soul. The presiding officer refused to accept his oath, given, he said, that the witness had destroyed in advance all the faith that could have been put in his words.[3] The newspapers reported the fact without commentary.

Americans so completely confuse Christianity and freedom in their minds

---

3. Here are the words in which the *New York Spectator* of August 23, 1831, reports the fact: "The court of common pleas of Chester county (New York) a few days since rejected a witness who declared his disbelief in the existence of God. The presiding judge remarked that he had not before been aware that there was a man living who did not believe in the existence of God; that this belief constituted the sanction of all testimony in a court of justice and that he knew of no case in a Christian country where a witness had been permitted to testify without such a belief." [Cited in English.]

that it is almost impossible to have them conceive of the one without the other; and among them, this is not one of those sterile beliefs that the past wills to the present and which seems less to live than to stagnate in the bottom of the soul.

I saw Americans associating to send priests into the new states of the West and to found schools and churches there; they fear that religion will be lost in the midst of the woods, and that the people growing up may not be as free as the one from which it has issued. I encountered wealthy inhabitants of New England who abandoned the land of their birth with the aim of going to lay the foundations of Christianity and freedom by the banks of the Mississippi or on the prairies of Illinois. Thus it is that in the United States religious zeal constantly warms itself at the hearth of patriotism. You think that these men act solely in consideration of the other life, but you are mistaken: eternity is only one of their cares. If you interrogate these missionaries of Christian civilization, you will be altogether surprised to hear them speak so often of the goods of this world, and to find the political where you believe you will see only the religious. "All American republics are in solidarity with one another," they will say to you; "if the republics of the West fell into anarchy or came under the yoke of despotism, the republican institutions that flourish on the edges of the Atlantic Ocean would be in great peril; we therefore have an interest in the new states' being religious so that they permit us to remain free."

Such are the opinions of Americans; but their error is clear: for, it is proven to me daily in a very learned manner that all is well in America except precisely the religious spirit that I admire; and I learn that on the other side of the ocean the freedom and happiness of the human species lack nothing except to believe with Spinoza in the eternity of the world and to assert with Cabanis that the brain secretes thought.* To that I have truly nothing to respond if not that those who hold to this language have not been in America, and have no more seen religious peoples than free peoples. I therefore await them on their return [from America].

There are people in France who consider republican institutions to be the temporary instrument of their greatness. They measure with their eyes the immense space that separates their vices and their miseries from power and wealth, and they would like to pile ruins into this abyss to try to fill it. Those people are to freedom what the condottieri of the Middle Ages were to the kings; they make war for their own account even as they bear his colors: the republic will at least live long enough to lift them out of their present

---

*The philosopher Benedict Spinoza (1632–1677) and the medical doctor Pierre-Jean Georges Cabanis (1757–1808), who authored several philosophic works.

degradation. It is not to them that I am speaking; but there are others who see in the republic a permanent and tranquil state, a necessary goal toward which ideas and mores carry modern societies each day, and who sincerely wish to prepare men to be free. When these attack religious beliefs, they follow their passions and not their interests. Despotism can do without faith, but freedom cannot. Religion is much more necessary in the republic they extol than in the monarchy they attack, and in democratic republics more than all others. How could society fail to perish if, while the political bond is relaxed, the moral bond were not tightened? And what makes a people master of itself if it has not submitted to God?

ON THE PRINCIPAL CAUSES THAT MAKE RELIGION POWERFUL IN AMERICA

Care that Americans have taken to separate church from state.—The laws, public opinion, the efforts of the priests* themselves cooperate to reach this result.—To this cause one must attribute the power that religion exerts over souls in the United States.—Why.—What is the natural state of men in the matter of religion in our day.—What particular and accidental cause is opposed in certain countries to men's conforming to this state.

The philosophers of the eighteenth century explained the gradual weakening of beliefs in an altogether simple fashion. Religious zeal, they said, will be extinguished as freedom and enlightenment increase. It is unfortunate that the facts do not accord with this theory.

There is a certain European population whose disbelief is equaled only by their brutishness and ignorance, whereas in America one sees one of the freest and most enlightened peoples in the world eagerly fulfill all the external duties of religion.

On my arrival in the United States it was the religious aspect of the country that first struck my eye. As I prolonged my stay, I perceived the great political consequences that flowed from these new facts.

Among us, I had seen the spirit of religion and the spirit of freedom almost always move in contrary directions. Here I found them united intimately with one another: they reigned together on the same soil.

I felt my desire to know the cause of this phenomenon growing daily.

To learn it, I interrogated the faithful of all communions; above all, I sought the society of priests, who keep the depositories of the different beliefs and who have a personal interest in their duration. The religion that I profess brought me together particularly with the Catholic clergy, and I was not slow to bond in a sort of intimacy with several of its members. To each of them I

---

*AT uses the term "priests" generally, referring to Protestant as well as Catholic clergy.

expressed my astonishment and exposed my doubts: I found that all these men differed among themselves only on details; but all attributed the peaceful dominion that religion exercises in their country principally to the complete separation of church and state. I do not fear to affirm that during my stay in America I did not encounter a single man, priest or layman, who did not come to accord on this point.

This led me to examine more attentively than I had until then the position that American priests occupy in political society. I learned with surprise that they did not fill any public post.[4] I did not see a single one in the administration, and I discovered that they were not even represented within the assemblies.

The law in several states had closed any political career to them;[5] opinion did so in all the others.

When I finally came to inquire what the mind of the clergy itself was, I perceived that most of its members seemed to distance themselves from power voluntarily and take a sort of professional pride in remaining strangers to it.

I heard them anathematize ambition and bad faith, whatever might be the political opinions with which these took care to cover themselves. But I learned in listening to them that men cannot be condemnable in the eyes of God because of these same opinions when they are sincere, and that there is no more sin in erring in matters of government than in being mistaken about the manner in which one must build a dwelling or plow a furrow.

I saw them separate themselves carefully from all parties, and avoid contact with them with all the ardor of personal interest.

These facts served to prove to me that I had been told the truth. Then I wanted to bring the facts back to the causes: I wondered how it could happen that in diminishing the apparent force of a religion one came to increase its real power, and I believed that it was not impossible to discover this.

The short space of sixty years will never confine the whole imagination of man; the incomplete joys of this world will never suffice for his heart. Alone

4. Unless one gives this name to the offices that many of them occupy in the schools. The greater part of education is entrusted to the clergy.

5. See the Constitution of New York [1821], art. 7, sec. 4; Constitution of North Carolina [1776], art. 31; Constitution of Virginia; Constitution of South Carolina [1790], art. 1, sec. 23; Constitution of Kentucky [1799], art. 2, sec. 26; Constitution of Tennessee [1796], art. 8, sec. 1; Constitution of Louisiana, art. 2, sec. 22. The article of the Constitution of New York is conceived thus:

Ministers of the Gospel, being by their profession consecrated to the service of God and given to the care of directing souls, ought not to be troubled in the exercise of these important duties; consequently no minister of the Gospel or priest, to whatever sect he may belong, shall be able to be vested with any public offices, civil or military.

among all the beings, man shows a natural disgust for existence and an immense desire to exist: he scorns life and fears nothingness. These different instincts constantly drive his soul toward contemplation of another world, and it is religion that guides it there. Religion is therefore only a particular form of hope, and it is as natural to the human heart as hope itself. Only by a kind of aberration of the intellect and with the aid of a sort of moral violence exercised on their own nature do men stray from religious beliefs; an invincible inclination leads them back to them. Disbelief is an accident; faith alone is the permanent state of humanity.

In considering religions from a purely human point of view, one can therefore say that all religions draw from man himself an element of strength that can never fail them, because it depends on one of the constituent principles of human nature.

I know that there are times when religion can add to the influence that is proper to it the artificial power of the laws and the support of the material powers that direct society. One has seen religions intimately united with earthly governments, dominating souls by terror and by faith at the same time; but when a religion contracts an alliance like this, I do not fear to say that it acts as a man would: it sacrifices the future with a view to the present, and in obtaining a power that is not due to it, it risks its legitimate power.

When a religion seeks to found its empire only on the desire for immortality that torments the hearts of all men equally, it can aim at universality; but when it comes to be united with a government, it must adopt maxims that are applicable only to certain peoples. So, therefore, in allying itself with a political power, religion increases its power over some and loses the hope of reigning over all.

As long as a religion is supported only by sentiments that are the consolation of all miseries, it can attract the hearts of the human race to it. Mixed with the bitter passions of this world, it is sometimes constrained to defend allies given it by interest rather than love; and it must repel as adversaries men who often still love it, while they are combating those with whom it has united. Religion, therefore, cannot share the material force of those who govern without being burdened with a part of the hatreds to which they give rise.

The political powers that appear the best established have as a guarantee of their longevity only the opinions of a generation, the interests of a century, often the life of one man. One law can modify the social state that seems the most definitive and the best consolidated, and with it everything changes.

The powers of society are all more or less fugitive, as are our years on earth; they rapidly succeed each other like the various cares of life; and no government has ever been seen to be supported by an invariable disposition of the human heart or founded on an immortal interest.

As long as a religion finds its force in the sentiments, instincts, and passions that one sees reproduced in the same manner in all periods of history, it defies the effort of time, or at least it can only be destroyed by another religion. But when religion wishes to be supported by the interests of this world, it becomes almost as fragile as all the powers on earth. Alone, it can hope for immortality; bound to ephemeral powers, it follows their fortune and often falls with the passions of a day that sustain them.

In uniting with different political powers, religion can therefore contract only an onerous alliance. It does not need their assistance to live, and in serving them it can die.

The danger that I have just pointed out exists in all times, but it is not always so visible.

There are centuries in which governments appear to be immortal, and others in which one would say that the existence of society is more fragile than that of one man.

Certain constitutions maintain citizens in a sort of lethargic slumber, and others deliver them to feverish agitation.

When governments seem so strong and laws so stable, men do not perceive the danger that religion can risk by uniting with power.

When governments show themselves so weak and laws so changeable, the peril strikes every eye, but then there is often no longer time to escape it. One must therefore learn to perceive it from afar.

Insofar as a nation takes on a democratic social state, and societies are seen to incline toward republics, it becomes more and more dangerous for religion to unite with authority; for the time approaches when power is going to pass from hand to hand, when political theories will succeed one another, when men, laws, and constitutions themselves will disappear or be modified daily—and this lasting not only for a time, but constantly. Agitation and instability are due to the nature of democratic republics, just as immobility and sleep form the law of absolute monarchies.

If the Americans, who change their head of state every four years, who every two years make a choice of new legislators and replace provincial administrators each year; if the Americans, who have delivered the political world to the attempts of innovators, had not placed their religion somewhere outside of that, what could it hold onto in the ebb and flow of human opinions? In the midst of the parties' struggle, where would the respect be that is due it? What would become of its immortality when everything around it was perishing?

American priests have perceived this truth before all others, and they conform their behavior to it. They saw that they had to renounce religious influence if they wanted to acquire a political power, and they preferred to lose the support of power rather than share in its vicissitudes.

In America, religion is perhaps less powerful than it has been in certain times and among certain peoples, but its influence is more lasting. It is reduced to its own strength, which no one can take away from it; it acts in one sphere only, but it covers the whole of it and dominates it without effort.

I hear voices in Europe arising from all sides; they deplore the absence of beliefs and they wonder what means will give back to religion some remnant of its former power.

It seems to me that one must first inquire attentively into what ought to be, in our day, *the natural state* of men in the matter of religion. Then, knowing what we can hope and have to fear, we would perceive clearly the goal toward which our efforts ought to tend.

Two great dangers menace the existence of religions: schisms and indifference.

In centuries of fervor, it sometimes happens that men abandon their religion, but they escape its yoke only to submit to that of another. Faith changes its object, it does not die. Then the old religion excites either ardent love or implacable hatred in all hearts; some quit it with anger, others attach themselves to it with a new ardor: beliefs differ, irreligion is unknown.

But it is not the same when a religious belief is undermined silently by doctrines that I shall call negative, since in affirming the falseness of one religion they do not establish the truth of any other.

Then prodigious revolutions are worked in the human mind without the apparent aid of man's passions and so to speak without his suspecting them. One sees men who let the object of their dearest hopes escape almost by forgetting. Carried along by an insensible current against which they do not have the courage to struggle and to which they nonetheless yield with regret, they abandon the faith that they love to follow the doubt that leads them to despair.

In the centuries we have just described, beliefs are abandoned in coldness rather than hate; they are not rejected, they leave you. In ceasing to believe religion true, the unbeliever continues to judge it useful. Considering religious beliefs under a human aspect, he recognizes their empire over mores, their influence on laws. He understands how they can make men live in peace and prepare them gently for death. He therefore regrets his faith after he has lost it, and deprived of a good of which he knows the entire value, he fears to take it away from those who still possess it.

For his part, he who continues to believe does not fear exposing his faith to all eyes. In those who do not share his hopes he sees unfortunates rather than adversaries; he knows that he can acquire their esteem without following their example; he is therefore not at war with anyone; and not considering the society in which he lives as an arena where religion must constantly struggle against a thousand relentless enemies, he loves his contemporaries at the same time that he condemns their weaknesses and is afflicted by their errors.

With those who do not believe hiding their disbelief and those who believe showing their faith, a public opinion in favor of religion is produced; people love it, sustain it, and honor it, and one must penetrate to the bottom of their souls to discover the wounds that it has received.

The mass of men, whom religious sentiment never abandons, see nothing, then, that turns them aside from established beliefs. The instinct for another life leads them without difficulty to the foot of altars and delivers their hearts to the precepts and consolations of faith.

Why is this picture not applicable to us?

I perceive men among us who have ceased to believe in Christianity without attaching themselves to any religion.

I see others who are halted in doubt and already no longer pretend to believe.

Further, I encounter Christians who still believe and do not dare to say it.

In the midst of these tepid friends and ardent adversaries, I finally discover a few of the faithful ready to brave all obstacles and scorn all dangers for their beliefs. They have done violence to human weakness in order to rise above common opinion. Carried away by this effort, they no longer know precisely where they ought to halt. As they have seen that in their native country the first use that man has made of independence was to attack religion, they fear their contemporaries and turn away in terror from the freedom that they pursue. Disbelief appears to them to be a new thing, and they envelop all that is new in the same hatred. They are therefore at war with their century and their country, and in each opinion professed there they see a necessary enemy of faith.

Such ought not to be the natural state of men in the matter of religion in our day.

One encounters among us, therefore, an accidental and particular cause that prevents the human spirit from following its inclination, and pushes it beyond the limits within which it ought naturally to halt.

I am profoundly convinced that this particular and accidental cause is the intimate union of politics and religion.

The unbelievers of Europe hound Christians as political enemies rather than as religious adversaries: they hate faith as the opinion of a party much more than as an erroneous belief; and it is less the representative of God that they repel in the priest than the friend of power.

In Europe, Christianity has permitted itself to be intimately united with the powers of the earth. Today these powers are falling and it is almost buried under their debris. It is a living [thing] that someone wanted to attach to the dead: cut the bonds that hold it back and it will rise again.

I am ignorant of what one would have to do to give back the energy of youth to European Christianity. God alone could do it; but at least it depends on men to allow to faith the use of all the strength it still preserves.

HOW THE ENLIGHTENMENT, THE HABITS, AND THE PRACTICAL EXPERIENCE OF THE AMERICANS CONTRIBUTE TO THE SUCCESS OF DEMOCRATIC INSTITUTIONS

What one ought to understand by the enlightenment of the American people.—The human mind has received a less profound culture in the United States than in Europe.— But no one has remained in ignorance.—Why.—Rapidity with which thought circulates in the half-wilderness states of the West.—How practical experience serves Americans even more than literary knowledge.

In a thousand places in this work I have had readers note what has been the influence exerted by the enlightenment and the habits of the Americans on the maintenance of their political institutions. Few new things, therefore, now remain for me to say.

Up to the present, America has had only a very few remarkable writers; it has not had great historians and does not count one poet. Its inhabitants look on literature properly so-called with a sort of disfavor; and there are towns of the third order in Europe that publish more literary works each year than the twenty-four states of the Union taken together.

The American mind turns away from general ideas; it does not direct itself toward theoretical discoveries. Politics itself and industry cannot bring it to them. In the United States, new laws are constantly made; but great writers have still not been found to inquire into the general principles of the laws.

The Americans have jurisconsults and commentators; they lack publicists;* and in politics they give to the world examples rather than lessons.

It is the same for the mechanical arts.

In America, they apply the inventions of Europe shrewdly, and after per-

---

*Jurisconsults are legal advisors or jurists; commentators are legal writers; publicists are experts in public or international law.

fecting them, they adapt them marvelously to the needs of the country. Men there are industrious, but they do not cultivate the science of industry. One finds good workers and few inventors. Fulton* hawked his genius among foreign peoples for a long time before being able to devote it to his country.

Whoever wants to judge what is the state of enlightenment among the Anglo-Americans, therefore, is exposed to seeing the same object under two different aspects. If he pays attention only to the learned, he will be astonished at their small number; and if he counts the ignorant, the American people will seem to him the most enlightened people on earth.

The population as a whole is placed between these two extremes; I have already said it elsewhere.†

In New England, each citizen receives the elementary notions of human knowledge; in addition, he learns what the doctrines and the proofs of his religion are: he is made familiar with the history of his native country and the principal features of the constitution that governs it. In Connecticut and Massachusetts, it is very rare to find a man who knows all these things imperfectly, and whoever is absolutely ignorant of them is in a way a phenomenon.

When I compare the Greek and Roman republics to these republics of America, the manuscript libraries of the first and their coarse populace, to the thousand newspapers that crisscross the second and the enlightened people who inhabit them; when I think next of all the efforts that are still made to judge the one with the aid of the others and to foresee by what happened two thousand years ago what will happen in our day, I am tempted to burn my books so as to apply only new ideas to a social state so new.

Furthermore, one must not extend indiscriminately to the whole Union what I say about New England. The farther one moves to the west or toward the south, the more instruction of the people diminishes. In the states that neighbor the Gulf of Mexico, as among us, a certain number of individuals are found who are strangers to the elements of human knowledge; but one would seek in vain in the United States for a single district that is plunged into ignorance. The reason for this is simple: the peoples of Europe have left the shadows and barbarism to advance toward civilization and enlightenment. Their progress has been unequal: some have run down this course, others have in a way only walked along it; several have halted and still sleep on the road.

It has not been the same in the United States.

---

*Robert Fulton (1765–1815) ran the first commercially successful steamboat, and is usually considered its inventor. See AT's marginal note in *Oeuvres* 2: 1018.

†*DA* I 1.3.

The Anglo-Americans arrived quite civilized on the soil that their posterity occupies; they did not have to learn, it was enough for them not to forget.
Now, it is the sons of these same Americans who, each year, bring knowledge
already acquired and esteem for learning, together with their dwellings, into
the wilderness. Education has made them feel the utility of enlightenment
and has put them in a position to transmit this same enlightenment to their
descendants. In the United States, therefore, society has no childhood; it is
born at the age of manhood.

Americans do not use the word "peasant"; they do not employ the word
because they do not have the idea; the ignorance of the first ages, the simplicity of the fields, the rusticity of the village have not been preserved among
them, and they conceive neither the virtues nor the vices, nor the coarse
habits, nor the naive graces of a civilization being born.

At the extreme limits of the confederated states, on the boundaries of
society and wilderness, stands a population of hardy adventurers who, in
order to flee the poverty ready to afflict them under their fathers' roofs, have
no fear of plunging into the solitudes of America and seeking a new native
country there. Scarcely arrived at a place that will serve as a refuge for him,
the pioneer hastily fells some trees and raises a cabin under the leaves. Nothing offers a more miserable aspect than these isolated dwellings. The traveler
who approaches them toward evening perceives from afar the flame of the
hearth glittering through the walls; and at night, if the wind comes up, he
hears the roof of foliage rustling in the midst of the trees of the forest. Who
would not believe that this poor cottage serves as a refuge for coarseness and
ignorance? Yet one must not establish any relation between the pioneer and
the place that serves as his refuge. All is primitive and savage around him,
but he is so to speak the result of eighteen centuries of work and experience.
He wears the clothing of the towns, he speaks their language; he knows the
past, is curious about the future, argues about the present; he is a very civilized man who, for a time, submits to living in the middle of the woods, and
who plunges into the wilderness of the New World with his Bible, a hatchet,
and newspapers.

It is difficult to imagine how incredibly rapidly thought circulates within
this wilderness.[6]

6. I traveled over a part of the frontiers of the United States in a kind of uncovered cart that
was called the mail coach. We advanced briskly night and day by scarcely cleared paths in the
middle of immense forests of green trees; when the darkness became impenetrable, my guide lit
branches of larch and we continued our route by their light. Here and there one encountered a
cottage in the middle of the woods: it was the post office. The courier threw an enormous packet
of letters at the door of the isolated dwelling and we resumed our course at a gallop, leaving to
each inhabitant in the neighborhood the care of coming to seek his part of the treasure.

I do not believe that so great an intellectual movement is produced in the most enlightened and most populated cantons of France.[7]

One cannot doubt that in the United States the instruction of the people serves powerfully to maintain a democratic republic. It will be so, I think, everywhere that the instruction that enlightens the mind is not separated from the education that regulates mores.

Still, I do not exaggerate this advantage and I am still further from believing, as do a great number of people in Europe, that it suffices to teach men to read and to write to make them citizens immediately.

Genuine enlightenment arises principally from experience, and if one had not habituated the Americans little by little to govern themselves, the literary knowledge that they possess would not greatly help them today to succeed in it.

I lived much with the people of the United States, and I cannot say how much I admired their experience and their good sense.

Do not lead an American to speak of Europe; he will ordinarily show great presumption and a rather silly pride. He will be content with those general and indefinite ideas that in all countries are of such great help to the ignorant. But ask him about his country, and you will see the cloud that envelops his intellect suddenly dissipate: his language becomes clear, clean, and precise, like his thought. He will teach you what his rights are and what means he will use to exercise them; he will know according to what usages the political world conducts itself. You will perceive that the rules of administration are known to him and that he has made himself familiar with the mechanisms of the laws. The inhabitant of the United States has not drawn his practical knowledge and positive notions from books: his literary education could prepare him to receive them, but it did not provide them to him.

It is from participating in legislation that the American learns to know the laws, from governing that he instructs himself in the forms of government. The great work of society is accomplished daily before his eyes and so to speak in his hands.

In the United States, the sum of men's education is directed toward poli-

---

7. In 1832 each inhabitant of Michigan furnished 1 franc 22 centimes for the tax on letters, and each inhabitant of Florida, 1 franc 5 centimes. (See *National Calendar*, 1833, p. 244.) [Force, *National Calendar*, 249.] In the same year, each inhabitant of the [French] Département du Nord paid to the state 1 franc 4 centimes for the same object. (See *Compte général de l'administration des finances*, 1833, p. 623.) Now, in this period Michigan still had only seven inhabitants per square league, and Florida, five: instruction was less widespread and activity less great in these two districts than in most of the states of the Union, whereas the Département du Nord, which contains 3,400 individuals per square league, forms one of the most enlightened and most industrial sections of France.

tics; in Europe, its principal goal is to prepare for private life. The action of citizens in affairs is a fact too rare to be foreseen in advance.

When one casts a glance at the two societies, these differences are revealed even in their external aspect.

In Europe we often have the ideas and habits of private existence enter into public life, and as we pass suddenly from the interior of the family into the government of the state, one often sees us discuss the great interests of society in the same manner as we converse with our friends.

Americans, on the contrary, almost always carry the habits of public life into private life. Among them the idea of the jury is discovered in school games, and one finds parliamentary forms even in the ordering of a banquet.

THAT THE LAWS SERVE TO MAINTAIN A DEMOCRATIC REPUBLIC IN THE UNITED STATES MORE THAN PHYSICAL CAUSES, AND MORES MORE THAN LAWS

All the peoples of America have a democratic social state.—Nonetheless, democratic institutions are sustained only among the Anglo-Americans.—The Spanish of South America, as favored by physical nature as the Anglo-Americans, cannot support a democratic republic.—Mexico, which adopted the Constitution of the United States, cannot do it.— Anglo-Americans in the West support it with more difficulty than in the East. Reasons for these differences.

I have said* that one must attribute the maintenance of democratic institutions in the United States to circumstances, to laws, and to mores.[8]

Most Europeans know only the first of these three causes, and they give it a preponderant importance that it does not have.

It is true that the Anglo-Americans brought equality of conditions to the New World. Never will one encounter among them either commoners or nobles; the prejudices of birth have always been as unknown there as professional prejudices. The social state thus being democratic, democracy had no trouble in establishing its empire.

But this fact is not particular to the United States; almost all the colonies of America were founded by men equal among themselves or who became so from inhabiting them. There is not a single part of the New World where Europeans have been able to create an aristocracy.

---

*At the beginning of this chapter.

8. I recall here to the reader the general sense in which I take the word *mores;* I understand by this word the sum of the intellectual and moral dispositions that men bring to the state of society.

Nevertheless democratic institutions prosper only in the United States.

The American Union has no enemies to combat. It is alone in the midst of the wilderness like an island in the ocean.

But nature had isolated the Spanish of South America in the same manner, and that isolation did not prevent them from keeping armies. They made war among themselves when foreigners were lacking. It is only Anglo-American democracy that, up to the present, has been able to maintain itself in peace.

The territory of the Union presents a boundless field to human activity; it offers inexhaustible nourishment for industry and work. Love of wealth therefore takes the place of ambition, and well-being extinguishes the ardor of parties.

But in what portion of the world does one encounter wilderness more fertile, greater rivers, wealth more intact and more inexhaustible than in South America? Nevertheless, South America cannot support democracy. If, for peoples to be happy, it were enough to have been placed in a corner of the universe and to be able to spread at will over uninhabited lands, the Spanish of southern America would not have to complain of their lot. And if they did not enjoy the same happiness as inhabitants of the United States, they ought at least to have made themselves envied by the peoples of Europe. There are nevertheless no nations on earth more miserable than those of South America.

Thus, not only can physical causes not lead to analogous results in Americans of the South and of the North, but they cannot even produce something in the former that is not inferior to what one sees in Europe, where these [causes] act in a contrary direction.

Physical causes therefore do not influence the destiny of nations as much as one supposes.

I met men in New England ready to abandon a native country where they had been able to find ease to go seek a fortune in the wilderness. Nearby, I saw the French population of Canada pressed into a space too narrow for it, when the same wilderness was close; and whereas the emigrant of the United States acquired a great domain at the price of a few days of work, the Canadian paid for land as dearly as if he still inhabited France.

Thus nature, in delivering to the Europeans the solitudes of the New World, offers them goods which they do not always know how to use.

I perceive in the other peoples of the New World the same conditions of prosperity as in the Anglo-Americans, minus their laws and their mores; and those peoples are miserable. The laws and mores of the Anglo-Americans therefore form the special reason for their greatness and the predominant cause that I seek.

I am far from claiming that there is an absolute good in American laws: I do not believe that they are applicable to all democratic peoples; and among them there are several that, in the United States itself, seem to me dangerous.

Nonetheless, one cannot deny that the legislation of the Americans, taken in its entirety, is well adapted to the genius of the people that it has to rule and to the nature of the country.

American laws are therefore good, and one must attribute to them a great part of the success that the government of democracy obtains in America; but I do not think that they are the principal cause of it. And if they seem to me to have more influence on the social happiness of Americans than the nature of the country itself, on the other hand I perceive reasons for believing that they exert less [influence] than mores.

Federal laws surely form the most important share of legislation of the United States.

Mexico, which is as happily situated as the Anglo-American Union, has appropriated these same laws, and it has not been able to become habituated to the government of democracy.

There is therefore a reason independent of physical causes and laws that enables democracy to govern the United States.

But here is what proves it still more. Almost all the men who inhabit the territory of the Union have issued from the same blood. They speak the same language, pray to God in the same manner, are subject to the same material causes, obey the same laws.

Whence therefore arise the differences that are to be observed among them?

Why, in the East of the Union, does republican government show itself strong and regular, and proceed maturely and slowly? What cause impresses a wise and lasting character on all its acts?

How is it, on the contrary, that in the West the powers of society seem to march haphazardly?

Why is there reigning in the movement of affairs there something disordered, passionate, one could almost say feverish, that does not foretell a long future?

I am no longer comparing the Anglo-Americans to foreign peoples; I am now opposing the Anglo-Americans to one another, and I inquire why they do not resemble each other. Here, I lack at the same time all arguments drawn from the nature of the country and from the difference of laws. One must recur to some other cause; and where shall I discover this cause if not in mores?

It is in the East that the Anglo-Americans have practiced the longest use of democratic government and have formed habits and conceived ideas most favorable to maintaining it. There, democracy has penetrated little by little into usages, into opinion, into forms; it is found in all the details of social life as in the laws. It is in the East that the literary instruction and the practical education of the people have been most perfected and that religion has best intermingled with freedom. What are all these habits, these opinions, these usages, these beliefs, if not what I have called mores?

In the West, on the contrary, a part of the same advantages is still lacking. Many Americans in the states of the West were born in the woods, and they mix with the civilization of their fathers the ideas and customs of the savage life. Among them, passions are more violent, religious morality less powerful, ideas less fixed. Men there exercise no control over one another, for they hardly know each other. The nations of the West therefore show, up to a certain point, the inexperience and unregulated habits of nascent peoples. Nevertheless, societies in the West are formed of old elements; but the assemblage is new.

It is therefore particularly mores that render the Americans of the United States, alone among all Americans, capable of supporting the empire of democracy; and it is again [mores] that make the various Anglo-American democracies more or less regulated and prosperous.

Thus, in Europe one exaggerates the influence that the geographic position of the country exerts on the longevity of democratic institutions. One attributes too much importance to laws, too little to mores. Without doubt, these three great causes serve to regulate and to direct American democracy; but if it were necessary to class them, I would say that physical causes contribute less than laws, and laws less than mores.

I am convinced that the happiest situation and the best laws cannot maintain a constitution despite mores, whereas the latter turn even the most unfavorable positions and the worst laws to good account. The importance of mores is a common truth to which study and experience constantly lead back. It seems to me that I have it placed in my mind as a central point; I perceive it at the end of all my ideas.

I have only one more word to say on this subject.

If, in the course of this work, I have not succeeded in making the reader feel the importance that I attribute to the practical experience of the Americans, to their habits, to their opinions—in a word, to their mores—in the maintenance of their laws, I have missed the principal goal that I proposed for myself in writing it.

WOULD LAWS AND MORES SUFFICE TO MAINTAIN DEMOCRATIC INSTITUTIONS ELSEWHERE THAN IN AMERICA?

The Anglo-Americans, transported to Europe, would be obliged to modify their laws.— One must distinguish between democratic institutions and American institutions.—One can conceive of better or at least different democratic laws than the ones American democracy has given itself.—The example of America proves only that one must not despair of regulating democracy with the aid of laws and mores.

I have said that the success of democratic institutions in the United States is due more to the laws themselves and to mores than to the nature of the country.

But does it follow that these same causes transported elsewhere would, alone, have the same power? and if the country cannot take the place of laws and mores, can laws and mores in their turn take the place of the country?

Here one will conceive without difficulty that we lack the elements of proof: there are other peoples in the New World than Anglo-Americans, and as those peoples are subject to the same material causes as the latter, I have been able to compare them.

But outside of America there are no nations that, deprived of the same physical advantages as Anglo-Americans, have nevertheless adopted their laws and mores.

Thus we have no object of comparison in this matter; one can only hazard opinions.

It seems to me, first, that one must carefully distinguish the institutions of the United States from democratic institutions in general.

When I think of the state of Europe, of its great peoples, of its populous cities, of its formidable armies, of the complications of its politics, I cannot believe that Anglo-Americans themselves, transported onto our soil with their ideas, their religion, their mores, could live on it without considerably modifying their laws.

But one can suppose a democratic people organized in another manner than the American people.

Is it therefore impossible to conceive of a government founded on the real will of the majority, but where the majority, doing violence to the instincts of equality that are natural to it in favor of the order and the stability of the state, would consent to vest one family or one man with all the prerogatives of executive power? Can one not imagine a democratic society where national forces would be more centralized than in the United States, where the people would exercise a less direct and less irresistible empire over general affairs, and where nevertheless each citizen, vested with certain rights, would take part, in his sphere, in the proceedings of the government?

What I have seen among the Anglo-Americans brings me to believe that democratic institutions of this nature, introduced prudently into society, that would mix little by little with habits and gradually blend with the very opinions of the people, could subsist elsewhere than in America.

If the laws of the United States were the only democratic laws that might be imagined or the most perfect that it is possible to encounter, I conceive that one could conclude that the success of the laws of the United States proves nothing for the success of democratic laws in general, in a country less favored by nature.

But if the laws of the Americans appear to me defective in many points and if it is easy for me to conceive of others, the special nature of the country does not prove to me that democratic institutions cannot succeed in a people where, physical circumstances being less favorable, the laws would be better.

If men showed themselves to be different in America from what they are elsewhere, if their social state gave rise to habits and opinions in them contrary to those that arise from this same social state in Europe, what takes place in the American democracies would teach nothing about what will take place in other democracies.

If Americans showed the same penchants as all other democratic peoples, and if their legislators had relied on the nature of the country and on the favor of circumstances to contain these penchants within just limits, the prosperity of the United States, having to be attributed to purely physical causes, would prove nothing in favor of peoples who would like to follow their example without having their natural advantages.

But neither one of these suppositions is found to be verified by the facts.

In America I have encountered passions analogous to those that we see in Europe: some depend on the very nature of the human heart; others, on the democratic social state of society.

Thus I found in the United States the restiveness of heart that is natural to men when, all conditions being nearly equal, each sees the same chances of rising. I encountered there the democratic sentiment of envy expressed in a thousand different manners. I remarked that the people often showed a great mixture of presumption and ignorance in the conduct of affairs, and I concluded from this that in America as among us, men are subject to the same imperfections and exposed to the same miseries.

But when I came to examine attentively the state of society, I discovered without difficulty that Americans had made great and fortunate efforts to combat these weaknesses of the human heart and to correct these natural defects of democracy.

Their various municipal laws appeared to me as so many barriers that keep the restive ambition of citizens within a narrow sphere and turn the very democratic passions that could overturn the state to the profit of the township. It seemed to me that American legislators had come, not without success, to oppose the idea of rights to sentiments of envy; to the continuous movements of the political world, the immobility of religious morality; the experience of the people, to its theoretical ignorance, and its habit of business, to the enthusiasm of its desires.

The Americans have therefore not relied on the nature of the country to combat the dangers that are born of their constitution and their political laws. To the ills that they share with all democratic peoples they have applied remedies which, up to now, they alone have noticed; and although they were the first to try them out, they have succeeded.

The mores and laws of the Americans are not the only ones that can suit democratic peoples; but the Americans have shown that one must not despair of regulating democracy with the aid of laws and mores.

If other peoples, borrowing this general and fruitful idea from America, without wanting in addition to imitate its inhabitants in the particular application that they made of it, attempted to make themselves appropriate to the social state that Providence imposes on men in our day, and thus sought to escape from the despotism or the anarchy that threaten them, what reasons do we have to believe that they would fail in their efforts?

The organization and establishment of democracy among Christians is the great political problem of our time. The Americans have doubtless not resolved this problem, but they furnish useful lessons to those who wish to resolve it.

IMPORTANCE OF WHAT PRECEDES IN RELATION TO EUROPE

One easily discovers why I have engaged in the preceding researches. The question I have raised interests not only the United States, but the entire world; not one nation, but all men.

If peoples whose social state is democratic could remain free only when they inhabit a wilderness, one would have to despair of the future lot of the human species; for men are advancing rapidly toward democracy and the wildernesses are filling up.

If it were true that laws and mores were insufficient to maintain democratic institutions, what other refuge would remain for nations if not the despotism of one alone?

I know that in our day there are many honest people whom this future scarcely frightens, and who, fatigued by freedom, would like to rest at last far from its storms.

But they know very poorly the port toward which they direct themselves. Preoccupied with their memories, they judge absolute power by what it was formerly, and not by what it could be in our day.

If absolute power came to be established anew among the democratic peoples of Europe, I do not doubt that it would take a new form, and that it would show itself with features unknown to our fathers.

There was a time in Europe when law, as well as the consent of the people, vested kings with an almost boundless power. But it almost never happened that they made use of it.

I shall not speak of the prerogatives of the nobility, of the authority of sovereign courts, of the right of corporations, of the privileges of the province, which, while absorbing the blows of authority, maintained a spirit of resistance in the nation.

Independent of these political institutions, which, often contrary to the freedom of particular persons, nevertheless served to maintain the love of freedom in souls, and whose utility in this relation is conceived without difficulty, opinions and mores raised less well-known but no less powerful barriers around the royal power.

Religion, love of subjects, the goodness of the prince, honor, the spirit of family, provincial prejudices, custom, and public opinion bounded the power of the kings and confined their authority within an invisible circle.

The constitutions of peoples then were despotic and their mores free. Princes had the right but neither the ability nor the desire to do everything.

Of the barriers that formerly stopped tyranny, what remains to us today?

Religion having lost its empire over souls, the most visible boundary that divided good and evil is overturned; all seems doubtful and uncertain in the moral world; kings and peoples advance in it haphazardly, and no one can say where the natural limits of despotism and the bounds of license are.

Long revolutions have destroyed forever the respect that used to surround heads of state. Unburdened of the weight of public esteem, princes from now on can indulge without fear in the intoxication of power.

When kings see into the hearts of the peoples who come before them, they are lenient, because they feel themselves strong; and they are careful with the love of their subjects because the love of subjects is the support of the throne. An exchange of sentiments is then established between prince and people, the mildness of which recalls to society the bosom of the family. While subjects murmur against the sovereign, they are still distressed to displease him, and the sovereign strikes his subjects with a light hand, as a father chastises his children.

But when once the prestige of royalty has vanished in the midst of the tumult of revolutions; when kings, succeeding each other on the throne, have by turns exposed to peoples the weakness of *right* and the hardness of *fact*, no one any longer sees in the sovereign the father of the state and everyone perceives a master there. If he is weak, one scorns him; one hates him if he is strong. He himself is full of anger and fear; he sees himself as a foreigner in his country, and he treats his subjects as having been defeated.

When provinces and towns formed so many different nations in the midst of the common native country, each of them had a particular spirit that opposed the general spirit of servitude; but today, when all the parts of the same empire, after having lost their franchises, their usages, their prejudices, and even their memories and their names, have become habituated to obeying the same laws, it is no more difficult to oppress them all together than to oppress one of them separately.

While the nobility enjoyed its power, and for a long time even after it had lost it, aristocratic honor gave an extraordinary strength to individual resistance.

Then one used to see men who, despite their powerlessness, still maintained a lofty idea of their individual worth and dared to resist in isolation the efforts of public power.

But in our day, when all classes end by being confused together, when the individual disappears more and more into the crowd and is easily lost in the midst of the common obscurity; today, when monarchic honor has almost lost its empire without being replaced by virtue, and nothing any longer sustains man above himself, who can say where the demands of power and the compliance of weakness would stop?

As long as the spirit of the family lasted, the man who struggled against tyranny was never alone; he found clients around him, hereditary friends, relations. And if he lacked this support, he still felt sustained by his ancestors and animated by his descendants. But when patrimonies are divided, and when in a few years the races intermingle, where does one place the spirit of the family?

What force remains to customs in a people that has entirely changed its face and that changes it constantly, when all acts of tyranny already have a precedent, when all crimes can be supported by an example, when nothing can be encountered old enough so that one fears to destroy it, nor nothing be conceived so new that one cannot dare it?

What resistance is offered by mores that have already bowed so many times?

What can public opinion itself do, when there do not exist *twenty* persons that a common bond unites;* when one encounters neither a man nor a

---

*Reference to a law of April 1834 in France, strongly opposed by AT, which forbade associations of more than twenty persons.

family nor a body nor a class nor a free association that can represent that opinion and make it act?

When each citizen, being equally powerless, equally poor, equally isolated, can only oppose his individual weakness to the organized force of the government?

To conceive something analogous to what would then take place among us, one ought not recur to our annals. One would perhaps have to inquire into the monuments of antiquity and think back to those frightful centuries of Roman tyranny, when mores were corrupt, memories effaced, habits destroyed, opinions wavering, and freedom, chased out of the laws, no longer knew where to take refuge to find an asylum; when nothing any longer stood guarantee for citizens and citizens no longer stood guarantee for themselves, one would see men make sport of human nature, and princes weary the clemency of the heavens rather than the patience of their subjects.

Those who think they can recover the monarchy of Henry IV or of Louis XIV seem to me blind indeed. As for me, when I consider the state at which several European nations have already arrived, and that to which all the others are tending, I feel myself brought to believe that there will soon no longer be room in them except for either democratic freedom or the tyranny of the Caesars.

Is this not worth thinking about? If men had to arrive, in effect, at the point where it would be necessary to make them all free or all slaves, all equal in rights or all deprived of rights; if those who govern societies were reduced to this alternative of gradually raising the crowd up to themselves or of letting all citizens fall below the level of humanity, would this not be enough to overcome many doubts, to reassure consciences well, and to prepare each to make great sacrifices readily?

Would it not then be necessary to consider the gradual development of democratic institutions and mores, not as the best, but as the sole means that remains to us to be free; and without loving the government of democracy, would one not be disposed to adopt it as the best applicable and the most honest remedy that one can oppose to the present ills of society?

It is difficult to make the people participate in government; it is more difficult still to furnish them with the experience and to give them the sentiments that they lack to govern well.

The will of democracy is changeable; its agents coarse; its laws imperfect; I agree with this. But if it were true that there would soon be nothing intermediate between the empire of democracy and the yoke of one alone, ought we not to tend toward the one rather than to submit voluntarily to the other? And if complete equality must finally arrive, would it not be better to let oneself be leveled by freedom than by a despot?

Those who, after having read this book, judged that in writing it I wanted to propose Anglo-American laws and mores for imitation by all peoples who have a democratic social state would have committed a great error; they would have become attached to the form, abandoning the very substance, of my thought. My goal has been to show, by the example of America, that laws and above all mores can permit a democratic people to remain free. I am, for the rest, very far from believing that we ought to follow the example that American democracy has given and to imitate the means it has used to attain that goal by its efforts; for I am not ignorant of the influence exerted by the nature of the country and antecedent facts on political constitutions, and I would regard it as a great misfortune for the human race if freedom had to be produced with the same features in all places.

But I think that if one does not come little by little to introduce and finally to found democratic institutions among us, and that if one renounces giving to all citizens ideas and sentiments that first prepare them for freedom and afterwards permit them the use of it, there will be independence for no one, neither for the bourgeois nor for the noble, nor for the poor man, nor for the rich man, but an equal tyranny for all; and I foresee that if one does not in time succeed in founding the peaceful empire of the greatest number among us, we shall arrive sooner or later at the *unlimited* power of one alone.

Chapter 10 SOME CONSIDERATIONS ON THE PRESENT STATE AND THE PROBABLE FUTURE OF THE THREE RACES THAT INHABIT THE TERRITORY OF THE UNITED STATES

The principal task that I imposed on myself is now fulfilled; I have shown, at least as far as I was able to succeed, what the laws of American democracy are; I have made known what its mores are. I could stop here, but the reader would perhaps find that I had not satisfied his expectations.

One encounters in America something more than an immense and complete democracy; the peoples who inhabit the New World can be envisaged from more than one point of view.

In the course of this work, my subject has often led me to speak of the

Indians and the Negroes, but I have never had the time to stop in order to show what position these two races occupy in the midst of the democratic people that I was occupied with depicting; I have said according to what spirit, with the aid of what laws the Anglo-American confederation was formed; I could indicate only in passing and in a very incomplete manner the dangers that threaten this confederation, and it has been impossible for me to set out in detail what, independently of laws and mores, are its chances of enduring. In speaking of the united republics, I did not hazard any conjecture about the permanence of republican forms in the New World, and while often alluding to the commercial activity that reigns in the Union, I nevertheless did not occupy myself with the future of the Americans as a trading people.

These objects, which touch on my subject, do not enter into it; they are American without being democratic, and it is above all democracy that I wanted to portray. I therefore had to turn away from them at first; but in ending I have to come back to them.

The territory occupied or claimed by the American Union in our day extends from the Atlantic Ocean to the shores of the South Sea.* To the east or to the west its limits are therefore the same as those of the continent; to the south it comes up against the border of the tropics, and then climbs back amidst the glaciers of the north.

The men spread over this space do not form, as in Europe, so many offshoots of the same family. From the first one finds in them three naturally distinct and, I could almost say, inimical races. Education, law, origin, and even the external form of their features have raised an almost insurmountable barrier between them; fortune has gathered them on the same soil, but it has mixed them without being able to intermingle them, and each pursues its destiny separately.

Among these men, so diverse, the first who attracts the eye, the first in enlightenment, in power, in happiness, is the white man, the European, man par excellence; below him appear the Negro and the Indian.

These two unfortunate races have neither birth, nor face, nor language, nor mores in common; only their misfortunes look alike. Both occupy an equally inferior position in the country that they inhabit; both experience the effects of tyranny; and if their miseries are different, they can accuse the same authors for them.

Would one not say, on seeing what takes place in the world, that the European is to men of other races what man himself is to the animals? He makes them serve his use, and when he cannot bend them, he destroys them.

*The Pacific Ocean.

Oppression has with one blow taken from the descendants of the Africans almost all the privileges of humanity! The Negro of the United States has lost even the memory of his country; he no longer understands the language that his fathers spoke; he has abjured their religion and forgotten their mores. In thus ceasing to belong to Africa, he has however acquired no right to the goods of Europe; but he has stopped between the two societies; he has remained isolated between the two peoples, sold by one and repudiated by the other, finding in the entire universe only the hearth of his master to offer him the incomplete image of a native country.

The Negro has no family; he cannot see in woman anything but the passing companion of his pleasures, and his sons, by being born, are his equals.

Shall I call a good deed of God or a final curse of his anger that disposition of soul which renders man insensitive to extreme miseries, and often even gives him a sort of depraved taste for the cause of his misfortunes?

Plunged into this abyss of evils, the Negro hardly feels his misfortune; violence had placed him in slavery, the habit of servitude has given him the thoughts and ambition of a slave; he admires his tyrants more than he hates them and finds his joy and his pride in servile imitation of those who oppress him.

His intellect has been debased to the level of his soul.

The Negro enters into servitude and into life at the same time. What am I saying? often one buys him in his mother's belly, and he begins so to speak to be a slave before he is born.

Without need as he is without pleasure, useless to himself, he comprehends by the first notions he receives of existence that he is the property of another, whose interest is to watch over his days; he perceives that the care of his own lot has not devolved on him; the very use of thought seems to him a useless gift of Providence, and he peacefully enjoys all the privileges of his baseness.

If he becomes free, independence then often appears to him a heavier chain than slavery itself; for in the course of his existence, he has learned to submit to everything except to reason; and when reason becomes his sole guide, he cannot recognize its voice. A thousand new needs besiege him, and he lacks the necessary knowledge and energy to resist them. Needs are masters that must be combated, and he has been taught only to submit and to obey. He has therefore arrived at this height of misery, that servitude brutalizes him and freedom makes him perish.

Oppression has not exerted less influence on the Indian races, but the effects are different.

Before the arrival of the whites in the New World, the men who inhabited

North America lived tranquilly in the woods. Left to the ordinary vicissitudes of savage life, they showed the vices and the virtues of uncivilized peoples. The Europeans, after having dispersed the Indian tribes far into the wilderness, condemned them to a wandering and vagabond life, full of inexpressible miseries.

Savage nations are governed only by opinions and mores.

In weakening sentiment for one's native country among the Indians of North America, in dispersing their families, in obscuring their traditions, in interrupting the chain of their memories, in changing all their habits, and in increasing their needs beyond measure, European tyranny has rendered them more disordered and less civilized than they already were. The moral condition and physical state of these peoples has not ceased to worsen at the same time, and they have become more barbarous to the degree they were more unfortunate. Still, the Europeans have not been able to modify the character of the Indians entirely, and together with the power to destroy them, they have never had that of civilizing* and subjugating them.

The Negro is placed at the ultimate bounds of servitude; the Indian at the extreme limits of freedom. Slavery scarcely produces more fatal effects in the first than does independence in the second.

The Negro has even lost ownership of his person, and he cannot dispose of his own existence without committing a sort of larceny.

The savage is delivered to himself as soon as he can act. He has hardly known the authority of the family; he has never bent his will before that of those like him; no one has taught him to distinguish voluntary obedience from shameful subjection, and he is ignorant even of the name of law. For him, to be free is to escape from almost all the bonds of society. He takes pleasure in this barbarous independence, and he would rather perish than sacrifice the least part of it. Civilization has little hold on such a man.

The Negro makes a thousand useless efforts to introduce himself into a society that repels him; he bows to the tastes of his oppressors, adopts their opinions, and in imitating them aspires to intermingle with them. He has been told since birth that his race is naturally inferior to that of the whites, and he is not far from believing it, so he is ashamed of himself. In each of his features he discovers a trace of slavery, and if he could, he would joyfully consent to repudiate himself as a whole.

The Indian, on the contrary, has an imagination filled up with the pretended nobility of his origin. He lives and dies in the midst of these dreams of his pride. Far from wanting to bend his mores to ours, he attaches himself

*Lit.: "policing."

to barbarism as a distinctive sign of his race, and he repels civilization perhaps less in hatred of it than in fear of resembling the Europeans.[1]

To the perfection of our arts he wants to oppose only the resources of the wilderness; to our tactics, only his undisciplined courage; to the profundity of our designs, only the spontaneous instincts of his savage nature. He succumbs in this unequal struggle.

The Negro would like to intermingle with the European, and he cannot. The Indian could up to a certain point succeed at it, but he disdains the attempt. The servility of the one delivers him to slavery, and the pride of the other to death.

I remember, while traveling through the forests that still cover the state of Alabama, that one day I came upon the hut of a pioneer. I did not want to enter the dwelling of the American, but I went to rest for some moments at the edge of a spring in the wood not far from there. While I was in this place, an Indian woman came (we were then near the territory occupied by the Creek nation); she was holding the hand of a girl of five or six, belonging to the white race, whom I supposed to be the daughter of the pioneer. A Negro woman followed them. A sort of barbarous luxury prevailed in the costume of the Indian: rings of metal were suspended from her nostrils and her ears; her hair, mixed with beads of glass, fell freely on her shoulders, and I saw that she was not a wife, for she still wore the shell necklace that virgins have

---

1. The native of North America preserves his opinions and his habits to the least detail with an inflexibility that has no example in history. For the more than two hundred years that the wandering tribes of North America have had daily relations with the white race, they have borrowed from it so to speak not one idea nor one usage. The men of Europe have nonetheless exerted a very great influence on the savages. They have made the Indian character more disordered, but they have not made it more European.

In the summer of 1831, finding myself on the far side of Lake Michigan, in a place named Green Bay, which serves as the extreme frontier to the United States alongside the Indians of the Northwest, I made the acquaintance of an American officer, Major H., who, one day, after having spoken much to me of the inflexibility of the Indian character, recounted to me the following fact: "I once knew, he said to me, a young Indian who had been schooled in a college in New England. He obtained great success there and had taken on the whole external aspect of a civilized man. When war broke out between us and the English in 1810, I again saw this young man; he then served in our army at the head of the warriors of his tribe. The Americans had admitted Indians into their ranks only on the condition that they would abstain from their horrible usage of scalping the defeated. The evening of the battle of ***, C... came to seat himself beside the fire in our bivouac; I asked him what had happened during the day; he recounted it to me, and becoming animated by degrees in the recollections of his exploits, he ended by half-opening his clothes and saying to me: 'Do not betray me, but see!' I saw, in fact, added Major H., between his body and his shirt, the hair of an Englishman still dripping with blood." [Major H. is identified as Major Lamard in AT's notebooks. See *Journey to America*, ed. J. P. Mayer (New Haven, 1959), 37.]

the custom of depositing on the nuptial bed; the Negro woman was clothed in European dress almost in shreds.

All three of them came to sit down on the edge of the spring, and the young savage, taking the child in her arms, lavished caresses on her that one could believe were dictated by the heart of a mother; for her part, the Negro woman sought by a thousand innocent artifices to attract the attention of the little Creole. The latter showed in her least movements a sentiment of superiority that contrasted strangely with her weakness and her age; one would have said that she used a sort of condescension in receiving the care of her companions.

Crouched before her mistress, watching for each of her desires, the Negro woman seemed equally divided between an almost maternal attachment and a servile fear; whereas one saw a free, proud, and almost ferocious air prevailing even in the effusion of tenderness from the savage woman.

I approached and contemplated this spectacle in silence; my curiosity doubtless displeased the Indian woman, for she rose brusquely, pushed the child far from her with a sort of rudeness, and after throwing an irritated glance at me, plunged into the woods.

It often happened that I saw individuals belonging to the three human races that people North America gathered in the same places; I had already recognized the preponderance exercised by the whites in a thousand diverse effects; but in the picture that I have just described there was something particularly touching: a bond of affection here united the oppressed to the oppressors, and nature, in striving to bring them together, rendered more striking still the immense space that prejudices and laws had put between them.

PRESENT STATE AND PROBABLE FUTURE OF THE INDIAN TRIBES THAT INHABIT THE TERRITORY POSSESSED BY THE UNION

Gradual disappearance of the native races.—How this works.—Miseries that accompany the forced migrations of the Indians.—The savages of North America had only two means of escaping destruction: war or civilization.—They can no longer make war.—Why they have not wanted to become civilized when they could do it and can no longer do it when they come to want to.—Example of the Creeks and the Cherokees.—Policy of the particular states toward these Indians.—Policy of the federal government.

All the Indian tribes that used to inhabit the territory of New England— the Narragansetts, the Mohicans, the Pequots—no longer live except in the memory of men; the Lenapes, who received Penn* a hundred and fifty years

*William Penn (1644–1718).

ago on the shores of the Delaware, have disappeared today. I met the last of the Iroquois: they asked for alms. All the nations that I have just named formerly extended to the shores of the sea; now one must go more than a hundred leagues into the interior of the continent to meet with an Indian. These savages have not only withdrawn, they are destroyed.[2] As the natives move away and die, an immense people comes constantly and grows larger in their place. A development so prodigious has never been seen among nations, nor a destruction so rapid.

It is easy to indicate the manner in which this destruction works.

When the Indians lived alone in the wilderness from which they are exiled today, their needs were few; they themselves manufactured their arms, the water of the rivers was their only drink, and for clothes they had the hides of the animals whose flesh served to nourish them.

The Europeans introduced firearms, iron, and brandy among the natives of North America; they taught them to replace with our fabrics the barbarous clothes with which Indian simplicity had been contented until then. While contracting new tastes, the Indians did not learn the art of satisfying them, and they had to resort to the industry of the whites. In return for goods which he himself did not know how to create, the savage could offer nothing but the rich furs that his woods still contained. From that moment, hunting not only had to provide for his needs, but also for the frivolous passions of Europe. He no longer pursued the beasts of the forests only to nourish himself, but in order to procure the sole objects of exchange that he could give us.[3]

2. In the thirteen original states, only 6,273 Indians remain. (See *Legislative Documents*, [House, "On Indian Affairs,"] 20th Congress, no. 117, p. 90.)

3. Mr. Clark and Mr. Cass, in their report to Congress, February 4, 1829, p. 23, said:

The time when the Indians generally could supply themselves with food and clothing, without any of the articles of civilized life, has long since passed away. The more remote tribes, beyond the Mississippi, who live where immense herds of buffalo are yet to be found, and who follow those animals in their periodical migrations, could, more easily than any others, recur to the habits of their ancestors, and live without the white man or any of his manufactures. But the buffalo is constantly receding [. . .]. The smaller animals, the bear, the deer, the beaver, the otter, the muskrat, &c. principally minister to the comfort and support of the Indians, and these cannot be taken without guns, ammunition, and traps [. . .].

Among the northwestern Indians particularly, the labor of supplying a family with food and clothing is excessive. Day after day is spent by the hunter without success, and during this interval his family must subsist upon bark or roots, or perish [. . .]. Many die every Winter from actual starvation.

The Indians do not want to live like the Europeans: nonetheless they can neither do without the Europeans nor live entirely like their fathers. One will judge by this single fact, knowledge of which I also draw from an official source. Some men belonging to an Indian tribe on the

While the needs of the natives were thus increasing, their resources did not cease to diminish.

From the day when a European settlement forms in the neighborhood of the territory occupied by Indians, the wild game takes alarm.[4] Thousands of savages, wandering in the forests without fixed dwellings, did not frighten it; but from the moment when the continuous noise of European industry made itself heard someplace, it began to flee and to retreat toward the west, where its instinct taught it that it would encounter still boundless wilderness. "The buffalo is constantly receding," say Mr. Cass and Mr. Clark in their report to Congress, February 4, 1829. "A few years since, they approached the base of the Allegheny, and a few years hence they may even be rare upon the immense plains which extend to the base of the Rocky Mountains."* I was assured that this effect of the approach of the whites was often felt at two hundred leagues from their frontier. Thus their influence is exerted on tribes whose names they hardly know, and who suffer the evils of usurpation long before recognizing its authors.[5]

Soon, hardy adventurers penetrate into Indian country; they advance to fifteen or twenty leagues from the whites' last frontier and go to build the dwelling of a civilized man in the very midst of barbarism. It is easy for them to do this: the boundaries of the territory of a hunting people are ill-secured. This territory, moreover, belongs to the nation as a whole and is not precisely the property of anyone; no part of it, therefore, is defended by individual interest.

A few European families, occupying well-separated points, then serve to chase out the wild animals, never to return, from all the intermediate space

---

*House, "On Indian Affairs," 24.

---

shore of Lake Superior had killed a European; the American government forbade trafficking with the tribe that the guilty were part of until the latter had been delivered to it: which took place. [House, "On Indian Affairs," 20th Cong., 2d sess., 1829, H. Doc. 117, serial 186, 23. Lewis Cass served as secretary of war from 1831 to 1836, previously having been governor of the Michigan territory.]

4. "Five years ago," says Volney in his *Tableau of the United States*, p. 370, "in going from Vincennes to Kaskaskia, a territory included in the state of Illinois today, then entirely savage (1797), one did not cross prairies without seeing herds of four to five hundred buffalo: today no more remain; they have passed the Mississippi by swimming, importuned by hunters and above all by the bells of American cows." [Constantin F. Volney, *Tableau du climat et du sol des Etats-Unis d'Amérique* (Paris: Boussangue Frères, 1822; originally published in 1803 by Courcier), 370.]

5. One can be convinced of the truth of what I advance here by consulting the general table of the Indian tribes contained within the limits claimed by the United States (*Legislative Documents,* [House, "On Indian Affairs,"] 20th Congress, no. 117, pp. 90–105). One will see that the tribes of the center of America are decreasing rapidly although the Europeans are still very far from them.

that extends between them. The Indians, who had lived until then in a sort of abundance, find it difficult to subsist, and have still more difficulty in procuring the objects of exchange they need. By making their game flee, it is as if one made the fields of our farmers sterile. Soon the means of existence are almost entirely lacking to them. One then encounters these unfortunates prowling like famished wolves in the midst of their wooded wilderness. An instinctive love of their native country attaches them to the soil that has seen them born,[6] and they now find nothing there but misery and death. Finally, they decide; they part, and following from a distance the elk, the buffalo, and the beaver in their flight, they leave to these wild animals the care of choosing a new native country for them. It is therefore not, properly speaking, the Europeans who chase the natives from America, it is famine: a happy distinction that had escaped ancient casuists, and that modern doctors have discovered.

One cannot imagine the frightful evils that accompany these forced migrations. At the moment when the Indians left their paternal fields, they were already exhausted and worn down. The country where they go to stay is occupied by small tribes who see the newcomers only with jealousy. Behind them is hunger, before them is war, everywhere is misery. In order to escape so many enemies, they divide up. Each of them seeks to isolate himself so as to find furtively the means of sustaining his existence and lives in the immensity of the wilderness like an outcast in the heart of civilized societies. The social bond, long since weakened, then breaks. Already there was no more native country for them, soon there will no longer be a people; families will scarcely remain; the common name is lost, the language is forgotten, traces of the origin disappear. The nation has ceased to exist. It scarcely lives in the memory of American antiquarians and is known only by a few scholars in Europe.

I would not want a reader to be able to believe that my picture here is overcharged. I saw with my own eyes several of the miseries that I have just described; I contemplated evils that would be impossible for me to recount.

At the end of the year 1831, I found myself on the left bank of the Mississippi, at a place named Memphis by the Europeans. While I was at this place, a numerous troop of Choctaws came (the French of Louisiana name them Chactas); the savages were leaving their country and sought to cross to the

6. The Indians, say Messrs. Clark and Cass in their report to Congress, p. 15, are attached to their country by the same feelings which bind us to ours; and besides, there are certain superstitious notions connected with the alienation of what the Great Spirit gave their ancestors, which operate strongly upon the tribes who have made few or no cessions, but which gradually weakened as our intercourse with them is extended. "We will not sell the spot which contains the bones of our fathers," is almost always the first answer to a proposition for a sale. [House, "On Indian Affairs," 15.]

right bank of the Mississippi, where they flattered themselves they would find the refuge that the American government promised them. It was then in the heart of winter, and the cold ravaged that year with an unaccustomed violence; snow had hardened on the ground, and the river carried along enormous pieces of ice. The Indians brought along their families with them; they dragged behind them the wounded, the ill, infants who had just been born, and the old who were going to die. They had neither tents nor carts, but only some provisions and arms. I saw them embark to cross the great river, and this solemn spectacle will never leave my memory. One heard neither tears nor complaints among this assembled crowd; they were silent. Their misfortunes were old, and they felt them to be irreparable. All the Indians had already entered the vessels that were to carry them; their dogs still remained on the shore; when the animals finally saw that they were going away forever, together they let out frightful howls, and dashing at once into the icy waters of the Mississippi, they followed their masters swimming.*

In our day the dispossession of the Indians often works in a regular and so to speak wholly legal manner.

When the European population begins to approach the wilderness occupied by a savage nation, the government of the United States commonly sends a solemn embassy to it; the whites assemble the Indians on a great plain, and after having eaten and drunk with them, they say to them: "What have you to do in the country of your fathers? Soon you must dig up their bones in order to live. How is the region that you inhabit worth more than any other? Are there woods, marshes, and prairies only where you are, and can you live only under your sun? Beyond those mountains that you see on the horizon, beyond that lake that borders your territory to the west, one encounters vast regions where wild beasts are still abundant; sell us your lands and go live happily in those places." After having held this discourse, they spread firearms, wool clothes, barrels of brandy, glass necklaces, tin bracelets, earrings, and mirrors[7] before the eyes of the Indians. If at the sight

---

*On this episode, see AT's letter to his mother of December 25, 1831. See also AT, *Oeuvres* 2: 1023 n. 1.

7. See in the *Legislative Documents of Congress*, Doc. 117, the narrative of what happens in these circumstances. This curious morsel is found in the report already cited, made by Mr. Clark and Mr. Lewis Cass to Congress on February 4, 1829. Today, Mr. Cass is secretary of war.

"The Indians, as has been stated, reach the treaty ground poor, and almost naked," say Mr. Clark and Mr. Cass. "Large quantities of goods are taken there by the traders, and are seen and examined by the Indians. The women and children become importunate to have their wants supplied, and their influence is soon exerted to induce a sale. Their improvidence is habitual and unconquerable. The gratification of his immediate wants and desires is the ruling passion of an Indian. The expectation of future advantages seldom produces much effect. The experience of the past is lost, and the prospects of the future disregarded. This is one of the most striking

of all these riches they still hesitate, it is insinuated to them that they cannot refuse the consent that is asked of them and that soon the government itself will be powerless to guarantee them enjoyment of their rights. What to do? Half-convinced, half-compelled, the Indians move out; they go to inhabit new wilderness, where the whites will hardly leave them in peace for ten years. Thus it is that Americans acquire at a cheap price entire provinces that the wealthiest sovereigns of Europe cannot pay for.[8]

I have just recounted great evils, I add that they appear to me to be irremediable. I believe that the Indian race of North America is condemned to perish, and I cannot prevent myself from thinking that on the day that the Europeans will have settled on the coast of the Pacific Ocean, it will have ceased to exist.[9]

The Indians of North America had only two options for salvation: war or

---

traits in their character, and is well known to all who have had much intercourse with them. It would be utterly hopeless to demand a cessation of land, unless the means were at hand of gratifying their immediate wants; and when their conditions and circumstances are fairly considered, it ought not to surprise us that they are so anxious to relieve themselves." [House, "On Indian Affairs," 15–16.]

8. On May 19, 1830, Mr. Ed. Everett affirmed before the House of Representatives that the Americans had already acquired by *treaty*, to the east and to the west of the Mississippi, 230,000,000 acres.

In 1808, the Osages ceded 48,000,000 acres for a rent of $1,000.

In 1818, the Quapaws ceded 20,000,000 acres for $4,000; they reserved for themselves a territory of 1,000,000 acres to hunt on. It had been solemnly sworn that it would be respected, but it was not long before it was invaded like the rest.

Mr. Bell, reporter for the Committee of Indian Affairs, in Congress, February 24, 1830, said, "To pay an Indian tribe what their ancient *hunting grounds* [in English also] are worth to them, after the game is fled or destroyed, as a mode of appropriating wild lands, claimed by Indians, has been found more convenient, and certainly more agreeable to the forms of justice, as well as more merciful, than to assert the possession of them by the sword. Thus, the practice of buying Indian titles is but the substitute which *humanity and expediency* [in English also] have imposed, in place of the sword, in arriving at the actual enjoyment of property claimed by the rights of discovery, and sanctioned by the natural superiority allowed to the claims of civilized communities over those of savage tribes.

"Up to the present time, so invariable has been the operation of certain causes, first in diminishing the value of forest lands to the Indians; and secondly, in disposing them to sell readily; that the plan of buying their *right of occupancy* [in English also] has never threatened to retard, in any perceptible degree, the prosperity of any of the States." (*Legislative Documents*, 21st Congress, no. 227, p. 6.) [House, "Removal of the Indians," 21st Cong., 1st sess., 1830, H. Rep. 227, serial 200, 6.]

9. This opinion has, in addition, appeared to us to be that of almost all American statesmen.

"Judging of the future by the past," said Mr. Cass to Congress, "we cannot err in anticipating a progressive diminution of their numbers, and their eventual extinction, unless our border should become stationary, and they be removed beyond it, or unless some radical change should take place in the principles of our intercourse with them, which it is easier to hope for than to expect." [House, "On Indian Affairs," 107.]

civilization; in other words, they had to destroy the Europeans or become their equals.

At the birth of the colonies it would have been possible for them, by uniting their forces, to deliver themselves from the few foreigners who came to land on the shores of the continent.[10] More than once they attempted it and were at the point of succeeding. Today the disproportion of resources is too great for them to be able to think of such an undertaking. Nevertheless, among the Indian nations men of genius still arise who foresee the final lot reserved to the savage populations and seek to unite all the Indian tribes in common hatred of the Europeans; but their efforts are impotent. The small tribes who neighbor the whites are already too weakened to offer an effective resistance; the others, indulging in the childish insouciance of the morrow that characterizes the savage nature, wait for the danger to arrive before occupying themselves with it; the ones cannot act, the others do not want to.

It is easy to foresee that the Indians will never want to become civilized, or that they will try it too late when they come to want it.

Civilization is the result of a long social endeavor that operates in one same place, and that different generations hand down, one to another, as they succeed each other. The peoples among whom civilization has the most difficulty founding its empire are hunting peoples. Tribes of shepherds change location, but they always follow a regular order in their migrations and constantly retrace their steps; the dwellings of hunters vary with those of the very animals they pursue.

Several times attempts have been made to bring enlightenment among the Indians while leaving them their vagabond mores; the Jesuits had undertaken it in Canada, the Puritans in New England. Neither did anything lasting.[11] Civilization was born in the hut and went to die in the woods. The great fault of these legislators for the Indians was not to understand that to succeed in civilizing a people, one must before everything else get them to settle, and one can only do that by cultivating the soil; it was therefore a question first of turning the Indians into farmers.

Not only do the Indians not possess this indispensable preliminary for civilization, but it is very difficult for them to acquire it.

Men who have once indulged in the idle and adventurous life of hunters feel an almost insurmountable disgust for the constant and regular labor that

10. See, among others, the war undertaken by the Wampanoags and the other confederated tribes under the leadership of Metacom in 1675 against the colonies of New England, and the one the English had to sustain in 1622 in Virginia.

11. See the different historians of New England. See also *Histoire de la Nouvelle-France*, by Charlevoix, and *Lettres édifiantes*. [The latter were reports by the Jesuits; which edition AT had in mind is not known.]

cultivation requires. That can be perceived within our societies, but it is still more visible in peoples for whom the habits of hunting have become national customs.

Independent of this general cause, there is one no less powerful that is encountered only among the Indians. I have already indicated it; I believe I ought to go back to it.

The natives of North America not only consider work as an evil, but as a dishonor, and their haughtiness struggles against civilization almost as obstinately as their laziness.[12]

There is no Indian so miserable who, in his bark hut, does not entertain a haughty idea of his individual worth; he considers the cares of industry to be demeaning occupations; he compares the farmer to the cow who plows a furrow, and in each of our arts he perceives nothing but the work of slaves. It is not that he has not conceived a very lofty idea of the power of the whites and the greatness of their intellect; but if he admires the result of our efforts, he scorns the means by which we have obtained it, and while submitting to our ascendancy, he still believes himself superior to us. Hunting and war seem to him the only cares worthy of a man.[13] The Indian, in the depth of his misery in his woods, therefore nourishes the same ideas, the same opinions as the noble of the Middle Ages in his fortified castle, and to resemble him completely he needs only to become a conqueror. What a singular thing! It is in the forests of the New World, and not among the Europeans who people its shores, that the old prejudices of Europe are still found today.

I have sought more than once in the course of this work to make understood the prodigious influence that the social state appears to me to exert on the laws and mores of men. Permit me to add only a word to this subject.

---

12. "In all the tribes," says Volney in his *Tableau of the United States,* p. 423, "a generation of old warriors still exists who, on seeing anyone handle a hoe, keep decrying the degradation of ancient mores and who claim that the savages owe their decadence only to these innovations, and that in order to recover their glory and power, it would suffice for them to go back to their primitive mores." [Volney, *Tableau du climat,* 466.]

13. In an official document one finds the following portrait:

Until a young man has been engaged with an enemy and can boast of his prowess, he is held in no estimation, and is considered little better than a woman.

At their great war dances, all the warriors in succession strike the post, as it is called and recount the feats they have done. The auditory, upon these occasions, is composed of the relations, the friends, and the companions of the narrator, and the intensity of their feelings is manifested by the deep silence with which they listen to his tale, and by the loud shouts with which he is hailed at the termination. Unfortunate is the young man who has no deeds of valor to recount at these assemblages; and instances are not wanting, where young warriors, in the excitement of their feelings, have departed alone from these dances, in search of trophies to exhibit, and of adventures to relate. [House, "On Indian Affairs," 40.]

When I perceive the resemblance that exists between the political institutions of our fathers, the Germans, and those of the wandering tribes of North America, between the customs recounted by Tacitus and those that I was sometimes able to witness, I cannot keep from thinking that in both hemispheres the same cause has produced the same effects, and that in the midst of the apparent diversity of human things, it is not impossible to find a few generative facts from which all the others flow. In all that we name Germanic institutions I am therefore tempted to see only the habits of barbarians, and the opinions of savages in what we call feudal ideas.

Whatever the vices and prejudices that prevent the Indians of North America from becoming farmers and civilized, necessity sometimes obliges them to it.

Several considerable nations of the South, among others the Cherokees and the Creeks,[14] have found themselves almost surrounded by Europeans who, disembarking on the shores of the ocean, descending the Ohio, and going up the Mississippi, arrived all around them at the same time. They were not chased from place to place, as were the tribes of the North, but little by little they were pressed together within narrowing limits, as hunters first make a wall around the underbrush before simultaneously breaking into the interior. The Indians, placed then between civilization and death, saw themselves reduced to living shamefully by their work like the whites; they have therefore become farmers; and without entirely dropping either their habits or their mores, have sacrificed of them what was absolutely necessary to their existence.

The Cherokees went further; they created a written language, established a stable enough form of government; and as everything moves at a hasty pace in the New World, they had a newspaper[15] before they all had clothes.

What has singularly favored the rapid development of European habits

14. These nations are contained today in the states of Georgia, Tennessee, Alabama, and Mississippi.

There were formerly four great nations in the South (one sees the remains of them): the Choctaws, the Chickasaws, the Creeks, and the Cherokees.

The remains of these four nations still formed about 75,000 individuals in 1830. It is reckoned that at present about 300,000 Indians are on the territory occupied or claimed by the Anglo-American union. (See *Proceedings of the Indian Board in the City of New York.*) [*Documents and Proceedings Relating to the Formation and Progress of a Board in the City of New York for the Emigration, Preservation, and Improvement of the Aborigines of America, July 22, 1829* (New York: Vanderpool and Cole, 1829).] Official documents furnished to Congress bring this number to 313,130. The reader who might be curious to know the name and strength of all the tribes that inhabit the Anglo-American territory should consult the documents that I have just indicated. (*Legislative Documents,* 20th Congress, no. 117, pp. 90–105.) [House, "On Indian Affairs," 90–105.]

15. I have brought one or two copies of this singular publication back to France.

among these Indians has been the presence of half-breeds.[16] Participating in the enlightenment of his father without entirely abandoning the savage customs of his maternal race, the half-breed forms the natural link between civilization and barbarism. Everywhere that half-breeds have multiplied, one has seen savages little by little modify their social state and change their mores.[17]

The success of the Cherokees therefore proves that the Indians have the ability to civilize themselves, but it does not at all prove that they can succeed at it.

The difficulty Indians have in submitting to civilization arises from a general cause that is almost impossible for them to escape.

If one turns an attentive regard to history, one discovers that in general, barbarian peoples have raised themselves to civilization little by little and by their own efforts.

When they happened to get enlightenment from a foreign nation, they then held towards them the rank of vanquishers, and not the position of the vanquished.

When the conquered people is enlightened and the conquering people half-savage, as in the invasion of the Roman Empire by the nations of the

16. See in the report of the Committee on Indian Affairs, 21st Congress, no. 227, p. 23, what made half-breeds multiply among the Cherokees; the principal cause goes back to the War of Independence. Many Anglo-Americans from Georgia, having taken the side of England, were compelled to withdraw among the Indians, and married there. [House, "Removal of the Indians," 23.]

17. Unhappily half-breeds were fewer and have exercised less influence in North America than anywhere else.

Two great nations of Europe have peopled this portion of the American continent: the French and the English.

The first did not take long to contract unions with the daughters of the natives; but as misfortune had it, there was a secret affinity between the Indian character and theirs. Instead of giving the barbarians the taste and habits of civilized life, they often attached themselves passionately to the savage life: they have become the most dangerous occupants of the wilderness and have won the friendship of the Indian by exaggerating his vices and his virtues. M. de Sénonville, governor of Canada, wrote to Louis XIV in 1685: "It has long been believed that it was necessary to bring the savages near to us in order to Frenchify them; everyone has had to recognize that they were mistaken. Those who have been brought near us have not been made French, and the French who have frequented them have become savages. They affect to dress like them, to live like them."(*History of New France,* by Charlevoix, vol. 2, p. 345.) [Charlevoix, *Histoire et description,* 345. AT misspells the name of his subject; M. de Denonville was governor of Canada from 1685 to 1689.]

The Englishman, on the contrary, staying obstinately attached to the opinions, the usages, and the least habits of his fathers, remained in the midst of the American solitudes what he was within the towns of Europe; he therefore did not want to establish any contact with the savages whom he despised, and he carefully avoided mixing his blood with that of barbarians.

Thus, whereas the Frenchman exerted no salutary influence on the Indians, the Englishman was always a stranger to them.

North, or in that of China by the Mongols, the power that victory assures to the barbarian suffices to hold him at the level of the civilized man and to permit him to advance as his equal until he becomes his model; the one has force on his behalf, the other intelligence; the first admires the sciences and the arts of the vanquished, the second envies the power of the vanquishers. In the end the barbarians introduce the well-ordered man into their palaces, and the well-ordered man in his turn opens his schools to them. But when the one who possesses material force enjoys intellectual preponderance at the same time, it is rare that the vanquished is civilized; he withdraws or is destroyed.

Thus it is that one can say in a general manner that savages go to seek enlightenment with arms in hand, but that they do not accept it [when imposed].

If the Indian tribes who now inhabit the center of the continent could find enough energy in themselves to undertake to become civilized, they would perhaps succeed at it. Superior, then, to the barbarian nations that would surround them, they would little by little get strength and experience, and when the Europeans finally appeared on their frontiers, they would be in a state, if not to maintain their independence, at least to have their rights to the soil recognized and to incorporate with the vanquishers. But the misfortune of the Indians is to enter into contact with the most civilized and, I shall add, the greediest people on the globe, when they themselves are still half-barbarian; to find masters in their instructors, and to receive oppression and enlightenment at the same time.

Living within the freedom of the woods, the Indian of North America was miserable, but he did not feel himself inferior to anyone; from the moment that he wants to enter into the social hierarchy of the whites, he can occupy only the lowest rank in it; for he enters ignorant and poor into a society where science and wealth reign. After having led an agitated life, full of ills and dangers, but at the same time filled with emotion and greatness,[18] he

18. In the adventurous life of hunting peoples there is a certain irresistible attraction that seizes the heart of man and carries him away despite his reason and experience. One can be convinced of this truth in reading the *Memoirs of Tanner*. [John Tanner, *A Narrative of the Captivity and Adventures of John Tanner, during Thirty Years Residence among the Indians in the Interior of North America* (New York: G. & C. & H. Carvill, 1830).]

Tanner is a European who had been carried off by Indians at the age of six and who remained with them in the woods for thirty years. It is impossible to see anything more frightful than the miseries he describes. He shows us tribes without chiefs, families without nations, isolated men, mutilated wreckage of powerful tribes, wandering haphazardly amid ice fields and among the desolate solitudes of Canada. Hunger and cold pursued them; each day life seemed ready to escape them. Among them mores have lost their empire, traditions are without power. Men become more and more barbarian. Tanner shares all these evils; he knows his European origin;

must submit to a monotonous, obscure, and degraded existence. To gain the bread that will nourish him by hard work and in the midst of ignominy: such is in his eyes the only result of the civilization that is extolled to him.

And he is not always sure of obtaining even this result.

When the Indians undertake to imitate their European neighbors and to cultivate the land like them, they immediately find themselves exposed to the effects of a very fatal competition. The white is master of the secrets of agriculture. The Indian makes a crude start in an art that he is ignorant of. The one makes great harvests grow without trouble, the other extracts fruits from the land only with a thousandfold effort.

The European is placed in the midst of a population whose needs he knows and shares.

The savage is isolated in the midst of an enemy people whose mores, language, and laws he knows incompletely and yet cannot do without. It is only in exchanging his products for the whites' that he can find comfort, for his compatriots are no more than feeble assistance to him.

So, therefore, when the Indian wants to sell the fruits of his labors, he does not always find the buyer that the European farmer discovers without trouble, and he can produce only at great cost what the other delivers at a low price.

The Indian has therefore escaped from the ills to which the barbarian nations are exposed only to submit to the greatest miseries of well-ordered

---

he is not held by force far from whites; on the contrary, he comes to trade with them each year, goes by their dwellings, sees their ease; he knows that from the day he wants to reenter the bosom of the civilized life he can easily do it, and he remains in the wilderness for thirty years. When he finally returns to the midst of a civilized society, he confesses that the existence whose miseries he described has secret charms for him that he cannot define; he constantly goes back after having left it and tears himself away from so many evils only with a thousand regrets; and when he has finally settled in the midst of whites, several of his children refuse to come to share his tranquillity and ease with him.

I myself encountered Tanner at the entrance of Lake Superior. He appeared to me still to resemble a savage much more than a civilized man.

In the work of Tanner one finds neither order nor taste; but without knowing it, the author makes a lively painting of the prejudices, the passions, the vices, and above all the miseries of those in whose midst he lived.

Viscount Ernest de Blosseville, author of an excellent work on the penal colonies of England, has translated the *Memoirs of Tanner*. [The work on penal colonies: Ernest de Blosseville, *Histoire des colonies pénales de l'Angleterre dans l'Australie*, 1830. The translation: *Mémoires de John Tanner; ou, Trente années dans les déserts de l'Amérique du Nord* (Paris: A. Bertrand, 1831).] M. Blosseville has added notes of great interest to his translation that permit the reader to compare the facts recounted by Tanner with those already related by a great number of ancient and modern observers.

All those who desire to know the current state and to foresee the future destiny of the Indian races of North America ought to consult the work of M. Blosseville.

peoples, and he encounters almost as many difficulties in living within our abundance as in the midst of his forests.

Nevertheless, the habits of the wandering life are still not destroyed in him. Traditions have not lost their empire; the taste for the hunt is not spent. The savage joys that he formerly experienced in the depth of the woods are then painted with more vivid colors in his troubled imagination; the privations that he endured there seem, on the contrary, less frightful to him, the perils that he encountered less great. The independence that he enjoyed among his equals contrasts with the servile position he occupies in a civilized society.

On the other hand, the solitude in which he lived free for so long is still near to him; a few hours' march can bring it back to him. For the half-cleared field from which he scarcely draws something to nourish himself, the whites who are his neighbors offer him a price that seems high to him. Perhaps the money the Europeans present to him would permit him to live happy and tranquil far from them. He leaves the plow, takes up his arms again, and goes back into the wilderness forever.[20]

One can judge of the truth of this sad picture by what is taking place among the Creeks and the Cherokees, whom I have mentioned.

20. This destructive influence that very civilized peoples exert on those who are less so may be remarked among the Europeans themselves.

Nearly a century ago, some French had founded the city of Vincennes on the Wabash in the midst of the wilderness. They lived in great abundance there until the arrival of American emigrants. These immediately began to ruin the former inhabitants by their competition; afterwards they bought their lands from them at a low price. At the moment in which Mr. Volney, from whom I borrow this detail, crossed Vincennes, the number of French had been reduced to a hundred individuals, most of whom were about to move to Louisiana or to Canada. These French were honest men, but without enlightenment and without industry; they had contracted a part of the habits of the savages. The Americans, who were perhaps their inferiors from a moral point of view, had an immense intellectual superiority over them; they were industrious, educated, wealthy, and habituated to governing themselves.

I myself saw in Canada, where the intellectual difference between the two races is much less pronounced, the Englishman, master of commerce and industry in the country of the [French] Canadian, spreading in every direction and pressing the Frenchman into very narrow limits.

Likewise, in Louisiana, almost all the commercial and industrial activity is concentrated in the hands of the Anglo-Americans.

Something more striking still is taking place in the province of Texas; the state of Texas, as we know, makes up a part of Mexico and serves as its frontier with the United States. [Texas became one of the United States in 1845.] For some years, the Anglo-Americans entered individually into this still ill-populated province, bought lands, took possession of industry, and rapidly substituted themselves for the original population. It can be foreseen that if Mexico does not hasten to halt this movement, it will not be long before Texas escapes from it.

If some comparatively unnoticeable differences in European civilization lead to such results, it is easy to comprehend what will happen when the most perfected civilization enters into contact with Indian barbarism.

These Indians, in the little they have done, have surely shown as much natural genius as the peoples of Europe in their vaster undertakings; but nations, like men, need time to learn, whatever their intelligence and their efforts might be.

While these savages worked to civilize themselves, the Europeans continued to envelop them from all sides and to press them in more and more. Today, the two races have finally met; they touch each other. The Indian has indeed become superior to his father, the savage, but he is still very inferior to the white, his neighbor. With the aid of their resources and their enlightenment, the Europeans have not been slow to appropriate most of the advantages that possession of the soil could furnish to the natives; they have settled in their midst, taken possession of the land or bought it at a low price, and ruined them by a competition that the latter could not in any way sustain. Isolated in their own country, the Indians no longer formed but a small colony of inconvenient foreigners in the midst of a numerous and dominant people.[20]

Washington had said in one of his messages to Congress: "We are more enlightened and more powerful than the Indian nations; it is to our honor to treat them with goodness and even with generosity."*

This noble and virtuous policy has not been followed.

The tyranny of the government is ordinarily added to the greed of the colonists. Though the Cherokees and the Creeks be settled on the soil that they inhabited before the arrival of the Europeans, although the Americans

---

*AT may be referring to the following sentence: "A System corresponding with the mild principles of Religion and Philanthropy towards an unenlightened race of Men, whose happiness materially depends on the conduct of the United States, would be as honorable to the national character as conformable to the dictates of sound policy." George Washington, *3rd Annual Message to Congress, October 25, 1791,* in Washington, *Writings* (New York: The Library of America, 1997), 788.

20. See in the Legislative Documents, 21st Congress, no. 89, the excesses of all kinds committed by the white population on the territory of the Indians. Sometimes the Anglo-Americans establish themselves on a part of the territory, as if land were lacking elsewhere, and the troops of Congress must come to expel them; sometimes they carry off the [Indians'] cattle, burn their homes, cut down the natives' crops, or do violence to their persons.

All these documents prove that each day the natives are victims of the abuse of force. The Union habitually maintains among the Indians an agent charged with representing it; the report of the agent of the Cherokees is found among the documents that I cite: the language of this official is almost always favorable to the savages. "I fear," he says, p. 12, "[. . .] a great number of white families [would] rush into and settle on the lands embraced [. . .] to the great annoyance, distress, and ruin of the poor, helpless and inoffensive Cherokees who inhabit them." One sees further on that the state of Georgia, wanting to shrink the limits of the Cherokees, proceeds to mark out a boundary; the federal agent points out that the demarcation, having been made only by the whites and not [being] contravened, is worth nothing. [House, "Intrusions on Cherokee Lands," 21st Cong., 1st sess., 1830, H. Doc. 89, serial 197, 12ff.]

have often dealt with them as with foreign nations, the states in whose midst they are have not wanted to recognize them as independent peoples, and they have undertaken to subject these men, scarcely come out of the forest, to their magistrates, their customs, and their laws.[21] Misery had driven these unfortunate Indians toward civilization; today oppression pushes them back toward barbarism. Many among them, leaving their half-cleared fields, resume the habits of savage life.

If one pays attention to the tyrannical measures adopted by the legislators of the southern states, to the conduct of their governors and to the acts of their courts, one will easily be convinced that the complete expulsion of the Indians is the final goal to which all of their efforts simultaneously tend. The Americans of this part of the Union look jealously on the lands that the natives possess;[22] they feel that the latter have still not completely abandoned the traditions of the savage life, and before civilization has attached them solidly to the soil, they want to reduce them to despair and to force them to move out.

Oppressed by the particular states, the Creeks and the Cherokees have addressed themselves to the central government. The latter is not insensitive to their ills; it sincerely would like to save the remnants of the natives and assure them free possession of the territory that it guaranteed to them itself;[23] but when it seeks to execute this design, the particular states put up a formidable resistance, and then it resolves without difficulty to let some already half-destroyed savage tribes perish in order not to put the American Union in danger.

Powerless to protect the Indians, the federal government would like at

21. In 1829 the state of Alabama divides the territory of the Creeks into counties and subjects the Indian population to European magistrates.

In 1830 the state of Mississippi assimilates Choctaws and Chickasaws to the whites and declares that those of them who take the title of chief will be punished by a $1,000 fine and one year of prison. When the state of Mississippi thus extended its laws to the Chactas Indians who lived within its limits, the latter assembled; their chief made known to them what the claim of the whites was and read to them some of the laws to which they wanted to subject them; the savages declared in a common voice that it would be better to sink back into the wilderness. (*Mississippi Papers.*) [See *Laws of the Colonial and State Governments Relating to Indians and Indian Affairs from 1633 to 1831 Inclusive* (Washington, D.C., 1832), 242ff.]

22. The Georgians, who find themselves so uncomfortable in the neighborhood of the Indians, occupy a territory that still does not count more than seven inhabitants per square mile. In France there are one hundred sixty-two individuals in the same space.

23. In 1818 Congress ordained that the territory of Arkansas would be visited by some American commissioners, accompanied by a deputation of Creeks, Choctaws, and Chickasaws. This expedition was commanded by Messrs. Kennerly, McCoy, Wash Hood, and John Bell. See the different reports of the commissioners and their journal in the papers of Congress, no. 87, *House of Representatives.* [AT may be referring to House, 20th Cong., 2d sess., 1828–1829, H. Rep. 87, serial 190.]

least to make their lot milder; with this aim it has undertaken to transport them at its expense to other places.

Between 33 and 37 degrees north latitude extends a vast region that has taken the name Arkansas from the principal river that waters it. It borders the frontiers of Mexico on one side, the banks of the Mississippi on the other. A multitude of streams and rivers crisscross from all directions; the climate is mild and the soil fertile. One encounters only a few wandering hordes of savages there. It is to a portion of this country, most closely neighboring Mexico, and at a great distance from American settlements, that the government of the Union wants to transport the remnants of the native populations of the South.

At the end of the year 1831 we were assured that 10,000 Indians had already descended on the shores of the Arkansas; others were arriving daily. But Congress still has not been able to create a unanimous will among those whose lot it wants to regulate: some consent with joy to move out of the abode of tyranny; the most enlightened refuse to abandon their growing crops and their new dwellings; they think that if the work of civilization is interrupted, it will no longer be taken up again; they fear that sedentary habits, barely contracted, will be lost forever in the midst of still savage countries where nothing has been prepared for the subsistence of a farming people; they know that they will find enemy hordes in this new wilderness, and to resist them they no longer have the energy of barbarism, without having yet acquired the force of civilization. Besides, the Indians have no difficulty detecting all that is provisional in the settlement that is proposed for them. Who will assure them that they can finally rest in peace in their new refuge? The United States engages itself to maintain them there; but the territory that they now occupy had formerly been guaranteed to them by the most solemn oaths.[24] Today, it is true, the American government does not take their lands away from them, but it allows them to be invaded. In a few years, doubtless, the same white population that now presses on them will be on their heels in the solitudes of Arkansas; then they will again meet the same ills without the

24. In the treaty made with the Creeks in 1790, one finds this clause: "The United States solemnly guarantees to the nation of the Creeks all the lands that it possesses in the territory of the Union."

The treaty concluded in July 1791 with the Cherokees contains the following: "The United States solemnly guarantees to the nation of the Cherokees all the lands that it has not previously ceded. If a citizen of the United States or anyone other than an Indian comes to settle on the territory of the Cherokees, the United States declares that it withdraws its protection from this citizen and delivers him to the nation of the Cherokees to punish him as it seems good to them." Art. 8. [*Indian Treaties and Laws and Regulations Relating to Indian Affairs,* ed. Samuel S. Hamilton (Washington, D.C., 1826), 117.]

same remedies; and as sooner or later they will run out of land, they will ever have to resign themselves to dying.

There is less cupidity and violence in the Union's manner of acting toward the Indians than in the policy followed by the states; but the two governments are equally lacking in good faith.

The states, in extending what they call the benefit of their laws to the Indians, reckon that the latter will rather move away than submit to them; and the central government, in promising to these unfortunates a permanent refuge in the West, is not ignorant that it cannot guarantee it to them.[25]

Thus the states, by their tyranny, force the savages to flee; the Union, by its promises and with the aid of its resources, makes flight easy. These are different measures tending to the same end.[26]

"By the will of our Father in Heaven, the Governor of the whole world," said the Cherokees in their petition to Congress,[27]

> the red man of America has become small, and the white man great and renowned.
>
> When the ancestors of the people of these United States first came to the shores of America, they found the red man strong—though he was ignorant and savage, yet he received them kindly, and gave them

25. This does not prevent it from promising [a refuge] to them in the most formal manner. See the letter of the president [Andrew Jackson] addressed to the Creeks, March 23, 1829 (*Proceedings of the Indian Board in the City of New York*, p. 5). [AT shortens the text. The original reads]: "Beyond the great river Mississippi, [. . .] your father," he says, "has provided a country large enough for all of you [. . .]. There your white brothers will not trouble you; they will have no claim to the land, and you can live upon it, you and all your children, as long as the grass grows or the water runs, in peace and plenty. To you, it will *belong forever*." [AT adds emphasis; *Documents and Proceedings*, 5.]

In a letter written to the Cherokees by the secretary of the Department of War, April 18, 1829, this official [John H. Eaton, secretary of war] declares to them that they ought not to flatter themselves that they will preserve the use of the territory they occupy at this moment, but he gives them this same positive assurance for the time that they will be on the other side of the Mississippi (ibid., p. 6): as if the power that it lacks now will not be lacking just as much then!

26. In order to form an exact idea of the policy followed by the particular states and by the Union regarding the Indians, one must consult: first, the laws of the particular states relative to the Indians (this collection is found in the legislative documents, 21st Congress, no. 319) [House, "Indians, Laws of Colonial and State Governments Relating to," 21st Cong., 1st sess., 1829–1830, H. Rep. 319, serial 201]; second, the laws of the Union relative to the same object, and in particular that of March 30, 1802 (these laws are found in the work of Mr. Story entitled *Laws of the United States*) [Story, *Public and General Statutes*]; third, finally, to know what is the current state of the relations of the Union with all the Indian tribes, see the report done by Mr. Cass, secretary of war, November 29, 1823.

27. November 19, 1829. This piece is translated word for word. [House, "Cherokee Indians, Memorial of, by the Delegation of," 21st Cong., 1st sess., 1829–1830, H. Rep. 311, serial 201, 7ff.]

dry land to rest their weary feet. They met in peace, and shook hands in token of friendship.

Whatever the white man wanted and asked of the Indian, the latter willingly gave. At that time the Indian was the lord, and the white man the suppliant. But now the scene has changed. The strength of the red man has become weakness. As his neighbors increased in numbers, his power became less and less, and now, of the many and powerful tribes who once covered these United States, only a few are to be seen—a few whom a sweeping pestilence has left. The Northern tribes, who were once so numerous and powerful, are now nearly extinct. Thus it has happened to the red man of America.

Shall we, who are remnants, share the same fate?

The land on which we stand we have received as an inheritance from our fathers, who possessed it from time immemorial, as a gift from our common Father in Heaven. We have already said, that, when the white man came to the shores of America, our ancestors were found in peaceable possession of this very land. They bequeathed it to us as their children, and we have sacredly kept it, as containing the remains of our beloved men. This right of inheritance we have never ceded, nor ever forfeited. Permit us to ask, what better right can the people have to a country, than the right of inheritance and immemorial peaceable possession? We know it is said of late by the State of Georgia, and by the Executive of the United States, that we have forfeited this right—but we think this is said gratuitously. At what time have we made the forfeit? What great crime have we committed, whereby we must forever be divested of our country and rights? Was it when we were hostile to the United States, and took part with the King of Great Britain, during the struggle for Independence? If so, why was not this forfeiture declared in the first treaty of peace between the United States and our beloved men? Why was not such an article as the following inserted in the treaty: "The United States give peace to the Cherokees, but, for the part they took in the late war, declare them to be but tenants at will, to be removed, when the convenience of the States within whose chartered limits they live, shall require it." That was the proper time to assume such a possession. But it was not thought of, nor would our forefathers have agreed to any treaty, whose tendency was to deprive them of their rights and their country.

Such is the language of the Indians: what they say is true; what they foresee seems to me inevitable.

From whatever side one views the destiny of the natives of North America, one sees only irreparable ills: if they remain savages, one drives them ahead as one advances; if they want to civilize themselves, contact with men more civilized than they delivers them to oppression and misery. If they continue to wander from wilderness to wilderness, they perish; if they undertake to settle, they still perish. They can only become enlightened with the aid of the Europeans, and the approach of the Europeans depraves them and pushes them back toward barbarism. As long as they are left in their solitudes, they refuse to change their mores, and there is no longer time to do that when they are finally compelled to want it.

The Spanish unleash their dogs on the Indians as on ferocious beasts; they pillage the New World like a town taken by assault, without discrimination and without pity; but one cannot destroy everything, fury has a limit: the remnant of the Indian populations escaping the massacres in the end mixes with those who have defeated it and adopts their religion and mores.[28]

The conduct of the Americans of the United States toward the natives, on the contrary, breathes the purest love of forms and legality. Provided that the Indians stay in the savage state, the Americans do not mix at all in their affairs and treat them as independent peoples; they do not permit themselves to occupy their lands without having duly acquired them by means of a contract; and if by chance an Indian nation can no longer live on its territory, they take it like a brother by the hand and lead it to die outside the country of its fathers.

The Spanish, with the help of unexampled monstrous deeds, covering themselves with an indelible shame, could not succeed in exterminating the Indian race, nor even prevent it from sharing their rights; the Americans of the United States have attained this double result with marvelous facility— tranquilly, legally, philanthropically, without spilling blood, without violating a single one of the great principles of morality[29] in the eyes of the world. One cannot destroy men while being more respectful of the laws of humanity.

28. Furthermore, one must not honor the Spanish for this result. If the Indian tribes had not already been settled on the soil through agriculture at the moment the Europeans arrived, they would doubtless have been destroyed in South America as in North America.

29. See among others the report made by Mr. Bell in the name of the Committee on Indian Affairs, February 24, 1830, in which it is established, p. 5, by very logical reasons and where it is proved very learnedly that: "The fundamental principle, that the Indians had no right by virtue of their ancient possession either of soil, or sovereignty, has never been abandoned expressly or by implication."[Quoted in English by AT; his translation is omitted. House, "Removal of the Indians," 5.]

In reading this report, written, moreover, by a skillful hand, one is astonished at the facility and the ease with which, from the first words, the author disposes of arguments founded on natural right and on reason, which he names abstract and theoretical principles. The more I think about it, the more I think that the only difference that exists between civilized man and one who is not, in relation to justice, is this: the one disputes the justice of the rights that the other is content to violate.

POSITION THAT THE BLACK RACE OCCUPIES IN THE UNITED STATES; [30] DANGERS INCURRED BY WHITES FROM ITS PRESENCE

Why it is more difficult to abolish slavery and to make all trace of it disappear among the moderns than among the ancients.—In the United States the prejudice of the whites against the blacks seems to strengthen to the degree that slavery is destroyed.—Situation of the Negroes in the northern and southern states.—Why the Americans abolish slavery.—Servitude, which brutalizes the slave, impoverishes the master.—Differences one remarks between the right bank and the left bank of the Ohio.—To what one must attribute them.—The black race is relegated to the South, as is slavery.—How this is to be explained.—Difficulties that the southern states encounter in abolishing slavery.—Dangers of the future.—Preoccupation of minds.—Founding of a black colony in Africa.— Why Americans of the South, at the same time that they are disgusted by slavery, increase its rigors.

The Indians will die in isolation as they have lived; but the destiny of the Negroes is in a way intertwined with that of the Europeans. The two races are bound to one another without being intermingled because of that; it is as difficult for them to separate themselves completely as to unite.

The most dreadful of all the evils that threaten the future of the United States arises from the presence of blacks on its soil. When one seeks the cause of the present troubles and future dangers of the Union, from whatever point one departs one almost always arrives at this first fact.

Men generally need great and constant efforts in order to create lasting evils; but there is one evil that enters the world furtively: at first one hardly perceives it in the midst of ordinary abuses of power; it begins with an individual whose name history does not preserve; it is deposited as a cursed seed on some point of the soil; then it nourishes itself, spreads without effort, and grows naturally with the society that has let it in: this evil is slavery.

Christianity had destroyed servitude; Christians of the sixteenth century reestablished it; they nevertheless accepted it only as an exception in their social system, and they took care to restrict it to a single one of the human

---

30. Before treating this matter, I owe a notice to the reader. In a book of which I have already spoken at the beginning of this work and which is about to appear, M. Gustave de Beaumont, my traveling companion, has the principal object of making known in France what is the position of the Negroes in the midst of the white population of the United States. M. Beaumont has treated deeply a question that my subject has only permitted me to touch on.

His book, of which the notes contain a very large number of very precious and entirely unknown legislative and historical documents, presents, in addition, pictures whose energy can only be equaled by their truth. M. Beaumont's work ought to be read by those who want to comprehend to what excesses of tyranny men are pushed little by little once they begin to get away from nature and humanity. [Gustave de Beaumont, *Marie; ou, L'esclavage aux Etats-Unis: Tableau de moeurs américaines* (Brussels: Louis Hauman, 1835).]

races. They thus made a wound in humanity less large, but infinitely more difficult to heal.

One must carefully distinguish two things: slavery in itself and its consequences.

The immediate evils produced by slavery were nearly the same among the ancients as among the moderns, but the consequences of these evils were different. Among the ancients, the slave belonged to the same race as his master, and often he was superior to him in education and enlightenment.[31] Freedom alone separated them; freedom once granted, they easily intermingled.

The ancients therefore had a very simple means of delivering themselves from slavery and its consequences; this means was emancipation, and when they employed it in a general manner, they succeeded.

It is not that in antiquity the traces of servitude did not still last for some time after servitude was destroyed.

There is a natural prejudice that brings man to scorn whoever has been his inferior, for a long time after he has become his equal; an imaginary inequality that has its roots in mores always follows upon the real inequality that fortune or law produces; but among the ancients this secondary effect of slavery had a limit. The freedman so strongly resembled men of free origin that it soon became impossible to distinguish him in their midst.

What was most difficult among the ancients was to modify the law; among the moderns it is to change mores, and for us, the real difficulty begins where antiquity saw it end.

This is because among the moderns the immaterial and fugitive fact of slavery is combined in the most fatal manner with the material and permanent fact of difference in race. The remembrance of slavery dishonors the race, and race perpetuates the remembrance of slavery.

There is no African who has come freely to the shores of the New World, from which it follows that all those found there in our day are slaves or freedmen. Thus the Negro transmits to all his descendants, with their existence, the external sign of his ignominy. The law can destroy servitude; but God alone can make the trace of it disappear.

The modern slave differs from the master not only by freedom, but also by origin. You can make the Negro free, but you cannot do it so that he is not in the position of a stranger vis-à-vis the European.

This is not yet all: this man who was born in baseness; this stranger, whom

---

31. It is known that several of the most celebrated authors of antiquity were or had been slaves: Aesop [ca. 620–ca. 560 B.C.] and Terence [ca. 190–159 B.C.] are in this number. Slaves were not always taken from among the barbarian nations: war put very civilized men in servitude.

servitude introduced among us, we hardly recognize in him the general features of humanity. His countenance appears hideous to us, his intelligence
seems limited to us, his tastes are base; we very nearly take him for a being
intermediate between brute and man.[32]

The moderns, after having abolished slavery, therefore have still to destroy
three prejudices much more intangible and more tenacious than it: the prejudice of the master, the prejudice of race, and finally the prejudice of the white.

It is very difficult for us, we who have had the happiness to be born in the
midst of men whom nature made like us and the law made our equals; it is
very difficult for us, I say, to comprehend what impassable space separates
the Negro of America from the European. But we can have a distant idea of
it from reasoning by analogy.

Formerly we saw great inequalities among us that had their beginnings*
only in legislation. What is more fictitious than a purely legal inequality!
What is more contrary to the instinct of man than permanent differences
established among people evidently alike! These differences have nonetheless
persisted for centuries; they still persist in a thousand places; everywhere they
have left traces that are imaginary, but that time can hardly efface. If inequality created solely by the law is so difficult to uproot, how does one destroy
that which seems, in addition, to have its immutable foundations in nature
itself?

As for me, when I consider the trouble that aristocratic corps, of whatever
nature they may be, have in mingling with the mass of people and the extreme care they take to preserve for centuries the imaginary† barriers that
separate them from it, I despair of seeing an aristocracy founded on visible
and imperishable signs disappear.

Those who hope that the Europeans will one day intermingle with Negroes therefore appear to me to cherish a chimera. My reason does not lead
me to believe it, and I see nothing in the facts that indicates it to me.

Until now, everywhere that whites have been most powerful, they have
held Negroes in degradation or in slavery. Everywhere that Negroes have
been strongest, they have destroyed whites; this is the only account that has
ever been opened between the two races.

If I consider the United States in our day, I see indeed that in a certain
part of the country the legal barrier that separates the two races tends to fall,

---

*Lit.: "principles."

†Lit.: "ideal."

32. In order that the whites abandon the opinion they have conceived of the intellectual and
moral inferiority of their former slaves, the Negroes would have to change, and they cannot
change as long as this opinion subsists.

but not that of mores: I perceive slavery receding; the prejudice to which it has given birth is unmoving.

In the portion of the Union where Negroes are no longer slaves, have they been brought closer to whites? Every man who has inhabited the United States will have noticed that a contrary effect has been produced.

Racial prejudice appears to me stronger in the states that have abolished slavery than in those where slavery still exists, and nowhere is it shown to be as intolerant as in states where servitude has always been unknown.

It is true that in the North of the Union the law permits Negroes and whites to contract legitimate alliances; but opinion declares the white man who would unite with a Negro woman to be infamous, and it would be very difficult to cite an example of such a deed.

In almost all the states where slavery was abolished, the Negro has been given electoral rights; but if he presents himself to vote, he runs a risk to his life. Oppressed, he can complain, but he finds only whites among his judges. The law does indeed open the jurors' bench to him, but prejudice repels him from it. His son is excluded from the school where the descendant of Europeans comes to be instructed. In theaters he cannot buy for the price of gold the right to be placed at the side of one who was his master; in hospitals he lies apart. The black is permitted to beseech the same God as whites, but not to pray to him at the same altar. He has his own priests and churches. One does not close the doors of Heaven to him: yet inequality hardly stops at the boundary of the other world. When the Negro is no longer, his bones are cast to one side, and the difference of conditions is still found even in the equality of death.

Thus the Negro is free, but he can share neither the rights, nor the pleasures, nor the labors, nor the grief, nor even the tomb of the one whose equal he has been declared; nowhere can he meet with him, neither in life nor in death.

In the South, where slavery still exists, Negroes are kept to one side less carefully; they sometimes share the labors of whites and their pleasures; one consents up to a certain point to mix with them; legislation is harder in regard to them; habits are more tolerant and milder.

In the South, the master does not fear lifting his slave up to himself because he knows that he will always be able, if he wishes, to throw him back into the dust. In the North, the white no longer perceives distinctly the barrier that will separate him from a debased race, and he draws back from the Negro with all the more care since he fears one day being intermingled with him.

In the American of the South, nature, sometimes recovering its rights, comes for a moment to reestablish equality between whites and blacks. In the North, pride silences even the most imperious passion of man. The American of the North would perhaps consent to make the Negro woman the passing companion of his pleasures if legislators had declared that she must not aspire to share his bed; but she can become his wife, and he draws back from her with a sort of horror.

Thus in the United States the prejudice that repels Negroes seems to grow as Negroes cease to be slaves, and inequality is engraved in mores in the same measure as it is effaced in the laws.

But if the relative position of the two races inhabiting the United States is such as I have just shown it to be, why have Americans abolished slavery in the North of the Union, why have they preserved it in the South, and how is it that they aggravate its rigors there?

It is easy to respond. It is not in the interest of Negroes, but of whites, that slavery is being destroyed in the United States.

The first Negroes were imported into Virginia around the year 1621.[33] In America, as on all the rest of the earth, servitude was therefore born in the South. From there it has advanced little by little; but as slavery spread toward the North, the number of slaves decreased;[34] one has always seen very few Negroes in New England.

The colonies were founded; a century had already passed, and an extraordinary fact began to strike the notice of all. The provinces that so to speak possessed no slaves grew in population, in wealth, and in well-being more rapidly than those that had them.

In the former, however, the inhabitant was obliged to cultivate the soil himself or to rent the services of another; in the latter he found at his disposi-

---

33. See *The History of Virginia*, by Beverley. See also, in the *Memoirs of Jefferson*, curious details about the introduction of the Negroes into Virginia and about the first act that prohibited their importation in 1778. [Beverley, *History*, 35–37. Conseil, *Mélanges politiques et philosophiques*, 197.]

34. The number of slaves was less in the North, but the advantages resulting from slavery were not more contested there than in the South. In 1740 the legislature of the state of New York declared that the greatest possible direct importation of slaves must be encouraged and that contraband must be severely punished as tending to discourage the honest trader. (Kent's *Commentaries*, vol. 2, p. 206).

In the Historical Collection of Massachusetts, vol. 4, p. 193, one finds some curious research of Belknap on slavery in New England. [Jeremy Belknap, *Queries Respecting the Slavery and Emancipation of the Negroes in Massachusetts, Proposed by the Hon. Judge Tucker of Virginia, and Answered by the Rev. Dr. Belknap*, in *Collections of the Massachusetts Historical Society for the Year 1795* (Boston: Samuel Hall, n.d.), 191–211.] From this it appears that Negroes were introduced as early as 1630, but that ever since then legislation and mores showed opposition to slavery.

In this [same] place, see also the manner in which public opinion, then the law, came to destroy servitude.

tion workers whose efforts were not remunerated. There was, therefore, work and expense on one side, leisure and economy on the other; the advantage, however, remained with the former.

This result appeared all the more difficult to explain as the emigrants, all belonging to the same European race, had the same habits, the same civilization, the same laws, and differed only by hardly perceptible nuances.

Time continued to march on: leaving the coast of the Atlantic Ocean, the Anglo-Americans plunged farther every day into the solitudes of the West; there they encountered new terrains and climates; there they had to defeat obstacles of a diverse nature; their races mixed, southerners went to the North, northerners descended to the South. In the midst of all these causes, the same fact recurred at each step; and, generally, the colonies where there were no slaves became more populated and more prosperous than those in which slavery was vigorous.

As one advanced, one therefore began to make out that servitude, while so cruel to the slave, was fatal to the master.

But this truth received its final demonstration when one reached the banks of the Ohio.

The river that the Indians had named for its excellence the Ohio, or Beautiful River, waters one of the most magnificent valleys in which man has ever made his stay. On both banks of the Ohio stretches undulating ground, where every day the soil offers inexhaustible treasures to the laborer: on both banks the air is equally healthful and the climate temperate; each of them forms the frontier of a vast state: the one that follows on the left the thousand windings that the Ohio describes in its course is named Kentucky; the other has borrowed its name from the river itself. The two states differ only on a single point: Kentucky has accepted slaves, the state of Ohio has rejected them all from its midst.[35]

The traveler who, placed in the middle of the Ohio, allows himself to be carried along by the current to the mouth of the river in the Mississippi, therefore, navigates so to speak between freedom and servitude; and he has only to cast glances around himself to judge in an instant which is more favorable to humanity.

On the left bank of the river, the population is sparse; from time to time one perceives a troop of slaves running through half-wild fields with an insouciant air; the primitive forest constantly reappears; one would say that society is asleep; man seems idle, nature offers the image of activity and of life.

35. Not only does Ohio not accept slavery, but it prohibits the entry of free Negroes into its territory, and forbids them to acquire anything in it. See the statutes of Ohio.

From the right bank, on the contrary, rises a confused noise that proclaims from afar the presence of industry; rich harvests cover the fields; elegant dwellings announce the taste and the care of the laborer; on all sides comfort reveals itself; man appears rich and content: he works.[36]

The state of Kentucky was founded in 1775, the state of Ohio only twelve years later: twelve years in America is more than a half-century in Europe. Today the population of Ohio already exceeds that of Kentucky by 250,000 inhabitants.[37]

These diverse effects of slavery and freedom are easily understood; they suffice to explain very well differences that are encountered between ancient civilization and that of our day.

On the left bank of the Ohio work is blended with the idea of slavery; on the right bank, with that of well-being and progress; there it is degraded, here they honor it; on the left bank of the river, one cannot find workers belonging to the white race, [for] they would fear resembling slaves; one must rely on the care of the Negroes; on the right bank one would seek in vain for an idle man: the white extends his activity and his intelligence to all his works.

So, therefore, the men in Kentucky who are charged with exploiting the natural riches of the soil have neither zeal nor enlightenment; while those who could have these two things do nothing, or cross over into Ohio in order to utilize their industry and to be able to exercise it without shame.

It is true that in Kentucky, masters make slaves work without being obliged to pay them, but they receive little fruit from their efforts, while the money that they would give to free workers would be recovered with interest from the value of their labors.

The free worker is paid, but he acts more quickly than the slave, and rapidity of execution is one of the great elements of economy. The white sells his assistance, but one buys it only when it is useful; the black has nothing to claim as the price of his services, but one is obliged to nourish him at all times; one must sustain him in his old age as in his mature age, in his sterile childhood as during the fruitful years of his youth, through sickness as in health. Thus, only by paying does one obtain the work of these two men: the free worker receives a wage; the slave an education, food, care, clothing; the money that the master spends to keep the slave is drained little by little and in detail; one hardly perceives it: the wage that one gives to the worker is

36. It is not only the individual man who is active in Ohio; the state itself has immense undertakings; the state of Ohio has established a canal between Lake Erie and the Ohio by means of which the valley of the Mississippi communicates with the river of the north. Thanks to this canal, goods from Europe that arrive in New York can descend by water to New Orleans across more than five hundred leagues of the continent.

37. The exact figure according to the census of 1830: Kentucky, 688,844; Ohio, 937,679.

delivered in one stroke, and it seems to enrich only the one who receives it; but in reality the slave has cost more than the free man and his work has been less productive.[38]

The influence of slavery extends further still; it penetrates to the very soul of the master and impresses a particular direction on his ideas and his tastes.

On the two banks of the Ohio, nature has given man an enterprising and energetic character; but on each side of the river he makes a different use of this common quality.

The white on the right bank, obliged to live by his own efforts, has placed in material well-being the principal goal of his existence; and as the country that he inhabits presents inexhaustible resources to his industry and offers ever renewed enticements to his activity, his ardor for acquiring has surpassed the ordinary bounds of human cupidity: tormented by the desire for wealth, one sees him enter boldly onto all the paths that fortune opens to him; he becomes indiscriminately a sailor, a pioneer, a manufacturer, a farmer, supporting the work or dangers attached to these different professions with equal constancy; there is something marvelous in the resources of his genius and a sort of heroism in his greed for gain.

The American on the left bank scorns not only work, but all the undertakings that work makes successful; living in idle ease, he has the tastes of idle men; money has lost a part of its worth in his eyes; he pursues fortune less than agitation and pleasure, and he applies in this direction the energy that his neighbor deploys elsewhere; he passionately loves hunting and war; he pleases himself with the most violent exercises of the body; the use of arms is familiar to him, and from his childhood he has learned to stake his life in single combat. Slavery, therefore, not only prevents whites from making a fortune; it diverts them from wanting it.

The same causes working in contrary directions continuously for two centuries in the English colonies of northern America have in the end made an enormous difference between the commercial capacity of the southerner and

38. Independent of these causes, which, everywhere free workers abound, render their work more productive and more economical than that of slaves, one must point out another one particular to the United States: over all the area of the Union a means of cultivating sugar cane with success has still not been found except on the banks of the Mississippi, near the mouth of this river in the Gulf of Mexico. In Louisiana the cultivation of cane is extremely advantageous: nowhere does the laborer get as high a price from his work; and, as there is always established a certain relation between the costs of production and the products, the price of slaves is very high in Louisiana. Now, Louisiana being among the number of confederated states, one can transport slaves from all parts of the Union to it; the price that one gives for a slave in New Orleans therefore raises the price of slaves in all other markets. The result is that in countries where the land brings in little, the costs of cultivation by slaves continue to be very considerable, which gives a great advantage to the competition of free workers.

that of the northerner. Today it is only the North that has ships, manufactures, railroads, and canals.

This difference is remarked not only in comparing the North and the South, but in comparing the inhabitants of the South among themselves. Almost all the men in the southernmost states of the Union who engage in commercial undertakings and seek to utilize slavery have come from the North; every day people from the North expand into this part of American territory where competition is less to be feared for them; they discover resources there that the inhabitants have not perceived, and bowing to a system that they disapprove of, they succeed in taking better advantage of it than those who still support it after having founded it.

If I wanted to push the parallel further, I would easily prove that almost all the differences remarked between Americans of the South and the North have arisen from slavery; but that would be to depart from my subject: at this moment I am not looking for all the effects of servitude, but for the effects it produces on the material prosperity of those who have accepted it.

The influence of slavery on the production of wealth could only be very imperfectly known in antiquity. Servitude existed then in the whole ordered universe, and peoples who did not know it were barbarians.

So Christianity destroyed slavery only by asserting the rights of the slave; in our day one can attack it in the name of the master: on this point interest and morality are in accord.

As these truths became obvious in the United States, one saw slavery receding little by little before the enlightenment of experience.

Servitude had begun in the South and was then extended toward the North; today it is retreating. Freedom, starting out from the North, is descending toward the South without a stop. Among the large states, Pennsylvania today forms the ultimate limit of slavery to the north, but within these very limits it is shaken; every day Maryland, which is immediately below Pennsylvania, is preparing itself to do without it, and already Virginia, which follows Maryland, is discussing its utility and its dangers.[39]

No great change in human institutions will be made without discovering estate law in the middle of the causes of that change.

39. There is a particular reason that serves to detach the last two states that I have just named from the cause of slavery.

The former wealth of this part of the Union was founded principally on the cultivation of tobacco. Slaves are particularly appropriate to this cultivation: now, it happens that for many years tobacco has been losing its monetary value; nonetheless, the value of slaves has remained the same. Thus the relation between the costs of production and the products has changed. The inhabitants of Maryland and Virginia therefore feel more disposed than they were thirty years ago either to do without slaves in the cultivation of tobacco or to abandon the cultivation of tobacco and slavery at the same time.

When inequality of [inherited] shares reigned in the South, each family was represented by a rich man who felt no more need than taste for work; around him the members of his family whom law had excluded from the common inheritance lived in the same manner, like so many parasitic plants; one then saw in all the families of the South what one still sees in our day in the noble families of certain countries of Europe, where the younger ones, without having the same wealth as the eldest, remain as idle as he. An effect like this was produced in America and in Europe by entirely analogous causes. In the South of the United States, the entire race of whites formed an aristocratic corps at the head of which stood a certain number of privileged individuals whose wealth was permanent and whose leisure was hereditary. These heads of the American nobility perpetuated the traditional prejudices of the white race in the body of which they were the representatives and kept idleness in honor. Within this aristocracy, one could encounter poor men, but not workers; misery appeared preferable to industry; Negro workers and slaves therefore found no competitors, and whatever opinion one could have about the utility of their efforts, it was indeed necessary to employ them, since they were the only ones.

From the moment when this estate law was abolished, all fortunes began to diminish simultaneously, all families were brought by the same movement to a state in which work became necessary to existence; many among them disappeared entirely; all foresaw the moment when it would be necessary for each to provide for his needs himself. Today one still sees wealthy men, but they no longer form a compact and hereditary corps; they could not adopt one spirit, persevere in it, and make it pervade through all ranks. The prejudice that vilified work therefore began to be abandoned by common accord; there were more poor men, and the poor could occupy themselves with the means of earning their living without blushing. Thus one of the quickest effects of equality of shares was to create a class of free workers. From the moment when the free worker entered into competition with the slave the inferiority of the latter made itself felt, and slavery was attacked in its very principle, which is the interest of the master.

As slavery recedes, the black race follows it in its backward march and returns with it to the tropics, from which it originally came.

This can appear extraordinary at first; [but] one will soon conceive why.

In abolishing the principle of servitude, Americans do not set the slaves free.

Perhaps one would comprehend only with difficulty what is going to follow if I did not cite an example: I shall choose the state of New York. In 1788, the state of New York prohibited the sale of slaves within it. That was a roundabout manner of prohibiting importation. From that time the number of Negroes no longer increased except with the natural increase of the black population. Eight years after, they took a more decisive measure, and declared that starting July 4, 1799, all children born to slave parents would be free. Every way to increase is then closed; there are still slaves, but one can say that servitude no longer exists.

From the time when a northern state thus prohibits the importation of slaves, one no longer withdraws blacks from the South to transport them to it.

From the moment when a northern state forbids the sale of Negroes, the slave, no longer able to leave the hands of whoever possesses him, becomes inconvenient property and one has an interest in transporting him to the South.

On the day when a northern state declares the son of the slave shall be born free, the latter loses a great part of his monetary value; for his posterity can no longer enter the market, and again one has a great interest in transporting him to the South.

Thus the same law prevents southern slaves from coming to the North and pushes northern ones toward the South.

But here is another cause more powerful than all those I have just spoken of.

As the number of slaves diminishes in a state, the need for free workers is felt. As free workers take hold of industry, the work of the slave being less productive, the latter becomes mediocre or useless property, and again it is to one's great interest to export him to the South, where competition is not to be feared.

The abolition of slavery, therefore, does not enable the slave to arrive at freedom; it only makes him change masters: from the North he passes to the South.

As for freed Negroes and those born after slavery has been abolished, they do not leave the North to go to the South, but they find themselves in a position analogous to that of the natives vis-à-vis the Europeans; they remain half-civilized and deprived of rights in the midst of a population that is infinitely superior to them in wealth and enlightenment; they come up against the tyranny of the laws[40] and the intolerance of mores. More unfortunate in a certain respect than the Indians, they have the remembrance of slavery [working] against them, and they cannot claim the possession of a single

40. The states in which slavery has been abolished ordinarily apply themselves to rendering the stay in their territory unpleasant to free Negroes; and as a sort of emulation is established on this point among the different states, the unfortunate Negroes can only choose among evils.

spot on the soil; many succumb to their misery;[41] the others concentrate in the towns, where, taking on the roughest work, they lead a precarious and miserable existence.

Besides, even if the number of Negroes should continue to grow in the same manner as in the period when they did not yet possess freedom, while the number of whites is rising at double their rate after the abolition of slavery, blacks would soon be almost engulfed within the torrents of a foreign population.

A country cultivated by slaves is generally less populated than a country cultivated by free men; in addition, America is a new region; therefore at the moment when a state abolishes slavery, it is still only half full. Scarcely has servitude been destroyed there, and the need for free workers made itself felt, when one sees a host of hardy adventurers from all parts of the country run to it; they come to profit from the new resources that are going to be opened to industry. The soil is divided up among them; on each portion a family of whites settles down to take possession of it. It is thus toward the free states that European emigration is directed. What would the poor man of Europe do if, coming to seek comfort and happiness in the New World, he went to inhabit a country where work is tainted with ignominy?

Thus the white population grows by its own natural motion and at the same time by an immense emigration, whereas the black population does not get emigrants and diminishes. Soon the proportion that existed between the two races is reversed. The Negroes form no more than unfortunate remnants, a small, poor, and nomadic tribe lost in the midst of an immense people that is master of the soil; and their presence is no longer perceived except by the injustices and the rigors of which they are the object.

In many of the western states the Negro race has never appeared; in all the northern states it is disappearing. The great question of the future therefore contracts into a narrow circle; it thus becomes less formidable but not easier to resolve.

As one descends toward the South, it is more difficult to abolish slavery usefully. This results from several material causes which it is necessary to develop.

41. A great difference in the mortality of whites and blacks exists in states where slavery has been abolished: from 1820 to 1831 only one white out of forty-two individuals belonging to the white race died in Philadelphia, whereas one Negro out of twenty-one individuals belonging to the black race died there. Mortality is not nearly as great among Negro slaves. (See *Emerson's Medical Statistics*, p. 28.) [Gouverneur Emerson, *Medical Statistics: Consisting of Estimates Relating to the Population of Philadelphia, with Its Changes as Influenced by the Deaths and Births, during Ten Years* (Philadelphia: Skerret, 1831), 28.]

The first is climate: it is certain that to the degree that Europeans approach the tropics, work becomes more difficult for them; many Americans even claim that below a certain latitude it is in the end fatal for them, whereas the Negro submits to it without dangers;[42] but I do not think that this idea, so favorable to the laziness of the southerner, is founded on experience. It is not warmer in the south of the Union than in the south of Spain and Italy.[43] Why can the European not execute the same work there? And if slavery has been abolished in Italy and Spain without the masters' perishing, why would the same not happen in the Union? I therefore do not believe that nature has forbidden the Europeans of Georgia or Florida, under pain of death, to derive their subsistence from the soil by themselves; but that work would surely be more painful and less productive[44] for them than for the inhabitants of New England. The free worker thus losing a part of his superiority over the slave in the South, it is less useful to abolish slavery.

All the plants of Europe grow in the north of the Union; the South has some special products.

It has been remarked that slavery is an extravagant means of cultivating cereal. Whoever grows wheat in a country where servitude is unknown habitually keeps a small number of workers in his service; in the period of the harvest and during sowings, it is true, he brings in many others; but they stay in his dwelling only temporarily.

To fill his granaries or to seed his fields, the farmer who lives in a slave state is obliged to maintain a great number of servants during the whole year, who are necessary to him only for a few days; for, as distinct from free workers, slaves cannot wait, while working for themselves, for the moment when one will come to hire their industry. One must buy them to make use of them.

Slavery, independent of its general inconveniences, is therefore naturally less suitable to countries where cereals are cultivated than to those where other products are grown.

The cultivation of tobacco, cotton, and above all sugar cane, on the con-

42. This is true in the places where rice is cultivated. Rice paddies, which are unhealthful in every country, are particularly dangerous in those that are struck by the burning sun of the tropics. Europeans would indeed have trouble in cultivating the land in this part of the New World if they wanted to persist in having it produce rice. But can one not do without rice paddies?

43. These states are nearer to the equator than Italy and Spain, but the continent of America is infinitely colder than Europe.

44. Spain formerly transported a certain number of peasants from the Azores into a district of Louisiana called Attakapas. Slavery was not introduced among them; it was a test. Today these men still cultivate the land without slaves; but their industry is so listless that it scarcely furnishes their needs.

trary, requires continuous care. One can employ women and children that one could not use in the cultivation of wheat. Thus, slavery is naturally more appropriate to countries where one extracts the products that I have just named.

Tobacco, cotton, and sugar cane grow only in the South; there they form the principal sources of the wealth of the country. By destroying slavery, southerners would find themselves in one of these alternatives: either they would be obliged to change their system of cultivation, and then they would enter into competition with northerners, more active and more experienced than they; or they would cultivate the same products without slaves, and then they would have to withstand the competition of other states in the South that had kept them.

Thus the South has particular reasons for keeping slavery that the North does not have.

But here is another motive, more powerful than all the others. The South, if it had to, could well abolish servitude; but how would it relieve itself of blacks? In the North, slavery and the slaves are driven out at the same time. In the South, one cannot hope at the same time to attain this double result.

In proving that servitude was more natural and more advantageous in the South than in the North, I indicated sufficiently that the number of slaves will be much greater there. It is to the South that the first Africans were brought; they have always arrived in greater number there. As one advances toward the South, the prejudice that holds idleness in honor gathers power. In the states most closely neighboring the tropics, there is no white who works. Negroes are therefore naturally more numerous in the South than in the North. Each day, as I said above, they become more so; for as slavery is destroyed at one end of the Union, Negroes accumulate at the other. Thus the number of blacks rises in the South, not only by the natural motion of the population, but also by the forced migration of Negroes from the North. The African race has causes to grow in this part of the Union analogous to those that make the European race in the North enlarge so quickly.

In the state of Maine, there is one Negro per three hundred inhabitants; in Massachusetts, one in a hundred; in the state of New York, two in a hundred; in Pennsylvania, three; in Maryland, thirty-four; forty-two in Virginia; and finally, fifty-five in South Carolina.[45] Such was the proportion of blacks

45. One reads what follows in the American work entitled *Letters on the Colonization Society*, by Carey, 1833: "In South Carolina, for forty years the black race has grown more quickly than that of the whites. In making a sum of the population of the five states of the South that have had slaves from the first," Mr. Carey also says, "Maryland, Virginia, North Carolina, South Carolina and Georgia, one discovers that from 1790 to 1830, whites have increased in the ratio of 80

in relation to that of whites in the year 1830. But this proportion changes constantly: every day it becomes smaller in the North and greater in the South.

It is evident that in the southernmost states of the Union, slavery cannot be abolished as has been done in the northern states without running very great dangers that the latter have not had to fear.

We have seen how the northern states managed the transition between slavery and freedom. They keep the present generation in irons and emancipate future races; in this manner, Negroes are introduced into society only little by little, and while the man who could make a bad use of his independence is kept in servitude, the one who can still learn the art of being free, before becoming master of himself, is set free.

It is difficult to apply this method to the South. When one declares that from a certain period on, the Negro's son shall be free, one introduces the principle and the idea of freedom into the very heart of servitude: the blacks that the legislator keeps in slavery and who see their sons leave it are astonished by this unequal partition that destiny makes among them; they become restive and angered. From then on, in their eyes slavery has lost the kind of moral power that time and custom gave it; it is reduced to being no more than a visible abuse of force. The North had nothing to fear from this contrast because in the North blacks were few and whites very many. But if this first dawn of freedom brought light to two million men at the same time, the oppressors would have to tremble.

After having freed their slaves' sons, Europeans of the South would soon be compelled to extend the same benefit to all of the black race.

In the North, as I said above, from the moment that slavery is abolished, and even from the moment that it becomes probable that the time of its abolition is approaching, a twofold movement takes place: slaves leave the region to be transported farther to the south; in their place whites from the northern states and emigrants from Europe pour in.

These two causes cannot operate in the same manner in the states farthest south. On the one hand, the mass of slaves is too great to enable one to hope to make them leave the region; on the other hand, the Europeans and Anglo-Americans of the North fear living in a place where work has still not been rehabilitated. Besides, they reasonably regard the states in which the propor-

---

per 100 in these states, and blacks in that of 112 per 100." [Only the last phrase is close to a direct quote; the rest are AT's summaries of Carey's tables.]

In the United States in 1830, men belonging to the two races were distributed in the following manner: states where slavery has been abolished, 6,565,434 whites, 120,520 Negroes. States where slavery still exists, 3,960,814 whites, 2,208,102 Negroes. [Matthew Carey, *Letters on the Colonization Society and on Its Probable Results* (Philadelphia: Johnson, 1833), 12.]

tion of Negroes surpasses or equals that of whites as threatened with great misfortunes, and they refrain from turning their industry in that direction.

Thus, in abolishing slavery, southerners would not, like their brothers in the North, succeed in having the Negroes arrive at freedom gradually; they would not appreciably diminish the number of blacks, and they alone would remain to check them. In the course of a few years, one would therefore see a great population of free Negroes placed in the midst of an approximately equal nation of whites.

In the South the same abuses of power that maintain slavery today would then become the source of the greatest dangers that the whites had to fear. Today the descendant of Europeans alone possesses land; he is absolute master of industry; he alone is wealthy, enlightened, armed. The black possesses none of the these advantages; but he can do without them, he is a slave. Having become free, charged with watching over his lot by himself, can he remain deprived of all these things without dying? What constituted the force of the white when slavery existed exposes it, therefore, to a thousand perils after slavery has been abolished.

Leaving the Negro in servitude, one can keep him in a state bordering on that of a brute; free, one cannot prevent him from instructing himself enough to appreciate the extent of his ills and to glimpse a remedy for them. There is, moreover, a singular principle of relative justice that one finds very deeply embedded in the human heart. Men are much more struck with the inequality existing inside the same class than with inequalities they remark between different classes. One comprehends slavery; but how does one conceive the existence of several million citizens eternally bowed under infamy and left to inherited miseries? In the North, a population of freed Negroes experiences these evils and feels these injustices; but it is weak and reduced; in the South it would be numerous and strong.

From the moment one accepts that whites and emancipated Negroes have been placed on the same soil as peoples foreign to one another, one will understand without difficulty that there are no more than two chances for the future: Negroes and whites must intermingle entirely or separate.

I have already expressed my conviction about the first means.[46] I do not think that the white race and the black race will come to live on a footing of equality anywhere.

46. This opinion, furthermore, is supported by authorities far more serious than mine. One reads in the *Memoirs of Jefferson* among others: "Nothing is more clearly written in the book of destinies than the freeing of the Blacks, and it is altogether as certain that the two races, equally free, cannot live under the same government. Nature, habit and opinion have established insurmountable barriers between them." (See *Extract of the Memoirs of Jefferson,* by M. Conseil.) [Conseil, *Mélanges politiques et philosophiques.*]

But I believe that the difficulty will be much greater in the United States than everywhere else. It happens that a man places himself outside the prejudices of religion, country, race—and if this man is a king, he can work surprising revolutions in society: a whole people cannot thus put itself in a way above itself.

A despot coming to intermingle the Americans and their former slaves under the same yoke would perhaps succeed in mixing them: as long as American democracy remains at the head of affairs, no one will dare to attempt such an undertaking, and one can foresee that the more the whites of the United States are free, the more they will seek to isolate themselves.[48]

I said elsewhere* that the genuine bond between the European and the Indian is the half-breed; likewise, the genuine transition between the white and the Negro is the mulatto: everywhere that a very great number of mulattoes are found, fusion between the two races is not impossible.

There are parts of America where the European and the Negro are so crossed that it is difficult to encounter a man who is either perfectly white or perfectly black: arrived at this point, one can really say that the two races are mixed; or rather, in their place, a third has come about that takes after the two without being precisely either the one or the other.

Of all Europeans, the English are those who have least mixed their blood with that of Negroes. One sees more mulattoes in the South of the Union than in the North, but infinitely fewer than in any other European colony; mulattoes are very few in number in the United States; they have no force by themselves, and in quarrels of the races, they ordinarily make common cause with the whites. Thus in Europe one often sees the lackeys of great lords play the noble with the people.

This haughtiness about origin, natural to the Englishman, is again singularly increased in the American by the individual haughtiness that democratic freedom gives birth to. The white man in the United States is proud of his race and proud of himself.

Besides, as whites and Negroes do not succeed in mixing in the North of the Union, how would they mix in the South? Can one suppose for an instant that the American of the South, placed, as he always will be, between the white man, in all his physical and moral superiority, and the Negro, can ever think of intermingling with the latter? The American of the South has two energetic passions that will always bring him to isolate himself: he fears

*Earlier in this chapter.

48. If the English of the West Indies had governed themselves, one can be sure that they would not have accorded the act of emancipation that the mother country has just imposed.

resembling the Negro, his former slave, and descending below his white neighbor.

If one absolutely had to foresee the future, I would say that, following the probable course of things, the abolition of slavery in the South will increase the repugnance for blacks felt by the white population. I base this opinion on what I have already remarked by analogy in the North. I said that white northerners draw back from Negroes all the more carefully as the legislator lessens the legal separation that exists between them: why would it not be the same in the South? In the North, when whites fear being intermingled with blacks, they are scared of an imaginary danger. In the South, where the danger would be real, I cannot believe that the fear would be less.

If, on the one hand, one recognizes (and the fact is not doubtful) that in the extreme South, blacks accumulate constantly and increase more quickly than whites; if on the other hand, one concedes that it is impossible to foresee the period when blacks and whites will come to be mixed and to get the same advantages from society, ought one not conclude that in the states of the South, blacks and whites will sooner or later end by entering into conflict?

What will the final result of this conflict be?

One will understand without difficulty that on this point one must wrap oneself in vague conjectures. The human mind succeeds only with difficulty in tracing a sort of great circle around the future; but within that circle vibrates chance, which escapes all efforts [of foresight]. In the picture of the future, chance always forms the obscure point where the eye of the intellect cannot penetrate. What one can say is this: in the West Indies, it is the white race that seems destined to succumb; on the continent, the black race.

In the West Indies, whites are isolated in the middle of an immense population of blacks; on the continent, blacks are placed between the sea and an innumerable people that already extends above them like a compact mass from the glaciers of Canada to the frontiers of Virginia, from the banks of the Missouri to the coast of the Atlantic Ocean. If the whites of North America remain united, it is difficult to believe that the Negroes can escape the destruction that threatens them; they will succumb to the sword or to misery. But the black populations gathered along the Gulf of Mexico have a chance of salvation if the struggle between the two races comes to develop at a time when the American confederation has dissolved. Once the federal link is broken, southerners would be wrong to count on lasting support on the part of their brothers in the North. The latter know that the danger can never reach them; if a positive duty does not constrain them to march to the assistance of the South, one can foresee that racial sympathies will be powerless.

Furthermore, whatever the period of the struggle may be, the whites of the South, should they be abandoned to themselves, will enter the lists with an immense superiority of enlightenment and of means; but the blacks will have numbers and the energy of despair working for them. These are great resources when one has arms in hand. Perhaps then what happened to the Moors in Spain will happen to the white race of the South. After having occupied the country for centuries, they will finally withdraw little by little toward the region from which their ancestors once came, abandoning to the Negroes possession of a country that Providence seems to destine for them, since they live in it without difficulty and work in it more easily than whites.

The more or less distant, but inevitable, danger of a struggle between the blacks and whites who populate the South of the Union constantly presents itself as a painful dream to the imagination of the Americans. Inhabitants of the North discuss these perils every day, although they have nothing to fear from them directly. They seek vainly to find a means of averting the misfortunes they foresee.

In the southern states people keep silent; they do not speak of the future to foreigners; they avoid explaining it to their friends; each so to speak hides it from himself. The silence of the South is something more frightening than the noisy fears of the North.

This general preoccupation of minds has given birth to an almost overlooked undertaking that may change the lot of a part of the human race.

Dreading the dangers that I have just described, a certain number of American citizens have united in a society with the goal of exporting at their expense to the coasts of Guinea the free Negroes who would like to escape the tyranny that weighs on them.[48]

In 1820, the society I am speaking of succeeded in founding a settlement in Africa, at 7 degrees north latitude, to which it gave the name *Liberia.* The latest news was announcing that two thousand five hundred Negroes were already gathered at this point. Transported to their former native country, blacks have introduced American institutions to it. Liberia has a representative system, Negro jurors, Negro magistrates, Negro priests; one sees churches and newspapers there, and, by a singular reversal of the vicissitudes of this world, it is forbidden to whites to settle within its precincts.[49]

48. This society took the name Society for the Colonization of Blacks.

See the annual reports, and notably the fifteenth. See also the already noted brochure entitled *Letters on the Colonization Society and on Its Probable Results,* by Mr. Carey. Philadelphia, April 1833.

49. This last rule was drawn up by the founders of the settlement themselves. They feared that something analogous to what is taking place on the frontiers of the United States would happen in Africa, and that the Negroes, like the Indians, as they entered into contact with a more enlightened race than theirs, would be destroyed before being able to civilize themselves.

There for sure is a strange play of fortune! Two centuries have passed since the day when the inhabitant of Europe undertook to remove the Negroes from their families and their country to transport them to the shores of North America. Today one encounters the European busy with carrying the descendants of those same Negroes across the Atlantic Ocean again so as to carry them back to the soil from which he had formerly dragged away their fathers. Barbarians have drawn the enlightenment of civilization from the midst of servitude and learned in slavery the art of being free.

Until our day, Africa was closed to the arts and sciences of whites. The enlightenment of Europe, brought in by Africans, will perhaps spread there. There is, therefore, a beautiful and great idea in the founding of Liberia; but this idea, which can become so fruitful for the Old World, is sterile for the New.

In twelve years, the Society for the Colonization of Blacks has transported two thousand five hundred Negroes to Africa. During the same space of time, around seven hundred thousand of them were born in the United States.

Should the colony of Liberia be in a position to receive thousands of new inhabitants each year and these be in a state to be taken there usefully; were the Union to put itself in the place of the Society and employ its treasures[50] and its vessels to export the Negroes to Africa annually, it still could not equal the natural progress alone of the population among blacks; and not removing as many men as come into the world each year, it would not even succeed in suspending the development of the evil that grows larger within it each day.[51]

The Negro race will not again depart the shores of the American continent, on which the passions and vices of Europe have set it down; it will disappear from the New World only by ceasing to exist. The inhabitants of the United States can put off the misfortunes they dread, but today they cannot destroy their cause.

I am obliged to avow that I do not consider the abolition of servitude as a means of delaying the struggle between the two races in the southern states.

Negroes can long remain slaves without complaint; but having joined the

50. Many other difficulties would also be encountered in such an undertaking. If in order to transport the Negroes of America to Africa, the Union undertook to buy the blacks from those whose slaves they are, the price of Negroes, growing in proportion to their rarity, would soon rise to enormous sums, and it is not believable that the states of the North would consent to make an expenditure like this, from which they would not collect the profit. If the Union took possession of the slaves of the South by force or acquired them at a low price fixed by it, it would create an insurmountable resistance among the states situated in that part of the Union. From both sides one ends at the impossible.

51. In 1830 there were 2,010,327 slaves in the United States and 319,439 freedmen; in all, 2,329,766 Negroes, who formed a little more than a fifth of the total population of the United States in the same period.

number of free men, they will soon become indignant at being deprived of almost all the rights of citizens; and not being able to become the equals of the whites, they will not be slow to show themselves their enemies.

In the North, one only profited by freeing slaves; one thus delivered one-self from slavery without having anything to fear from free Negroes. These were too few in number ever to claim their rights. It is not the same in the South.

The question of slavery was, for masters in the North, a commercial and manufacturing question; in the South, it is a question of life or death. One must therefore not confuse slavery in the North and the South.

May God keep me from seeking, as do certain American authors, to justify the principle of Negro servitude; I say only that all those who have once accepted this frightful principle are not equally free today to depart from it.

I confess that when I consider the state of the South, I discover in it only two manners of acting for the white race that inhabits those regions: free the Negroes and mingle them with it; remain isolated from them and hold them in slavery for the longest possible time. Intermediate measures appear to me to lead directly to the most horrible of all civil wars, and perhaps to the ruin of one of the two races.

Americans of the South envision the question from this point of view, and they act accordingly. Not wanting to mingle with the Negroes, they do not want to set them free.

It is not that all inhabitants of the South regard slavery as necessary to the wealth of the master; on this point many of them are in accord with north-erners and willingly admit with them that servitude is an evil; but they think that one must preserve this evil in order to live.

Enlightenment is increasing in the South, and it has made the inhabitants of that part of the territory perceive that slavery is harmful to the master, and this same enlightenment shows them, more clearly than they had seen before, the near impossibility of destroying it. Hence a singular contrast: slavery is more and more established by the laws as its utility is more contested; and while its principle is gradually being abolished in the North, in the South one draws more and more rigorous consequences from this same principle.

The legislation of the southern states relative to slaves in our day presents a sort of unheard-of atrocity, and that alone serves to reveal some profound perturbation in the laws of humanity. It suffices to read the legislation of the southern states to judge the desperate position of the two races that inhabit them.

It is not that Americans of this part of the Union have precisely increased the rigors of servitude; they have, on the contrary, made the material lot of the slaves milder. The ancients knew only irons and death to maintain slavery; Americans of the South of the Union have found more intellectual guarantees for the longevity of their power. They have, if I can express myself so, spiritualized despotism and violence. In antiquity, one sought to prevent the slave from breaking his irons; in our day, one has undertaken to remove his desire for it.

The ancients chained the slave's body, but they left his spirit free and permitted him to enlighten himself. In that they were consistent with themselves; there was then a natural way out of servitude: from one day to another a slave could become free and equal to his master.

Americans of the South, who do not think that Negroes can be intermingled with them in any period, have forbidden, under severe penalties, teaching them to read and to write. Not wanting to elevate them to their level, they hold them down as close as possible to the brute.

In all times, the hope of freedom had been placed in the bosom of slavery in order to make its rigors milder.

Americans of the South have understood that emancipation would always offer dangers, when the freedman could not succeed in assimilating himself one day to the master. To give a man freedom and to leave him in misery and ignominy—what is this to do, if not to furnish a future chief to a slave revolt? Moreover, it had long been noticed that the presence of the free Negro stirred a vague restiveness in the bottom of the souls of those who were not [free], and made the idea of their rights enter, like an uncertain glimmer. Americans of the South have in most cases taken away from masters the ability to emancipate.[52]

I encountered an old man in the South of the Union who had formerly lived in illegitimate commerce with one of his Negro women. He had had several children from [the illegitimate commerce] who, in coming into the world, had become slaves of their father. Several times he had thought of at least willing them their freedom, but years passed before he could remove the obstacles set by the legislator to emancipation. During that time old age had come, and he was going to die. He then pictured to himself his sons dragged from market to market and passing from paternal authority to the whip of a stranger. These horrible images threw his dying imagination into delirium. I saw him racked by the anguish of despair, and I then understood that nature knew how to avenge herself for wounds the laws had given her.

These evils are doubtless frightening; but are they not the foreseen and necessary consequence of the very principle of servitude among the moderns?

From the moment that the Europeans took their slaves from within a race of men different from theirs, which many of them considered inferior to the

52. Emancipation is not forbidden, but subject to formalities that render it difficult.

other human races, and to which all viewed with horror the idea of ever assimilating, they supposed slavery eternal; for, between the extreme inequality that servitude creates and the complete equality that independence naturally produces among men, there is no lasting intermediate state. The Europeans have vaguely felt this truth, but without avowing it. Every time that it has been a question of Negroes, they have been seen to obey sometimes their interest or pride, sometimes their pity. They have violated all the rights of humanity towards the black, and then they have instructed him in the worth and the inviolability of these rights. They have opened their ranks to their slaves, and when the latter attempted to enter them, they chased them away with ignominy. Though wanting servitude, they have allowed themselves to be carried along, despite themselves or without knowing it, toward freedom, without having the courage to be either completely iniquitous or entirely just.

If it is impossible to foresee a period when Americans of the South will mix their blood with that of the Negroes, can they, without exposing themselves to perishing, permit the latter to come to freedom? And if they are obliged to want to keep them in irons to save their own race, ought one not to excuse them for taking the most efficacious means to succeed in that?

What is taking place in the South of the Union seems to me at once the most horrible and the most natural consequence of slavery. When I see the order of nature reversed, when I hear humanity crying and struggling in vain under the laws, I avow that I cannot find the indignation to stigmatize the men of our day, authors of these outrages; but I gather all my hatred against those who, after more than a thousand years of equality, introduced servitude into the world once again.

Furthermore, whatever the efforts of Americans of the South to preserve slavery, they will not succeed at it forever. Slavery contracted to a single point on the globe, attacked by Christianity as unjust, by political economy as fatal; slavery, in the midst of the democratic freedom and enlightenment of our age, is not an institution that can endure. It will cease by the deed of the slave or the master. In both cases, one must expect great misfortunes.

If one refuses freedom to Negroes in the South, they will in the end seize it violently themselves; if one grants it to them, they will not be slow to abuse it.

WHAT ARE THE CHANCES THAT THE AMERICAN UNION WILL LAST? WHAT DANGERS THREATEN IT?

What makes preponderant force reside in the states rather than in the Union.—The confederation will last only as long as all the states that compose it wish to be part of it.—

*Causes that will bring them to remain united.—Utility of being united so as to resist foreigners and not to have foreigners in America.—Providence has not placed natural barriers between the different states.—No material interests exist that divide them.— Interest that the North has in the prosperity of and union with the South and the West; the South with the North and the West; the West with the other two.—Immaterial interests that unite the Americans.—Uniformity of opinions.—The dangers for the confederation arise from the difference in the character of the men who compose it and from their passions.—Character of southerners and northerners.—The rapid growth of the Union is one of its greatest perils.—Advance of the population toward the Northwest.—Gravitation of power to this side.—Passions that these rapid movements of fortune give rise to.— If the Union continues, will its government tend to take on force or to weaken?—Various signs of weakening.—*Internal improvements.*—Wilderness lands.—Indians.—Affair of the Bank.—Affair of the tariff.—General Jackson.*

On the existence of the Union depends in part the maintenance of whatever exists in each of the states that compose it. One must therefore first examine what the probable fate of the Union is. But, before everything, it is good to fix on one point: if the current confederation came to be broken, it appears incontestable to me that the states that make up parts of it would not return to their first individuality. In place of the Union, several would be formed from it. I do not intend to inquire on what bases these new unions would come to be established; I want to show what the causes are that can lead to the dismemberment of the current confederation.

To come to this, I am going to be obliged to travel once again some of the routes I have previously entered. I shall have to expose to view several objects that are already known. I know that in doing so, I expose myself to reproaches from the reader; but the importance of the matter that remains for me to treat is my excuse. I prefer to repeat myself sometimes than not to be understood, and I would rather harm the author than the subject.

The legislators who formed the Constitution of 1789[†] strove to give the federal power separate existence and preponderant force.

But they were limited by the very conditions of the problem that they had to resolve. They had not been charged with constituting the government of a unitary people, but with regulating the association of several peoples; and whatever their desires were, they still had in the end to partition the exercise of sovereignty.

In order to understand well what the consequences of this partition were, it is necessary to make a brief distinction among the acts of sovereignty.

There are objects that are national by their nature, which is to say, those

---

*English in the original.

†The American constitution, framed in 1787, went into effect in 1789; see *DA* I 1.8.

that relate only to the nation taken as a body and that can be entrusted only to the man or the assembly representing the entire nation most completely. I shall put in this number war and diplomacy.

There are others that are provincial in their nature, which is to say, those that relate only to certain localities and that can only be conveniently treated in the locality itself. Such is the budget of townships.

One finally encounters objects that have a mixed nature: they are national in that they interest all individuals who compose the nation; they are provincial in that there is no necessity that the nation itself provide for them. These are, for example, the rights that regulate the civil and political state of citizens. No social state exists without civil and political rights. These rights therefore interest all citizens equally; but it is not always necessary for the existence and prosperity of the nation that these rights be uniform and, consequently, that they be regulated by the central power.

Among the objects with which sovereignty is occupied there are therefore two necessary categories; they are found in all well-constituted societies, whatever may be the basis on which the social pact has been established.

Between these two extreme points, like a floating mass, are located general, but not national, objects that I have called mixed. These objects being neither exclusively national nor entirely provincial, the care of providing for them can be attributed to the national government or to the provincial government, according to the conventions of those who associate, without failing to attain the goal of the association.

Most often, mere individuals unite to form the sovereign, and their union composes a people. Below the general government that they have given themselves, one then encounters only individual forces or collective powers, each of which represents a very minimal fraction of the sovereign. Then also it is the general government that is most naturally called to regulate not only objects national in their essence, but the greater part of the mixed objects of which I have already spoken. Localities are reduced to the portion of sovereignty that is indispensable to their well-being.

Sometimes, by a previous fact of association, the sovereign finds itself composed of already organized political bodies; then it happens that the provincial government takes charge of providing not only for objects exclusively provincial in their nature, but also for all or a part of the mixed objects just considered. For confederated nations, which themselves formed sovereigns before their union, and which continue to represent a very considerable fraction of the sovereign, although they may be united, have intended to cede to the general government only the exercise of rights indispensable to the union.

When the national government, independently of the prerogatives inherent in its nature, finds itself vested with the right to regulate the mixed objects of sovereignty, it possesses a preponderant force. Not only does it have many rights, but the rights that it does not have are at its mercy, and it is to be feared that it may come to take away from the provincial governments their natural and necessary prerogatives.

When, on the contrary, the provincial government finds itself vested with the right to regulate mixed objects, an opposite tendency reigns in society. Then preponderant force resides in the province, not in the nation; and one must fear that the national government will in the end be stripped of the privileges necessary to its existence.

Unitary peoples are therefore naturally brought toward centralization, and confederations toward dismemberment.

It remains only to apply these general ideas to the American Union.

To the particular states fell perforce the right to regulate purely provincial objects.

Moreover, these same states retained the right to fix the civil and political capacity of citizens, to regulate the relations of men among themselves, and to render justice to them; rights that are general in their nature, but that do not necessarily belong to the national government.

We have seen that the power to give orders in the name of the entire nation was delegated to the government of the Union in cases where the nation would have to act as one and the same individual. It represented the nation in regard to foreigners; it directed the common forces against the common enemy. In a word, it occupied itself with objects that I have called exclusively national.

In this partition of the rights of sovereignty, the part of the Union at first still seems greater than that of the states; a somewhat deeper examination demonstrates that, in fact, it is less.

The government of the Union executes vaster undertakings, but one rarely feels it acting. The provincial government does smaller things, but it never rests and it reveals its existence at each instant.

The government of the Union watches over the general interests of the country; but the general interests of a people have only a questionable influence over individual happiness.

On the contrary, the affairs of the province visibly influence the well-being of those who inhabit it.

The Union assures the independence and greatness of the nation, things that do not immediately touch particular persons. The state maintains freedom, regulates rights, guarantees the fortune, secures the life, the whole future of each citizen.

The federal government is located at a great distance from its subjects; the provincial government is within reach of all. It is enough to raise one's voice in order to be heard by it. The central government has on its behalf the passions of some superior men who aspire to direct it: on the side of the provincial government is the interest of men of the second order who hope to obtain power only in their state; and it is the latter who, located near to the people, exert the most power over it.

Americans therefore have much more to expect and to fear from the state than from the Union; and following the natural course of the human heart, they will be attached in a much more lively way to the first than to the second.

In this, habits and sentiments are in accord with interests.

When a compact nation splits its sovereignty and arrives at a state of confederation, memories, usages, and habits struggle for a long time against the laws and give the central government a force refused it by the laws. When confederated peoples are united into a single sovereignty, the same causes act in a contrary direction. I do not doubt that if France became a confederated republic like that of the United States, the government would at first show itself more energetic than that of the Union; and if the Union constituted itself as a monarchy like France, I think that the American government would remain weaker than ours for some time. At the moment when national life was created among the Anglo-Americans, provincial existence was already old, necessary relations had been established between the townships and individuals of the same states; one had become habituated to considering certain objects from a common point of view, and to occupying oneself exclusively with certain undertakings as representing a special interest.

The Union is an immense body that offers a vague object for patriotism to embrace. The state has fixed forms and circumscribed boundaries; it represents a certain number of things known and dear to those who inhabit it. It is intermingled with the very image of the soil, identified with property, with the family, with memories of the past, with the travails of the present, with dreams of the future. Patriotism, which most often is only an extension of individual selfishness, has therefore remained in the state and has not so to speak passed to the Union.

Thus interests, habits, sentiments combine to concentrate genuine political life in the state, and not in the Union.

One can easily judge the difference in strength of the two governments by seeing each of them move within the circle of its power.

Every time a state government addresses a man or an association of men, its language is clear and imperative; it is the same for the federal government when it speaks to individuals; but when it finds itself before a state, it begins to parley: it explains its motives and justifies its conduct; it argues, it counsels—it hardly orders. Should it raise doubts about the limits of the constitutional powers of each government, the provincial government claims its right boldly and takes prompt and energetic measures to sustain it. During this time the government of the Union reasons; it appeals to the good sense of the nation, to its interests, to its glory; it temporizes, it negotiates; it is only when reduced to the last extremity that it finally determines to act. At first, one could believe that the provincial government is armed with the strength of the whole nation and that Congress represents one state.

The federal government, despite the efforts of those who constituted it, is, therefore, as I have already said elsewhere,* by its very nature a weak government that, more than any other, needs the free concurrence of the governed in order to subsist.

It is easy to see that its object is to actualize readily the will of the states to remain united. This first condition fulfilled, it is wise, strong, and agile. It was organized in a manner so as habitually to confront individuals only and to overcome easily the resistance that someone might want to oppose to the common will; but the federal government was not established in anticipation that the states or several among them would cease wishing to be united.

If the sovereignty of the Union entered into a struggle with that of the states today, one could easily foresee that it would succumb; I even doubt that the combat would ever be engaged in a serious manner. Every time that one opposes a relentless resistance to the federal government, one will see it yield. Experience has proven until now that when a state obstinately wanted a thing and resolutely demanded it, it never failed to obtain it; and that when it clearly refused to act,[53] it was allowed the freedom to do so.

If the government of the Union had a force of its own, the material situation of the country would make the use of it very difficult.[54]

The United States cover an immense territory; long distances separate them; the population is scattered through a country still half wilderness. If the Union undertook to maintain the confederates in their duty by arms, it would be found in a position analogous to that of England during the War of Independence.

Moreover, even if a government were strong, it could only with difficulty

---

*DA I 1.8.

53. See the conduct of the northern states in the War of 1812. "During this war," said Jefferson in a letter of March 17, 1817, to General La Fayette, "four of the Eastern states were no longer bound to the remainder of the Union except as cadavers to living men." (*Correspondence of Jefferson*, published by M. Conseil.) [Conseil, *Mélanges politiques et philosophiques*. See also *Writings of Thomas Jefferson* (Washington, D.C., 1905), 115.]

54. The state of peace in which the Union finds itself gives it no pretext for having a permanent army. Without a permanent army, a government has nothing prepared in advance to profit from a favorable moment, to overcome resistance, and to take away a sovereign power by surprise.

escape the consequences of a principle when once it itself accepted this principle as the foundation of the public right that ought to rule it. The confederation was formed by the free will of the states; they did not lose their nationality in uniting and were not blended into one and the same people. If today one of these same states wanted to withdraw its name from the contract, it would be quite difficult to prove to it that it could not do so. To combat it, the federal government would have no evident support in either force or right.

In order that the federal government triumph easily over the resistance that some of its subjects might oppose to it, the particular interest of one or several of them would have to be intimately bound to the existence of the Union, as has often been seen in the history of confederations.

Let me suppose that among those states that the federal bond unites, there are some that themselves alone enjoy the principal advantages of union, or for whom prosperity depends entirely on the fact of union; it is clear that the central power will find a very great support in them to keep the others in obedience. But then it will no longer get its force from itself; it will draw it from a principle that is contrary to its nature. Peoples confederate only to derive equal advantages from union, and in the case cited above, it is because inequality reigns among the nations united that the federal government is powerful.

Let me suppose again that one of the confederated states has acquired a great enough preponderance to take possession of the central power by itself; it will consider the other states as its subjects and will make its own sovereignty respected in the pretended sovereignty of the union. It will then do great things in the name of the federal government, but to tell the truth, that government will no longer exist.[55]

In these two cases, the power that acts in the name of the confederation becomes all the stronger as one moves further away from the natural state and the recognized principle of confederations.

In America the present union is useful to all the states, but it is not essential to any of them. Should several states break the federal bond, the fate of the others would not be compromised, although the sum of their happiness would be less. As there is no state whose existence or prosperity is entirely bound to the present confederation, neither is there any that is disposed to make very great personal sacrifices to preserve it.

---

55. Thus it is that the province of Holland, in the republic of the Netherlands, and the emperor in the German Confederation sometimes put themselves in the place of the union and exploit federal power in their particular interest.

On the other hand, one perceives no state that has, for the present, a great ambitious interest in maintaining the confederation such as we see it in our day. Doubtless, all do not exert the same influence in federal councils, but one sees none of them that might flatter itself that it dominates there, and that can treat its confederates as inferiors or subjects.

It therefore appears certain to me that if one portion of the Union seriously wanted to separate from the other, not only could one not prevent it, but one would not even attempt to do so. The present Union will therefore last only as long as all the states that compose it continue to want to be part of it.

This point fixed, we are more at ease: it is no longer a question of inquiring if the presently confederated states can separate, but if they will want to remain united.

Among all the reasons that render the present union useful to Americans, one encounters two principal ones readily evident to all eyes.

Although Americans are so to speak alone on their continent, commerce makes all the peoples with whom they traffic into neighbors. Despite their apparent isolation, Americans therefore need to be strong, and they can be strong only when all remain united.

In disuniting, the states would not only diminish their force in regard to foreigners, they would create foreigners on their own soil. From then on, they would enter a system of internal customs; they would divide valleys by imaginary lines; they would imprison the course of rivers and hinder in every manner the exploitation of the immense continent that God has granted them as a domain.

Today they have no invasion to fear, consequently no armies to maintain, no taxes to raise; if the Union came to be broken, the need of all these things would perhaps not be slow to make itself felt.

The Americans therefore have an immense interest in remaining united.

On the other hand, it is almost impossible to discover what kind of material interest one portion of the Union would have, for the present, in separating from the others.

When one casts one's eyes on a map of the United States, and when one perceives the chain of the Allegheny Mountains, running from the northeast to the southwest, and running through the country over an extent of 400 leagues, one is tempted to believe that the goal of Providence was to raise between the basin of the Mississippi and the coast of the Atlantic Ocean one of those natural barriers that, opposing itself to permanent relations of men among themselves, forms as it were the necessary limits of different peoples.

But the average height of the Alleghenies does not exceed 800 meters.[57] Their rounded summits and the spacious valleys that they enclose within their contours provide easy access in a thousand places. There, in addition, the principal rivers that pour their waters into the Atlantic Ocean, the Hudson, the Susquehanna, the Potomac, have their sources beyond the Alleghenies, on an open plateau that borders the basin of the Mississippi. Departing from that region,[58] they open their way across the rampart that seemed bound to throw them back to the West, and trace natural routes through the mountains always open to man.

No barrier, therefore, is raised between the different parts of the country occupied by the Anglo-Americans in our day. Far from the Alleghenies serving as limits on peoples, they are not even boundaries of states. New York, Pennsylvania, Virginia contain them within their precincts and extend as much to the west as to the east of these mountains.[59]

The territory occupied in our day by the twenty-four states of the Union and the three great districts that are still not included among the number of states, although they already have inhabitants, covers an area of 131,144 square leagues;[60] that is to say, it already provides an area almost equal to five times that of France. Within these limits one encounters varied soil, different temperatures, and very diverse products.

This great extent of territory occupied by the Anglo-American republics has given birth to doubts about the maintenance of their Union. Here one must distinguish: sometimes contrary interests are created in the different provinces of a vast empire and in the end come into conflict: then it is that the greatness of the state is what most compromises its longevity. But if the men who cover this vast territory do not have contrary interests among them, its very extent will serve their prosperity, for the unity of the government singularly favors the exchange that can be made of different products of the soil, and in rendering their flow easier, it increases their value.

Now, I see well different interests in the different parts of the Union, but I find none that are contrary to one another.

57. Average height of the Alleghenies, according to Volney (*Tableau of the United States*, p. 33), 700 to 800 meters; 5,000 to 6,000 feet, according to Darby: the greatest height of the Vosges is 1,400 meters above sea level.

58. See *View of the United States*, by Darby, pp. 64 and 79.

59. The chain of the Alleghenies is no higher than the Vosges and does not offer as many obstacles to the efforts of human industry as the latter. The country situated on the eastern side of the Alleghenies is therefore as naturally bound to the valley of the Mississippi as Franche-Comté, upper Burgundy, and Alsace are to France.

60. 1,002,600 square miles. See *View of the United States*, by Darby, p. 435.

The southern states are almost exclusively farming; the northern states are particularly manufacturing and trading; the western states are at the same time manufacturing and farming. In the South, tobacco, rice, cotton, and sugar are grown; in the North and the West, corn and wheat. Here are diverse sources of wealth; but in order to draw from these sources, there is a common means equally favorable to all, which is the Union.

The North, which carries the wealth of the Anglo-Americans to all parts of the world and the wealth of the globe into the heart of the Union, has an evident interest in having the confederation subsist as it is in our day, so that the number of American producers and consumers that it is called upon to serve remains the greatest possible. The North is the most natural go-between for the South and the West of the Union, on the one hand, and on the other, the rest of the world; the North therefore ought to desire that the South and the West remain united and prosperous so that they furnish raw materials for its manufactures and freight for its vessels.

The South and the West have, on their side, a still more direct interest in the preservation of the Union and in the prosperity of the North. The products of the South are to a great extent exported across the seas; the South and the West therefore need the commercial resources of the North. They ought to want the Union to be a great maritime power in order to be able to protect them effectively. The South and the West ought to contribute willingly to the expense of a navy, although they have no vessels; for if European fleets came to blockade the ports of the South and the Mississippi delta, what would become of the rice of the Carolinas, the tobacco of Virginia, the sugar and the cotton that grow in the valleys of the Mississippi? There is therefore no portion of the federal budget that does not apply to the preservation of a material interest common to all the confederates.

Independently of this commercial utility, the South and the West of the Union find great political advantage in remaining united between themselves and with the North.

The South contains within it an immense population of slaves, a population threatening in the present and more threatening still in the future.

The western states occupy the bottom of a single valley. The rivers that water the territory of these states, departing from the Rocky Mountains or the Alleghenies, all mix their waters with those of the Mississippi and run with it toward the Gulf of Mexico. The western states are by their situation entirely isolated from the traditions of Europe and from the civilization of the Old World.

The inhabitants of the South will therefore desire to preserve the Union so as not to live alone faced with the blacks, and the inhabitants of the West, so that they do not find themselves confined in the heart of America without free communication with the globe.

The North, for its part, will want the Union not to divide in order to remain the link that joins this great body to the rest of the world.

A tight bond therefore exists among the material interests of all parts of the Union.

I shall say as much for the opinions and sentiments that one could call the immaterial interests of man.

The inhabitants of the United States speak much of their love for their native country; I avow that I do not trust this reflective patriotism founded on interest, and which interest, by changing its object, can destroy.

Nor do I attach very great importance to the language of the Americans when they express the intention daily of preserving the federal system that their fathers adopted.

What maintains a great number of citizens under the same government is much less the reasoned will to live united than the instinctive and in a way involuntary accord resulting from similarity of sentiments and resemblance of opinions.

I shall never agree that men form a society by the sole fact that they recognize the same head and obey the same laws; there is a society only when men consider a great number of objects under the same aspect; when on a great number of subjects they have the same opinions; when, finally, the same facts give rise in them to the same impressions and the same thoughts.

Looking at the question from this point of view, whoever would study what has taken place in the United States would discover without difficulty that its inhabitants, divided as they are into twenty-four distinct sovereignties, nevertheless constitute a unitary people; and perhaps he would even come to think that the state of society is more real in the Anglo-American Union than among certain nations of Europe that nonetheless have only a single [system of] legislation and submit to a single man.

Although the Anglo-Americans have several religions, they all have the same manner of viewing religion.

They do not always agree on the means to take in order to govern well, and they differ on some of the forms suitable to give to government, but they are in accord on the general principles that ought to rule human societies. From Maine to Florida, from Missouri to the Atlantic Ocean, they believe that the origin of all legitimate powers is in the people. They conceive the same ideas about freedom and equality; they profess the same opinions about the press, the right of association, the jury, the responsibility of agents of power.

If we pass from political and religious ideas to the philosophical and moral opinions that rule the daily actions of life and direct [one's] entire conduct, we shall remark the same agreement.

The Anglo-Americans[60] place moral authority in universal reason, as they do political power in the universality of citizens, and they reckon that one must rely on the sense of all to discern what is permitted or forbidden, what is true or false. Most of them think that the knowledge of one's self-interest well understood is enough to lead man toward the just and the honest. They believe that at birth each has received the ability to govern himself, and that no one has the right to force one like himself to be happy. All have a lively faith in human perfectibility; they judge that the diffusion of enlightenment will necessarily produce useful results, that ignorance will bring fatal effects; all consider society as a body in progress; humanity as a changing picture, in which nothing is or ought to be fixed forever, and they admit that what seems good to them today can be replaced tomorrow by the better that is still hidden.

I do not say that all these opinions are correct, but they are American.

At the same time that the Anglo-Americans are united among themselves in this way by common ideas, they are separated from all other peoples by a sentiment of pride.

For fifty years it has been constantly repeated to the inhabitants of the United States that they form the only religious, enlightened, and free people. They see that up to now, democratic institutions have prospered among them, while they have failed in the rest of the world; they therefore have an immense opinion of themselves, and they are not far from believing that they form a species apart in the human race.

So, therefore, the dangers by which the American Union is threatened arise no more from the diversity of opinions than from that of interests. One must seek them in the variety of characters and in the passions of Americans.

The men who inhabit the immense territory of the United States have almost all come from a common stock; but in the long term, climate and above all slavery have introduced marked differences between the character of the English in the South of the United States and the character of the English in the North.

Among us, it is generally believed that slavery gives to one portion of the Union interests contrary to those of the other. I did not remark that this was so. Slavery has not created interests contrary to those of the North; but it has modified the character of the inhabitants of the South and given them different habits.

---

60. I have no need, I think, to say that by this expression, *the Anglo-Americans*, I intend to speak only of the great majority. Outside this majority there are always some isolated individuals.

Elsewhere I have made known the influence that servitude has exerted on the commercial capacity of the Americans of the South;* this same influence extends also to their mores.

The slave is a servant who does not debate and submits to everything without murmuring. Sometimes he assassinates his master, but he never resists him. In the South there are no families so poor as to have no slaves. The American of the South, from his birth, finds himself invested with a sort of domestic dictatorship; the first notions that he receives from life make him know that he is born to command, and the first habit that he contracts is that of dominating without difficulty. Education therefore tends powerfully to make the American of the South a man high-minded, prompt, irascible, violent, ardent in his desires, impatient of obstacles; but easy to discourage if he cannot triumph with the first stroke.

The American of the North does not see slaves running around his cradle. He does not even encounter free servants, for most often he is reduced to providing for his needs himself. Scarcely is he in the world before the idea of necessity comes from all sides to present itself to his mind; he therefore learns early to know by himself exactly the natural limit of his power; he does not expect to bend by force wills that are opposed to his, and he knows that in order to obtain the support of those like him, he must before all gain their favor. He is therefore patient, reflective, tolerant, slow to act, and persevering in his designs.

In the southern states the most pressing needs of man are always satisfied. Thus the American of the South is not preoccupied with the material needs of life; someone else takes charge of thinking of them for him. Free on this point, his imagination is directed toward other greater objects, less exactly defined. The American of the South loves greatness, luxury, glory, noise, pleasures, above all idleness; nothing constrains him to make efforts in order to live, and as he has no necessary work, he falls asleep and does not even undertake anything useful.

Since equality of fortunes reigns in the North and slavery no longer exists there, man finds himself absorbed by those same material cares that the white in the South disdains. Since childhood he has been occupied with combating misery, and he learns to place ease above all the enjoyments of mind and heart. Concentrated on the small details of life, his imagination is extinguished, his ideas are less numerous and less general, but they become more practical, more clear, and more precise. As he directs all the efforts of his intellect toward the single study of well-being, he is not slow to excel at it; he knows admirably how to take advantage of nature and of men to produce

*In the preceding section of this chapter.

wealth; he understands marvelously the art of making society cooperate for the prosperity of each of its members and for extracting from individual selfishness the happiness of all.

The man of the North has not only experience, but know-how; nevertheless, he does not prize science as a pleasure, he esteems it as a means, and he greedily grasps only the useful applications of it.

The American of the South is more spontaneous, more spiritual, more open, more generous, more intellectual, and more brilliant.

The American of the North is more active, more reasonable, more enlightened, and more skillful.

The one has the tastes, prejudices, weaknesses, and greatness of all aristocracies.

The other, the qualities and defects that characterize the middle class.

Bring together two men in society, give to these two men the same interests and in part the same opinions; if their character, their enlightenment, and their civilization differ, there are many chances that they will not agree. The same remark is applicable to a society of nations.

Slavery therefore does not attack the American confederation directly by its interests, but indirectly by its mores.

The states adhering to the federal pact in 1790 were thirteen in number; the confederation amounts to twenty-four today. The population that amounted to nearly four million in 1790 had quadrupled in the space of forty years; in 1830 it rose to nearly thirteen million.[61]

Such changes cannot be worked without danger.

For a society of nations as for a society of individuals, there are three principal chances for longevity: the wisdom of the members, their individual weakness, and their small number.

The Americans who move away from the coast of the Atlantic Ocean to plunge into the West are adventurers impatient with every kind of yoke, greedy for wealth, often thrown out by the states that saw them born. They arrive in the middle of the wilderness without knowing one another. There they find neither traditions, nor family spirit, nor examples to check them. For them the empire of law is weak, and that of mores weaker still. The men who populate the valleys of the Mississippi every day are therefore inferior in all regards to Americans who live within the old limits of the Union. Nevertheless they already exert a great influence in its councils, and they come to the government of common affairs before having learned to direct themselves.[62]

61. Census of 1790, 3,929,328; of 1830, 12,856,165.
62. This, it is true, is only a passing peril. I do not doubt that with time, society will come to be settled and to regulate itself in the West as it has already done on the shores of the Atlantic Ocean.

The more the members are individually weak, the more society has a chance of longevity, for they then have security only in remaining united. When in 1790 the most populous of the American republics did not have 500,000 inhabitants,[63] each of them felt its insignificance as an independent people, and this thought made obedience to federal authority easier for it. But when one of the confederated states has 2,000,000 inhabitants like the state of New York and covers a territory whose area is equal to a quarter of France,[64] it feels strong by itself, and if it continues to desire union as useful to its well-being, it no longer regards it as necessary to its existence; it can do without it; and, as it consents to remain in it, it is not slow to want to predominate there.

Multiplying the members of the Union would alone tend powerfully to break the federal bond. All men placed at the same point of view do not envision the same objects in the same manner. This is so with greater reason when the point of view is different. Therefore as the number of American republics increases, one sees the chance of gathering the assent of all to the same laws diminish.

Today the interests of the different parts of the Union are not contrary to one another; but who can foresee the diverse changes that an impending future will give rise to in a country where each day creates cities and each five years, nations?

Since the English colonies were founded, the number of inhabitants has doubled nearly every twenty-two years; I do not perceive any causes from here on for another century that will halt this progressive movement of the Anglo-American population. Before a hundred years have passed, I think that the territory occupied or claimed by the United States will be covered by more than a hundred million inhabitants and divided into forty states.[65]

Let me assume that these hundred million men do not have different interests; on the contrary, let me grant them all an equal advantage in re-

63. Pennsylvania had 431,373 inhabitants in 1790.

64. Area of the state of New York, 6,213 square leagues (500 square miles). See *View of the United States,* by Darby, p. 435. [500 should read 50,000. See AT, *Oeuvres* 2: 1036 (note to p. 438).]

65. If the population continues to double in twenty-two years for a century more, as it has done for two hundred years, in 1852 there will be twenty-four million inhabitants in the United States, forty-eight in 1874, and ninety-six in 1896. It would be so even if one encountered lands on the eastern side of the Rocky Mountains that resisted cultivation. The lands already occupied can very easily contain this number of inhabitants. A hundred million men spread over the soil occupied at this moment by the twenty-four states and the three territories of which the Union is composed would give only 762 individuals per square league, which would still be far from the average population of France, which is 1,006; from that of England, which is 1,457; and which would remain even below the population of Switzerland. Switzerland, despite its lakes and mountains, has 783 inhabitants per square league. See Malte-Brun, vol. 6, p. 92. [Malte-Brun, *Annales des voyages,* 6: 92.]

maining united, and I say that by the very fact that they are a hundred million forming forty distinct and unequally powerful nations, maintaining the federal government is no more than a happy accident.

I want very much to put faith in human perfectibility; but until men should have changed in nature and have been completely transformed, I shall refuse to believe in the longevity of a government whose task is to hold together forty diverse peoples spread over an area equal to half of Europe,[66] to avoid rivalries, ambition, and conflicts among them, and to unite the action of their independent wills toward the accomplishment of the same designs.

But the greatest peril that the Union risks in becoming more numerous comes from the continuous displacement of forces that works within it.

From the shores of Lake Superior to the Gulf of Mexico, as the crow flies, it is around four hundred French leagues. The frontier of the United States winds along the length of this immense line; sometimes it returns inside these limits, most often it penetrates well beyond into the wilderness. It has been calculated that each year, whites have advanced, on average, seven leagues over all this vast front.[67] From time to time an obstacle presents itself: an unproductive district, a lake, an Indian nation unexpectedly encountered in its path. The column then stops for a instant; its two extremities bend around themselves and, after they have been rejoined, the advance begins again. In this gradual and continual march of the European race toward the Rocky Mountains there is something providential: it is like a flood of men which is constantly rising and which the hand of God whips up every day.

Inside this first line of conquerors, towns are built and vast states are founded. In 1790 scarcely a few thousand pioneers were found spread over the valleys of the Mississippi; today, these same valleys contain as many men as the whole Union included in 1790. The population there has risen to nearly four million inhabitants.[68] The city of Washington was founded in 1800, at the very center of the American confederation; now, it is located at one of its extremities. The representatives from the latest states of the West,[69] in order to come occupy their seats in Congress, are already obliged to make a journey as long as a traveler would take from Vienna to Paris.

66. The territory of the United States has an area of 295,000 square leagues; that of Europe, according to Malte-Brun, vol. 6, p. 4, is 500,000.

67. See *Legislative Documents,* 20th Congress, no. 117, p. 105. [House, "On Indian Affairs," 105.]

68. 3,672,317, enumeration of 1830.

69. From Jefferson, capital of the state of Missouri, to Washington, it is 1,019 miles, or 420 leagues of postal route. (*American Almanac,* 1831, p. 48.) [*American Almanac and Repository of Useful Knowledge for the Year 1831* (Boston: Gray and Bowen, 1831), 44.]

All the states of the Union are carried along toward fortune at the same time; but all cannot grow and prosper to the same degree.

In the North of the Union, detached branches of the Allegheny chain advancing as far as the Atlantic Ocean form spacious harbors and ports always open to the largest vessels. From the Potomac, on the contrary, and following the American coast as far as the delta of the Mississippi, one encounters nothing more than flat and sandy terrain. In this part of the Union, the mouths of almost all the rivers are obstructed, and the ports opened at long intervals in the midst of these lagoons do not provide the same depth to vessels as in the North and offer much less facility to commerce.

To this first inferiority born of nature another is added that comes from the laws.

We have seen that slavery, which was abolished in the North, still exists in the South, and I have shown the fatal influence that it exerts on the well-being of the master himself.

The North is bound, therefore, to be more commercial[70] and more industrious than the South. It is natural that population and wealth accumulate there more rapidly.

The states situated on the shores of the Atlantic Ocean are already half-populated. Most of the lands have a proprietor;* they therefore cannot receive the same number of emigrants as the states of the West, which still make available a boundless field to industry. The basin of the Mississippi is infinitely more fertile than the coast of the Atlantic Ocean. This reason,

*Lit.: "master."

70. To judge the difference that exists between the commercial movement of the South and that of the North, it suffices to cast an eye on the following tableau:

In 1829 the vessels of great and small commerce belonging to Virginia, to the two Carolinas, and to Georgia (the four great states of the South) measured only 5,243 tons.

In the same year, the ships of the state of Massachusetts alone measured 17,322 tons. (*Legislative Documents,* 21st congress, 2d session, no. 140, p. 244.) [House, "Commerce and Navigation of U.S.," 21st Cong., 2d sess., 1830, H. Doc. 140, serial 209, 284—note page correction.]

Thus the state of Massachusetts alone had three times more vessels than the four above-named states.

Nonetheless, the state of Massachusetts is only 959 square leagues in area (7,335 square miles) and 610,014 inhabitants, whereas the four states I am speaking of have 27,204 square leagues (210,000 miles) and 3,047,767 inhabitants. Thus the area of the state of Massachusetts forms only a thirtieth part of the area of the four states, and its population is five times less great than theirs. (*View of the United States,* by Darby.) Slavery injures the commercial prosperity of the South in several ways: it diminishes the spirit of enterprise among whites and it prevents them from finding at their disposal the seamen whom they would need. Sailors are generally recruited only from the lowest class of the population. Now, it is slaves who, in the South, form this class, and it is difficult to utilize them at sea: their service would be inferior to that of whites, and one would always have to fear that they would revolt in the middle of the Ocean or take flight when landing on foreign shores.

added to all the others, drives the Europeans forcefully toward the West. This is rigorously demonstrated by the figures.

If one works from the entirety of the United States, one finds that in forty years the number of inhabitants has about tripled. But if one views only the basin of the Mississippi, one finds that in the same space of time, the population[71] has become thirty-one times greater.[72]

The center of federal power is shifting daily. Forty years ago, the majority of the citizens of the Union were on the seacoast in the environs of the place where Washington is built today; now, they have gone farther inland and more to the north; one cannot doubt that before twenty years they will be on the other side of the Alleghenies. If the Union persists, the basin of the Mississippi, by its fertility and its extent, is necessarily called upon to become the permanent center of federal power. In thirty or forty years, the basin of the Mississippi will have taken its natural rank. It is easy to calculate that its population then, compared to that of the states located on the Atlantic coast, will be in the proportion of nearly 40 to 11. In a few years more, the direction of the Union will therefore completely escape the states that founded it, and the population of the valleys of the Mississippi will dominate in federal councils.

This continuous gravitation of strength and federal influence toward the northwest is revealed every ten years when, after having taken a general census of the population, the number of representatives that each state will send to Congress is fixed anew.[73]

In 1790, Virginia had nineteen representatives in Congress. That number continued to grow until 1813, when it was seen to reach the figure of twenty-three. Since that period, it has begun to diminish. It was no more than twenty-one in 1833.[74] During this same period, the state of New York followed a contrary progression: in 1790 it had ten representatives in Congress; in 1813,

71. *View of the United States,* by Darby, p. 444.

[To be precise, Darby's figures show that over a period of thirty-eight years the U.S. population more than tripled, "from four to thirteen millions," and that over the same period the population of the Mississippi Basin grew thirty-three times greater.]

72. Notice that, when I speak of the basin of the Mississippi, I do not include the portion of the states of New York, Pennsylvania, and Virginia located to the west of the Alleghenies, which one ought nevertheless to consider as also making up part of it.

73. One then perceives that during the ten years that have just passed, such and such a state has increased its population by 5 percent, like Delaware; another by 250 percent, like the territory of Michigan. Virginia discovers that during the same period, it has increased the number of its inhabitants by 13 percent, while the adjacent state of Ohio has increased its number by 61 percent. See the general table contained in the *National Calendar;* you will be struck by what inequality there is in the fortunes of the different states. [Force, *National Calendar,* 49–79.]

74. One is going to see further on that during the latest period the population of Virginia grew in the proportion of 13 to 100. [But see n. 77 below.] It is necessary to explain how the

twenty-seven; in 1823, thirty-four; in 1833, forty. Ohio had only a single representative in 1803; in 1833 the count was nineteen.

It is difficult to conceive of a lasting union between two peoples when one
is poor and weak, the other wealthy and strong, even if it should be proven
that the force and wealth of the one were not the cause of the weakness and
poverty of the other. Union is still more difficult to maintain at a time when
one is losing force and the other acquiring it.

The rapid and disproportionate increase of certain states threatens the
independence of the others. If New York, with its two million inhabitants
and its forty representatives, wanted to lay down the law in Congress, it
would perhaps succeed. But even if the most powerful states should not seek
to oppress the least, the danger would still exist, for it is in the potentiality of
the fact almost as much as in the fact itself.

The weak rarely have confidence in the justice and reason of the strong.
States that grow less quickly than others therefore cast glances of distrust and
envy toward those whom fortune favors. Hence that profound malaise and
vague restiveness that one remarks in one part of the Union, which contrast
with the well-being and confidence that reign in the other. I think that the
hostile attitude that the South has taken has no other cause.

Southerners are, of all Americans, those who ought most to hold on to
the Union, for it is they above all who would suffer in being abandoned to
themselves; nevertheless, it is they alone who threaten to break up the bundle
of the confederation. How does that come about? It is easy to say: the South,
which has furnished four presidents to the confederation,[75] that today knows
that federal power is escaping it, that each year sees the number of its repre-

---

number of representatives of a state can decrease when the population of the state, far from
decreasing itself, is increasing.

I take for an object of comparison Virginia, which I have already cited. The number of
representatives from Virginia in 1823 was in proportion to the total number of representatives
of the Union; the number of representatives from Virginia in 1833 is likewise in proportion to
the total number of representatives of the Union in 1833, and in relation to its population, increased during these ten years. The relation between the new number of representatives from
Virginia and the old will therefore be proportionate, in one regard, to the relation between the
new total number of representatives and the old, and in the other regard, to the ratios of increase
between Virginia and the whole Union. Thus, in order that the number of representatives from
Virginia remain stationary, it suffices that the relation of the proportion of increase in the small
area to that of the large be the inverse of the relation of the new total number of representatives
to the old; and even if the ratio of the proportion of increase of the population of Virginia to
the proportion of increase in the whole Union is only a little less than [that of] the new number
of representatives in the Union to the old, the number of representatives of Virginia will be diminished.

75. Washington, Jefferson, Madison, Monroe.

sentatives in Congress diminish and those of the North and the West grow—the South, populated by ardent and irascible men, is irritated and restive. With chagrin it turns its regard on itself; questioning the past, it wonders every day if it is not oppressed. If it comes to find that a law of the Union is not evidently favorable to it, it cries out against an abuse of force in its regard; it speaks up ardently, and if its voice is not listened to, it becomes indignant and threatens to withdraw from a society in which it bears the burden without getting any profit.

"Can it excite any surprise, that under the operation of the Protecting System," said the inhabitants of Carolina in 1832, "the manufacturing States should be constantly increasing in riches and growing in strength, with an inhospitable climate and barren soil, while the Southern States, the natural garden of America, should be rapidly falling into decay?"[76]

If the changes I have spoken of worked gradually, in such a manner that each generation at least had the time to pass on, together with the order of things to which it had been witness, the danger would be less; but there is something precipitous, I could almost say revolutionary, in the progress that society makes in America. The same citizen could see his state march at the head of the Union and afterwards become powerless in federal councils. An Anglo-American republic may have grown up as quickly as a man, being born, raised, and come to maturity in thirty years.

One must not, however, imagine that states that lose power are depopulated or in decline; their prosperity does not halt; they grow even more swiftly than any realm in Europe.[77] But to them it seems that they are getting poor because they are not getting rich as quickly as their neighbors, and they believe that they are losing their power because they suddenly come into contact with a power greater than theirs:[78] it is, therefore, their sentiments and their passions more than their interests that are wounded. But is that not

76. See the report made by its committee at the convention that proclaimed nullification in South Carolina. [Thomas Cooper, *The Statutes at Large of South Carolina*, vol. 1 (Columbia, S.C., 1836), 316.]

77. The population of a country surely forms the first element of its wealth. During this same period from 1820 to 1832, during which Virginia lost two representatives in Congress, its population increased in the proportion of 13.7 percent; that of the Carolinas in the relation of 15 percent, and that of Georgia in the proportion of 51.5 percent. (See *American Almanac*, 1832, p. 162.) Now, Russia, which is the country in Europe where the population grows most quickly, only increases the number of its inhabitants in the proportion of 9.5 percent in ten years; France by 7 percent, and Europe en masse by 4.7 percent (see Malte-Brun, vol. 6, p. 95).

78. One must nonetheless admit that the depreciation in the price of tobacco that has been at work for fifty years has notably diminished the comfort of the farmers of the South; but this fact is independent of the will of men in the North, as of theirs.

enough for the confederation to be in peril? If, since the beginning of the world, peoples and kings had had only their real utility in view, one would hardly know what war is among men.

Thus the greatest danger that threatens the United States arises from its very prosperity; in several of the confederates, it tends to create the intoxication that accompanies a rapid increase of fortune, and among the others, the envy, distrust, and regret that most often follow the loss of it.

Americans rejoice in contemplating this extraordinary movement; they ought, it seems to me, to view it with regret and fear. Americans of the United States, whatever they do, will become one of the greatest peoples of the world; with their offspring they will cover almost all of North America; the continent that they inhabit is their domain, it cannot escape them. What presses them, therefore, to get possession of it from today? Wealth, power, and glory cannot be lacking to them one day, and they rush toward that immense fortune as if only a moment remained for them to seize it.

I believe I have demonstrated that the existence of the current confederation depends entirely on all the confederates' agreeing in the wish to remain united; and, starting from that given, I inquired what are the causes that could bring the different states to want to separate. But there are two ways for the Union to perish: one of the confederated states can wish to withdraw from the contract and thus break the common bond violently; it is to that case that most of the remarks that I have previously made relate; [or] the federal government can lose its power progressively by a simultaneous tendency in the united republics to take back the use of their independence. The central power, deprived successively of all its prerogatives, reduced to powerlessness by a tacit agreement, would become unable to fulfill its objective, and the second Union would perish like the first by a sort of senile imbecility.

Moreover, the gradual weakening of the federal bond, leading finally to the abolition of the Union, is in itself a distinct fact that can bring many other less extreme results before producing that one. The confederation would still exist, while the weakness of its government could already reduce the nation to powerlessness, causing anarchy inside it and the slowing of general prosperity in the country.

After having inquired what brings the Anglo-Americans to disunite, it is therefore important to examine whether, while the Union subsists, their government is enlarging the sphere of its action or shrinking it, whether it is becoming more energetic or weaker.

Americans are evidently preoccupied with one great fear. They perceive that among most peoples of the world, the exercise of the rights of sovereignty tends to be concentrated in few hands, and they are frightened at the idea that it in the end it will be so with them. Statesmen themselves feel these terrors, or at least feign to feel them; for in America, centralization is not popular, and one cannot court the majority more skillfully than by rising up against the alleged encroachments of the central power. Americans refuse to see that in countries where this frightening centralizing tendency manifests itself, one encounters only a single people, whereas the Union is a confederation of different peoples; a fact that is enough to upset all forecasts founded on analogy.

I avow that I consider these fears of many Americans to be entirely imaginary. Far from dreading with them the consolidation of sovereignty in the hands of the Union, I believe that the federal government is becoming visibly weaker.

To prove what I advance on this point, I shall not have recourse to old facts, but to those I was able to be a witness to, or that have taken place in our time.

When one examines attentively what is coming to pass in the United States, one discovers without difficulty the existence of two contrary tendencies; they are like two currents running in opposite directions through the same bed.

For the forty-five years the Union has existed, time has done justice upon a host of provincial prejudices that at first militated against it. The patriotic sentiment attaching each American to his state has become less exclusive. Coming to know each other better, the various parties of the Union have been brought together. The mail, that great bond of minds, today reaches to the end of the wilderness;[80] each day steamboats make all points of the coast communicate with one another. Commerce goes up and down the rivers of the interior with unexampled rapidity.[81] To the opportunities created by nature and art are added the instability of desires, the restiveness of spirit, the love of wealth that constantly push an American out of his dwelling, putting him in communication with a great number of his fellow citizens. He travels through his country in all directions; he visits all the populations inhabiting it. One does not encounter a province in France whose inhabitants

80. In 1832 the district of Michigan, with only 31,639 inhabitants, forming still only a hardly cleared wilderness, showed 940 miles of mail routes developed. The almost entirely wild territory of Arkansas was already crossed by 1,938 miles of mail routes. See *The Report of the Postmaster General*, November 30, 1833. The postage for newspapers alone in the entire Union brings in 254,796 dollars per year. [*Report of the Postmaster General*, Nov. 30, 1833, in Force, *National Calendar*, 244ff.]

81. In the course of ten years, from 1821 to 1831, 271 steamboats have been launched on the rivers that flow in the valley of the Mississippi alone. In 1829, there were 256 steamboats in the United States. See *Legislative Documents*, no. 140, p. 274. [House, "Commerce and Navigation," 285—note page correction.]

know one another as perfectly as the 13 million men who cover the area of the United States.

At the same time that Americans mix together, they assimilate to one another; the differences that climate, origin, and institutions have put between them diminish. More and more all are brought together into a common type. Each year thousands of men who have left the North spread into all parts of the Union: they bring with them their beliefs, their opinions, their mores; and as their enlightenment is superior to that of the men among whom they go to live, they are not slow to take hold of affairs and to modify society to their profit. This continuous emigration from the North toward the South singularly favors the fusion of all provincial characters into a single national character. The civilization of the North seems destined, therefore, to become the common measure by which all the rest will be regulated one day.

As the industry of Americans makes progress, one sees the commercial bonds that unite all the confederated states tighten, and after having existed in opinions, the Union enters into habits. Time, in passing, makes a host of fantastic terrors disappear that tormented the imaginations of men in 1789. Federal power has not become an oppressor; it has not destroyed the independence of the states; it does not lead the confederates to monarchy; under the Union, small states have not fallen into dependence on large ones. The confederation has continued to grow constantly in population, wealth, and power.

I am therefore convinced that in our time Americans have fewer natural difficulties in living united than they had in 1789; the Union has fewer enemies than then.

And yet, if one wants to study carefully the history of the United States for forty-five years, one will be convinced without any trouble that federal power is decreasing.

It is not difficult to point out the causes of this phenomenon.

At the moment when the Constitution of 1789 was promulgated, everything was perishing in anarchy; the Union that succeeded this disorder excited much fear and hatred; but it had ardent friends because it was the expression of a great need. Although more attacked then than it is today, federal power thus rapidly attained the maximum of its power, as ordinarily happens to a government that triumphs after having roused its forces in struggle. In that period the interpretation of the Constitution seemed to extend rather than narrow federal sovereignty, and in several respects the Union presented the spectacle of one and the same people, directed, inside as outside, by one government.

But to arrive at that point, the people had put itself in a way above itself.

The Constitution had not destroyed the individuality of the states, and all bodies, whatever they may be, have a secret instinct that carries them toward independence. This instinct is still more pronounced in a country like America, where each village forms a sort of republic habituated to governing itself.

There was therefore an effort on the part of the states that submitted to federal preponderance. And every effort, even if it is crowned with great success, cannot fail to be weakened together with the cause that has given birth to it.

As the federal government consolidated its power, America retook its rank among nations, peace returned on its frontiers, public credit rose; settled order succeeded confusion, permitting individual industry to follow its natural course and to develop in freedom.

It was this very prosperity that began to make people lose sight of the cause that had produced it; the danger having passed, Americans no longer found in themselves the energy and patriotism that had helped to ward it off. Delivered from the fears that had preoccupied them, they readily reverted to the course of their habits and abandoned themselves without resistance to the ordinary tendency of their penchants. From the moment that a strong government no longer seemed necessary, they again began to think it was a hindrance. Everything prospered with the Union, and no one detached himself from the Union; but they hardly wanted to feel the action of the power representing it. Generally, people desired to remain united, but each particular fact tended to make them independent again. Each day the principle of the confederation was more readily accepted and less applied; thus the federal government, by creating order and peace, itself brought on its decline.

As soon as this disposition of spirits began to be outwardly manifest, party men, who live on the passions of the people, began exploiting it to their profit.

From then on, the federal government found itself in a very critical situation; its enemies had popular favor, and it was by promising to weaken it that one obtained the right to direct it.

From that period, every time that the government of the Union has entered the lists with those of the states, it has almost never ceased to retreat. When an interpretation of the terms of the federal constitution has taken place, most often the interpretation has been contrary to the Union and favorable to the states.

The Constitution gave to the federal government the care of providing for national interests: it was for the federal government, it was thought, to make or favor great internal undertakings that were of a nature to increase the prosperity of the Union as a whole ("internal improvements"), such as, for example, canals.

The states were frightened at the idea of seeing another authority than theirs dispose of a portion of their territory in this way. They feared that the central power, in this manner acquiring formidable patronage in their own midst, would come to exert an influence there that they wished to reserve wholly to their own agents.

The democratic party, which had always been opposed to all developments of federal power, therefore raised its voice; it accused Congress of usurpation; the head of state, of ambition. The central government, intimidated by these clamors, in the end recognized its error itself, and confined itself exactly to the sphere that was traced for it.

The Constitution gives to the Union the privilege of treating with foreign peoples. The Union had generally considered the Indian tribes that bordered the frontiers of its territory from this point of view. As long as the savages consented to flee before civilization, the federal right was not contested; but from the day that an Indian tribe undertook to settle on one spot of soil, the surrounding states claimed a right of possession over these lands and a right of sovereignty over the men holding them. The central government hastened to recognize both, and after having treated with the Indians as with independent peoples, it left them subject to the legislative tyranny of the states.[81]

Among the states that had formed on the Atlantic coast, several extended indefinitely to the west into wilderness where Europeans had still not penetrated. Those whose limits had been irrevocably fixed saw with a jealous eye the immense future open to their neighbors. The latter, in a spirit of conciliation, and to facilitate the action of the Union, consented to draw up limits for themselves and abandoned to the confederation all the territory that could be found beyond them.[82]

Since that period, the federal government has become owner of all the uncultivated terrain to be found outside the thirteen states originally confederated. It takes charge of dividing and selling it, and the money that comes from it goes exclusively into the Union's treasury. With the aid of this revenue, the federal government buys the Indians' lands from them, opens routes in the new districts, and facilitates with all its power the rapid development of society.

Now, it happened that in time new states were formed in the same wilderness formerly ceded by inhabitants of the Atlantic coast. To the profit of the

81. See, in the legislative documents that I have already cited in the chapter on the Indians, the letter from the President of the United States to the Cherokees, his correspondence on this subject with his agents, and his messages to Congress. [House, "Cherokee Indians."]

82. The first act of transfer took place on the part of the state of New York in 1780; Virginia, Massachusetts, Connecticut, South Carolina, North Carolina followed this example at different periods, Georgia was the last; its act of transfer goes back only to 1802.

nation as a whole, Congress has continued to sell the uncultivated lands that these states still enclose within them. But today the latter claim that once they have been constituted, they ought to have the exclusive right to apply the product of these sales to their own use. These claims having become more and more threatening, Congress believed it had to take away from the Union a part of the privileges which it had enjoyed until then, and at the end of 1832 it passed a law by which, without ceding to the new republics of the West ownership of their uncultivated lands, it nevertheless reserved the greatest part of the revenue drawn from them for their profit alone.[83]

It suffices to travel through the United States to appreciate the advantages that the country derives from the Bank. These advantages are of several sorts; but there is one above all that strikes the foreigner: bills from the Bank of the United States are accepted at the frontier of the wilderness for the same value as in Philadelphia, where the seat of its operations is.[84]

The Bank of the United States is nevertheless the object of great hatred. Its directors have pronounced against the president, and they are accused, not implausibly, of having abused their influence to hinder his election. The president therefore attacks the institution that they represent with all the ardor of personal enmity. What encourages the president to pursue his vengeance in this way is that he feels himself supported by the secret instincts of the majority.

The Bank forms the great monetary bond of the Union just as Congress is the great legislative bond, and the same passions that tend to make the states independent of the central power tend to the destruction of the Bank.

The Bank of the United States always holds in its hands many bills belonging to provincial banks; each day it can oblige them to repay their bills in cash. For it, on the contrary, such a danger is not to be feared; the greatness of its disposable resources permits it to face all exigencies. Their existence thus threatened, the provincial banks are forced to use restraint and to put into circulation only the number of bills proportional to their capital. The provincial banks suffer this salutary control with impatience. The newspapers that have sold out to them, and the president, whom interest has rendered their organ, attack the Bank therefore with a sort of fury. They stir up local passions and the country's blind democratic instinct against it. According to them, the directors of the Bank form an aristocratic and perma-

83. The president, it is true, refused to sanction this law, but he accepted the principle of it completely. See *Message of December 8, 1833*.

84. The current Bank of the United States was created in 1816, with a capital of $35,000,000 (185,500,000 F): its privilege expires in 1836. Last year, Congress passed a law to renew it; but the president refused his sanction. Today the struggle is engaged on both sides with extreme violence, and it is easy to predict the impending fall of the Bank.

nent body whose influence cannot fail to make itself felt in the government and will sooner or later alter the principles of equality on which American society rests.

The struggle of the Bank against its enemies is only one incident in the great combat that the provinces fight against the central power in America; the spirit of independence and of democracy against the spirit of hierarchy and of subordination. I do not claim that the enemies of the Bank of the United States are precisely the same individuals who attack the federal government on other points; but I do say that the attacks against the Bank of the United States are the product of the same instincts that militate against the federal government, and that the great number of enemies of the first is a distressing symptom of the weakness of the second.

But never has the Union shown itself to be weaker than in the famous tariff affair.[85]

The wars of the French Revolution and of 1812, by preventing free communication between America and Europe, had created manufactures in the North of the Union. When peace reopened the path to the New World for the products of Europe, Americans believed that they should establish a system of customs that could at once protect their nascent industry and pay off the amount of the debts that war had made them contract.

The southern states, which did not have manufactures to encourage, being only agricultural, were not slow to complain of this measure.

I do not claim to examine here what could have been imaginary or real in their complaints; I am speaking of the facts.

As long ago as the year 1820, South Carolina declared in a petition to Congress that the tariff law was *unconstitutional, oppressive,* and *unjust.** Afterwards, Georgia, Virginia, North Carolina, the state of Alabama, and that of Mississippi made more or less energetic claims in the same sense.

Far from taking account of this grumbling, in the years 1824 and 1828 Congress again raised tariff duties and again sanctioned their principle.

Then a celebrated doctrine that took the name of *nullification* was produced, or rather recalled, in the South.

I have shown in its place that the goal of the federal constitution was not to establish a league, but to create a national government.[†] Americans of the United States, in all the cases foreseen by their constitution, formed but one

*English in the original.

†*DA* I 1.8.

85. For the details of this affair, see principally the *Legislative Documents,* 22d Congress, 2d session, no. 30. [Senate, "Presidential Message with Proclamations, Proceedings, and Documents, on Measures of South Carolina and General Government on Nullification," 22d Cong., 2d sess., 1832–1833, Sen. Doc. 30, serial 230.]

and the same people. On all those points, the national will was expressed, as among all constitutional peoples, with the aid of a majority. Once the majority has spoken, the duty of the minority is to submit.

Such is the legal doctrine, the only one that is in accord with the text of the Constitution and the known intention of those who established it.

The *nullifiers* of the South claim, on the contrary, that Americans, in uniting, did not understand that they were blending into one and the same people, but that they wanted only to form a league of independent peoples; hence it follows that each state, having preserved its complete sovereignty if not in action at least in principle, has the right to interpret the laws of Congress and to suspend execution within it of those that seem to it opposed to the Constitution or to justice.

The whole doctrine of nullification is summed up in a sentence pronounced by Mr. Calhoun, the avowed chief of the nullifiers of the South, before the Senate of the United States in 1833:

"The Constitution," he says, "is a contract in which the states have appeared as sovereigns. Now, every time that a contract intervenes between parties that do not acknowledge a common arbiter, each of them retains the right to judge by itself the extent of its obligation."*

It is manifest that such a doctrine in principle destroys the federal bond and in fact brings back the anarchy from which the Constitution of 1789 had delivered Americans.

When South Carolina saw that Congress showed itself deaf to its complaints, it threatened to apply the doctrine of the nullifiers to the federal tariff law. Congress persisted in its system; finally, the storm broke.

In the course of 1832, the people of South Carolina[86] named a national convention to decide the extraordinary means that remained to be taken; and on November 24 of the same year that convention published, under the name of an ordinance, a law that rendered void the federal tariff law, forbade the deduction of duties that were imposed by it, and [forbade] the acceptance of appeals that could be made to the federal courts.[87] This ordinance was not to

---

*John C. Calhoun (1782–1850) makes similar statements in Senate, "Resolutions," 22d Cong., 2d sess., 1832–1833, Sen. Docs. 42, 47, 57, serial 230.

86. That is to say a majority of the people, for the opposing party, named the *Union Party,* long had a very strong and very active minority in its favor. Carolina may have around 47,000 electors; 30,000 were favorable to nullification and 17,000 opposed.

87. This ordinance was preceded by a report of the committee charged with preparing the draft of it: this report contained the explication and goal of the law. One reads in it, p. 34:

When the rights reserved to the several States are deliberately invaded, it is their right and their duty to "interpose for the purpose of arresting the progress of the evil of usurpation, and to maintain, within their respective limits, the authorities and privileges belonging to them as *independent sovereignties.*" If the several States do not possess this

be put into effect until the month of February following, and it was indicated that if Congress modified the tariff before that period, South Carolina would consent not to follow up its threats. Later they expressed the desire, in a vague and indeterminate manner, to submit the question to an extraordinary assembly of all the confederated states.

While waiting, South Carolina armed its militia and prepared for war.

What did Congress do? Congress, which had not listened to its suppliant subjects, lent its ear to their complaints when it saw them with arms in hand.[88] It passed a law[89] according to which the duties brought in by the tariff would be reduced progressively for ten years until they had been brought down so as not to exceed the needs of government. Thus Congress completely abandoned the principle of the tariff. For a duty to protect industry it substituted a purely fiscal measure.[90] To conceal its defeat, the government of the Union had recourse to an expedient that is much used by weak governments: while yielding on the facts, it showed itself inflexible on the principles. At the same time that Congress changed the tariff legislation, it passed another law in virtue of which the president was invested with an extraordinary power to overcome by force resistance that from then on was no longer to be feared.

South Carolina did not even consent to allow the Union these weak appearances of victory; the same national convention that had rendered the tariff law void, when assembled anew, accepted the concession that was offered to it; but at the same time it declared it was only persisting with more force in the doctrine of the nullifiers and, to prove it, it annulled the law that conferred extraordinary powers on the president, although it was very certain that it would not have been used.

---

right, it is in vain that they claim to be sovereign [. . .]. South Carolina claims to be a sovereign State. She recognizes no tribunal upon earth as above her authority. It is true, she has entered into *a solemn compact of Union* [quoted in English] with other sovereign States, but she claims, and will exercise the right to determine the extent of her obligations under that compact, nor will she consent that any other power shall exercise the right of judgment for her. And when that compact is violated by her co-States, or by the Government which they have created, she asserts her *unquestionable* [quoted in English] right to judge of the infractions, as well as of the mode and measure of redress. [Senate, "Presidential Message," 34–35.]

88. What served to determine Congress in this measure was a demonstration from the powerful state of Virginia, whose legislature offered to serve as arbiter between the Union and South Carolina. Until then the latter had appeared entirely abandoned, even by the states who had made demands with it.

89. Law of March 2, 1833.

90. This law was suggested by Mr. Clay and passed in four days in the two houses of Congress by an immense majority.

Almost all the actions I have just spoken of took place under the presidency of General [Andrew] Jackson. One cannot deny that in the tariff affair, he sustained the rights of the Union with skill and vigor. I nevertheless believe that one must put among a number of dangers incurred by the federal power today the very conduct of the one who represents it.

Some persons in Europe have formed an opinion about the influence that General Jackson can exert in the affairs of his country that appears quite extravagant to those who have seen things at close hand.

One has heard it said that General Jackson has won battles, that he is an energetic man, brought on by character and habit to the use of force, desirous of power and a despot by taste. All that is perhaps true, but the consequences that have been drawn from these truths are great errors.

It has been imagined that General Jackson wants to establish a dictatorship in the United States, that he is going to make the military spirit reign there and extend the central power so as to endanger provincial freedoms. In America, the time for undertakings like this and the century of such men have not yet come: if General Jackson had wished to dominate in this manner, he would surely have lost his political position and compromised his life: so he has not been imprudent enough to attempt it.

Far from wanting to extend federal power, the current president represents, on the contrary, the party that wants to restrict that power to the clearest and most precise terms of the Constitution, and that does not ever accept any interpretation favorable to the government of the Union; far from presenting himself as the champion of centralization, General Jackson is the agent of provincial jealousies; it is (if I can express myself so) *decentralizing* passions that brought him to sovereign power. He maintains himself and prospers by flattering these passions daily. General Jackson is the slave of the majority: he follows it in its wishes, its desires, its half-uncovered instincts, or rather he divines it and runs to place himself at its head.

Every time that the governments of the states enter into a struggle with the Union, it is rare that the president is not the first to doubt his right; he almost always anticipates the legislative power; when there is room for interpretation of the extent of federal power, he ranges himself in a way against himself; he diminishes himself, hides himself, effaces himself. It is not that he is naturally weak or an enemy of the Union; when the majority had pronounced against the claims of the nullifiers of the South, one saw him put himself at its head, formulate cleanly and energetically the doctrines that it professed, and be the first to call it to [the use of] force. General Jackson, to make use of a comparison borrowed from the vocabulary of the American parties, seems to me *federal* by taste and *republican* by calculation.

After having thus abased himself before the majority to gain its favor,

General Jackson picks himself up; he then advances toward the objects it pursues itself, or those that it does not see with a jealous eye, overturning all obstacles before him. Made strong with support that his predecessors did not have, he rides roughshod over his personal enemies everywhere he finds them, with a facility that no president has hit upon; he takes under his responsibility measures that no one before him would ever have dared to take; he even comes to treat the national representatives with a sort of almost insulting disdain; he refuses to sign the laws of Congress and often omits to respond to that great body. He is a favorite who sometimes bullies his master. The power of General Jackson constantly increases, therefore; but that of the president diminishes. In his hands, the federal government is strong; it will pass to his successor enfeebled.

Either I am strangely mistaken or the federal government of the United States tends to weaken daily; it successively withdraws from affairs, it contracts the sphere of its action more and more. Naturally weak, it even abandons appearances of force. On the other hand, I believed I saw in the United States that the sentiment of independence became more and more lively in the states, the love of provincial government more and more pronounced.

They want the Union, but reduced to a shadow: they want it strong in certain cases and weak in all the others; they pretend that in time of war it can gather the national strength and all the resources of the country in its hands, and that in time of peace it so to speak does not exist, as if this alternation of debility and vigor were [to be found] in nature.

I see nothing for the present that can arrest this general movement of minds; the causes that have given rise to it will not cease working in the same direction. It will therefore continue, and one can predict that if some extraordinary circumstance does not occur, the government of the Union will go on weakening every day.

I nevertheless believe that we are still far from the time when the federal power, incapable of protecting its own existence and of giving peace to the country, will be extinguished in some way by itself. The Union is [established] in mores, it is desired; its results are evident, its benefits visible. When it is perceived that the weakness of the federal government compromises the existence of the Union, I do not doubt that a movement of reaction in favor of its force will be seen to arise.

The government of the United States is, of all the federal governments that have been established up to our day, the one that is most naturally destined to act: as long as one does not attack it in an indirect manner by interpreting its laws, as long as one does not alter its substance profoundly, a change of opinion, an internal crisis, a war could suddenly give it back the vigor it needs.

What I wanted to state is only this: many people among us think that in the United States there is a movement of minds that favors the centralization of power in the hands of the president and Congress. I claim that a contrary movement there is obvious to remark. Far from the federal government's gaining force with age and threatening the sovereignty of the states, I say that it tends to weaken each day and that the sovereignty of the Union alone is in peril. That is what the present reveals. What will be the final result of this tendency, what events can halt, delay, or hasten the movement that I have described? The future hides them, and I do not claim to be able to sweep away its veil.

ON REPUBLICAN INSTITUTIONS IN THE UNITED STATES; WHAT ARE THEIR CHANCES OF LONGEVITY?

The Union is only an accident.—Republican institutions have more of a future.—The republic is, for the present, the natural state of the Anglo-Americans.—Why.—In order to destroy it, one would have to change all the laws and modify all mores at the same time. Difficulties that the Americans meet with in creating an aristocracy.

The dismemberment of the Union, by introducing war within the states to-day confederated, and with it permanent armies, dictatorship and taxes, could in the long term compromise the fate of republican institutions there.

One must nevertheless not confuse the future of the republic with that of the Union.

The Union is an accident that will last only as long as circumstances favor it, but a republic seems to me to be the natural state of the Americans; and only the continuous action of contrary causes, acting always in the same direction, could substitute monarchy for it.

The Union exists principally in the law that created it. A single revolution, a change in public opinion can break it apart forever. The republic has more profound roots.

What one understands by republic in the United States is the slow and tranquil action of society on itself. It is a regular state really founded on the enlightened will of the people. It is a conciliating government, in which resolutions ripen for a long time, are discussed slowly and executed only when mature.

Republicans in the United States prize mores, respect beliefs, recognize rights. They profess the opinion that a people ought to be moral, religious, and moderate to the degree it is free. What one calls a republic in the United States is the tranquil reign of the majority. The majority, after it has had the time to recognize itself and to certify its existence, is the common source of powers. But the majority itself is not all-powerful. Above it in the moral world are humanity, justice, and reason; in the political world, acquired rights. The majority recognizes these two barriers, and if it happens to cross them, it is because it has passions, like each man, and because like him, it can do evil while discerning the good.

But we in Europe have made strange discoveries.

A republic, according to some among us, is not the reign of the majority, as has been believed until now, it is the reign of those who are strongly for the majority. It is not the people who direct these sorts of governments, but those who know the greatest good of the people: a happy distinction that permits one to act in the name of nations without consulting them and to claim their recognition while riding roughshod over them. A republican government is, furthermore, the only one in which one must recognize the right to do everything, and which can scorn what men have respected up to the present, from the highest laws of morality to the vulgar rules of common sense.

Until our time, it had been thought that despotism was odious, whatever its forms were. But in our day it has been discovered that there are legitimate tyrannies and holy injustices in the world, provided that one exercises them in the name of the people.

The ideas of a republic that the Americans have made for themselves singularly facilitate their use of it and assure its longevity. Among them, if the practice of republican government is often bad, at least the theory is good, and in the end the people always conform their acts to it.

At the origin it was impossible, and it would still be very difficult, to establish a centralized administration in America. Men are dispersed over too great a space and separated by too many natural obstacles for one alone to be able to undertake to direct the details of their existence. America is therefore the country par excellence of provincial and township government.

To this cause, whose action is equally felt by all Europeans of the New World, the Anglo-Americans have added several others that were particular to them.

When the colonies of North America were established, municipal freedom had already penetrated into English laws as well as mores, and the English emigrants adopted it not only as a necessary thing, but as a good that all knew the value of.

In addition, we have seen in what manner the colonies had been founded. Each province, and so to speak each district, was peopled separately by men who were strangers to one another or associated in different goals.

The English of the United States have therefore found themselves, from the origin, divided into a great number of distinct little societies that were not attached to any common center, and each of these little societies had to occupy itself with its own affairs, since nowhere did they perceive a central authority that naturally would and easily could provide for them.

Thus the nature of the country, the very manner in which the English colonies had been founded, the habits of the first emigrants—all united to develop communal and provincial freedoms there to an extraordinary degree.

In the United States, the sum of the institutions of the country is therefore essentially republican; to destroy in a lasting fashion the laws that found the republic, one would in a way have to abolish all the laws at once.

If in our day a party undertook to found a monarchy in the United States, it would be in a still more difficult position than one that might wish to proclaim a republic from now on in France. Royalty would not find legislation prepared in advance for it, and then one would really see a monarchy surrounded by republican institutions.

The monarchical principle would have just as much difficulty penetrating the mores of the Americans.

In the United States, the dogma of the sovereignty of the people is not an isolated doctrine that is joined neither to habits nor to the sum of dominant ideas; on the contrary, one can view it as the last link in a chain of opinions that envelops the Anglo-American world as a whole. Providence has given to each individual, whoever he may be, the degree of reason necessary for him to be able to direct himself in things that interest him exclusively. Such is the great maxim on which civil and political society in the United States rests: the father of a family applies it to his children, the master to his servants, the township to those under its administration, the province to the townships, the state to the provinces, the Union to the states. Extended to the entirety of the nation, it becomes the dogma of the sovereignty of the people.

Thus, in the United States, the generative principle of the republic is the same one that regulates most human actions. Therefore the republic penetrates, if I can express myself so, the ideas, the opinions, and all the habits of the Americans at the same time as it establishes itself in their laws; and to come to change the laws, [the Americans] would have to come in a way to the point of wholly changing themselves. In the United States, even the religion of the greatest number is itself republican; it submits the truths of the other world to individual reason, as politics abandons to the good sense of all the care of their interests, and it grants that each man freely take the way that will lead him to Heaven, in the same manner that the law recognizes in each citizen the right to choose his government.

Evidently, it is only a long series of facts, all having the same tendency, that might be able to substitute for this sum of laws, opinions and mores, a sum of contrary mores, opinions and laws.

If republican principles are to perish in America, they will succumb only after a long social travail, frequently interrupted, often resumed; they will seem to be reborn several times, and they will disappear without return only when an entirely new people has taken the place of the one that exists in our day. Now, nothing can presage a revolution like this, no sign announces it.

What strikes you most on your arrival in the United States is the kind of tumultuous movement within which political society is placed. The laws change constantly, and at first it seems impossible that a people so little sure of its will would not soon come to substitute for its current form of government an entirely new form. These fears are premature. In the case of political institutions, there are two kinds of instability that must not be confused: one attaches to secondary laws; it can reign for a long time within a well-established society; the other constantly shakes the very bases of the constitution and attacks the generative principles of the laws; this is always followed by troubles and revolutions; the nation that suffers it is in a violent and transitory state. Experience makes known that these two kinds of legislative instability have no necessary connection between them, for they have been seen to exist jointly or separately according to times and places. The first is encountered in the United States, but not the second. Americans frequently change the laws, but the foundation of the Constitution is respected.

In our day, the republican principle reigns in America as the monarchical principle dominated in France under Louis XIV. The French of that time were not only friends of the monarchy, but also they did not imagine that one could put anything in its place; they accepted it as one accepts the course of the sun and the changes of the seasons. Among them, royal power had no more advocates than adversaries.

Thus a republic exists in America without combat, without opposition, without proof, by a tacit accord, a sort of *consensus universalis.*

Still, I think that in changing their administrative processes as often as they do, the inhabitants of the United States compromise the future of republican government.

Constantly hindered in their projects by the continuous volatility of legislation, it is to be feared that men will in the end consider the republic as an inconvenient way of living in society; the evil resulting from the instability of secondary laws would then put the existence of fundamental laws in question, and would indirectly bring a revolution; but that period is still very far from us.

What one can foresee at present is that in emerging from a republic, the Americans would pass rapidly to despotism, without stopping very long at monarchy. Montesquieu says that there is nothing more absolute than the authority of a prince who succeeds a republic, the indefinite powers that were given over without fear to an elective magistrate then being placed in the hands of an hereditary chief.* This is generally true, but particularly applicable to a democratic republic. In the United States, magistrates are not elected by a particular class of citizens, but by the majority of the nation; they represent the passions of the multitude immediately and depend entirely on its will; they therefore inspire neither hatred nor fear: thus I remarked how little care had been taken to limit their power in drawing the boundaries of its action and what an immense part had been left to their arbitrary [will]. This order of things has created habits that would survive it. While ceasing to be responsible, the American magistrate would keep his undefined power, and it is impossible to say where tyranny would then halt.

There are people among us who expect to see aristocracy arise in America, and who already foresee exactly the period in which it will take possession of power.

I have already said, and I repeat, that the current movement of American society seems to me to be more and more democratic.

Nevertheless, I do not claim that Americans will not come, one day, to restrict the sphere of political rights among them, or to confiscate these same rights to the profit of one man; but I cannot believe that they will ever entrust their exclusive use to a particular class of citizens or, in other words, that they will found an aristocracy.

An aristocratic corps is composed of a certain number of citizens who, without being placed very far from the crowd, are nevertheless elevated above it in a permanent manner; [a corps] that one touches and cannot strike, with which one mixes daily and cannot intermingle.

It is impossible to imagine anything more contrary to the nature and the secret instincts of the human heart than a subjection of this kind: left to themselves, men will always prefer the arbitrary power of a king to the regular administration of nobles.

An aristocracy, in order to last, needs to found inequality in principle, to legalize it in advance, to introduce it into the family at the same time that it spreads it over society: all things so strongly repugnant to natural equity that one can obtain them from men only by constraint.

Since human societies have existed, I do not believe one can cite the example of a single people that, left to itself and by its own efforts, has created an aristocracy at its heart: all the aristocracies of the Middle Ages were daughters of conquest. The vanquisher was the noble, the vanquished the

---

*See Montesquieu, *On the Greatness and Decadence of the Romans,* XV 13.

serf. Force then imposed the inequality that, once entered into mores, maintained itself and passed naturally into the laws.

One has seen societies that, due to events prior to their existence, were so to speak born aristocratic, and that each century afterwards led back toward democracy. Such was the lot of the Romans, and that of the barbarians who settled after them. But a people starting from civilization and democracy that would bring itself by degrees to inequality of conditions and in the end establish inviolable privileges and exclusive categories in its heart—that would be something new in the world.

Nothing indicates that America is destined to be first to give such a spectacle.

SOME CONSIDERATIONS ON THE CAUSES OF THE COMMERCIAL GREATNESS OF THE UNITED STATES

The Americans are called by nature to be a great maritime people.—Extent of their shores.—Depth of the ports.—Greatness of the rivers.—It is nevertheless much less to physical causes than to intellectual and moral causes that the commercial superiority of the Anglo-Americans should be attributed.—Reason for this opinion.—Future of the Anglo-Americans as a trading people.—The ruin of the Union would not halt the maritime surge of the peoples who compose it.—Why.—The Anglo-Americans are naturally called upon to serve the needs of the inhabitants of South America.—They, like the English, will become the carriers for a great part of the world.

From the Bay of Fundy to the Sabine River in the Gulf of Mexico, the coast of the United States extends over a length of nearly nine hundred leagues.

These shores form a single uninterrupted line, all placed under the same domination.

There is no people in the world that can offer to commerce deeper, vaster, and safer ports than the Americans.

The inhabitants of the United States compose a great civilized nation that fortune has placed in the midst of the wilderness at twelve hundred leagues from the principal hearth of civilization. America therefore has daily need of Europe. With time, Americans will undoubtedly come to produce or to manufacture at home most of the objects that are necessary to them, but the two continents will never be able to live entirely independent of one another: too many natural bonds exist between their needs, their ideas, their habits, and their mores.

The Union has produce that has become necessary to us and that our soil entirely refuses to supply or can provide only at great expense. Americans consume only a very small part of these products; they sell us the rest.

Europe is therefore the market of America, as America is the market of Europe; and maritime commerce is as necessary to inhabitants of the United States to bring their raw materials to our ports as to carry our manufactured objects to them.

The United States had, therefore, to have furnished a great fuel to the industry of maritime peoples, if they themselves renounced commerce, as the Spanish of Mexico have done up to the present; or had to have become one of the first maritime powers of the globe: this alternative was inevitable.

At all times the Anglo-Americans have shown a decided taste for the sea. Independence, in breaking off the commercial bonds that united them to England, gave a new and powerful surge to their maritime genius. Since that period the number of vessels in the Union has increased in a progression almost as rapid as the number of its inhabitants. Today it is Americans themselves who carry home nine-tenths of the products of Europe.[91] It is again Americans who bring three-quarters of the exports of the New World to consumers in Europe.[92]

United States vessels fill the ports of Le Havre and Liverpool. One sees only a few English or French bottoms in the port of New York.[93]

Thus not only does the American trader brave competition on his own soil, but he also does combat with foreigners advantageously on theirs.

This is readily explained: of all the vessels in the world, United States ships cross the seas most cheaply. As long as the United States merchant marine preserves this advantage over others, not only will it keep what it has conquered, but it will augment its conquests every day.

The problem of knowing why the Americans navigate at a lower price than other men is a difficult one to resolve: one is at first tempted to attribute this superiority to a few material advantages that nature has put within their sole reach; but that is not so.

91. The total value of imports in the year ending September 30, 1832, was $101,129,266. Imports made on foreign ships came only to a sum of $10,731,039, about a tenth.

92. The total value of exports during the same year was $87,176,943; the value exported on foreign vessels was $21,036,183, or nearly a quarter (*Williams' Register*, 1833, p. 398). [*Williams' Register*, 399.]

93. During the years 1829, 1830, 1831, ships measuring 3,307,719 tons altogether entered the ports of the Union. Foreign ships furnished only 544,571 tons of this total. They were therefore a fraction of nearly 16 percent (*National Calendar*, 1833, p. 304). [Force, *National Calendar*, 305.]

In the years 1820, 1826, and 1831, English vessels entering the ports of London, Liverpool, and Hull measured 443,800 tons. Foreign vessels entering the same ports during the same years measured 159,431 tons. The relation between them was therefore nearly 36 to 100 (*Companion to the Almanac*, 1834, p. 169).

In the year 1832 the ratio of foreign bottoms to English bottoms entered into the ports of Great Britain was 29 to 100.

American vessels are almost as dear to build as ours;[94] they are not better constructed and generally do not last as long.

The wages of the American seaman are higher than those of the European seaman; what proves it is the great number of Europeans that one encounters in the merchant marine of the United States.

How is it, therefore, that Americans navigate more cheaply than we do?

I think that one would seek in vain the causes of this superiority in material advantages; it is due to purely intellectual and moral qualities.

Here is a comparison that will shed light on my thought:

During the wars of the Revolution, the French introduced a new tactic into the military art that troubled the most aged generals and nearly destroyed the oldest monarchies of Europe. They undertook for the first time to do without a host of things that until then had been judged indispensable to war; they required new efforts of their soldiers that well-ordered nations had never demanded of theirs; one saw them do everything on the run and without hesitation risk the lives of men with a view to the result to be obtained.

The French were fewer and less wealthy than their enemies; they possessed infinitely fewer resources; nevertheless they were constantly victorious until the latter decided to imitate them.

The Americans have introduced something analogous into commerce. What the French did for victory, they do for low cost.

The European navigator ventures on the seas only with prudence; he departs only when the weather invites him to; if an unforeseen accident comes upon him, he enters into port at night, he furls a part of his sails, and when he sees the ocean whiten at the approach of land, he slows his course and examines the sun.

The American neglects these precautions and braves these dangers. He departs while the tempest still roars; at night as in day he opens all his sails to the wind; while on the go, he repairs his ship, worn down by the storm, and when he finally approaches the end of his course, he continues to fly toward the shore as if he already perceived the port.

The American is often shipwrecked; but there is no navigator who crosses the seas as rapidly as he does. Doing the same things as another in less time, he can do them at less expense.

Before reaching the end of a voyage with a long course, the European navigator believes he ought to land several times on his way. He loses precious time in seeking a port for relaxation or in awaiting the occasion to leave it, and he pays each day for the right to remain there.

---

94. Raw materials generally cost less in America than in Europe, but the price of labor is much higher there.

The American navigator leaves Boston to go to buy tea in China. He arrives at Canton, remains there a few days and comes back. In less than two years he has run over the entire circumference of the globe, and he has seen land only a single time. During a crossing of eight to ten months, he has drunk brackish water and lived on salted meat; he has struggled constantly against the sea, against illness, against boredom; but on his return he can sell the pound of tea for one penny less than the English merchant: the goal is attained.

I cannot express my thought better than by saying that the Americans put a sort of heroism into their manner of doing commerce.

It will always be very difficult for the European trader to follow his American competitor on the same course. The American, in acting in the manner that I described above, not only follows a calculation, he obeys, above all, his nature.

The inhabitant of the United States feels all the needs and desires that an advanced civilization gives rise to, and he does not find around him, as in Europe, a society knowledgeably organized to satisfy them; he is therefore often obliged to procure by himself the diverse objects that his education and habits have rendered necessary to him. In America, it sometimes happens that the same man plows his field, builds his dwelling, fashions his tools, makes his shoes, and weaves with his hands the coarse fabric that will cover him. This detracts from the perfection of industry, but serves powerfully to develop the intellect of the worker. There is nothing that tends more than the great division of labor to materialize man and to deny even the trace of a soul in his works. In a country like America, where specialists are so rare, one cannot require a long apprenticeship of each of those who embrace a profession. Americans therefore have a great facility in changing their status, and they take advantage of it according to the needs of the moment. One encounters some who have been successively attorneys, farmers, traders, evangelical ministers, doctors. If the American is less skillful than the European in each industry, there is almost none that is entirely foreign to him. His capacity is more general, the sphere of his intellect is more extensive. The inhabitant of the United States is therefore never stopped by any axiom of status; he escapes all the prejudices of profession; he is no more attached to one system of operation than to another; he feels no more bound to an old method than to a new one; he has not created any habit, and he readily escapes from the empire that foreign habits would exercise over his mind, for he knows that his country resembles no other and that his situation is new in the world.

The American inhabits a land of prodigies, around him everything is constantly moving, and each movement seems to be progress. The idea of the

new is therefore intimately bound in his mind to the idea of the better. Nowhere does he perceive any boundary that nature can have set to the efforts
of man; in his eyes, what is not is what has not yet been attempted.

The universal movement reigning in the United States, the frequent turns
of fortune, the unforeseen displacement of public and private wealth—all
unite to keep the soul in a sort of feverish agitation that admirably disposes
it to every effort and maintains it so to speak above the common level of
humanity. For an American, one's entire life is spent as a game of chance, a
time of revolution, a day of battle.

These same causes operating at the same time on all individuals in the
end impress an irresistible impulse on the national character. The American
taken randomly will therefore be a man ardent in his desires, enterprising,
adventurous—above all, an innovator. This spirit is in fact found in all his
works; he introduces it into his political laws, his religious doctrines, his theories of social economy, his private industry; he brings it with him everywhere, into the depth of the woods as into the heart of towns. It is this same
spirit, applied to maritime commerce, that makes the American navigate
more quickly and more cheaply than all the traders of the world.

As long as the sailors of the United States keep these intellectual advantages and the practical superiority derived from them, not only will they
continue to provide by themselves for the needs of the producers and the
consumers of their country, but they will tend more and more to become,
like the English,[95] the carriers for other peoples.

This is beginning to be realized before our eyes. Already we are seeing
American navigators introduce themselves into the commerce of several nations of Europe as intermediate agents;[96] America offers them a still greater
future.

The Spanish and the Portuguese founded great colonies in South America
that have since become empires. Today civil war and despotism desolate these
vast regions. The movement of the population halts, and the few men who
inhabit them, absorbed in the care of defending themselves, hardly feel the
need to improve their lot.

But it cannot be so forever. Europe, left to itself, succeeded in piercing the
darkness of the Middle Ages with its own efforts; South America is Christian

95. One must not believe that English vessels are occupied only in transporting foreign
products to England or in transporting English products among foreigners; in our day the merchant marine of England forms a great enterprise of public vehicles, ready to serve all the producers of the world and to have all peoples communicate among themselves. The maritime
genius of Americans brings them to start a rival enterprise to the English.

96. A part of the commerce of the Mediterranean is already done on American vessels.

like us; it has our laws, our usages; it contains all the seeds of civilization that have been developed within the European nations and their offshoots; besides, South America has our example: why should it remain ever barbaric?

Here it is evidently only a question of time: a period more or less distant will doubtless come in which South Americans will form flourishing and enlightened nations.

But when the Spanish and the Portuguese of southern America begin to experience the needs of well-ordered peoples, they will still be far from being able to satisfy them themselves; last-born of civilization, they will submit to the superiority already acquired by their elders. They will be farmers long before being manufacturers and traders, and they will need the intervention of foreigners to go beyond the seas to sell their products and to get in exchange the objects whose new necessity will make itself felt.

One cannot doubt that Americans of the north of America are called upon to provide one day for the needs of the South Americans. Nature has placed them nearby. It has thus furnished them with great abilities to learn and appreciate the latter's needs, to bond with these peoples in permanent relations, and gradually to gain control of their market. The trader from the United States could only lose these natural advantages if he were very inferior to the trader from Europe, and he is, on the contrary, superior at several points. Americans of the United States already exert a great moral influence over all the peoples of the New World. It is with them that enlightenment starts. All the nations that inhabit the same continent are already habituated to considering them as the most enlightened offspring, the most powerful and wealthiest of the great American family. They constantly turn their regard toward the Union, therefore, and they assimilate themselves, as much as is in their power, to the peoples that compose it. They come daily to draw political doctrines from the United States and to borrow laws from it.

Americans of the United States find themselves, vis-à-vis the peoples of South America, in precisely the same position as their fathers, the English, vis-à-vis the Italians, the Spanish, the Portuguese, and all those peoples of Europe who, being less advanced in civilization and in industry, receive most of the objects of consumption from their hands.

England is today the natural seat of commerce for almost all the nations that lie close to it; the American Union is called upon to fill the same role in the other hemisphere. Each people that is born or grows up in the New World is therefore born and grows up there in a way to the profit of the Anglo-Americans.

If the Union came to be dissolved, the commerce of the states that had formed it would doubtless be slowed in its surge for some time; still, less than one thinks. It is evident that, whatever happens, the trading states will remain united. They all touch each other; among them there is a perfect identity of opinions, interests, and mores, and alone, they can make up a very great maritime power. Even if the South of the Union were to become independent of the North, the result would not be that it could do without it. I have said that the South is not commercial; nothing yet indicates that it will become so. The Americans of the South of the United States will therefore be obliged for a long time to have recourse to foreigners to export their products and to bring to them the objects that are necessary to their needs. Now, of all the intermediaries that they can use, their neighbors to the north are surely those who can serve them most cheaply. Therefore they will serve them, for low cost is the supreme law of commerce. There is no sovereign will nor national prejudices that can struggle for long against low cost. One cannot see a hatred more envenomed than the one existing between Americans of the United States and the English. Despite these hostile sentiments, the English never-theless furnish most manufactured objects to the Americans for the sole rea-son that they make them pay less than do other peoples. The growing pros-perity of America thus turns, despite the desire of the Americans, to the profit of the manufacturing industry of England.

Reason indicates and experience proves that there is no lasting commer-cial greatness if it cannot unite in case of need with military power.

This truth is as well understood in the United States as everywhere else. The Americans are already in a state to make their flag respected; soon they will be able to make it feared.

I am convinced that the dismemberment of the Union, far from diminish-ing the naval forces of the Americans, would tend strongly to increase them. Today the trading states are bound to those that are not, and often only with regret do the latter lend themselves to increasing a maritime power from which they profit only indirectly.

If, on the contrary, all the trading states of the Union formed but one and the same people, commerce would become a national interest of the first order for them; they would therefore be disposed to make very great sacri-fices to protect their vessels, and nothing would prevent them from following their desires on this point.

I think that nations, like men, almost always indicate the principal features of their destiny in their youth. When I see the spirit in which the Anglo-Americans carry on commerce, the opportunities that they find to do it, the success that they obtain in it, I cannot prevent myself from believing that one day they will become the first maritime power on the globe. They are driven to gain control of the seas, as the Romans were to conquer the world.

CONCLUSION

Here I approach the end. Up to now, in speaking of the future destiny of the United States, I have striven to divide my subject into various parts in order to study each of them more carefully.

Now I would like to gather all of them under a single point of view. What I shall say will be less detailed, but surer. I shall perceive each object less distinctly; I shall embrace the general facts with more certainty. I shall be like the voyager who, in going outside of the walls of a vast city, climbs the nearest hill. As he moves away, the men he has just left disappear before his eyes; their dwellings intermingle; he no longer sees public squares; he discerns the trace of streets with trouble; but his eye follows the contours of the town more easily, and for the first time, he grasps the form of it. It seems to me that I likewise discover before me the entire future of the English race in the New World. The details of this immense picture have remained in the shadow; but my regard comprehends the sum of them, and I conceive a clear idea of the whole.

The territory occupied or possessed in our day by the United States of America forms nearly a twentieth part of inhabited lands.

However extensive these limits are, one would be wrong to believe that the Anglo-American race will always be contained within them; it already extends well beyond.

There was a time when we as well could have created a great French nation in the American wilderness and, with the English, held the balance of the destinies of the New World. France once possessed a territory in North America almost as vast as all of Europe. The three greatest rivers of the continent then flowed wholly under our laws. The Indian nations who lived from the mouth of the St. Lawrence to the delta of the Mississippi heard only our language spoken; all the European settlements spread over this immense space recalled the memory of the native country: there were Louisbourg, Montmorency, Duquesne, Saint Louis, Vincennes, New Orleans, all names dear to France and familiar to our ears.

But a concurrence of circumstances that would be too long to list[97] deprived us of this magnificent inheritance. Everywhere that the French were few in number and badly settled, they have disappeared. The rest are collected in a small space and have passed under other laws. The four hundred

---

97. In the first rank is this: free peoples habituated to a municipal regime succeed much more easily than others in creating flourishing colonies. The habit of thinking by oneself and governing oneself is indispensable in a new country, where success necessarily depends to a large extent on the individual efforts of the colonists.

thousand French of Lower Canada today form the debris of an old people lost in the midst of the flood of a new nation. Around them the foreign population grows larger constantly; it extends on all sides; it penetrates into the ranks of the former masters of the land, dominates their towns, and denatures their language. This population is identical to that of the United States. I am therefore right to say that the English race does not halt at the limits of the Union, but advances well beyond toward the northeast.

To the northwest one encounters only a few Russian settlements without importance; but to the southwest, Mexico presents itself as a barrier to the march of the Anglo-Americans.

So, to tell the truth, there are only two rival races that share the New World today, the Spanish and the English.

The limits separating these two races have been fixed by a treaty. But however favorable this treaty should be to the Anglo-Americans, I do not doubt that they will soon come to infringe it.

Beyond the frontiers of the Union toward Mexico extend vast provinces that still lack inhabitants. The men of the United States will penetrate into these solitudes even before those who have the right to occupy them. They will appropriate the soil, they will establish a society on it, and when the legitimate proprietor finally presents himself, he will find the desert fertilized and foreigners sitting tranquilly on his inheritance.

The land of the New World belongs to the first occupant, and empire over it is the prize in the race.

Countries already populated will themselves have trouble safeguarding themselves from invasion.

I have spoken previously of what is taking place in the province of Texas.* Each day, little by little, inhabitants of the United States are introducing themselves into Texas; they are acquiring lands there, and while submitting to the laws of the country, they are founding an empire of their language and mores there. The province of Texas is still under the domination of Mexico; but soon Mexicans, so to speak, will no longer be found in it. A similar thing is happening at all points where the Anglo-Americans enter into contact with populations of another origin.

One cannot conceal from oneself the fact that the English race has acquired an immense preponderance over all the other European races of the New World. It is very superior to them in civilization, industry, and power. As long as it has before it wilderness or thinly inhabited country, as long as it does not encounter aggregated populations in its path, across which it

*See note 19 in this chapter.

would be impossible to clear itself a passage, one will see it expand constantly. It will not stop at lines drawn in treaties, but it will overflow these imaginary dikes on all sides.

This rapid development of the English race in the New World is marvelously facilitated by the geographic position that it occupies.

When one heads north, above its northern frontiers, one encounters polar ice, and when one descends some degrees below its southern limits, one is in the midst of the fires of the equator. The English of America are therefore located in the most temperate zone and the most habitable portion of the continent.

One may imagine that the enormous movement to be remarked in the increase of the population in the United States dates only from independence: that is an error. The population grew as quickly under the colonial system as in our day; it too nearly doubled in twenty-two years. But then it was occurring in thousands of inhabitants; now it is millions. The same fact that passed unnoticed a century ago strikes all minds today.

The English of Canada, who obey a king, increase in number and extend almost as quickly as the English of the United States, who live under a republican government.

In the eight years that the War of Independence lasted, the population did not cease increasing at the rate previously indicated.

Although great Indian nations, allied with the English, existed then on the frontiers of the West, the movement of emigration westward was so to speak never slowed. While the enemy ravaged the coasts of the Atlantic, Kentucky, the western districts of Pennsylvania, the state of Vermont, and that of Maine were filling with inhabitants. Nor did the disorder that followed the war prevent the population from growing, or stop its progressive march into the wilderness. Thus, differences of laws, the state of peace or the state of war, order or anarchy, have influenced the continuing development of the Anglo-Americans only in an imperceptible manner.

This may be understood without difficulty: causes general enough to make themselves felt at all points of such an immense territory at once do not exist. Thus there is always a great portion of the country where one is sure of finding shelter from the calamities that strike another, and however great the ills may be, the remedy available is always greater still.

One must therefore not believe that it is possible to stop the surge of the English race in the New World. The dismemberment of the Union, by bringing war to the continent, the abolition of the republic, by introducing tyranny to it, can delay these developments, but not prevent it from attaining the necessary completion of its destiny. No power on earth can close off, before the march of the emigrants, this fertile wilderness, which is open on every side to industry and offers a refuge in all miseries. Future events, whatever they may be, will not take away from Americans their climate, or their internal seas, or their great rivers, or the fertility of their soil. Bad laws, revolutions, and anarchy cannot destroy among them the taste for well-being and the spirit of enterprise that seems to be the distinctive characteristic of their race, nor can they absolutely extinguish the lights that enlighten them.

Thus, in the midst of an uncertain future, there is at least one event that is certain. At a period that we can call imminent, since it is a question here of the life of peoples, the Anglo-Americans will alone cover the whole immense space included between the polar ice and the tropics; they will spread from the shores of the Atlantic Ocean to the shores of the South Sea.*

I think that the territory over which the Anglo-American race will one day spread will equal three-quarters of Europe.[98] The climate of the Union is, all in all, preferable to that of Europe; its natural advantages are as great; it is evident that its population cannot fail to be proportionate one day to ours.

Europe, divided among so many diverse peoples; Europe, through the constantly renewed wars and barbarism of the Middle Ages, has come to have four hundred ten inhabitants[99] per square league. What cause as powerful could prevent the United States from having as many one day?

Many centuries will pass before the various offspring of the English race in America cease to present a common visage. One cannot foresee a period when man will be able to establish a permanent inequality of conditions in the New World.

Whatever may be the differences, therefore, that peace or war, freedom or tyranny, prosperity or misery, make in the destiny of the various offspring of the great Anglo-American family one day, they will all preserve at least an analogous social state and will have in common the usages and the ideas that flow from the social state.

The bond of religion alone was enough in the Middle Ages to gather the diverse races that peopled Europe into one same civilization. The English of the New World have a thousand other bonds between them, and they live in a century in which everything aims to become equal among men.

The Middle Ages were a period of fragmentation. Each people, each province, each city, each family tended strongly at that time to express its individ-

---

*The Pacific Ocean.

98. The United States alone already covers a space equal to half of Europe. The area of Europe is 500,000 square leagues; its population, 205,000,000 inhabitants. Malte-Brun, vol. 6, bk. 114, p. 4.

99. See Malte-Brun, vol. 6, bk. 116, p. 92.

uality. In our day, a contrary movement is felt; peoples seem to march toward unity. Intellectual bonds unite the most distant parts of the land, and men cannot remain strangers to one another for a single day or ignorant of what is taking place in any corner of the globe whatsoever: thus one remarks less difference today between Europeans and their descendants in the New World, despite the ocean that divides them, than between certain towns of the thirteenth century that were separated only by a river.

If this movement of assimilation brings foreign peoples together, with still greater reason it opposes the offspring of the same people becoming strangers to one another.

A time will arrive, therefore, when one can see one hundred fifty million men[100] in North America, equal among themselves, who all belong to the same family, who have the same point of departure, the same civilization, the same language, the same religion, the same habits, the same mores, and through whom thought will circulate in the same form and be painted in the same colors. All the rest is doubtful, but this is certain. Now, here is a fact entirely new in the world, of which the imagination itself cannot grasp the range.

There are two great peoples on the earth today who, starting from different points, seem to advance toward the same goal: these are the Russians and the Anglo-Americans.

Both have grown larger in obscurity; and while men's regards were occupied elsewhere, they have suddenly taken their place in the first rank of nations, and the world has learned of their birth and of their greatness almost at the same time.

All other peoples appear to have nearly reached the limits that nature has drawn and to have nothing more to do than preserve themselves; but these are growing:[101] all the others have halted or advance only with a thousand efforts; these alone march ahead at an easy and rapid pace on a course whose bounds the eye cannot yet perceive.

The American struggles against the obstacles that nature opposes to him; the Russian grapples with men. The one combats the wilderness and barbarism, the other, civilization vested with all its arms: thus the conquests of the American are made with the plowshare of the laborer, those of the Russian, with the sword of the soldier.

To attain his goal, the first relies on personal interest and allows the force and the reason of individuals to act, without directing them.

---

100. This is the population proportionate to that of Europe, taking the mean of 410 men per square league.

101. Russia is, of all the nations of the Old World, the one whose population increases proportionately the most rapidly.

The second in a way concentrates all the power of society in one man.

The one has freedom for his principal means of action; the other servitude.

Their point of departure is different, their ways are diverse; nonetheless, each of them seems called by a secret design of Providence to hold the destinies of half the world in its hands one day.

DEMOCRACY IN AMERICA

Volume

NOTICE

The Americans have a democratic social state that has naturally suggested to them certain laws and political mores.

This same social state has, in addition, given birth to a multitude of sentiments and opinions among them that were unknown in the old aristocratic societies of Europe. It has destroyed or modified relations that formerly existed, and established new ones. The aspect of civil society has met with change no less than the visage of the political world.

I treated the first subject in the work I published on American democracy five years ago. The second is the object of the present book. The two parts complete one another and form a single work.

I must warn the reader right away against an error that would be very prejudicial to me.

In seeing me attribute so many diverse effects to equality, he could conclude that I consider equality to be the unique cause of all that happens in our day. That would be to suppose that I had a very narrow view.

There are a host of opinions, sentiments, and instincts in our time that owe their birth to facts alien or even contrary to equality. So if I took the United States, for example, I would easily prove that the nature of the country, the origin of its inhabitants, the religion of its first founders, their acquired enlightenment, their prior habits did and still do exert, independently of democracy, an immense influence on their manner of thinking and feeling. Different causes, also distinct from the fact of equality, would be encountered in Europe and would explain a great part of what is taking place there.

I recognize the existence of all these different causes and their power, but to speak of them is not my subject. I have not undertaken to show the reason for all our penchants and ideas; I only wanted to bring out the extent to which equality has modified the one and the other.

One will perhaps be astonished that, while I am firmly of the opinion that the democratic revolution to which we are witness is an irresistible fact against which it would be neither desirable nor wise to struggle, in this book I often come to address such severe words to the democratic societies this revolution has created.

I shall respond simply that it is because I was not an adversary of democracy that I wanted to be sincere with it.

Men do not receive the truth from their enemies, and their friends scarcely offer it to them; that is why I have spoken it.

I thought that many would take it upon themselves to announce the new goods that equality promises to men, but that few would dare to point out from afar the perils with which it threatens them. It is therefore principally at those perils that I have directed my regard, and believing that I have uncovered them clearly I was not so cowardly as to be silent about them.

I hope that the impartiality that people appear to have remarked in the first work will again be found in this second one. Placed in the midst of the contradictory opinions that divide us, I have tried for the moment to destroy the favorable sympathies or contrary instincts that each of these opinions inspires in my heart. If those who read my book find a single sentence in it whose object is to flatter one of the great parties that have agitated our country or one of the little factions that, in our day, vex and enervate it, let these readers raise their voices and accuse me.

The subject I wanted to embrace is immense; for it comprehends most of the sentiments and ideas to which the new state of the world gives birth. Such a subject surely exceeds my strength, and in treating it I have not managed to satisfy myself.

But if I have been unable to attain the goal I strove for, readers will at least do me this justice: I have conceived and pursued my enterprise in the spirit that could make me worthy of success.

Influence of
Democracy on
Intellectual Movement
in the
United States

Chapter 1 ON THE PHILOSOPHIC
METHOD OF THE AMERICANS

I think there is no country in the civilized world where they are less occupied with philosophy than the United States.

The Americans have no philosophic school of their own, and they worry very little about all those that divide Europe; they hardly know their names.

It is easy to see, nevertheless, that almost all the inhabitants of the United States direct their minds in the same manner and conduct them by the same rules; that is to say, they possess a certain philosophic method, whose rules they have never taken the trouble to define, that is common to all of them.

To escape from the spirit of system, from the yoke of habits, from family maxims, from class opinions, and, up to a certain point, from national prejudices; to take tradition only as information, and current facts only as a useful study for doing otherwise and better; to seek the reason for things by themselves and in themselves alone, to strive for a result without letting themselves be chained to the means, and to see through the form to the foundation: these are the principal features that characterize what I shall call the philosophic method of the Americans.

If I go still further and seek among these diverse features the principal one that can sum up almost all the others, I discover that in most of the operations of the mind, each American calls only on the individual effort of his reason.

America is therefore the one country in the world where the precepts of Descartes* are least studied and best followed. That should not be surprising.

Americans do not read Descartes's works because their social state turns them away from speculative studies, and they follow his maxims because this same social state naturally disposes their minds to adopt them.

Amidst the continual movement that reigns in the heart of a democratic society, the bond that unites generations is relaxed or broken; each man easily loses track of the ideas of his ancestors or scarcely worries about them.

Men who live in such a society can no longer draw their beliefs from the opinions of the class to which they belong, for there are, so to speak, no longer any classes, and those that still exist are composed of elements that

---

*René Descartes (1596–1650), French philosopher, founder of modern rationalism, and author of *Discourse on Method* and *Meditations on First Philosophy*.

move so much that the body can never exert a genuine power over its members.

As for the action that the intellect of one man can have on another, it is necessarily very restricted in a country where citizens, having become nearly the same, all see each other from very close, and, not perceiving in anyone among themselves incontestable signs of greatness and superiority, are constantly led back toward their own reason as the most visible and closest source of truth. Then not only is trust in such and such a man destroyed, but the taste for believing any man whomsoever on his word.

Each therefore withdraws narrowly into himself and claims to judge the world from there.

The American way of taking the rule of their judgment only from themselves leads to other habits of mind.

As they see that they manage to resolve unaided all the little difficulties that practical life presents, they easily conclude that everything in the world is explicable and that nothing exceeds the bounds of intelligence.

Thus they willingly deny what they cannot comprehend: that gives them little faith in the extraordinary and an almost invincible distaste for the supernatural.

Since they customarily rely on their own witness, they like to see the object that occupies them very clearly; so they take off its wrapping as far as they can; they put to the side all that separates them from it and remove all that hides it from their regard in order to see it more closely and in broad daylight. This disposition of their minds soon leads them to scorn forms, which they consider useless and inconvenient veils placed between them and the truth.

Thus Americans have not needed to draw their philosophic method from books; they have found it in themselves. I shall say as much for what has happened in Europe.

The same method was established and vulgarized in Europe only as conditions there became more equal and men more alike.

Let us consider for a moment the chain of events:

In the sixteenth century, the reformers submit to individual reason some of the dogmas of the ancient faith; but they continue to exclude all others from discussion. In the seventeenth, Bacon,* in the natural sciences, and Descartes, in philosophy properly so-called, abolish the received formulas, destroy the empire of traditions, and overturn the authority of the master.

The philosophers of the eighteenth century, finally generalizing the same

---

*Francis Bacon (1561–1626), English philosopher and statesman, and author of *The Advancement of Learning* and *Novum Organum.*

principle, undertake to submit the objects of all beliefs to the individual examination of each man.

Who does not see that Luther,* Descartes, and Voltaire† made use of the same method, and that they differ only in the greater or lesser use that they claimed one might make of it?

How is it that the reformers so narrowly confined themselves within the circle of religious ideas? Why did Descartes, wanting to make use of his method only in certain matters even though he had put it in such a way that it applied to all, declare that one must judge for oneself only philosophical, and not political, matters? How did it happen that in the eighteenth century all at once they derived from the same method general applications that Descartes and his predecessors had not perceived or had refused to uncover? How is it, finally, that only in that period did the method we are speaking of suddenly leave the schools to penetrate society and become the common rule of intelligence, and that, after having become popular with the French, it was either openly adopted or secretly followed by all the peoples of Europe?

The philosophic method in question could be born in the sixteenth century and be clarified and generalized in the seventeenth; but it could not be commonly adopted in either of the two. Political laws, the social state—the habits of mind that flow from these first causes—were opposed to it.

It had been discovered in a period when men were beginning to be equal and to resemble each other. It could only be generally followed in centuries when conditions had finally become nearly the same and men almost alike.

The philosophic method of the eighteenth century is therefore not only French, but democratic, which explains why it was so easily accepted in all of Europe, whose face it has contributed so much to changing. It is not because the French changed their ancient beliefs and modified their ancient mores that they turned the world upside down; it is because they were the first to generalize and to bring to light a philosophic method with whose aid one could readily attack all ancient things and open the way to all new ones.

If someone were now to ask me why in our day this same method is followed more rigorously and applied more often by the French than by the Americans, among whom equality is nevertheless as complete and more ancient, I shall respond that it is partly due to two circumstances that it is necessary to make understood in the first place.

It is religion that gave birth to the Anglo-American societies: one must never forget this; in the United States religion is therefore intermingled with

*Martin Luther (1483–1546), German theologian and religious reformer who initiated the Protestant Reformation.

†Assumed name of François Marie Arouet (1694–1778), French writer and Enlightenment philosopher.

all national habits and all the sentiments to which a native country gives birth; that gives it a particular strength.

To this powerful reason add another no less so: in America religion itself has so to speak set its own limits; the religious order there has remained entirely distinct from the political order, in such a way that ancient laws could easily be changed without shaking ancient beliefs.

Christianity has therefore preserved a great empire over the American mind, and what I especially want to note is that it reigns not only as a philosophy that is adopted after examination, but as a religion that is believed without discussion.

In the United States, Christian sects vary infinitely and are constantly modified, but Christianity itself is an established and irresistible fact that no one undertakes either to attack or defend.

The Americans, having accepted the principal dogmas of the Christian religion without examination, are obliged to receive in the same manner a great number of moral truths that flow from them and depend on them. That restricts the action of individual analysis within narrow limits and spares from it several of the most important human opinions.

The other circumstance I spoke of is this:

The Americans have a democratic social state and constitution, but they did not have a democratic revolution. They arrived on the soil they occupy nearly as we see them. That is very important.

There are no revolutions that do not disrupt ancient beliefs, weaken authority, and obscure common ideas. Therefore every revolution has the effect, more or less, of delivering men over to themselves and of opening a wide and almost limitless space before the mind of each.

When conditions become equal following a prolonged conflict between the different classes forming the old society, envy, hatred and scorn of one's neighbor, haughtiness, and exaggerated self-confidence invade, so to speak, the human heart and make their home there for a time. This, independent of equality, contributes powerfully to dividing men, to making them distrust the judgment of one another and seek enlightenment in themselves alone.

Each then undertakes to be self-sufficient and finds his glory in making for himself beliefs that are his own about all things. Men are no longer bound except by interests, not by ideas; and one could say that human opinions form no more than a sort of intellectual dust that is blown around on all sides and cannot gather and settle.

Thus the independence of mind that equality supposes is never so great, and never appears so excessive, as at the moment when equality begins to be established and during the painful work of founding it. One ought therefore to distinguish carefully the kind of intellectual freedom that equality can provide from the anarchy that revolution brings. One must consider each of these two things separately so as not to conceive exaggerated hopes and fears for the future.

I believe that the men who will live in the new societies will often make use of their individual reason; but I am far from believing that they will often abuse it.

This is due to a cause more generally applicable to all democratic countries and which in the long term will restrain individual independence of thought within fixed and sometimes narrow limits.

I am going to speak of it in the chapter that follows.

౿ఴ ౿ఴ

Chapter 2 ON THE PRINCIPAL SOURCE OF BELIEFS AMONG DEMOCRATIC PEOPLES

Dogmatic beliefs are more or less numerous according to the times. They are born in different manners and can change form and object; but one cannot make it so that there are no dogmatic beliefs, that is, opinions men receive on trust without discussing them. If each undertook himself to form all his opinions and to pursue the truth in isolation down paths cleared by him alone, it is not probable that a great number of men would ever unite in any common belief.

Now it is easy to see that there is no society that can prosper without such beliefs, or rather there is none that could survive this way; for without common ideas there is no common action, and without common action men still exist, but a social body does not. Thus in order that there be society, and all the more, that this society prosper, it is necessary that all the minds of the citizens always be brought and held together by some principal ideas; and that cannot happen unless each of them sometimes comes to draw his opinions from one and the same source and unless each consents to receive a certain number of ready-made beliefs.

If I now consider man separately, I find that dogmatic beliefs are no less indispensable to him for living alone than for acting in common with those like him.

If man were forced to prove to himself all the truths he makes use of every day, he would never finish; he would exhaust himself in preliminary demonstrations without advancing; as he does not have the time because of the short span of life, nor the ability because of the limits of his mind, to act that way, he is reduced to accepting as given a host of facts and opinions that he has neither the leisure nor the power to examine and verify by himself, but that the more able have found or the crowd adopts. It is on this first foundation that he himself builds the edifice of his own thoughts. It is not his will that brings him to proceed in this manner; the inflexible law of his condition constrains him to do it.

There is no philosopher in the world so great that he does not believe a million things on faith in others or does not suppose many more truths than he establishes.

This is not only necessary, but desirable. A man who would undertake to examine everything by himself could accord but little time and attention to each thing; this work would keep his mind in a perpetual agitation that would prevent him from penetrating any truth deeply and from settling solidly on any certitude. His intellect would be at the same time independent and feeble. It is therefore necessary that he make a choice among the various objects of human opinions and that he adopt many beliefs without discussing them in order better to fathom a few he has reserved for examination.

It is true that every man who receives an opinion on the word of another puts his mind in slavery; but it is a salutary servitude that permits him to make good use of his freedom.

It is therefore always necessary, however it happens, that we encounter authority somewhere in the intellectual and moral world. Its place is variable, but it necessarily has a place. Individual independence can be more or less great; it cannot be boundless. Thus, the question is not that of knowing whether an intellectual authority exists in democratic centuries, but only where it is deposited and what its extent will be.

In the preceding chapter I showed how equality of conditions makes men conceive a sort of instinctive incredulity about the supernatural and a very high and often much exaggerated idea of human reason.

Men who live in times of equality are therefore only with difficulty led to place the intellectual authority to which they submit outside of and above humanity. It is in themselves or in those like themselves that they ordinarily seek the sources of truth. That would be enough to prove that a new religion cannot be established in these centuries, and that all attempts to cause one to be born would be not only impious, but ridiculous and unreasonable. One can foresee that democratic peoples will not readily believe in divine missions, that they will willingly laugh at new prophets, and that they will want to find the principal arbiter of their beliefs within the limits of humanity, not beyond it.

When conditions are unequal and men are not alike, there are some individuals who are very enlightened, very learned, and of very powerful intellect, and a multitude who are very ignorant and very limited. People who live in aristocratic times are therefore naturally brought to take the superior reason of one man or one class as a guide for their opinions, while they are little disposed to recognize the infallibility of the mass.

The opposite happens in centuries of equality.

As citizens become more equal and alike, the penchant of each to believe blindly a certain man or class diminishes. The disposition to believe the mass is augmented, and more and more it is opinion that leads the world.

Not only is common opinion the sole guide that remains for individual reason among democratic peoples; but it has an infinitely greater power among these peoples than among any other. In times of equality, because of their similarity, men have no faith in one another; but this same similarity gives them an almost unlimited trust in the judgment of the public; for it does not seem plausible to them that when all have the same enlightenment, truth is not found on the side of the greatest number.

When the man who lives in democratic countries compares himself individually to all those who surround him, he feels with pride that he is the equal of each of them; but when he comes to view the sum of those like him and places himself at the side of this great body, he is immediately overwhelmed by his own insignificance and his weakness.

The same equality that makes him independent of each of his fellow citizens in particular leaves him isolated and without defense against the action of the greatest number.

The public therefore has a singular power among democratic peoples, the very idea of which aristocratic nations could not conceive. It does not persuade [one] of its beliefs, it imposes them and makes them penetrate souls by a sort of immense pressure of the minds of all on the intellect of each.

In the United States, the majority takes charge of furnishing individuals with a host of ready-made opinions, and it thus relieves them of the obligation to form their own. There are a great number of theories on matters of philosophy, morality, or politics that everyone thus adopts without examination, on the faith of the public; and if one looks very closely, one will see that religion itself reigns there much less as revealed doctrine than as common opinion.

I know that among Americans political laws are such that the majority reigns sovereign over society, which greatly increases the empire it naturally exercises over the intellect. For nothing is more familiar to man than to recognize superior wisdom in whoever oppresses him.

This political omnipotence of the majority in the United States in effect augments the influence that the opinions of the public would otherwise obtain over the mind of each citizen; but it does not found it. It is in equality itself that one must seek the sources of that influence, and not in the more or less popular institutions that equal men can give themselves. It is to be believed that the intellectual empire of the greatest number would be less absolute in a democratic people subject to a king than in the heart of a pure democracy; but it will always be very absolute, and whatever political laws regulate men in centuries of equality, one can foresee that faith in common opinion will become a sort of religion whose prophet will be the majority.

Thus intellectual authority will be different, but it will not be less; and so far am I from believing that it will disappear that I augur that it might readily become too great, and that it could be that it might in the end confine the action of individual reason within narrower limits than befit the greatness and happiness of the human species. I see very clearly two tendencies in equality: one brings the mind of each man toward new thoughts, and the other would willingly induce it to give up thinking. And I perceive how, under the empire of certain laws, democracy would extinguish the intellectual freedom that the democratic social state favors, so that the human spirit, having broken all the shackles that classes or men formerly imposed on it, would be tightly chained to the general will of the greatest number.

If democratic peoples substituted the absolute power of a majority in place of all the diverse powers that hindered or retarded beyond measure the ascent of individual reason, the evil would have done nothing but change its character. Men would not have found the means of living independently; they would only have discovered—a difficult thing—a new face for servitude. That, I cannot repeat too often, is something to cause profound reflection by those who see in the freedom of the intellect something holy and who hate not only the despot but despotism. As for me, when I feel the hand of power weighing on my brow, it matters little to know who oppresses me, and I am no more disposed to put my head in the yoke because a million arms present it to me.

☙ ☙ ☙ ☙ ☙ ☙ ☙ ☙ ☙ ☙ ☙ ☙ ☙ ☙ ☙ ☙ ☙ ☙ ☙ ☙

Chapter 3 WHY THE AMERICANS SHOW MORE APTITUDE AND TASTE FOR GENERAL IDEAS THAN THEIR ENGLISH FATHERS

God does not ponder the human race in general. At a single glance he sees separately all of the beings of which humanity is composed, and he perceives each of them with the similarities that bring [each one] closer to all and the differences that isolate [each one] from [everyone else].

God therefore has no need of general ideas; that is to say, he never feels the necessity of enclosing a very great number of analogous objects under the same form so as to think about them more conveniently.

It is not so with man. If the human mind undertook to examine and judge individually all the particular cases that strike it, it would soon be lost in the midst of the immensity of detail and would no longer see anything; in this extremity it has recourse to an imperfect but necessary process that both aids it in its weakness and proves its weakness.

After having superficially considered a certain number of objects and remarking that they resemble each other, he gives them all the same name, puts them aside, and continues on his route.

General ideas do not attest to the strength of human intelligence, but rather to its insufficiency, because there are no beings in nature exactly alike: no identical facts, no rules indiscriminately applicable in the same manner to several objects at once.

General ideas are admirable in that they permit the human mind to bring rapid judgments to a great number of objects at one time; but on the other hand, they never provide it with anything but incomplete notions, and they always make it lose in exactness what they give it in extent.

As societies age, they acquire knowledge of new facts and each day take hold, almost without knowing it, of some particular truths.

As man grasps more truths of this species, he is naturally led to conceive a greater number of general ideas. One cannot see a multitude of particular facts separately without finally discovering the common bond that brings them together. Several individuals make the notion of species perceptible; several species lead necessarily to that of genus. The habit of and taste for general ideas will therefore always be the greater in a people as its enlightenment is more ancient and more manifold.

But there are still other reasons that push men to generalize their ideas or that move them away from doing so.

Americans make use much more often than do the English of general ideas and take more pleasure in them; that appears very singular at first, if one considers that these two peoples have the same origin, that they lived for centuries under the same laws, and that they still constantly pass their opinions and mores on to each other. The contrast appears much more striking when one focuses one's attention on our Europe and compares the two most enlightened peoples who inhabit it to one another.

One would say that for the English, the human mind is torn from the contemplation of particular facts only with regret and sorrow to ascend from there to causes and that it generalizes only despite itself.

It seems, on the contrary, that among us the taste for general ideas has become such a frenetic passion that one must satisfy it at every turn. Each morning on awakening I learn that someone has just discovered some general and eternal law that I had never heard spoken of until then. There is no writer so mediocre that it is enough for him to discover truths applicable to a great realm in his first attempt, and who does not remain discontented with himself if he has been unable to enclose the human race in the subject of his discourse.

Such a dissimilarity between two very enlightened peoples astonishes me. If finally I bring my mind back toward England and I remark what has taken place within it in the last half century, I believe I can affirm that the taste for general ideas is developing as the ancient constitution of the country weakens.

Therefore, the more or less advanced state of enlightenment alone is not enough to explain what suggests the love of general ideas to the human mind or averts it from them.

When conditions are very unequal and the inequalities are permanent, individuals little by little become so unalike that one would say there are as many distinct humanities as there are classes; one always discovers only one of them at a time, and losing sight of the general bond that brings all together in the vast bosom of the human race, one ever views only some men, not man.

Those who live in these aristocratic societies, therefore, never conceive very general ideas relative to themselves, and that is enough to give them an habitual distrust of these ideas and an instinctive distaste for them.

On the contrary, the man who inhabits democratic countries finds near to him only beings who are almost the same; he therefore cannot consider any part whatsoever of the human species without having his thought enlarge and dilate to embrace the sum. All the truths applicable to himself appear to him to apply equally and in the same manner to each of his fellow citizens and to those like him. Having contracted the habit of general ideas in the one study with which he most occupies himself and which most interests him, he carries this same habit over to all the others, and thus the need to discover common rules for all things, to enclose many objects within the same form, and to explain a collection of facts by a single cause becomes an ardent and often blind passion of the human mind.

Nothing shows better the truth of the preceding than the opinions of antiquity relative to slaves.

The most profound and vast geniuses of Rome and Greece were never able to arrive at the idea, so general but at the same time so simple, of the similarity of men and of the equal right to freedom that each bears from birth; and they did their utmost to prove that slavery was natural and that it would always exist. Even more, everything indicates that even those of the ancients who were slaves before becoming free, several of whom have left us beautiful writings,* themselves viewed servitude in the same light.

All the great writers of antiquity were a part of the aristocracy of masters, or at least they saw that aristocracy established without dispute before their eyes; their minds, after expanding in several directions, were therefore found limited in that one, and it was necessary that Jesus Christ come to earth to make it understood that all members of the human species are naturally alike and equal.

In centuries of equality all men are independent of one another, isolated and weak; one does not see anyone whose will directs the movements of the crowd in a permanent fashion; in these times, humanity always seems to run by itself. To explain what happens in the world, one is therefore reduced to searching for a few great causes which, acting in the same manner on each of those like us, thus bring all to follow the same route voluntarily. That also naturally leads the human mind to conceive general ideas and brings it to contract a taste for them.

Previously I showed how equality of conditions brought each to seek the truth by himself.† It is easy to see that such a method will imperceptibly make the human mind tend toward general ideas. When I repudiate the traditions of class, profession, and family, when I escape the empire of example to seek by the effort of my reason alone the path to follow, I am inclined to draw the

---

*In *DA* I 2.10, AT mentions Aesop and Terence; another famous example is the Greek Stoic philosopher Epictetus (55?–135?).

†*DA* II 1.1.

grounds of my opinions from the very nature of man, which necessarily leads me, almost without my knowing it, toward a great number of very general notions.

All that precedes serves to explain why the English show much less aptitude and taste for the generalization of ideas than their sons, the Americans, and above all their neighbors, the French, and why the English of our day show more of these than their fathers had done.

The English have long been a very enlightened people and at the same time very aristocratic; their enlightenment made them tend constantly toward very general ideas, and their aristocratic habits held them to very particular ideas. Hence the philosophy, at once audacious and timid, broad and narrow, that has dominated England until now and that still keeps so many minds confined and immobile.

Independent of the causes I have shown above, one encounters still others less apparent, but not less effective, that produce among almost all democratic peoples the taste and often the passion for general ideas.

One must carefully distinguish among these sorts of ideas. There are those that are products of a slow, detailed, conscientious work of intelligence; and they enlarge the sphere of human knowledge.

There are others that are readily born of a first rapid effort of the mind and lead only to very superficial and very uncertain notions.

Men who live in centuries of equality have much curiosity and little leisure; their life is so practical, so complicated, so agitated, so active that little time remains to them for thinking. Men of democratic centuries like general ideas because they exempt them from studying particular cases; they contain, if I can express myself so, many things in a small volume and give out a large product in a little time. When, therefore, after an inattentive and brief examination, they believe they perceive a common relation among certain objects, they do not push their research further, and without examining in detail how these various objects resemble each other or differ, they hasten to arrange them under the same formula in order to get past them.

One of the distinctive characteristics of democratic centuries is the taste all men experience for easy successes and present enjoyments. This is found in intellectual careers as well as all others. Most of those who live in times of equality are full of an ambition that is at once lively and soft; they want to obtain great success right away, but they would like to exempt themselves from great efforts. These contrary instincts lead them directly to the search for general ideas, with the aid of which they flatter themselves by painting very vast objects at small cost and attracting public attention without trouble.

And I do not know if they are wrong to think like that; for their readers are as afraid of going into depth as they themselves can be, and they ordinarily seek in the works of the mind only easy pleasures and instruction without work.

If aristocratic nations do not make enough use of general ideas and often show them an inconsiderate scorn, it happens, on the contrary, that democratic peoples are always ready to abuse these sorts of ideas and indiscreetly to become inflamed over them.

Chapter 4 WHY THE AMERICANS HAVE NEVER BEEN AS PASSIONATE AS THE FRENCH FOR GENERAL IDEAS IN POLITICAL MATTERS

I said previously that Americans show a less lively taste than the French for general ideas. That is above all true of general ideas relative to politics.

Although Americans have infinitely more general ideas enter into legislation than the English, and although they are much more concerned with adjusting the practice of human affairs to theory, political bodies in the United States have never been as enamored of general ideas as were our Constituent Assembly and Convention;* never has the whole American nation become passionate for these sorts of ideas in the same manner as the French people in the eighteenth century, nor has it displayed as blind a faith in the goodness and absolute truth of any theory.

This difference between the Americans and us arises from several causes, but from this one principally:

The Americans form a democratic people that has always directed public affairs by itself, and we are a democratic people who for a long time could only dream of a better manner of conducting them.

Our social state had already brought us to conceive very general ideas in matters of government while our political constitution still prevented us from rectifying these ideas through experience and from discovering their

---

*The Constituent Assembly ruled revolutionary France from 1789 to 1791, drew up a new constitution, and issued the Declaration of the Rights of Man and Citizen. The Convention came to power in 1792, made a new constitution and suspended it immediately, ruled by means of the "Terror" and revolutionary war, and came to an end in 1795.

insufficiency little by little, whereas with the Americans these two things were balanced constantly and corrected naturally.

It seems at first that this is much opposed to what I said previously, that democratic nations draw the love they show for theories from the very agitations of their practical life. A more attentive examination makes one discover that there is nothing contradictory here.

Men who live in democratic countries are very avid for general ideas because they have little leisure and these ideas free them from wasting their time in examining particular cases; that is true, but it must be understood to be so only in matters that are not habitual and necessary objects of their thoughts. Those in commerce will readily seize all the general ideas one presents to them relative to philosophy, politics, the sciences, and the arts without looking at them closely; but they will entertain those that have reference to commerce only after examination and will accept them only with reservation.

The same thing happens to men of state when it is a question of general ideas relative to politics.

Therefore, when there is a subject on which it is particularly dangerous for democratic peoples to indulge in general ideas blindly and beyond measure, the best corrective that one can employ is to have them occupy themselves with it every day in a practical manner; they will then be forced to enter into the details, and the details will make them perceive the weak sides of the theory.

The remedy is often painful, but its effect is sure.

Thus it is that democratic institutions, which force each citizen to occupy himself practically with government, moderate the excessive taste for general theories in political matters that equality puts forward.

ൟ ൟ

Chapter 5 HOW, IN THE UNITED STATES, RELIGION KNOWS HOW TO MAKE USE OF DEMOCRATIC INSTINCTS

I established in one of the preceding chapters* that men cannot do without dogmatic beliefs and that it was even very much to be wished that they have them. I add here that among all dogmatic beliefs the most desirable seem to me to be dogmatic beliefs in the matter of religion; that may be deduced very clearly even if one wants to pay attention only to the interests of this world.

There is almost no human action, however particular one supposes it, that does not arise from a very general idea that men have conceived of God, of his relations with the human race, of the nature of their souls, and of their duties toward those like them. One cannot keep these ideas from being the common source from which all the rest flow.

Men therefore have an immense interest in making very fixed ideas for themselves about God, their souls, their general duties toward their Creator and those like them; for doubt about these first points would deliver all their actions to chance and condemn them to a sort of disorder and impotence.

That, therefore, is the matter about which it is most important that each of us have fixed ideas; and unfortunately it is also the one in which it is most difficult for each person, left to himself, to come to fix his ideas solely by the effort of his reason.

Only minds very free of the ordinary preoccupations of life, very penetrating, very agile, very practiced, can, with the aid of much time and care, break through to these so necessary truths.

Still we see that these philosophers themselves are almost always surrounded by uncertainties; that at each step the natural light that enlightens them is obscured and threatens to be extinguished, and that despite all their efforts, they still have been able to discover only a few contradictory notions, in the midst of which the human mind has constantly floated for thousands of years without being able to seize the truth firmly or even to find new errors. Such studies are much above the average capacity of men, and even if most men should be capable of engaging in them, it is evident that they would not have the leisure for it.

Some fixed ideas about God and human nature are indispensable to the

---

*DA II 1.2.

daily practice of their lives, and that practice keeps them from being able to acquire them.

That appears to me to be unique. Among the sciences there are some that are useful to the crowd and are within its reach; others are accessible only to a few persons and are not cultivated by the majority, who need only their most remote applications; but the daily use of this [science] is indispensable to all, though its study is inaccessible to most.

General ideas relative to God and human nature are therefore, among all ideas, the ones it is most fitting to shield from the habitual action of individual reason and for which there is most to gain and least to lose in recognizing an authority.

The first object and one of the principal advantages of religions is to furnish a solution for each of these primordial questions that is clear, precise, intelligible to the crowd, and very lasting.

There are religions that are very false and very absurd; nevertheless one can say that every religion that remains within the circle I have just indicated and that does not claim to leave it, as several have attempted to do, in order to stop the free ascent of the human mind in all directions, imposes a salutary yoke on the intellect; and one must recognize that if it does not save men in the other world, it is at least very useful to their happiness and their greatness in this one.

That is above all true of men who live in free countries.

When religion is destroyed in a people, doubt takes hold of the highest portions of the intellect and half paralyzes all the others. Each becomes accustomed to having only confused and changing notions about matters that most interest those like him and himself; one defends one's opinions badly or abandons them, and as one despairs of being able to resolve by oneself the greatest problems that human destiny presents, one is reduced, like a coward, to not thinking about them at all.

Such a state cannot fail to enervate souls; it slackens the springs of the will and prepares citizens for servitude.

Not only does it then happen that they allow their freedom to be taken away, but often they give it over.

When authority in the matter of religion no longer exists, nor in the matter of politics, men are soon frightened at the aspect of this limitless independence. This perpetual agitation of all things makes them restive and fatigues them. As everything is moving in the world of the intellect, they want at least that all be firm and stable in the material order; and as they are no longer able to recapture their former beliefs, they give themselves a master.

As for me, I doubt that man can ever support a complete religious independence and an entire political freedom at once; and I am brought to think that if he has no faith, he must serve, and if he is free, he must believe.

I do not know, however, whether this great utility of religions is not still more visible among peoples where conditions are equal than among all others.

One must recognize that equality, which introduces great goods into the world, nevertheless suggests to men very dangerous instincts, as will be shown hereafter;* it tends to isolate them from one another and to bring each of them to be occupied with himself alone.

It opens their souls excessively to the love of material enjoyments.

The greatest advantage of religions is to inspire wholly contrary instincts. There is no religion that does not place man's desires beyond and above earthly goods and that does not naturally raise his soul toward regions much superior to those of the senses. Nor is there any that does not impose on each some duties toward the human species or in common with it, and that does not thus draw him, from time to time, away from contemplation of himself. This one meets even in the most false and dangerous religions.

Religious peoples are therefore naturally strong in precisely the spot where democratic peoples are weak; this makes very visible how important it is that men keep to their religion when becoming equal.

I have neither the right nor the will to examine the supernatural means God uses to make a religious belief reach the heart of man. For the moment I view religions only from a purely human point of view; I seek the manner in which they can most easily preserve their empire in the democratic centuries that we are entering.

I have brought out how, in times of enlightenment and equality, the human mind consents to receive dogmatic beliefs only with difficulty and feels the need of them keenly only in the case of religion. This indicates first that in those centuries more than in all others religions ought to keep themselves discreetly within the bounds that are proper to them and not seek to leave them; for in wishing to extend their power further than religious matters, they risk no longer being believed in any matter. They ought therefore to trace carefully the sphere within which they claim to fix the human mind, and beyond that to leave it entirely free to be abandoned to itself.

Mohammed had not only religious doctrines descend from Heaven and placed in the Koran, but political maxims, civil and criminal laws, and scientific theories. The Gospels, in contrast, speak only of the general relations of men to God and among themselves. Outside of that they teach nothing and

*See especially *DA* II 2.2.

oblige nothing to be believed. That alone, among a thousand other reasons, is enough to show that the first of these two religions cannot dominate for long in enlightened and democratic times, whereas the second is destined to reign in these centuries as in all the others.

If I continue this same inquiry further, I find that for religions to be able, humanly speaking, to maintain themselves in democratic centuries, they must not only confine themselves carefully to the sphere of religious matters; their power depends even more on the nature of the beliefs they profess, the external forms they adopt, and the obligations they impose.

What I said previously, that equality brings men to very general and vast ideas, ought to be understood principally in the matter of religion.* Men who are alike and equal readily conceive the notion of a single God imposing the same rules on each of them and granting them future happiness at the same price. The idea of the unity of the human race constantly leads them back to the idea of the unity of the Creator, whereas on the contrary, men very separate from one another and very unalike willingly come to make as many divinities as there are peoples, castes, classes and families, and to trace a thousand particular paths for going to Heaven.

One cannot deny that Christianity itself has in some fashion come under the influence exerted over religious beliefs by the social and political state.

At the moment when the Christian religion appeared on earth, Providence, which was undoubtedly preparing the world for its coming, had united a great part of the human species, like an immense flock, under the scepter of the Caesars. The men who composed that multitude differed much from one another, but they nevertheless had this common point: they all obeyed the same laws; and each of them was so weak and small in relation to the greatness of the prince that they all appeared equal when one came to compare them to him.

One must recognize that this new and particular state of humanity ought to have disposed men to receive the general truths taught by Christianity, and serves to explain the easy and rapid manner with which it then penetrated the human mind.

The corresponding proof came after the destruction of the Empire.

As the Roman world was then shattering, so to speak, into a thousand shards, each nation returned to its former individuality. Inside those nations, ranks were soon graduated to infinity; races were marked out, castes partitioned each nation into several peoples. In the midst of this common effort that seemed to bring human societies to subdivide themselves into as many

*DA II 1.3.

fragments as it was possible to conceive, Christianity did not lose sight of the principal general ideas it had brought to light. But it nonetheless appeared to lend itself, as much as it could, to the new tendencies arising from the fragmentation of the human species. Men continued to adore one God alone as creator and preserver of all things; but each people, each city, and so to speak each man, believed himself able to obtain some separate privilege and to create for himself particular protectors before the sovereign master. Unable to divide the Divinity, they at least multiplied it and magnified its agents beyond measure; the homage due to angels and saints became an almost idolatrous worship for most Christians, and one could fear a moment might come when the Christian religion would regress to the religions it had defeated.

It appears evident to me that the more the barriers that separate nations within humanity and citizens within the interior of each people tend to disappear, the more the human mind is directed, as if by itself, toward the idea of a single omnipotent being, dispensing the same laws to each man equally and in the same manner. It is therefore particularly in centuries of democracy that it is important not to allow the homage rendered to secondary agents to be confused with the worship that is due only the Creator.

Another truth appears very clear to me: that religions should be less burdened with external practices in democratic times than in all others.

I have brought out, concerning the philosophic method of the Americans, that nothing revolts the human mind more in times of equality than the idea of submitting to forms.* Men who live in these times suffer [representational] figures with impatience; symbols appear to them to be puerile artifices that are used to veil or adorn for their eyes truths it would be more natural to show to them altogether naked and in broad daylight; the sight of ceremonies leaves them cold, and they are naturally brought to attach only a secondary importance to the details of worship.

Those charged with regulating the external form of religions in democratic centuries ought indeed to pay attention to these natural instincts of human intelligence in order not to struggle unnecessarily against them.

I believe firmly in the necessity of forms; I know that they fix the human mind in the contemplation of abstract truths, and by aiding it to grasp them forcefully, they make it embrace them ardently. I do not imagine that it is possible to maintain a religion without external practices; but on the other hand, I think that in the centuries we are entering, it would be particularly dangerous to multiply them beyond measure; that one must rather restrict

*DA II 1.1.

them, and that one ought to retain only what is absolutely necessary for the perpetuation of the dogma itself, which is the substance of religions,[1] whereas worship is only the form. A religion that would become more minute, inflexible, and burdened with small observances at the same time that men were becoming more equal would soon see itself reduced to a flock of impassioned zealots in the midst of an incredulous multitude.

I know that one will not fail to object that since all religions have general and eternal truths for their object, they cannot so yield to the inconstant instincts of each century without losing the character of certainty in the eyes of men: I shall still respond here that one must distinguish very carefully the principal opinions that constitute a belief and that form what theologians call articles of faith, from the accessory notions that are linked to them. Religions are obliged always to hold firm in the first, whatever the particular spirit of the times may be; but they would do well to keep from binding themselves in the same manner to the second in centuries in which everything constantly changes place and in which the mind, habituated to the moving spectacle of human things, suffers itself to be held fixed only with regret. Immobility in external and secondary things appears to me to have a chance of lasting only when civil society itself is immobile; everywhere else, I am brought to believe that it is a peril.

We shall see* that among all the passions that equality gives birth to or favors, there is one that it renders particularly keen and that it sets in the hearts of all men at the same time: the love of well-being. The taste for well-being forms the salient and indelible feature of democratic ages.

One may believe that a religion that undertook to destroy this mother passion would in the end be destroyed by it; if it wanted to tear men entirely from contemplation of the goods of this world to deliver them solely to the thought of those of the other world, one can foresee that their souls would finally escape from its hands to go plunge themselves, far away from it, only in material and present enjoyments.

The principal business of religions is to purify, regulate, and restrain the too ardent and too exclusive taste for well-being that men in times of equality feel; but I believe that they would be wrong to try to subdue it entirely and to destroy it. They will not succeed in turning men away from love of wealth; but they can still persuade them to enrich themselves only by honest means.

This leads me to a final consideration that in some fashion comprises all the others. As men become more alike and equal, it is more important that

---

*DA II 2.10.

1. In all religions there are ceremonies that are inherent in the very substance of belief and in which one must indeed guard against changing anything. That is seen particularly in Catholicism, in which the form and the foundation are often so tightly united that they are one.

religions, while carefully putting themselves out of the way of the daily movement of affairs, not collide unnecessarily with the generally accepted ideas and permanent interests that reign among the mass; for common opinion appears more and more as the first and most irresistible of powers; there is no support outside of it strong enough to permit long resistance to its blows. That is no less true in a democratic people subject to a despot than in a republic. In centuries of equality, kings often make one obey, but it is always the majority that makes one believe; it is therefore the majority that one must please in all that is not contrary to the faith.

I showed in my first work how American priests keep their distance from public affairs.* This is the most striking, but not the only, example of their restraint. In America religion is a world apart, where the priest reigns, but which he is careful never to leave; within its limits he guides intelligence; outside of it, he leaves men to themselves and abandons them to the independence and instability that are proper to their nature and to the times. I have not seen a country where Christianity wraps itself less in forms, practices, and [representational] figures than the United States, and presents ideas more clearly, simply, and generally to the human mind. Although Christians of America are divided into a multitude of sects, they all perceive their religion in the same light. This applies to Catholicism as well as to other beliefs. There are no Catholic priests who show less taste for small, individual observances, for extraordinary and particular methods of gaining salvation, or who cling more to the spirit of the law and less to its letter, than the Catholic priests of the United States; nowhere does one teach more clearly or follow better the doctrine of the Church that forbids rendering to saints the worship that is reserved only for God. Nevertheless, Catholics of America are very submissive and very sincere.

Another remark is applicable to the clergy of all communions: American priests do not try to attract and fix all the attentions of man on the future life; they willingly abandon a part of his heart to present cares; they seem to consider the goods of the world as important although secondary objects; if they do not associate themselves with industry, they are at least interested in its progress and applaud it, and while constantly showing to the faithful the other world as the great object of their hopes and fears, they do not forbid them from honestly searching for well-being in this one. Far from bringing out how these two things are divided and contrary, they rather apply themselves to finding the spot at which they touch and are bound to each other.

All American priests know the intellectual empire the majority exercises and respect it. They never support any but necessary struggles against it.

* *DA* I 2.9.

They do not mix in the quarrels of the parties, but they willingly adopt the general opinions of their country and time, and they let themselves go without resistance in the current of sentiments and ideas that carries away all things around them. They strive to correct their contemporaries, but they do not separate themselves from them. Public opinion is never, therefore, their enemy; rather it supports and protects them, and their beliefs reign both by the forces that are proper to them and by those of the majority that they borrow.

Thus it is in respecting all the democratic instincts that are not contrary to it and in taking aid from several of them that religion succeeds in struggling to its advantage against the spirit of individual independence that is the most dangerous of all to it.

᪥ ᪥

Chapter 6 ON THE PROGRESS OF CATHOLICISM IN THE UNITED STATES

America is the most democratic land on earth, and it is at the same time the country where, according to trustworthy reports, the Catholic religion is making most progress. At first sight that is surprising.

One must distinguish two things well: equality disposes men to want to judge for themselves; but on the other hand, it gives them the taste for and idea of a single social power that is simple and the same for all. Men living in democratic centuries are therefore strongly inclined to eschew all religious authority. But if they do consent to submit to an authority like this, they at least want it to be one and uniform; religious powers that do not all end at one and the same center naturally shock their intelligence, and they are almost as ready to conceive that there is no religion as that there are several.

In our day more than in earlier periods, one sees Catholics who become nonbelievers and Protestants who make themselves Catholics. If one considers Catholicism internally it seems to lose; if one looks outside it, it is gaining. That may be explained.

Men of our day are naturally little disposed to believe; but when they have a religion they immediately encounter a hidden instinct in themselves that pushes them without their knowing it toward Catholicism. Several of the doctrines and usages of the Roman Church astonish them; but they feel a secret admiration for its government, and its great unity attracts them.

If Catholicism finally succeeded in escaping from the political hatreds to which it gave birth, I hardly doubt that this same spirit of the century that seems so contrary to it would become very favorable to it, and that all at once it would make great conquests.

It is one of the most familiar weaknesses of the human intellect to want to reconcile contrary principles and to buy peace at the expense of logic. Therefore there always have been and always will be men who, after having submitted some of their religious beliefs to an authority, want to spare several others and let their minds float at random between obedience and freedom. But I am brought to believe that the number of these will be smaller in democratic than in other centuries and that our descendants will tend more and more to be divided into only two parts, those leaving Christianity entirely and others entering into the bosom of the Roman Church.

ꗦ ꗦ

Chapter 7 WHAT MAKES THE MIND OF DEMOCRATIC PEOPLES LEAN TOWARD PANTHEISM

Later I shall show how the predominant taste of democratic peoples for very general ideas is found in politics as well;* but right now I want to indicate its principal effect on philosophy.

It cannot be denied that pantheism has made great progress in our day. The writings of a portion of Europe visibly bear its imprint. The Germans introduce it into philosophy, the French into literature.† Among the works of the imagination published in France, most either contain some opinions or depictions borrowed from pantheistic doctrines or allow one to perceive a sort of tendency toward these doctrines in their authors. This does not appear to me to come only by accident, but to be due to a lasting cause.

DA II 1.20.

†Pantheism is most commonly associated with the teachings of the Dutch philosopher Benedict Spinoza (1632–1677). Among German philosophers, the teachings of Gottfried Wilhelm von Leibnitz (1646–1716), Johann Gottlieb Fichte (1762–1814), and Georg Wilhelm Friedrich Hegel (1770–1831) contain pantheistic elements, and a philosophic school contemporary with AT known as the "Young Hegelians" goes further in this direction; the French writers Alphonse de Lamartine (1790–1869) and Edgar Quinet (1803–1869) helped to introduce pantheism into literature.

As conditions become more equal and each man in particular becomes more like all the others, weaker and smaller, one gets used to no longer viewing citizens so as to consider only the people; one forgets individuals so as to think only of the species.

In these times the human mind loves to embrace a host of diverse objects at once; it constantly aspires to be able to link a multitude of consequences to a single cause.

The idea of unity obsesses [the mind]; it seeks it on all sides, and when it believes it has found it, it willingly wraps it in its bosom and rests with it. Not only does it come to discover only one creation and one Creator in the world; this first division of things still bothers it, and it willingly seeks to enlarge and simplify its thought by enclosing God and the universe within a single whole. If I encounter a philosophic system according to which the things material and immaterial, visible and invisible that the world includes are considered as no more than diverse parts of an immense being which alone remains eternal in the midst of the continual change and incessant transformation of all that composes it, I shall have no trouble concluding that such a system, although it destroys human individuality, or rather because it destroys it, will have secret charms for men who live in democracy; all their intellectual habits prepare them to conceive it and set them on the way to adopting it. It naturally attracts their imagination and fixes it; it nourishes the haughtiness and flatters the laziness of their minds.

Among the different systems with whose aid philosophy seeks to explain the universe, pantheism appears to me one of the most appropriate to seduce the human mind in democratic centuries; all who remain enamored of the genuine greatness of man should unite and do combat against it.

Chapter 8 HOW EQUALITY SUGGESTS TO THE AMERICANS THE IDEA OF THE INDEFINITE PERFECTIBILITY OF MAN

Equality suggests several ideas to the human mind that would not otherwise have come to it, and it modifies almost all those already there. I take as an example the idea of human perfectibility because it is one of the principal ones that intelligence can conceive and because it alone constitutes in itself a great philosophic theory whose consequences are displayed at each instant in the practice of affairs.

Although man resembles the animals in several points, one feature is peculiar to him alone: he perfects himself and they do not perfect themselves. The human species could not fail to discover this difference from the outset. The idea of perfectibility is therefore as old as the world; equality did not give birth to it, but it gives it a new character.

When citizens are classed according to rank, profession or birth, and all are constrained to follow the track at the entrance to which chance has placed them, each believes that he perceives the furthest boundaries of human power near himself, and none seeks any longer to struggle against an inevitable destiny. It is not that aristocratic peoples absolutely deny man the faculty of self-perfection. They do not judge it to be indefinite; they conceive of improvement, not change; they imagine the condition of coming societies as better, but not different; and all the while admitting that humanity has made great progress and that it can make still more, they confine it in advance within certain impassable limits.

They therefore do not believe they have arrived at the sovereign good and the absolute truth (what man or what people has ever been senseless enough to imagine it?), but they like to persuade themselves that they have attained nearly the degree of greatness and knowledge that our imperfect nature permits; and as nothing around them is moving, they willingly fancy that everything is in its place. It is then that the legislator claims to promulgate eternal laws, that peoples and kings want to raise only monuments [lasting] for centuries, and that the present generation takes on the charge of sparing future generations the care of regulating their destinies.

As castes disappear, as classes get closer to each other, as men are mixed tumultuously, and their usages, customs, and laws vary, as new facts come up, as new truths are brought to light, as old opinions disappear and others take their place, the image of an ideal and always fugitive perfection is presented to the human mind.

Continual changes then pass at each instant before the eyes of each man. Some worsen his position, and he understands only too well that a people or an individual, however enlightened [it or] he may be, is not infallible. Others improve his lot, and he concludes from this that man in general is endowed with the indefinite faculty of perfecting himself. His reverses make him see that no one can flatter himself with having discovered the absolute good; his successes inflame him to pursue it without respite. Thus, always seeking, falling, righting himself, often disappointed, never discouraged, he tends ceaselessly toward the immense greatness that he glimpses confusedly at the end of the long course that humanity must still traverse.

One cannot believe how many facts naturally flow from this philosophic theory according to which man is indefinitely perfectible, and what a prodigious influence it exerts even on those who, always being occupied only with acting and not thinking, seem to conform their actions to it without knowing it.

I meet an American sailor and I ask him why his country's vessels are built to last a short time, and he replies to me without hesitation that the art of navigation makes such rapid progress daily that the most beautiful ship would soon become almost useless if its existence were prolonged beyond a few years.

In these words pronounced at random by a coarse man concerning a particular fact I perceive the general and systematic idea according to which a great people conducts all things.

Aristocratic nations are naturally brought to contract the limits of human perfectibility too much, and democratic nations sometimes extend them beyond measure.

Chapter 9 HOW THE EXAMPLE OF THE AMERICANS DOES NOT PROVE THAT A DEMOCRATIC PEOPLE CAN HAVE NO APTITUDE AND TASTE FOR THE SCIENCES, LITERATURE, AND THE ARTS

One must recognize that among the civilized peoples of our day there are few in whom the advanced sciences have made less progress than in the United States, and who have furnished fewer great artists, illustrious poets, and celebrated writers.

Several Europeans, struck by this spectacle, have considered it a natural and inevitable result of equality, and they have thought that if a democratic social state and institutions once came to prevail over all the earth, the human mind would see the lights that enlighten it gradually dimmed, and men would fall back into darkness.

Those who reason thus, I think, confuse several ideas that it would be important to divide and examine separately. Without wishing to, they mix what is democratic with what is only American.

The religion that the first emigrants professed and which they bequeathed to their descendants, simple in its worship, austere and almost savage in its principles, hostile to external signs and to the pomp of ceremonies, is naturally little favorable to the fine arts and permits literary pleasures only with regret.

The Americans are a very old and very enlightened people who encountered a new and immense country in which they can spread out at will and which they make fruitful without trouble. That is without example in the world. In America, therefore, each finds easy ways, unknown elsewhere, to make his fortune or to increase it. Cupidity is always breathless there, and the human mind, distracted at every moment from pleasures of the imagination and works of the intellect, gets carried away only in the pursuit of wealth. Not only does one see industrial and commercial classes in the United States, as in all other countries; but what has never been encountered—all men simultaneously occupied with industry and commerce.

I am nevertheless convinced that if the Americans had been alone in the universe, with the freedoms and enlightenment acquired by their fathers and the passions that were their own, they would not have been slow to discover that one cannot make progress in the practice of the sciences for long without cultivating the theory; that all the arts are perfected by one another, and however absorbed they might have been in the pursuit of the principal object of their desires, they would soon have recognized that one must turn aside from it from time to time, the better to attain it.

Besides, the taste for pleasures of the mind is so natural to the heart of civilized man that in the polite nations that are the least disposed to indulge it, a certain number of citizens who conceive it are always to be found. This intellectual need, once felt, would soon have been satisfied.

But at the same time that Americans were naturally brought to demand of science only its particular applications to the arts and the means of rendering life easy, learned and literary Europe was taking charge of going back to the general sources of truth, and at the same time it was perfecting all that can contribute to the pleasures as well as all that will serve the needs of man.

At the head of the enlightened nations of the Old World the inhabitants of the United States distinguished one in particular to which a common origin and similar habits united them closely. Among this people they found celebrated scholars, skillful artists, and great writers; and they could collect the treasures of the intellect without having need to work to amass them.

I cannot consent to separate America from Europe, despite the ocean that divides them. I consider the people of the United States as the portion of the English people charged with exploiting the forests of the New World while the rest of the nation, provided with more leisure and less preoccupied with the material cares of life, can be engaged in thought and develop the human mind in all directions.

The situation of the Americans is therefore entirely exceptional, and it is to be believed that no [other] democratic people will ever be placed in it. Their wholly Puritan origin; their uniquely commercial habits; the very country they inhabit, which seems to turn their intelligence away from the study of the sciences, letters, and arts; the proximity of Europe, which permits them not to study these without falling back into barbarism; a thousand particular causes, of which I could make only the principal ones known, must have concentrated the American mind in a singular manner on caring for purely material things. Their passions, needs, education, circumstances—all in fact seem to cooperate in making the inhabitant of the United States incline toward the earth. Religion alone, from time to time, makes him raise passing, distracted glances toward Heaven.

Let us therefore cease to see all democratic nations in the shape of the American people and try finally to view them with their own features.

One can conceive of a people within which there would be neither castes, nor hierarchy, nor classes; where the law, recognizing no privileges, would apportion inheritances equally, and which would at the same time be deprived of enlightenment and freedom. This is not a vain hypothesis: a despot might find that his interest lies in making his subjects equal and leaving them ignorant in order to keep them more easily as slaves.

Not only will a democratic people of this species not show an aptitude or taste for the sciences, literature, and the arts, but it is to be believed that it will never come to show any.

Estate law itself would take charge of destroying fortunes in each generation, and no one would create new ones. The poor man, deprived of enlightenment and freedom, would not even conceive the idea of raising himself toward wealth, and the wealthy man would let himself be carried along toward poverty without knowing how to defend himself. A complete and invincible equality between these two citizens would soon be established. No one would then have either the time or the taste to engage in the works and pleasures of the intellect. But all would dwell numbly in the same ignorance and in an equal servitude.

When I come to imagine a democratic society of this kind, I immediately believe I feel myself in one of those low, dark, stifling places where enlightenment, brought from outside, soon fades and is extinguished. It seems to me that a sudden weight is crushing me, and I drag myself in the midst of the darkness that surrounds me to find the way out that would to bring me back to the air and broad daylight. But all this cannot be applied to men already enlightened who remain free after having destroyed the particular and hereditary rights among them that settled goods in the hands of certain individuals or certain bodies in perpetuity.

When men who live in the heart of a democratic society are enlightened, they discover without difficulty that nothing limits or fixes them and forces them to content themselves with their present fortune.

They therefore all conceive the idea of increasing it, and if they are free, they all try to do it, but all do not succeed at it in the same manner. The legislature, it is true, no longer grants privileges, but nature gives them. Natural inequality being very great, fortunes become unequal from the moment that each makes use of all his faculties to enrich himself.

Estate law is still opposed to what wealthy families are founded on, but it no longer prevents there being [persons] who are wealthy. It constantly brings citizens back toward a common level from which they constantly escape; they become more unequal in goods in proportion as their enlightenment is more extensive and their freedom greater.

In our day a sect arose,* celebrated for its genius and its extravagances, that intended to concentrate all goods in the hands of a central power and then to charge it with distributing them to all particular persons according to merit. In this manner they would have avoided the complete and eternal equality that seems to threaten democratic societies.

There is another simpler and less dangerous remedy, which is to grant privilege to no one, to give equal enlightenment and an equal independence to all, and to leave to each the care of marking out his own place. Natural inequality will soon see the light of day, and wealth will proceed by itself in the direction of the most skillful.

Democratic and free societies will therefore always contain within themselves a multitude of people who are opulent or well-to-do. These wealthy will not be bound as closely among themselves as the members of the former aristocratic class; they will have different instincts and will almost never possess a leisure as secure and as complete; but they will be infinitely more numerous than those who composed that class could be. These men will not be closely confined to the preoccupations of material life and they will be able, although in different degrees, to engage in the works and pleasures of the intellect: they therefore will engage in them; for if it is true that the human mind leans at one extreme toward the bounded, material, and useful, at the other it naturally rises toward the infinite, immaterial, and beautiful. Physical needs tie it to the earth, but as soon as it is no longer restrained, it rights itself.

---

*A reference to the school of Henri de Saint-Simon (1760–1825), with which AT was acquainted through his cousin and friend Louis de Kergorlay, who had connections to members of the sect.

Not only will the number of those who can be interested in the works of the mind be greater, but the taste for intellectual pleasures will descend by degrees even to those who in aristocratic societies do not seem to have either the time or the capacity to engage in them.

When there are no longer inherited wealth, class privileges, and prerogatives of birth, and each draws his force only from himself, it becomes visible that what makes the principal difference among the fortunes of men is intelligence. All that serves to fortify, enlarge, and adorn intelligence immediately brings a high price.

The utility of knowledge is revealed with a very particular clarity even to the eyes of the crowd. Those who do not taste its charms prize its effects and make efforts to attain it.

In democratic, enlightened, and free centuries, men have nothing separating them or keeping them in their place; they rise or fall with singular rapidity. All classes see each other constantly because they are very close. They communicate and mix with each other every day, they imitate and envy each other; that suggests a host of ideas, notions, and desires to people that they would not have had if ranks had been fixed and society immobile. In these nations the servant never considers himself entirely a stranger to the pleasures and works of the master, nor the poor man to those of the rich; the man in the fields strives to resemble someone in the towns, and the provinces, the metropolis.

Thus no one easily lets himself be reduced to the mere material cares of life, and the most humble artisan casts some eager and furtive glances at the superior world of the intellect from time to time. They do not read in the same spirit and manner as in aristocratic peoples; but the circle of readers is constantly extended and in the end contains all citizens.

From the moment when the crowd begins to be interested in works of the mind, it is discovered that a great means of acquiring glory, power, or wealth is to excel in some of them. The restive ambition equality gives birth to is immediately turned in this direction as in all others. The number of those who cultivate the sciences, letters, and arts becomes immense. A prodigious activity is awakened in the world of the intellect; each one seeks to open a path to it and strives to bring the public eye in his wake. Something analogous to what happens in the United States in political society takes place; works are often imperfect, but they are innumerable; and although the results of individual efforts are ordinarily very small, the general result is always very great.

It is therefore not true to say that men who live in democratic centuries are naturally indifferent to the sciences, letters, and arts; one must only recognize that they cultivate them in their own manner, and that they bring in this way the qualities and faults that are their own.

æ æ

Chapter 10 WHY THE AMERICANS APPLY THEMSELVES TO THE PRACTICE OF THE SCIENCES RATHER THAN TO THE THEORY

If the democratic social state and institutions do not stop the ascent of the human mind, it is at least incontestable that they steer it in one direction rather than another. Their efforts, thus limited, are still very great, and I hope I will be pardoned if I stop for a moment to contemplate them.

When we treated the philosophic method of the Americans* we made several remarks of which we must take advantage here.

Equality develops the desire in each man to judge everything by himself; it gives him in all things a taste for the tangible and real and a contempt for traditions and forms. These general instincts are displayed principally in the particular object of this chapter.

Those who cultivate the sciences in democratic peoples always fear losing themselves in utopias. They distrust systems, they like to hold themselves very close to the facts and to study them by themselves; as they do not allow themselves to be easily filled with respect for the name of anyone like themselves, they are never disposed to swear by the word of the master; on the contrary, one sees them occupied constantly with seeking the weak side of his doctrine. Scientific traditions hold little dominion over them; they never stop for long at the subtleties of a school and they are not easily fobbed off with big words; they penetrate as much as they can to the principal parts of the subject that occupies them, and they like to expose them in vulgar language. The sciences therefore have a freer and surer but less lofty style.

The mind, it seems to me, can divide science in three parts.

The first contains the most theoretical principles, the most abstract notions, those whose application is not known or is very distant.

The second is composed of general truths which, still depending on pure theory, nevertheless lead by a direct, short path to practice.

DA II 1.1.

The processes of application and the means of execution fill out the third.

Each of these different portions of science can be cultivated apart, even though reason and experience make it known that none of them can prosper for long when it is absolutely separated from the other two.

In America the purely practical part of the sciences is cultivated admirably, and people attend carefully to the theoretical portion immediately necessary to application; in this way the Americans display a mind that is always clear, free, original, and fertile; but there is almost no one in the United States who gives himself over to the essentially theoretical and abstract portion of human knowledge. In this the Americans show the excess of a tendency which I think will again be found in all democratic peoples, though to a lesser degree.

Nothing is more necessary to the cultivation of the advanced sciences or of the elevated portion of sciences than meditation, and there is nothing less fit for meditation than the interior of a democratic society. One does not encounter there, as in aristocratic peoples, a numerous class that stays at rest because it finds itself well-off and another that does not move because it despairs of being better off. Everyone is agitated: some want to attain power, others to take possession of wealth. In the midst of this universal tumult, the repeated collision of contrary interests, the continual advance of men toward fortune, where does one find the calm necessary to the profound combinations of the intellect? how does each man bring his thought to a stop at such and such a point, when everything moves around him and he himself is carried along and tossed about every day in the impetuous current that swirls all things along?

One must discriminate well between the kind of permanent agitation that reigns in the heart of a tranquil, already constituted democracy and the tumultuous, revolutionary movements that almost always accompany the birth and development of a democratic society.

When a violent revolution takes place among a very civilized people, it cannot fail to give a sudden thrust to sentiments and ideas.

This is above all true of democratic revolutions, which, while stirring up at once all the classes of which a people is composed, give birth at the same time to immense ambitions in the heart of each citizen.

If the French suddenly made such admirable progress in the exact sciences at the very moment when they were succeeding in destroying the remains of the old feudal society, one must attribute this sudden fruitfulness not to democracy, but to the unexampled revolution that accompanied its developments. What came about then was a particular case; it would be imprudent to see in it the indication of a general law.

Great revolutions are no more common in democratic peoples than in other peoples; I am even brought to believe that they are less so. But a slight, bothersome movement reigns within these nations, a sort of incessant rotation of men over one another that troubles and distracts the mind without animating or elevating it.

Not only do men living in democratic societies give themselves over to meditation with difficulty, but they naturally have little esteem for it. The democratic social state and institutions bring most men to act continually; yet the habits of mind suited to action are not always suited to thought. The man who acts is often reduced to contenting himself with what is nearly so because he would never arrive at the end of his design if he wished to perfect every detail. He must constantly rely on ideas that he has not had the leisure to fathom, for it is much more the timeliness of the idea he makes use of than its rigorous exactness that helps him; and all in all, there is less risk for him in making use of some false principles than in wasting his time in establishing the truth of all his principles. It is not by long and learned demonstrations that the world is led. There, the quick look at a particular fact, the daily study of the changing passions of the crowd, the chance of the moment and the skill to seize it decide all affairs.

In centuries in which almost everyone acts, one is therefore generally brought to attach an excessive value to rapid sparks and superficial conceptions of the intellect and, on the contrary, to depreciate immoderately its profound, slow work.

This public opinion influences the judgment of men who cultivate the sciences; it persuades them that they can succeed at them without meditation or it diverts them from those sciences that require it.

There are several manners of studying the sciences. In a crowd of men one encounters a selfish, mercenary, industrial taste for the discoveries of the mind which must not be confused with the disinterested passion that lights up in the hearts of a few; there is a desire to utilize knowledge and a pure desire to know. I do not doubt that an ardent and inexhaustible love of truth that nourishes itself and enjoys itself incessantly without being able to satisfy itself arises now and then in some men. It is that ardent, haughty, and disinterested love of the true that guides men to the abstract sources of truth from which to draw out mother ideas.

If Pascal* had envisaged only some great profit, or even if he had been moved by the desire for glory alone, I cannot believe that he would ever have been able to assemble, as he did, all the powers of his intellect in order better to discover the most hidden secrets of the Creator. When I see him tear his

---

*Blaise Pascal (1623–1662), French philosopher, mathematician, and physicist, and author of the *Pensées* and *Provincial Letters*.

soul in a way from the midst of the cares of life to tie it wholly to that search, prematurely breaking the bonds that hold it to the body, so as to die of old age before forty, I halt in bewilderment and understand that it is no ordinary cause that can produce such extraordinary efforts.

The future will prove whether those passions, so rare and fruitful, are born and developed as easily in the midst of democratic societies as within aristocracies. As for me, I avow that I have trouble believing it.

In aristocratic societies the class that directs opinion and leads affairs, placed in a permanent and hereditary manner above the crowd, naturally conceives a high-minded idea of itself and of man. It willingly imagines glorious enjoyments for him and fixes magnificent goals for his desires. Aristocracies often do very tyrannical and very inhuman deeds, but they rarely conceive base thoughts, and they show a certain haughty disdain for little pleasures, even when they indulge in them; this lifts all souls to a very high tone. In aristocratic times one generally makes for oneself very vast ideas of the dignity, power, and greatness of man. These opinions influence those who cultivate the sciences as well as all others; they facilitate the natural spark of the mind toward the highest regions of thought and naturally dispose it to conceive a sublime and almost divine love of truth.

The learned of those times are therefore carried along toward theory, and it often even happens that they conceive an inconsiderate scorn for practice. "Archimedes," says Plutarch, "had a heart so lofty that he never deigned to leave any work in writing on the manner of erecting all the machines of war; and holding the whole science of inventing and composing machines and generally every art that ascribes some utility to putting it in practice to be vile, low, and mercenary, he applied his mind and his study to writing only things whose beauty and subtlety were not at all mixed with necessity."* That is the aristocratic aim of the sciences.

It cannot be the same in democratic nations.

Most men who compose these nations are very eager for present material enjoyments; as they are always discontented with the position they occupy and always free to leave it, they dream only of the means of changing their fortune or of increasing it. For minds so disposed, every new method that leads to wealth by a shorter path, every machine that shortens work, every instrument that diminishes the costs of production, every discovery that facilitates pleasures and augments them seems to be the most magnificent effort of human intelligence. It is principally in this way that democratic

---

*Cf. "Life of Marcellus," in Plutarch's *Lives of the Noble Grecians and Romans* (New York: Modern Library, n.d.), p. 378. Archimedes (ca. 287–212 B.C.) was a Greek mathematician and inventor, and author of important works on geometry, arithmetic, and mechanics.

peoples apply themselves to the sciences, understand them, and honor them. In aristocratic centuries, enjoyments of the mind are particularly demanded of the sciences; in democratic, those of the body.

Reckon that the more a nation is democratic, enlightened, and free, the more the number of these interested appreciators of scientific genius is going to be increasing and the more the discoveries immediately applicable to industry will bestow profit, glory, and even power on their authors; for in democracies, the working class takes part in public affairs, and those who serve it have to expect honors as well as money from it.

One can easily conceive that in a society organized in this manner, the human mind is insensibly guided to neglect theory and that it must, on the contrary, feel impelled with unparalleled energy toward application or, at the very least, toward the portion of theory that is necessary to those who apply it.

In vain does an instinctive penchant elevate [the mind] toward the highest spheres of the intellect; interest leads it back toward the middle ones. There it deploys its force and restive activity, and begets marvels. The same Americans who have not discovered a single general law of mechanics have introduced a new machine into navigation that is changing the face of the world.*

Certainly I am far from claiming that democratic peoples of our day are destined to see the transcendent lights of the human mind extinguished, or even that new ones may not be illuminated within them. In our age of the world, and among so many literate nations that the ardor of industry incessantly stirs, the bonds that unite the different parts of science among themselves cannot fail to strike their regard; and the very taste for practice, if it is enlightened, will bring men not to neglect theory. In the midst of so many attempts at application, of so many experiences repeated daily, it is almost impossible that very general laws should not often make their appearance, so that great discoveries would be frequent even though great inventors would be rare.

Moreover, I believe in advanced scientific vocations. If democracy does not bring men to cultivate the sciences for [the sciences'] sake, on the other hand it increases immensely the number of those who cultivate them. It is not to be believed that among such a great multitude some speculative genius whom the singular love of truth inflames will not be born from time to time. One can be assured that he will strive to penetrate the most profound mysteries of nature, whatever the spirit of his country and his times should be. There is no need to aid his ascent; it is enough not to stop it. All that I

---

*The first steamboat was launched by the American John Fitch in 1786. In 1807 American inventor Robert Fulton built his first successful paddle-wheel boat, and boats of this type were soon used extensively in the United States and Great Britain.

want to say is this: permanent inequality of conditions brings men to confine themselves to the haughty, sterile search for abstract truths, whereas the democratic social state and institutions disposes them to demand of the sciences only their immediate, useful applications.

This tendency is natural and inevitable. It is interesting to know and perhaps necessary to point out.

If those who are called upon to direct the nations of our day perceived clearly and from afar the new instincts that will soon be irresistible, they would understand that with enlightenment and freedom, men who live in democratic centuries cannot fail to perfect the industrial portion of the sciences, and that from now on all the effort of the social power must be brought to sustain advanced studies and to create great scientific passions.

In our day one must detain the human mind in theory; it runs of itself to practice, and instead of constantly leading it back toward the detailed examination of secondary effects, it is good to distract it from them sometimes in order to raise it to the contemplation of first causes.

Because Roman civilization died following the barbarian invasions, we are perhaps too much inclined to believe that civilization cannot die in any other way.

If the lights that enlighten us ever came to be extinguished, they would be obscured little by little and as if by themselves. By dint of being confined to application, one would lose sight of the principles, and when one had entirely forgotten the principles one would follow the methods derived from them badly; one would no longer be able to invent new ones, and one would employ without intelligence and without art the erudite procedures that one would no longer understand.

When the Europeans landed in China three hundred years ago, they found that almost all the arts there had reached a certain degree of perfection, and they were astonished that having arrived at that point, they had not gone further. Later they discovered the vestiges of some advanced knowledge that had been lost. The nation was industrial; most of the scientific methods had been preserved within it; but science itself no longer existed. That explained to them the singular kind of immobility in which they had found the minds of this people. The Chinese, in following the trail of their fathers, had forgotten the reasons that had directed them. They still made use of the formula without seeking the sense of it; they kept the instrument and no longer possessed the art of modifying and reproducing it. Therefore the Chinese could not change anything. They had to renounce improvement. They were forced to imitate their fathers always and in everything, so as not to be cast into impenetrable darkness if they strayed for an instant from the path these latter had traced. The source of human knowledge had almost dried up; and although the river still flowed, it could no longer swell its waters or change its course.

Nevertheless, China subsisted peacefully for centuries; its conquerors had adopted its mores; order reigned there. A sort of material well-being let itself be perceived on all sides. Revolutions were very rare, and war was so to speak unknown.

One must therefore not reassure oneself by thinking that the barbarians are still far from us; for if there are peoples who allow the light to be torn from their hands, there are others who stifle it themselves under their feet.

Chapter 11 IN WHAT SPIRIT THE AMERICANS CULTIVATE THE ARTS

I would believe I was wasting readers' time and my own if I applied myself to showing how the general mediocrity of fortunes, the absence of superfluity, the universal desire for well-being, and the constant efforts in which each engages to procure it for himself, make the taste for the useful predominate over the love of the beautiful in the heart of man. Democratic nations, in which all these things are encountered, will therefore cultivate the arts that serve to render life convenient in preference to those whose object is to embellish it; they will habitually prefer the useful to the beautiful and they will want the beautiful to be useful.

But I intend to go further, and after having indicated the first feature, to sketch several others.

It ordinarily happens in centuries of privilege that the exercise of almost all the arts becomes a privilege and that each profession is a world apart where not everyone is permitted to enter. And even though industry is free, the natural immobility of aristocratic nations makes all those who are occupied with the same art nonetheless in the end form a distinct class always composed of the same families, all of whose members know each other and in which a public opinion and a corporate pride are soon born. In an industrial class of this kind, each artisan has not only his fortune to make but his status to guard. It is not only his interest that makes the rule for him, nor even that of the buyer, but that of the corporation, and the interest of the corporation is that each artisan produce masterpieces. In aristocratic centuries, the aim of the arts is therefore to make the best possible, not the quickest or the cheapest.

When, on the contrary, each profession is open to all, when the crowd constantly enters and leaves it, when its different members become strangers, indifferent and almost invisible to one another because of their multitude, the social bond is destroyed, and each worker, led back toward himself, seeks only to gain the most money possible at the least cost; there is nothing more than the will of the consumer to limit him. Now it happens that at the same time a corresponding revolution makes itself felt in the latter.

In countries where wealth, like power, is concentrated in a few hands and does not leave them, the use of most of the goods of this world belongs to a few individuals who are always the same; necessity, opinion, and moderation of desires turn all the others away from it.

As this aristocratic class is held immobile at the point of greatness where it is placed, without either contracting or expanding, it always experiences the same needs and feels them in the same manner. The men who compose it naturally draw from the superior and hereditary position they occupy the taste for what is very well made and very durable.

That gives a general turn to the ideas of the nation in the case of the arts.

It often happens in these peoples that the peasant himself would rather be deprived entirely of the objects he covets than to acquire imperfect ones.

In aristocracies, workers therefore work only for a limited number of buyers who are very difficult to satisfy. The gain the workers expect principally depends on the perfection of their works.

It is no longer so when, all privileges being destroyed, ranks are mixed and all men are constantly falling and rising on the social scale.

One always encounters a crowd of citizens within a democratic people whose patrimonies are being divided and are decreasing. In better times they contracted certain needs that remain after the ability to satisfy them no longer exists, and they look restively to see whether there would not be some roundabout means of providing them.

On the other hand, in democracies one always sees a very great number of men whose fortune grows, but whose desires grow much more quickly than their fortune and who devour with their eyes the goods it promises long before it delivers them. These seek in all directions to open shorter paths to nearby enjoyments. From the combination of these causes, it results that in democracies one always encounters a multitude of citizens whose needs are above their resources and who would willingly consent to be incompletely satisfied rather than to renounce absolutely the object of their covetousness.

The worker easily understands these passions because he himself shares them: in aristocracies he sought to sell his products very dear to some; he now conceives that there might be a more expeditious means of enriching himself, which would be to sell them cheaply to all.

Now, there are only two manners of lowering the price of merchandise.

The first is to find better means—shorter and more skillful—of producing it. The second is to manufacture a greater quantity of objects, nearly alike, but of less value. In democratic peoples, all the intellectual faculties of the worker are directed toward these two points.

He strives to invent processes that permit him to work not only better, but more quickly and with less cost, and if he cannot succeed at this, to diminish the intrinsic qualities of the thing he makes without rendering it entirely unfit for the use for which it is destined. When it was only the rich who had watches, they were almost all excellent. Scarcely any but mediocre ones are made any longer, but everyone has one. Thus democracy not only tends to direct the human mind toward the useful arts, it brings artisans to make many imperfect things very rapidly, and the consumer to content himself with these things.

It is not that in democracies art is not capable of producing marvels in case of need. That is sometimes discovered when buyers present themselves who consent to pay for the time and trouble. In this struggle in all industries, in the midst of this immense competition and these innumerable attempts, excellent workers who penetrate to the furthest limits of their profession are formed; but they rarely have the occasion to show what they know how to do: they are carefully sparing in their efforts; they keep themselves in a skillful mediocrity that judges itself and that, though being capable of reaching beyond the goal it proposes for itself, aims only at the goal it reaches for. In aristocracies, on the contrary, workers always do all they know how to do, and when they stop it is because they are at the end of their science.

When I arrive in a country and see the arts yielding some admirable products, that teaches me nothing about the social state and political constitution of the country. But if I perceive that the products of the arts there are generally imperfect, in very great number and at a low price, I am assured that among the people where this happens, privileges are weakened, and the classes are beginning to mix and are soon going to be confused with one another.

Artisans who live in democratic centuries not only seek to put their useful products within the reach of all citizens, they also strive to give all their products brilliant qualities that they do not have.

In the confusion of all classes each hopes to be able to appear what he is not and engages in great efforts to succeed at this. Democracy does not give birth to this sentiment, which is only too natural to the heart of man; but it applies it to material things: there is hypocrisy of virtue in all times; that of luxury belongs more particularly to democratic centuries.

To satisfy these new needs of human vanity, there are no impostures to which the arts do not have recourse; industry sometimes goes so far in this sense that it comes to harm itself. They have already succeeded so perfectly at imitating a diamond that it is easy to mistake it. From the moment when the art of manufacturing false diamonds so that one can no longer distinguish them from genuine ones is invented, both will probably be abandoned and they will again become pebbles.

This leads me to speak of those arts that have been named par excellence fine arts.

I do not believe that the necessary effect of the democratic social state and institutions is to diminish the number of men who cultivate the fine arts; but these causes powerfully influence the manner in which they are cultivated. Since most of those who had already contracted the taste for the fine arts are becoming poor, and on the other hand, many of those not yet rich are beginning to conceive a taste for the fine arts by imitation, the quantity of consumers generally increases, and very rich and very refined consumers become rarer. In the fine arts, something analogous then takes place to what I already brought out when I spoke of the useful arts. They multiply their works and diminish the merit of each of them.

No longer able to aim at the great, they seek the elegant and pretty; they strive less for reality than for appearance.

In aristocracies, a few great pictures are done, and in democratic countries, a multitude of small paintings. In the first they raise statues of bronze and in the second they pour out statues of plaster.

When I arrived for the first time in New York by the part of the Atlantic Ocean named the East River, I was surprised to perceive along the bank at some distance from town a certain number of small palaces of white marble, several of which had an antique architecture; the next day, having been to consider more closely the one that had particularly attracted my regard, I found that its walls were whitewashed bricks and its columns painted wood. It was the same with all the monuments I had admired the day before.

In addition, the democratic social state and institutions give to all the imitative arts certain particular tendencies that are easy to point out. They often turn them from the depiction of the soul to apply themselves only to the body; and they substitute the representation of motions and sensations for that of sentiments and ideas; finally, in place of the ideal they put the real.

I doubt that Raphael* made as profound a study of the smallest springs of the human body as have the draftsmen of our day. He did not attach the same importance as they to rigorous exactitude on this point, for he claimed

---

*Raphael (1483–1520), Italian Renaissance painter.

to surpass nature. He wanted to make of man something that was superior to man. He undertook to embellish beauty itself.

David* and his students were, on the contrary, as good anatomists as painters. They represented the models they had before their eyes marvelously well, but it was rare that they imagined anything beyond that; they followed nature exactly, whereas Raphael sought better than that. They left us an exact depiction of man, but the first made us glimpse divinity in his works.

One can apply even to the choice of subject what I have said of the manner of treating it.

The painters of the Renaissance ordinarily sought great subjects above themselves, or far from their times, that left a vast course to their imaginations. Our painters often put their talent to reproducing exactly the details of the private life that they have constantly before their eyes, and they copy from all sides small objects of which they have only too many originals in nature.

Chapter 12 WHY THE AMERICANS AT THE SAME TIME RAISE SUCH LITTLE AND SUCH GREAT MONUMENTS

I have just said that in democratic centuries the monuments of the arts tend to become more numerous and less great. I hasten to indicate myself the exception to this rule.

In democratic peoples individuals are very weak; but the state, which represents all and holds all in its hand, is very strong. Nowhere do citizens appear smaller than in a democratic nation. Nowhere else does the nation itself seem greater, nor does the mind more readily make a vast picture of it. In democratic societies the imagination of men contracts when they consider themselves; it extends indefinitely when they think of the state. Hence it happens that the same men who live cramped in narrow dwellings often aim at the gigantic when it is a question of public monuments.

On the site they wanted to make their capital Americans have placed the precincts of an immense city which today is still scarcely more populated

*Jacques-Louis David (1748–1825), French neoclassical painter.

than Pontoise,* but which according to them will one day contain a million inhabitants; they have already uprooted trees for ten leagues around lest they should become inconvenient to the future citizens of this imaginary metropolis. In the center of the city they have raised a magnificent palace to serve as the seat of Congress, and they have given it the pompous name of Capitol.

Every day the several states themselves conceive and execute prodigious undertakings that would astonish the genius of the great nations of Europe.

Thus democracy not only brings men to make a multitude of minute works; it also brings them to raise a few very great monuments. But between these two extremes there is nothing. Some sparse remains of very vast edifices therefore tell nothing about the social state and institutions of the people that raised them.

I add, although it departs from my subject, that they do not make its greatness, enlightenment, and real prosperity any better known.

Every time any power whatever is capable of making a whole people combine in a single undertaking, it will succeed with little science and much time in getting something immense from the combination of such great efforts without anyone's having to conclude, because of this, that the people is very happy, very enlightened, or even very strong. The Spanish found Mexico City full of magnificent temples and vast palaces, which did not prevent Cortés† from conquering the empire of Mexico with six hundred infantry and sixteen horses.

If the Romans had known the laws of hydraulics better, they would not have raised all the aqueducts that surround the ruins of their cities, and they would have made a better use of their power and wealth. If they had discovered the steam engine, perhaps they would not have spread to the extremities of their empire the long artificial rock masses named Roman roads.

These things are magnificent testimonies to their ignorance at the same time as to their greatness.

A people that left no vestiges of its passage other than some lead pipes in the earth and iron rods on its surface could have been more a master of nature than the Romans.

---

*A town in France, near Paris.
†Hernando Cortés (1485–1547), Spanish explorer and conqueror of the Aztec Empire.

ఆ ఆ

Chapter 13 THE LITERARY FACE OF DEMOCRATIC CENTURIES

When one enters the shop of a bookseller in the United States and inspects the American books that fill the shelves, the number of works there appears very great, whereas that of known authors seems, on the contrary, very small.

First, one finds a multitude of elementary treatises meant to give first notions of human knowledge. Most of these works have been composed in Europe. The Americans reprint them, adapting them to their use. Afterwards comes an almost innumerable quantity of religious books, Bibles, sermons, pious anecdotes, disputations, accounts of charitable institutions. Finally, the long catalogue of political pamphlets appears: in America the parties do not produce books in order to fight each other, but brochures that circulate with an incredible rapidity, live for a day, and die.

In the midst of all these obscure productions of the human mind appear the more remarkable works of a few authors who alone are known to Europeans or who ought to be.*

Although America is perhaps the civilized country of our day where people are least occupied with literature, one nevertheless meets a great quantity of individuals there who are interested in things of the mind and who make them if not the study of their whole lives, at least the charm of their leisure. But England furnishes them most of the books they demand. Almost all the great English works are reproduced in the United States. The literary genius of Great Britain still casts its rays deep in the forests of the New World. There is scarcely a pioneer's cabin where one does not encounter some odd volumes of Shakespeare. I recall having read the feudal drama of *Henry V* for the first time in a *log-house.*†

Not only do Americans draw every day on treasures from English literature, but one can truthfully say that they find the literature of England on their own soil. Among the few men in the United States who are occupied in composing works of literature, most are English at bottom and above all in form. Thus they transport into the midst of democracy the ideas and literary usages that are current in the aristocratic nation they have taken for a model. They paint with colors borrowed from foreign mores; almost never repre-

---

*In sentences crossed out before his manuscript was published, AT specified "the works of Mr. [Washington] Irving, the novels of Mr. [James Fenimore] Cooper, the eloquent treatises of Dr. [William Ellery] Channing."

†AT's English.

senting in its reality the country that has seen them born, they are rarely popular there.

Citizens of the United States themselves seem so convinced that books are not published for them, that before settling on the merit of one of their writers, they ordinarily wait for him to have been sampled in England. As in the case of pictures, one willingly leaves to the author of the original the right to judge the copy.

The inhabitants of the United States, therefore, still do not have a literature, properly speaking. The only authors I recognize as Americans are journalists. These are not great writers, but they speak the language of the country and make themselves understood by it. I see in the others only strangers. They are for the Americans what the imitators of Greeks and Romans in the period of the renaissance of letters were for us, an object of curiosity, not of general sympathy. They amuse the mind and do not act on mores.

I have already said that this state of things is very far from depending only on democracy and that one must search for its causes in several particular circumstances independent of [democracy].*

If the Americans, while preserving their social state and their laws, had another origin and found themselves transported to another country, I do not doubt that they would have had a literature. Such as they are, I am sure that in the end they will have one; but it will have a character different from the one that is manifest in the American writings of our day, and it will be proper to it. It is not impossible to trace this character in advance.

Let me suppose an aristocratic people in which letters are cultivated; the works of the intellect, like the affairs of government, are regulated in it by a sovereign class. Literary life, like political existence, is almost entirely concentrated in this class or in those most closely adjoining it. This is enough for me to have the key to all that remains.

When a few men, always the same, are occupied at the same time with the same objects, they readily understand each other and decide in common certain principal rules that will direct each of them. If the object that attracts the attention of these men is literature, works of the mind will soon be submitted by them to some precise laws from which it will no longer be permitted to deviate.

If these men occupy an hereditary position in the country, they will naturally be inclined not only to adopt a certain number of fixed rules for themselves, but to follow those that their ancestors imposed; their legislation will be at once rigorous and traditional.

As they are not necessarily preoccupied with material things, as they have

*DA II 1.9.

never been and their fathers were no more so, they could have been interested in works of the mind for several generations. They have understood the literary art, and in the end they love it for itself and take a scholar's pleasure in seeing that it is conformed to.

This is still not all: the men I am speaking of began their lives and finished them in ease or wealth; they therefore naturally conceived a taste for studied enjoyments and a love of refined and delicate pleasures.

Even more, a certain softness of spirit and heart, which they often contract in the midst of this long and peaceful use of so many goods, brings them to exclude from their very pleasures whatever could be encountered in them that is too unexpected or too lively. They prefer being amused to being moved in a lively way; they want to be interested, but not to be carried away.

Now imagine a great number of literary works executed by the men I have just depicted, or for them, and you will conceive without difficulty a literature in which all will be regular and coordinated in advance. The least work will be groomed in its smallest details; art and work will be shown in all things; each genre will have its particular rules from which it will not be permissible to deviate and which will isolate it from all the others.

Style will appear in it almost as important as the idea, the form as the content; the tone will be polished, moderate, sustained. The spirit will always have a noble step, rarely a lively pace, and writers will apply themselves more to perfecting than producing.

It will sometimes happen that the members of the literate class, living only among themselves and writing only for themselves, will entirely lose sight of the rest of the world, which will throw them into the studied and the false; they themselves will impose little literary rules for their own sole use, which will turn them away insensibly from good sense and finally lead them outside of nature.

By dint of wanting to speak otherwise than the vulgar, they will come to a sort of aristocratic jargon that is scarcely less distant from beautiful language than the patois of the people.

These are the natural shoals for literature in aristocracies.

Every aristocracy that sets itself entirely apart from the people becomes impotent. That is true in letters as well as in politics.[1]

1. All this is above all true of aristocratic countries that have long been peacefully subject to the power of a king.

When freedom reigns in an aristocracy, the upper classes are constantly obliged to make use of the lower; and in making use of them, they are brought closer to them. That often makes something of the democratic spirit penetrate to them. Besides, energy and a habit of enterprise, a taste for movement and for noise, develop in a privileged body that governs, which cannot fail to influence all literary works.

Let us now turn the picture over and consider the reverse.

Let us transport ourselves to the heart of a democracy whose old traditions and present enlightenment render it responsive to enjoyments of the mind. Ranks in it are mixed and confused; knowledge, like power, is infinitely divided and, I dare say, scattered in all directions.

Here is a confused crowd whose intellectual needs are to be satisfied. These new lovers of the pleasures of the mind have not all received the same education; they do not possess the same enlightenment, they do not resemble their fathers, and at each instant they differ from themselves; for they constantly change places, sentiments, and fortunes. The mind of each of them is therefore not bound to those of all the others by common traditions and habits, and they have never had the power, the will, or the time to understand each other.

Nonetheless, in the heart of this incoherent and agitated multitude authors are born, and it distributes profits and glory to them.

I have no trouble understanding that with things being so, I should expect to encounter in the literature of such a people only a few of those rigorous conventions that readers and writers in aristocratic centuries recognize. If it happened that the men of a period reached agreement on some, that would still prove nothing for the following period; for in democratic nations each new generation is a new people. In these nations, therefore, literature can be subjected to strict rules only with difficulty, and it is almost impossible that it ever be subjected to permanent rules.

In democracies, it is far from the case that all men who are occupied with literature have received a literary education, and among those of them who have some tincture of belles-lettres, most follow a political career or embrace a profession from which they can turn aside only in moments to taste the pleasures of the mind furtively. They therefore do not make these pleasures the principal charm of their existence; but they consider them as a passing and necessary relaxation in the midst of the serious work of life: such men can never acquire a profound enough knowledge of the literary art to feel its delicacies; the little nuances elude them. Having only a very short time to give to letters, they want to put it wholly to profit. They like books that are procured without trouble, that are quickly read, that do not require learned research to be understood. They demand facile beauties that deliver themselves and that one can enjoy at that instant; above all the unexpected and new are necessary to them. Habituated to an existence that is practical, contested, and monotonous, they need lively and rapid emotions, sudden clarity, brilliant truths or errors that instantly pull them from themselves and introduce them suddenly, almost violently, into the midst of the subject.

What more need I say about this? and who does not understand what is going to follow without my expressing it?

Taken in its entirety, literature in democratic centuries cannot present the image of order, of regularity, of science, and of art as in aristocratic times; in it, form will ordinarily be found neglected and sometimes scorned. Style will often show itself bizarre, incorrect, overloaded, and soft, and almost always bold and vehement. Authors will aim more at rapidity of execution than at perfection of details. Small writings will be more frequent than large books, spirit than erudition, imagination than profundity; an uncultivated and almost savage force will reign in thought, and often a very great variety and a singular fruitfulness in its products. One will try to astonish rather than to please, and one will strive to carry away passions more than to charm taste.

Without doubt writers will be encountered now and then who will want to take another path, and if they have superior merit, they will succeed in getting themselves read in spite of their defects and their [good] qualities; but these exceptions will be rare, and these very ones who have departed in this way from common usage in the entirety of their works will always return to it in some details.

I have just painted two extreme states; but nations do not go all at once from the first to the second; they only arrive at it gradually and through infinite nuances. In the transition that leads a literate people from the one to the other, a moment almost always comes when, as the literary genius of democratic nations meets that of aristocracies, both seem to want to reign in accord over the human mind.

Those are passing, but very brilliant periods: then one has fertility without exuberance and movement without confusion. Such was French literature in the eighteenth century.

I would go further than my thought if I said that the literature of a nation is always subordinate to its social state and its political constitution. I know that independent of these causes, there are several others that give certain characteristics to literary works; but these appear to me the principal ones.

The relations existing between the social and political state of a people and the genius of its writers are always very numerous; he who knows the one is never completely ignorant of the other.

Chapter 14   ON THE LITERARY INDUSTRY

Democracy not only makes the taste for letters penetrate the industrial classes, it introduces the industrial spirit into the heart of literature.

In aristocracies readers are difficult and few; in democracies it is less hard to please them and their number is enormous. Hence the result is that in aristocratic peoples, one may hope to succeed only with immense efforts, and these efforts, which can give much glory, can never procure much money; whereas in democratic nations a writer can flatter himself that he may get a mediocre renown and a great fortune cheaply. For that it is not necessary that one admire him; it is enough that one have a taste for him.

The ever-growing crowd of readers and the continual need they have of the new assure the sale of a book that they scarcely esteem.

In democratic times, the public often acts with authors as kings ordinarily do with their courtiers; they enrich them and scorn them. What more is necessary to venal souls who are born in courts or who are worthy of living there?

Democratic literatures always swarm with these authors who perceive in letters only an industry; and for the few great writers that one sees there, one counts vendors of ideas by the thousands.

Chapter 15   WHY THE STUDY OF GREEK AND LATIN LITERATURE IS PARTICULARLY USEFUL IN DEMOCRATIC SOCIETIES

What was called the people in the most democratic republics of antiquity scarcely resembled what we name the people. In Athens all citizens took part in public affairs; but there were only twenty thousand citizens out of more than three hundred fifty thousand inhabitants; all the others were slaves and fulfilled most of the functions that in our day belong to the people and even to the middle classes.

Athens, with its universal suffrage, was therefore, after all, only an aristocratic republic in which all the nobles had an equal right to the government.

One must consider the struggle of the patricians and plebeians of Rome in the same light and see in it only an internal quarrel between the juniors and seniors of the same family. All in fact held to aristocracy and had its spirit.

One ought to remark, furthermore, that in all of antiquity books were rare and expensive, and great difficulty was experienced in reproducing them and having them circulate. These circumstances came to concentrate the taste for and use of letters in a few men, who formed almost a small literary aristocracy of the elite of a great political aristocracy. Thus nothing argues that, among the Greeks and Romans, letters were ever treated as an industry.

These peoples, who not only formed aristocracies, but who were also very well-ordered and very free nations, ought therefore to have imparted to their literary productions the particular vices and special qualities that characterize literature in aristocratic centuries.

In fact, it is enough to cast one's eyes on the writings left us by antiquity to discover that if the writers sometimes lacked variety and fecundity in their subjects, and boldness, movement, and generalization in their thought, they always displayed an admirable art and care in the details; nothing in their works seems done in haste or haphazardly; everything there is written for connoisseurs, and the search for ideal beauty constantly shows itself. There is no literature that puts the qualities naturally lacking in the writers of democracies more in relief than that of the ancients. Thus there exists no literature better suited for study in democratic centuries. That study is the most fitting of all to combat the literary defects inherent in these centuries; as for their natural qualities, they will indeed arise by themselves without its being necessary to learn to acquire them.

It is here that one needs to be well understood.

A study can be useful to the literature of a people and not be appropriate to its social and political needs.

If one persisted in teaching only belles-lettres in a society where each one was habitually led to make violent efforts to increase his fortune or to maintain it, one would have very polite but very dangerous citizens; for every day the social and political state would give them needs that they would never learn to satisfy by education, and they would trouble the state in the name of the Greeks and Romans instead of making it fruitful by their industry.

It is evident that in democratic centuries the interest of individuals as well as the security of the state requires that the education of the greatest number be scientific, commercial, and industrial rather than literary.

Greek and Latin ought not to be taught in all schools; but it is important that those whose nature or whose fortune destines them to cultivate letters or predisposes them to that taste find schools in which one can be made a perfect master of ancient literature and wholly steeped in its spirit. To attain this result, a few excellent universities would be worth more than a multitude of bad colleges where superfluous studies that are done badly prevent necessary studies from being done well.

All those who have the ambition to excel in letters in democratic nations ought to be nourished often from the works of antiquity. It is a salutary diet.

It is not that I consider the literary productions of the ancients irreproachable. I think only that they have special qualities that can serve marvelously to counterbalance our particular defects. They prop us up on the side where we lean.

Chapter 16 HOW AMERICAN DEMOCRACY HAS MODIFIED THE ENGLISH LANGUAGE

If what I said previously about letters in general* was well understood by the reader, he will conceive without difficulty what kind of influence the democratic social state and institutions can exert on language itself, which is the first instrument of thought.

American authors, to tell the truth, live more in England than in their own country since they constantly study English writers and take them for a model every day. It is not so for the population itself, which is more immediately subject to the particular causes that can act on the United States. It is therefore not to the written language, but to the spoken language, that one must pay attention if one wants to perceive the modifications that the idiom of an aristocratic people can undergo in becoming the language of a democracy.

Educated Englishmen and those who appreciate these delicate nuances more competently than I myself have often assured me that the enlightened classes of the United States differ notably in their language from the enlightened classes of Great Britain.

They not only complained that the Americans had put many new words

DA II 1.13.

into use—the difference and the distance between the countries would have sufficed to explain that—but that the new words were in particular borrowed either from the jargon of the parties or from the mechanical arts or from the language of business. They added that old English words were often taken by the Americans in a new meaning. They said, finally, that the inhabitants of the United States frequently interwove styles in a singular manner and that they sometimes placed together words that in the language of the mother country were customarily kept separate.

These remarks, which were made to me on several occasions by people who appeared to me worthy of belief, brought me to reflect on this subject myself, and my reflections led me by theory to the same point at which they had arrived by practice.

In aristocracies, language will naturally participate in the repose in which all things are held. One makes few new words because few new things are made; and if one made new things, one would strive to depict them with known words whose sense tradition had fixed.

If it happens that the human mind finally becomes agitated on its own or is awakened by light penetrating from outside, the new expressions that one creates have a learned, intellectual, and philosophical character indicating that they do not owe their birth to a democracy. When the fall of Constantinople* made the sciences and letters flow back toward the West, the French language was invaded all at once by a multitude of new words that had their roots in Greek and Latin. One then saw an erudite neologism in France that was intended only for the enlightened classes and whose effects were never felt by the people or reached them only at length.

All the nations of Europe provided the same spectacle in succession. Milton† alone introduced more than six hundred words into the English language, almost all taken from Latin, Greek, and Hebrew.

The perpetual movement that reigns at the heart of a democracy tends, on the contrary, to renew constantly the face of language like that of business. In the midst of this general agitation and combination of all minds, a great number of new ideas are formed; old ideas are lost or reappear; or else they are subdivided into infinitely small nuances.

One therefore often finds words that will go out of use and others that must be brought into it.

Democratic nations, moreover, like movement for itself. That is seen in language as well as in politics. Even when they do not have the need to change words, they sometimes feel the desire to do it.

---

*Constantinople, the capital of the Byzantine Empire, fell to the Turks in 1453.
†John Milton (1608–1674), English poet and author of *Paradise Lost*.

The genius of democratic peoples manifests itself not only in the great number of new words they put into use, but also in the nature of the ideas these new words represent.

In these peoples the majority make the law in the matter of language just as in everything else. Their spirit is revealed there as elsewhere. Now, the majority are more occupied with business than with studies, with political and commercial interests than with philosophical speculations or belles-lettres. Most of the words created or accepted by them will bear the imprint of these habits; they will serve mainly to express the needs of industry, the passions of the parties, or the details of public administration. The language will constantly stretch in that direction, whereas on the contrary it will abandon little by little the terrain of metaphysics and theology.

As for the source from which democratic nations draw their new words and the manner in which they go about manufacturing them, it is easy to say.

Men who live in democratic countries scarcely know the language that was spoken in Rome or Athens, and they do not care about going back to antiquity to find the expression they lack. If they sometimes have recourse to learned etymologies, it is ordinarily vanity that makes them seek deeply in dead languages, and not erudition that naturally offers them to their minds. It sometimes even happens that the most ignorant among them make the most use of them. The quite democratic desire to move out of one's sphere often brings them to want to enhance a very coarse profession with a Greek or Latin name. The more the job is low and distant from science, the more the name is pompous and erudite. Thus it is that our rope dancers are transformed into acrobats and funambulists.

For want of dead languages democratic peoples willingly borrow the words of living languages; for they communicate constantly between themselves, and men of different countries imitate each other willingly because each day they resemble each other more.

But it is principally within their own languages that democratic peoples seek the means of innovating. From time to time they take up forgotten expressions in their vocabulary and restore them to light, or else they draw from a particular class of citizens a term proper to it, so as to make it enter habitual language with a figurative sense; a multitude of expressions that first belonged only to the special language of a party or a profession are thus carried into general circulation.

The most ordinary expedient that democratic peoples employ to innovate in the case of language consists in giving to an expression already in use a sense not in use. That method is very simple, very prompt, and very convenient. One does not need science to make good use of it, and ignorance even facilitates its employment. But it makes the language run great risks. In thus doubling the sense of a word, democratic peoples sometimes render doubtful the one they leave to it and the one they give to it.

An author begins by turning a known expression away from its primary sense a little, and after having modified it so, he does his best to adapt it to his subject. Another comes up who pulls the meaning from another direction; a third drags it with him on another route; and as there is no common arbitrator, no permanent tribunal, that can fix the sense of the word definitively, it is left in a mobile situation. That makes writers almost never look as if they apply themselves to a single thought; they always seem to aim at a group of ideas, leaving to the reader the care of judging which of them is hit.

This is a distressing consequence of democracy. I would rather that the language be bristling with Chinese, Tartar, or Huron words than that the sense of French words be rendered uncertain. Harmony and homogeneity are only secondary beauties of language. There is much convention in these sorts of things, and strictly one can do without them. But there is no good language without clear terms.

Equality necessarily brings several other changes to language.

In aristocratic centuries, when each nation tends to hold itself apart from all the others and likes to have a physiognomy that is its own, it often happens that several peoples who have a common origin nevertheless become quite foreign to one another, so that, without ceasing to be able to understand each other, they no longer all speak in the same manner.

In these same centuries, each nation is divided into a certain number of classes that see each other little and do not mix; each of these classes takes on and preserves without variation intellectual habits peculiar to it and adopts out of preference certain words and certain terms that pass afterwards from generation to generation like inheritances. One then encounters in the same idiom a language of the poor and a language of the rich, a language of commoners and a language of nobles, a learned language and a vulgar language. The more profound the divisions are and the more impassable the barriers, the more it will be so. I would willingly bet that among the castes of India, language varies enormously and that one finds almost as much difference between the language of an untouchable and that of a Brahmin as between their clothes.

When, on the contrary, men no longer kept in their places see each other and communicate constantly, when castes are destroyed and classes are made anew and intermingle, all words in the language mix together. Those that cannot suit the greatest number perish; the rest form a common mass in which everyone takes hold almost at random. Almost all the different dialects that used to divide the idioms of Europe tend visibly to fade away; there is no patois in the New World, and they are disappearing each day from the Old.

This revolution in the social state influences style as well as language.

Not only does everyone make use of the same words, but they get used to employing each of them indifferently. The rules that style had created are almost destroyed. One scarcely ever encounters expressions that by their nature seem vulgar and others that appear distinguished. As individuals coming out of diverse ranks have brought with them to wherever they have arrived the expressions and terms that they were used to, the origin of words, like that of men, has been lost, and confusion has been produced in language as in society.

I know that in the classification of words one encounters rules that do not depend on one form of society rather than on another, but that derive from the very nature of things. There are expressions and turns that are vulgar because the sentiments they are supposed to express are really low, and there are others that are elevated because the objects they want to depict are naturally very high.

The mixing of ranks will never make these differences disappear. But equality cannot fail to destroy what is purely conventional and arbitrary in the forms of thought. I do not know whether even the necessary classification I indicated above will not always be less respected in a democratic people than in another; because in such a people one does not find men whose education, enlightenment, and leisure dispose them in a permanent manner to study the natural laws of language and who make them respected by observing them themselves.

I do not want to abandon this subject without depicting one last feature of democratic languages that will characterize them perhaps more than all the others.

I showed previously that democratic peoples have the taste and often the passion for general ideas;* that is due to qualities and defects proper to them. This love of general ideas manifests itself in democratic languages in the continual use of generic terms and abstract words, and in the manner in which they are employed. That is the great merit and the great weakness of these languages.

Democratic peoples passionately love generic terms and abstract words because these expressions enlarge thought, and, by permitting the inclusion of many objects in a small space, they aid the work of the intellect.

A democratic writer will willingly say in an abstract manner *capacities* for

*DA II 1.3.

capable men, without entering into the details of the things to which this capacity applies. He will speak of *actualities* to paint in a single stroke things that pass before his eyes in that moment, and he will comprehend under the word *eventualities* all that can happen in the universe starting from the moment in which he speaks.

Democratic writers constantly make abstract words of this kind, or they take the abstract words of the language in a more and more abstract sense.

Even more, to render discourse more rapid, they personify the object of these abstract words and make it act like a real individual. They will say that *the force of things wants capacities to govern.*

I do not ask more than to explain my thought by my own example:

I have often made use of the word equality in an absolute sense; I have, in addition, personified equality in several places, and so I have come to say that equality does certain things or abstains from certain others. One can affirm that the men of the century of Louis XIV* would not have spoken in this way; it would never have come into the mind of any of them to use the word equality without applying it to a particular thing, and they would sooner have renounced the use of it than have consented to make equality into a living person.

These abstract words that fill democratic languages, and of which use is made at every turn without linking them to any particular fact, enlarge and veil a thought; they render the expression more rapid and the idea less clear. But in the case of language, democratic peoples prefer obscurity to workmanship.

Besides, I do not know whether the vague does not have a certain secret charm for those who speak and write among these peoples.

Men who live among them, being often left to the individual efforts of their intellect, are almost always nagged by doubt. Furthermore, as their situation changes constantly, they are never held firmly to any of their opinions by the very immobility of their fortune.

Men who inhabit democratic countries therefore often have vacillating thoughts; they must have very large expressions to contain them. As they never know if the idea they are expressing today will suit the new situation they will have tomorrow, they naturally conceive a taste for abstract terms. An abstract word is like a box with a false bottom: one puts in it the ideas one desires and one takes them out without anyone's seeing it.

Among all peoples, generic and abstract terms form the foundation of language; I therefore do not claim that one encounters these words only in democratic languages; I say only that the tendency of men in times of equal-

*King of France from 1643 to 1715.

ity is in particular to increase the number of words of this kind; always to take them in isolation, in their most abstract meaning, and to make use of them at every turn even if they are not required to meet the need of the discourse.

Chapter 17 ON SOME SOURCES OF POETRY IN DEMOCRATIC NATIONS

Several very diverse meanings have been given to the word poetry.

It would be fatiguing to readers to inquire with them which of these different senses is most suitable to choose; I prefer to say right away which I have chosen.

Poetry in my eyes is the search for and depiction of the ideal.

The one who, by cutting out a part from what exists, by adding some imaginary features to the picture, and by combining certain circumstances that are real but are not found together in conjunction, completes and enlarges nature—that is the poet. Thus poetry will not have for its goal to represent the true, but to adorn it, and to offer a superior image to the mind.

Verses appear to me as the beautiful ideal of language, and in this sense they will be eminently poetic; but by themselves they will not constitute poetry.

I want to inquire whether among the actions, sentiments, and ideas of democratic peoples, some are not encountered that lend themselves to the imagination of the ideal, and that one ought to consider for this reason as natural sources of poetry.

One must first recognize that the taste for the ideal and the pleasure one takes in seeing it depicted are never as lively and as widespread in a democratic people as within an aristocracy.

In aristocratic nations, it sometimes happens that the body acts as if by itself, while the soul is plunged into a repose that weighs on it. In these nations the people themselves often display poetic tastes and their spirits sometimes soar beyond and above what surrounds them.

But in democracies, the love of material enjoyments, the idea of the better, the competition, and the imminent charm of success are like so many spurs that hasten the steps of each man down the course he has embraced and forbid him from deviating from it for a single moment. The principal effort of the soul goes in this direction. Imagination is not extinguished, but it is given over almost exclusively to conceiving the useful and representing the real.

Equality not only diverts men from depiction of the ideal; it diminishes the number of objects to depict.

Aristocracy, in holding society immobile, favors the firmness and duration of positive religions as well as the stability of political institutions.

Not only does it maintain the human mind in faith, but it disposes it to adopt one faith rather than another. An aristocratic people will always be inclined to place intermediary powers between God and man.

One can say that in this, aristocracy shows itself very favorable to poetry. When the universe is peopled with supernatural beings who do not come before the senses, but which the mind discovers, imagination feels itself at ease, and poets, finding a thousand diverse subjects to depict, meet innumerable spectators ready to be interested in their pictures.

In democratic centuries, on the contrary, it sometimes happens that beliefs are as much afloat as are laws. Doubt then brings the imagination of poets back to earth and confines them to the visible and real world.

Even if equality does not shake religions, it simplifies them; it turns attention away from secondary agents to bring it principally to the sovereign master.

Aristocracy naturally leads the human mind to contemplation of the past and fixes it there. Democracy, on the contrary, gives men a sort of instinctive distaste for what is old. In that, aristocracy is much more favorable to poetry: for things ordinarily become larger and are veiled as they move away; and in this double relation they lend themselves more to the depiction of the ideal.

After having removed the past from poetry, equality takes away a part of the present.

In aristocratic peoples, there exist a certain number of privileged individuals whose existence is so to speak outside and above the human condition; power, wealth, glory, spirit, delicacy, and distinction in all things appear to belong exclusively to them. The crowd never sees them from close up, or it does not follow them in detail; one has little to do to make the depiction of these men poetic.

On the other hand, there exist in these same peoples ignorant, humble, and subjugated classes; and these lend themselves to poetry by the very excess of their coarseness and misery as do the others by their refinement and greatness. Furthermore, since the different classes of which an aristocratic people is composed are very separate from one another and know one another poorly, in representing them the imagination can always add to or take away something from the real.

In democratic societies where men are all very small and very much alike, each one, while viewing himself, sees all the others at that instant. Poets who live in democratic centuries can therefore never take one man in particular for the subject of their picture; for an object of mediocre size that is perceived distinctly from all sides will never lend itself to the ideal.

Thus equality, in establishing itself on the earth, dries up most of the old sources of poetry.

Let us try to show how it uncovers new ones.

When doubt had depopulated Heaven and the progress of equality had reduced each man to better known and smaller proportions, the poets, still not imagining what they could put in place of the great objects that were fleeing with aristocracy, turned their eyes toward inanimate nature. Losing sight of heroes and gods, they undertook at first to depict rivers and mountains.

In the last century that gave birth to the poetry one called preeminently descriptive.

Some thought that this depiction, embellishing the material, inanimate things that cover the earth, was the poetry proper to democratic centuries; but I think that is an error. I believe that it represents only a passing phase.

I am convinced that in the long term democracy turns the imagination away from all that is external to man to fix it only on man.

Democratic peoples can amuse themselves well for a moment in considering nature; but they only become really animated at the sight of themselves. It is in this way alone that the natural sources of poetry are found among these peoples, and one may believe that all poets who do not wish to draw from them will lose all dominion over the souls of those they intend to charm and in the end will no longer have any but cold witnesses to their transports.

I have brought out how the idea of progress and of the indefinite perfectibility of the human species is proper to democratic ages.*

Democratic peoples scarcely worry about what has been, but they willingly dream of what will be, and in this direction their imagination has no limits; here it stretches and enlarges itself beyond measure.

This offers a vast course to poets and permits them to move their picture far back from the eye. Democracy, which closes the past to poetry, opens the future to it.

All citizens who compose a democratic society being almost equal and alike, poetry cannot apply itself to any one of them; but the nation offers itself to the brush. The similarity of all individuals that renders each of them separately unsuitable to become the object of poetry permits poets to include

*DA II 1.8.

all of them in the same image and finally to consider the people itself. Democratic nations perceive more clearly than all others their own shape, and that great shape lends itself marvelously to the depiction of the ideal.

I shall readily agree that the Americans have no poets; I cannot likewise admit that they have no poetic ideas.

Europe is much occupied with the wilderness of America, but the Americans themselves scarcely think of it. The marvels of inanimate nature find them insensible, and they so to speak perceive the admirable forests that surround them only at the moment at which they fall by their strokes. Their eyes are filled with another spectacle. The American people sees itself advance across this wilderness, draining swamps, straightening rivers, peopling the solitude, and subduing nature. This magnificent image of themselves is not offered only now and then to the imagination of the Americans; one can say that it follows each of them in the least of his actions as in his principal ones, and that it is always there, dangling before his intellect.

One can conceive of nothing so small, so dull, so filled with miserable interests, in a word, so antipoetic, as the life of a man in the United States; but among the thoughts that direct it one always meets one that is full of poetry, and that one is like the hidden nerve that gives vigor to all the rest.

In aristocratic centuries, each people, like each individual, is inclined to keep itself immobile and separated from all the others.

In democratic centuries, the extreme mobility of men and their impatient desires make them change place constantly, and the inhabitants of different countries mix with each other, see each other, listen to each other, and borrow from each other. Therefore not only do members of the same nation become alike; nations themselves are assimilated, and in the eye of the spectator all together form nothing more than a vast democracy of which each citizen is a people. That puts the shape of the human race in broad daylight for the first time.

All that relates to the existence of the human race taken as a whole, its vicissitudes, its future, becomes a very rich mine for poetry.

Poets who lived in aristocratic ages made admirable depictions by taking certain incidents in the life of one people or one man for their subjects; but none of them ever dared to include the destiny of the human species in his picture, whereas the poets who write in democratic ages can undertake that.

At the same time that each one, by raising his eyes above his country, finally begins to perceive humanity itself, God manifests himself more and more to the human spirit in his full and entire majesty.

If in democratic centuries faith in positive religions is often faltering, and beliefs in intermediate powers, whatever name one gives them, are obscured, men are, on the other hand, disposed to conceive a much vaster idea of divinity itself, and its intervention in human affairs appears to them in a new and greater light.

Perceiving the human race as a single whole, they easily conceive that one same design presides over its destiny, and they are brought to recognize in the actions of each individual the tracing of a general and constant plan according to which God guides the species.

This can still be considered as a very abundant source of poetry that opens up in these centuries.

Democratic poets will always appear small and cold if they try to give corporeal forms to gods, demons, or angels, and if they seek to make them descend from Heaven to contend for the earth.

But if they wish to link the great events they sketch back to the general designs of God for the universe, and, without showing the hand of the sovereign master, enable one to penetrate his thought, they will be admired and understood, for the imagination of their contemporaries follows this route by itself.

One can foresee equally that poets who live in democratic ages will depict passions and ideas rather than persons and deeds.

The language, customs, and daily actions of men in democracies reject the imagination of the ideal. These things are not poetic in themselves, and besides, they would cease to be so for the reason that they are too well known by all those to whom one would undertake to speak of them. That forces poets constantly to pierce beneath the exterior surface disclosed by the senses in order to catch a glimpse of the soul itself. For there is nothing that lends itself more to depiction of the ideal than man so viewed in the depths of his immaterial nature.

I have no need to travel through heaven and earth to discover a marvelous object full of contrasts, of infinite greatness and pettiness, of profound obscurities and singular clarity, capable of giving birth at once to pity,* admiration, scorn, and terror. I have only to consider myself: man comes from nothing, traverses time, and is going to disappear forever into the bosom of God. One sees him for only a moment wandering, lost, between the limits of the two abysses.

If man were completely ignorant of himself, he would not be poetic; for one cannot depict what one has no idea of. If he saw himself clearly, his imagination would remain idle and would have nothing to add to the picture. But man is uncovered enough to perceive something of himself and veiled enough so that the rest is sunk in impenetrable darkness, into which he

---

*Or, "piety."

plunges constantly and always in vain, in order to succeed in grasping himself.

One must therefore not expect poetry in democratic peoples to live on legends, to be nourished by traditions and ancient memories, to try to repopulate the universe with supernatural beings in which readers and poets themselves no longer believe, nor to personify coldly virtues and vices that one can see in their own form. It lacks all these resources; but man remains, and he is enough for it. Human destinies, man, taken apart from his time and his country and placed before nature and God with his passions, his doubts, his unheard-of prosperity, and his incomprehensible miseries, will become the principal and almost unique object of poetry for these peoples; and one can already be assured of this if one considers what the greatest poets have written who have appeared as the world succeeds in turning to democracy.

The writers who in our day have so admirably reproduced the features of Childe Harold, René, and Jocelyn* have not claimed merely to relate one man's actions; they wished to illuminate and enlarge certain still obscure sides of the human heart.

These are the poems of democracy.

Therefore equality does not destroy all the objects of poetry; it makes them less numerous and more vast.

☙ ☙ ☙ ☙ ☙ ☙ ☙ ☙ ☙ ☙ ☙ ☙ ☙ ☙ ☙ ☙ ☙ ☙ ☙ ☙

Chapter 18 WHY AMERICAN WRITERS AND ORATORS ARE OFTEN BOMBASTIC

I have often remarked that Americans, who generally treat affairs in a clear and dry language deprived of every ornament, whose extreme simplicity is often vulgar, willingly run to bombast when they want to enter into poetic style. Then they show themselves relentlessly pompous from one end of the speech to the other, and to see them thus squander images at every turn one would believe that they have never said anything simply.

The English more rarely fall into a defect like this.

The cause of this can be indicated without much difficulty.

---

*These are *Childe Harold's Pilgrimmage* (1812–1818), a poem by Byron; *René* (1802), a novel by Chateaubriand; and *Jocelyn* (1836), a poem by Lamartine.

In democratic societies each citizen is habitually occupied in contemplating a very small object, which is himself. If he comes to raise his eyes higher, he then perceives only the immense image of society or the still greater figure of the human race. He has only very particular and very clear ideas, or very general and very vague notions; the intermediate space is empty.

When he has been drawn out of himself, he therefore always expects that he is going to be offered some enormous object to look at, and it is only at this price that he consents to tear himself for a moment from the small, complicated cares that agitate and charm his life.

This appears to me to explain well enough why men of democracies, who generally have such slight affairs, demand from their poets conceptions so vast and depictions so excessive.

For their part, writers hardly fail to obey the instincts they share: they constantly swell their imaginations, and as they extend them beyond measure, they make them reach the gigantic, for which they often forsake the great.

In this manner they hope to attract the regard of the crowd right away and to fix it readily around themselves, and they often succeed in doing so; for the crowd, which only seeks very vast objects in poetry, does not have the time to measure exactly the proportions of all the objects presented to it, nor a taste sure enough to perceive easily how they are disproportionate. The author and the public corrupt one another at the same time.

We have seen, moreover, that in democratic peoples the sources of poetry are beautiful but not abundant. In the end one soon exhausts them. Not finding more material for the ideal in the real and true, poets leave them entirely and create monsters.

I am not afraid that the poetry of democratic peoples will prove timid or that it will stay very close to the earth. I am apprehensive rather that it will lose itself in the clouds at each moment and that in the end it will depict entirely imaginary regions. I fear that the works of democratic poets will often offer immense and incoherent images, overloaded depictions, and bizarre composites, and that the fantastic beings issuing from their minds will sometimes make one long for the real world.

తా తా తా తా తా తా తా తా తా తా తా తా తా తా తా తా తా తా తా

Chapter 19 SOME OBSERVATIONS ON THE THEATER OF DEMOCRATIC PEOPLES

When the revolution that has changed the social and political state of an aristocratic people begins to come to light in literature, it is generally first produced by the theater, and there it remains always visible.

The spectator of a dramatic work is in a way taken unawares by the impression that is suggested to him. He has no time to question his memory or to consult the experts; he does not think of combating the new literary instincts that are beginning to be manifest in him; he yields to them before he knows them.

Authors are not slow to discover the side to which public taste thus secretly inclines. They turn their works to that side; and the plays, after having served to make one perceive the literary revolution being prepared, soon succeed in accomplishing it. If you want to judge in advance the literature of a people that is turning to democracy, study its theater.

In aristocratic nations themselves, moreover, plays form the most democratic portion of literature. There is no literary enjoyment more within reach of the crowd than those one experiences in sight of the stage. Neither preparation nor study is necessary to feel them. They seize you in the midst of your preoccupations and your ignorance. When love of the pleasures of the mind, still half coarse, begins to penetrate a class of citizens, it immediately drives them toward the theater. The theaters of aristocratic nations have always been filled with spectators who did not belong to the aristocracy. Only in the theater have the upper classes mixed with the middle and lower and consented if not to accept their advice, at least to suffer their giving it. It is at the theater that the erudite and literate have always had the most trouble making their taste prevail over the people's and refraining from being carried along themselves by it. The pit has often made the law for the boxes.

If it is difficult for an aristocracy not to allow the theater to be invaded by the people, one readily understands that the people will reign there as masters when, democratic principles having penetrated laws and mores, ranks are confused and intellects come closer together as do fortunes, and the upper class loses its power, its traditions, and its leisure, together with its hereditary wealth.

The tastes and instincts natural to democratic peoples in the case of literature will therefore be manifest first at the theater, and one can foresee that they will be introduced there with violence. In writings, the literary laws of aristocracy will be modified little by little in a gradual and so to speak legal manner. At the theater, they will be overturned by riots.

The theater puts in relief most of the qualities and almost all the vices inherent in democratic literatures.

Democratic peoples have only a very mediocre esteem for erudition, and they scarcely care about what took place in Rome and Athens; they mean to be spoken to about themselves, and they demand a picture of the present.

And so when the heroes and mores of antiquity are reproduced often on the stage, and care is taken to remain very faithful to ancient traditions, that is enough for one to conclude that the democratic classes are not yet dominant in the theater.

Racine excuses himself very humbly in the preface to *Britannicus* for having made Junia enter into the number of vestal virgins when, according to Aulus Gellius, he says, "no one under six years or above ten was accepted."* One may believe that he would not have dreamed of accusing himself or of defending himself from such a crime if he had written in our day.

A fact like this enlightens me not only about the state of literature in the time it takes place but also about that of society itself. A democratic theater does not prove that the nation is a democracy; for as we have just seen, even in aristocracies it can happen that democratic tastes influence the stage; but when the spirit of aristocracy reigns alone at the theater, that demonstrates invincibly that society as a whole is aristocratic, and one can boldly conclude that the same erudite and literate class that directs authors commands citizens and leads affairs.

It is indeed rare that the refined tastes and haughty penchants of the aristocracy, when it rules the theater, do not bring it to make, so to speak, a choice in human nature. It is principally interested in certain social conditions, and it is pleased to find them depicted on the stage; certain virtues and even certain vices appear to it to deserve more particularly to be reproduced; it accepts the picture of these, while it moves all others away from its eyes. At the theater, as elsewhere, it wants to encounter only great lords and it is moved only on behalf of kings. So with styles. An aristocracy willingly imposes certain manners of speaking on dramatic authors; it wishes everything to be said in this tone.

The theater thus often comes to depict only one side of man, or sometimes even to represent what is not encountered in human nature; it lifts itself above and departs from it.

In democratic societies, spectators have no such preferences, and they

---

Britannicus, Première Préface, in Racine, *Oeuvres complètes*, vol. 1, édition Pléiade (Paris, 1950), 388. Jean Baptiste Racine (1639–1699) was a French classical poet and dramatist.

rarely display antipathies like these; they like to find on the stage the confused mixture of conditions, sentiments, and ideas that they encounter before their eyes; the theater becomes more striking, more vulgar, and more true.

Sometimes, however, those who write for the theater in democracies also depart from human nature, but it is through another extreme than their predecessors'. By wanting to reproduce minutely the little singularities of the present moment and the particular physiognomy of certain men, they forget to trace the general features of the species.

When the democratic classes reign at the theater, they introduce as much freedom into the manner of treating the subject as into the choice of subject.

Love of the theater being of all literary tastes the most natural to democratic peoples, the number of authors and of spectators constantly increases in these peoples, as does the number of spectacles. Such a multitude, composed of elements so diverse and spread out in so many different places, cannot recognize the same rules and submit itself to the same laws. There is no accord possible between the very many judges who, not knowing where to find each other, bring forth their rulings separately. If the effect of democracy generally is to make rules and literary conventions doubtful, at the theater it abolishes them entirely in order to substitute the caprice of each author and each public.

It is also in the theater above all that what I have already said elsewhere in a general manner concerning style and art in democratic literatures is displayed.* When one reads the criticisms to which the dramatic works of the century of Louis XIV gave rise, one is surprised to see the great esteem of the public for plausibility and the importance placed in a man's always remaining consistent with himself and doing nothing that could not be readily explained and understood. It is equally surprising how high a price was then put on the forms of language and what petty quarrels over words were made with dramatic authors.

It seems that men of the century of Louis XIV attached a much exaggerated value to these details, which are perceived in one's study, but which elude one on the stage. For after all, the principal object of a play is to be performed, and its first merit is to move. [The exaggerated value attached to details] came from the fact that the spectators of this period were at the same time readers. On leaving the performance, they waited for the writer at home in order to finish judging him.

In democracies one listens to plays at the theater, but one does not read them. Most of those who attend the acting on the stage do not seek pleasures of the mind, but lively emotions of the heart. They do not expect to find a

*DA II 1.13.

work of literature but a spectacle, and provided that the author speaks the language of the country correctly enough to make himself understood, and that his characters excite curiosity and awaken sympathy, they are content; without demanding anything more of the fiction, they immediately reenter the real world. Style is therefore less necessary; for on the stage these rules are even less observed.

As for plausibility, it is impossible often to be new, unexpected, and rapid while remaining faithful to it. Therefore one neglects it, and the public gives its pardon. One can reckon that [the public] will not become restive because of the paths by which you have conducted it if you finally bring it before an object that touches it. It will never reproach you for having moved it despite the rules.

The Americans bring the different instincts I have just depicted into broad daylight when they go to the theater. But one must recognize that there are still only a few of them who go there. Although spectators and spectacles have increased enormously in the United States in the last forty years, the population still indulges in this genre of amusement only with extreme restraint.

That is due to particular causes that the reader already knows, and it is enough to remind him in a few words.*

The Puritans who founded the American republics were not only enemies of pleasures; they further professed an altogether special horror of the theater. They considered it an abominable diversion, and as long as their spirit reigned undivided, dramatic performances were absolutely unknown among them. The opinions of the first fathers of the colony left profound marks on the spirit of their descendants.

Moreover, the extreme regularity of habit and great rigidity of mores seen in the United States have, up to now, hardly favored the development of the theatrical art.

There are no subjects for drama in a country that has not been witness to great political catastrophes and where love always leads by a direct and easy path to marriage. People who spend every day of the week making a fortune and Sundays praying to God do not lend themselves to the comic muse.

A single fact is enough to show that the theater is hardly popular in the United States.

Americans, whose laws authorize freedom and even license of speech in all things, have nonetheless subjected dramatic authors to a sort of censorship. Theatrical performances can only take place when the administrators of the township permit them. This shows well that peoples are like individuals.

*See *DA* I 1.2; II 1.1.

They indulge themselves unsparingly in their principal passions, and then they take good care not to yield too much to the attraction of tastes they do not have.

There is no portion of literature that is linked by stricter and more numerous bonds to the current state of society than the theater.

The theater of one period can never suit the following period if, between the two, an important revolution has changed mores and laws.

One still studies the great writers of another century. But one no longer goes to plays written for another public. Dramatic authors of a time past live only in books.

The traditional taste of some men, vanity, fashion, the genius of an actor can for a time sustain or revive an aristocratic theater within a democracy; but soon it falls by itself. It is not overturned, it is abandoned.

Chapter 20   ON SOME TENDENCIES PARTICULAR TO HISTORIANS IN DEMOCRATIC CENTURIES

Historians who write in aristocratic centuries ordinarily make all events depend on the particular wills and humors of certain men, and they willingly tie the most important revolutions to the least accidents. With sagacity they bring out the smallest causes, and often they do not perceive the greatest.

Historians who live in democratic centuries show altogether contrary tendencies.

Most of them attribute almost no influence to the individual over the destiny of the species or to citizens over the fate of the people. But, in reverse, they give great general causes to all the little particular facts. These opposed tendencies explain themselves.

When historians of aristocratic centuries cast their eyes on the theater of the world, they perceive first of all a very few principal actors who guide the whole play. These great personages, who are kept at the front of the stage, arrest their sight and fix it: while they apply themselves to unveiling the secret motives that make them act and speak, they forget the rest.

The importance of the things they see done by some men gives them an exaggerated idea of the influence that a man can exert and naturally disposes them to believe that one must always go back to the particular action of an individual to explain the movements of the crowd.

When, on the contrary, all citizens are independent of one another, and each of them is weak, one finds none who exert a very great or above all a very lasting power over the mass. At first sight, individuals seem absolutely powerless over it, and one would say that society advances all by itself—by the free and spontaneous concourse of all the men who compose it.

That naturally brings the human mind to search for the general reason that could strike so many intellects at once and turn them simultaneously in the same direction.

I am very convinced that in democratic nations themselves, the genius, the vices, or the virtues of certain individuals slow or hasten the natural course of the destiny of the people; but these sorts of fortuitous and secondary causes are infinitely more varied, more hidden, more complicated, less powerful, and consequently more difficult to unravel and follow in times of equality than in centuries of aristocracy, when it is only a question of analyzing the particular action of a single man or of a few in the midst of the general facts.

The historian is soon fatigued by such work; his mind is lost in the middle of this labyrinth, and, as he is unable to perceive clearly individual influences and bring them sufficiently to light, he denies them. He prefers to speak to us of the nature of races, the physical constitution of the country, or the spirit of the civilization. That shortens his work and, at less cost, satisfies the reader better.

M. de La Fayette said somewhere in his *Mémoires* that the exaggerated system of general causes procures marvelous consolations for mediocre public men.* I add that it gives admirable ones to mediocre historians. It always furnishes them some great reasons that quickly pull them through the most difficult spot in their book and supports the weakness or laziness of their minds, all the while doing honor to their profundity.

As for me, I think that there is no period in which it is not necessary to attribute one part of the events of this world to very general facts and another to very particular influences. These two causes are always met with; only their relationship differs. General facts explain more things in democratic centuries than in aristocratic centuries, and particular influences fewer. In aristocratic times, it is the contrary: particular influences are stronger and

---

*Marquis de Lafayette, *Mémoires, correspondance et manuscrits du général Lafayette* (H. Fournier, 1837–1838), 6 vols. This remark is cited by Sainte-Beuve in his account of Lafayette's *Mémoires* (*Revue des deux mondes*, 4th series, vol. 15, 1838, pp. 355–381), p. 359. Lafayette (1757–1834) was a French military leader and statesman; called "the hero of two worlds," he fought on the side of the colonists in the American Revolution and played a prominent part in the French Revolution.

general causes are weaker, unless one considers as a general cause the very fact of inequality of conditions that permits some individuals to oppose the natural tendencies of all the others.

Historians who seek to depict what happens in democratic societies are therefore right to allow a large part to general causes, and to apply themselves principally to uncovering them; but they are wrong to deny the particular action of individuals entirely because it is not easy to find and follow it.

Not only are historians who live in democratic centuries drawn to assign a great cause to each fact, but they are also brought to link the facts among themselves and make a system issue from them.

In aristocratic centuries, when the attention of historians is diverted to individuals at every moment, the sequence of events eludes them, or rather they do not believe in a sequence like this. The thread of history seems to them broken at each instant by the passage of one man.

In democratic centuries, on the contrary, the historian, who sees the actors much less and the acts much more, can readily establish a relationship and a methodical order among them.

Ancient literature, which left us such beautiful histories, does not offer a single great historical system, whereas the most miserable modern literature swarms with them. It seems that ancient historians did not make enough use of the general theories that ours are always near to abusing.

Those who write in democratic centuries have another, more dangerous tendency.

When any trace of the action of individuals on nations is lost, it often happens that one sees the world moving without discovering its motor. As it becomes very difficult to perceive and analyze the reasons that, acting separately on the will of each citizen, in the end produce the movement of the people, one is tempted to believe that this movement is not voluntary and that, without knowing it, societies obey a superior, dominating force.

Even if one should discover on earth the general fact that directs the particular wills of all individuals, that does not save human freedom. A cause vast enough to be applied to millions of men at once and strong enough to incline all together in the same direction easily seems irresistible; after having seen that one yields to it, one is quite close to believing that one cannot resist it.

Historians who live in democratic times, therefore, not only deny to a few citizens the power to act on the destiny of a people, they also take away from peoples themselves the ability to modify their own fate, and they subject them either to an inflexible providence or to a sort of blind fatality. According to them, each nation is invincibly attached, by its position, its origin, its antecedents, its nature, to a certain destiny that all its efforts cannot change. They render generations interdependent on one another, and thus going back from age to age and from necessary events to necessary events up to the origin of the world, they make a tight and immense chain that envelopes the whole human race and binds it.

It is not enough for them to show how the facts have come about; they also take pleasure in making one see that it could not have happened otherwise. They consider a nation that has reached a certain place in its history and affirm that it was constrained to follow the path that led it there. That is easier than instructing us on how it could have acted to take a better route.

In reading the historians of aristocratic ages and particularly those of antiquity, it seems that to become master of his fate and to govern those like him, a man has only to know how to subdue himself. In running through the histories written in our time, one would say that man can do nothing either about himself or his surroundings. Historians of antiquity instruct on how to command, those of our day teach hardly anything other than how to obey. In their writings, the author often appears great, but humanity is always small.

If this doctrine of fatality, which has so many attractions for those who write history in democratic times, passed from writers to their readers, thus penetrating the entire mass of citizens and taking hold of the public mind, one can foresee that it would soon paralyze the movement of the new societies and reduce Christians to Turks.

I shall say, furthermore, that such a doctrine is particularly dangerous in the period we are in; our contemporaries are only too inclined to doubt free will because each of them feels himself limited on all sides by his weakness, but they still willingly grant force and independence to men united in a social body. One must guard against obscuring this idea, for it is a question of elevating souls and not completing their prostration.

Chapter 21 ON PARLIAMENTARY ELOQUENCE IN THE UNITED STATES

In aristocratic peoples all men are joined and depend on one another; a hierarchical bond exists among all with the aid of which one can keep each in his place and the entire body in obedience. Something analogous is always found within the political assemblies of these peoples. Their parties are naturally arranged under certain chiefs, whom they obey by a sort of instinct that is only the result of habits contracted elsewhere. They bring into a small society the mores of the larger.

In democratic countries, it often happens that a great number of citizens are directed toward the same point; but each advances to it, or at least flatters himself that he advances to it, only by himself. Habituated to regulating his movements only by following his personal impulses, he bows uneasily when receiving regulation from the outside. This taste for and use of independence follow him into the national councils. If he consents to associate with others there for the pursuit of the same design, he at least wants to remain his own master in cooperating for the common success in his own manner.

Hence it is that parties in democratic lands tolerate direction with impatience and only prove to be subordinate when the peril is very great. Still, the authority of chiefs, which in these circumstances can go as far as making them act and speak, almost never extends to the power of making them keep silent.

Among aristocratic peoples, members of political assemblies are at the same time members of the aristocracy.

Each of them possesses an elevated and stable rank by himself, and the place he occupies in the assembly is often less important in his eyes than the one he fills in the country. That consoles him for not playing a role in the discussion of affairs there and disposes him not to search with too much ardor for a mediocre one.

In America it ordinarily happens that the deputy is nothing but for his position in the assembly. He is therefore constantly tormented by the need to acquire importance there, and he feels a petulant desire to put forth his ideas in broad daylight at every moment.

He is driven in this direction not only by his own vanity, but by that of his electors and by the continual necessity of pleasing them.

In aristocratic peoples, the member of the legislature is rarely in a strict dependence on electors; often he is in some fashion a necessary representative for them; sometimes he keeps them in a strict dependence, and if they finally come to refuse him their vote, he easily gets himself named elsewhere; or, renouncing a public career, he withdraws into an idleness that still has splendor.

In a democratic country like the United States, the deputy almost never has a lasting hold on the minds of his electors. However small the electoral body is, democratic instability makes it change its face constantly. He must therefore captivate it every day. He is never sure of them; and if they abandon him, he is immediately without resources; for he does not naturally have a position elevated enough to be perceived easily by those who are not close to him; and in the complete independence in which citizens live, he cannot hope that his friends or the government will easily impose him on an electoral body that does not know him. It is therefore in the district he represents that all the seeds of his fortune are deposited; it is from this corner of earth that he must go out to raise himself to command the people and influence the destinies of the world.

Thus it is natural that in democratic countries the members of political assemblies think more of their electors than of their party, while in aristocracies they are occupied more with their party than with their electors.

Now, what one must say to please electors is not always the fit thing to do to serve well the political opinion that they profess.

The general interest of a party is often that the deputy who is a member of it never speak of great affairs that he understands badly; that he speak little of the small ones by which the advance of the great ones would be hampered, and finally, that he most often be entirely silent. To keep silent is the most useful service that a mediocre talker can render to the public.

But electors do not understand it this way.

The population of a district charges a citizen with taking part in the government of the state because it has conceived a very vast idea of his merit. Since men appear greater in proportion as they are surrounded by smaller objects, one may believe that the opinion held of the agent will be higher as talents are rarer among those he represents. It will therefore often happen that electors hope all the more from their deputy as they have less to expect from him; and however incapable he may be, they cannot fail to require outstanding efforts from him corresponding to the rank they give him.

In addition to legislator of the state, electors also see in their representative the natural protector of the district before the legislature; they are not even far from considering him as the proxy of each of those who elected him, and they flatter themselves that he will use no less ardor to put forward their particular interests than the country's.

Thus the electors consider themselves assured in advance that the deputy they choose will be an orator; that he will speak often if he can, and that in case he must refrain, he will at least strive to include in his rare discourses an examination of all the great affairs of state joined to an exposition of all the little grievances they themselves have to complain of, in such fashion that, while unable to show himself often, on each occasion he will display what he knows how to do, and instead of being endlessly profuse, from time to time he will compress himself as a whole into a small volume, thus furnishing a sort of brilliant and complete summation of his constituents and himself. At this price they promise their next vote.

This drives to despair honest mediocrities who, knowing themselves, would not have come forth on their own. The deputy, thus incited, takes the floor to the great chagrin of his friends, and imprudently projecting himself into the midst of the most celebrated orators, he muddles the debate and tires the assembly.

All laws that tend to render the elected more dependent on the elector therefore modify not only the conduct of legislators, as I have pointed out elsewhere,* but their language as well. They influence affairs and the manner of speaking about them at the same time.

There is so to speak no member of Congress who consents to go back home without having at least one speech preceding him there, or who suffers being interrupted before having been able to include within the limits of his harangue all that one can say of use to the twenty-four states of which the Union is composed, and especially to the district he represents. He therefore parades successively before the minds of his listeners great general truths that he himself often does not perceive and that he indicates only confusedly, and very slender little particulars that he does not have much facility for uncovering and setting forth. Thus it very often happens that discussion becomes vague and embarrassed within this great body, and it seems to drag itself toward the goal proposed rather than march to it.

Something analogous will, I think, always be displayed in the public assemblies of democracies.

Fortunate circumstances and good laws could succeed in attracting much more remarkable men to the legislature of a democratic people than those who are sent by the Americans to Congress; but one will never prevent the mediocre men who are there from exhibiting themselves complacently on all sides in broad daylight.

The evil does not appear to me entirely curable, because it is due not only to the regulation of the assembly, but to its constitution and even to that of the country.

The inhabitants of the United States themselves seem to consider the thing from this point of view, and they bear witness to their long practice of parliamentary life not in abstaining from bad speeches, but in courageously submitting to hearing them. They resign themselves as to an evil that experience has made them recognize as inevitable.

We have shown the petty side of political discussions in democracies; let us bring out the great.

For one hundred fifty years what has happened in the Parliament of England has never had great repercussions outside; the ideas and sentiments expressed by the orators have always found little sympathy in the very peoples

*DA I 1.8.

who were placed nearest to the great theater of British freedom, whereas from the first debates that took place in the little colonial assemblies of America in the period of the Revolution, Europe was moved.

That was due not only to particular and fortuitous circumstances, but to general and lasting causes.

I see nothing more admirable or more powerful than a great orator discussing great affairs within a democratic assembly. As there is never a class that has charged its representatives with asserting its interests, it is always to the whole nation in the name of the whole nation that one speaks. That enlarges thought and elevates language.

As precedents have little dominion; as there are no longer privileges attached to certain goods, nor rights inherent in certain bodies or certain men, the mind is obliged to go back to general verities drawn from human nature in order to treat the particular affair that occupies it. Hence in the political discussions of a democratic people, however small it is, a character of generality arises that often makes them attractive to the human race. All men are interested in them because it is a question of man, who is the same everywhere.

In the greatest aristocratic peoples, on the contrary, the most general questions are almost always treated with some particular reasons derived from the usages of a period or the rights of a class, which interests only the class in question or at the very most the people within whom this class is found.

It is to this cause as much as to the greatness of the French nation and to the favorable dispositions of the people who listen to it that one must attribute the great effect that our political discussions sometimes produce in the world.

Our orators often speak to all men even when they are only addressing their fellow citizens.

PART TWO

Influence of
Democracy on
the Sentiments
of the Americans

Chapter 1 WHY DEMOCRATIC PEOPLES SHOW A MORE ARDENT AND MORE LASTING LOVE FOR EQUALITY THAN FOR FREEDOM

The first and most lively of the passions to which equality of conditions gives birth, I have no need to say, is the love of this same equality. One will therefore not be astonished if I speak of that before all the others.

Everyone has remarked that in our time, and especially in France, this passion for equality holds a greater place in the human heart each day. It has been said a hundred times that our contemporaries have a much more ardent and tenacious love for equality than for freedom, but I do not find that anyone has yet gone back sufficiently to the causes of this fact. I am going to try.

One can imagine an extreme point at which freedom and equality touch each other and intermingle.

Let me suppose that all citizens concur in the government and that each has an equal right to concur in it.

Then with none differing from those like him, no one will be able to exercise a tyrannical power; men will be perfectly free because they will all be entirely equal; and they will all be perfectly equal because they will be entirely free. This is the ideal toward which democratic peoples tend.

That is the most complete form that equality can take on earth; but there are a thousand others, not as perfect, that are scarcely less dear to these peoples.

Equality can be established in civil society and not reign in the political world. One can have the right to indulge in the same pleasures, to enter the same professions, to meet in the same places; in a word, to live in the same manner and pursue wealth by the same means, without having all take the same part in government.

A sort of equality can even be established in the political world although there may be no political freedom. One might be equal to all those like him except the one who is, without any distinction, the master of all and who picks the agents of his power equally from among all.

It would be easy to make several other hypotheses by which a very great quantity [of equality] could easily be combined with more or less free institutions or even with institutions that were not free at all.

Although men cannot become absolutely equal without being entirely free, and consequently equality in its most extreme degree becomes confused with freedom, yet there is a foundation for distinguishing one from the other.

The taste that men have for freedom and the one they feel for equality are in fact two distinct things, and I do not fear to add that among democratic peoples they are two unequal things.

If one wishes to pay attention to it, one will see that in each century one encounters a singular and dominating fact to which all the others are connected; this fact almost always gives rise to a mother idea, or a principal passion, that in the end attracts and carries along in its course all sentiments and all ideas. It is like a great river toward which each of the surrounding streams seems to run.

Freedom has manifested itself to men in different times and in different forms; it is not attached exclusively to one social state, and one encounters it elsewhere than in democracies. It therefore cannot form the distinctive characteristic of democratic centuries.

The particular and dominating fact that makes those centuries unique is equality of conditions; the principal passion that agitates men in those times is the love of this equality.

Do not ask what unique charm men in democratic ages find in living as equals, or the particular reasons that they can have for being so obstinately attached to equality rather than to the other goods that society presents to them: equality forms the distinctive characteristic of the period they live in; that alone is enough to explain why they prefer it to all the rest.

But independent of this reason, there are several others that will usually bring men in all times to prefer equality to freedom.

If a people could ever succeed by itself in destroying or even diminishing the equality that reigned within it, it would arrive at that only by long and painful efforts. It would have to modify its social state, abolish its laws, renew its ideas, change its habits, alter its mores. But to lose political freedom, it is enough not to hold on to it, and it escapes.

Men, therefore, do not hold to equality only because it is dear to them; they are also attached to it because they believe that it will last forever.

Political freedom in its excesses is able to compromise the tranquillity, the patrimony, the lives of particular persons—and one encounters no men so limited and so flighty as not to realize this. On the contrary, only attentive and clairvoyant people perceive the perils with which equality threatens us, and ordinarily they avoid pointing them out. They know that the miseries they fear are remote, and flatter themselves that they will overtake only generations to come, which the present generation scarcely worries about. The evils that freedom brings are sometimes immediate; they are visible to all, and all more or less feel them. The evils that extreme equality can produce become manifest only little by little; they insinuate themselves gradually into the social body; one sees them only now and then, and at the moment when they have become most violent, habit has already made them no longer felt.

The goods that freedom brings show themselves only in the long term, and it is always easy to fail to recognize the cause that gives birth to them.

The advantages of equality make themselves felt from now on, and each day one sees them flow from their source.

From time to time political freedom gives a certain number of citizens sublime pleasures.

Equality furnishes a multitude of little enjoyments daily to each man. The charms of equality are felt at all moments, and they are within reach of all; the noblest hearts are not insensitive to them, and the most vulgar souls get their delights from them. The passion to which equality gives birth will therefore be both energetic and general.

Men cannot enjoy political freedom unless they purchase it with some sacrifices, and they never get possession of it except with many efforts. But the pleasures brought by equality offer themselves. Each little incident of private life seems to give birth to them, and to taste them, one needs only to be alive.

Democratic peoples love equality at all times, but in certain periods, they press the passion they feel for it to delirium. This happens at the moment when the old social hierarchy, long threatened, is finally destroyed after a last internecine struggle, and the barriers that separated citizens are finally overturned. Then men rush at equality as at a conquest, and they become attached to it as to a precious good someone wants to rob them of. The passion for equality penetrates all parts of the human heart; there it spreads, and fills it entirely. Do not say to men that in giving themselves over so blindly to an exclusive passion, they compromise their dearest interests; they are deaf. Do not show them that freedom escapes from their hands while they are looking elsewhere; they are blind, or rather they perceive only one good in the whole universe worth longing for.

What precedes applies to all democratic nations. What follows regards only us.

In most modern nations and in particular in all the peoples of the continent of Europe, the taste for and idea of freedom began to arise and to develop only at the moment when conditions began to be equalized and as a consequence of that very equality. It was the absolute kings who worked the most at leveling the ranks among their subjects. In these peoples, equality preceded freedom; equality was therefore an old fact when freedom was still a new thing; the one had already created opinions, usages, laws proper to it when the other was produced alone and for the first time in broad daylight.

Thus the latter existed still only in ideas and tastes, whereas the former had already penetrated habits, taken hold of mores, and given a particular turn to the least acts of life. How be astonished if men of our day prefer the one to the other?

I think that democratic peoples have a natural taste for freedom; left to themselves they seek it, they love it, and they will see themselves parted from it only with sorrow. But for equality they have an ardent, insatiable, eternal, invincible passion; they want equality in freedom, and, if they cannot get it, they still want it in slavery. They will tolerate poverty, enslavement, barbarism, but they will not tolerate aristocracy.

This is true in all times, and above all in ours. All men and all powers that wish to struggle against this irresistible power will be overturned and destroyed by it. In our day freedom cannot be established without its support, and despotism itself cannot reign without it.

Chapter 2 ON INDIVIDUALISM IN DEMOCRATIC COUNTRIES

I have brought out how, in centuries of equality, each man seeks his beliefs in himself;* I want to show how, in the same centuries, he turns all his sentiments toward himself alone.

Individualism is a recent expression† arising from a new idea. Our fathers knew only selfishness.

Selfishness is a passionate and exaggerated love of self that brings man to relate everything to himself alone and to prefer himself to everything.

Individualism is a reflective and peaceable sentiment that disposes each citizen to isolate himself from the mass of those like him and to withdraw to one side with his family and his friends, so that after having thus created a little society for his own use, he willingly abandons society at large to itself.

Selfishness is born of a blind instinct; individualism proceeds from an erroneous judgment rather than a depraved sentiment. It has its source in the defects of the mind as much as in the vices of the heart.

---

*DA II 1.1.

†This is the first occurrence in *DA* of the word "individualism," a new word not coined by AT, but defined and developed by him. See Schleifer, *The Making of Tocqueville's "Democracy in America,"* 251–259.

Selfishness withers the seed of all the virtues; individualism at first dries up only the source of public virtues; but in the long term it attacks and destroys all the others and will finally be absorbed in selfishness.

Selfishness is a vice as old as the world. It scarcely belongs more to one form of society than to another.

Individualism is of democratic origin, and it threatens to develop as conditions become equal.

In aristocratic peoples, families remain in the same state for centuries, and often in the same place. That renders all generations so to speak contemporaries. A man almost always knows his ancestors and respects them; he believes he already perceives his great-grandsons and he loves them. He willingly does his duty by both, and he frequently comes to sacrifice his personal enjoyments for beings who no longer exist or who do not yet exist.

In addition, aristocratic institutions have the effect of binding each man tightly to several of his fellow citizens.

Classes being very distinct and immobile within an aristocratic people, each of them becomes for whoever makes up a part of it a sort of little native country, more visible and dearer than the big one.

As in aristocratic societies all citizens are placed at a fixed post, some above the others, it results also that each of them always perceives higher than himself a man whose protection is necessary to him, and below he finds another whom he can call upon for cooperation.

Men who live in aristocratic centuries are therefore almost always bound in a tight manner to something that is placed outside of them, and they are often disposed to forget themselves. It is true that in these same centuries the general notion of *those like oneself* is obscure and that one scarcely thinks of devoting oneself to the cause of humanity; but one often sacrifices oneself for certain men.

In democratic centuries, on the contrary, when the duties of each individual toward the species are much clearer, devotion toward one man becomes rarer: the bond of human affections is extended and loosened.

In democratic peoples, new families constantly issue from nothing, others constantly fall into it, and all those who stay on change face; the fabric of time is torn at every moment and the trace of generations is effaced. You easily forget those who have preceded you, and you have no idea of those who will follow you. Only those nearest have interest.

As each class comes closer to the others and mixes with them, its members become indifferent and almost like strangers among themselves. Aristocracy had made of all citizens a long chain that went from the peasant up to the king; democracy breaks the chain and sets each link apart.

As conditions are equalized, one finds a great number of individuals who, not being wealthy enough or powerful enough to exert a great influence over the fates of those like them, have nevertheless acquired or preserved enough enlightenment and goods to be able to be self-sufficient. These owe nothing to anyone, they expect so to speak nothing from anyone; they are in the habit of always considering themselves in isolation, and they willingly fancy that their whole destiny is in their hands.

Thus not only does democracy make each man forget his ancestors, but it hides his descendants from him and separates him from his contemporaries; it constantly leads him back toward himself alone and threatens finally to confine him wholly in the solitude of his own heart.

Chapter 3 HOW INDIVIDUALISM IS GREATER AT THE END OF A DEMOCRATIC REVOLUTION THAN IN ANY OTHER PERIOD

It is above all at the moment when a democratic society succeeds in forming itself on the debris of an aristocracy that this isolation of men from one another and the selfishness resulting from it strike one's regard most readily.

These societies not only contain many independent citizens, they are filled daily with men who, having arrived at independence yesterday, are drunk with their new power: these conceive a presumptuous confidence in their strength, and not imagining that from now on they could need to call upon the assistance of those like them, they have no difficulty in showing that they think only of themselves.

An aristocracy ordinarily succumbs only after a prolonged struggle, during which implacable hatreds among the different classes are ignited. These passions survive victory, and one can follow their track in the midst of the democratic confusion that succeeds it.

Those among the citizens who were the first in the hierarchy that has been destroyed cannot immediately forget their former greatness; for a long time they consider themselves strangers within the new society. They see all the equals that this society gives them as oppressors whose destiny cannot excite their sympathy; they have lost sight of their former equals and no longer feel bound by a common interest to their fates; each, in withdrawing separately, therefore believes himself reduced to being occupied only with himself. Those, on the contrary, who were formerly placed at the bottom of the social scale, and whom a sudden revolution has brought to the common level, enjoy their newly acquired independence only with a sort of secret restiveness; if they find some of their former superiors at their side, they cast looks of triumph and fear at them, and draw apart from them.

It is, therefore, ordinarily at the origin of democratic societies that citizens show themselves the most disposed to isolate themselves.

Democracy inclines men not to get close to those like themselves; but democratic revolutions dispose them to flee each other and to perpetuate in the heart of equality the hatreds to which inequality gave birth.

The great advantage of the Americans is to have arrived at democracy without having to suffer democratic revolutions, and to be born equal instead of becoming so.

Chapter 4 HOW THE AMERICANS COMBAT INDIVIDUALISM WITH FREE INSTITUTIONS

Despotism, which in its nature is fearful, sees the most certain guarantee of its own duration in the isolation of men, and it ordinarily puts all its care into isolating them. There is no vice of the human heart that agrees with it as much as selfishness: a despot readily pardons the governed for not loving him, provided that they do not love each other. He does not ask them to aid him in leading the state; it is enough that they do not aspire to direct it themselves. He calls those who aspire to unite their efforts to create common prosperity turbulent and restive spirits, and changing the natural sense of words, he names those who confine themselves narrowly to themselves good citizens.

Thus the vices to which despotism gives birth are precisely those that equality favors. These two things complement and aid each other in a fatal manner.

Equality places men beside one another without a common bond to hold them. Despotism raises barriers between them and separates them. Equality disposes them not to think of those like themselves, and for them despotism makes a sort of public virtue of indifference.

Despotism, which is dangerous in all times, is therefore particularly to be feared in democratic centuries.

It is easy to see that in these same centuries men have a particular need of freedom.

When citizens are forced to be occupied with public affairs, they are necessarily drawn from the midst of their individual interests, and from time to time, torn away from the sight of themselves.

From the moment when common affairs are treated in common, each man perceives that he is not as independent of those like him as he at first fancied, and that to obtain their support he must often lend them his cooperation.

When the public governs, there is no man who does not feel the value of public benevolence and who does not seek to capture it by attracting the esteem and affection of those in the midst of whom he must live.

Several of the passions that chill and divide hearts are then obliged to withdraw to the bottom of the soul and hide there. Haughtiness dissimulates; contempt does not dare come to light. Selfishness is afraid of itself.

Under a free government, since most public functions are elective, men who by the loftiness of their souls or the restiveness of their desires are cramped in private life, feel every day that they cannot do without the populace surrounding them.

It then happens that through ambition one thinks of those like oneself, and that often one's interest is in a way found in forgetting oneself. I know that one can object to me here with all the intrigues that arise in an election, the shameful means the candidates often make use of, and the calumnies their enemies spread. These are occasions for hatred, and they present themselves all the more often as elections become more frequent.

These evils are undoubtedly great, but they are passing, whereas the goods that arise with them stay.

The longing to be elected can momentarily bring certain men to make war on each other, but in the long term this same desire brings all men to lend each other a mutual support; and if it happens that an election accidentally divides two friends, the electoral system brings together in a permanent manner a multitude of citizens who would have always remained strangers to one another. Freedom creates particular hatreds, but despotism gives birth to general indifference.

The Americans have combated the individualism to which equality gives birth with freedom, and they have defeated it.

The legislators of America did not believe that, to cure a malady so natural to the social body in democratic times and so fatal, it was enough to accord to the nation as a whole a representation of itself; they thought that, in addition, it was fitting to give political life to each portion of the territory in order to multiply infinitely the occasions for citizens to act together and to make them feel every day that they depend on one another.

This was wisely done.

The general affairs of a country occupy only the principal citizens. They assemble in the same places only from time to time; and as it often happens that afterwards they lose sight of each other, lasting bonds among them are not established. But when it is a question of having the particular affairs of a district regulated by the men who inhabit it, the same individuals are always in contact and they are in a way forced to know each other and to be pleasing to each other.

Only with difficulty does one draw a man out of himself to interest him in the destiny of the whole state, because he understands poorly the influence that the destiny of the state can exert on his lot. But should it be necessary to pass a road through his property, he will see at first glance that he has come across a relation between this small public affair and his greatest private affairs, and he will discover, without anyone's showing it to him, the tight bond that here unites a particular interest to the general interest.

Thus by charging citizens with the administration of small affairs, much more than by leaving the government of great ones to them, one interests them in the public good and makes them see the need they constantly have for one another in order to produce it.

One can capture the favor of a people all at once by a striking action; but to win the love and respect of the populace that surrounds you, you must have a long succession of little services rendered, obscure good offices, a constant habit of benevolence, and a well-established reputation of disinterestedness.

Local freedoms, which make many citizens put value on the affection of their neighbors and those close to them, therefore constantly bring men closer to one another, despite the instincts that separate them, and force them to aid each other.

In the United States, the most opulent citizens take much care not to isolate themselves from the people; on the contrary, they constantly come close to them, they gladly listen to them and speak to them every day. They know that the rich in democracies always need the poor, and that in democratic times one ties the poor to oneself more by manners than by benefits. The very greatness of the benefits, which brings to light the difference in conditions, causes a secret irritation to those who profit from them; but simplicity of manners has almost irresistible charms: their familiarity carries one away and even their coarseness does not always displease.

At first this truth does not penetrate the minds of the rich. They ordinarily resist it as long as the democratic revolution lasts, and they do not accept it immediately even after this revolution is accomplished. They willingly consent to do good for the people, but they want to continue to hold them carefully at a distance. They believe that is enough; they are mistaken. They would thus ruin themselves without warming the hearts of the population that surrounds them. It does not ask of them the sacrifice of their money, but of their haughtiness.

One would say that in the United States there is no imagination that does not exhaust itself in inventing the means of increasing wealth and satisfying the needs of the public. The most enlightened inhabitants of each district constantly make use of their enlightenment to discover new secrets appropriate to increasing the common prosperity; and when they have found any, they hasten to pass them along to the crowd.

When examining up close the vices and weakness often displayed in America by those who govern, one is astonished at the growing prosperity of the people—and one is wrong. It is not the elected magistrate who makes American democracy prosper; but it prospers because the magistrate is elective.

It would be unjust to believe that the patriotism of the Americans and the zeal that each of them shows for the well-being of his fellow citizens have nothing real about them. Although private interest directs most human actions, in the United States as elsewhere, it does not rule all.

I must say that I often saw Americans make great and genuine sacrifices for the public, and I remarked a hundred times that, when needed, they almost never fail to lend faithful support to one another.

The free institutions that the inhabitants of the United States possess and the political rights of which they make so much use recall to each citizen constantly and in a thousand ways that he lives in society. At every moment they bring his mind back toward the idea that the duty as well as the interest of men is to render themselves useful to those like them; and as he does not see any particular reason to hate them, since he is never either their slave or their master, his heart readily leans to the side of benevolence. One is occupied with the general interest at first by necessity and then by choice; what was calculation becomes instinct; and by dint of working for the good of one's fellow citizens, one finally picks up the habit and taste of serving them.

Many people in France consider equality of conditions as the first evil and political freedom as the second. When they are obliged to submit to the one, they strive at least to escape the other. And I say that to combat the evils that equality can produce there is only one efficacious remedy: it is political freedom.

Chapter 5 ON THE USE THAT THE
AMERICANS MAKE OF ASSOCIATION
IN CIVIL LIFE

I do not wish to speak of those political associations with the aid of which men seek to defend themselves against the despotic action of a majority or against the encroachments of royal power. I have already treated this subject elsewhere.* It is clear that if each citizen, as he becomes individually weaker and consequently more incapable in isolation of preserving his freedom, does not learn the art of uniting with those like him to defend it, tyranny will necessarily grow with equality.

Here it is a question only of the associations that are formed in civil life and which have an object that is in no way political.

The political associations that exist in the United States form only a detail in the midst of the immense picture that the sum of associations presents there.

Americans of all ages, all conditions, all minds constantly unite. Not only do they have commercial and industrial associations in which all take part, but they also have a thousand other kinds: religious, moral, grave, futile, very general and very particular, immense and very small; Americans use associations to give fêtes, to found seminaries, to build inns, to raise churches, to distribute books, to send missionaries to the antipodes; in this manner they create hospitals, prisons, schools. Finally, if it is a question of bringing to light a truth or developing a sentiment with the support of a great example, they associate. Everywhere that, at the head of a new undertaking, you see the government in France and a great lord in England, count on it that you will perceive an association in the United States.

In America I encountered sorts of associations of which, I confess, I had no idea, and I often admired the infinite art with which the inhabitants of the United States managed to fix a common goal to the efforts of many men and to get them to advance to it freely.

I have since traveled through England,† from which the Americans took some of their laws and many of their usages, and it appeared to me that there they were very far from making as constant and as skilled a use of association.

*DA I 2.4, 2.6.
†AT visited England in 1833 and 1835; see his *Journeys to England and Ireland*, J. P. Mayer, ed. (Garden City, N.Y.: Anchor Books [Doubleday], 1968).

It often happens that the English execute very great things in isolation, whereas there is scarcely an undertaking so small that Americans do not unite for it. It is evident that the former consider association as a powerful means of action; but the latter seem to see in it the sole means they have of acting.

Thus the most democratic country on earth is found to be, above all, the one where men in our day have most perfected the art of pursuing the object of their common desires in common and have applied this new science to the most objects. Does this result from an accident or could it be that there in fact exists a necessary relation between associations and equality?

Aristocratic societies always include within them, in the midst of a multitude of individuals who can do nothing by themselves, a few very powerful and very wealthy citizens; each of these can execute great undertakings by himself.

In aristocratic societies men have no need to unite to act because they are kept very much together.

Each wealthy and powerful citizen in them forms as it were the head of a permanent and obligatory association that is composed of all those he holds in dependence to him, whom he makes cooperate in the execution of his designs.

In democratic peoples, on the contrary, all citizens are independent and weak; they can do almost nothing by themselves, and none of them can oblige those like themselves to lend them their cooperation. They therefore all fall into impotence if they do not learn to aid each other freely.

If men who live in democratic countries had neither the right nor the taste to unite in political goals, their independence would run great risks, but they could preserve their wealth and their enlightenment for a long time; whereas if they did not acquire the practice of associating with each other in ordinary life, civilization itself would be in peril. A people among whom particular persons lost the power of doing great things in isolation, without acquiring the ability to produce them in common, would soon return to barbarism.

Unhappily, the same social state that renders associations so necessary to democratic peoples renders them more difficult for them than for all others.

When several members of an aristocracy want to associate with each other they easily succeed in doing so. As each of them brings great force to society, the number of members can be very few, and, when the members are few in number, it is very easy for them to know each other, to understand each other, and to establish fixed rules.

The same facility is not found in democratic nations, where it is always necessary that those associating be very numerous in order that the association have some power.

I know that there are many of my contemporaries whom this does not embarrass. They judge that as citizens become weaker and more incapable, it is necessary to render the government more skillful and more active in order that society be able to execute what individuals can no longer do. They believe they have answered everything in saying that. But I think they are mistaken.

A government could take the place of some of the greatest American associations, and within the Union several particular states already have attempted it. But what political power would ever be in a state to suffice for the innumerable multitude of small undertakings that American citizens execute every day with the aid of an association?

It is easy to foresee that the time is approaching when a man by himself alone will be less and less in a state to produce the things that are the most common and the most necessary to his life. The task of the social power will therefore constantly increase, and its very efforts will make it vaster each day. The more it puts itself in place of associations, the more particular persons, losing the idea of associating with each other, will need it to come to their aid: these are causes and effects that generate each other without rest. Will the public administration in the end direct all the industries for which an isolated citizen cannot suffice? and if there finally comes a moment when, as a consequence of the extreme division of landed property, the land is partitioned infinitely, so that it can no longer be cultivated except by associations of laborers, will the head of the government have to leave the helm of state to come hold the plow?

The morality and intelligence of a democratic people would risk no fewer dangers than its business and its industry if the government came to take the place of associations everywhere.

Sentiments and ideas renew themselves, the heart is enlarged, and the human mind is developed only by the reciprocal action of men upon one another.

I have shown that this action is almost nonexistent in a democratic country. It is therefore necessary to create it artificially there. And this is what associations alone can do.

When the members of an aristocracy adopt a new idea or conceive a novel sentiment, they place it in a way next to themselves on the great stage they are on, and in thus exposing it to the view of the crowd, they easily introduce it into the minds or hearts of all those who surround them.

In democratic countries, only the social power is naturally in a state to act like this, but it is easy to see that its action is always insufficient and often dangerous.

A government can no more suffice on its own to maintain and renew the circulation of sentiments and ideas in a great people than to conduct all its industrial undertakings. As soon as it tries to leave the political sphere to project itself on this new track, it will exercise an insupportable tyranny even without wishing to; for a government knows only how to dictate precise rules; it imposes the sentiments and the ideas that it favors, and it is always hard to distinguish its counsels from its orders.

This will be still worse if it believes itself really interested in having nothing stir. It will then hold itself motionless and let itself be numbed by a voluntary somnolence.

It is therefore necessary that it not act alone.

In democratic peoples, associations must take the place of the powerful particular persons whom equality of conditions has made disappear.

As soon as several of the inhabitants of the United States have conceived a sentiment or an idea that they want to produce in the world, they seek each other out; and when they have found each other, they unite. From then on, they are no longer isolated men, but a power one sees from afar, whose actions serve as an example; a power that speaks, and to which one listens.

The first time I heard it said in the United States that a hundred thousand men publicly engaged not to make use of strong liquors, the thing appeared to me more amusing than serious, and at first I did not see well why such temperate citizens were not content to drink water within their families.

In the end I understood that those hundred thousand Americans, frightened by the progress that drunkenness was making around them, wanted to provide their patronage to sobriety. They had acted precisely like a great lord who would dress himself very plainly in order to inspire the scorn of luxury in simple citizens. It is to be believed that if those hundred thousand men had lived in France, each of them would have addressed himself individually to the government, begging it to oversee the cabarets all over the realm.

There is nothing, according to me, that deserves more to attract our regard than the intellectual and moral associations of America. We easily perceive the political and industrial associations of the Americans, but the others escape us; and if we discover them, we understand them badly because we have almost never seen anything analogous. One ought however to recognize that they are as necessary as the first to the American people, and perhaps more so.

In democratic countries the science of association is the mother science; the progress of all the others depends on the progress of that one.

Among the laws that rule human societies there is one that seems more precise and clearer than all the others. In order that men remain civilized or become so, the art of associating must be developed and perfected among them in the same ratio as equality of conditions increases.

Chapter 6 ON THE RELATION BETWEEN ASSOCIATIONS AND NEWSPAPERS

When men are no longer bound among themselves in a solid and permanent manner, one cannot get many to act in common except by persuading each of them whose cooperation is necessary that his particular interest obliges him voluntarily to unite his efforts with the efforts of all the others.

That can be done habitually and conveniently only with the aid of a newspaper; only a newspaper can come to deposit the same thought in a thousand minds at the same moment.

A newspaper is a counselor that one does not need to go seek, but that presents itself of its own accord and that speaks to you briefly each day and of common affairs without disturbing your particular affairs.

Newspapers therefore become more necessary as men are more equal and individualism more to be feared. It would diminish their importance to believe that they serve only to guarantee freedom; they maintain civilization.

I shall not deny that in democratic countries newspapers often bring citizens to make very inconsiderate undertakings in common; but if there were no newspapers, there would almost never be common action. The ill they produce is therefore much less than the one they cure.

A newspaper not only has the effect of suggesting the same design to many men; it furnishes them the means of executing in common the designs they themselves had already conceived.

The principal citizens who live in an aristocratic country perceive each other from afar; and if they want to unite their forces, they move toward one another carrying along a multitude in their train.

It often happens in democratic countries, on the contrary, that many men who have the desire or the need to associate cannot do it, because all being very small and lost in the crowd, they do not see each other and do not know where to find each other. Up comes a newspaper that exposes to their view the sentiment or the idea that had been presented to each of them simultaneously but separately. All are immediately directed toward that light, and those wandering spirits who had long sought each other in the shadows finally meet each other and unite.

The newspaper has brought them nearer, and it continues to be necessary to them to keep them together.

In order that an association in a democratic people have some power, it must be numerous. Those who compose it are therefore dispersed over a great space, and each of them is kept in the place he inhabits by the mediocrity of his fortune and by the multitude of little cares that it requires. They must find a means of speaking to each other every day without seeing each other and of moving in accord without being united. Thus there is scarcely a democratic association that can do without a newspaper.

There exists, therefore, a necessary relation between associations and newspapers: newspapers make associations, and associations make newspapers; and if it was true to say that associations must be multiplied as conditions are equalized, it is no less certain that the number of newspapers must be increased as associations are multiplied.

Thus in America one encounters at once more associations and more newspapers than any other country in the world.

This relation between the number of newspapers and that of associations leads us to uncover another one between the state of the periodical press and the form of the administration of the country, and tells us that the number of newspapers will diminish or grow in a democratic people in proportion as administrative centralization is greater or less. For in democratic peoples, one cannot entrust the exercise of local powers to the principal citizens as in aristocracies. One must abolish these powers or hand over the use of them to a very great number of men. These then form a genuine association established by law in a permanent manner to administer a portion of territory, and they need a newspaper to come to find them each day in the midst of their small affairs and tell them the state of public affairs. The more numerous these local powers are, the greater the number of those that the law calls to exercise them, and, as this necessity is felt at every moment, the more newspapers proliferate.

It is the extraordinary fragmentation of administrative power, much more than the great political freedom and absolute independence of the press, that so singularly multiplies the number of newspapers in America. If all the inhabitants of the Union were electors under the dominion of a system that limited their electoral right to the choice of the legislators of the state,* they would need only a few newspapers because they would have only some very important, but very rare, occasions to act together; but inside the great national association, the law has established in each province, in each city, and so to speak in each village, small associations having local administration as an object. The legislator has in this manner forced each American to cooperate daily with some of his fellow citizens in a common work, and each of them must have a newspaper to tell him what the others are doing.

*That is, the federal government.

I think that a democratic people[1] that did not have any national representation, but many small local powers, would in the end possess more newspapers than another in which a centralized administration existed next to an elective legislature. What best explains to me the prodigious development that the daily press has enjoyed in the United States is that among the Americans I see the greatest national freedom combined with local freedoms of every kind.

In France and England it is generally believed that to increase newspapers indefinitely, it is enough to abolish the taxes that weigh on the press. This is to exaggerate greatly the effects of a reform like this. Newspapers multiply not only relative to their cheapness, but relative to the more or less repeated need of many men to communicate together and to act in common.

I would equally attribute the growing power of newspapers to more general reasons than those often used to explain it.

A newspaper can only exist on condition that it reproduce a doctrine or a sentiment common to many men. A newspaper therefore always represents an association of which its habitual readers are the members.

That association can be more or less defined, more or less narrow, more or less numerous, but at least the seed of it exists in minds, by which alone the newspaper does not die.

This leads us to a final reflection that will end this chapter.

The more conditions become equal, and the less men are individually strong, the more they easily let themselves go with the current of the crowd and have trouble holding alone an opinion that it has abandoned.

The newspaper represents the association; one can say that it speaks to each of its readers in the name of all the others, and it carries them along the more easily as individuals are weaker.

The empire of newspapers should therefore grow as men become equal.

---

1. I say a *democratic people.* Administration can be very decentralized in an aristocratic people without making the need for newspapers felt, because local powers are then in the hands of a very few men who act in isolation or who know each other and can easily see each other and agree.

Chapter 7 RELATIONS BETWEEN CIVIL ASSOCIATIONS AND POLITICAL ASSOCIATIONS

There is only one nation on earth where the unlimited freedom to associate for political views is used daily. That same nation is the only one in the world whose citizens have imagined making a continuous use of the right of association in civil life, and have come in this manner to procure for themselves all the goods that civilization can offer.

Among all the peoples where political association is prohibited, civil association is rare.

It is hardly probable that this is the result of an accident; and one ought rather to conclude that a natural and perhaps necessary relation exists between these two types of association.

By chance, some men have a common interest in a certain affair. It is a question of a commercial undertaking to direct, of an industrial operation to conclude; they meet each other and unite; in this manner they familiarize themselves little by little with association.

The more the number of these small common affairs increases, the more do men, even without their knowing it, acquire the ability to pursue great ones in common.

Civil associations therefore facilitate political associations; but, on the other hand, political association singularly develops and perfects civil association.

In civil life, each man can, if he must, fancy that he is in a state of self-sufficiency. In politics he can never imagine it. When a people has a public life, the idea of association and the desire to associate with each other are therefore presented daily to the minds of all citizens: whatever natural repugnance men have for acting in common, they will always be ready to do it in the interest of a party.

Thus politics generalizes the taste for and habit of association; it makes a crowd of men who would otherwise have lived alone desire to unite, and teaches the art of doing it.

Politics not only gives birth to many associations, it creates vast associations.

In civil life it is rare that the same interest naturally attracts many men toward a common action. Only with much art can one come to create [an interest] like this.

In politics, the occasion offers itself at every moment. For it is only in large associations that the general worth of associations is manifest. Individually weak citizens do not get in advance a clear idea of the force they can acquire in uniting; for them to understand it, one must show it to them. Hence it is that it is often easier to assemble a multitude for a common goal than a few men; a thousand citizens cannot see the interest they have in uniting; ten thousand perceive it. In politics, men unite for great undertakings, and the advantage they derive from association in important affairs teaches them in a practical manner the interest they have in aiding each other in lesser ones.

A political association draws a multitude of individuals outside themselves at the same time; however separated they are naturally by age, mind, fortune, it brings them together and puts them in contact. They meet each other once and learn to find each other always.

One can be engaged in most civil associations only by risking a portion of one's patrimony; so it is for all industrial and commercial companies. When men are still little versed in the art of associating and they are ignorant of the principal rules, they dread, in associating in this manner for the first time, paying dearly for the experience. Therefore they would rather be deprived of a powerful means of success than risk the dangers that accompany it. But they hesitate less to take part in political associations, which appear to them to be without peril, because in them they do not risk their money. Now, they cannot take part in those associations for a long time without discovering how to maintain order among a great number of men and with what procedure one succeeds in getting them to advance in accord and methodically toward the same goal. They learn to submit their will to that of all the others and to subordinate their particular efforts to the common action—all things it is no less necessary to know in civil associations than in political associations.

Political associations can therefore be considered great schools, free of charge, where all citizens come to learn the general theory of associations.

Even if political association did not directly serve the progress of civil association, one would still do harm to the latter in destroying the former.

When citizens can only associate in certain cases, they regard association as a rare and singular procedure and they scarcely ever dare to think of it.

When they are allowed to associate freely in all things, in the end they see in association the universal, and so to speak the unique, means of which men can make use to attain the different ends they propose for themselves.

Each new need immediately awakens the idea of it. The art of association then becomes, as I said above, the mother science;* all study it and apply it.

When certain associations are forbidden and others permitted, it is difficult to distinguish in advance the first from the second. When in doubt, one abstains from all, and a sort of public opinion is established that tends to make one consider any association whatsoever as a bold and almost illicit undertaking.[1]

It is therefore a chimera to believe that the spirit of association, compromised on one point, will be left to develop with the same vigor on all others, and that it will suffice to permit men to execute certain undertakings in common for them to hasten to attempt it. When citizens have the ability and the habit of associating for all things, they will as willingly associate for small ones as for great. But if they can only associate for small ones, they will not even have the desire and the capacity to do so. In vain will you allow them entire freedom to engage in common in their trade: they will use only halfheartedly the rights that are granted them, and after you are exhausted by efforts to turn them away from forbidden associations, you will be surprised at not being able to persuade them to form permitted associations.

I do not say that there cannot be civil associations in a country where political association is prohibited; for men can never live in society without engaging in some common undertaking. But I maintain that in a country like this, civil associations will always be very few in number, weakly conceived, unskillfully conducted, and that they will never embrace vast designs or will fail when they want to execute them.

This naturally leads me to think that freedom of association in political matters is not as dangerous for public tranquillity as is supposed, and that it could happen that after having shaken up the state for some time, it would consolidate it.

---

*DA II 2.5.

1. That is above all true when it is the executive power that is charged with permitting or forbidding associations according to its arbitrary will.

When the law is limited to prohibiting certain associations and leaves to the courts the care of punishing those who disobey, the evil is much less great: each citizen then knows almost in advance what to count on; he judges for himself in some way before his judges do, and avoiding forbidden associations, he turns to permitted associations. It is thus that all free peoples have always understood that one could restrain the right of association. But if it happened that the legislator charged one man with sorting out in advance which are the dangerous and useful associations and left him free to destroy the seed of all associations or to let them spring up, no one being able to foresee in advance in which case one can associate and in which one must abstain, the spirit of association would be wholly stricken with inertia. The first of these two laws attacks only certain associations; the second is addressed to society itself and hurts it. I conceive that an acknowledged government may have recourse to the first, but I recognize in no government the right to bring on the second.

In democratic countries, political associations form so to speak the only powerful particular persons who aspire to regulate the state. So governments in our day consider these kinds of association with the same eye that the kings of the Middle Ages regarded the great vassals of the crown: they feel a sort of instinctive horror of them and combat them at every encounter.

They have, on the contrary, a natural benevolence toward civil associations because they have readily discovered that, instead of directing the minds of citizens toward public affairs, these serve to distract them and, engaging them more and more in projects that cannot be accomplished without public peace, turn them away from revolutions. But they do not take note that political associations multiply civil associations and facilitate them enormously, and in avoiding a dangerous evil, they deprive themselves of an efficacious remedy. When you see Americans associate freely every day for the goal of making a public opinion prevail, of elevating a statesman to the government, or of taking away power from someone, you have trouble comprehending that men so independent do not fall into license at every moment.

If you come, on the other hand, to consider the infinite number of industrial undertakings that are pursued in common in the United States, and if you perceive Americans on all sides working without relaxation in the execution of some important and difficult design that the least revolution could confound, you easily conceive why people so well occupied are not tempted to trouble the state or to destroy a public repose from which they profit.

Is it enough to perceive these things separately, or must one not discover the hidden knot that binds them? It is within political associations that Americans of all conditions, of all minds, and of all ages get the general taste for association daily and familiarize themselves with its use. There they see each other in great number, speak to each other, understand each other, and in common become animated for all sorts of undertakings. Afterwards, they carry into civil life the notions they have acquired and make them serve a thousand uses.

It is therefore while enjoying a dangerous freedom that Americans learn the art of rendering the perils of freedom less great.

If one chooses a certain moment in the existence of a nation, it is easy to prove that political associations trouble the state and paralyze industry; but should one take the whole life of a people, it will perhaps be easy to demonstrate that freedom of association in political matters is favorable to the well-being and even to the tranquillity of citizens.

I said in the first part of this work:* "Unlimited freedom of association

---

*DA I 2.4. In volume 1 the first sentence in the passage begins "But unlimited freedom of association cannot be *entirely* confused with the freedom to write" [emphasis added].

cannot be confused with the freedom to write: the former is at once less necessary and more dangerous. A nation can set bounds for it without ceasing to be master of itself; it sometimes must do that to continue to be such." And further on I added: "One cannot conceal from oneself that unlimited freedom of association in political matters is, of all freedoms, the last that a people can tolerate. If it does not make it fall into anarchy, it makes it so to speak touch it at each instant."

Thus, I do not believe that a nation is always so much a master as to allow citizens the absolute right to associate in political matters, and I even doubt that there is any country, in any period, in which it would not be wise to set bounds for freedom of association.

Such and such a people, it is said, cannot maintain peace within itself, inspire respect for the laws, or found a lasting government if it does not confine the right of association within narrow limits. Such goods are doubtless precious, and I conceive that to acquire them or preserve them a nation consents to impose great hindrances temporarily; but still it is good for it to know precisely what these goods cost it.

If to save the life of a man one cuts off his arm, I understand it; but I do not want someone to assure me that he is going to show himself as adroit as if he were not one-armed.

Chapter 8 HOW THE AMERICANS COMBAT INDIVIDUALISM BY THE DOCTRINE OF SELF-INTEREST WELL UNDERSTOOD*

When the world was led by a few powerful and wealthy individuals, these liked to form for themselves a sublime idea of the duties of man; they were pleased to profess that it is glorious to forget oneself and that it is fitting to do good without self-interest like God himself. This was the official doctrine of the time in the matter of morality.

I doubt that men were more virtuous in aristocratic centuries than in

---

*"Self-interest" translates the French *intérêt* when unmodified.

others, but it is certain that the beauties of virtue were constantly spoken of then; only in secret did they study the side on which it is useful. But as the imagination takes a less lofty flight and each man concentrates on himself, moralists become frightened at this idea of sacrifice and they no longer dare to offer it to the human mind; therefore they are reduced to inquiring whether the individual advantage of citizens would not be to work for the happiness of all, and when they have discovered one of the points where particular interest happens to meet the general interest and to be confounded with it, they hasten to bring it to light; little by little such observations are multiplied. What was only an isolated remark becomes a general doctrine, and one finally believes one perceives that man, in serving those like him, serves himself, and that his particular interest is to do good.

I have already shown in several places in this work how the inhabitants of the United States almost always know how to combine their own well-being with that of their fellow citizens.* What I want to remark here is the general theory by the aid of which they come to this.

In the United States it is almost never said that virtue is beautiful. They maintain that it is useful and they prove it every day. American moralists do not claim that one must sacrifice oneself to those like oneself because it is great to do it; but they say boldly that such sacrifices are as necessary to the one who imposes them on himself as to the one who profits from them.†

They have perceived that in their country and their time, man had been led back toward himself by an irresistible force, and losing hope of stopping him, they no longer dreamed of doing more than guiding him.

They therefore do not deny that each man can follow his interest, but they do their best to prove that the interest of each is to be honest.

I do not want to enter here into the details of their reasons, which would divert me from my subject; it suffices for me to say that they have convinced their fellow citizens.

Long ago Montaigne said, "When I do not follow the right path for the sake of righteousness, I follow it for having found by experience that all things considered, it is commonly the happiest and most useful."‡

The doctrine of self-interest well understood is therefore not new;§ but among Americans of our day it has been universally accepted; it has become

* *DA* I 2.4, 2.6.

†The name of Benjamin Franklin is so obvious among these "American moralists" as to obscure all others.

‡Montaigne, "Of Glory," *Essays*, II 16.

§The actual phrase "self-interest well understood" was apparently first used by Etienne de Condillac in 1798; see his *Traité des animaux*, vol. 3, 453.

popular there: one finds it at the foundation of all actions; it pierces into all discussions. It is encountered not less in the mouth of the poor man than in that of the rich.

In Europe the doctrine of self-interest is much coarser than in America, but at the same time it is less widespread and above all shown less, and among us one still feigns great devotions every day that one has no longer.

Americans, on the contrary, are pleased to explain almost all the actions of their life with the aid of self-interest well understood; they complacently show how the enlightened love of themselves constantly brings them to aid each other and disposes them willingly to sacrifice a part of their time and their wealth to the good of the state. I think that in this it often happens that they do not do themselves justice; for one sometimes sees citizens in the United States as elsewhere abandoning themselves to the disinterested and unreflective sparks that are natural to man; but the Americans scarcely avow that they yield to movements of this kind; they would rather do honor to their philosophy than to themselves.

I could halt here and not try to judge what I have just described. The extreme difficulty of the subject would be my excuse. But I do not want to avail myself of that; and I prefer that my readers see my goal clearly and refuse to follow me rather than that I leave them in suspense.

Self-interest well understood is a doctrine not very lofty, but clear and sure. It does not seek to attain great objects; but it attains all those it aims for without too much effort. As it is within the reach of all intellects, each seizes it readily and retains it without trouble. Marvelously accommodating to the weaknesses of men, it obtains a great empire with ease, and preserves it without difficulty because it turns personal interest against itself, and to direct the passions, it makes use of the spur that excites them.

The doctrine of self-interest well understood does not produce great devotion; but it suggests little sacrifices each day; by itself it cannot make a man virtuous; but it forms a multitude of citizens who are regulated, temperate, moderate, farsighted, masters of themselves; and if it does not lead directly to virtue through the will, it brings them near to it insensibly through habits.

If the doctrine of self-interest well understood came to dominate the moral world entirely, extraordinary virtues would without doubt be rarer. But I also think that gross depravity would then be less common. The doctrine of self-interest well understood perhaps prevents some men from mounting far above the ordinary level of humanity; but many others who were falling below do attain it and are kept there. Consider some individuals, they are lowered. View the species, it is elevated.

I shall not fear to say that the doctrine of self-interest well understood seems to me of all philosophic theories the most appropriate to the needs of men in our time, and that I see in it the most powerful guarantee against themselves that remains to them. The minds of the moralists of our day ought to turn, therefore, principally toward it. Even should they judge it imperfect, they would still have to adopt it as necessary.

I do not believe that, all in all, there is more selfishness among us than in America; the only difference is that there it is enlightened and here it is not. Each American knows how to sacrifice a part of his particular interests to save the rest. We want to keep everything, and often everything eludes us.

I see around me only people who seem to want to teach their contemporaries every day by their word and their example that the useful is never dishonest. Shall I therefore finally discover none who undertake to make them understand how honesty can be useful?

There is no power on earth that can prevent the growing equality of conditions from bringing the human spirit toward searching for the useful and from disposing each citizen to shrink within himself.

One must therefore expect that individual interest will become more than ever the principal if not the unique motive of men's actions; but it remains to know how each man will understand his individual interest.

If in becoming equal, citizens remained ignorant and coarse, it is difficult to foresee what stupid excess their selfishness could be brought to, and one cannot say in advance into what shameful miseries they would plunge for fear of sacrificing something of their well-being to the prosperity of those like them.

I do not believe that the doctrine of self-interest such as it is preached in America is evident in all its parts; but it contains a great number of truths so evident that it is enough to enlighten men so that they see them. Enlighten them, therefore, at any price; for the century of blind devotions and instinctive virtues is already fleeing far from us, and I see the time approaching when freedom, public peace, and social order itself will not be able to do without enlightenment.

Cᴿᴰᴼ Cᴿᴰᴼ Cᴿᴰᴼ Cᴿᴰᴼ Cᴿᴰᴼ Cᴿᴰᴼ Cᴿᴰᴼ Cᴿᴰᴼ Cᴿᴰᴼ Cᴿᴰᴼ Cᴿᴰᴼ Cᴿᴰᴼ Cᴿᴰᴼ Cᴿᴰᴼ Cᴿᴰᴼ Cᴿᴰᴼ Cᴿᴰᴼ Cᴿᴰᴼ Cᴿᴰᴼ Cᴿᴰᴼ

Chapter 9 HOW THE AMERICANS APPLY THE DOCTRINE OF SELF-INTEREST WELL UNDERSTOOD IN THE MATTER OF RELIGION

If the doctrine of self-interest well understood had only this world in view, it would be far from sufficient; for there are a great number of sacrifices that can find their recompense only in the other world; and whatever effort of mind that one makes to prove the utility of virtue, it will always be hard to make a man who does not wish to die live well.

It is therefore necessary to know if the doctrine of self-interest well understood can be easily reconciled with religious beliefs.

The philosophers who teach this doctrine say to men that to be happy in life one ought to watch over one's passions and carefully repress their excesses; that one can acquire a lasting happiness only in refusing a thousand passing enjoyments, and finally that one must constantly triumph over oneself to serve oneself better.*

The founders of almost all religions have held to nearly the same language. Without indicating another route to men they have only moved the goal back; instead of placing the prize for the sacrifices they impose in this world, they have put it in the other.

Still, I refuse to believe that all those who practice virtue out of a spirit of religion act only in view of recompense.

I have encountered zealous Christians who constantly forget themselves in order to work with more ardor for the happiness of all, and I have heard them claim that they were only acting this way in order to merit the goods of the other world; but I cannot prevent myself from thinking that they deceive themselves. I respect them too much to believe them.

It is true that Christianity tells us that one must prefer others to oneself to gain Heaven; but Christianity tells us as well that one ought to do good to those like oneself out of love of God. That is a magnificent expression; man penetrates Divine thought by his intelligence; he sees that the goal of God is

---

*See among others, Descartes, *The Passions of the Soul*, 41, 48–50; Thomas Hobbes, *Leviathan*, 15, 30, 31; John Locke, *An Essay concerning Human Understanding*, I 3, II 21; Montesquieu, *The Spirit of the Laws*, XXI 20; David Hume, *A Treatise of Human Nature*, III 2.1; Adam Smith, *The Wealth of Nations*, II 3, IV 9, *The Theory of Moral Sentiments*, III 1, 5.

order; he freely associates himself with that great design; and all the while sacrificing his particular interests to the admirable order of all things, he expects no other recompense than the pleasure of contemplating it.

I therefore do not believe that the sole motive of religious men is interest; but I think that interest is the principal means religions themselves make use of to guide men, and I do not doubt that it is only from this side that they take hold of the crowd and become popular.

I therefore do not see clearly why the doctrine of self-interest well understood would turn men away from religious beliefs, and it seems to me, on the contrary, that I am sorting out how it brings them near to them.

I suppose that to attain happiness in this world, a man resists instinct in all encounters and reasons coldly about all the acts of his life, that instead of blindly yielding to the enthusiasm of his first desires, he has learned the art of combating them, and that he has been habituated to sacrificing without effort the pleasure of the moment to the permanent interest of his whole life.

If such a man has faith in the religion that he professes, it will scarcely cost him to submit himself to the hindrances that it imposes. Reason itself counsels him to do it, and custom has prepared him in advance to suffer it.

If he has conceived doubts about the object of his hopes, he will not easily allow them to stop him, and he will judge that it is wise to risk some of the goods of this world to preserve his rights to the immense inheritance that he has been promised in the other.

"In being deceived by believing the Christian religion to be true," Pascal said, "there is nothing great to lose, but what unhappiness in being wrong about believing it false!"*

Americans do not affect a coarse indifference to the other life; they do not put on a puerile pride by scorning the perils from which they hope to escape.

They therefore practice their religion without shame and without weakness; but one ordinarily sees even in the midst of their zeal something so tranquil, so methodical, so calculated, that it seems to be reason much more than heart that leads them to the foot of the altar.

Not only do Americans follow their religion out of interest, but they often place in this world the interest that one can have in following it. In the Middle Ages priests spoke only of the other life; they scarcely worried about proving that a sincere Christian can be a happy man here below.

But American preachers constantly come back to earth and only with great trouble can they take their eyes off it. To touch their listeners better, they make them see daily how religious beliefs favor freedom and public or-

---

*See Pascal, *Pensées*, 233 Br., for "Pascal's bet." But the words AT quotes were not found.

der, and it is often difficult to know when listening to them if the principal object of religion is to procure eternal felicity in the other world or well-being in this one.

ॐ ॐ

Chapter 10 ON THE TASTE FOR MATERIAL WELL-BEING IN AMERICA

In America the passion for material well-being is not always exclusive, but it is general; if all do not experience it in the same manner, all do feel it. The care of satisfying the least needs of the body and of providing the smallest comforts of life preoccupies minds universally.

Something like this is more and more to be seen in Europe.

Among the causes that produce these similar effects in the two worlds there are several that come close to my subject and that I will point out.

When wealth is settled by inheritance in the same families, one sees a great number of men who enjoy material well-being without feeling the exclusive taste for well-being.

What attaches the human heart most keenly is not the peaceful possession of a precious object, but the imperfectly satisfied desire to possess it and the incessant fear of losing it.

In aristocratic societies the rich, never having known a state different from their own, do not fear changing it; they hardly imagine another. Material well-being is therefore not the goal of life for them; it is a manner of living. They consider it in a way like existence and enjoy it without thinking about it.

The natural and instinctive taste that all men feel for well-being thus being satisfied without trouble and without fear, their souls transport themselves elsewhere and apply themselves to some more difficult and greater undertaking that animates them and carries them along.

Thus even in the midst of material enjoyments, the members of an aristocracy often display a haughty scorn of these same enjoyments and find singular strength when they must at last be deprived of them. All revolutions that have troubled or destroyed aristocracies have shown with what facility people accustomed to the superfluous can do without the necessary, whereas men who have laboriously arrived at ease can hardly live after having lost it.

If I pass from the superior ranks to the lower classes, I shall see analogous effects produced by different causes.

In nations where the aristocracy dominates society and holds it immobile, the people in the end become habituated to poverty like the rich to their opulence. The latter are not preoccupied with material well-being because they possess it without trouble; the former do not think about it because they despair of acquiring it and because they are not familiar enough with it to desire it.

In these sorts of societies the imagination of the poor is thrown back upon the other world; the miseries of real life repress it, but it escapes them and goes to seek its enjoyments outside of it.

When, on the contrary, ranks are confused and privileges destroyed, when patrimonies are divided and enlightenment and freedom are spread, the longing to acquire well-being presents itself to the imagination of the poor man, and the fear of losing it, to the mind of the rich. A multitude of mediocre fortunes is established. Those who possess them have enough material enjoyments to conceive the taste for these enjoyments and not enough to be content with them. They never get them except with effort, and they indulge in them only while trembling.

They therefore apply themselves constantly to pursuing or keeping these enjoyments that are so precious, so incomplete, and so fleeting.

I seek a passion that is natural to men who are excited and limited by the obscurity of their origin or the mediocrity of their fortune, and I find none more appropriate than the taste for well-being. The passion for material well-being is essentially a middle-class passion; it grows larger and spreads with this class; it becomes preponderant with it. From there it reaches the higher ranks of society and descends within the people.

I did not encounter a citizen in America so poor that he did not cast a glance of hope and longing on the enjoyments of the rich and whose imagination was not seized in advance by the goods that fate was obstinately refusing him.

On the other hand, I never perceived that high-minded disdain for material well-being among the rich of the United States that is sometimes shown even within the most opulent and most dissolute aristocracies.

Most of these rich have been poor; they have felt the sting of need; they have long combated adverse fortune, and, now that victory is gained, the passions that accompanied the struggle survive it; they stand as if intoxicated in the midst of the little enjoyments that they have pursued for forty years.

It is not that in the United States as elsewhere one does not encounter a great enough number of the rich who, holding their goods by inheritance, possess effortlessly an opulence that they have not acquired. But even they do not show themselves less attached to the enjoyments of material life. Love of well-being has become the national and dominant taste; the great current of human passions bears from this direction; it carries everything along in its course.

Chapter 11   ON THE PARTICULAR EFFECTS THAT THE LOVE OF MATERIAL ENJOYMENTS PRODUCES IN DEMOCRATIC CENTURIES

One could believe, from what precedes, that the love of material enjoyments must constantly carry Americans along toward disorder in mores, trouble their families, and finally compromise the fate of society itself.

But it is not so: the passion for material enjoyments produces different effects within democracies than in aristocratic peoples.

It sometimes happens that the lassitude of affairs, the excess of wealth, the ruin of beliefs, the decadence of the state turn the heart of an aristocracy little by little toward material enjoyments alone. At other times, the power of the prince or the weakness of the people, without robbing the nobles of their fortune, forces them to turn away from power and, closing their way to great undertakings, abandons them to the restiveness of their desires; they then fall back heavily on themselves, and they seek forgetfulness of their past greatness in enjoyments of the body.

When the members of an aristocratic body thus turn exclusively toward love of material enjoyments, they ordinarily gather on this side alone all the energy that the long habit of power has given them.

For such men the search for well-being is not enough; they must have a sumptuous depravity and a brilliant corruption. They render magnificent worship to the material and they seem to want to vie with each other to excel in the art of besotting themselves.

The stronger, more glorious, and freer an aristocracy has been, the more it will then show itself depraved, and whatever the splendor of its virtues has been, I dare to predict that it will always be surpassed by the brilliance of its vices.

The taste for material enjoyments does not bring democratic peoples to similar excesses. There, the love of well-being shows itself to be a tenacious, exclusive, universal, but contained passion. It is not a question of building vast palaces, of vanquishing and outwitting nature, of depleting the universe in order better to satiate the passions of a man; it is about adding a few toises to one's fields, planting an orchard, enlarging a residence, making life easier and more comfortable at each instant, preventing inconvenience, and satisfying the least needs without effort and almost without cost. These objects are small, but the soul clings to them: it considers them every day and from very close; in the end they hide the rest of the world from it, and they sometimes come to place themselves between it and God.

This, one will say, can only be applied to those citizens whose fortune is mediocre; the rich will show tastes analogous to those they used to display in aristocratic centuries. I contest that.

In the case of material enjoyments, the most opulent citizens of a democracy will not show tastes very different from those of the people, whether, having come from within the people, they really share them, or whether they believe they ought to submit to them. In democratic societies, the sensuality of the public has taken a certain moderate and tranquil style, to which all souls are held to conform. It is as difficult to escape the common rule by one's vices as by one's virtues.

The rich who live in the midst of democratic nations therefore aim at the satisfaction of their least needs rather than at extraordinary enjoyments; they gratify a multitude of small desires and do not give themselves over to any great disordered passion. They fall into softness rather than debauchery.

The particular taste that men of democratic centuries conceive for material enjoyments is not naturally opposed to order; on the contrary, it often needs order to be satisfied. Nor is it the enemy of regular mores; for good mores are useful to public tranquillity and favor industry. Often, indeed, it comes to be combined with a sort of religious morality; one wishes to be the best possible in this world without renouncing one's chances in the other.

Among material goods there are some whose possession is criminal; one takes care to abstain from them. There are others the use of which is permitted by religion and morality; to these one's heart, one's imagination, one's life are delivered without reserve; and in striving to seize them, one loses sight of the more precious goods that make the glory and the greatness of the human species.

What I reproach equality for is not that it carries men away in the pursuit of forbidden enjoyments; it is for absorbing them entirely in the search for permitted enjoyments.

Thus there could well be established in the world a sort of honest materialism that does not corrupt souls, but softens them and in the end quietly loosens all their tensions.

Chapter 12 WHY CERTAIN AMERICANS DISPLAY SUCH AN EXALTED SPIRITUALISM

Although the desire to acquire the goods of this world may be the dominant passion of Americans, there are moments of respite when their souls seem all at once to break the material bonds that restrain them and to escape impetuously toward Heaven.

In all the states of the Union, but principally in the half-populated regions of the West, one sometimes encounters itinerant preachers who peddle the divine word from place to place.

Entire families, the aged, women, and children cross difficult places and penetrate the woods of the wilderness, coming from very far to hear them; and when they have met them, while listening to them they forget for several days and nights the care of their affairs and even the most pressing needs of the body.

One finds here and there in the heart of American society souls altogether filled with an exalted and almost fierce spiritualism that one scarcely encounters in Europe. From time to time bizarre sects arise that strive to open extraordinary roads to eternal happiness. Religious follies are very common there.

This should not surprise us.

Man did not give himself the taste for the infinite and the love of what is immortal. These sublime instincts are not born of a caprice of his will: they have their immovable foundation in his nature; they exist despite his efforts. He can hinder and deform them, but not destroy them.

The soul has needs that must be satisfied; and whatever care one takes to distract it from itself, it soon becomes bored, restive, and agitated amid enjoyments of the senses.

If the minds of the great majority of the human race were ever concentrated on the search for material goods alone, one can expect that an enormous reaction would be produced in the souls of some men. The latter would throw themselves head over heels into the world of spirits for fear of remaining encumbered in the too narrow fetters that the body wants to impose on them.

One should therefore not be astonished if, in the heart of a society that thought only of the earth, one encountered a few individuals who wished to regard only Heaven. I would be surprised if mysticism did not soon make progress in a people uniquely preoccupied with its own well-being.

It is said that the persecutions of the emperors and the tortures of the circus peopled the deserts of the Thebaid;* but I think that it was rather the delights of Rome and the Epicurean philosophy of Greece.

If the social state, circumstances, and laws did not restrain the American spirit so closely in the search for well-being, one might believe that when it came to be occupied with immaterial things, it would show more reserve and more experience and would moderate itself without trouble. But it feels itself imprisoned within limits from which it is seemingly not allowed to leave. As soon as it passes these limits, it does not know where to settle, and it often runs without stopping beyond the bounds of common sense.

Chapter 13 WHY THE AMERICANS SHOW THEMSELVES SO RESTIVE IN THE MIDST OF THEIR WELL-BEING

One still sometimes encounters small populations in certain secluded districts of the Old World that have been almost forgotten in the midst of the universal tumult and that have remained immobile when everything around them was moving. Most of these peoples are very ignorant and very miserable; they do not meddle in the affairs of government and often governments oppress them. Nevertheless, they ordinarily show a serene countenance, and they often let a playful humor appear.

In America I saw the freest and most enlightened men placed in the happiest condition that exists in the world; it seemed to me that a sort of cloud habitually covered their features; they appeared to me grave and almost sad even in their pleasures.

The principal reason for this is that the first do not think of the evils they endure, whereas the others dream constantly of the goods they do not have.

It is a strange thing to see with what sort of feverish ardor Americans pursue well-being and how they show themselves constantly tormented by a vague fear of not having chosen the shortest route that can lead to it.

---

*A region of Egypt, which was a province of the Roman Empire.

The inhabitant of the United States attaches himself to the goods of this world as if he were assured of not dying, and he rushes so precipitately to grasp those that pass within his reach that one would say he fears at each instant he will cease to live before he has enjoyed them. He grasps them all but without clutching them, and he soon allows them to escape from his hands so as to run after new enjoyments.

In the United States, a man carefully builds a dwelling in which to pass his declining years, and he sells it while the roof is being laid; he plants a garden and he rents it out just as he was going to taste its fruits; he clears a field and he leaves to others the care of harvesting its crops. He embraces a profession and quits it. He settles in a place from which he departs soon after so as to take his changing desires elsewhere. Should his private affairs give him some respite, he immediately plunges into the whirlwind of politics. And when toward the end of a year filled with work some leisure still remains to him, he carries his restive curiosity here and there within the vast limits of the United States. He will thus go five hundred leagues in a few days in order better to distract himself from his happiness.

Death finally comes, and it stops him before he has grown weary of this useless pursuit of a complete felicity that always flees from him.

One is at first astonished to contemplate the singular agitation displayed by so many happy men in the very midst of their abundance. This spectacle is, however, as old as the world; what is new is to see a whole people show it.

The taste for material enjoyments must be considered as the first source of this secret restiveness revealed in the actions of Americans and of the inconstancy of which they give daily examples.

He who has confined his heart solely to the search for the goods of this world is always in a hurry, for he has only a limited time to find them, take hold of them, and enjoy them. His remembrance of the brevity of life constantly spurs him. In addition to the goods that he possesses, at each instant he imagines a thousand others that death will prevent him from enjoying if he does not hasten. This thought fills him with troubles, fears, and regrets, and keeps his soul in a sort of unceasing trepidation that brings him to change his designs and his place at every moment.

If a social state in which law or custom no longer keeps anyone in his place is joined to the taste for material well-being, this too greatly excites further restiveness of spirit: one will then see men change course continuously for fear of missing the shortest road that would lead them to happiness.

Besides, it is easy to conceive that if men who passionately search for material enjoyments desire keenly, they will be easily discouraged; the final object being to enjoy, the means of arriving at it must be prompt and easy, without which the trouble of acquiring the enjoyment would surpass the enjoyment. Most souls are, therefore, at once ardent and soft, violent and enervated. Often one dreads death less than continuing efforts toward the same goal.

Equality leads men by a still more direct path to several of the effects that I have just described.

When all the prerogatives of birth and fortune are destroyed, when all professions are open to all, and when one can reach the summit of each of them by oneself, an immense and easy course seems to open before the ambition of men, and they willingly fancy that they have been called to great destinies. But that is an erroneous view corrected by experience every day. The same equality that permits each citizen to conceive vast hopes renders all citizens individually weak. It limits their strength in all regards at the same time that it permits their desires to expand.

Not only are they impotent by themselves, but at each step they find immense obstacles that they had not at first perceived.

They have destroyed the annoying privileges of some of those like them; they come up against the competition of all. The barrier has changed form rather than place. When men are nearly alike and follow the same route, it is difficult indeed for any one of them to advance quickly and to penetrate the uniform crowd that surrounds him and presses against him.

The constant opposition reigning between the instincts that equality gives birth to and the means that it furnishes to satisfy them is tormenting and fatiguing to souls.

One can conceive of men having arrived at a certain degree of freedom that satisfies them entirely. They then enjoy their independence without restiveness and without ardor. But men will never found an equality that is enough for them.

Whatever a people's efforts, it will not succeed in making conditions perfectly equal within itself; and if it had the misfortune to reach this absolute and complete leveling, the inequality of intellects would still remain, which, coming directly from God, will always escape the laws.

However democratic the social state and political constitution of a people may be, one can therefore count on the fact that each of its citizens will always perceive near to him several positions in which he is dominated, and one can foresee that he will obstinately keep looking at this side alone. When inequality is the common law of a society, the strongest inequalities do not strike the eye; when everything is nearly on a level, the least of them wound it. That is why the desire for equality always becomes more insatiable as equality is greater.

In democratic peoples, men easily obtain a certain equality; they cannot attain the equality they desire. It retreats before them daily but without ever evading their regard, and, when it withdraws, it attracts them in pursuit. They constantly believe they are going to seize it, and it constantly escapes their grasp. They see it from near enough to know its charms, they do not approach it close enough to enjoy it, and they die before having fully savored its sweetness.

It is to these causes that one must attribute the singular melancholy that the inhabitants of democratic lands often display amid their abundance, and the disgust with life that sometimes seizes them in the midst of an easy and tranquil existence.

In France one complains that the number of suicides is increasing; in America suicide is rare, but one is sure that madness is more common than everywhere else.

Those are different symptoms of the same malady.

Americans do not kill themselves, however agitated they may be, because religion forbids them from doing so, and because materialism so to speak does not exist among them, although the passion for material well-being is general.

Their will resists, but often their reason gives way.

In democratic times, enjoyment is keener than in aristocratic centuries, and above all the number of those who taste it is infinitely greater; but on the other hand, one must recognize that hopes and desires are more often disappointed, souls more aroused and more restive, and cares more burning.

Chapter 14 HOW THE TASTE FOR MATERIAL ENJOYMENTS AMONG AMERICANS IS UNITED WITH LOVE OF FREEDOM AND WITH CARE FOR PUBLIC AFFAIRS

When a democratic state turns to absolute monarchy, the activity previously directed to public and private affairs comes all at once to be concentrated on the latter, and for some time, great material prosperity results; but soon the movement slows and the development of production comes to a stop.

I do not know if one can cite a single manufacturing and commercial people, from the Tyrians* to the Florentines to the English, that has not been a free people. There is therefore a tight bond and a necessary relation between these two things: freedom and industry.

That is generally true of all nations, but especially of democratic nations.

I have brought out above how men who live in centuries of equality have a continuous need of association in order to procure for themselves almost all the goods they covet, and I have shown, on the other hand, how great political freedom perfects and popularizes the art of association within them.† In these centuries, therefore, freedom is particularly useful to the production of wealth. One can see, on the contrary, that despotism is its particular enemy.

The nature of absolute power in democratic centuries is neither cruel nor savage, but it is minute and vexatious. Although despotism of this kind does not ride roughshod over humanity, it is directly opposed to the genius of commerce and the instincts of industry.

Thus men of democratic times need to be free in order to procure more easily for themselves the material enjoyments for which they constantly sigh.

It sometimes happens, however, that the excessive taste they conceive for these same enjoyments delivers them to the first master who presents himself. The passion for well-being is then turned against itself and, without perceiving it, drives away the object of its covetousness.

There is, in fact, a very perilous passage in the life of democratic peoples.

When the taste for material enjoyments develops in one of these peoples more rapidly than enlightenment and the habits of freedom, there comes a moment when men are swept away and almost beside themselves at the sight of the new goods that they are ready to grasp. Preoccupied with the sole care of making a fortune, they no longer perceive the tight bond that unites the particular fortune of each of them to the prosperity of all. There is no need to tear from such citizens the rights they possess; they themselves willingly allow them to escape. The exercise of their political duties appears to them a distressing contretemps that distracts them from their industry. If it is a question of choosing their representatives, of giving assistance to authority, of treating the common thing in common, they lack the time; they cannot waste their precious time in useless work. These are games of the idle that do not suit grave men occupied with the serious interests of life. These people believe they are following the doctrine of interest, but they have only a coarse idea of it, and to watch better over what they call their affairs, they neglect the principal one, which is to remain masters of themselves.

*Inhabitants of Tyre, an ancient Phoenician city.
†DA II 2.5–7.

Since the citizens who work do not wish to think of the public, and the class that could take charge of this care to occupy its leisure no longer exists, the place of government is almost empty.

If, at this critical moment, an ambitious, able man comes to take possession of power, he finds the way open to every usurpation.

Let him see to it for a time that all material interests prosper, they will easily release him from the rest. Let him above all guarantee good order. Men who have a passion for material enjoyments ordinarily find out how the agitations of freedom trouble their well-being before perceiving how freedom serves to procure it for them; and at the least noise from public passions that penetrate into the midst of the little enjoyments of their private lives, they wake up and become restive; for a long time, fear of anarchy holds them constantly in suspense and always ready to throw out their freedom at the first disorder.

I shall acknowledge without difficulty that public peace is a great good; but I nevertheless do not want to forget that it is through good order that all peoples have arrived at tyranny. It surely does not follow that peoples ought to scorn public peace; but they must not let it suffice for them. A nation that demands of its government only the maintenance of order is already a slave at the bottom of its heart; it is a slave to its well-being, and the man who is to put it in chains can appear.

The despotism of factions is no less to be dreaded there than that of one man.

When the mass of citizens wants to be occupied only with private affairs, the smallest parties should not despair of becoming masters of public affairs.

At that time it is not rare to see on the vast stage of the world, as well as in our theaters, a multitude represented by a few men. They alone speak in the name of an absent or inattentive crowd; they alone act in the midst of universal immobility; they dispose of all things according to their whim, they change laws and tyrannize at will over mores; and one is astonished at seeing the small number of weak and unworthy hands into which a great people can fall.

Up to now, the Americans have happily avoided all the shoals that I have just indicated; and in that they genuinely deserve to be admired.

There is perhaps no country on earth where fewer idle people are encountered than in America, and where all those who work are more inflamed by the search for well-being. But if the passion of the Americans for material enjoyments is violent, at least it is not blind, and reason, though powerless to moderate it, directs it.

An American occupies himself with his private interests as if he were alone in the world, and a moment later, he gives himself over to the public as if he had forgotten them. He sometimes appears animated by the most selfish cupidity and sometimes by the most lively patriotism. The human heart cannot be divided in this manner. Inhabitants of the United States bear witness alternatively to a passion so strong and so similar for their well-being and for their freedom that it is to be believed these passions are united and intermingled at some place in their souls. In fact, Americans see in their freedom the best instrument and the greatest guarantee of their well-being. They love these two things for each other. They therefore do not think that meddling in the public is not their affair; they believe, on the contrary, that their principal affair is to secure by themselves a government that permits them to acquire the goods they desire and that does not prevent them from enjoying in peace those they have acquired.

Chapter 15 HOW RELIGIOUS BELIEFS AT TIMES TURN THE SOULS OF AMERICANS TOWARD IMMATERIAL ENJOYMENTS

In the United States, when the seventh day of each week arrives, the commercial and industrial life of the nation seems suspended; all noise ceases. A deep repose, or rather a sort of solemn meditation, follows; the soul finally comes back into possession of itself and contemplates itself.

During this day, places devoted to commerce are deserted; each citizen, surrounded by his children, goes to a church; there strange discourses are held for him that seem hardly made for his ears. He is informed of the innumerable evils caused by pride and covetousness. He is told of the necessity of regulating his desires, of the delicate enjoyments attached to virtue alone, and of the true happiness that accompanies it.

Once back in his dwelling, one does not see him run to his business accounts. He opens the book of the Holy Scriptures; in it he finds sublime or moving depictions of the greatness and the goodness of the Creator, of the infinite magnificence of the works of God, of the lofty destiny reserved for men, of their duties, and of their rights to immortality.

Thus at times the American in a way steals away from himself, and as he is torn away for a moment from the small passions that agitate his life and the passing interests that fill it, he at once enters into an ideal world in which all is great, pure, eternal.

In another place in this work* I sought the causes to which one must attribute the maintenance of Americans' political institutions, and religion appeared to me one of the principal ones. Now that I am occupied with individuals, I find it again and I perceive that it is not less useful to each citizen than to the entire state.

Americans show by their practice that they feel every necessity of making democracy more moral by means of religion. What they think in this regard about themselves is a truth with which every democratic nation ought to be instilled.

I do not doubt that the social and political constitution of a people disposes it to certain beliefs and tastes which then become abundant without difficulty; whereas these same causes turn it away from certain opinions and penchants without working at it and so to speak without suspecting it.

The whole art of the legislator consists in discerning well and in advance these natural inclinations of human societies in order to know when one must aid the efforts of citizens and when it would rather be necessary to slow them down. For these obligations differ according to the times. Only the goal toward which the human race should always tend is unmoving; the means of getting it there vary constantly.

If I had been born in an aristocratic century, in the midst of a nation where the hereditary wealth of some and the irremediable poverty of others equally turned men from the idea of [something] better and held their souls almost numb in the contemplation of another world, I would wish it possible for me to stimulate the sentiment of needs among such a people; I would think of discovering the most rapid and easiest means of satisfying the new desires that I had made to arise, and, turning the greatest efforts of the human mind toward physical studies, I would try to excite it with the search for well-being.

If it happened that some men were inflamed inconsiderately by the pursuit of wealth and displayed an excessive love for material enjoyments, I would not be alarmed; these particular features would soon disappear in the common physiognomy [of men].

Legislators of democracies have other cares.

Give democratic peoples enlightenment and freedom and leave them alone. With no trouble they will succeed in taking all the goods from this world that it can offer; they will perfect each of the useful arts and render life more comfortable, easier, milder every day; their social state naturally pushes them in this direction. I do not fear they will stop.

But while man takes pleasure in this honest and legitimate search for well-

---

*DA I 2.9.

being, it is to be feared that he will finally lose the use of his most sublime faculties, and that by wishing to improve everything around him, he will finally degrade himself. The peril is there, not elsewhere.

Legislators of democracies and all honest and enlightened men who live in them must therefore apply themselves relentlessly to raising up souls and keeping them turned toward Heaven. It is necessary for all those who are interested in the future of democratic societies to unite, and for all in concert to make continuous efforts to spread within these societies a taste for the infinite, a sentiment of greatness, and a love of immaterial pleasures.

If one encounters among the opinions of a democratic people some of those harmful theories that tend to make it believed that everything perishes with the body, consider the men who profess them as the natural enemies of this people.

There are many things that offend me in the materialists. Their doctrines appear to me pernicious and their haughtiness revolts me. If their system could be of some utility to man, it seems that it would be in giving him a modest idea of himself. But they do not make anyone see that this should be so; and when they believe they have sufficiently established that they are only brutes, they show themselves as proud as if they had demonstrated they were gods.

Materialism is a dangerous malady of the human mind in all nations; but one must dread it particularly in a democratic people because it combines marvelously with the most familiar vice of the heart in these peoples.

Democracy favors the taste for material enjoyments. This taste, if it becomes excessive, soon disposes men to believe that all is nothing but matter; and materialism in its turn serves to carry them toward these enjoyments with an insane ardor. Such is the fatal circle into which democratic nations are propelled. It is good for them to see the peril and restrain themselves.

Most religions are only general, simple, and practical means of teaching men the immortality of the soul. That is the greatest advantage that a democratic people derives from beliefs, and it is what renders them more necessary to such a people than to all others.

Therefore when any religion whatsoever has cast deep roots within a democracy, guard against shaking it; but rather preserve it carefully as the most precious inheritance from aristocratic centuries; do not seek to tear men from their old religious opinions to substitute new ones, for fear that, in the passage from one faith to another, the soul finding itself for a moment empty of belief, the love of material enjoyments will come to spread through it and fill it entirely.

Surely, metempsychosis is not more reasonable than materialism; however, if a democracy absolutely had to make a choice between the two, I would not hesitate, and I would judge that its citizens risk brutalizing themselves less by thinking that their soul is going to pass into the body of a pig than in believing it is nothing.

Belief in an immaterial and immortal principle, united for a time with matter, is so necessary to the greatness of man that it produces beautiful effects even when one does not join to it an opinion in favor of rewards and punishments, and when one is limited to believing that after death the divine principle contained in man is absorbed into God or is going to animate another creature.

Even these latter consider the body the secondary and inferior portion of our nature; and they scorn it even as they fall under its influence, whereas they have a natural esteem and a secret admiration for the immaterial part of man even though they sometimes refuse to submit to its empire. This is enough for it to give a certain elevated turn to their ideas and their tastes, and to make them strive disinterestedly and almost by themselves toward pure sentiments and great thoughts.

It is not certain that Socrates and his school had decided opinions about what would happen to man in the other life; but the sole belief on which they were settled, that the soul has nothing in common with the body and that it survives it, was enough to give to Platonic philosophy the sort of sublime spark that distinguishes it.

When one reads Plato, one perceives that in the times prior to him, and in his time, many writers existed who extolled materialism. These writers have not come down to us or have come only very incompletely. Thus it has been in almost all centuries: most of the great literary reputations have been joined to spiritualism. The instinct and taste of the human race sustain this doctrine; they often preserve it despite men themselves, and they make the names of those attached to it persist. One must therefore not believe that, at any time and in whatever political condition, the passion for material enjoyments and the opinions attached to it can be enough for a whole people. The human heart is vaster than one supposes; it can at once contain a taste for the goods of the earth and a love of those of Heaven; sometimes it seems to give itself over frantically to one of the two; but it is never long before it thinks of the other.

If it is easy to see that it is particularly important in times of democracy to make spiritualist opinions reign, it is not easy to say what those who govern democratic peoples ought to do to make them reign.

I do not believe in the prosperity any more than the longevity of official philosophies, and as for state religions, I have always thought that if sometimes they could temporarily serve the interests of political power, they would always sooner or later become fatal to the Church.

Nor am I in the number of those who judge that to elevate religion in the eyes of peoples and to put the spiritualism that it professes in honor, it is good to give its ministers indirectly a political influence that the law refuses them.

I feel myself so sensitive to the almost inevitable dangers that beliefs risk when their interpreters mix in public affairs, and I am so convinced that one must maintain Christianity within the new democracies at all cost, that I would rather chain priests in the sanctuary than allow them to leave it.

What means, therefore, remain to authority to bring men back toward spiritualist opinions or to keep them in the religion that evokes them?

What I am going to say is indeed going to harm me in the eyes of politicians. I believe that the only efficacious means governments can use to put the dogma of the immortality of the soul in honor is to act every day as if they themselves believed it; and I think it is only in conforming scrupulously to religious morality in great affairs that they can flatter themselves they are teaching citizens to know it, love it, and respect it in small ones.

Chapter 16 HOW THE EXCESSIVE LOVE OF WELL-BEING CAN BE HARMFUL TO WELL-BEING

There is more of a bond than one would think between perfecting the soul and improving the goods of the body; man can leave these two things distinct and view each of them alternately; but he cannot separate them entirely without finally losing sight of both.

Beasts have the same senses as we and nearly the same lusts: there are no material passions that are not common to us and them, of which the seed is not as much in a dog as in ourselves.

How, therefore, does it come about that animals know only how to provide for their first and coarsest needs, whereas we vary our enjoyments infinitely and increase them constantly?

What renders us superior to the beasts in this is that we employ our souls in finding the material goods toward which instinct alone leads them. In men, the angel teaches the brute the art of satisfying itself. It is because man is capable of elevating himself above the goods of the body and of scorning even life—of which beasts do not have any idea—that he knows how to multiply these same goods to a degree that they cannot conceive of.

All that elevates, enlarges, extends the soul renders it more capable of succeeding in the very one of its undertakings that does not concern it.

All that enervates it, on the contrary, or debases it, weakens it for all things, the principal ones as well as the least, and threatens to render it almost as powerless for the latter as for the former. Thus the soul must remain great and strong, if only to be able from time to time to put its force and its greatness in the service of the body.

If men ever came to be contented with material goods, it is to be believed that little by little they would lose the art of producing them, and that in the end they would enjoy them without discernment and without progress, like brutes.

෴ ෴

Chapter 17 HOW IN TIMES OF EQUALITY AND DOUBT IT IS IMPORTANT TO MOVE BACK THE OBJECT OF HUMAN ACTIONS

In centuries of faith the final goal of life is placed after life.

Men of those times are therefore accustomed naturally, and so to speak without wanting it, to consider for a long succession of years an unmoving object toward which they constantly advance, and they learn by insensible progressions to repress a thousand little passing desires the better to succeed in satisfying the great and permanent desire that torments them. When the same men want to occupy themselves with earthly things, these habits are found again. They willingly settle on a general and certain goal for their actions here below, toward which all their efforts are directed. One does not see them engage in new attempts every day; but they have fixed designs that they do not grow weary of pursuing.

This explains why religious peoples have often accomplished such lasting things. In occupying themselves with the other world they encountered the great secret of succeeding in this one.

Religions supply the general habit of behaving with a view to the future. In this they are no less useful to happiness in this life than to felicity in the other. It is one of their greatest political aspects.

But as the lights of faith are obscured, men's view shrinks and one would say that the object of human actions appears closer to them each day.

When they are once accustomed to no longer being occupied with what will happen after their lives, one sees them fall back easily into a complete brutish indifference to the future that conforms only too well to certain instincts of the human species. As soon as they have lost the habit of placing their principal hopes in the long term, they are naturally brought to want to realize their least desires without delay, and it seems that from the moment they despair of living an eternity, they are disposed to act as if they will exist for only a single day.

In centuries of disbelief it is therefore always to be feared that men will constantly give themselves over to the daily chance of their desires and that, as they renounce entirely the obtaining of what cannot be acquired without long effort, they will found nothing great, peaceful, and lasting.

If it happens that the social state of a people so disposed becomes democratic, the danger I point out is increased.

When each seeks constantly to change place, when an immense competition is open to all, when wealth is accumulated and dissipated in a few instants amid the tumult of democracy, the idea of sudden and easy fortune, of great goods easily acquired and lost, the image of chance in all its forms presents itself to the human mind. The instability of the social state comes to favor the natural instability of desires. Amid these perpetual fluctuations of fate the present grows large; it hides the future that is being effaced, and men want to think only of the next day.

In these countries, where irreligion and democracy meet in an unhappy convergence, philosophers and those who govern ought constantly to apply themselves to moving back the object of human actions in the eyes of men; it is their great business.

The moralist, enclosing himself in the spirit of his century and country, must learn to defend himself there. He must strive daily to show his contemporaries how, in the very midst of the perpetual movement surrounding them, it is easier than they suppose to conceive and execute long-term undertakings. He must make them see that although humanity has changed its face, the methods with which men can procure prosperity for themselves in this world have remained the same and that, in democratic peoples as elsewhere, it is only by resisting a thousand particular little everyday passions that they can come to satisfy the general passion for happiness that torments them.

The task of those who govern is no less delineated.

In all times it is important that those who direct nations conduct themselves with a view to the future. But that is still more necessary in centuries of democracy and disbelief than in all others. In acting so, the heads of democracies not only make public affairs prosper, but by their example they also teach particular persons the art of conducting private affairs.

They must strive above all to banish chance as much as possible from the political world.

The sudden and unmerited elevation of a courtier produces only a passing impression in an aristocratic country because the sum of institutions and beliefs habitually forces men to advance slowly on paths from which they cannot depart.

But there is nothing more pernicious than such examples offered to the regard of a democratic people. They serve to hasten its heart down a slope along which everything is carrying it. It is therefore principally in times of skepticism and equality that one ought carefully to avoid that the favor of the people or that of the prince—which chance favors you with or deprives you of—take the place of science and of services rendered. It is to be wished that each instance of progress appear to be the fruit of an effort, so that no greatness be too easy and that ambition be forced to fix its eye on the goal for a long time before attaining it.

Governments must apply themselves to giving back to men this taste for the future which is no longer inspired by religion and the social state, and without saying so, they must teach citizens practically every day that wealth, renown, and power are the prizes of work; that great successes are found at the end of long-lasting desires, and that one gets nothing lasting except that which is acquired with difficulty.

When men have become accustomed to foreseeing from very far what should happen to them here below, and to nourishing themselves on hopes for it, it becomes difficult for them always to arrest their spirits at the precise boundaries of life, and they are very ready to cross these limits to cast their regard beyond.

I therefore do not doubt that in habituating citizens to think of the future in this world, one would bring them little by little and without their knowing it to religious beliefs.

Thus the means that permit men up to a certain point to do without religion is perhaps, after all, the only one remaining to us to lead the human race by a long detour back toward faith.

∓ ∓ ∓ ∓ ∓ ∓ ∓ ∓ ∓ ∓ ∓ ∓ ∓ ∓ ∓ ∓ ∓ ∓ ∓ ∓

Chapter 18 WHY AMONG THE AMERICANS ALL HONEST PROFESSIONS ARE REPUTED HONORABLE

In democratic peoples, where there is no hereditary wealth, everyone works to live, or has worked, or was born of people who worked. The idea of work as a necessary, natural, and honest condition of humanity is therefore offered to the human mind on every side.

Not only is work not held in dishonor among these peoples, but it is held in honor; the prejudice is not against it but for it. In the United States, a rich man believes that he owes it to public opinion to devote his leisure to some operation of industry or commerce or to some public duty. He would deem himself disreputable if he used his life only for living. It is to escape this obligation of work that so many rich Americans come to Europe: there they find the debris of aristocratic societies among which idleness is still honored.

Equality not only rehabilitates the idea of work, it uplifts the idea of working to procure lucre.

In aristocracies, it is not precisely work that is scorned, but work with a view to profit. Work is glorious when ambition or virtue alone makes one undertake it. Under aristocracy, nevertheless, it constantly happens that he who works for honor is not insensitive to the lure of gain. But these two desires meet only in the depth of his soul. He takes much care to conceal from all regard the place where they unite. He willingly hides it from himself. In aristocratic countries there is scarcely a public official who does not claim to serve the state without interest. Their wages are a detail they sometimes think little of and always affect not to think of.

Thus the idea of gain remains distinct from that of work. No matter that they are joined in fact, the past separates them.

In democratic societies, these two ideas are, on the contrary, always visibly united. As the desire for well-being is universal, as fortunes are mediocre and transient, as each needs to increase his resources or to prepare new ones for his children, all see very clearly that gain is, if not all, at least part of what brings them to work. The very ones who act principally with a view to glory are bound to be tamed with the thought that they do not act solely with this in view, and they discover, despite their wishes, that the desire to live is mixed with the desire to give luster to their lives.

From the moment when, on the one hand, work seems to all citizens an honorable necessity of the human condition, and when, on the other hand, work is always visibly done wholly or in part for the consideration of a wage, the immense space that separated the different professions in aristocratic societies disappears. If they are not all similar, they at least have one like feature.

There is no profession in which one does not work for money. The wage common to all gives a family resemblance to all.

This serves to explain the opinions that Americans entertain relative to the various professions.

American servants do not believe themselves degraded because they work; for everyone around them works. They do not feel themselves debased by the idea that they receive a wage, for the President of the United States works for a wage as well. He is paid to command just as they are to serve.

In the United States professions are more or less onerous, more or less lucrative, but they are never high or low. Every honest profession is honorable.

Chapter 19   WHAT MAKES ALMOST ALL AMERICANS INCLINE TOWARD INDUSTRIAL PROFESSIONS

I do not know if agriculture, of all the useful arts, is not the one perfected least quickly in democratic nations. Often one would even say that it is stationary because several others seem to run ahead.

On the contrary, almost all the tastes and habits that are born of equality naturally lead men toward commerce and industry.

Let me imagine a man who is active, enlightened, free, at ease, full of desires. He is too poor to be able to live in idleness; he is rich enough to feel himself above the immediate fear of need, and he thinks of improving his lot. This man has conceived the taste for material enjoyments; a thousand others abandon themselves to this taste before his eyes; he himself has begun to indulge it, and he burns to increase the means of satisfying it more. Nevertheless, life passes, time presses. What is he to do?

Cultivation of the earth promises almost certain, but slow, results for his efforts. One is enriched by it only little by little and with difficulty. Agriculture suits only the rich who already have a great superfluity, or the poor who ask only to live. His choice is made: he sells his field, quits his residence, and goes out to engage in some hazardous, but lucrative, profession.

Now, democratic societies abound with people of this kind; and as equality of conditions becomes greater, their host increases.

Democracy therefore not only multiplies the number of workers; it brings men to one work rather than to another; and whereas it gives them a distaste for agriculture, it directs them toward commerce and industry.[1]

This spirit is displayed in the wealthiest citizens themselves.

In democratic countries a man, however opulent one supposes him, is almost always discontented with his fortune, because he finds himself less wealthy than his father and he fears that his sons will be less so than he. Most of the rich in democracies therefore dream constantly of means of acquiring wealth, and they naturally turn their eyes toward commerce and industry, which appear to them the promptest and most powerful means of getting it. On this point they share the instincts of one who is poor without having his needs, or rather they are pushed by the most imperious of all needs: that of not sinking.

In aristocracies the rich are at the same time those who govern. The attention that they constantly give to great public affairs turns them from the little cares that commerce and industry demand. If the will of one of them is nonetheless directed by chance toward trade, the will of the [aristocratic] corps immediately blocks the route for him; for no matter how one rises up against the empire of number, one never completely escapes its yoke, and within the very aristocratic corps that refuse most insistently to recognize the rights of the national majority, a particular majority that governs is formed.[2]

In democratic countries, where money does not take the one who possesses it to power, but often keeps him from it, the rich do not know what to do with their leisure. The restiveness and the greatness of their desires, the extent of their resources, the taste for the extraordinary that those who raise

1. It has been remarked several times that industrialists and men of commerce are possessed of an immoderate taste for material enjoyments, and commerce and industry have been blamed for that; I believe that here the effect has been taken for the cause.

It is not commerce and industry that prompt a taste for material enjoyments in men, but rather this taste that brings men to industrial and commercial careers, where they hope to satisfy themselves more completely and more quickly.

If commerce and industry cause the desire for well-being to increase, that comes from the fact that every passion is fortified as one is more occupied with it and is increased by all the efforts by which one attempts to assuage it. All the causes that make love of the goods of this world predominate in the human heart develop industry and commerce. Equality is one of these causes. It favors commerce not only directly in giving men a taste for trade, but indirectly in fortifying and generalizing the love of well-being in their souls.

2. See the note at the end of the volume [XIX, page 699].

themselves above the crowd in any manner whatsoever almost always feel press them to act. The route of commerce alone is open to them. In democracies there is nothing greater nor more brilliant than commerce; it is what attracts the regard of the public and fills the imagination of the crowd; all energetic passions are directed toward it. Nothing can prevent the rich from engaging in it, neither their own prejudices nor those of anyone else. The rich in democracies never form a corps that has its own mores and policing; the particular ideas of their class do not stop them and the general ideas of their country push them ahead. Moreover, since the great fortunes that one sees within a democratic people almost always have a commercial origin, several generations must succeed one another before their possessors have entirely lost the habits of trade.

Compressed in the narrow space that politics leaves for them, the rich in democracies therefore throw themselves into commerce on all sides; there they can extend themselves and use their natural advantages; and in a way one ought to judge from the very audacity and the greatness of their industrial undertakings how little they would have made of industry if they had been born within an aristocracy.

One further remark is similarly applicable to all men of democracies, whether poor or rich.

Those who live amid democratic instability constantly have the image of chance before their eyes, and in the end they love all undertakings in which chance plays a role.

They are therefore all brought into commerce, not only because of the gain it promises them, but for love of the emotions that it gives them.

The United States of America emerged from the colonial dependence in which England held them only a half-century ago; the number of great fortunes there is very small and capital is still rare. There is nevertheless no people on earth that has made as rapid progress as the Americans in commerce and industry. Today they form the second maritime nation in the world; and although their manufactures have to struggle against almost insurmountable natural obstacles, they continue to make new developments daily.

In the United States the greatest industrial enterprises are executed without difficulty, because the population as a whole is involved in industry and because the poorest as well as the most opulent citizen willingly unite their efforts in this. One is therefore astonished daily to see immense works executed without trouble by a nation that includes so to speak no rich men. Americans arrived only yesterday on the soil they inhabit, and they have already overturned the whole order of nature to their profit. They have united the Hudson to the Mississippi and linked the Atlantic Ocean with the Gulf of Mexico across more than five hundred leagues of continent that separate these two seas. The longest railroads that have been made up to our day are in America.

But what strikes me most in the United States is not the extraordinary greatness of a few industrial enterprises, it is the innumerable multitude of small enterprises.

Almost all the farmers in the United States have joined some commerce to agriculture; most have made a commerce of agriculture.

It is rare that an American cultivator settles forever on the soil he occupies. In the new provinces of the West especially, a field is cleared to be resold and not to be harvested; a farm is built in the anticipation that, as the state of the country will soon change as a consequence of an increase of inhabitants, one can obtain a good price for it.

Every year a swarm of inhabitants from the North descend toward the South and settle in regions where cotton and sugar cane grow. These men cultivate the earth with the goal of making it produce in a few years whatever will enrich them, and they already glimpse the moment when they can return to their native country to enjoy the ease thus acquired. Americans therefore transport the spirit of trade into agriculture, and their industrial passions show themselves there as elsewhere.

Americans make immense progress in industry because they are all occupied with industry at the same time; and for this same cause they are subject to very unexpected and very formidable industrial crises.

As they are all in commerce, commerce among them is subject to such numerous and such complicated influences that it is impossible to foresee in advance the obstacles that can arise. As each of them is more or less involved in industry, at the least shock that affairs experience there, all particular fortunes stumble at the same time and the state totters.

I believe that the return of industrial crises is an endemic malady in the democratic nations of our day. One can render it less dangerous, but not cure it, because it is due not to an accident, but to the very temperament of these peoples.

ॐ ॐ

Chapter 20 HOW ARISTOCRACY COULD ISSUE FROM INDUSTRY

I have shown how democracy favors developments in industry and multiplies the number of industrialists without measure; we are going to see the path by which industry in its turn could well lead men back to aristocracy.

It has been recognized that when a worker is occupied every day with the same detail, the general production of the work comes more easily, more rapidly, and with more economy.*

It has also been recognized that the more an industry is a large-scale undertaking with great capital and great credit, the cheaper are its products.

These truths have been glimpsed for a long time, but in our day they have been demonstrated. They have already been applied to several very important industries, and in turn the least are taking hold of them.

I see nothing in the political world that should preoccupy the legislator more than these two new axioms of industrial science.

When an artisan engages constantly and uniquely in the manufacture of a single object, in the end he performs this work with singular dexterity. But at the same time he loses the general faculty of applying his mind to the direction of the work. Each day he becomes more skillful and less industrious, and one can say that the man in him is degraded as the worker is perfected.

What should one expect from a man who has used twenty years of his life in making pinheads? And to what, in him, can that powerful human intelligence which has often moved the world be applied from now on if not to the search for the best means of making pinheads!

When a worker has consumed a considerable portion of his existence in this manner, his thought is forever halted at the daily object of his labors; his body has contracted certain fixed habits from which he is no longer permitted to depart. In a word, he no longer belongs to himself, but to the profession he has chosen. In vain have laws and mores taken care to break all the barriers around this man and to open a thousand different paths to fortune for him in all directions; an industrial theory more powerful than mores and laws attaches him to a trade and often to a place that he cannot quit. It has assigned him a certain position in society which he cannot leave. In the midst of universal movement it has made him immobile.

---

*See Adam Smith, *The Wealth of Nations,* I 1.

As the principle of the division of labor is more completely applied, the worker becomes weaker, more limited, and more dependent. The art makes progress, the artisan retrogresses. On the other hand, as it is more plainly discovered that the products of an industry are so much more perfect and less dear as manufacture is vaster and capital greater, very wealthy and very enlightened men come forward to exploit industries which, until then, had been left to ignorant or awkward artisans. They are attracted by the greatness of the necessary efforts and the immensity of the results to be obtained.

So, therefore, at the same time that industrial science constantly lowers the class of workers, it elevates that of masters.

While the worker brings his intelligence more and more to the study of a single detail, each day the master casts his eye over a more far-reaching ensemble, and his mind extends as the worker's shrinks. Soon the latter will have to have only physical force without intelligence; the former will need science and almost genius to succeed. The one resembles more and more the administrator of a vast empire, the other a brute.

Master and worker here have nothing alike, and each day they differ more. They are joined only as two links at the extremes of a long chain. Each occupies a place that is made for him and that he cannot leave. The one is in a continual, strict, and necessary dependence on the other, and he seems born to obey as the latter is to command.

What is this if not aristocracy?

With conditions coming to be more and more equalized in the body of the nation, the need for manufactured objects becomes more general and increases in it, and the cheapness that puts these objects within the reach of mediocre fortunes becomes a greater element in success.

Each day, therefore, one finds that more opulent and more enlightened men devote their wealth and their science to industry and seek to satisfy the new desires that are manifest in all parts by opening great workshops and by dividing work strictly.

Thus as the mass of the nation turns to democracy, the particular class occupied with industry becomes more aristocratic. Men show themselves more and more alike in the one, and more and more different in the other, and inequality increases in the small society as it decreases in the great.

Thus, when one goes back to the source, it seems that one sees aristocracy issue by a natural effort from within the very heart of democracy.

But this aristocracy does not resemble those that have preceded it.

One will remark at first that in being applied only to industry and to some of the industrial professions, it is an exception, a monster, in the entirety of the social state.

The small aristocratic societies that certain industries form amid the immense democracy of our day contain, like the great aristocratic societies of former times, some very opulent men and a very miserable multitude.

The poor have few means of leaving their condition and of becoming rich, but the rich constantly become poor or quit trade after they have realized their profits. Thus the elements that form the class of the poor are nearly fixed; but the elements that compose the class of the rich are not. To tell the truth, although there are rich, the class of the rich does not exist; for the rich have neither common spirit nor objects, neither common traditions nor hopes. There are then members, but no corps.

Not only are the rich not solidly united among themselves, but one can say that there is no genuine bond between one who is poor and one who is rich.

They are not fixed in perpetuity, the one next to the other; at each instant interest brings them together and separates them. The worker depends generally on masters, but not on such and such a master. These two men see each other at the factory and do not know each other elsewhere, and while they touch each other at one point they remain very distant at all others. The manufacturer asks of the worker only his work, and the worker expects only a wage from him. The one is not engaged to protect, nor the other to defend, and they are not bound in a permanent manner either by habit or by duty.

The aristocracy founded by trade almost never settles in the midst of the industrial population that it directs; its goal is not to govern the latter, but to make use of it.

An aristocracy thus constituted cannot have a great hold on those it employs; and, should it come to seize them for a moment, they will soon escape it. It does not know what it wants and cannot act.

The territorial aristocracy of past centuries was obliged by law or believed itself to be obliged by mores to come to the aid of its servants and to relieve their miseries. But the manufacturing aristocracy of our day, after having impoverished and brutalized the men whom it uses, leaves them to be nourished by public charity in times of crisis. This results naturally from what precedes. Between worker and master relations are frequent, but there is no genuine association.

I think that all in all, the manufacturing aristocracy that we see rising before our eyes is one of the hardest that has appeared on earth; but it is at the same time one of the most restrained and least dangerous.

Still, the friends of democracy ought constantly to turn their regard with anxiety in this direction; for if ever permanent inequality of conditions and aristocracy are introduced anew into the world, one can predict that they will enter by this door.

PART THREE

Influence of Democracy on Mores Properly So-Called

Chapter 1 HOW MORES BECOME MILDER AS CONDITIONS ARE EQUALIZED

We perceive that for several centuries conditions have been becoming more equal and we discover at the same time that mores have been becoming milder. Are these two things only contemporaneous or does some secret bond exist between them so that the one cannot advance without setting the other in motion?

There are several causes that can cooperate to render the mores of a people less rude; but among all these causes the most powerful appears to me to be equality of conditions. Equality of conditions and the greater mildness of mores are therefore not only contemporaneous events in my eyes; they are also correlative facts.

When the makers of fables want to interest us in the actions of animals, they give them human ideas and passions. So do poets when they speak of genies and angels. There are no miseries so profound nor felicities so pure that they can arrest our minds and seize our hearts unless we are represented to ourselves with different features.

This very much applies to the subject presently occupying us.

When all men are ranked in an irrevocable manner according to their profession, their goods, and their birth within an aristocratic society, the members of each class, considering themselves all as children of the same family, feel a continual and active sympathy for one another that can never be encountered to the same degree among citizens of a democracy.

But it is not the same for the different classes vis-à-vis one another.

In an aristocratic people each caste has its own opinions, sentiments, rights, mores, and separate existence. Thus the men who compose it do not resemble everyone else; they do not have the same manner of thinking or of feeling, and they scarcely believe themselves to be a part of the same humanity.

Therefore they cannot understand well what the others feel, or judge them by themselves.

Yet one sometimes sees them lending mutual aid to each other with ardor; but that is not contrary to the preceding.

The same aristocratic institutions that had rendered beings of the same species so different had nevertheless united them to one another by a very tight political bond.

Although the serf was not naturally interested in the lot of the nobles, he did not believe himself less obliged to devote himself to whoever among them was his chief; and although the noble believed himself to be of another nature than the serfs, he nonetheless judged that his duty and his honor constrained him to defend, at the peril of his own life, those who lived on his domains.

It is evident that these mutual obligations did not arise from natural right, but from political right, and that society obtained more than humanity alone could have done. It was not to a man that one believed oneself bound to lend support; it was to a vassal or a lord. Feudal institutions rendered one very sensitive to the ills of certain men, but not to the miseries of the human species. They gave generosity rather than mildness to mores, and although they prompted great devotion, they did not give birth to genuine sympathy; for there is real sympathy only among people who are alike; and in aristocratic centuries one sees those like oneself only in the members of one's caste.

When the chroniclers of the Middle Ages, who all belonged by their birth or their habits to the aristocracy, relate the tragic end of a noble, it is with infinite sorrow; whereas they recount the massacre and tortures of men of the people all in one breath and without a frown.

It is not that these writers felt an habitual hatred or a systematic scorn for the people. War between the various classes of the state had not yet been declared. They obeyed an instinct rather than a passion; as they did not form a clear idea for themselves of the sufferings of the poor man, they had a weak interest in his lot.

It was so with men of the people as soon as the feudal bond came to be broken. The same centuries that saw so much heroic devotion on the part of vassals for their lords were witness to unheard-of cruelties exercised from time to time by the lower classes on the higher.

One should not believe that this mutual insensitivity was due solely to lack of order and enlightenment; for one finds signs of it in following centuries which, while becoming regulated and enlightened, still remained aristocratic.

In the year 1675 the lower classes of Brittany became aroused over a new tax. These tumultuous movements were repressed with an unexampled atrocity. Here is how Madame de Sévigné,* witness to these horrors, tells her daughter of them:

---

*Marie de Rabutin-Chantal, marquise de Sévigné (1626–1696), wrote approximately 1,700 letters to her daughter. See Sévigné, *Correspondance* (Paris: Gallimard, 1978), 3: 146–147, 171. AT constructs these quotations from passages in the letters of October 30 and November 24, 1675.

Rochers, October 3, 1675

My God, daughter, how amusing your letter from Aix is! At least reread your letters before sending them. Let yourself be surprised at their agreeableness and console yourself by this pleasure for the trouble of writing so many of them. So you have kissed all Provence? There would not be satisfaction in kissing all Brittany unless one loved to smell wine. Do you want to know the news from Rennes? They have passed a tax of 100,000 ecus, and if this sum is not found in 24 hours it will be doubled and exacted by soldiers. They have expelled and exiled all from a great street and forbidden the inhabitants to gather under pain of death, so that all those miserable people, women in confinement, old men and children, were seen wandering in tears at leaving the town without knowing where to go, having neither food nor any place to lodge. The day before yesterday, the fiddler who had begun the dance and the stealing of stamped paper was broken on the wheel; he was quartered and his four quarters exposed in the four corners of the town. They took sixty townspeople and tomorrow they begin the hanging. This province is a beautiful example for the others, above all of respecting governors and governors' wives and of not throwing stones in their gardens.[1]

Mme de Tarente was in her woods yesterday in delightful weather. There's no question of a room or a meal. She enters by the gate and returns in the same way . . .

In another letter she adds:

You speak to me quite jokingly of our miseries; we are no longer broken so much on the wheel; one per week to maintain justice. It is true that hanging now appears to me a refreshment. I have got a wholly different idea of justice since I have been in this [part of the] country. Your galley slaves appear to me a society of honest people who have withdrawn from the world to lead a mild life.

One would be wrong to believe that Madame de Sévigné, who wrote these lines, was a selfish and barbaric creature: she loved her children passionately and showed herself very sensitive to the distress of her friends; and one even perceives in reading her that she treated her vassals and servants with goodness and indulgence. But Madame de Sévigné did not clearly conceive what it was to suffer when one was not a gentleman.

In our day the hardest man, writing to the most insensitive person, would not dare engage in cold blood in the cruel banter that I have just reproduced,

---

1. To appreciate the relevance of this last joke, one must recall that Mme. de Grignan was wife of the governor of Provence.

and even if his particular mores would permit him to do it, the general mores of the nation would forbid it to him.

How has that come about? Do we have more sensitivity than our fathers? I do not know, but surely our sensitivity bears on more objects.

When ranks are almost equal in a people, all men having nearly the same manner of thinking and feeling, each of them can judge the sensations of all the others in a moment: he casts a rapid glance at himself; that is enough for him. There is therefore no misery he does not conceive without trouble and whose extent a secret instinct does not discover for him. It makes no difference whether it is a question of strangers or of enemies: imagination immediately puts him in their place. It mixes something personal with his pity and makes him suffer himself while the body of someone like him is torn apart.

In democratic centuries, men rarely devote themselves to one another; but they show a general compassion for all members of the human species. One does not see them inflict useless evils, and when they can relieve the sorrows of another without denying themselves much, they take pleasure in doing it; they are not disinterested, but they are mild.

Although the Americans have so to speak reduced selfishness to a social and philosophical theory, they do not show themselves any less accessible to pity.

There is no country where criminal justice is administered with more kindness than in the United States. Whereas the English seem to want to preserve carefully the bloody traces of the Middle Ages in their penal legislation, the Americans have almost made the death penalty disappear from their codes.

North America is, I think, the sole region on earth where for fifty years the life of not a single citizen has been taken for political offenses.

What serves to prove that this singular mildness of the Americans comes principally from their social state is the manner in which they treat their slaves.

Perhaps, taken as a whole, there is no European colony in the New World where the physical condition of blacks is less hard than in the United States. Nevertheless the slaves there still experience frightful miseries and are constantly exposed to very cruel punishments.

It is easy to discover that the lot of these unfortunates inspires little pity in their masters, and that they see in slavery not only a fact from which they profit, but also an ill that scarcely touches them. Thus the same man who is full of humanity for those like him when they are at the same time his equals becomes insensitive to their sorrows as soon as equality ceases.

It is therefore still more to this equality that one must attribute his mildness than to his civilization and enlightenment.

What I have just said of individuals applies up to a certain point to peoples.

When each nation has its separate opinions, beliefs, laws, and usages, it considers itself as if, by itself alone, it formed humanity as a whole, and feels itself touched only by its own sorrows. If war is ignited between two peoples disposed in this manner, it cannot fail to be fought with barbarity.

At the time of their greatest enlightenment, the Romans cut the throats of enemy generals after having dragged them in triumph behind a chariot and delivered prisoners over to beasts for the amusement of the people. Cicero,* who utters such great groans at the idea of a citizen crucified, finds nothing to reproach in these atrocious abuses of victory. It is evident that in his eyes a foreigner is not of the same human species as a Roman.

On the contrary, as peoples become more like one another, they show themselves reciprocally more compassionate regarding their miseries, and the law of nations becomes milder.

Chapter 2 HOW DEMOCRACY RENDERS THE HABITUAL RELATIONS OF THE AMERICANS SIMPLER AND EASIER

Democracy does not attach men strongly to one another, but it renders their habitual relations easier.

Two Englishmen encounter each other by chance at the antipodes; they are surrounded by foreigners whose language and mores they scarcely know.

These two men at first consider each other very curiously and with a sort of secret anxiety; then they turn aside, or if they meet, they take care to speak to each other only with a constrained and distracted air and to say things of little importance.

Nevertheless no enmity exists between them; they have never seen each other and they mutually hold each other to be quite honest. Why therefore do they take such care to avoid each other?

One must return to England to understand it.

When it is birth alone, independent of wealth, that classes men, each knows precisely the point that he occupies on the social scale; he does not

*Marcus Tullius Cicero (106–43 B.C.), Roman statesman, orator, and writer.

seek to climb and he does not fear to descend. In a society so organized, men of different castes communicate little with one another, but when chance puts them in contact they meet willingly without hoping or dreading to be confused. Their relations are not based on equality; but they are not constrained.

When an aristocracy of wealth succeeds an aristocracy of birth, it is no longer the same.

The privileges of some are still very great, but the possibility of acquiring them is open to all; hence it follows that those who possess them are constantly preoccupied with the fear of losing them or of seeing them partitioned; and those who do not yet have them want at all cost to possess them, or if they cannot succeed at this, to appear to—which is not impossible. As the social value of men is no longer fixed in an obvious and permanent manner by blood, and as it varies infinitely according to wealth, ranks still exist, but one no longer sees those who occupy them clearly at first glance.

A muted war among all citizens is immediately established; some strive by a thousand artifices to penetrate, in reality or in appearance, among those who are above them; others constantly do combat to repel these usurpers of their rights—or rather the same man does both things, and while he seeks to be introduced into the higher circle, he struggles without respite against the effort that comes from below.

Such is the state of England in our day, and I think that it is principally to this state that one must relate the preceding.

As aristocratic haughtiness is still very great among the English and the limits of the aristocracy have become doubtful, each fears at each instant that his familiarity may be taken unawares. Not being able to judge at first glance what is the social situation of those whom he encounters, he prudently avoids entering into contact with them. He dreads forming an ill-suited friendship despite himself by rendering slight services; he fears good offices, and he avoids the indiscreet gratitude of a stranger as carefully as his hatred.

There are many people who explain this singular unsociability and reserved and taciturn humor of the English by purely physical causes. I am very willing to have blood in fact be something of it; but I believe that the social state is much more. The example of the Americans comes to prove it.

In America, where privileges of birth have never existed and where wealth gives no particular right to one who possesses it, strangers willingly gather in the same places and find neither advantage nor peril in freely communicating their thoughts to each other. When meeting each other by chance, they neither seek nor avoid each other; their approach is therefore natural, frank, and open; one sees that there is almost nothing they either hope for or fear from one another, and that they strive no more to show than to hide the position they occupy. If their countenances are often cold and serious, they are never haughty or constrained, and when they do not address a word to each other, it is that they are not in a humor to speak, and not that they believe they have an interest in keeping silent.

In a foreign country, two Americans are friends right away for the sole reason that they are Americans. There is no prejudice that repels them, and the community of their native country attracts them. For two Englishmen, the same blood is not enough: the same rank must bring them together.

The Americans notice as well as we do this unsociable humor of the English among themselves, and they are no less astonished by it than we are. Nevertheless the Americans are joined to England by origin, religion, language, and in part mores; they differ only by their social state. It is therefore permissible to say that the reserve of the English flows from the constitution of the country much more than from that of the citizens.

క్రా క్రా క్రా క్రా క్రా క్రా క్రా క్రా క్రా క్రా క్రా క్రా క్రా క్రా క్రా క్రా క్రా క్రా క్రా క్రా

Chapter 3   WHY THE AMERICANS HAVE SO LITTLE OVERSENSITIVITY IN THEIR COUNTRY AND SHOW THEMSELVES TO BE SO OVERSENSITIVE IN OURS

Like all serious and reflective peoples, Americans have a vindictive temperament. They almost never forget an offense; but it is not easy to offend them, and their resentment is as slow to ignite as to be extinguished.

In aristocratic societies, where a few individuals direct all things, external relations among men are subject to nearly fixed conventions. Each then believes he knows in a precise manner by what sign it is fitting to show respect or to signal good will, and etiquette is a science of which one does not assume ignorance.

These usages in the first class then serve as a model for all the others, and further, each of these makes a separate code for itself to which all its members are held to conform.

Thus the rules of politeness form a complicated [body of] legislation which is difficult to possess completely and from which one is nonetheless not permitted to deviate without risk; in this way men are constantly exposed each day to giving or receiving cruel wounds involuntarily.

But as ranks are effaced, as men diverse in their education and birth are mixed and confused in the same places, it is almost impossible to agree on the rules of social graces. The law being uncertain, disobeying it is not a crime even in the eyes of those who know it; one becomes attached, therefore, to the substance of actions rather than to the form, and one is at once less civil and less quarrelsome.

There are a host of small respects on which an American does not insist; he judges that they are not owed to him or he supposes that one is ignorant that they are owed to him. So he does not perceive that one is failing him or rather he pardons it; his manners become less courteous and his mores simpler and more manly.

The reciprocal indulgence that Americans display and the virile confidence they show result again from a more general and more profound cause. I have already pointed it out in the previous chapter.

In the United States, ranks differ only very little in civil society and not at all in the political world; therefore, an American does not believe himself bound to provide particular care to any of those like him nor does he dream of requiring it for himself. As he does not see that his interest is in ardently seeking the company of some fellow citizens, only with difficulty does he fancy that his [company] is being rejected; as he does not scorn anyone because of his condition, he does not imagine that anyone scorns him for the same cause, and until he has clearly perceived the injury he does not believe that anyone wants to insult him.

The social state naturally disposes Americans not to be easily offended in little things. And on the other hand, the democratic freedom they enjoy makes this indulgence pass into the national mores.

The political institutions of the United States constantly put citizens of all classes in contact and force them to pursue great undertakings in common. People thus occupied scarcely have time to think of the details of etiquette, and besides they have too much interest in living in accord to be stopped by them. So they easily become accustomed to considering sentiments and ideas rather than manners in those whom they meet, and they do not allow themselves to be aroused by trivialities.

I remarked many times in the United States that it is not an easy thing to make a man understand that his presence is unwelcome. To come to that, roundabout ways do not always suffice.

I contradict an American at every turn in order to make him feel that his discourses fatigue me; and at each instant I see him make new efforts to convince me; I keep an obstinate silence, and he imagines that I am reflecting deeply on the truths that he presents to me; and when finally I suddenly escape his pursuit, he supposes that a pressing affair calls me elsewhere. This man will not comprehend that he exasperates me without my telling him, and I cannot save myself from him without becoming his mortal enemy.

What is surprising at first is that this same man, transported to Europe, suddenly becomes meticulous and difficult company, to the point that I often encounter as much difficulty in not offending him as I had used to find in displeasing him. These two such different effects are produced by the same cause.

Democratic institutions generally give men a vast idea of their native country and of themselves.

The American leaves his country with his heart inflated with pride. He arrives in Europe and first perceives that they are not as much preoccupied there as he imagined with the United States and the great people that inhabits it. This begins to arouse him.

He has heard it said that conditions are not equal in our hemisphere. He perceives in fact that among the nations of Europe traces of rank have not been entirely effaced; that wealth and birth preserve uncertain privileges there—which is as difficult for him to fail to recognize as it is to define. This spectacle surprises him and makes him anxious, because it is entirely new for him; nothing of what he has seen in his own country helps him to comprehend it. He is therefore profoundly ignorant of the place that is fitting for him to occupy in this half-destroyed hierarchy, among classes that are distinct enough to hate and scorn each other and close enough together so that he is always prone to confuse them. He fears placing himself too high and especially being ranked too low: this double peril continually tortures his mind and constantly embarrasses his actions as well as his discourse.

Tradition has taught him that in Europe ceremony varied infinitely according to conditions; this remembrance of another time serves to trouble him, and he dreads not obtaining the respect that is due him all the more as he does not know precisely what it consists in. So he always proceeds like a man surrounded by ambushes; society is not relaxation for him, but serious work. He weighs your least moves, questions your glances, and carefully analyzes all your discourses for fear that they contain some hidden allusions that wound him. I do not know if there has ever been encountered a country gentleman more punctilious than he is on the detail of good manners; he strives to obey the least laws of etiquette himself, and he does not suffer being neglected on any concerning him; he is at once full of scruple and exactness; he would desire to do enough, but fears doing too much, and as he does not know well the limits of either, he holds to an embarrassed and lofty reserve.

Nor is this all, and here indeed is another twist of the human heart.

An American speaks every day of the admirable equality that reigns in the United States; he prides himself highly on his country; but he is secretly distressed for himself and aspires to show that, as for himself, he makes an exception to the general order he extols.

One scarcely encounters an American who does not want to owe something of his birth to the first founders of the colonies, and as for offshoots of the great families of England, America seemed to me to be entirely covered with them.

When an opulent American lands in Europe, his first care is to surround himself with all the wealth of luxury; and he has so great a fear of being taken for a simple citizen of a democracy that he twists himself in a hundred ways to present you with a new view of his wealth every day. He ordinarily finds lodging in the most conspicuous quarter of the town; he has numerous servants who constantly surround him.

I heard an American complain that in the principal salons of Paris one met only mixed society. The taste that reigns there did not appear pure enough for him, and he adroitly allowed it to be heard that in his opinion distinction in manners was lacking. He was not in the habit of seeing the mind thus hide itself in such vulgar forms.

Such contrasts should not be surprising.

If the trace of old aristocratic distinctions were not so completely effaced in the United States, Americans would show themselves less simple and tolerant in their country, less exacting and affected in ours.

Chapter 4 CONSEQUENCES OF THE PRECEDING THREE CHAPTERS

When men feel a natural pity for one another in their ills, when easy and frequent relations bring them together daily without any oversensitivity to divide them, it is easy to understand that they will mutually lend each other their aid when in need. When an American calls for the cooperation of those like him, it is rare indeed that they refuse it to him, and I often observed that they spontaneously afforded it with great zeal.

Should some unforeseen accident come up on a public road, they come running from all around—whoever the victim may be; should some great unforeseen misfortune strike a family, the purses of a thousand strangers open up without trouble; modest but very numerous gifts come to its assistance in its misery.

In the most civilized nations on the globe it often happens that an unfortunate man is as isolated in the midst of the crowd as a savage in the woods; that is almost unseen in the United States. Americans, who are always cold in their manner and often coarse, almost never show themselves insensitive, and if they do not hasten to offer services, they do not refuse to provide them.

All this is not contrary to what I said previously about individualism. I even see that these things are in accord and far from conflicting.

At the same time that equality of conditions makes men feel their independence, it shows them their weakness; they are free but exposed to a thousand accidents, and experience is not slow to teach them that although they do not have an habitual need of assistance from others, some moment almost always arrives when they cannot do without it.

We see every day in Europe that men of the same profession willingly aid each other; they are all exposed to the same ills; that is enough to get them to seek mutual guarantees for each other, however hard or selfish they are otherwise. So when one of them is in danger, and when the others can shield him from it by a small passing sacrifice or a sudden impulse, they do not fail to attempt it. It is not that they are profoundly interested in his fate; for if by chance the efforts they make to assist him are useless they forget him immediately and return to themselves; but a sort of tacit and almost involuntary accord is made between them according to which each owes the others a momentary support which he himself will be able to call for in his turn.

Extend to a people what I say of only one class and you will comprehend my thought.

In fact a convention analogous to the one I am speaking of exists among all citizens of a democracy; all feel themselves to be subject to the same weakness and the same dangers, and their interest as well as their sympathy makes it a law for them to lend each other mutual assistance when in need.

The more conditions become alike, the more men allow this reciprocal disposition to be seen to obligate them.

In democracies, where they scarcely provide great benefits, they constantly render good offices. It is rare that a man shows himself devoted, but all are serviceable.

Chapter 5 HOW DEMOCRACY
MODIFIES THE RELATIONS OF SERVANT
AND MASTER

An American who had traveled for a long time in Europe said to me one day:

"The English treat their servants with a haughtiness and a peremptory manner that surprise us; but on the other hand, the French sometimes use a familiarity with them or show a politeness with regard to them that we cannot conceive of. One would say that they fear to command. The attitude of superior and inferior is poorly kept."

This remark is just and I myself have made it many times.

I have always considered England to be the country in the world where, in our time, the bond of domestic service is the tightest and France the region on earth where it is most relaxed. Nowhere has the master appeared to me to be higher or lower than in these two countries.

It is between these extremes that the Americans take their place.

That is the superficial and apparent fact. One must go very far back to discover the causes of it.

Societies have not yet been seen where conditions were so equal that one encountered neither rich nor poor and, consequently, neither masters nor servants.

Democracy does not prevent these two classes of men from existing; but it changes their spirit and modifies their relations.

In aristocratic peoples, servants form a particular class that does not vary any more than that of masters. A fixed order is not slow to arise; in the former as in the latter, a hierarchy is soon seen to appear, with numerous classifications and marked ranks, and generations succeed each other without changing their positions. They are two societies superimposed on one another, always distinct, but regulated by analogous principles.

This aristocratic constitution influences the ideas and mores of servants scarcely less than those of masters, and while the effects are different it is easy to recognize the same cause.

They both form small nations in the midst of the great one; and in the end certain permanent notions in the matter of justice and injustice arise in their midst. They view the different acts of human life in a particular light that does not change. In the society of servants as in that of masters, men exert a great influence on one another. They recognize fixed rules and, for want of law, they encounter a public opinion that directs them; regulated habits, orderliness reign there.

These men whose destiny is to obey undoubtedly do not understand glory, virtue, honesty, or honor in the same manner as the masters. But they have made for themselves a glory, virtues, and an honesty of servants, and they conceive, if I can so express myself, a sort of servile honor.[1]

One must not believe that because a class is base, all those who are part of it have base hearts. That would be a great error. However inferior it may be, whoever is first in it and has no idea of leaving it finds himself in an aristocratic position that suggests elevated sentiments to him, a ferocious pride, and a respect for himself that make him fit for great virtues and uncommon actions.

Among aristocratic peoples, it was not rare to find noble and vigorous souls in the service of the great who bore servitude without feeling it and submitted to the will of their master without being afraid of his anger.

But it was almost never so in the inferior ranks of the domestic class. One conceives that whoever occupies the last step in a hierarchy of valets is base indeed.

The French had created a very definite word for this last of the servants of aristocracy. They called him lackey.

The word lackey served as an extreme term, when all others were lacking, to represent human baseness; under the old monarchy when one wanted to paint a vile and degraded being in a moment, one said of him that he had the *soul of a lackey*. That alone sufficed. The sense was complete and understood.

Permanent inequality of conditions not only gives servants certain particular virtues and vices, it places them in a particular position vis-à-vis masters.

Among aristocratic peoples the poor man is trained from childhood with the idea of being commanded. In whatever direction he turns his glance he immediately sees the image of hierarchy and the aspect of obedience.

In countries where a permanent inequality of conditions reigns, the master therefore readily obtains a prompt, complete, respectful, and easy obedience from his servants because they revere not only the master in him, but the class of masters. He weighs on their will with all the weight of the aristocracy.

He commands their acts; he also directs their thoughts up to a certain point. The master in aristocracies often exercises even without his knowing

1. If one comes to examine up close and in detail the principal opinions that direct men, the analogy appears more striking still, and one is astonished to find among them as well as among the most lofty members of a feudal hierarchy, pride of birth, respect for ancestors and descendants, scorn of the inferior, fear of contact, a taste for etiquette, for traditions, and for antiquity.

it a prodigious dominion over the opinions, habits, and mores of those who obey him, and his influence extends much further than his authority.

In aristocratic societies, not only are there hereditary families of valets as well as hereditary families of masters, but the same families of valets are settled for several generations beside the same families of masters (they are like parallel lines that neither meet nor separate), which changes the mutual relations of these two orders of persons prodigiously.

Thus, although under aristocracy the master and the servant have no natural resemblance between them; although on the contrary, fortune, education, opinions, and rights place them at an immense distance on the scale of beings, nevertheless, in the end time binds them together. A long community of memories connects them, and however different they may be, they assimilate; whereas in democracies, where they are naturally almost alike, they always remain strangers to one another.

Among aristocratic peoples, the master therefore comes to view his servants as an inferior and secondary part of himself, and he often interests himself in their lot by a final effort of selfishness.

For their part, servants are not far from considering themselves from the same point of view, and they sometimes identify themselves with the person of the master in such a way that they finally become his accessory in their own eyes as in his.

In aristocracies, the servant occupies a subordinate position that he cannot leave; next to him is another man who holds a superior rank he cannot lose. On the one side, obscurity, poverty, obedience in perpetuity; on the other, glory, wealth, command in perpetuity. These conditions are always diverse and always close, and the bond that unites them is as lasting as they are.

In this extremity, the servant is in the end uninterested in himself; he becomes detached from himself; in a way he deserts himself, or rather he transports himself entirely to his master; there he creates an imaginary personality for himself. He complacently adorns himself with the wealth of those who command him; he glorifies himself with their glory, enhances himself with their nobility, and constantly feeds on a borrowed greatness on which he often puts a higher price than do those who have full and genuine possession of it.

There is something at once touching and ridiculous in such a strange confusion of two existences.

The passions of masters transported to the souls of valets take the natural dimensions of the place they occupy; they shrink and fall away. What was pride in the former becomes puerile vanity and miserable pretension in the latter. Servants of a great man ordinarily show themselves to be very punctilious about the regard one owes him, and they hold more to his least privileges than he himself does.

One sometimes still meets one of these old servants of the aristocracy among us; he survives his race and will soon disappear with it.

In the United States I saw no one who resembles him. Not only are Americans unfamiliar with the man in question, but one has great trouble in getting them to understand his existence. They find scarcely less difficulty in conceiving of him than we ourselves have in imagining what a slave was among the Romans or a serf in the Middle Ages. All these men are in fact, although to different degrees, the products of the same cause. Together they recede from our regard and each day flee into the obscurity of the past together with the social state that gave birth to them.

Equality of conditions makes new beings of servant and master and establishes new relations between them.

When conditions are almost equal, men constantly change place; there is still a class of valets and a class of masters; but it is not always the same individuals, and above all not the same families, that compose them; and there is no more perpetuity in command than in obedience.

As servants do not form a separate people, they do not have usages, prejudices, or mores that are their own; one does not remark a certain turn of mind or a particular way of feeling among them; they know neither the vices nor the virtues of their state, but they share the enlightenment, ideas, sentiments, virtues, and vices of their contemporaries; and they are honest or roguish in the same manner as masters.

Conditions are no less equal among servants than among masters.

As one finds neither marked ranks nor a permanent hierarchy in the class of servants, one must not expect to encounter the vileness and the greatness there that are displayed in aristocracies of valets as well as in all other [aristocracies].

I never saw anything in the United States that could recall to me the idea of the elite servant, of whom we in Europe have preserved the memory; but neither did I find the idea of the lackey. Any trace of either one or the other is lost there.

In democracies not only are servants equal among themselves; one can say that they are in a way the equals of their masters.

This needs to be explained to be well understood.

At each instant the servant can become a master and aspire to become one; the servant, therefore, is not another man than the master.

Why therefore does the first have the right to command and what forces the second to obey? The temporary and free accord of their two wills. One is not naturally inferior to the other; he only becomes so temporarily by the fact of a contract. Within the limits of this contract the one is the servant and the other the master; outside of it they are two citizens, two men.

What I beg the reader to consider well is that this is not only the notion that servants form for themselves of their state. Masters consider domestic service in the same light, and the precise boundaries of command and obedience are as well fixed in the mind of the one as in that of the other.

When most citizens have long since attained an almost like condition, and equality is an old and accepted fact, the public sense, which exceptions never influence, assigns in a general manner certain limits to the value of man above or below which it is difficult for any man to stay for long.

In vain do wealth and poverty, command and obedience accidentally put great distances between two men; public opinion, which is founded on the ordinary order of things, brings them near to the common level and creates a sort of imaginary equality between them despite the real inequality of their conditions.

This all-powerful opinion in the end penetrates the very souls of those whom interest could arm against it; it modifies their judgment at the same time that it subjugates their wills.

At the bottom of their souls, master and servant no longer perceive a profound dissimilarity between them, and they neither hope nor dread ever to encounter it. They are therefore without scorn and without anger, and in regarding each other they find themselves neither humble nor proud.

The master judges that the sole origin of his power is in the contract, and the servant discovers in it the sole cause of his obedience. They do not dispute between themselves the reciprocal positions they occupy; but each readily sees his and holds to it.

In our armies the soldier is taken from almost the same classes as the officers and can attain the same posts; outside of the ranks, he considers himself perfectly equal to his chiefs and in fact he is; but under the flag he has no difficulty in obeying, and his obedience, though it is voluntary and defined, is no less prompt, clear, and easy.

This gives one an idea of what takes place in democratic societies between servant and master.

It would be senseless to believe that there could ever arise between these two men any of the ardent and profound affections that are sometimes kindled within aristocratic domestic service, or that one should see striking examples of devotion appear.

In aristocracies servant and master perceive each other only now and then, and often they speak to each other only through an intermediary. Nevertheless they ordinarily hold firmly to one another.

Among democratic peoples servant and master are very close; their bodies constantly touch, their souls do not mix; they have common occupations, they almost never have common interests.

Among these peoples the servant always considers himself a passerby in the dwelling of his masters. He did not know their ancestors and he will not see their descendants; he has nothing lasting to expect from them. Why would he confuse his existence with theirs, and where would that singular abandonment of himself come from? The reciprocal position has changed; their relations must too.

I would like to be able to support myself in all that precedes with the example of the Americans; but I cannot do so without carefully distinguishing persons and places.

In the South of the Union slavery exists. All that I have just said therefore cannot apply to it.

In the North most servants are freedmen or the sons of freedmen. These men occupy a contested position in public esteem: the law brings them near the level of their master; mores obstinately repel them from it. They themselves do not clearly discern their place, and they almost always show themselves insolent or cringing.

But in these same provinces of the North, particularly in New England, one encounters a fairly large number of whites who consent to submit temporarily to the will of those like themselves in return for a wage. I heard it said that these servants ordinarily fulfill the duties of their state exactly and intelligently, and that without believing themselves naturally inferior to whoever commands them, they submit without trouble to obey him.

It seemed to me I saw that they carried into servitude some of the virile habits to which independence and equality had given birth. Having once chosen a hard condition, they do not seek to escape it indirectly, and they respect themselves enough not to refuse their masters an obedience that they have freely promised.

For their part, masters require of their servants only faithful and rigorous execution of the contract; they do not demand respect; they claim neither their love nor their devotion; for them it is enough to find them punctual and honest.

It would therefore not be true to say that under democracy relations between servant and master are disordered; they are ordered in another manner; the rule is different, but there is a rule.

I have not inquired here whether this new state that I have just described is inferior to the one that preceded it or whether it is only otherwise. It is enough for me that it be regulated and fixed; for what is most important to encounter among men is not one certain order, but order.

But what shall I say of the sad and turbulent periods in which equality is founded amid the tumult of a revolution, when democracy, having been established in the social state, still struggles with difficulty against prejudices and mores?

Already the law, and in part opinion, proclaim that a natural and permanent inferiority between servant and master does not exist. But this new faith has not yet penetrated to the depth of the mind of the latter, or rather his heart rejects it. In the secrecy of his soul the master still deems himself to be of a particular, superior species; but he does not dare to say it, and he lets himself be drawn down, trembling, toward the same level. His command becomes at once timid and harsh; already he no longer feels the protective and benevolent sentiments for his servants to which long, uncontested power always gives rise, and he is astonished that, having changed himself, his servant changes; he wants the latter, while making him only so to speak pass through domestic service, to contract the regular and permanent habits of it; to show himself to be satisfied and proud in a servile position which sooner or later he will leave; to devote himself to a man who can neither protect him nor ruin him, and finally to attach himself by an eternal bond to beings who are like him and who last no longer than he does.

In aristocratic peoples it often happens that the state of domestic service does not debase the souls of those who submit to it because they are familiar with it and imagine no other, and because the enormous inequality that one sees between them and the master seems to them the necessary and inevitable effect of some hidden law of Providence.

Under democracy the state of domestic service has nothing degrading because it is chosen freely and adopted temporarily, because public opinion does not stigmatize it, and because it does not create any permanent inequality between servant and master.

But during the passage from one social condition to another, a moment almost always comes in which the spirit of men vacillates between the aristocratic notion of subjugation and democratic notion of obedience.

Then obedience loses its morality in the eyes of whoever obeys; he no longer considers it as a sort of divine obligation, and he does not yet see it in its purely human aspect; it is neither holy nor just in his eyes, and he submits to it as a degrading but useful fact.

At this moment a confused and incomplete image of equality is presented to the minds of servants; they do not at first discern whether it is in the state of domestic service itself or outside it that the equality they have a right to is located, and from the bottom of their hearts they revolt against an inferiority to which they themselves have submitted and from which they profit. They consent to serve and they are ashamed to obey; they love the advantages of servitude, but not the master, or, to say it better, they are not sure that they should not be the masters and they are disposed to consider whoever commands them as the unjust usurper of their right.

It is then that one sees in the dwelling of each citizen something analogous to the sad spectacle that political society presents. There a muted civil war is constantly pursued between ever suspicious and rival powers: the master shows himself malevolent and mild, the servant malevolent and intractable; the one wants constantly, by dishonorable restrictions, to escape from the obligation of protecting and remunerating, the other from that of obeying. Between them hang the reins of domestic administration that each strives to seize. The lines that divide authority from tyranny, freedom from license, and right from fact appear to their eyes entangled and confused, and no one knows precisely what he is, what he can do, or what he should do.

Such a state is not democratic, but revolutionary.

Chapter 6 HOW DEMOCRATIC INSTITUTIONS AND MORES TEND TO RAISE THE PRICE AND SHORTEN THE DURATION OF LEASES

What I have said about servants and masters applies up to a certain point to property owners and tenant farmers. Nevertheless, the subject deserves to be considered separately.

In America there are so to speak no tenant farmers; every man is the owner of the field he cultivates.

One must recognize that democratic laws tend powerfully to increase the number of property owners and diminish that of tenant farmers. Still, what happens in the United States ought to be attributed much less to the institutions of the country than to the country itself. In America land costs little and each man easily becomes a property owner. It yields little, and only with difficulty can its products be divided between a property owner and a tenant farmer.

America is therefore unique in this as in other things; and one would err in taking it as an example.

I think that in democratic countries as well as in aristocracies, property owners and tenant farmers will be encountered; but property owners and tenant farmers will not be bound in the same manner.

In aristocracies, farm rents are discharged not only in money, but in respect, affection, and services. In democratic countries, they are paid only in money. When patrimonies are divided and change hands, and the permanent relation that existed between families and the land disappears, it is no more than chance that puts the property owner and the tenant farmer in contact. They are joined for a moment to negotiate the conditions of the contract, and afterwards they lose sight of each other. They are two strangers whom interest brings together and who rigorously discuss between themselves an affair whose sole subject is money.

As goods are partitioned and wealth is dispersed here and there over all the area of the country, the state is filled with people whose former opulence is in decline and with the newly enriched whose needs grow more quickly than their resources. For all these, the least profit is of consequence, and none among them feels himself disposed to allow any of his advantages to escape or to lose any portion whatsoever of his revenue.

As ranks are being confused and very great as well as very small fortunes are becoming rarer, one finds less distance between the social condition of the property owner and that of the tenant farmer every day; the one naturally has no uncontested superiority over the other. Now between two equal and uneasy men, what could the matter of the rental contract be, if not money?

A man who has an entire district for his property and possesses a hundred small farms understands that it is a question of gaining the hearts of several thousand men at a time; this appears to him to be worth applying himself to. To attain such a great object he readily makes sacrifices.

One who possesses a hundred acres is not burdened with such cares; it scarcely matters to him to win the particular benevolence of his tenant farmer.

An aristocracy does not die like a man in one day. Its principle is destroyed slowly at the bottom of souls before being attacked in the laws. Long before the war against it breaks out, therefore, one sees the bond that until then had united the upper classes to the lower loosen little by little. Indifference and scorn betray themselves on one side; on the other jealousy and hatred: relations between poor and rich become rarer and less mild; the price of leases rises. This is not yet the result of the democratic revolution, but its certain announcement. For an aristocracy that has definitively allowed the heart of the people to escape from its hands is like a tree dead in its roots, which the wind overturns all the more easily the taller it is.

For fifty years the price of farm rents has increased enormously not only in France but in the greatest part of Europe. The singular progress that agriculture and industry have made during the same period is not enough, in my view, to explain this phenomenon. One must recur to some other more powerful and more hidden cause. I think this cause ought to be sought in the democratic institutions that several European peoples have adopted and in the democratic passions that agitate more or less all the others.

I have often heard great English property owners congratulate themselves on the fact that in our day they get more money from their domains than their fathers did.

Perhaps they are right to rejoice; but surely they do not know what they are rejoicing about. They believe they are making a clear profit and they are only making an exchange. It is their influence that they cede for petty cash; and what they gain in money they are soon going to lose in power.

There is yet another sign by which one can readily recognize that a great democratic revolution is being accomplished or prepared.

In the Middle Ages, almost all lands were rented in perpetuity or at least for very long terms. When one studies the domestic economy of this time, one sees that ninety-nine-year leases were then more frequent than twelve-year ones are in our day.

Then they believed in the immortality of families; conditions seemed forever fixed, and the whole society appeared so immobile that one did not imagine that anything would ever stir within it.

In centuries of equality, the human spirit takes another turn. It readily fancies that nothing stays put. The idea of instability possesses it.

In this mood the property owner and the tenant farmer himself feel a sort of instinctive horror of long-term obligations; they are afraid of finding themselves limited some day by the agreement from which they profit today. They wait vaguely for some sudden and unforeseen change in their condition. They dread themselves; they fear that when their taste comes to change they will be distressed by not being able to give up what was the object of their covetousness, and they are right to fear it; for in democratic centuries, what is most in motion amid the motion of all things is the heart of man.

Chapter 7 INFLUENCE OF DEMOCRACY ON WAGES

Most of the remarks that I made previously in speaking of servants and masters can be applied to masters and workers.

As the rules of social hierarchy are less observed, while the great are pulled down, while the small rise and poverty as well as wealth ceases to be hereditary, one sees the distance in fact and in opinion that separates the worker from the master decrease each day.

The worker conceives a more elevated idea of his rights, of his future, of himself; a new ambition, new desires fill him, new needs besiege him. At every moment he turns looks full of covetousness at the profits of his employer; in order to come to share them, he strives to set his work at a higher price, and in the end he ordinarily succeeds in this.

In democratic countries, as elsewhere, most industries are conducted at little cost by men whom wealth and enlightenment do not place above the common level of those they employ. These entrepreneurs of industry are very numerous; their interests differ; they therefore cannot readily agree among themselves and combine their efforts.

On the other hand, workers almost all have some secure resources that permit them to refuse their services when one does not want to accord them what they consider a just reward for their work.

In the continuous struggle over wages which these two classes are given to, forces are therefore divided and success alternates.

It is even to be believed that in the long term the interest of the workers will prevail; for the raise in wages they have already obtained renders them less dependent on their masters each day, and as they become more independent they can more easily obtain a raise in wages.

I shall take as an example the industry that in our time is still the most practiced among us as well as in almost all the nations of the world: the cultivation of land.

In France most of those who rent out their services to cultivate the soil themselves possess some parcels of it which permit them to subsist, if really necessary, without working for another. When they come to offer [the labor of] their arms to a large property owner or a neighboring tenant farmer and he refuses to accord them a certain wage, they go back to their little domains and wait for another occasion to present itself.

I think that taking all things together, one can say that the slow and progressive rise in wages is one of the general laws that regulate democratic societies. As conditions become more equal, wages rise, and as wages go higher, conditions become more equal.

But in our day one encounters a great and unfortunate exception.

I showed in a previous chapter how aristocracy, driven out of political society, had withdrawn into certain parts of the industrial world and established its empire there in another form.*

This powerfully influences wage rates.

*DA II 2.20.

As one must already be very wealthy to undertake the great industries I am speaking of, the number of those who undertake them is very small. Being few, they can easily league together and fix the price they please for work.

Their workers are, by contrast, very many in number, and the quantity of them grows constantly; for from time to time an extraordinary prosperity comes, during which wages rise beyond measure and attract the surrounding population into manufactures. Now, once men have entered into this career, we have seen that they cannot leave it because they are not slow to pick up habits of body and mind from it that render them unsuited for every other labor. These men generally have little enlightenment, industry, and resources; they are therefore almost at the mercy of their master. When competition, or some other fortuitous circumstance, decreases the latter's gains, he can restrict their wages almost as he pleases and easily recover from them what fortune takes away from him.

If they should refuse work by common accord, the master, who is a rich man, can easily wait for necessity to bring them back to him without being ruined; but they must work every day in order not to die; for they have scarcely any property other than [the labor of] their arms. They have long been impoverished by oppression, and they are easier to oppress as they become poorer. It is a vicious circle they can in no way escape.

One ought therefore not to be surprised if wages, after having sometimes suddenly risen, fall in a permanent manner here, whereas in other professions the price of work, which generally grows only little by little, constantly increases.

This state of dependence and misery in which a part of the industrial population in our time finds itself is an exceptional fact and contrary to everything that surrounds it; but for this very reason there is none graver or that deserves more to attract the particular attention of the legislator; for it is difficult, when the entire society is moving, to hold one class immobile, and when the greatest number constantly open new paths to fortune for themselves, to make a few bear their needs and desires in peace.

చేం చేం చేం చేం చేం చేం చేం చేం చేం చేం చేం చేం చేం చేం చేం చేం చేం చేం చేం చేం

Chapter 8 INFLUENCE OF DEMOCRACY ON THE FAMILY

I have just examined how among democratic peoples, and among Americans in particular, equality of conditions modifies the relations of citizens among themselves.

I want to penetrate more deeply and enter into the bosom of the family. My goal here is not to seek new truths but to show how already known facts are linked to my subject.

Everyone has remarked that in our day new relations between the different members of the family have been established, that the distance that formerly separated a father from his sons has diminished, and that paternal authority has been, if not destroyed, at least altered.

Something analogous but still more striking is seen in the United States.

In America, the family, taking this word in its Roman and aristocratic sense, does not exist. One only finds some vestiges of it during the first years following the birth of the children. The father exercises at that time, without opposition, the domestic dictatorship that the weakness of his sons renders necessary and which their interest as well as his incontestable superiority justifies.

But from the moment when the young American approaches manhood, the bonds of filial obedience are loosened day by day. Master of his thoughts, he is soon after master of his conduct. In America there is, to tell the truth, no adolescence. On leaving his first years the man shows himself and begins to trace out his path by himself.

It would be wrong to believe that this happens following an internal struggle in which the son has obtained, by a sort of moral violence, the freedom his father refused him. The same habits, the same principles that impel the one to seize independence dispose the other to consider the use of it as an incontestable right.

Therefore one remarks in the former none of the hateful and disordered passions that still agitate men long after they have escaped from an established power. The latter does not feel the regrets full of bitterness and anger that ordinarily survive after one has been deprived of power: the father has perceived from afar the boundaries at which his authority will come to expire; and when its time has approached these limits, he abdicates without difficulty. The son has foreseen in advance the precise period when his own will becomes his rule, and he takes possession of his freedom without haste and without effort, as a good that is due him and of which no one seeks to rob him.[1]

It is perhaps not useless to bring out how the changes that have taken place in the family are tightly bound to the social and political revolution that is finally being accomplished before our eyes.

There are certain great social principles that a people makes pervasive everywhere or allows to subsist nowhere.

In countries organized aristocratically and hierarchically, power is never directly addressed to the entirety of the governed. Since men are joined to one another, one limits oneself to guiding the first ones. The rest follow. This applies to the family as to all associations that have a head. In aristocratic peoples, society knows, to tell the truth, only the father. It holds the sons only by the hands of the father; it governs him and he governs them. The father therefore does not have only a natural right. He is given a political right to command. He is the author and the sustainer of the family; he is also its magistrate.

In democracies, where the arm of the government goes to seek each man particularly in the midst of the crowd to bend him, in isolation, to the common laws, it has no need of an intermediary like this; in the eyes of the law, the father is only an older and richer citizen than his sons.

When most conditions are very unequal and the inequality of conditions is permanent, the idea of a superior grows large in the imagination of men; should the law not accord him prerogatives, custom and opinion concede

1. Americans, however, have not yet imagined, as we have done in France, taking away one of the principal elements of power from fathers by denying them their freedom to dispose of their goods after death. In the United States the ability to make a will is unlimited.

In that, as in almost all the rest, it is easy to remark that if the political legislation of the Americans is much more democratic than ours, our civil legislation is infinitely more democratic than theirs. That one conceives without trouble.

Our civil legislation had for its author a man who saw his interest in satisfying the democratic passions of his contemporaries in all that was not directly and immediately hostile to his power. He willingly permitted some popular principles to regulate goods and govern families, provided that one did not claim to introduce them into the direction of the state. While the democratic torrent flooded over civil laws, he hoped to keep political laws easily sheltered. This view is at once full of skill and of selfishness, but such a compromise could not be lasting. For, in the long term, political society cannot fail to become the expression and image of civil society; and it is in this sense that one can say that there is nothing more political in a people than civil legislation.

[The Napoleonic, or Civil, Code to which AT refers was enacted in France in 1804. Claiming to be based on the dictates of reason rather than custom, it established uniformity of law throughout the country. The Code guaranteed the equality of all citizens, abolished hereditary nobility and class privileges, and replaced primogeniture, requiring fathers to distribute their estates among all sons equally. In practice, however, exceptions to equality of inheritance were frequent. See *DA* I 1.3 above, on estate law.]

them to him. When, on the contrary, men differ little one from another and do not remain always unalike, the general notion of a superior becomes weaker and less clear; in vain does the will of the legislator strive to place one who obeys much below one who commands; mores bring the two men together and each day draw them toward the same level.

Therefore, if I do not see particular privileges accorded to the head of the family in the legislation of an aristocratic people, I shall not cease to be assured that his power is much respected and more extensive than within a democracy, for I know that whatever the laws may be, a superior will always appear higher and an inferior lower in aristocracies than among democratic peoples.

When men live in the remembrance of what has been rather than in the preoccupation with what is, when they worry much more about what their ancestors thought than they seek to think for themselves, the father is the natural and necessary bond between the past and the present, the link at which these two chains end and are joined. In aristocracies the father is therefore not only the political head of the family; he is the organ of tradition, the interpreter of custom, the arbiter of mores. He is listened to with deference, approached only with respect; and the love one bears for him is always tempered by fear.

As the social state becomes democratic and men adopt for their general principle that it is good and legitimate to judge all things by oneself, taking old beliefs as information and not as a rule, the power of opinion exercised by the father over the sons becomes less great, as does his legal power.

The division of patrimonies to which democracy leads contributes perhaps more than everything else to changing relations between father and children.

When the father of a family has few [material] goods, he and his son live in the same place constantly and are occupied in common with the same work. Habit and need bring them together and force them to communicate with one another at each instant; therefore there cannot fail to be established between them a sort of familiar intimacy that renders authority less absolute and that ill accommodates to external forms of respect.

Now among democratic peoples, the class that possesses these small fortunes is precisely the one that gives power to ideas and sets the tone of mores. It makes its opinions predominate everywhere at the same time as its will, and even those who are most inclined to resist its commands allow themselves in the end to be carried away by its examples. I have seen fiery enemies of democracy who have gotten used to being addressed familiarly by their children.

Thus at the same time as power is slipping away from the aristocracy, one sees what there used to be of the austere, the conventional, and the legal in paternal power disappearing, and a sort of equality being established around the domestic hearth.

I do not know if, all in all, society loses by this change; but I am brought to believe that the individual gains by it. I think that as mores and laws become more democratic, the relations of father and son become more intimate and sweeter;* rule and authority are met with less; confidence and affection are often greater; and it seems that the natural bond tightens while the social bond is loosened.

In the democratic family the father exercises hardly any power other than that which one is pleased to accord to tenderness and to the experience of an old man. His orders would perhaps be neglected; but his counsels are ordinarily full of power. If he is not surrounded with official respect, his sons at least approach him with confidence. There is no recognized formula for addressing words to him; but they speak to him constantly and willingly consult him daily. The master and the magistrate have disappeared; the father remains.

To judge the difference between the two social states on this point, it suffices to run through the domestic correspondence that aristocracies have left us. Their style is always correct, ceremonious, rigid, and so cold that the natural warmth of the heart can hardly be felt through the words.

Among democratic peoples, on the contrary, in all the words that a son addresses to his father there reigns something at once free, familiar, and tender that makes one discover from the first that new relations have been established in the bosom of the family.

An analogous revolution modifies the mutual relations of children.

In the aristocratic family as well as in aristocratic society, all places are marked out. Not only does the father occupy a separate rank in it and enjoy immense privileges, the children are not equal among themselves: age and sex irrevocably fix the rank of each and assure him certain prerogatives. Democracy overturns or lowers most of these barriers.

In the aristocratic family, the eldest son, inheriting the greatest part of the goods and almost all the rights, becomes the chief, and up to a certain point the master, of his brothers. To him go greatness and power, to them mediocrity and dependence. Still, it would be wrong to believe that among aristocratic peoples the privileges of the eldest are advantageous to him alone and that they excite only envy and hatred around him.

The eldest ordinarily strives to procure wealth and power for his brothers

---

*Or "milder." *Doux* has sometimes been translated as "sweet," as in this chapter on the family; it is usually translated as "mild," for example in the chapter on mild despotism, *DA* II 4.6.

because the general brilliance of the house reflects on the one who represents it; and the younger ones seek to facilitate all the undertakings of the eldest because the greatness and force of the head of the family put him more and more in a state to elevate all the offspring.

The various members of the aristocratic family are therefore very tightly bound to one another; their interests are joined, their minds are in accord; but it is rare that their hearts agree.

Democracy also attaches brothers to one another; but it goes about it in another manner.

Under democratic laws children are perfectly equal and consequently independent; nothing forces them to come together, but also nothing draws them apart; and as they have a common origin, are raised under the same roof, are the object of the same cares, and are not distinguished or separated by any particular prerogative, one sees the sweet, childlike intimacy of the first years arise easily among them. With the bond thus formed at the beginning of life, there are scarcely any occasions to break it, for fraternity brings them together daily without hindrance.

It is therefore not by interests but by community of memories and free sympathy of opinions and tastes that democracy attaches brothers to one another. It divides their inheritance, but it permits their souls to intermingle.

The sweetness of these democratic mores is so great that even partisans of aristocracy allow themselves to be taken by it, and after tasting it for some time, they are not tempted to return to the respectful and cold forms of the aristocratic family. They would willingly preserve the domestic habits of democracy provided that they could reject its social state and laws. But these things are joined, and one cannot enjoy the one without suffering the other.

What I have just said of filial love and fraternal tenderness ought to be understood of all the passions that spontaneously have their source in nature itself.

When a certain manner of thinking or feeling is the product of a particular state of humanity, and that state comes to change, nothing remains. Thus it is that the law can very tightly attach two citizens to one another; when the law is abolished, they separate. There was nothing tighter than the knot that united vassal to lord in the feudal world. Now these two men no longer know each other. The fear, recognition, and love that formerly bound them have disappeared. One does not find a trace of them.

But it is not the same with sentiments natural to the human species. It is rare that the law, in striving to bend these in a certain manner, does not enervate them; that in wishing to add to them it does not take away something, and that they are not always stronger left to themselves.

Democracy, which destroys or obscures almost all the old social conventions and prevents men from readily fastening on new ones, makes most of the sentiments that arise from these conventions disappear entirely. But it only modifies the others, and often it gives them an energy and a sweetness they did not use to have.

I think it is not impossible to contain all the sense of this chapter and several others that precede it in a single sentence. Democracy loosens social bonds, but it tightens natural bonds. It brings relatives together at the same time that it separates citizens.

Chapter 9 EDUCATION OF GIRLS IN THE UNITED STATES

There have never been free societies without mores, and as I said in the first part of this work,* it is woman who makes mores. Therefore, all that influences the condition of women, their habits, and their opinions has great political interest in my eyes.

In almost all Protestant nations, girls are infinitely more mistresses of their actions than in Catholic peoples.

This independence is still greater in Protestant countries like England which have preserved or acquired the right to govern themselves. Freedom then penetrates the family through political habits and religious beliefs.

In the United States, the doctrines of Protestantism come to combine with a very free constitution and a very democratic social state; and nowhere is the girl more promptly or more completely left to herself.

Long before the young American woman has attained the age of puberty, one begins to free her little by little from maternal tutelage; before she has entirely left childhood she already thinks for herself, speaks freely, and acts alone; the great picture of the world is constantly exposed before her; far from seeking to conceal the view of it from her, they uncover more and more of it to her regard every day and teach her to consider it with a firm and tranquil eye. Thus the vices and perils that society presents are not slow to be revealed to her; she sees them clearly, judges them without illusion, and faces them without fear; for she is full of confidence in her strength, and her confidence seems to be shared by all those who surround her.

*See *DA* I 2.9.

Therefore one must almost never expect to encounter in the girl of America the virginal candor in the midst of nascent desires or the naive and artless graces that ordinarily accompany the passage from childhood to youth in the European woman. It is rare that the American woman, whatever her age, shows a puerile timidity and ignorance. Like the European girl, she wants to please, but she knows precisely at what price. If she does not indulge in evil she at least knows what it is; she has pure mores rather than a chaste mind.

I was often surprised and almost frightened on seeing the singular dexterity and happy audacity with which these girls of America knew how to conduct their thoughts and words amid the pitfalls of a playful conversation; a philosopher would have stumbled a hundred times on the narrow path that they traveled without accident and without trouble.

It is in fact easy to recognize that in the very midst of the independence of her first youth, the American woman never entirely ceases to be mistress of herself; she enjoys all permitted pleasures without abandoning herself to any of them, and her reason does not drop the reins although it often seems to let them dangle.

In France, where we still mix debris from all ages in our opinions and tastes in such a strange manner, we often give women a timid, withdrawn, and almost cloistered education as in aristocratic times, and afterwards we suddenly abandon them, without a guide and without assistance, in the midst of the disorders inseparable from a democratic society.

The Americans are in better accord with themselves.

They have seen that within a democracy, individual independence could not fail to be very great, youth premature, tastes badly controlled, custom changing, public opinion often uncertain or impotent, paternal authority weak, and marital power contested.

They have judged that in this state of things there were few chances of being able to repress in woman the most tyrannical passions of the human heart, and that it was surer to teach her the art of combating them herself. As they could not prevent her virtue from often being in peril, they wanted her to know how to defend it, and they counted more on the free effort of her will than on shaky or destroyed barriers. Instead of keeping her in mistrust of herself, therefore, they constantly seek to increase her confidence in her own strength. Having neither the possibility nor the desire to keep a girl in perpetual and complete ignorance, they have hastened to give her a precocious knowledge of all things. Far from hiding the corruptions of the world from her, they wanted her to see them right away and to exert herself to flee them; and they would rather safeguard her honesty than respect her innocence too much.

Although Americans are a very religious people, they have not relied on religion alone to defend the virtue of woman; they have sought to arm her reason. In this as in many other circumstances they have followed the same method. They have first made incredible efforts to get individual independence to rule itself, and it is only when they have reached the last limits of human force that they have finally called religion to aid them.

I know that such an education is not without danger; nor am I ignorant that it tends to develop judgment at the expense of imagination and to make women honest and cold rather than tender spouses and amiable companions of man. If society is more tranquil and better regulated for it, private life often has fewer charms. But those are secondary evils that ought to be faced for a greater interest. Having come to the point where we are, we are no longer permitted to make a choice: we need a democratic education to safeguard woman from the perils with which the institutions and mores of democracy surround her.

❧ ❧ ❧ ❧ ❧ ❧ ❧ ❧ ❧ ❧ ❧ ❧ ❧ ❧ ❧ ❧ ❧ ❧ ❧ ❧

Chapter 10 HOW THE GIRL IS FOUND BENEATH THE FEATURES OF THE WIFE

In America the independence of woman is irretrievably lost within the bonds of marriage. If the girl is less constrained there than everywhere else, the wife submits to stricter obligations. The one makes of the paternal home a place of freedom and pleasure, the other lives in her husband's dwelling as in a cloister.

These two so different states are perhaps not so contrary as is supposed, and it is natural that Americans pass through the one to arrive at the other.

Religious peoples and industrial nations have a particularly serious idea of marriage. The first consider the regularity of a woman's life as the best safeguard and most certain sign of the purity of her morals. The latter see in it a sure pledge of the order and prosperity of the home.

The Americans form at once a Puritan nation and a commercial people; their religious beliefs as well as their industrial habits therefore bring them to exact from woman a self-abnegation and a continual sacrifice of her pleasures to her business that is rare to demand of her in Europe. Thus an inexorable public opinion reigns in the United States that carefully confines woman within the small circle of interests and domestic duties, and forbids her to leave it.

On her entrance into the world, the young American woman finds these notions firmly established; she sees the rules that flow from them; she is not slow to be convinced that she cannot for a moment escape the usages of her contemporaries without immediately putting her tranquillity, her honor, and even her social existence in peril; and she finds the energy to submit to them in the firmness of her reason and in the virile habits her education has given her.

One can say that it is in the use of independence that she drew the courage to undergo the sacrifice without struggle and without murmur when the moment came for it to be imposed on her.

The American woman, moreover, never falls into the bonds of marriage as into a trap set for her simplicity and ignorance. She has been taught in advance what is expected of her, and she freely places herself in the yoke on her own. She tolerates her new condition courageously because she has chosen it.

As paternal discipline is very lax in America and the conjugal bond very strict, it is only with circumspection and fear that a girl contracts for it. One scarcely sees any precocious unions there. Therefore American women marry only when their reason is exercised and mature, while elsewhere most women ordinarily begin to exercise their reason and become mature in it only within marriage.

Furthermore, I am very far from believing that the great change that occurs in all the habits of women in the United States as soon as they are married ought to be attributed only to the constraint of public opinion. Often they impose it on themselves by the sole effort of their will.

When the time has come to choose a spouse, the cold and austere reason that has been enlightened and steadied by a free view of the world indicates to the American woman that a light and independent spirit within the bonds of marriage is a subject of eternal trouble, not of pleasure; that the amusements of a girl cannot become the relaxations of a wife, and that for woman the sources of happiness are within the conjugal dwelling. Seeing clearly in advance the sole path that can lead to domestic felicity, she enters on it with her first steps and follows it to the end without seeking to turn back.

This same strength of will that the young wives of America display in bowing all at once, without complaint, to the austere duties of their new state is, furthermore, found also in all the great trials of their lives.

There is no country in the world where particular fortunes are more unstable than in the United States. It is not rare that in the course of his existence the same man rises and falls back through all the stages that lead from opulence to poverty.

The women of America tolerate these revolutions with tranquil and indomitable energy. One would say that their desires contract with their fortunes as easily as they expand.

Most of the adventurers who come each year to populate the solitudes of the West belong, as I said in my first work,* to the old Anglo-American race of the North. Some of these men who run with so much audacity toward wealth already enjoyed ease in their own land. They bring their companions with them and make them share the innumerable perils and miseries that always signal the beginning of such undertakings. I often met young women at the utmost limits of the wilderness who, after having been raised in the midst of all the delicacies of the great cities of New England, had passed almost without transition from the rich dwellings of their parents to leaky huts in the middle of a forest. Fever, solitude, and tedium had not broken the springs of their courage. Their features seemed altered and faded, but their look was firm. They appeared at once sad and resolute.

I do not doubt that these young American women had gathered from their early education the internal force they made use of then.

It is therefore the girl who is found again beneath the features of the wife in the United States; the role has changed, the habits differ, the spirit is the same.†

༄ ༄

Chapter 11 HOW EQUALITY OF CONDITIONS CONTRIBUTES TO MAINTAINING GOOD MORES‡ IN AMERICA

There are philosophers and historians who have said or let it be understood that women are more or less severe in their mores according to whether they live more or less far from the equator.§ This is getting out of the difficulty cheaply, and by this account a globe and a compass would suffice to resolve in an instant one of the most difficult problems that humanity presents.

I do not see that this materialist doctrine is established by the facts.

The same nations have shown themselves to be chaste or dissolute at

---

*DA I 2.10.
†See AT's note XX, page 699.
‡Or "morals," throughout this chapter.
§Montesquieu, *The Spirit of the Laws,* XVI 9, 12.

different periods in their history. The regularity or disorder of their mores therefore depended on some changing causes and not only on the nature of the country, which did not change.

I will not deny that in certain climates the passions that arise from the reciprocal attraction of the sexes are particularly ardent; but I think that this natural ardor can always be excited or contained by the social state and political institutions.*

Although travelers who have visited North America differ among themselves on several points, they all agree in remarking that mores are infinitely more severe there than everywhere else.

It is evident that on this point the Americans are much superior to their fathers, the English. A superficial view of the two nations suffices to show that.

In England as in all other countries of Europe, public ill will is constantly exercised over the weaknesses of women. One often hears philosophers and men of state complain that mores are not regular enough, and every day literature makes one assume it.

In America all books, not excepting novels, assume women chaste, and no one tells of gallant adventures in them.

This great regularity of American mores is doubtless due in part to the country, race, and religion. But all these causes, which are encountered elsewhere, are still not enough to explain it. For that, one must have recourse to some particular reason.

That reason appears to me to be equality and the institutions that flow from it.

Equality of conditions does not produce regularity of mores by itself alone; but one cannot doubt that it facilitates and adds to it.

In aristocratic peoples, birth and fortune often make man and woman such different beings that they can never come to be united to one another. Passions bring them together, but the social state and the ideas it suggests prevent them from bonding in a permanent and open manner. Hence a great number of passing and clandestine unions necessarily arise. Nature compensates itself in secret for the constraint that the laws impose on it.

One does not see this same thing when equality of conditions has brought down all the imaginary or real barriers that separate man from woman. Then there is no girl who does not believe she can become the wife of the man who prefers her, which makes disorder in mores before marriage very difficult. For whatever the credulity of passions may be, there is scarcely a means by which a woman may be persuaded that you love her when you are perfectly free to marry her and do not do it.

*See AT's note XXI, page 701.

The same cause operates within marriage, although in a more indirect manner.

Nothing serves better to legitimate illegitimate love in the eyes of those who feel it or of the crowd that contemplates it than unions that are forced or made haphazardly.[1]

In a country where a woman always exercises her choice freely, and where education has put her in a state to choose well, public opinion is inexorable toward her faults.

The rigor of the Americans arises in part from that. They consider marriage as an often onerous contract of which one is nonetheless strictly held to execute all the clauses because [the parties] were able to know them all in advance and because they enjoyed the complete freedom of not obligating themselves to anything.

What renders fidelity more obligatory renders it easier.

In aristocratic countries, marriage has the purpose of uniting goods rather than persons; so it sometimes happens that the husband is picked while in school and the wife at the wet nurse. It is not surprising that the conjugal bond that keeps the fortunes of the two spouses united leaves their hearts to wander about aimlessly. This flows naturally from the spirit of the contract.

When, on the contrary, each always chooses his companion by himself without having anything external to hinder him or even direct him, it is ordinarily only similarity of tastes and ideas that brings man and woman together; and that same similarity keeps and fixes them beside one another.

Our fathers conceived a singular opinion in regard to marriage.

As they had perceived that the few marriages by inclination that were made in their time had almost always had a fatal issue, they resolutely concluded that in such a matter it was very dangerous to consult one's own heart. Chance appeared to them to be more perceptive than choice.

It was not very difficult to see, however, that the examples they had before their eyes proved nothing.

I shall first remark that if democratic peoples accord to women the right

---

1. It is easy to be convinced of this truth by studying the different literatures of Europe.

When a European wants to retrace in his fiction some of the great catastrophes that are so often displayed in the bosom of marriage among us, he takes care to excite the pity of the reader in advance by showing him ill-matched or constrained beings. Although a long tolerance relaxed our mores long ago, he would with difficulty succeed in interesting us in the misfortunes of these personages if he did not begin by making their fault excusable. This artifice scarcely ever fails to work. The daily spectacle to which we are witness prepares us from afar for indulgence.

American writers cannot render such excuses plausible in the eyes of their readers; their usages and laws resist it, and as they despair of making disorder likable, they do not portray it. It is in part to this cause that one must attribute the small number of novels published in the United States.

to choose their husbands freely, they take care in advance to furnish to their minds the enlightenment, and to their wills the force, that can be necessary for such a choice; whereas among aristocratic peoples, girls who furtively escape paternal authority to throw themselves into the arms of a man whom they have been given neither the time to know nor the capacity to judge lack all these safeguards. One cannot be surprised that they make a bad use of their free will the first time they use it, nor that they fall into such cruel errors when they want to follow the customs of democracy in marrying, without having received a democratic education.

But there is more.

When a man and a woman want to come together across the inequalities of the aristocratic social state, they have immense obstacles to overcome. After having broken or loosened the bonds of filial obedience, they must escape the empire of custom and the tyranny of opinion by a last effort; and when they have finally come to the end of that harsh undertaking, they find themselves almost strangers amid their natural friends and near relations: the prejudice they have overstepped separates them. This situation does not take long to bring down their courage and embitter their hearts.

If it therefore happens that spouses united in this manner are at first unhappy, and then guilty, one must not attribute it to their having freely chosen each other but rather to their living in a society that does not admit such choices.

One ought not to forget, moreover, that the same effort that makes a man violently take leave of a common error almost always carries him beyond reason; that to dare to declare a war, even a legitimate one, on the ideas of one's century and one's country, one must have a certain violent and adventurous disposition of spirit, and people of this character, whatever direction they take, rarely come to happiness and virtue. And it is this, one may say in passing, that explains why so few moderate and honest revolutionaries are encountered in the most necessary and holy revolutions.

Thus if in an aristocratic century a man by chance takes it into his head to consult no other propriety than his particular opinion and taste in a conjugal union, and afterwards disorder of mores and misery are not slow to be introduced into his household, one must not be surprised. But when this same manner of acting is in the natural and ordinary order of things; when the social state facilitates it; when paternal power is lent to it and public opinion recommends it, one ought not to doubt that the internal peace of families will become greater and that conjugal faith will be better kept.

Almost all men in democracies follow a political career or exercise a profession, and, on the other hand, the mediocrity of fortunes obliges a woman to confine herself inside her dwelling every day in order to preside herself very closely over the details of domestic administration.

All these distinct, compulsory tasks are like so many natural barriers which, by separating the sexes, make solicitations from the one rarer and less lively and the resistance of the other easier.

It is not that equality of conditions can ever come to make man chaste; but it gives a less dangerous character to the disorder of his mores. As no one then any longer has the leisure or the occasion to attack virtues that want to defend themselves, one sees at once a great number of courtesans and a multitude of honest women.

Such a state of things produces deplorable individual miseries, but it does not prevent the social body from being fit and strong; it does not destroy family bonds and does not enervate national mores. What puts society in danger is not the great corruption of some, it is the laxity of all. In the eyes of the legislator, prostitution is much less to be feared than intrigue.

This tumultuous and constantly vexed life, which equality gives to men, not only turns them away from love by taking away the leisure to indulge in it, but it also diverts them by a more secret, yet surer path.

All men who live in democratic times contract more or less the intellectual habits of the industrial and commercial classes; their minds take a serious, calculating, and positive turn; they willingly turn themselves away from the ideal to direct themselves toward some visible and proximate goal that presents itself as the natural and necessary object of their desires. Equality does not destroy imagination in this way, but limits it and permits it to fly only while skimming the earth.

None are less dreamers than citizens of a democracy, and one scarcely sees any of them who want to abandon themselves to the idle and solitary contemplation that ordinarily precedes and produces great agitations of the heart.

It is true that they put much value on procuring for themselves the sort of profound, regular, and peaceful affection that makes up the charm and security of life; but they do not willingly run after the violent and capricious emotions that trouble and shorten it.

I know that all the preceding applies completely only to America and for the present cannot be extended in a general manner to Europe.

In the half century in which laws and habits have pushed several peoples of Europe toward democracy with unequaled energy, one has not seen the relations of man and woman in those nations becoming more regular and more chaste. The contrary is even perceived in some places. Certain classes are better regulated; general morality appears more lax. I shall not fear to remark on it, for I do not feel myself more disposed to flatter my contemporaries than to speak ill of them.

This spectacle ought to be distressing, but not surprising.

The fortunate influence that a democratic social state can exert on regularity of habits is one of those facts that can only be discovered in the long term. If equality of conditions is favorable to good morals, the social travail that renders conditions equal is quite fatal to them.

In the fifty years that France has been transforming itself, we have rarely had freedom, but always disorder. In the midst of this universal confusion of ideas and general shaking of opinions, amid this incoherent mixture of just and unjust, of true and false, of right and fact, public virtue has become uncertain and private morality unsteady.

But all revolutions, whatever their object and their agents might have been, have at first produced effects like these. The very ones that have ended by tightening the bond of morals have begun by loosening it.

The disorders to which we are often witness therefore do not seem to me to be a durable fact. Some curious indications already announce it.

There is nothing more miserably corrupt than an aristocracy that preserves its wealth while losing its power and which, though reduced to vulgar enjoyments, still possesses immense leisure. The energetic passions and great thoughts that formerly animated it then disappear, and one encounters scarcely more than a multitude of gnawing little vices that attach themselves to it like worms to a cadaver.

No one disputes that the French aristocracy of the last century was very dissolute, whereas old habits and aged beliefs still maintained respect for morals in the other classes.

Nor will one have any trouble reaching agreement that in our time a certain severity of principles is displayed amid the debris of that same aristocracy, instead of the disorder of morals that appears to have spread in the middle and inferior ranks of society. In such a way the same families that showed themselves to be the most lax fifty years ago show themselves to be the most exemplary today, and democracy seems to have made only the aristocratic classes more moral.

The Revolution, by dividing the fortunes of the nobles, by forcing them to occupy themselves assiduously with their affairs and their families, by confining them with their children under the same roof, finally by giving their thoughts a more reasonable and serious turn, prompted in them, without their having perceived it themselves, a respect for religious beliefs and a love of order, of peaceful pleasures, of domestic joys, and of well-being; whereas the rest of the nation, which naturally had these same tastes, was carried along toward disorder by the very effort that had to be made to overthrow laws and political customs.

The old French aristocracy has suffered the consequences of the Revolution, and it neither experienced the revolutionary passions nor shared the often anarchic transports that produced it; it is easy to conceive that it feels the salutary influence of this revolution in its morals before the very ones who made it.

It is therefore permissible to say, although the thing appears surprising at first sight, that in our day it is the most antidemocratic classes of the nation that best display the species of morality that it is reasonable to expect from democracy.

I cannot prevent myself from believing that when we have obtained all the effects of the democratic revolution, after having left the tumult to which it gave birth, what is true only of a few today will little by little become true of all.

CRES CRES CRES CRES CRES CRES CRES CRES CRES CRES CRES CRES CRES CRES CRES CRES CRES CRES CRES CRES

Chapter 12 HOW THE AMERICANS UNDERSTAND THE EQUALITY OF MAN AND WOMAN

I have brought out how democracy is destroying or modifying the various inequalities to which society gives birth; but is that all, or will it not come finally to act on the great inequality of man and woman, which until our day has seemed to have its eternal foundations in nature?

I think that the social movement that brings son and father, servant and master, and, in general, inferior and superior closer to the same level elevates woman and must, more and more, make her the equal of man.

But it is here, more than ever, that I feel the need to be well understood; for there is no subject on which the coarse and disordered imagination of our century has given itself freer rein.

There are people in Europe who, confusing the diverse attributes of the sexes, intend to make man and woman into beings not only equal, but alike.*

---

*AT may be referring to followers of Saint-Simon, who advocated a scientific organization of industry and society aimed at helping the poorest classes. His writings included arguments for women's equality.

They give both the same functions, impose the same duties on them, and accord them the same rights; they mix them in all things—labors, pleasures, affairs. One can easily conceive that in thus striving to equalize one sex with the other, one degrades them both; and that from this coarse mixture of nature's works, only weak men and disreputable women can ever emerge.

This is not the way Americans have understood the kind of democratic equality that can be established between woman and man. They have thought that since nature had established such great variation between the physical and moral constitution of man and that of woman, its clearly indicated goal was to give a diverse employment to their different faculties; and they have judged that progress did not consist in making two unlike beings do nearly the same things, but in getting each of them to acquit its task as well as possible. Americans have applied to the two sexes the great principle of political economy that dominates industry in our day. They have carefully divided the functions of man and woman in order that the great social work be better done.

America, among the world's countries, is the one where they have taken the most continual care to draw cleanly separated lines of action for the two sexes, and where they have wanted them both to march at an equal pace but on ever different paths. You do not see American women directing the external affairs of the family, conducting a business, or indeed entering the political sphere; but neither do you encounter any of them who are obliged to engage in the rough work of plowing or in any painful exertions that require the development of physical force. There are no families so poor as to make an exception to this rule.

If the American woman cannot escape from the peaceful circle of domestic occupations, she is, on the other hand, never constrained to leave it.

Hence it is that American women, who often display a manly reason and a wholly virile energy, generally preserve a very delicate appearance and always remain women in their manners, although they sometimes show themselves to be men in mind and heart.

Neither have Americans ever imagined that democratic principles should have the consequence of overturning marital power and introducing confusion of authorities in the family. They have thought that every association, to be efficacious, must have a head, and that the natural head of the conjugal association is the man. They therefore do not deny him the right to direct his mate; and they believe that in the little society of husband and wife, as well as in the great political society, the object of democracy is to regulate and legitimate necessary powers, not to destroy all power.

This is not an opinion particular to one sex and fought by the other.

I did not remark that American women considered conjugal authority as a happy usurpation of their rights, or that they believed they were debasing themselves in submitting to it. On the contrary, it seemed evident to me that they made a sort of glory for themselves out of the voluntary abandonment of their wills, and that they found their greatness in submitting on their own to the yoke and not in escaping from it. That is at least the sentiment that the most virtuous women express: the others are silent, and one does not hear in the United States of an adulterous wife noisily claiming the rights of woman while riding roughshod over her most hallowed duties.*

It has often been remarked that in Europe a certain scorn is disclosed in the very midst of the flatteries that men lavish on women: although the European often makes himself the slave of woman, one sees that he never sincerely believes her his equal.

In the United States women are scarcely praised, but it is shown daily that they are esteemed.

Americans constantly display a full confidence in the reason of their mate and a profound respect for her freedom. They judge that her mind is as capable as a man's of discovering the naked truth, and her heart firm enough to follow it; and they have never sought to place the virtue of the one more than the other under the shelter of prejudices, ignorance, or fear.

It seems that in Europe, where they submit so readily to the despotic empire of women, they nevertheless deny them some of the greatest attributes of the human species, and consider them as seductive and incomplete beings; and what one cannot find too astonishing is that women in the end see themselves in the same light, and that they are not far from considering as a privilege the ability left to them of showing themselves futile, weak, and fearful. American women do not claim rights like these.

One would say, on the other hand, that on the question of morals we have granted the man a sort of singular immunity, in such a way that there is almost one virtue for his use and another for his mate; and that according to public opinion, the same act can be alternatively a crime or only a fault.

Americans do not know this iniquitous division of duties and rights. Among them the seducer is as dishonored as his victim.

It is true that Americans rarely show women the ready attentions with which one is pleased to surround them in Europe; but they always show by their conduct that they suppose them virtuous and delicate; and they have such a great respect for their moral freedom that in their presence each

---

*AT may be referring to Mary Wollstonecraft (1759–1797), an English writer who argued for women's equality while leading a scandalous private life.

watches his discourse carefully for fear that they be forced to hear language that offends them. In America a girl undertakes a long voyage alone without fear.

The legislators of the United States, who have made almost all the provisions of the penal code milder, punish rape with death; and there is no crime that public opinion pursues with more inexorable ardor. That can be explained: as the Americans conceive of nothing more precious than the honor of woman and nothing so respectable as her independence, they deem no chastisement too severe for those who take them away from her against her will.

In France, where the same crime is punished with much milder penalties, it is often difficult to find a jury that convicts. Would this be contempt for chastity or contempt for woman? I cannot keep myself from believing that it is both.

Thus Americans do not believe that man and woman have the duty or the right to do the same things, but they show the same esteem for the role of each of them, and they consider them as beings whose value is equal although their destiny differs. They do not give the same form or the same employment to the courage of woman as to that of man, but they never doubt her courage; and if they deem that man and his mate should not always employ their intelligence and reason in the same manner, they at least judge that the reason of one is as sure as that of the other, and her intelligence as clear.

Americans, who have allowed the inferiority of woman to subsist in society, have therefore elevated her with all their power to the level of man in the intellectual and moral world; and in this they appear to me to have admirably understood the true notion of democratic progress.

As for me, I shall not hesitate to say it: although in the United States the woman scarcely leaves the domestic circle and is in certain respects very dependent within it, nowhere does her position seem higher to me; and now that I approach the end of this book where I have shown so many considerable things done by Americans, if one asked me to what do I think one must principally attribute the singular prosperity and growing force of this people, I would answer that it is to the superiority of its women.

Chapter 13 HOW EQUALITY NATURALLY
DIVIDES THE AMERICANS INTO
A MULTITUDE OF PARTICULAR
LITTLE SOCIETIES

One might be brought to believe that the ultimate consequence and necessary effect of democratic institutions is to intermingle citizens in private life
as well as in public life and to force them all to lead a common existence.

This is to understand the equality to which democracy gives birth in a
coarse and tyrannical form indeed.

Neither a social state nor laws can render men so alike that education,
fortune, and tastes do not put some difference between them, and if different
men can sometimes find their interest in doing the same things in common,
one must believe that they will never find pleasure in it. They will therefore
always escape the hand of the legislator, whatever one may do; and, by stealing off to some spot away from the circle in which one seeks to confine them,
they will establish, alongside the great political society, small private societies
in which similarity of conditions, habits, and mores will be the bond.

In the United States, citizens have no preeminence over one another; they
reciprocally owe each other neither obedience nor respect; together they administer justice and govern the state, and in general they all gather to treat
of the affairs that influence their common destiny; but I never heard anyone
claim that all of them should be brought to amuse themselves in the same
manner or to enjoy themselves when intermingled in the same places.

Americans, who so easily mix with each other in the precincts of political
assemblies and law courts, divide themselves, on the contrary, with great care
into very distinct little associations to taste the enjoyments of private life
separately. Each of them willingly recognizes all his fellow citizens as his
equals, but he never receives any but a very few of them among his friends
and guests.

That seems very natural to me. As the circle of public society grows larger,
one must expect that the sphere of private relations will narrow: instead of
imagining that citizens of the new societies are going to end by living in
common, I indeed fear that they will finally come to form no more than very
small coteries.

In aristocratic peoples, the different classes are like vast precincts that cannot be left and cannot be entered. The classes do not communicate between

themselves; but inside each of them, men are forced to deal with each other every day. Even if they would not naturally be suited to each other, the general suitability of the same condition brings them together.

But when neither law nor custom takes charge of establishing frequent and habitual relations among certain men, accidental resemblance of opinions and penchants decides them, which makes particular societies vary infinitely.

In democracies, where citizens never differ much from one another and naturally find themselves so close that at each instant all can come to be intermingled in a common mass, a multitude of artificial and arbitrary classifications are created, with the aid of which each seeks to set himself apart, out of fear of being carried away into the crowd despite himself.

It can never fail to be so; for one can change human institutions, but not man: whatever may be the general effort of a society to render citizens equal and alike, the particular pride of individuals will always seek to escape the [common] level and wish to form an inequality somewhere from which it profits.

In aristocracies, men are separated from one another by high, immovable barriers; in democracies, they are divided by a multitude of small, almost invisible threads that are broken at every moment and are constantly changed from place to place.

Thus, whatever the progress of equality may be, a great number of small private associations in the midst of the great political society will always be formed in democratic peoples. But none of these will resemble in its manners the upper class that directs aristocracies.

Chapter 14 SOME REFLECTIONS ON AMERICAN MANNERS

There is nothing, at first sight, that seems less important than the external form of human actions, and there is nothing to which men attach more value; they become accustomed to everything except living in a society that does not have their manners. The influence that the social and political state exerts on manners is therefore worth the trouble of serious examination.

Manners generally issue from the very substance of mores; and in addition, they sometimes result from an arbitrary convention among certain men. They are at the same time natural and acquired.

When some men perceive that without contest and without trouble they are first, when they daily have before their eyes great objects with which they are occupied, leaving the details to others, and when they live amid wealth they have not acquired and do not fear to lose, one conceives that they experience a sort of superb disdain for the little interests and material cares of life, and that they have a natural grandeur of thought that their words and manners reveal.

In democratic countries, manners ordinarily have little grandeur because private life there is very petty. They are often vulgar because thought has but few occasions to raise itself above preoccupation with domestic interests.

Genuine dignity of manners consists in always showing oneself in one's place, neither higher nor lower; that is within the reach of the peasant as of the prince. In democracies, all places appear doubtful; hence it happens that manners, which are often haughty, are rarely dignified. In addition, they are never either well regulated or well informed.

Men who live in democracies are too mobile for a certain number of them to succeed in establishing a code of social graces and to be able to keep it in hand so that it is followed. Each therefore acts nearly as he pleases, and a certain incoherence in manners always reigns because they conform to the sentiments and individual ideas of each rather than to an ideal model given in advance for imitation by all.

Still, this is felt much more at the moment when aristocracy has fallen than when it has long been destroyed.

New political institutions and new mores unite at that moment in the same places men whom education and habits still render prodigiously unlike each other and often force them to live in common; this makes great variations emerge at every moment. One still remembers that a precise code of politeness existed, but already one no longer knows either what it contains or where it is. Men have lost the common law of manners and they have not yet resolved to do without it; but each strives to form a certain arbitrary and changing rule with the debris of former usages, so that manners have neither the regularity nor the grandeur that they often display among aristocratic peoples, nor the simple and free turn that one sometimes remarks in them in democracy; they are all at once constrained and without constraint.

That is not a normal state.

When equality is complete and long-standing, all men, having nearly the same ideas and doing nearly the same things, do not need to agree or to copy each other in order to act and speak in the same way; one constantly sees a multitude of small dissimilarities in their manners, but one does not perceive great differences. They never resemble each other perfectly, because they do not have the same model; they are never very dissimilar, because they have the same condition. At first sight one would say that the manners of all Americans are exactly the same. Only in considering them very closely does one perceive the particularities by which all differ.

The English amuse themselves very much at the expense of American manners; and what is particular about this is that most of those who draw such a comical picture for us belong to the English middle classes, to whom this same picture is very applicable. So these pitiless detractors ordinarily present an example of what they find fault with in the United States; they do not perceive that they are making fun of themselves, to the great delight of the aristocracy in their country.

Nothing does more harm to democracy than the external form of its mores. Many people who cannot tolerate its manners would willingly accommodate themselves to its vices.

I cannot allow, however, that that there is nothing to praise in the manners of democratic peoples.

In aristocratic nations all those close to the first class ordinarily strive to resemble it, which produces very ridiculous and very flat imitations. If democratic peoples do not possess in themselves a model of grand manners, they at least escape the daily obligation of seeing wretched copies of them.

In democracies, manners are never so refined as among aristocratic peoples; but neither do they ever show themselves as coarse. One hears neither the coarse words of the populace nor the noble and select expressions of great lords. There is often triviality in mores, but no brutality or baseness.

I have said that democracies cannot form a precise code in the case of social graces. This has its inconveniences and its advantages. In aristocracies, the rules of polite society impose the same appearance on each; they render all the members of the same class alike despite their particular penchants; they adorn the natural and conceal it. In democratic peoples, manners are neither so learned nor so regular; but they are often more sincere. They form as it were a light and poorly woven veil, through which the genuine sentiments and individual ideas of each man are allowed to be seen easily. The form and substance of human actions are therefore often encountered there in an intimate relation, and if the great picture of humanity is less ornate, it is truer. Thus one can say in a sense that the effect of democracy is not precisely to give men certain manners but to prevent them from having manners.

One can sometimes find in a democracy the sentiments, passions, virtues, and vices of aristocracy, but not its manners. These are lost and disappear, never to return, when the democratic revolution is complete.

It seems that there is nothing more durable than the manners of an aristocratic class, for it still keeps them for some time after having lost its goods and its power; nor so fragile, for hardly have they disappeared when the trace of them can no longer be found, and it is difficult to say what they were from the moment they are no more. A change in the social state works this prodigy; a few generations suffice for it.

The principal features of aristocracy remain engraved in history when aristocracy is destroyed, but the delicate and slight forms of its mores disappear from the memories of men almost immediately after its fall. They cannot conceive of [the forms] when they no longer have them before their eyes. They escape them without either seeing or feeling that they do. For to experience the kind of refined pleasure procured by distinction and choice in manners, habit and education must prepare the heart, and one easily loses the taste along with the use of them.

Thus not only are democratic peoples unable to have the manners of aristocracy, but they can neither conceive of them nor desire them; they do not imagine them; for [these peoples], it is as if they had never been.

One must not attach too much importance to this loss; but it is permissible to regret it.

I know that it has happened more than once that the same men have had very distinguished mores and very vulgar sentiments: the interiors of courts have made it sufficiently evident that great external appearances can often hide very base hearts. But if the manners of aristocracy did not make virtue, they sometimes adorned virtue itself. A numerous and powerful class in which all the external acts of life seemed at each instant to reveal the natural loftiness of sentiments and thoughts, the delicacy and regularity of tastes, the urbanity of mores, was no ordinary spectacle.

The manners of aristocracy placed beautiful illusions over human nature; and although the picture was often deceptive, one felt a noble pleasure in regarding it.

☙ ☙

Chapter 15 ON THE GRAVITY OF THE AMERICANS AND WHY IT DOES NOT PREVENT THEIR OFTEN DOING ILL-CONSIDERED THINGS

Men who live in democratic countries do not prize the sorts of naive, unruly, and coarse entertainments that the people give themselves over to in aristocracies: they find them puerile or insipid. They scarcely show more taste for the intellectual and refined amusements of the aristocratic classes; they must have something more productive and substantial in their pleasures, they want to mix satisfaction with their joy.

In aristocratic societies, the people willingly abandon themselves to the impulses of a tumultuous and noisy gaiety that abruptly tears them away from the contemplation of their miseries; the inhabitants of democracies do not like to feel themselves violently pulled outside of themselves in this way, and when they lose sight of themselves it is always with regret. To these frivolous transports they prefer grave and silent relaxations that resemble business and do not make them entirely forget it.

There is a sort of American who, instead of going to dance joyously in the public square in his leisure moments, as people of his profession continue to do in a great part of Europe, goes off alone to the depth of his home to drink. This man enjoys two pleasures at once: he dreams of his trade and gets drunk decently within the family home.

I believed that the English formed the most serious nation there was on earth, but I have seen the Americans, and I have changed my opinion.

I do not want to say that temperament does not count for much in the character of the inhabitants of the United States. Yet I think that political institutions contribute still more to it.

I believe that the gravity of the Americans arises in part from their pride. In democratic countries, the poor man himself has a lofty idea of his personal worth. He contemplates himself with complacency and willingly believes that others are looking at him. In this mood he watches his words and actions carefully and does not reveal himself for fear of exposing what he lacks. He fancies that to appear dignified he must remain grave.

But I perceive another more intimate and powerful cause that instinctively produces in Americans the gravity that astonishes me.

Under despotism, peoples from time to time indulge in bursts of mad joy; but generally they are gloomy and concentrated, because they are afraid.

In the absolute monarchies that custom and mores temper, they often display an even and cheerful humor because, having some freedom and great enough security, they are diverted from the most important cares of life; but all free peoples are grave because their minds are habitually absorbed in the view of some dangerous or difficult project.

It is above all so with free peoples who are constituted as democracies. Then one encounters an infinite number of people in all classes who are constantly preoccupied with the serious affairs of government, and those who do not think of directing the public fortune are left wholly to the cares of increasing their private fortunes. In such a people gravity is no long particular to certain men; it becomes a national habit.

One speaks of the small democracies of antiquity, whose citizens used to go to the public square with crowns of roses and passed almost all their time in dances and spectacles.* I no more believe in republics like these than in Plato's; or if things took place there as recounted to us, I do not fear to affirm that these alleged democracies were formed of very different elements than ours, and that they had nothing in common with ours except the name.

Furthermore, one must not believe that in the midst of all their labors, the people who live in democracies judge they have anything to complain of: one remarks the contrary. There are no men who hold as much to their condition as these. They would find life without savor if they were delivered from the cares that torment them, and they show themselves more attached to their worries than are aristocratic peoples to their pleasures.

I wonder why these same democratic peoples, who are so grave, sometimes conduct themselves in such an ill-considered manner.

Americans, who almost always keep a controlled bearing and a cold air, nonetheless often allow themselves to be taken far indeed from the limits of reason by a sudden passion or an unreflective opinion, and they come to perform seriously acts of a singular absentmindedness.

This contrast ought not to be surprising.

There is a sort of ignorance that is born of extreme publicity. In despotic states men do not know how to act because one says nothing to them; in democratic nations they often act at random because one wanted to say everything to them. The former do not know, the latter forget. The principal features of each picture disappear for the latter among the multitude of details.

---

*See Rousseau, *Letter to M. d'Alembert on the Theatre*, 11.

One is astonished at all the imprudent proposals that a public man, in free states and above all in democratic states, is sometimes permitted without being compromised by them; whereas in absolute monarchies a few words that escape haphazardly are enough to unveil him forever and to ruin him irremediably.

That is explained by what precedes. When one speaks in the midst of a great crowd, many words are not heard or are immediately erased from the memories of those who hear them; but in the silence of a mute and immobile multitude, the least whispers strike the ear.

In democracies men are never settled; a thousand accidents make them change place constantly, and there almost always reigns something unforeseen and so to speak improvised in their lives. Thus they are often forced to do what they have learned badly, to speak of what they scarcely understand, and to engage in work for which they have not been prepared by a long apprenticeship.

In aristocracies each one has only a single goal that he constantly pursues, but in democratic peoples the existence of man is more complicated; it is rare that the same mind does not embrace several objects at once, and often objects very foreign to one another. As he cannot know them all well, he is easily satisfied with imperfect notions.

When the inhabitant of democracies is not pressed by his needs, he is so at least by his desires; for among all the goods that surround him, he sees none that is entirely out of his reach. He therefore does all things in haste, contents himself with approximations, and never stops but for a moment to consider each of his acts.

His curiosity is at once insatiable and satisfied at little cost, for he insists on knowing very quickly rather than on knowing well.

He scarcely has the time and he soon loses the taste for going into depth.

So therefore, democratic peoples are grave because their social and political state constantly brings them to occupy themselves with serious things; and they perform ill-considered acts because they give only little time and attention to each of those things.

The habit of inattention ought to be considered the greatest vice of the democratic mind.

Chapter 16 WHY THE NATIONAL VANITY OF THE AMERICANS IS MORE RESTIVE AND MORE QUARRELSOME THAN THAT OF THE ENGLISH

All free peoples appear glorious to themselves; but national pride does not manifest itself among all in the same manner.*

Americans, in their relations with foreigners, appear impatient at the least censure and insatiable for praise. The slimmest eulogy is agreeable to them and the greatest is rarely enough to satisfy them; they pester you at every moment to get you to praise them; and if you resist their entreaties, they praise themselves. One would say that, doubting their own merit, they want to have a picture of it before their eyes at each instant. Their vanity is not only greedy, it is restive and envious. It grants nothing while demanding constantly. It is entreating and quarrelsome at the same time.

I say to an American that the country he inhabits is beautiful; he replies: "It is true, there is none like it in the world!" I admire the freedom that the inhabitants enjoy, and he responds to me: "What a precious gift freedom is! but there are few peoples indeed who are worthy of enjoying it." I remark on the purity of morals that reigns in the United States: "I conceive," he says, "that a foreigner who has been struck by the corruption that is displayed in all other nations may be astonished by this spectacle." Finally, I abandon him to the contemplation of himself; but he comes back to me and does not leave me until he has succeeded in making me repeat what I just said to him. One cannot imagine a more disagreeable and talkative patriotism. It fatigues even whose who honor it.

It is not so with the English. The Englishman quietly enjoys the advantages, real or imaginary, that his country possesses in his eyes. If he grants nothing to other nations, neither does he ask anything for his. The criticism of foreigners does not move him and their praise scarcely flatters him. He holds himself toward the entire world in a reserve full of disdain and ignorance. His pride has no need of nutriment; it lives on itself.

That two people lately come from the same stock show themselves so opposed to one another in their manner of feeling and speaking is remarkable.

In aristocratic countries, the great possess immense privileges, on which

*See AT's note XXII, page 701.

their pride rests, without seeking to be nourished on any trifling related advantages. These privileges having come to them by inheritance, they consider them in a way as a part of themselves or at least as a natural right inherent in their persons. They therefore have a calm sense of their superiority; they do not think of vaunting the prerogatives that everyone perceives and that no one denies to them. They are not surprised enough by them to speak of them. They remain immobile in the midst of their solitary greatness, sure that all the world sees them there without their seeking to show themselves, and that no one will undertake to make them leave it.

When an aristocracy conducts public affairs, its national pride naturally takes this reserved, insouciant, and haughty form, and all the other classes of the nation imitate it.

When, on the contrary, conditions differ little, the least advantages gain importance. As each sees a million people around him who possess [advantages] that are wholly alike or analogous, pride becomes demanding and jealous; it becomes attached to pittances and defends them stubbornly.

In democracies, with conditions very mobile, men have almost always recently acquired the advantages they possess, which makes them feel an infinite pleasure in exposing them to view in order to show to others and to bear witness to themselves that they do enjoy them; and as it can happen at any instant that these advantages may escape them, they are in constant alarm and strive to make one see that they still have them. Men who live in democracies love their country in the same manner that they love themselves, and they carry the habits of their private vanity over to their national vanity.

The restive and insatiable vanity of democratic peoples is so much due to the equality and the fragility of conditions that the members of the proudest nobility show absolutely the same passion in the little portions of their existence where there is something unstable and contested.

An aristocratic class always differs profoundly from the other classes of the nation by the extent and the perpetuity of its prerogatives; but it sometimes happens that several of its members differ among themselves only by little, fleeting advantages that they can lose and acquire every day.

Members of a powerful aristocracy, gathered in a capital or a court, have been seen disputing tenaciously the frivolous privileges that depend on the caprice of fashion or on the will of the master. They then showed precisely the same puerile jealousies toward one another that animate men in democracies, the same ardor to gain the least advantages that their equals contested, and the same need to expose those that they enjoyed to the view of all.

If courtiers ever considered having national pride, I do not doubt that they would display one quite similar to that of democratic peoples.

*

༄ ༄

Chapter 17 HOW THE ASPECT OF SOCIETY IN THE UNITED STATES IS AT ONCE AGITATED AND MONOTONOUS

It seems that nothing is more apt to excite and nourish curiosity than the aspect of the United States. Fortunes, ideas, and laws there vary constantly. One would say that unmoving nature itself is moving, so much is it transformed daily by the hand of man.

In the long term, however, the sight of such an agitated society appears monotonous, and after having contemplated this picture of such movement for some time, the spectator gets bored.

In aristocratic peoples, each man is nearly fixed in his sphere; but men are prodigiously unalike; they have essentially diverse passions, ideas, habits, and tastes. Nothing moves, everything differs.

In democracies, on the contrary, all men are alike and do things that are nearly alike. They are subject, it is true, to great and continual vicissitudes; but as the same successes and the same reverses come back continually, the name of the actors alone is different, the play is the same. The aspect of American society is agitated because men and things change continuously; and it is monotonous because all the changes are similar.

Men who live in democratic times have many passions; but most of their passions end in love of wealth or issue from it. That comes from the fact not that their souls are smaller, but that the importance of money really is greater then.

When fellow citizens are all independent and indifferent, it is only by paying them that one can obtain the cooperation of each; this infinitely multiplies the use of wealth and increases the value of it.

The prestige that attached to old things having disappeared, birth, condition, and profession no longer distinguish men or hardly distinguish them; there remains scarcely anything but money that creates very visible differences between them and that can set off some from their peers. The distinction that arises from wealth is increased by the disappearance and diminution of all the others.

In aristocratic peoples, money leads only to some points on the vast circumference of desires; in democracies, it seems to conduct one to all.

Ordinarily, therefore, one finds love of wealth, as principal or accessory, at the bottom of the actions of Americans; this gives all their passions a family resemblance, and is not slow to make of them a tiresome picture.

This perpetual return of the same passion is monotonous; the particular techniques that this passion employs to satisfy itself are equally so.

In a constituted and peaceful democracy like that of the United States, where one can enrich oneself neither by war nor by public posts nor by political confiscations, love of wealth directs men principally toward industry. Now industry, which often brings such great disorders and such great disasters, can nevertheless prosper only with the aid of very regular habits and by a long succession of very uniform little actions. The habits are all the more regular and the actions more uniform as the passion is more lively. One can say that it is the very violence of their desires that renders the Americans so methodical. It troubles their souls, but it arranges their lives.

Furthermore, what I say of America applies to almost all men of our day. Variety is disappearing from within the human species; the same manner of acting, thinking, and feeling is found in all the corners of the world. That comes not only from the fact that all peoples deal with each other more and copy each other more faithfully, but from the fact that in each country, men diverge further and further from the particular ideas and sentiments of a caste, a profession, or a family and simultaneously arrive at what depends more nearly on the constitution of man, which is everywhere the same. They thus become alike even though they have not imitated each other. They are like travelers dispersed in a great forest in which all the paths end at the same point. If all perceive the central point at once and direct their steps in this direction, they are insensibly brought nearer to one another without seeking each other, without perceiving and without knowing each other, and they will finally be surprised to see themselves gathered in the same place. All peoples who take for the object of their studies and imitation, not such and such a man, but man himself, will in the end encounter each other in the same mores, like these travelers at the center.

Chapter 18 ON HONOR IN THE UNITED STATES AND IN DEMOCRATIC SOCIETIES[1]

It seems that men make use of two very distinct methods in the public judgment that they bring to the actions of those like them: sometimes they judge them according to the simple notions of the just and the unjust that are widespread over all the earth; sometimes they appraise them with the aid of very particular notions that belong only to one country and one period. Often it happens that these two rules differ; sometimes they combat each other; but they are never entirely confused with each other, nor do they ever destroy each other.

Honor, at the time of its greatest power, rules the will more than belief, and even when men submit without hesitation and without murmur to its commandments, they still feel, by a sort of obscure but powerful instinct, that there exists a more general, older, and more holy law which they sometimes disobey without ceasing to recognize. There are actions that have been judged at once honest and dishonoring. The refusal of a duel has often been such a case.

I believe that these phenomena can be explained otherwise than by the caprice of certain individuals and certain peoples, as has been done up to now.

The human race feels permanent and general needs that have given birth to moral laws; all men have naturally attached in all places and all times the idea of blame and of shame to the nonobservance of them. Evading them they have called *to do evil,* submitting to them, *to do good.*

Within the vast human association, more restricted associations are also established, which are named peoples, and amid the latter, others smaller still, called classes or castes.

Each of these associations forms almost a particular species of the human race, and although it does not differ essentially from the mass of men, it holds itself a little apart from it and feels needs of its own. These special

---

1. The word *honor* is not always taken in the same sense in French.

(1) It signifies first the esteem, the glory, the consideration that one obtains from those like oneself: it is in this sense that one says *to win honor.*

(2) Honor also signifies the sum of rules with the aid of which one obtains this glory, esteem, and consideration. Thus it is that one says *that a man has always conformed strictly to the laws of honor: that he has forfeited honor.* In writing the present chapter I have always taken the word *honor* in this latter sense.

needs modify, in some fashion and in certain countries, the manner of viewing human actions and the esteem it is suitable to have for them.

The general and permanent interest of the human race is that men not kill one another, but it can happen that the particular and temporary interest of a people or a class in certain cases is to excuse and even to honor homicide.

Honor is nothing other than that particular rule, founded on a particular state, with the aid of which a people or a class distributes blame or praise.

There is nothing more unproductive for the human mind than an abstract idea. I therefore hurry to run toward the facts. An example will shed light on my thought.

I shall choose the most extraordinary species of honor that has ever appeared in the world and the one that we know the best: the aristocratic honor born in the bosom of feudal society. I shall explain it with the aid of the preceding and I shall explain the preceding by it.

I do not have to inquire here when and how the aristocracy of the Middle Ages was born, why it so profoundly separated itself from the rest of the nation, what founded and consolidated its power. I find it standing, and I seek to comprehend why it considered most human actions in such a particular light.

What strikes me at first is that in the feudal world actions were not always praised or blamed because of their intrinsic value, but it sometimes happened that they were prized solely in relation to whoever their author or object was, which is repugnant to the general conscience of the human race. Certain actions that dishonored a noble were therefore indifferent on the part of a commoner; others changed character according to whether the person who suffered from them belonged to the aristocracy or lived outside of it.

When these different opinions were born, the nobility formed a separate body amidst the people, which it dominated from the inaccessible heights to which it had withdrawn. To maintain the particular position that made up its force, it had need not only of political privileges: it had to have virtues and vices for its use.

That this virtue or that vice belonged to the nobility rather than to the commoners, that an action was indifferent when it had a villein for its object, or condemnable when it was a question of a noble—that was often arbitrary; but that one attached honor or shame to the actions of a man according to his condition—that resulted from the very constitution of an aristocratic society. This was in fact seen in all countries that had an aristocracy. As long as a single vestige of it remains, these singularities are found: to debauch a girl of color hardly harms the reputation of an American; to marry her dishonors him.

In certain cases, feudal honor prescribed vengeance and stigmatized pardon of injuries; in others it imperiously commanded men to overcome themselves, it ordered the forgetting of oneself. It made neither humanity nor mildness a law; but it vaunted generosity; it prized liberality more than beneficence, it permitted one to enrich oneself by gambling, by war, but not by work; it preferred great crimes to small gains. Cupidity appalled it less than avarice; violence often agreed with it, whereas guile and treason always appeared despicable to it.

These bizarre notions did not arise only from the caprice of those who had conceived them.

A class that has come to put itself at the head and above all the others, and that makes constant efforts to maintain itself in this superior rank, must particularly honor the virtues that have greatness and luster and that can be readily combined with pride and love of power. It is not afraid to disturb the natural order of conscience so as to place those virtues before all others. One even conceives that it willingly elevates certain audacious and brilliant vices above peaceful and modest virtues. It is in a way constrained by its condition to do so.

Before all virtues and in place of many of them, the nobles of the Middle Ages put military courage.

That again was a singular opinion that was bound to arise from the singularity of the social state.

Feudal aristocracy was born of war and for war; it had found its power in arms and it maintained it by arms; nothing therefore was more necessary to it than military courage; and it was natural that it glorified that above all the rest. All that manifested this outwardly, even at the expense of reason and humanity, was therefore approved and often commanded by it. The fantasies of men were found only in the details.

That a man regarded it as an enormous injury to receive a blow on the cheek and was obliged to kill in single combat whoever had thus lightly struck him, that was arbitrary; but that a noble could not receive an injury peacefully and was dishonored if he allowed himself to be struck without doing combat, this issued from the very principles and the needs of a military aristocracy.

It was therefore true up to a certain point to say that honor had its capricious aspects; but the caprices of honor were always confined within certain necessary limits. That particular rule called honor by our fathers is so far from appearing to me an arbitrary law that without trouble I would undertake to link its most incoherent and most bizarre prescriptions to a few fixed and invariable needs of feudal societies.

If I followed feudal honor onto the field of politics, I would have no more trouble in explaining its attitudes there.

The social state and the political institutions of the Middle Ages were such that the national power never directly governed citizens. This latter so to speak did not exist in their eyes; each one knew only a certain man whom he was obliged to obey. It was by him that, without knowing it, one was joined to all the others. In feudal societies all public order, therefore, turned on the sentiment of fidelity to the very person of the lord. That destroyed, they immediately fell into anarchy.

Moreover, fidelity to the political chief was a sentiment whose value all members of the aristocracy perceived every day, for each of them was at once lord and vassal and had to command as well as to obey.

To remain faithful to one's lord, to sacrifice oneself for him in case of need, to share his good or bad fortune, to aid him in his undertakings whatever they were, such were the first prescriptions of feudal honor in political matters. The treason of a vassal was condemned by opinion with an extraordinary rigor. A particularly infamous name was created for it; it was called *felony.*

On the contrary, one finds in the Middle Ages barely a trace of a passion that gave life to ancient societies. I mean patriotism. The very name of patriotism is not old in our idiom.[2]

Feudal institutions concealed the native country from the eye; they rendered love of it less necessary. They made one forget the nation by developing a passion for one man. Thus feudal honor was never seen to make it a strict law to remain faithful to one's country.

It is not that love of native country did not exist in the hearts of our fathers; but it formed only a sort of weak and obscure instinct that has become clearer and stronger as classes have been destroyed and power centralized.

This is seen well in the contrary judgments that the peoples of Europe bring to the different facts of their history, according to the generation that judges them. What principally dishonored the Constable of Bourbon in the eyes of his contemporaries was that he bore arms against his king; what dishonors him more in our eyes is that he made war against his country.* We stigmatize him[†] as much as our ancestors, but for other reasons.

I have chosen feudal honor to clarify my thought because feudal honor

---

*AT refers to Charles III, eighth duke of Bourbon (1490–1527). Early in life he served King Francis I as constable of France, but later he became a leading general for Francis's enemy, the Holy Roman Emperor Charles V.

†The text says "them," but the sense seems to require "him."

2. The word *patrie* [native country] itself is found in French authors only from the sixteenth century on.

has more and better marked features than any other; if I had taken my example from elsewhere, I would have arrived at the same goal by another path.

Although we are less well acquainted with the Romans than with our ancestors, we nevertheless know that there existed among them particular opinions, in point of glory and dishonor, that did not flow solely from general notions of good and evil. Many human actions were considered by them in a different light according to whether it was a question of a citizen or a foreigner, a free man or a slave; they glorified certain vices, they elevated certain virtues beyond all others.

"Now in those times," says Plutarch in his *Life of Coriolanus,* "prowess was honored and prized at Rome above all the other virtues. That is authenticated by the fact that it was named *virtus,* from the very name for virtue, attributing the name of the common genus to a particular species. So much was this so that 'virtue' in Latin was as much as to say 'valor.'"* Who does not recognize there the particular need of this singular association that was formed for the conquest of the world?

Each nation will lend analogous observations; for as I said above, every time men are gathered in a particular society, an honor is immediately established among them, that is to say, a set of their own opinions about what one ought to praise or blame; and these particular rules always have their source in the special habits and special interests of the association.

That applies in a certain measure to democratic societies as to others. We are going to find the proof of this among the Americans.[3]

One still encounters, scattered among the opinions of the Americans, some notions taken from the old aristocratic honor of Europe. These traditional opinions are very few; they have few roots and little power. It is a religion some of whose temples are left standing, but in which one no longer believes.

In the midst of these half-effaced notions of an exotic honor appear some new opinions that constitute what in our day we would call American honor.

I have shown how Americans are unceasingly impelled toward commerce and industry. Their origin, their social state, the political institutions, the very place that they inhabit, carry them irresistibly in this direction. They therefore presently form an almost exclusively industrial and commercial association, placed in the bosom of a new and immense country whose exploitation is its principal object. Such is the characteristic feature that in our day most particularly distinguishes the American people from all others.

---

*See Plutarch, *Lives of the Noble Grecians and Romans* (New York: Modern Library, 1932), 263.

3. I speak here of the Americans who inhabit the regions where slavery does not exist. Only they can present the complete image of a democratic society.

All the peaceful virtues that tend to give a regular pace to the social body and to favor trade must therefore be specially honored among this people, and one cannot neglect them without falling into public contempt.

On the contrary, all the turbulent virtues that often dazzle, but still more often bring trouble in society, occupy a subordinate rank in the opinion of this same people. One can neglect them without losing the esteem of one's fellow citizens, and by acquiring them one would perhaps expose oneself to losing it.

Americans make a no less arbitrary classification among vices.

There are certain penchants, condemnable in the eyes of the general reason and the universal conscience of the human race, that are in accord with the particular and momentary needs of the American association; and it reproves them only feebly, and sometimes it praises them; I shall cite particularly love of wealth and the secondary penchants that are linked to it. To clear, to make fruitful, to transform the vast uninhabited continent that is his domain, the American needs the daily support of an energetic passion; that passion can only be love of wealth; the passion for wealth is therefore not stigmatized in America, and provided that it does not exceed the limits that public order assigns to it, it is honored. The American calls noble and estimable ambition that which our fathers in the Middle Ages named servile cupidity, just as he gives the name of blind and barbaric fury to the conquering ardor and warlike humor that threw them into new combats each day.

In the United States, fortunes are destroyed and rebuilt without trouble. The country is boundless and full of inexhaustible resources. The people have all the needs and all the appetites of a being that is growing, and whatever efforts they make, they are always surrounded with more goods than they can seize. What is to be feared in such a people is not the ruin of some individuals, soon repaired; it is the inactivity and softness of all. Audacity in industrial undertakings is the first cause of its rapid progress, its force, its greatness. Industry is like a vast lottery for it, in which a few men lose every day, but the state gains constantly; a people like this must therefore see audacity with favor and honor it in matters of industry. Now, every audacious undertaking jeopardizes the fortune of whoever engages in it and the fortune of all those who trust him. Americans, who make a sort of virtue of commercial recklessness, cannot in any case stigmatize the reckless.

Hence the so singular indulgence shown in the United States for anyone in commerce who goes bankrupt: his honor does not suffer from such an accident. In that, the Americans differ not only from European peoples but from all the commercial nations of our day—as by their position and their needs, they resemble none of them.

In America they treat with a severity unknown in the rest of the world all the vices that are of a nature to adulterate the purity of morals and to destroy the conjugal union. That contrasts strangely, at first appearance, with the tolerance shown there on other points. One is surprised to encounter a morality so relaxed and so austere in the same people.

These things are not as incoherent as one supposes. Public opinion in the United States only gently represses love of wealth, which serves the industrial greatness and the prosperity of the nation; and it particularly condemns the bad morals that distract the human mind from the search for well-being and trouble the internal order of the family, so necessary to success in business. To be esteemed by those like themselves the Americans are therefore constrained to bow to regular habits. It is in this sense that one can say that they put their honor in being chaste.

American honor accords with the old honor of Europe on one point: it puts courage at the head of the virtues and makes it the greatest of moral necessities for man; but it does not view courage from the same aspect.

In the United States, warlike valor is little prized; the courage that is best known and most esteemed is that which makes one brave the furies of the ocean to arrive sooner in port, to tolerate without complaint the miseries of the wilderness, and the solitude, more cruel than all its miseries; the courage that renders one almost insensitive to the sudden reversal of a painfully acquired fortune and immediately prompts new efforts to construct a new one. Courage of this kind is principally necessary to the maintenance and prosperity of the American association, and it is particularly honored and glorified by it. One cannot show oneself to be lacking it without dishonor.

I find a final feature; it will serve to put the idea of this chapter into relief.

In a democratic society like that of the United States, where fortunes are small and ill-secured, everyone works and work leads to everything. That has turned around the point of honor and directed it against idleness.

In America I sometimes met rich young people, enemies by temperament of every painful effort, who had been forced to take up a profession. Their nature and their fortune permitted them to remain idle; public opinion imperiously forbade it to them, and they had to obey. I have often seen, on the contrary, in European nations, where aristocracy is still struggling against the torrent that carries it away, I have seen, I say, men whose needs and desires constantly spurred them on remain in idleness in order not to lose the esteem of their equals, and submit more easily to boredom and discomfort than to work.

Who does not perceive in these two so contrary obligations two different rules that nonetheless both emanate from honor?

What our fathers called honor par excellence was, to tell the truth, only one of its forms. They gave a generic name to what was only a species. Honor is therefore found in democratic centuries as in aristocratic times. But it will not be difficult to show that in the former it presents another face.

Not only are its prescriptions different; we are going to see that they are less numerous and less clear and that one follows its laws more loosely.

A caste is always in a much more particular situation than a people. There is nothing in the world more exceptional than a small society always composed of the same families, like the aristocracy of the Middle Ages, for example, and whose object is to concentrate enlightenment, wealth, and power in its bosom and to keep them exclusively and by heredity.

Now the more exceptional the position of a society is, the greater in number are its special needs, and the more the notions of its honor, which correspond to its needs, increase.

Prescriptions of honor will therefore always be less numerous in a people that is not partitioned into castes than in any other. If nations in which it is even difficult to find classes come to be established, honor will be limited to a few precepts, and these precepts will be less and less distant from the moral laws adopted by common humanity.

Thus prescriptions of honor will be less peculiar and less numerous in a democratic nation than in an aristocracy.

They will be more obscure as well; that necessarily results from what precedes.

The characteristic features of honor being fewer and less singular, it will often be difficult to discern them.

There are still other reasons.

In the aristocratic nations of the Middle Ages, generations succeeded one another in vain; each family was like an immortal and perpetually immobile man; ideas hardly varied more than conditions.

Each man therefore always had the same objects before his eyes, which he envisaged from the same point of view; his eye penetrated little by little into the least details and his perception could not fail in the long term to become clear and distinct. Thus not only did men in feudal times have very extraordinary opinions that constituted their honor, but each of these opinions was groomed in their minds into a clean and precise form.

It can never be the same in a country like America, where all citizens are on the move; where society, modifying itself every day, changes its opinions with its needs. In such a country one glimpses the rule of honor; one rarely has the leisure to consider it fixedly.

Should society be immobile, it would still be difficult to settle the sense that ought to be given to the word honor.

In the Middle Ages, when each class had its own honor, the same opinion was never adopted at once by a very great number of men, which permitted giving it a settled and precise form—all the more since all those who adopted it, having all a perfectly identical and very exceptional position, would find a natural disposition to agree on the prescriptions of a law that had been made for them alone.

Honor thus became a complete and detailed code in which all was foreseen and ordered in advance, and which presented a fixed and always visible rule of human actions. In a democratic nation like the American people, where ranks are confused and where the entire society forms a single mass, all the elements of which are analogous without being entirely alike, one can never agree in advance on exactly what is permitted and forbidden by honor.

There indeed exist within this people certain national needs that give rise to common opinions in the matter of honor; but these like opinions never present themselves at the same time, in the same manner, and with an equal force to the minds of all citizens; the law of honor exists, but it often lacks interpreters.

The confusion is much greater still in a democratic country like ours, where the different classes that composed the former society come to mix together without yet being able to blend with each other, and introduce diverse and often contrary notions of their honor to one another every day; where each man, following his caprices, abandons one part of the opinions of his fathers and retains another, so that in the midst of so many arbitrary measures a common rule can never be established. Then it is almost impossible to say in advance which actions will be honored or stigmatized. These are miserable times, but they do not last.

Honor in democratic nations, being ill-defined, is necessarily less powerful; for it is difficult to apply certainly and firmly a law that is imperfectly known. Public opinion, the natural and sovereign interpreter of the law of honor, does not see distinctly in which direction it is fitting to make blame or praise incline, and pronounces its decision only with hesitation. Sometimes it comes to contradict itself; often it holds itself immobile and lets things be.

The relative weakness of honor in democracies is due to several other causes as well.

In aristocratic countries, the same honor is only adopted by a certain number of men, often restricted and always separated from the rest of those like themselves. Honor is therefore easily mixed and confused in their minds with the idea of all that distinguishes them. It appears to them as the distinctive feature of their physiognomy; they apply its different rules with all the ardor of personal interest and, if I can express myself so, they put passion into obeying it.

This truth is brought out very clearly when one reads the customary [laws] of the Middle Ages on the article of judicial duels. One sees there that in their quarrels the nobles were required to make use of the lance and the sword, whereas villeins used the stick among themselves, "considering," added the custom, "*that villeins do not have honor.*" This did not mean, as one might imagine in our day, that these men were contemptible; it signified only that their actions were not judged according to the same rules as those of the aristocracy.

What is astonishing at first is that when honor reigns with this full power, its prescriptions are generally very strange, so that it seems to be better obeyed the more it appears to deviate from reason; from this it has sometimes come to be concluded that honor is strong because of its very extravagance.

In fact these two things have the same origin; but they do not flow one from the other.

Honor is peculiar to the degree that it represents more particular needs and is felt by fewer men; and it is because it represents needs of this kind that it is powerful. Honor is therefore not powerful because it is peculiar; but it is peculiar and powerful for the same cause.

I shall make another remark.

In aristocratic peoples all ranks differ, but all ranks are fixed; each occupies a place in his sphere that he cannot leave, where he lives in the midst of other men around him attached in the same manner. In these nations, therefore, no one can hope or fear not to be seen; he encounters no man placed so low that he has no theater, who will escape blame or praise by his obscurity.

In democratic states, on the contrary, where all citizens are confused in the same crowd and constantly act on each other, public opinion has no hold; its object disappears at each instant and escapes it. Honor will therefore always be less imperious and less pressing there; for honor only acts in public view, differing in that from simple virtue, which lives on itself and is satisfied with its own witness.

If the reader has indeed grasped all that precedes, he will have understood that there exists a tight and necessary relation between inequality of conditions and what we have called honor, which, if I am not mistaken, has not yet been clearly indicated. I must therefore make a last effort to bring it well to light.

A nation places itself apart in the human race. It has its particular interests and needs independent of certain general needs inherent in the human species. It immediately establishes within it certain opinions that are its own, in matters of blame and praise, and that its citizens call honor.

Within this same nation a caste comes to be established which, separating itself in its turn from all other classes, contracts particular needs, and these in their turn give rise to special opinions. The honor of this caste, a peculiar composite of the particular notions of the nation and the still more particular notions of the caste, will move as far as one can imagine from the simple and general opinions of men. We have reached the extreme point; let us go back.

Ranks are mixed, privileges are abolished. The men who compose the nation having again become alike and equal, their interests and needs are intermingled, and all the singular notions that each caste called honor are seen to vanish successively; honor flows from nothing more than the particular needs of the nation itself; it represents its individuality among peoples.

If it were finally permissible to suppose that all races should intermingle and all the peoples of the world should come to the point of having the same interests and the same needs, and of no longer distinguishing themselves from one another by any characteristic feature, one would cease entirely to attribute conventional value to human actions; all would view them in the same light; the general needs of humanity that conscience reveals to each man would be the common measure. Then one would no longer encounter in this world any but simple and general notions of good and evil, to which ideas of praise or of blame would be attached by a natural and necessary bond.

Thus, finally to include all my thought in a single formula, it is the dissimilarities and inequalities of men that have created honor; it is weakened insofar as these differences are effaced, and it should disappear with them.

Chapter 19 WHY ONE FINDS SO MANY AMBITIOUS MEN IN THE UNITED STATES AND SO FEW GREAT AMBITIONS

The first thing that strikes one in the United States is the innumerable multitude of those who seek to get out of their original condition; and the second is the small number of great ambitions that make themselves noticed in the midst of this universal movement of ambition. There are no Americans who do not show that they are devoured by the desire to rise, but one sees almost none of them who appear to nourish vast hopes or to aim very high. All want constantly to acquire goods, reputation, power; few envision all these things on a grand scale. And this is surprising at first sight, since one does not perceive anything, either in the mores or in the laws of America, that would limit desires and prevent them from soaring in all directions.

It seems difficult to attribute this singular state of things to equality of conditions; for at the moment when that same equality was established among us, it immediately made ambitions bloom almost without limit. Nevertheless, I believe that it is principally in the social state and democratic mores of the Americans that the cause of the preceding should be sought.

Every revolution enlarges the ambition of men. That is above all true of the revolution that overturns an aristocracy.

As the former barriers that separated the crowd from renown and power are suddenly lowered, an impetuous and universal movement of ascent is made toward this long-envied greatness, whose enjoyment is finally permitted. In this first exaltation of triumph, nothing seems impossible to anyone. Not only do desires have no bounds, but the power to satisfy them has almost none. In the midst of this general and sudden renovation of customs and laws, in this vast confusion of all men and all rules, citizens raise themselves and fall with unheard-of rapidity, and power passes so quickly from hand to hand that no one must despair of seizing it in his turn.

Moreover, one must remember well that people who destroy an aristocracy have lived under its laws; they have seen its splendors and they have allowed themselves, without knowing it, to be pervaded with the sentiments and ideas that it had conceived. Therefore, at the moment when an aristocracy is dissolved, its spirit still drifts over the mass, and its instincts are preserved long after it has been defeated.

Ambitions therefore always show themselves to be very great as long as the democratic revolution lasts; it will be the same for some time after it has ended.

The remembrance of the extraordinary events to which they have been witness is not effaced from the memory of men in a day. The passions that the revolution had prompted do not disappear with it. The sense of instability is perpetuated in the midst of order. The idea of easy success survives the strange vicissitudes that had given rise to it. Desires remain vast though the means of satisfying them diminish daily. The taste for great fortunes subsists even though great fortunes become rare, and on all sides one sees disproportionate and unfortunate ambitions ignited that burn secretly and fruitlessly in the hearts that contain them.

Little by little, however, these last traces of the struggle are effaced; the remains of aristocracy finally disappear. One forgets the great events that accompanied its fall; repose succeeds war, the empire of rules reigns within the new world; its desires become proportionate to its means; needs, ideas, and sentiments are linked; men have leveled themselves: a democratic society is finally seated.

If we consider a democratic people which has come to this permanent and normal state, it will present us with a very different spectacle from the one that we have just been contemplating, and we shall be able to judge without trouble whether, if ambition becomes great while conditions are being equalized, it loses this character when they are equal.

As great fortunes are partitioned and science is spread, no one is absolutely deprived of enlightenment or goods; the privileges and incapacities of classes being abolished and men having broken forever the bonds that held them immobile, the idea of progress offers itself to the mind of each of them; the longing to rise is born in all hearts at once; each man wants to leave his place. Ambition is the universal sentiment.

But if equality of conditions gives some resources to all citizens, it prevents any of them from having very extensive resources, which necessarily confines desires within fairly narrow limits. In democratic peoples, ambition is therefore ardent and continuous but it cannot habitually aim very high; and life is ordinarily passed in eagerly coveting petty objects that one sees within one's reach.

What above all turns men of democracies away from great ambition is not the smallness of their fortune, but the violent effort they make every day to better it. They compel the soul to employ all its strength in doing mediocre things—which cannot fail soon to limit its view and circumscribe its power. They could be much poorer and still be greater.

The few opulent citizens found within a democracy are no exception to this rule. A man who raises himself by degrees to wealth and power contracts habits of prudence and restraint in this long work from which he cannot afterwards depart. One does not gradually enlarge one's soul like one's house.

An analogous remark is applicable to the sons of this same man. They are born, it is true, into an elevated position, but their parents have been humble; they have grown up in the midst of sentiments and ideas from which it is later difficult for them to escape; and it is to be believed that they will inherit the instincts of their father and his goods at the same time.

It can happen, on the contrary, that the poorest offspring of a powerful aristocracy displays a vast ambition, because the traditional opinions of his race and the general spirit of his caste still sustain him for some time above his fortune.

What also prevents men of democratic times from easily giving themselves over to an ambition for great things is the time that they foresee must elapse before they are in a state to undertake them. "It is a great advantage," said Pascal, "to have the quality that puts a man as far on his way at eighteen or twenty years as another could be at fifty; these are thirty years gained without trouble."* Those thirty years are ordinarily lacking to the ambitious in democracies. Equality, which allows to each the ability to succeed at everything, prevents one from becoming great quickly.

In a democratic society, as elsewhere, there are only a certain number of great fortunes to be made; and as the careers that lead to them are open indiscriminately to each citizen, the progress of all must be slowed. As the candidates appear nearly similar, and as it is difficult to make a choice among them without violating the principle of equality, which is the supreme law of democratic societies, the first idea that presents itself is to make all advance at the same pace and to subject all to the same tests.

Therefore, as men become more alike and the principle of equality penetrates more peacefully and more deeply into institutions and mores, the rules of advancement become more inflexible and advancement slower; the difficulty of quickly reaching a certain degree of greatness increases.

By hatred of privilege and embarrassment over choosing, one comes to compel all men, whatever their stature might be, to pass through the same filter, and one subjects them all indiscriminately to a multitude of little preliminary exercises in the midst of which their youth is lost and their imagination extinguished; so they despair of ever being able to enjoy fully the goods that are offered to them; and when they finally come to be able to do extraordinary things, they have lost the taste for them.

In China, where equality of conditions is very great and very old, a man passes from one public office to another only after submitting to a competition. This test is encountered at each step in his career, and the idea of it is so well introduced into mores that I remember having read a Chinese novel in which the hero after many vicissitudes finally touches the heart of his mistress by passing an examination well. Great ambitions breathe uneasily in such an atmosphere.

What I say about politics extends to all things; equality produces the same effects everywhere; wherever the law does not take charge of regulating and slowing the movement of men, competition suffices for it.

In a well-established democratic society, great and rapid rises are therefore rare; they form exceptions to the common rule. It is their singularity that makes one forget their small number.

Men of democracies in the end catch a glimpse of all these things; they perceive at length that the legislator opens an unlimited field before them on which all can easily take some steps, but which no one flatters himself he can run through quickly. Between themselves and the vast and final object of

*Pascal, *Pensées*, 322 Br., quoted with slight changes.

their desires they see a multitude of small intermediate barriers, which they clear only slowly; this view tires their ambition in advance and sickens it. They therefore renounce these distant and doubtful hopes to seek less lofty and easier enjoyments near to them. The law does not bound their horizon, but they shrink it themselves.

I have said that great ambitions are rarer in democratic centuries than in aristocratic times; I add that when they arise despite these natural obstacles, they wear another face.

In aristocracies the arena of ambition is often extensive, but its boundaries are fixed. In democratic countries it ordinarily moves on a narrow field; but should it come to leave that, one would say there is no longer anything to limit it. As men there are weak, isolated, and on the move; as precedents have little empire and laws little duration, resistance to novelties is weak and the social body never appears very upright or quite firm in its seat. So when once the ambitious have power in hand, they believe they can dare all; and when it escapes them, they immediately think of overturning the state to get it back.

That gives a violent and revolutionary character to political ambition that is rare to see to the same degree in aristocratic societies.

A multitude of small, very sensible ambitions in the midst of which some badly regulated great desires burst out from to time: such is ordinarily the picture that democratic nations present. A proportionate ambition, moderate yet vast, is scarcely ever encountered in them.

I have shown elsewhere by what secret force equality makes the passion for material enjoyments and the exclusive love of the present predominate in the human heart;* these different instincts mix with the sentiment of ambition and tinge it, so to speak, with their colors.

I think that in democracies the ambitious are less preoccupied than all others with the interests and judgments of the future: the present moment alone occupies and absorbs them. They finish many undertakings rapidly rather than raise a few long-lasting monuments; they love success much more than glory. What they ask of men, above all, is obedience. What they want before everything is dominion. Their mores have almost always been less high than their condition, which very often makes them bring very vulgar tastes to extraordinary fortune, and they seem to raise themselves to sovereign power only to procure small and coarse pleasures more easily.

I believe that in our day it is very necessary to purify, to regulate, and to keep in proportion the sentiment of ambition, but that it would be very dangerous to want to impoverish and constrict it beyond measure. One must

* *DA* II 2.10–11.

try to pose the farthest boundaries for it in advance that it will never be permitted to cross; but one ought to guard against hindering its ascent too much within the permitted limits.

I avow that for democratic societies I dread the audacity much less than the mediocrity of desires; what seems to me most to be feared is that in the midst of the small incessant occupations of private life, ambition will lose its spark and its greatness; that human passions will be appeased and debased at the same time, so that each day the aspect of the social body becomes more tranquil and less lofty.

I think therefore that the heads of these new societies would be wrong to want to put citizens to sleep in a happiness too even and peaceful, and that it is good to give them difficult and perilous affairs sometimes in order to elevate ambition and to open a theater for it.

Moralists constantly complain that the favorite vice of our period is pride.

That is true in a certain sense: there is, in fact, no one who does not believe himself to be worth more than his neighbor and who consents to obey his superior; but that is very false in another; for this same man, who can tolerate neither subordination nor equality, nonetheless despises himself to the point that he believes himself made only to taste vulgar pleasures. He willingly settles into mediocre desires without daring to enter upon lofty undertakings: he hardly imagines them.

Therefore, far from believing that one must recommend humility to our contemporaries, I should want one to strive to give them a vaster idea of themselves and of their species; humility is not healthy for them; what they lack most, in my opinion, is pride. I would willingly trade several of our small virtues for this vice.

൧ ൧

Chapter 20 ON THE INDUSTRY IN PLACE-HUNTING IN CERTAIN DEMOCRATIC NATIONS

In the United States, as soon as a citizen has some enlightenment and some resources, he seeks to enrich himself in commerce and industry, or better, he buys a field covered with forests and makes himself a pioneer. All that he demands of the state is that it not come to trouble him in his labors, and that it assure him the fruits of them.

Among most European peoples, when a man begins to feel his strength and to extend his desires, the first idea that presents itself to him is to obtain a public post. These different effects, issuing from the same cause, merit our stopping here for a moment to consider them.

When public offices are few, poorly paid, unstable, and when, on the other hand, industrial careers are numerous and productive, it is toward industry and not the administration that the new and impatient desires born daily of equality are directed on all sides.

But if, at the same time that ranks are being equalized, enlightenment remains incomplete or spirits timid, or if commerce and industry, hindered in their development, offer only difficult and slow means of making a fortune, citizens, despairing of improving their lot by themselves, rush tumultuously toward the head of state and demand his aid. To be put more at ease at the expense of the public treasury appears to them to be, if not the sole way they have, at least the easiest and the best way open to all to leave a condition that no longer suffices for them: the search for places becomes the most practiced industry of all.

It will be so above all in great centralized monarchies, where the number of paid offices is immense and the life of officials assured enough so that no one despairs of obtaining a post and of enjoying it peacefully like a patrimony.

I shall not say that this universal and immoderate desire for public offices is a great social evil; that it destroys the spirit of independence in each citizen and spreads a venal and servile humor in the whole body of the nation; that it suffocates the virile virtues; nor shall I have it observed that an industry of this kind creates only an unproductive activity and agitates the country without making it fruitful: all that is easily understood.

But I want to remark that the government that favors a tendency like this risks its tranquillity and puts its very life in great peril.

I know that in a time like ours, when one sees the love and respect that were formerly attached to power being extinguished, it can appear necessary to those who govern to chain each man more tightly by his interest, and that it seems convenient for them to make use of his very passions to hold him in order and silence; but it cannot be so for long, and what can appear to be a cause of strength for a certain period surely becomes a great subject of trouble and weakness in the long term.

In democratic peoples as in all others, the number of public posts in the end has bounds; but in these same peoples the number of the ambitious has none; it increases constantly by a gradual and irresistible movement as conditions are equalized; it is bounded only when men are lacking.

Therefore, when ambition has no outlet but in administration alone, the government in the end necessarily encounters a permanent opposition; for its task is to satisfy with limited means desires that multiply without limits. One must indeed be convinced that of all peoples of the world, the most difficult to contain and direct is a people of place-hunters.* Whatever efforts its chiefs make, they can never satisfy it, and one should always be apprehensive that it will finally overturn the constitution of the country and change the face of the state solely out of the need to make some places vacant.

Princes in our time who strive to attract to themselves alone all the new desires that equality sparks, and to satisfy them, will therefore end, if I am not mistaken, by repenting of having engaged in such an undertaking; one day they will discover that they have risked their power in rendering it so necessary, and that it would have been more honest and more sure to teach each of their subjects the art of being self-sufficient.

Chapter 21 WHY GREAT REVOLUTIONS WILL BECOME RARE

A people that has lived under the regime of castes and classes for centuries comes to a democratic social state only through a long series of more or less painful transformations, with the aid of violent efforts and after numerous vicissitudes during which goods, opinions, and power change place rapidly.

Even when this great revolution is ended, one still sees the revolutionary habits created by it endure for a long time, and profound agitations succeed it.

As all this takes place at the moment when conditions are becoming equal, one concludes that a hidden relation and secret bond between equality itself and revolutions exists so that one cannot exist without giving rise to the other.

On this point reasoning seems in accord with experience.

In a people in which ranks are nearly equal, no apparent bond unites men and holds them firm in their places. None of them has either the permanent right or the power to command, and none has to obey because of his condition; but each, finding himself provided with some enlightenment and some resources, can choose his path and proceed separately from all those like him.

---

*Lit.: "solicitors."

The same causes that render citizens independent of one another push them every day toward new and restive desires and spur them constantly.

It therefore seems natural to believe that in a democratic society, ideas, things, and men must change forms and places eternally and that democratic centuries will be times of rapid and incessant transformations.

Is that in fact so? does equality of conditions bring men in an habitual and permanent manner to revolutions? does it contain some disruptive principle that prevents society from establishing itself and that disposes citizens constantly to renovate their laws, their doctrines, and their mores? I do not believe it. The subject is important; I beg the reader to follow me well.

Almost all the revolutions that have changed the face of peoples have been made in order to consecrate or to destroy equality. Put aside the secondary causes that have produced the great agitations of men and you will almost always arrive at inequality. It is the poor who have wanted to rob the goods of the rich or the rich who have tried to put the poor in chains. Therefore if you can found a state of society in which each has something to keep and little to take, you will have done much for the peace of the world.

I am not ignorant of the fact that in a great democratic people, very poor and very rich citizens are always to be found; but the poor, instead of forming the immense majority of the nation, as always happens in aristocratic societies, are few, and the law has not attached them to one another with the bonds of irremediable and hereditary misery.

The rich, for their part, are scattered and impotent; they do not have privileges that attract regard; their wealth itself, no longer incorporated in the land and represented by it, is elusive and almost invisible. Just as there are no longer races of the poor, there are no longer races of the rich; the latter issue from within the crowd each day and return to it constantly. They therefore do not form a separate class that one can easily define and despoil; and besides, as they adhere to the mass of their fellow citizens by a thousand secret threads, the people can scarcely strike at them without hitting themselves. Between these two extremes in democratic societies is found an innumerable multitude of almost similar men who, without being precisely either rich or poor, possess enough goods to desire order and do not have enough of them to excite envy.

These latter are naturally enemies of violent movements; their immobility keeps in repose all who are above and below them and secures the social body in its seat.

It is not that they themselves are satisfied with their present fortune or that they feel a natural horror for a revolution in which they would share in the spoils without experiencing the evils; on the contrary, they desire to enrich themselves with an unequaled ardor; but the trouble is knowing from whom to take. The same social state that constantly suggests desires to them confines these desires within necessary limits. It gives men more freedom to change and less interest in change.

Not only do men of democracies not naturally desire revolutions, but they fear them.

There is no revolution that does not more or less threaten acquired property. Most of those who inhabit democratic countries are property owners; they not only have property, they live in the condition in which men attach the most value to their property.

If one considers attentively each of the classes of which society is composed, it is easy to see that there is none in which the passions to which property gives rise are more fierce and more tenacious than in the middle classes.

Often the poor scarcely care for what they possess because they suffer much more from what they lack than they enjoy the little they have. The rich have many other passions to satisfy than that for wealth, and besides, the long and painful employment of a great fortune sometimes in the end renders them almost insensitive to its sweetness.

But men who live in an ease equally distant from opulence and misery put an immense value on their goods. As they are still very near to poverty, they see its rigors from close by and they dread them; between it and them there is nothing but a small patrimony on which they immediately fix their fears and their hopes. At each instant they become more interested in it by the continual worries it gives them, and they become attached to it by the daily efforts they make to augment it. The idea of yielding the least part of it is intolerable to them, and they consider its entire loss as the ultimate misfortune. Now, the number of these eager and anxious small proprietors is constantly increased by equality of conditions.

Thus in democratic societies the majority of citizens do not see clearly what they could gain by a revolution, and they feel at each instant and in a thousand ways what they could lose from one.

I have said in another place in this work how equality of conditions naturally pushes men toward industrial and commercial careers and how it increases and diversifies landed property; finally I have brought out how it inspires in each man an eager and constant desire to augment his well-being.* There is nothing more contrary to revolutionary passions than all these things.

It can happen that a revolution serves industry and commerce by its final

---

*DA II 2.11, 19.

result; but its first effect will almost always be to ruin the industrialists and businessmen, because it cannot fail to change the general state of consumption right from the first and to overturn momentarily the existing proportion between production and needs.

Moreover, I know of nothing more opposed to revolutionary mores than commercial mores. Commerce is naturally the enemy of all violent passions. It likes even tempers, is pleased by compromise, very carefully flees anger. It is patient, supple, insinuating, and it has recourse to extreme means only when the most absolute necessity obliges it. Commerce renders men independent of one another; it gives them a high idea of their individual worth; it brings them to want to handle their own affairs and teaches them to succeed at them; it therefore disposes them to freedom but moves them away from revolutions.

In a revolution, the possessors of movable goods have more to fear than all others; for on the one hand, their property is often easy to seize, and on the other hand, it can disappear completely at every moment; landed proprietors have less to dread; while losing the revenue of their lands, they at least hope to hold on to the land itself through vicissitudes. Thus one sees that the former are much more frightened than the latter at the appearance of revolutionary movements.

Peoples are therefore less disposed to revolutions as movable goods are multiplied and diversified among them and as the number of those who possess them becomes larger.

Besides, whatever may be the profession that men embrace and the kind of goods they enjoy, one feature is common to them all.

None is fully satisfied with his present fortune, and all strive daily to increase it by a thousand diverse means. Consider each one among them in whatever period of his life, and you will see him preoccupied with some new plans whose object is to increase his ease; do not speak to him of the interests and rights of the human race; that little domestic enterprise absorbs all his thoughts for the moment and makes him wish to put off public agitations to some other time.

Not only does that prevent them from making revolutions, but it diverts them from wishing for them. Violent political passions have little hold on men who have so attached their whole soul to the pursuit of well-being. The ardor they put into small affairs calms them in great ones.

It is true that from time to time in democratic societies there arise enterprising and ambitious citizens whose immense desires cannot be satisfied by following the common route. They love revolutions and call for them; but they have great trouble in giving rise to them if extraordinary events do not come to their aid.

No one struggles to advantage against the spirit of his century and country; and a man, however powerful one supposes him, only with difficulty makes his contemporaries share sentiments and ideas that the sum of their desires and sentiments repels. One must therefore not believe that when equality of conditions, once having become an old and uncontested fact, has impressed its character on mores, men will easily allow themselves to be rushed into taking risks by following an imprudent chief or bold innovator.

It is not that they resist him in an open manner with the aid of studied combinations or even by a premeditated design of resisting. They do not combat him energetically, they sometimes even applaud him, but they do not follow him. To his impetuosity they secretly oppose their inertia; to his revolutionary instincts, their conservative interests, their homebody tastes to his adventurous passions; their good sense to the leaps of his genius; to his poetry, their prose. He arouses them for a moment with a thousand efforts, but soon after they get away from him, and, as if dragged down by their own weight, they fall back. He exhausts himself in the wish to animate this indifferent and distracted crowd, and finally he sees himself reduced to powerlessness, not because he is defeated, but because he is alone.

I do not claim that men who live in democratic societies are naturally immobile; I think, on the contrary, that an eternal motion reigns in the heart of such a society and that no one knows repose in it; but I believe that men in it are agitated within certain limits that they scarcely ever exceed. They vary, alter, or renovate secondary things every day; they take great care not to touch the principal ones. They love change, but they dread revolutions.

Although the Americans constantly modify or abrogate some of their laws, they are far indeed from displaying revolutionary passions. It is easy to discover, in the promptness with which they stop and calm themselves when public agitation begins to become threatening and at the very moment when passions seem the most excited, that they dread a revolution as the greatest of misfortunes and that each of them is internally resolved to make great sacrifices to avoid it. There is no country in the world where the sentiment for property shows itself more active and more restive than in the United States, and where the majority evinces less inclination to doctrines that threaten to alter the constitution of goods in any manner whatsoever.

I often remarked that theories that are revolutionary by their nature, in that they cannot be realized except by a complete and sometimes sudden change in the state of property and of persons, are infinitely less in favor in the United States than in the great monarchies of Europe. If a few men profess them, the mass repels them with a sort of instinctive horror.

I do not fear to say that most of the maxims that one is accustomed to calling democratic in France would be proscribed by the democracy of the

United States. That is easily understood. In America they have democratic ideas and passions; in Europe we still have revolutionary passions and ideas.

If America ever experiences great revolutions, they will be brought about by the presence of blacks on the soil of the United States: that is to say, it will not be the equality of conditions, but on the contrary, their inequality, that will give rise to them.

When conditions are equal, each man willingly isolates himself within himself and forgets the public. If the legislators of democratic peoples did not seek to correct this fatal tendency or favored it, with the thought that it diverts citizens from political passions and thus leads them away from revolutions, it could possibly be that in the end they themselves would produce the evil that they want to avoid, and a moment might arrive in which the disordered passions of some men, aided by the unintelligent selfishness and pusillanimity of the greater number, would in the end compel the social body to undergo strange vicissitudes.

In democratic societies there are scarcely any but small minorities that desire revolutions; but minorities can sometimes make them.

Therefore I do not say that democratic nations are sheltered from revolutions, I say only that the social state of these nations does not bring them to revolutions, but rather moves them away from them. Democratic peoples, left to themselves, do not easily engage in great adventures; they are only carried along toward revolutions without their knowing it; they sometimes undergo them but they do not make them. And I add that when they are permitted to acquire enlightenment and experience, they do not allow them to be made.

I know very well that in this matter public institutions themselves can do much; they favor or constrain the instincts that arise from the social state. Therefore I do not maintain, I repeat, that a people is sheltered from revolutions by the sole fact that within it conditions are equal; but I believe that whatever the institutions of such a people may be, great revolutions will always be infinitely less violent and rarer in it than one supposes; and I easily glimpse such a political state that, when it comes to be combined with equality, would render society more stationary than it has ever been in our West.

What I have just said of deeds applies in part to ideas.

Two things are astonishing in the United States: the great mobility of most human actions and the singular fixity of certain principles. Men move constantly, the human mind seems almost immobile.

When once an opinion has extended over the American soil and has taken root, one would say that no power on earth is in a position to extirpate it. In the United States, general doctrines in the matter of religion, of philosophy, of morality, and even of politics do not vary, or at least they are modified

only after a hidden and often insensible travail; the coarsest prejudices themselves are effaced only with inconceivable slowness in the midst of this fric-
tion of things and men repeated a thousand times.

I hear it said that it is in the nature and in the habits of democracies to
change their sentiments and thoughts at every moment. That can be true of
small democratic nations, like those of antiquity, that gathered as a whole in
the public square and were then agitated at the will of an orator. I saw nothing like this within the great democratic people that occupies the opposite
shores of our ocean. What struck me in the United States is the trouble one
experiences in disabusing the majority of an idea it has conceived and of
detaching it from a man whom it adopts. Writings or discourses can scarcely
succeed at this; experience alone overcomes it; sometimes it must be repeated.

That is astonishing at first; a more attentive examination explains it.

I do not believe that it is as easy as one imagines to uproot the prejudices
of a democratic people; to change its beliefs; to substitute new religious, philosophical, political, and moral principles for them once they have been established; in a word, to make great and frequent revolutions in intellect. It is not
that the human mind there is idle; it is constantly agitated; but it exerts itself
in varying to infinity the consequences of known principles and in discovering new consequences rather than seeking new principles. It turns on
itself with agility rather than dashing ahead by a rapid and direct effort; it
extends its sphere little by little with continuous and precipitate small movements; it does not displace it all at once.

Men equal in rights, in education, in fortune, and to say it all in a word,
of similar condition, necessarily have needs, habits, and tastes barely unalike.
As they perceive objects under the same aspect, their minds naturally incline
toward analogous ideas, and although each of them can diverge from his
contemporaries and make his own beliefs for himself, in the end, without
knowing it and without wishing it, all meet each other in a certain number
of common opinions.

The more I consider attentively the effects of equality on the intellect, the
more I persuade myself that the intellectual anarchy to which we are witness
is not, as some suppose, the natural state of democratic peoples. I believe
that one must consider it rather as a particular accident of their youth, and
that it is shown only in that period of passage when men have already broken
the old bonds that attached them to one another, and still differ tremendously in origin, education, and mores; so that, having preserved very diverse
ideas, instincts, and tastes, nothing any longer prevents them from producing
them. The principal opinions of men become alike as conditions become

alike. Such appears to me to be the general and permanent fact; the rest is fortuitous and transient.

I believe it will rarely happen within a democratic society that a man comes to conceive in a single stroke a system of ideas very far removed from that which his contemporaries have adopted; and if a such an innovator presented himself, I imagine that he would in the first place have great trouble in making himself heard, and more still in making himself believed.

When conditions are almost alike, one man does not easily allow himself to be persuaded by another. As all see each other from very close, as they have together learned the same things and lead the same life, they are not naturally disposed to take one among them for a guide and to follow him blindly: one scarcely believes one's like or one's equal at his word.

It is not only confidence in the enlightenment of certain individuals that is weakened in democratic nations; as I have said elsewhere, the general idea of the intellectual superiority that any man whatsoever can acquire over all the others is not slow to be obscured.*

As men resemble each other more, the dogma of the equality of the intellect insinuates itself little by little into their beliefs, and it becomes more difficult for an innovator, whoever he may be, to acquire and exercise great power over the mind of a people. In such societies sudden intellectual revolutions are therefore rare; for if one casts a glance over the history of the world, one sees that it is much less the force of reasoning than the authority of a name that has produced great and rapid mutations in human opinions.

Remark, moreover, that as men who live in democratic societies are not attached to one another by any bond, one must convince each of them. Whereas in aristocratic societies it is enough to be able to act on the minds of a few; all the others follow. If Luther had lived in a century of equality, and if he had not had lords and princes for listeners, he would perhaps have found more difficulty in changing the face of Europe.

It is not that men in democracies are naturally very convinced of the certainty of their opinions and very firm in their beliefs; they often have doubts that in their eyes no one can resolve. It sometimes happens in those times that the human mind would willingly change its position, but since nothing either pushes it powerfully or directs it, it oscillates within itself and does not move.[1]

---

*DA II 1.1–2.

1. If I inquire what is the society most favorable to great revolutions of the intellect, I find that one encounters it somewhere between complete equality of all citizens and absolute separation of classes.

Under a regime of castes, generations succeed each other without men's changing their posi-

When one has acquired the confidence of a democratic people, it is still a great affair to get its attention. It is very difficult to make men who live in democracies listen when one is not talking to them about themselves. They do not listen to the things that are said to them because they are always very preoccupied with the things they are doing.

One encounters, in fact, few idle men in democratic nations. Life goes on in the midst of motion and noise, and men are so busy acting that little time remains to them for thinking. What I want to remark above all is that not only are they occupied, but they have a passion for their occupations. They are perpetually in action, and each of their actions absorbs their soul; the fire they put into affairs prevents them from being inflamed by ideas.

I think that it is very difficult to excite the enthusiasm of a democratic people for any theory whatsoever that has no visible, direct, and immediate relation to the daily practice of its life. Such a people does not easily abandon its old beliefs. For it is enthusiasm that precipitates the mind of man beyond beaten paths and that makes great intellectual revolutions as well as great political revolutions.

Thus democratic peoples have neither the leisure nor the taste to go in search of new opinions. Even if they come to doubt those they possess, they preserve them nonetheless because they would need too much time and examination to change them; they keep them not as certain, but as established.

There are still other, more powerful reasons opposed to working a great change easily in the doctrines of a democratic people. I have already pointed to them at the beginning of this book.*

If, within a people like this, individual influences are weak and almost nothing, the power exercised by the mass on the mind of each individual is very great. I have given the reasons for this elsewhere.† What I want to say

---

*DA II 1.1–2.
†DA I 2.7.

---

tion; some wait for nothing more and others hope for nothing better. The imagination goes to sleep in the midst of this silence and this universal immobility, and the very idea of movement no longer offers itself to the human mind.

When classes have been abolished and conditions have become almost equal, all men are constantly agitated, but each of them is isolated, independent, and weak. This last state differs tremendously from the first; nonetheless, it is analogous on one point. Great revolutions of the human mind are very rare in it.

But between these two extremes in the history of peoples, an intermediate age is encountered, a glorious and troubled period in which conditions are not fixed enough for the intellect to sleep and in which they are unequal enough for men to exercise a very great power over the minds of one another, and for some to be able to modify the beliefs of all. It is then that powerful reformers arise and that new ideas change the face of the world all at once.

at this moment is that one would be wrong to believe that this depends uniquely on the form of government and that the majority would lose its intellectual empire with its political power.

In aristocracies, men often have a greatness and a force that are their own. When they find themselves in contradiction with the greater number of those like them, they withdraw into themselves, and sustain and console themselves. There is nothing like this among democratic peoples. Among them, public favor seems as necessary as the air that one breathes, and to be in disagreement with the mass is, so to speak, not to live. [The mass] does not need to use the laws to bend those who do not think like it. It is enough for it to disapprove of them. Their sense of isolation and their impotence immediately overwhelms them and drives them to despair.

In all times when conditions are equal, general opinion puts an immense weight on the mind of each individual; it envelops it, directs it, and oppresses it: that is due to the very constitution of society much more than to its political laws. As all men resemble each other more, each feels himself more and more weak in the face of all. Not discovering anything that elevates him very much above them and distinguishes him from them, he distrusts himself when they are at war with him; not only does he doubt his strength, but he comes to doubt his right to it, and he is very near to recognizing that he is wrong when the greater number affirms it. The majority does not need to constrain him; it convinces him.

In whatever manner the powers of a democratic society are organized and however they are balanced, therefore, it will always be very difficult to believe in what the mass rejects and to profess what it condemns.

This marvelously favors the stability of beliefs.

When an opinion has gotten a foothold in a democratic people and has established itself in the minds of the greater number, it then subsists by itself and perpetuates itself effortlessly because no one attacks it. Those who had at first rejected it as false in the end receive it as general, and those who continue to war with it at the bottom of their hearts make nothing visible; they take good care not to engage in a dangerous and useless struggle.

It is true that when the majority of a democratic people changes its opinion, it can work strange and rapid revolutions at will in the world of the intellect; but it is very difficult to change its opinion and almost as difficult to ascertain that it has changed.

It sometimes happens that time, events, or the individual and solitary effort of intellects in the end shakes or destroys a belief little by little without anything appearing on the outside. They do not combat it openly. They do not unite to make war on it. Its sectarians quit it one by one without a sound;

but each day some abandon it, until finally it is no longer shared except by the few.

In this state it still reigns.

As its enemies continue to be silent or to communicate their thoughts with each other only furtively, for a long time they themselves are unable to assure themselves that a great revolution has been accomplished, and in their doubt they remain motionless. They observe and stay silent. The majority no longer believes; but it still looks like it believes and this vain phantom of a public opinion is enough to chill innovators and to keep them in silence and respect.

We live in a period that has seen the most rapid changes work on the minds of men. Nevertheless, it could soon happen that the principal human opinions are more stable than they have been in previous centuries of our history; this time has not come, but perhaps it approaches.

As I examine the needs and the natural instincts of democratic peoples more closely, I am persuaded that, if equality is ever established in a general and permanent manner in the world, great intellectual and political revolutions will become more difficult and rarer than one supposes.

Because men in democracies always appear excited, uncertain, breathless, ready to change will and place, one fancies that they are suddenly going to abolish their laws, to adopt new beliefs, and to take up new mores. One does not consider that if equality brings men to change, it suggests interests and tastes to them that need stability to be satisfied; it pushes them and at the same time it stops them, it spurs them and attaches them to the earth; it inflames their desires and limits their strength.

This is what is not discovered at first: the passions that turn citizens away from one another in a democracy make themselves manifest. But one does not perceive at first glance the hidden force that holds them back and keeps them together.

Dare I say it in the midst of the ruins that surround me? What I dread most for the generations to come are not revolutions.

If citizens continue to confine themselves more and more narrowly in the circle of small domestic interests, there to become agitated without rest, one can apprehend that in the end they will become almost inaccessible to those great and powerful public emotions that trouble peoples, but develop and renew them. When I see property become so mobile and the love of property so anxious and so ardent, I cannot prevent myself from fearing that men will arrive at the point of looking on every new theory as a peril, every innovation as a distressing trouble, every social progress as a first step toward a revolution, and that they will altogether refuse to move for fear that they will be carried away. I tremble, I confess, that they will finally allow themselves to be so much possessed by a relaxed love of present enjoyments that interest in their own future and that of their descendants will disappear, and they will rather follow the course of their destiny weakly than make a sudden and energetic effort when needed to redress it.

People believe that the new societies are going to change face daily, and I am afraid that in the end they will be too unchangeably fixed in the same institutions, the same prejudices, the same mores, so that the human race will stop and limit itself; that the mind will fold and refold itself around itself eternally without producing new ideas, that man will exhaust himself in small, solitary, sterile motions, and that, while constantly moving, humanity will no longer advance.

ᐧᐧ ᐧᐧ

Chapter 22   WHY DEMOCRATIC PEOPLES NATURALLY DESIRE PEACE AND DEMOCRATIC ARMIES NATURALLY [DESIRE] WAR

The same interests, the same fears, the same passions that divert democratic peoples from revolutions keep them away from war; the military spirit and the revolutionary spirit are weakened at the same time and by the same causes.

The always growing number of property owners friendly to peace; the development of movable wealth, which war devours so rapidly; the indulgence of mores, the softness of heart, the disposition to pity that equality inspires; the coldness of reason that renders one barely sensitive to the poetic and violent emotions that arise among arms—all these causes unite to extinguish the military spirit.

I believe that one can accept as a general and constant rule that among civilized peoples, warlike passions will become more rare and less lively as conditions are more equal.

War, however, is an accident to which all peoples are subject, democratic peoples as well as others. Whatever taste these nations may have for peace, they must keep themselves ready to repel war, or in other words, they must have an army.

Fortune, which has done such particular things in favor of the inhabitants of the United States, has placed them in the midst of a wilderness where they have, so to speak, no neighbors. A few thousand soldiers are enough for them, but this is American and not democratic.

The equality of conditions, and the mores as well as the institutions that derive from it, do not shield a democratic people from the obligation of maintaining armies, and its armies always exert a very great influence on its fate. It is therefore singularly important to inquire what are the natural instincts of those who compose them.

In aristocratic peoples, above all in those where birth alone regulates rank, inequality is found in the army as well as in the nation; the officer is the noble, the soldier is the serf. The one is necessarily called to command, the other, to obey. In aristocratic armies the ambition of the soldier, therefore, has very narrow boundaries.

That of officers is not unlimited either.

An aristocratic body is not only part of a hierarchy; it always contains a hierarchy within it; the members that compose it are placed one above another in a certain manner that does not vary. This one is naturally called by birth to command a regiment, and that one a company; arrived at these extreme ends of their hopes, they stop and hold themselves satisfied with their lot.

There is, first, one great cause which, in aristocracies, cools the desire for advancement in the officer.

In aristocratic peoples, the officer, independent of his rank in the army, also occupies an elevated rank in society; in his eyes, the first is almost always only an accessory to the second; the noble, in embracing the career of arms, still obeys ambition less than a sort of duty that his birth imposes on him. He enters into the army in order to employ the idle years of his youth honorably in it, and to be able to relate some honorable memories of military life at his hearth and among his peers; but his principal object is not to acquire goods, consideration, and power there; for he possesses these advantages by himself and enjoys them without leaving his home.

In democratic armies, all soldiers can become officers, which generalizes the desire for advancement and extends the limits of military ambition almost to infinity.

For his part, the officer sees nothing that naturally and inevitably stops him at one rank rather than another, and each rank has an immense price in his eyes because his rank in society almost always depends on his rank in the army.

In democratic peoples it often happens that the officer has nothing except his pay and can expect no consideration except his military honors. Every time he changes post, he also changes fortune, and he is in a way another man. What was the accessory of existence in aristocratic armies has thus become the principal, the whole—existence itself.

Under the old French monarchy, officers were addressed only by their title of nobility. In our day they are addressed only by their military title. This little change of the forms of language suffices to indicate that a great revolution has been worked in the constitution of society and of the army.

Within democratic armies, the desire to advance is almost universal; it is ardent, tenacious, continual; it is increased by all the other desires and is extinguished only with life. Now it is easy to see that of all the armies in the world, those in which advancement will be the slowest in times of peace are democratic armies. The number of ranks being naturally limited, the number of competitors almost innumerable, and the inflexible law of equality weighing on all, none can make rapid progress and many cannot budge from their place. Thus the need to advance is greater and the ability to advance less than elsewhere.

All the ambitious men that a democratic army contains therefore wish vehemently for war, because war empties places and finally permits violation of that right of seniority that is the sole privilege natural to democracy.

Thus we arrive at this singular consequence, that of all armies those that desire war most ardently are democratic armies, and that among peoples, those that love peace the most are democratic peoples; and what serves to make the thing extraordinary is that equality produces these contrary effects at the same time.

Every day, citizens, being equal, conceive the desire and discover the possibility of changing their condition and of increasing their well-being: that disposes them to love peace, which makes industry prosper and permits each to advance his little undertakings tranquilly to their end; and, on the other hand, this same equality, by increasing the value of military honors in the eyes of those who follow the career of arms, and by making honors accessible to all, makes soldiers dream of battlefields. On both sides the heart's restiveness is the same, the taste for enjoyments is as insatiable, the ambition equal; only the means of satisfying it is different.

These opposed dispositions of the nation and the army make democratic societies risk great dangers.

When military spirit abandons a people, a military career immediately ceases to be honored and men of war fall to the last rank of public officials. They are little esteemed and no longer understood. Then the contrary of what is seen in aristocratic centuries occurs. It is no longer the principal citizens who enter into the army, but the least. One gives oneself to military ambition only when no other is permitted. This forms a vicious circle one has trouble escaping. The elite of the nation avoids a military career because this career is not honored; and it is not honored because the elite of the nation no longer enters it.

One must therefore not be surprised if democratic armies often show themselves restive, grumbling, and ill satisfied with their lot, although their physical condition is ordinarily much milder and the discipline less rigid than in all others. The soldier feels himself in an inferior position, and his wounded pride serves to give him a taste for war, which renders him necessary, or a love of revolutions, during which he would hope to capture, arms in hand, the political influence and the individual consideration that people contest him.

The composition of democratic armies makes this last peril much to be feared.

In democratic society, almost all citizens have property to preserve; but democratic armies are generally led by proletarians. Most of them have little to lose in civil troubles. The mass of the nation naturally fears revolutions much more than in centuries of aristocracy; but the chiefs of the army dread them much less.

In addition, since in democratic peoples, as I said above, the wealthiest, the best instructed, the most capable citizens scarcely enter upon a military career, it happens that the entire army in the end makes up a separate little nation in which intelligence is less extensive and habits coarser than in the larger one. But this uncivilized little nation possesses arms, and it alone knows how to make use of them.

What in fact increases the peril that the military and turbulent spirit of the army makes democratic peoples risk is the peaceable humor of the citizens; there is nothing so dangerous as an army in the heart of a nation that is not warlike; the excessive love of all citizens in it for tranquillity puts the constitution at the mercy of the soldiers every day.

One can therefore say in a general manner that if democratic peoples are naturally brought toward peace by their interests and their instincts, they are constantly drawn to war and revolutions by their armies.

Military revolutions, which are almost never to be feared in aristocracies, are always to be dreaded in democratic nations. These perils ought to be ranked among the most dreadful of all those that their future contains; the attention of statesmen must be applied relentlessly to finding a remedy for them.

When a nation feels the restive ambition of its army at work internally, the first thought that presents itself is to give this inconvenient ambition war for an object.

I do not wish to speak ill of war; war almost always enlarges the thought of a people and elevates its heart. There are cases where only it can arrest the excessive development of certain penchants that equality naturally gives rise to, and where, for certain deep-seated maladies to which democratic societies are subject, it must be considered almost necessary.

War has great advantages; but one must not flatter oneself that it diminishes the peril that has just been pointed out. It only suspends it, and it comes back more terrible after the war, for the army suffers peace much more impatiently after having tasted war. War would only be a remedy for a people that always wanted glory.

I foresee that all the warlike princes who arise within great democratic nations will find that it is easier for them to win with their army than to make it live in peace after victory. There are two things that a democratic people will always have much trouble doing: beginning a war and ending it.

Moreover, if war has particular advantages for democratic peoples, on the other hand it makes them risk certain perils that aristocracies do not have to fear to the same degree. I shall cite only two.

If war satisfies the army, it hinders and often drives to despair that innumerable crowd of citizens whose small passions need peace every day to be satisfied. It therefore risks giving birth under another form to the disorder that it ought to prevent.

There is no long war that does not put freedom at great risk in a democratic country. It is not that one must precisely fear to see winning generals take possession of sovereign power by force after each victory, in the manner of Sulla and Caesar.* The peril is of another sort. War does not always give democratic peoples over to military government; but it cannot fail to increase immensely the prerogatives of civil government in these peoples; it almost inevitably centralizes the direction of all men and the employment of all things in its hands. If it does not lead one to despotism suddenly by violence, it leads to it mildly through habits.

All those who seek to destroy freedom within a democratic nation ought to know that the surest and shortest means of succeeding at this is war. There is the first axiom of the science.

A remedy seems to offer itself when the ambition of officers and soldiers comes to inspire fear, which is to increase the number of places to be given by enlarging the army. This relieves the present ill, but stakes the future all the more.

To enlarge the army can produce a lasting effect in an aristocratic society, because in these societies military ambition is limited to a single kind of man, and for each man, stops at a certain boundary, so that one can come to content nearly all those who feel it.

---

*Sulla (138–78 B.C.) and Julius Caesar (ca. 100–44 B.C.), Roman generals and statesmen.

But in a democratic people, one gains nothing by increasing the army, because the number of the ambitious is always increased in exactly the same proportion as the army itself. Those whose wishes you have fulfilled in creating new posts are immediately replaced by a new crowd that you cannot satisfy, and the first soon begin to complain again themselves; for the same agitation of spirit that reigns among the citizens of a democracy is displayed in the army; what one wishes is not to gain a certain rank, but always to advance. If desires are not very vast, they are constantly reborn. A democratic people that enlarges its army can therefore make the ambition of men of war milder only for a moment; soon it becomes more formidable because those who feel it are more numerous.

I think, for my part, that a restive and turbulent spirit is an ill inherent in the very constitution of democratic armies, and that one ought to renounce hope of curing it. Legislators of democracies must not pride themselves on finding a military organization that by itself has the strength to calm men of war and make them content; they would exhaust themselves in vain efforts before they attained it.

It is not in the army that the remedy for the vices of the army can be encountered, but in the country.

Democratic peoples naturally fear trouble and despotism. It is only a question of making reflective, intelligent, and stable tastes out of these instincts. When citizens have finally learned to make a peaceful and useful use of freedom and have felt its benefits; when they have contracted a virile love of order and have voluntarily bowed to its rule, these same citizens, as they enter the career of arms, bring these habits and mores to it without their knowing it and almost despite themselves. The general spirit of the nation, penetrating the particular spirit of the army, tempers the opinions and the desires that the military state gives rise to, or, through the all-powerful force of public opinion, it compromises them. Have enlightened, regulated, steadfast, and free citizens, and you will have disciplined and obedient soldiers.

Every law that, in repressing the turbulent spirit of the army, would tend to diminish the spirit of civil freedom in the heart of the nation and to obscure in it the idea of right and of rights, would therefore go against its object. It would favor the establishment of a military tyranny much more than it would nullify it.

After all, and whatever one might do, a great army in the heart of a democratic people will always be a great peril; and the most efficacious means of diminishing that peril will be to reduce the army; but this is not a remedy all peoples can use.

☙ ☙

Chapter 23 WHICH IS THE MOST WARLIKE AND THE MOST REVOLUTIONARY CLASS IN DEMOCRATIC ARMIES

It is of the essence of a democratic army to be very numerous relative to the people that furnishes it; I shall speak of the reasons further on.

On the other hand, men who live in democratic times hardly ever choose a military career.

Democratic peoples are therefore soon led to renounce voluntary recruitment and to have recourse to compulsory enlistment. The necessity of their condition obliges them to take this last means, and one can easily predict that all will adopt it.

Military service being compulsory, the burden is shared indiscriminately and equally by all citizens. That again necessarily springs from the condition of these peoples and from their ideas. Government can do nearly what it wants, provided that it addresses itself to everyone at once; it is the inequality of its weight, and not its weight, that ordinarily makes one resist it.

Now, military service being common to all citizens, it evidently results from this that each of them remains under the flag for only a few years.

Thus in the nature of things the soldier will be in the army only in passing, whereas in most aristocratic nations, military status is a job that the soldier takes on, or that is imposed on him, for all his life.

This has great consequences. Among soldiers who compose a democratic army, some are attached to military life; but the greater number, thus brought to serve under the flag despite themselves and always ready to return to their homes, do not consider themselves seriously engaged in a military career and think only of leaving it. They do not contract the needs and never share but halfway in the passions that this career gives rise to. They bow to their military duties, but their souls remain attached to the interests and desires they were filled with in civil life. They therefore do not take up the spirit of the army; rather, they bring the spirit of society within the army and preserve it there. In democratic peoples it is the plain soldiers who most remain citizens; it is over them that national habits keep the best hold and public opinion has the most power. It is through the soldiers above all that one can pride oneself on having a democratic army pervaded by the love of freedom and the respect for rights that one was able to inspire in the people themselves. The contrary happens in aristocratic nations, where in the end soldiers have nothing more in common with their fellow citizens and live in their midst as strangers and often as enemies.

In aristocratic armies, the conservative element is the officer, because the officer alone has kept tight bonds with civil society and never abandons his wish of coming back sooner or later to retake his place there; in democratic armies, it is the soldier, and for causes altogether alike.

It often happens, on the contrary, that in these same democratic armies, the officer contracts tastes and desires entirely separate from those of the nation. That is understandable.

In democratic peoples the man who becomes an officer breaks all the bonds that attached him to civil life; he leaves it forever and he has no interest in reentering it. His genuine native country is the army, as he is nothing but the rank he occupies there; he therefore follows the fortune of the army, ascends or falls with it, and from then on, he directs his hopes toward it alone. The officer, having needs very distinct from those of the country, can be made to desire war ardently or to work for a revolution at the very moment that the nation most aspires to stability and peace.

Still, there are causes that temper the warlike and restive humor in him. If ambition is universal and continuous in democratic peoples, we have seen that it is rarely great there. The man who, having come from the secondary classes of the nation, has come through the inferior ranks of the army up to the rank of officer has already taken an immense step. He has gotten a foothold in a sphere superior to the one he occupied within civil society, and there he has acquired rights that most democratic nations will always consider inalienable.[1] After this great effort he willingly stops and thinks about enjoying his conquest. The fear of compromising what he already possesses weakens the longing in his heart to acquire what he does not have. After having cleared the first and greatest obstacle that arrested his progress, he is resigned less impatiently to the slowness of his advance. This cooling of ambition increases as he rises in rank and finds he has more to lose from risks. If I am not mistaken, the least warlike as well as the least revolutionary part of a democratic army will always be the head.

What I have just said about the officer and the soldier is not applicable to a numerous class which in all armies occupies the intermediate place between them; I mean the noncommissioned officer.

This class of noncommissioned officers, which had not yet appeared in

---

1. The position of officer is, in fact, much more secure in democratic peoples than in others. The less the officer is on his own, the more the rank has comparative value, and the more the legislator finds it just and necessary to ensure enjoyment of it.

history before the present century, is, I think, called upon to play a role in it from now on.

Like the officer, the noncommissioned officer has in his thinking broken all the bonds that attached him to civil society; like him, he has made the military his career, and perhaps more than he, he has directed all his desires in this direction alone; but he has not yet attained, as has the officer, an elevated and solid position where it is permissible for him to stop and breathe at ease while waiting to be able to climb higher.

By the very nature of his functions, which cannot change, the noncommissioned officer is condemned to lead an obscure, narrow, uneasy, and precarious existence. He still sees only perils in a military status. He knows only privations and obedience, more difficult to tolerate than the perils. He suffers all the more from his present miseries as he knows that the constitution of society and that of the army permit him to free himself from them; in fact, from one day to the next he can become an officer. Then he would command, have honors, independence, rights, satisfactions; not only does this object of his hopes appear immense to him, but before he seizes it, he is never sure of attaining it. His rank is not at all irrevocable; he is left wholly to the arbitrariness of his chiefs every day; the needs of discipline imperatively require that it be so. A slight fault, a caprice, can always make him lose in a moment the fruit of several years of work and effort. Until he arrives at the rank he covets, he has therefore done nothing. There only does he seem to enter his career. In a man spurred so constantly by his youth, his needs, his passions, the spirit of his times, his hopes and his fears, a desperate ambition cannot fail to ignite.

The noncommissioned officer therefore wants war, he wants it always and at any price, and if he is refused war, he desires revolutions that suspend the authority of rules in the midst of which he hopes, thanks to the confusion and to political passions, to chase his officer out and take his place; and it is not impossible that he will give rise to them, because he exerts a great influence over the soldiers through their common origin and habits, although he differs much from them by passions and desires.

It would be wrong to believe that these diverse dispositions of the officer, the noncommissioned officer, and the soldier are tied to one time or to one country. They will be displayed in all periods and in all democratic nations.

In every democratic army it will always be the noncommissioned officer who least represents the peaceable and regular spirit of the country and the soldier who best represents it. The soldier brings into his military career the strength or weakness of national mores: there he will display a faithful image of the nation. If it is ignorant and weak, he will allow himself to be led away to disorder by his chiefs, without knowing it or despite himself. If it is enlightened and energetic, he himself will keep them in order.

Chapter 24 WHAT MAKES DEMOCRATIC ARMIES WEAKER THAN OTHER ARMIES WHEN ENTERING INTO A CAMPAIGN AND MORE FORMIDABLE WHEN WAR IS PROLONGED

Every army that enters into a campaign after a long peace risks being defeated; every army that has made war for a long time has a great chance of winning: this truth is particularly applicable to democratic armies.

In aristocracies, military status, being a privileged career, is honored even in times of peace. Men who have great talents, great enlightenment, and great ambition embrace it; the army is, in all things, at the level of the nation; often it even surpasses it.

On the contrary, we have seen how in democratic peoples the elite of the nation turns away little by little from a military career to seek consideration, power, and above all wealth, by other paths. After a long peace—and in democratic times a peace lasts long—the army is always inferior to the country itself. War finds it in this state; and until war has changed it, there is peril for the country and for the army.

I have brought out how in democratic armies and in times of peace, the right of seniority is the supreme and inflexible law of advancement.* That flows not only from the constitution of these armies, as I have said, but from the very constitution of the people, and it will always be so.

In addition, as in these peoples the officer is something in his country only by his military position, from which he draws all his consideration and all his ease, he retires or is excluded from the army only at the extreme end of his life.

From these two causes it results that when a democratic people finally takes up arms after a long repose, all the chiefs of its army are found to be old men. I speak not only of generals, but of subordinate officers, of whom most have remained stationary or have been able to advance only step by step. If one considers a democratic army after a long peace, one sees with surprise that all the soldiers are near to childhood and all the chiefs in decline, so that the first lack experience and the second, vigor.

*DA II 3.22.

That is a great cause of setbacks; for the first condition for conducting war well is to be young; I would not dare to say this if the greatest captain of modern times had not said it.*

These two causes do not act in the same manner on aristocratic armies.

As one advances in them by right of birth much more than by right of seniority, a certain number of young men, who bring to war all the first energy of body and soul, are always to be encountered in all ranks.

Furthermore, as the men who seek military honors in an aristocratic people have a secure position in civil society, they rarely wait in the army for the approach of old age to overtake them. After devoting the most vigorous years of their youth to the career of arms, they retire of their own accord and go to spend the rest of their mature age at home.

A long peace not only fills democratic armies with elderly officers, it also gives to all officers habits of body and mind that render them little suited for war. He who has long lived in the midst of the peaceful and lukewarm atmosphere of democratic mores bends uneasily at first to the rude work and austere duties that war imposes. If he does not absolutely lose the taste for arms, he at least takes to it fashions of living that prevent him from winning.

In aristocratic peoples, the softness of civil life exerts less influence on military mores because in these peoples it is the aristocracy that leads the army. Now, an aristocracy, however immersed in delights it may be, always has several other passions than those of well-being, and it willingly makes a temporary sacrifice of its well-being to satisfy those passions better.

I have shown how, in times of peace, advancement in democratic armies is extremely slow. At first, officers tolerate this state of things with impatience; they become agitated, restive, and desperate; but, in the long term, most of them become resigned. Those who have the most ambition and resources leave the army; the others, at last making their tastes and their desires proportionate to the mediocrity of their lot, end by considering military status from a civil aspect. What they prize most in it is the ease and stability that accompanies it; on the assurance of this small fortune they found the whole image of their future, and they ask only to be able to enjoy it peacefully.

Thus not only does a long peace fill democratic armies with elderly officers, but it often gives the instincts of old men to those who are still of a vigorous age.

I have also brought out how in democratic nations, in times of peace, a military career is little honored and ill pursued.

*This citation, presumably from Napoleon, was not found.

This public disfavor is a very heavy burden that weighs on the spirit of the army. Their souls are almost bent over by it; and when war finally arrives, they cannot regain their elasticity and their vigor in a moment.

One does not meet with a cause of moral weakness like this in aristocratic armies. Their officers are never debased in their own eyes and in those of others like themselves, because they are great in themselves, independently of their military greatness.

Should the influence of peace make itself felt by the two armies in the same manner, the results would still be different.

When the officers of an aristocratic army have lost a warlike spirit and the desire to elevate themselves through arms, a certain respect for the honor of their order and an age-old habit of being first and setting an example do still remain to them. But when the officers of a democratic army no longer have a love of war and military ambition, nothing remains.

I think therefore that a democratic people that undertakes a war after a long peace risks being defeated much more than any other; but it ought not to allow itself to be easily beaten down by setbacks, for the chances of its army are increased by the very duration of the war.

When prolonged, war finally tears all citizens away from their peaceful work and makes their small enterprises fail; and the same passions that made them attach such a price to peace turn them toward arms. After having destroyed all industries, war itself becomes the great and the sole industry, and then the ardent and ambitious desires that equality has given birth to are directed on all sides toward it alone. That is why the same democratic nations that are so difficult to get onto the battlefield sometimes do prodigious things when one has finally succeeded in putting arms in their hands.

As war more and more attracts all eyes toward the army, as one sees it create great reputations and great fortunes in little time, the elite of the nation takes up the career of arms; all the naturally enterprising, proud, and warlike spirits, which not only aristocracy but the entire country produces, are drawn in this direction.

As the number of competitors for military honors is immense and war rudely pushes each into his place, great generals are always found in the end. A long war produces for a democratic army what a democratic revolution produces for the people themselves. It breaks the rules and makes all the extraordinary men surge forward. Officers whose souls and bodies have grown old during peace are pushed aside, retire, or die. In their place presses a crowd of young men whom war has already hardened and whose desires it has stretched and inflamed. They want to become great at any price and they want it constantly; after them come others who have the same passions and the same desires; and after those others, others still, meeting no limits but those of the army. Equality permits ambition to all, and death takes charge of furnishing a chance for every ambition. Death constantly opens ranks, empties places, closes a career and opens it.

There is, moreover, a hidden relation between military mores and democratic mores that war uncovers.

Men of democracies naturally have a passionate desire to acquire quickly the goods that they covet and to enjoy them easily. Most of them adore chance and fear death much less than trouble. In this spirit they lead commerce and industry; and this same spirit, transported by them onto the battlefield, brings them willingly to expose their lives so as to be assured, in a moment, of the prizes of victory. There is no greatness that satisfies the imagination of a democratic people more than military greatness—brilliant and sudden greatness obtained without work, by risking only one's life.

Thus, whereas interest and tastes turn the citizens of a democracy away from war, the habits of their souls prepare them to fight it well; they easily become good soldiers as soon as one has been able to tear them from their business and their well-being.

If peace is particularly harmful to democratic armies, then war secures advantages to them that other armies never have; and these advantages, though hardly felt at first, cannot fail to give them victory in the long term.

An aristocratic people that, in conflict with a democratic nation, does not succeed in ruining it on the first campaigns always takes much risk of being defeated by it.*

Chapter 25 ON DISCIPLINE IN DEMOCRATIC ARMIES

It is a very widespread opinion, above all among aristocratic peoples, that the great equality reigning within democracies makes the soldier, in the long term, independent of the officer and thus destroys the bond of discipline.

This is an error. There are, in fact, two kinds of discipline that must not be confused.

When the officer is a noble and the soldier a serf, the one rich and the other poor; when the first is enlightened and strong and the second, ignorant

*See AT's note XXIII, page 702.

and weak, it is easy to establish the strictest bond of obedience between these two men. The soldier bows to military discipline, so to speak, before entering the army, or rather military discipline is only a perfecting of social servitude. In aristocratic armies, the soldier comes easily enough to be almost insensitive to all things except the orders of his chiefs. He acts without thinking, triumphs without ardor, and dies without complaining. In this state he is no longer a man, but he is still a very formidable animal trained for war.

Democratic peoples must despair of ever obtaining from their soldiers the blind, minute, resigned, and always equable obedience that aristocratic peoples impose on theirs without trouble. The state of society does not prepare it: they would risk losing their natural advantages if they wished to acquire that one artificially. In democratic peoples military discipline ought not to try to negate the free flight of souls; it can only aspire to direct it; the obedience that it creates is less exact, but more impetuous and more intelligent. Its root is in the very will of the one who obeys; it is supported not solely by his instinct, but by his reason; so it often tightens itself as danger renders it necessary. The discipline of an aristocratic army is easily relaxed in war because this discipline is founded on habits, and war disturbs these habits. The discipline of a democratic army is on the contrary steadied before the enemy, because then each soldier sees very clearly that he must be silent and obey in order to be able to win.

Peoples who have done the most considerable things by war have known no other discipline than the one I am speaking of. Among the ancients, only free men and citizens, who differed little from one another and were accustomed to treating each other as equals, were accepted in the armies. In this sense one can say that the armies of antiquity were democratic although they came from the heart of an aristocracy; so a sort of familiar fraternity between officer and soldier reigned within these armies. Of this one is convinced in reading Plutarch's *The Lives of the Great Captains*.* In that, soldiers speak constantly and very freely to their generals, and the latter listen willingly to the discourse of their soldiers and respond to it. They lead them by words and examples much more than by constraint and chastisements. One would say they were as much companions as chiefs.

I do not know if Greek and Roman soldiers ever perfected the little details of military discipline to the same point as the Russians; but that did not prevent Alexander† from conquering Asia, and Rome, the world.

---

*The correct title is *Parallel Lives* or *Lives;* AT adds "*of the Great Captains.*"
†Alexander III of Macedon, known as Alexander the Great, 356–323 B.C.

🌿 🌿 🌿 🌿 🌿 🌿 🌿 🌿 🌿 🌿 🌿 🌿 🌿 🌿 🌿 🌿 🌿 🌿 🌿 🌿

Chapter 26 SOME CONSIDERATIONS ON WAR IN DEMOCRATIC SOCIETIES

When the principle of equality develops not only in one nation, but in several neighboring peoples at the same time, as seen in our day in Europe, the men who inhabit these diverse countries, despite the disparity of tongues, usages and laws, still resemble each other inasmuch as they equally dread war and conceive the same love of peace.[1] In vain does ambition or anger arm princes; a sort of apathy and universal benevolence pacifies them despite themselves and makes their swords fall from their hands: wars become rarer.

In proportion as equality, developing at the same time in several countries, simultaneously pushes the men who inhabit them toward industry and commerce, not only do their tastes resemble each other's, but their interests mix and become entangled so that no nation can inflict ills on others that do not come back to it, and so that in the end all consider war as a calamity almost as great for the winner as for the defeated.

Thus, in democratic centuries it is very difficult, on the one hand, to bring peoples to combat each other, but on the other hand, it is almost impossible for two among them to make war in isolation. The interests of all are so intertwined, their opinions and their needs so similar, that none can keep itself at rest when the others are agitated. Wars therefore become rarer, but when they arise, they have a vaster field.

Democratic peoples who neighbor each other not only become alike on some points, as I have just said; in the end they resemble each other on almost all.[2]

1. The fear of war that European peoples show is due not only to the progress that equality has made among them; I think I do not need to make the reader remark this. Independent of this permanent cause there are several accidental ones that are very powerful. I shall cite, before all others, the extreme lassitude that the wars of the Revolution and the Empire have left.

2. This does not come uniquely from the fact that these peoples have the same social state, but from the fact that this same social state is such that it naturally brings men to imitate each other and to intermingle with each other.

When citizens are divided into castes and classes, not only do they differ from one another, but they have neither the taste nor the desire to resemble each other; on the contrary, each one seeks more and more to keep his own opinions and habits intact and to remain himself. The spirit of individuality is very keen.

When a people has a democratic social state, which is to say, that neither castes nor classes any longer exist within it, and when all citizens there are nearly equal in enlightenment and in goods, the human spirit moves in a contrary direction. Men resemble each other and, in addition, they suffer in a way from not resembling each other. Far from wanting to preserve what

Now, as to war, this similarity of peoples has very important consequences.

When I wonder why the Swiss confederation of the fifteenth century made the greatest and most powerful nations of Europe tremble, whereas in our day its power is in exact relation to its population, I find that the Swiss have become like all the men surrounding them, and the latter, like the Swiss; so that number alone makes the difference between them, and victory necessarily belongs to the biggest battalions. One result of the democratic revolution that has been operating in Europe is, therefore, to make numerical force prevail on all battlefields and to compel all small nations to incorporate into the great ones, or at least to come under their policy.

The decisive reason for victory being number, it results that each people will strain with all its efforts to bring the most men possible onto the battlefield.

When one species of troops superior to all the others could be enlisted under the flag, like the Swiss infantry or the French cavalry of the sixteenth century, one did not deem it necessary to raise very large armies; but it is no longer so when all soldiers have the same value.

The same cause that gives rise to this new need furnishes the means of satisfying it as well. For, as I have said, when all men are alike, they are all weak.* The social power is naturally much stronger in democratic peoples than everywhere else. At the same time that these peoples feel the desire to call all their male population to arms, they therefore have the ability to unite it: which makes armies, in centuries of equality, seem to grow as military spirit is being extinguished.

In the same centuries, the manner of making war changes as well, for the same causes.

Machiavelli says in his book *The Prince* that "it is much more difficult to

---

* *DA* II 3.4.

---

can still single out each of them, they ask only to lose it, so as to be blended into the common mass, which alone represents right and force in their eyes. The spirit of individuality is almost destroyed.

In aristocratic times the very ones who are naturally similar aspire to create imaginary differences among themselves. In democratic times the very ones who do not naturally resemble each other ask only to become alike and copy each other, so much is the spirit of each man always carried along in the general movement of humanity.

Something like this is equally to be remarked from people to people. Should two peoples have the same aristocratic social state, they could remain quite distinct and very different, because the spirit of aristocracy is to individualize. But two neighboring peoples cannot have the same democratic social state without immediately adopting like opinions and mores, because the spirit of democracy makes men strain to assimilate to each other.

subjugate a people that has a prince and barons for chiefs than a nation that is led by a prince and slaves."* In order to offend no one, let us put public officials in place of slaves, and we shall have a great truth, very applicable to our subject.

It is very difficult for a great aristocratic people to conquer its neighbors and to be conquered by them. It cannot conquer them because it can never gather all its forces and hold them together for long; and it cannot be conquered because the enemy finds little hotbeds of resistance everywhere that stop it. I shall compare war in an aristocratic country to war in a country of mountains: at each instant the defeated find occasion to rally in new positions and to hold them firm.

Precisely the contrary is seen in democratic nations.

These easily bring all their disposable forces onto the field of battle, and, when the nation is wealthy and numerous, it easily becomes a conqueror; but once it has been defeated and its territory penetrated, few resources remain to it, and if one gets so far as to take possession of its capital, the nation is lost. That may be very well explained: each citizen being individually very isolated and very weak, none can either defend himself or constitute a base of support for others. There is nothing strong in a democratic country but the state; when the military force of the state is destroyed by the destruction of its army and its civil power is paralyzed by the taking of its capital, the rest forms only a multitude without rule and force that cannot struggle against an organized power attacking it; I know that one can reduce the peril by creating freedoms and, consequently, provincial entities, but this remedy will always be insufficient.

Not only will the population no longer be able to continue the war then, but it is to be feared that it will not want to attempt it.

According to the law of nations adopted by civilized nations, wars do not have the goal of appropriating the goods of particular persons, but only of taking possession of political power. They destroy private property only occasionally in order to attain the second object.

When an aristocratic nation is invaded after the defeat of its army, the nobles, although they are at the same time the rich, would rather continue to defend themselves individually than to submit; for, if the winner remained master of the country, he would take their political power away from them, which they cling to even more than their goods: they therefore prefer combat

* From Niccolò Machiavelli, *The Prince*, chapter 4, but not a quotation. Machiavelli says that a state consisting of a prince and barons is easier to acquire, but harder to keep, than one with a prince and slaves (or servants).

to conquest, which is the greatest of misfortunes for them, and they easily carry the people with them, because the people have long contracted the usage of following and obeying them and, besides, have almost nothing to risk in war.

In a nation where equality of conditions reigns, each citizen, on the contrary, has only a small part in political power and often takes no part in it; on the other hand, all are independent and have goods to lose, so that they fear conquest much less and war much more than an aristocratic people. It will always be very difficult to make a democratic population determined to take up arms when war is brought to its territory. That is why it is necessary to give rights to these peoples and a political spirit that suggests to each citizen some of the interests that make nobles in aristocracies act.

Princes and other chiefs in democratic nations must indeed recall this: only the passion and the habit of freedom can compete with advantage against the habit and the passion of well-being. I imagine nothing better prepared for conquest, in case of setbacks, than a democratic people that does not have free institutions.

Formerly one entered a campaign with few soldiers; one joined small combats and made long sieges. Now great battles are joined, and as soon as one can advance ahead freely, one rushes to the capital in order to finish the war in a single stroke.

Napoleon, it is said, invented this new system. It did not depend on one man, whoever he might be, to create a system like this. The manner in which Napoleon made war was suggested to him by the state of society in his time, and it succeeded for him because it was marvelously appropriate to that state and because he put it in use for the first time. Napoleon was the first who at the head of an army traveled a path through all the capitals. But it was the ruin of feudal society that had opened this route for him. One is permitted to believe that if this extraordinary man had been born three hundred years ago, he would not have reaped the same fruits from his method, or rather he would have had another method.

I shall not add more than a word relative to civil wars, for I fear to test the patience of the reader.

Most of the things I said regarding foreign wars apply even more strongly to civil wars. Men who live in democratic countries do not naturally have a military spirit: they sometimes take it up when they are brought despite themselves onto the fields of battle; but to rise en masse by oneself and to expose oneself voluntarily to the miseries of war, and above all those that civil war brings, is an option to which man in democracies does not resolve himself. It is only the most adventurous citizens who consent to throw themselves into a hazard like this; the mass of the population remains unmoved.

Even if it should wish to act, it would not come to it easily, for it does not find within itself old and well-established influences to which it wishes to submit, no already known chiefs to assemble malcontents, rule them, and lead them; no political powers placed below the national power that come effectively to support the resistance that one opposes to it.

In democratic lands the moral power of the majority is immense, and the material strength at its disposal is out of proportion with that which it is at first possible to gather against it. The party that sits in the seat of the majority, that speaks in its name and employs its power, therefore triumphs over all particular resistances in a moment and without trouble. It does not even allow them time to arise; it nips them in the bud.

Those who want to make a revolution by arms among these peoples have, therefore, no other resource than unexpectedly to take possession of the machinery of government, all set up, which can be executed by a coup rather than by a war; for from the moment there is a regular war, the party that represents the state is almost always sure to win.

The only case in which a civil war could arise would be one in which, the army being divided, one part would raise the standard of revolt and the other would remain faithful. An army forms a small, very tightly bound, and very vital society, which is sometimes in a position to be self-sufficient for some time. The war could be bloody; but it would not be long; for either the rebel army would attract the government to it solely by the demonstration of its strength or by its first victory, and the war would be ended; or else the struggle would be joined and the part of the army that did not depend on the organized power of the state would soon disperse by itself or be destroyed.

One can therefore accept as a general truth that in centuries of equality, civil wars will become much rarer and shorter.[3]

---

3. It is understood that I speak here of *unitary* democratic nations and not of confederated democratic nations. In confederations, the preponderant power always resides, despite fictions, in the state governments and not in the federal government, and civil wars are only disguised foreign wars.

PART FOUR

On the Influence
That Democratic Ideas
and Sentiments Exert
on Political Society

I would fulfill the objective of this book badly if, after having shown the ideas and sentiments that equality suggests, I did not, in concluding, bring out the general influence that these same sentiments and ideas can exert on the government of human societies.

To succeed at this, I shall often be obliged to retrace my steps. But I hope that the reader will not refuse to follow me when paths known to him lead him to some new truth.

༜ ༜

Chapter 1 EQUALITY NATURALLY GIVES MEN THE TASTE FOR FREE INSTITUTIONS

Equality, which renders men independent of one another, makes them contract the habit and taste of following their will alone in their particular actions. This entire independence, which they enjoy continually vis-à-vis their equals and in the practice of private life, disposes them to consider all authority with the eye of a malcontent and soon suggests to them the idea and love of political freedom. Men who live in these times therefore advance on a natural slope directing them toward free institutions. Take one of them at random; go back, if possible, to his primitive instincts: you will discover that among the different governments, the one he conceives of first and prizes most is the government whose head he has elected and whose actions he controls.

Of all the political effects that equality of conditions produces, it is this love of independence that first strikes one's regard and which most frightens timid spirits, and one cannot say that they are absolutely wrong to be so, for anarchy has more frightening features in democratic countries than elsewhere. As citizens do not have any influence over one another, it seems that disorder will immediately go to the limit at the instant when the national power keeping them all in place happens to fail, and that, as each citizen strays off in his own direction, the social body is going to be reduced to dust all at once.

Yet I am convinced that anarchy is not the principal evil that democratic centuries will have to fear, but the least.

Equality produces, in fact, two tendencies: one leads men directly to independence and can drive them all at once into anarchy, the other conducts them by a longer, more secret, but surer path toward servitude.

Peoples easily see the first and resist it; they allow themselves to be carried along by the other without seeing it; to show it is therefore particularly important.

For me, far from reproaching equality for the intractability it inspires, I praise it principally for that. I admire it as I see it deposit that obscure notion and instinctive penchant for political independence at the bottom of the mind and heart of each man, thus preparing the remedy for the evil to which it gives birth. It is on this side that I cling to it.

Chapter 2 THAT THE IDEAS OF DEMOCRATIC PEOPLES IN THE MATTER OF GOVERNMENT ARE NATURALLY FAVORABLE TO THE CONCENTRATION OF POWERS

The idea of secondary powers, placed between sovereign and subjects, naturally presented itself to the imagination of aristocratic peoples because those powers contained within them individuals or families whom birth, enlightenment, and wealth held up as without peer and who seemed destined to command. For contrary reasons, this same idea is naturally absent from the minds of men in centuries of equality; it can only be introduced artificially then, and it is retained only with difficulty; whereas they conceive, so to speak without thinking about it, the idea of a lone central power that leads all citizens by itself.

In politics, moreover, as in philosophy and religion, the intellect of democratic peoples receives simple and general ideas with delight. Complicated systems repel it, and it is pleased to imagine a great nation in which all of the citizens resemble a single model and are directed by a single power.

After the idea of a lone central power, the one that presents itself most spontaneously to the minds of men in centuries of equality is the idea of uniform legislation. As each of them sees himself little different from his neighbors, he hardly understands why the rule that is applicable to one man should not be equally so to all others. The least privileges, therefore, are repugnant to his reason. The slightest dissimilarities in the political institutions of the same people wound him, and legislative uniformity appears to him to be the first condition of a good government.

I find, on the contrary, that this same notion of a uniform rule equally imposed on all members of the social body is foreign, as it were, to the human mind in aristocratic centuries. It does not receive it or it rejects it.

These opposing penchants of the intellect end on both sides by becoming such blind instincts and such invincible habits that they still direct actions despite particular facts. In spite of the immense variety of the Middle Ages, individuals perfectly alike were sometimes encountered: this did not prevent the legislator from assigning diverse duties and different rights to each of them. And, on the contrary, in our day governments exhaust themselves to impose the same usages and the same laws on populations that do not yet resemble each other.

As conditions are equalized in a people, individuals appear smaller and society seems greater, or rather, each citizen, having become like all the others, is lost in the crowd, and one no longer perceives [anything] but the vast and magnificent image of the people itself.

This naturally gives men in democratic times a very high opinion of the privileges of society and a very humble idea of the rights of the individual. They readily accept that the interest of the former is everything and that of the latter, nothing. They willingly enough grant that the power representing society possesses much more enlightenment and wisdom than any of the men who compose it, and that its duty as well as its right is to take each citizen by the hand and lead him.

If one wants to examine well our contemporaries from up close and to pierce through to the root of their political opinions, there one will find some of the ideas I have just reproduced, and one will perhaps be astonished to encounter so much accord among people who so often make war on each other.

Americans believe that in each state the social power ought to emanate directly from the people; but once that power is constituted, they imagine so to speak no limits to it; they willingly recognize that it has the right to do everything.

As for the particular privileges granted to towns, families, or individuals, they have lost even the idea of them. Their minds have never foreseen that one might not apply the same law uniformly to all parts of the same state and to all men inhabiting it.

These same opinions are spreading more and more in Europe; they are introduced into the very heart of the nations that repel the dogma of the sovereignty of the people most violently. The latter give another origin to power than the Americans, but they view power with the same features. In all of them, the notion of intermediate power is obscured and effaced. The idea of a right inherent in certain individuals is rapidly disappearing from the minds of men; the idea of the all-powerful and so to speak unique right of society comes to fill its place. These ideas take root and grow as conditions become more equal and men more alike; equality gives birth to them, and they in their turn hasten the progress of equality.

In France, where the revolution I am speaking of is more advanced than in any other people in Europe, these same opinions have entirely taken possession of intellects. Should one listen attentively to the voice of our different parties, one will see that there is not one of them that does not adopt them. Most deem that the government acts badly; but all think that the government ought to be acting constantly and to take everything in hand. The very ones who make war on each other most roughly do not fail to agree on this point. The unity, ubiquity, and omnipotence of the social power, the uniformity of its rules, form the salient feature characterizing all newly born political systems of our day. One finds them at the foundation of the most bizarre utopias. The human mind pursues these images even when it dreams.

If such ideas present themselves spontaneously in the minds of particular persons, they offer themselves still more readily to the imagination of princes.

While the old social state of Europe is altering and dissolving, sovereigns develop new beliefs regarding their faculties and their duties; for the first time they comprehend that the central power they represent can and ought to administer all affairs and all men by itself, and on a uniform plan. This opinion, which, I dare to say, had never been conceived before our time by the kings of Europe, penetrates the intelligence of these princes most profoundly; there it stands firm amid the agitation of all other [opinions].

Men of our day are therefore much less divided than one imagines; they dispute constantly to know into whose hands sovereignty will be delivered, but they easily agree on the duties and rights of sovereignty. All conceive the government in the image of a lone, simple, providential, and creative power.

All secondary ideas in the matter of politics are mobile; that one remains settled, unalterable, and like unto itself. Publicists and statesmen adopt it, the crowd seizes it avidly; the governed and those governing are in accord in pursuing it with the same ardor; it comes first; it seems innate.

It therefore does not issue from a caprice of the human mind, but is a natural condition of the current state of men.*

╔═╗ ╔═╗ ╔═╗ ╔═╗ ╔═╗ ╔═╗ ╔═╗ ╔═╗ ╔═╗ ╔═╗ ╔═╗ ╔═╗ ╔═╗ ╔═╗ ╔═╗ ╔═╗ ╔═╗ ╔═╗ ╔═╗ ╔═╗

Chapter 3 THAT THE SENTIMENTS OF DEMOCRATIC PEOPLES ARE IN ACCORD WITH THEIR IDEAS IN BRINGING THEM TO CONCENTRATE POWER

If, in centuries of equality, men easily perceive the idea of a great central power, one cannot doubt, moreover, that their habits and sentiments predispose them to recognize such a power and to lend it a hand. One can demonstrate this in few words, most of the reasons having already been given elsewhere.

Men who inhabit democratic countries, having neither superiors nor inferiors nor habitual and necessary associates, willingly fall back on themselves and consider themselves in isolation. I have had occasion to show this at great length when individualism was in question.†

It is therefore never effortless for these men to tear themselves away from their particular affairs to occupy themselves with common affairs; their natural inclination is to abandon the care of the latter to the sole visible and permanent representative of collective interests, which is the state.

Not only do they not naturally have the taste to occupy themselves with the public, but often they lack the time to do it. Private life is so active in democratic times, so agitated, so filled with desires and work, that hardly any energy or leisure remains to each man for political life.

That such penchants are not invincible I shall not deny, since my principal goal in writing this book has been to combat them. I only maintain that in our day a secret force constantly develops them in the human heart, and that not to stop them is enough for them to fill it up.

I have also had occasion to show how the growing love of well-being and the mobile nature of property make democratic peoples dread material disorder.‡ Love of public tranquillity is often the sole political passion that these

*See AT's note XXIV, page 703.
†*DA* II 2.2.
‡*DA* II 3.21.

peoples preserve, and it becomes more active and powerful in them as all the others are weakened and die; this naturally disposes citizens constantly to give the central power new rights, or to allow it to take them; it alone seems to them to have the interest and the means to defend them from anarchy by defending itself.

As in centuries of equality no one is obliged to lend his force to those like him and no one has the right to expect great support from those like him, each is at once independent and weak. These two states, which must neither be viewed separately nor confused, give the citizen of democracies very contrary instincts. His independence fills him with confidence and pride among his equals, and his debility makes him feel, from time to time, the need of the outside help that he cannot expect from any of them, since they are all impotent and cold. In this extremity, he naturally turns his regard to the immense being that rises alone in the midst of universal debasement. His needs and above all his desires constantly lead him back toward it, and in the end he views it as the unique and necessary support for individual weakness.[1]

This serves to make understandable what often happens in democratic peoples, where one sees men who so uneasily tolerate superiors patiently suffer a master, and show themselves proud and servile at the same time.

The hatred that men bear for privilege is increased as privileges become rarer and less great, so that one would say that democratic passions are more inflamed in the very times in which they find the least nourishment. I have already given the reason for this phenomenon.* When all conditions are unequal, there is no inequality great enough to offend the eye, whereas the

---

*DA II 2.13.

1. In democratic societies only the central power has some stability in its seat and some permanence in its undertakings. All citizens are constantly on the move and transforming themselves. Now, it is in the nature of all government to wish to enlarge its sphere continuously. It is therefore very difficult for it not to succeed in the long term, since it acts with a fixed thought and a continuous will on men whose position, ideas, and desires vary every day.

Often it happens that citizens work for [the central power] without wanting to.

Democratic centuries are times of attempts, innovations, and adventures. There is always a multitude of men engaged in a difficult or new undertaking that they pursue separately, without bothering themselves about those like them. They do indeed accept for a general principle that the public power ought not to intervene in private affairs, but each of them desires that it aid him as an exception in the special affair that preoccupies him, and he seeks to attract the action of the government to his side, all the while wanting to shrink it for everyone else.

Since a multitude of people have this particular view of a host of different objects all at once, the sphere of the central power spreads insensibly on all sides even though each of them wishes to restrict it. A democratic government therefore increases its prerogatives by the sole fact that it endures. Time works for it; all accidents profit it; individual passions aid it without even knowing it, and one can say that it becomes all the more centralized as democratic society gets older.

smallest dissimilarity appears shocking in the midst of general uniformity; the sight of it becomes more intolerable as uniformity is more complete. It is therefore natural that the love of equality grow constantly with equality itself; in satisfying it, one develops it.

This immortal hatred, more and more afire, which animates democratic peoples against the slightest privileges, particularly favors the gradual concentration of all political rights in the hands of the sole representative of the state. The sovereign, being necessarily above all citizens and uncontested, does not excite the envy of any of them, and each believes he deprives his equals of all the prerogatives he concedes to it.

Man in democratic centuries obeys his neighbor, who is his equal, only with extreme repugnance; he refuses to recognize in him any enlightenment superior to his own; he distrusts his justice and looks on his power with jealousy; he fears and scorns him; he loves to make him feel at each instant the common dependence of them both on the same master.

Every central power that follows these natural instincts loves equality and favors it; for equality singularly facilitates the action of such a power, extends it, and secures it.

It can also be said that every central government adores uniformity; uniformity spares it the examination of an infinity of details with which it would have to occupy itself if it were necessary to make a rule for men, instead of making all men pass indiscriminately under the same rule. Thus the government loves what citizens love, and it naturally hates what they hate. This community of sentiments which, in democratic nations, continuously unites each individual and the sovereign in the same thought, establishes a secret and permanent sympathy between them. The government is pardoned for its faults for the sake of its tastes, public confidence abandons it only with difficulty in the midst of its excesses or errors, and it returns to it when it is recalled. Democratic peoples often hate the depositories of the central power; but they always love this power itself.

Thus I have come by two diverse paths to the same goal. I have shown that equality suggests to men the thought of a lone, uniform, and strong government. I have just brought out that it gives them the taste for it; the nations of our day tend therefore toward a government of this kind. The natural inclination of their minds and hearts leads them to it, and it is enough that they not be held back for them to arrive at it.

I think that in the democratic centuries that are going to open up, individual independence and local liberties will always be the product of art. Centralization will be the natural government.*

*See AT's note XXV, page 703.

Chapter 4 ON SOME PARTICULAR AND ACCIDENTAL CAUSES THAT SERVE TO BRING A DEMOCRATIC PEOPLE TO CENTRALIZE POWER OR TURN IT AWAY FROM THAT

If all democratic peoples are instinctively drawn toward the centralization of powers, they tend to it in an unequal manner. That depends on particular circumstances that can develop or restrict the natural effects of the social state. These circumstances are very large in number; I shall speak only of some.

Among men who have lived free for a long time before becoming equal, the instincts given by freedom combat up to a certain point the penchants that equality suggests; and although the central power increases its privileges among them, particular persons never entirely lose their independence.

But when equality develops in a people that has never known freedom or that has not known it for a long time, as is seen on the continent of Europe, the old habits of the nation come to be combined suddenly and by a sort of natural attraction with the new habits and doctrines to which the social state has given birth, and all powers seem of themselves to rush toward the center; there they accumulate with surprising rapidity, and all at once the state attains the extreme limit of its force while particular persons let themselves sink in one moment to the last degree of weakness.

The English who came three centuries ago to found a democratic society in the wilderness of the New World had all been habituated in the mother country to take part in public affairs; they knew the jury; they had freedom of speech and of the press, individual freedom, the idea of right and the practice of resorting to it. They transported these free institutions and virile mores to America, and these sustained them against the encroachments of the state.

Among the Americans, therefore, freedom is old; equality is comparatively new. The contrary obtains in Europe, where equality, introduced by absolute power and under the eye of the kings, had already penetrated the habits of peoples long before freedom had entered into their ideas.

I have said that in democratic peoples government is naturally presented to the human mind only in the form of a lone central power, and that the notion of intermediate powers is not familiar to it. That is particularly applicable to democratic nations that have seen the principle of equality triumph with the aid of a violent revolution. Since the classes that directed local affairs disappear all at once in this storm and the confused mass that remains still has neither the organization nor the habits that permit it to take the administration of its own affairs in hand, one no longer perceives anything but the state itself that can take charge of all the details of government. Centralization becomes a sort of necessary fact.

One must neither praise nor blame Napoleon for having concentrated almost all administrative powers in his hands alone; for after the abrupt disappearance of the nobility and the haute bourgeoisie, these powers came to him of themselves; it would have been almost as difficult for him to repel them as to take them up. A necessity like this was never felt by the Americans, who, not having had a revolution and having governed themselves from their origin, never had to burden the state with serving them temporarily as their schoolmaster.

Thus centralization does not develop in a democratic people only according to the progress of equality, but also according to the manner in which that equality is founded.

At the beginning of a great democratic revolution, when the war between the different classes has only just arisen, the people strive to centralize public administration in the hands of the government in order to tear direction of local affairs from the aristocracy. Toward the end of this same revolution, on the contrary, it is ordinarily the defeated aristocracy that tries to deliver the direction of all affairs to the state because it dreads the petty tyranny of the people, which has become its equal and often its master.

Thus it is not always the same class of citizens that applies itself to increasing the prerogatives of power; but as long as the democratic revolution lasts, there will always be found in the nation one class, powerful by its number or by its wealth, whose special passions and particular interests bring it to centralize public administration, independently of the hatred for government by one's neighbor, which is a general and permanent sentiment in democratic peoples. One can remark that in our time it is the lower classes of England that work with all their strength to destroy local independence and to transfer administration from all points of the circumference to the center, whereas the upper classes strive to retain this same administration within its former limits. I dare predict that a day will come when an altogether contrary spectacle will be seen.

What precedes makes it well understood why social power will always be stronger and the individual weaker in a democratic people that has arrived at equality by long and painful social travail than in a democratic society where citizens have always been equal from its origin. This is what the example of the Americans serves to prove.

Men who inhabit the United States have never been separated by any privilege; they have never known the reciprocal relation of inferior and master, and as they neither dread nor hate one another, they have never known the need to call in the sovereign to direct the details of their affairs. The destiny of the Americans is singular: they have taken from the English aristocracy the idea of individual rights and the taste for local freedoms; and they have been able to preserve both because they have not had to combat an aristocracy.

If in all times enlightenment serves men to defend their independence, that is above all true in democratic centuries. It is easy, when all men resemble each other, to found a single, all-powerful government; instinct suffices. But men must have much intelligence, science, and art, in the same circumstances, to organize and maintain secondary powers and in the midst of the independence and individual weakness of citizens to create free associations that are in a position to struggle against tyranny without destroying order.

Concentration of powers and individual servitude therefore grow in democratic nations not only in proportion to equality but owing to ignorance.

It is true that in barely enlightened centuries the government often lacks the enlightenment to perfect despotism, as do citizens to evade it. But the effect is not equal on both sides.

However coarse a democratic people is, the central power that directs it is never completely deprived of enlightenment, because it readily attracts to itself the little that is found in the country and because, if need be, it goes to seek it outside. In a nation that is ignorant as well as democratic, therefore, an enormous difference between the intellectual capacity of the sovereign and that of each of its subjects cannot fail to become manifest soon. That readily serves to concentrate all powers in its hands. The administrative power of the state constantly spreads because no one but it is skilled enough to administer.

Aristocratic nations, however little enlightened one supposes them, never present the same spectacle, because enlightenment there is equally enough distributed between the prince and the principal citizens.

The pasha who reigns over Egypt today found the population of that country composed of very ignorant and very equal men, and he appropriated the science and intelligence of Europe to govern it. The particular enlightenment of the sovereign thus coming to be combined with the ignorance and democratic weakness of the subjects, the furthest limit of centralization has been attained with no difficulty, and the prince has been able to make his country into his factory and its inhabitants into his workers.

I believe the extreme centralization of political power in the end enervates society and thus at length weakens the government itself. But I do not deny that a centralized social force is in a position to execute great undertakings easily at a given time and on a determined point. That is above all true in war, where success depends much more on the facility one has in bringing all one's resources rapidly upon a certain point than on the extent of those resources. It is therefore principally in war that peoples feel the desire and often the need to increase the prerogatives of the central power. All geniuses of war love centralization, which increases their strength, and all centralizing geniuses love war, which obliges nations to draw tight all powers in the hands of the state. Thus, the democratic tendency that brings men constantly to multiply the privileges of the state and to restrict the rights of particular persons is much more rapid and more continuous in democratic peoples subject by their position to great and frequent wars, and whose existence can often be put in peril, than in all others.

I have said how fear of disorder and love of well-being insensibly bring democratic peoples to augment the prerogatives of the central government, the sole power that appears to them in itself strong enough, intelligent enough, stable enough to protect them against anarchy. I hardly need to add that all the particular circumstances that tend to render the state of a democratic society troubled and precarious augment this general instinct and bring particular persons, more and more, to sacrifice their rights to their tranquillity.

A people is therefore never so disposed to increase the prerogatives of the central power as on emerging from a long and bloody revolution which, after having torn the goods from the hands of their former owners, has shaken all beliefs and filled the nation with furious hatreds, opposed interests, and contrary factions. The taste for public tranquillity then becomes a blind passion, and citizens are subject to being overcome with a very disordered love for order.

I have just examined several accidents that all combine to aid the centralization of power. I have not yet spoken of the principal one.

The first of the accidental causes that, in democratic peoples, can draw the direction of all affairs into the hands of the sovereign is the origin of this sovereign itself and its penchants.

Men who live in centuries of equality naturally love the central power and willingly extend its privileges; but if it happens that this same power faithfully represents their interests and exactly reproduces their instincts, the confidence they bring to it has almost no bounds, and they believe that all that they give they accord to themselves.

The attraction of administrative powers toward the center will always be less easy and less rapid with kings who still hold on to some place in the old aristocratic order than with new princes, sons of their own works, whose birth, prejudices, instincts, and habits seem to be bound indissolubly to the cause of equality. I do not want to say that princes of aristocratic origin who live in centuries of democracy do not seek to centralize. I believe that they busy themselves at it as diligently as all others. For them, the sole advantages of equality are in this direction; but their opportunities are fewer, because citizens, instead of naturally anticipating their desires, often lend themselves to them only with difficulty. In democratic societies centralization will always be greater as the sovereign is less aristocratic: that is the rule.

When an old race of kings directs an aristocracy, since the natural prejudices of the sovereign are in perfect accord with the natural prejudices of the nobles, the vices inherent in aristocratic societies develop freely and do not find remedy. The contrary happens when the offshoot of feudal stock is placed at the head of a democratic people. Each day the prince inclines by his education, his habits, and his memories toward the sentiments that inequality of conditions suggests; and the people constantly tend by their social state toward the mores that equality gives birth to. Then it often happens that citizens seek to contain the central power, much less as it is tyrannical than as it is aristocratic; and they firmly maintain their independence, not only because they want to be free, but above all because they intend to remain equal.

A revolution that overturns an old family of kings to place new men at the head of a democratic people can weaken the central power momentarily; but however anarchic it appears at first, one ought not hesitate to predict that its final and necessary result will be to extend and secure the prerogatives of this same power.

The first, and in a way the only, necessary condition for arriving at centralizing public power in a democratic society is to love equality or to make it believed [that one does]. Thus the science of despotism, formerly so complicated, is simplified: it is reduced, so to speak, to a single principle.

Chapter 5 THAT AMONG EUROPEAN NATIONS OF OUR DAY SOVEREIGN POWER INCREASES ALTHOUGH SOVEREIGNS ARE LESS STABLE

If one comes to reflect on what precedes, one will be surprised and frightened to see how in Europe everything seems to combine to increase the prerogatives of the central power indefinitely and each day to render individual existence weaker, more subordinate, and more precarious.

The democratic nations of Europe have all the same general and permanent tendencies that carry Americans toward the centralization of powers and, in addition, they are subject to a multitude of secondary and accidental causes that Americans do not know. One would say that each step they take toward equality brings them closer to despotism.

It is enough to cast a glance around us and at ourselves to be convinced of it.

During the aristocratic centuries that preceded ours the sovereigns of Europe had been deprived of or had relinquished several of the inherent rights of their power. It was not a hundred years ago that one still found in most European nations particular persons or almost independent bodies that administered justice, raised and maintained soldiers, collected taxes, and often even made or explained the law. Everywhere the state has retaken these natural attributes of sovereign power for itself alone; in all that has a relation to government, it no longer puts up with an intermediary between it and the citizens, and it directs them by itself in general affairs. I am very far from criticizing this concentration of powers; I limit myself to showing it.

In the same period there existed in Europe many secondary powers that represented local interests and administered local affairs. Most of these local authorities have already disappeared; all tend rapidly to disappear or to fall into the most complete dependence. From one end of Europe to the other, the privileges of lords, the freedoms of towns, the provincial administrations are, or are going to be, destroyed.

For a half century Europe has experienced many revolutions and counter-revolutions that have moved it in contrary directions. But all these movements resemble each other on one point: all have shaken or destroyed secondary powers. Local privileges that the French nation had not abolished in the countries conquered by it have finally succumbed under the efforts of the princes who defeated it. These princes have rejected all the novelties that the revolution had created among them except centralization: it is the sole thing they consented to keep.

What I want to remark is that all the diverse rights that in our time have been successively taken away from classes, from corporations, from men, have not served to elevate new secondary powers on a more democratic base, but have been concentrated on all sides in the hands of the sovereign. Everywhere the state comes more and more to direct the least citizens by itself and alone to conduct each of them in the least affairs.[1]

Almost all the charitable establishments of old Europe were in the hands of particular persons or corporations; they have all more or less fallen into dependence on the sovereign, and in several countries they are governed by it. The state has undertaken almost alone to give bread to those who are hungry, aid and refuge to the ill, work to the idle; it has made itself almost the sole reliever of all miseries.

Education as well as charity has become a national affair among most peoples of our day. The state receives and often takes the child from the arms of his mother to entrust him to its agents; it takes charge of inspiring sentiments in each generation and furnishing it with ideas. Uniformity reigns in studies as in all the rest; diversity like freedom disappears from them each day.

Nor do I fear to set forth that in almost all Christian nations of our day, Catholic as well as Protestant, religion is threatened with falling into the hands of the government. It is not that sovereigns show themselves very jealous of fixing dogma by themselves; but more and more they take hold of the will of whoever explains it: they take away property from the clergyman, assign him a salary, divert and use to their sole profit the influence the priest possesses; they make him one of their officials and often one of their servants, and with him they penetrate the depths of the soul of each man.[2]

1. This gradual weakening of the individual compared with society is manifest in a thousand ways. I shall cite among others the one related to testaments.

In aristocratic countries one ordinarily professes a profound respect for the last will of men. This sometimes even went as far as superstition among the ancient peoples of Europe: the social power, far from hindering the caprices of the dying man, lent its force to the least of them; it assured him a perpetual power.

When all the living are weak, the will of the dead is less respected. A very narrow circle is traced for it, and if it leaves that, the sovereign annuls or controls it. In the Middle Ages the power to make a will had so to speak no bounds. Among the French of our day one cannot distribute one's patrimony among one's children without having the state intervene. After having regimented life as a whole, it still wants to regulate the final act.

2. As the prerogatives of the central power increase, the number of officials that represent it rises. They form a nation within each nation, and as the government lends them its stability, they more and more replace the aristocracy in each.

Almost everywhere in Europe the sovereign dominates in two ways: it leads one part of the

But that is still only one side of the picture.

Not only has the power of the sovereign been extended, as we have just seen, into the entire sphere of former powers; this is no longer enough to contain it; it overflows on every side and goes on to spread over the domain that individual independence had reserved for itself until now. A multitude of actions that formerly escaped the control of society entirely have been subjected to it in our day, and their number constantly increases.

In aristocratic peoples, the social power was ordinarily limited to directing and overseeing citizens in all that had a direct and visible relation to the national interest; it willingly abandoned them to their free will in all the rest. In these peoples the government often seemed to forget that there is a point at which the faults and miseries of individuals compromise universal well-being, and that to prevent the ruin of a particular person ought sometimes to be a public affair.

Democratic nations in our time incline toward a contrary excess.

It is evident that most of our princes not only want to direct the people as a whole; one would say that they judge themselves responsible for the actions and the individual destinies of their subjects, that they have undertaken to guide and to enlighten each of them in the different acts of his life and, if need be, to render him happy despite himself.

For their part, particular persons more and more view the social power in the same light; in all their needs they call it to their aid, and at every moment they fasten their regard on it as on a preceptor or guide.

I assert that there is no country in Europe where public administration has not become not only more centralized, but more inquisitive and detailed; everywhere it penetrates further into private affairs than formerly; in its manner it regulates more actions, and smaller actions, and it establishes itself more every day beside, around, and above each individual to assist him, counsel him, and constrain him.

Formerly the sovereign lived on the revenue of its lands or on the income from taxes. Since today its needs have grown with its power, that is no longer the case. In the same circumstances in which formerly a prince established a new tax, today it has recourse to a loan. Thus, little by little the state becomes a debtor to most of the wealthy, and it centralizes the greatest capital sums in its own hands.

It attracts the lesser sums in another manner.

As men are mixed and conditions are equalized, the poor man has more resources, enlightenment, and desires. He conceives the idea of improving

---

citizens by the fear that they feel of its agents, and the other by the hope they conceive of becoming its agents.

his lot, and he seeks to come to this by saving. Saving therefore gives birth daily to an infinite number of small capital sums, slow and successive fruits of work; they increase constantly. But the greater number would remain unproductive if they stayed scattered. This has given birth to a philanthropic institution that, if I am not mistaken, will soon become one of our greatest political institutions. Some charitable men have conceived the thought of collecting the savings of the poor man and using the income from them. In some countries these beneficent associations have remained entirely distinct from the state; but in almost all they tend visibly to be blended with it, and there are even some in which the government has replaced them and has undertaken the immense task of centralizing in a single place and putting to work the daily savings of several million workers by its hands alone.

Thus the state attracts to itself the money of the wealthy by loans, and by savings banks it disposes to its liking of the money of the poor man. The wealth of the country constantly rushes to it and into its hands; it accumulates there all the more as equality of conditions becomes greater; for in a democratic nation there is only the state to inspire the confidence of particular persons, because only it appears to them to have some force and some duration.[3]

Thus the sovereign is not limited to directing the public fortune; it is introduced into private fortunes; it is the chief of each citizen and often his master, and in addition, it makes itself his paymaster and his banker.

Not only does the central power alone fill the entire sphere of former powers, extend it, and surpass it, but it moves in it with more agility, force, and independence than it formerly did.

All the governments of Europe have perfected administrative science prodigiously in our time; they do more things and they do each thing with more order, more rapidity, and less cost; they seem constantly to enrich themselves with all the enlightenment they have taken away from particular persons. Each day the princes of Europe hold their delegates in a stricter dependence, and they invent new methods to direct them more closely and oversee them with less trouble. It is not enough for them to conduct all affairs by their agents; they undertake to direct the conduct of their agents in all their affairs; so that public administration not only depends on the same power, it is compressed more and more in the same place and is concentrated in fewer hands.

---

3. On the one hand, the taste for well-being constantly increases, and on the other hand, the government takes hold more and more of all the sources of well-being.

Men therefore come by two diverse paths toward servitude. The taste for well-being turns them away from being involved in government, and the love of well-being puts them in an ever stricter dependence on those who govern.

The government centralizes its action at the same time that it increases its prerogatives: a double cause of force.

When one examines the constitution that the judicial power formerly had in most of the nations of Europe, two things are striking: the independence of that power and the extent of its prerogatives.

Not only did the courts of justice decide almost all quarrels between particular persons; in a great number of cases they served as arbiters between each individual and the state.

I do not want to speak here of the political and administrative prerogatives that the courts had usurped in some countries, but of the judicial prerogatives they possessed in all. In all the peoples of Europe, there were and there still are many individual rights, most linked to the general right of property, that were placed under the safeguard of the judge and that the state could not violate without his permission.

It is this semipolitical power that principally distinguished the courts of Europe from all others; for all peoples have had judges, but all have not given judges the same privileges.

If one now examines what is taking place in the democratic nations of Europe that are called free, as well as in the others, one sees on all sides that alongside these courts, others, more dependent, are being created, the particular object of which is to decide exceptionally the contentious questions that can arise between the public administration and citizens. Independence is left to the former judicial power, but its jurisdiction is narrowed and it tends more and more to be made only an arbiter between particular interests.

The number of these special courts constantly increases, and their prerogatives grow. The government is therefore escaping more each day from the obligation to have its will and its rights sanctioned by another power. Unable to do without judges, it wishes at least to choose its judges itself and to keep them always in hand; that is to say that between it and particular persons it puts the image of justice rather than justice itself.

Thus it is not enough for the state to attract all business to itself; it also comes more and more to decide everything by itself without control and without recourse.[4]

In the modern nations of Europe there is one great cause that, indepen-

---

4. In France they have a singular sophism on this subject. When a case between the administration and a particular person arises, they refuse to submit it to the examination of an ordinary judge, in order, they say, not to mix administrative power and judicial power. As if that were not to mix these two powers, and to mix them in the most perilous and most tyrannical fashion, by vesting the government with the right to judge and administer at the same time.

dently of all those I have just indicated, contributes constantly to extending the action of the sovereign or increasing its prerogatives; people have not been watchful enough of it. This cause is the development of industry, which is favored by the progress of equality.

Industry ordinarily groups a multitude of men together in the same place; it establishes new and complicated relations among them. It exposes them to great and sudden alternations of abundance and misery, during which public tranquillity is threatened. It can finally happen that this work compromises the health and even the lives of those who profit from it or those who engage in it. Thus the industrial class needs to be regulated, overseen, and contained more than other classes, and it is natural that the prerogatives of government grow with it.

This truth is generally applicable; but here is what relates more particularly to the nations of Europe.

In the centuries that preceded those in which we live, the aristocracy possessed the soil and was in a position to defend it. Real property was therefore surrounded with guarantees, and its possessors enjoyed a great independence. This created laws and habits that were perpetuated despite the division of lands and the ruin of nobles; and in our day landowners and farmers are still, of all citizens, those who escape the control of the social power most easily.

In these same aristocratic centuries, in which all the sources of our history are found, movable property had little importance and its possessors were scorned and weak; industrialists formed an exceptional class in the midst of the aristocratic world. As they had no secure patronage, they were not protected, and often they could not protect themselves.

It therefore became habit to consider industrial property as a good of a particular nature, which did not merit the same respect and ought not to obtain the same guarantees as property in general, and industrialists as a small class apart in the social order, whose independence had little value and which it was fit to abandon to the regulatory passion of princes. If in fact one turns to the codes of the Middle Ages, one is astonished to see how in these centuries of individual independence, industry was constantly regulated by the kings down to the least details; on this point centralization is as active and as detailed as it can be.

Since that time, a great revolution has taken place in the world; industrial property, which was only a seed, has been developed—it covers Europe; the industrial class has been extended—it has been enriched from the debris of all the others; it has grown in number, in importance, in wealth; it grows constantly; almost all those who are not part of it are linked to it, at least at some place; after having been the exceptional class, it threatens to become the principal class, and so to speak, the sole class; nevertheless, the ideas and political habits to which it had formerly given birth have stayed on. Those ideas and habits have not changed, because they are old, and also because they are in perfect harmony with the new ideas and general habits of men of our day.

Industrial property therefore does not add to its rights with its importance. In becoming more numerous, the industrial class does not become less dependent; but one would say, on the contrary, that it carries despotism within itself and that despotism naturally spreads as it develops.[5]

In proportion as the nation becomes more industrial, it feels a greater need for roads, canals, ports, and other works of a semipublic nature that facilitate the acquisition of wealth, and in proportion as it is more democratic, particular persons experience more difficulty in executing such works and the state has more facility in performing them. I do not fear to assert that the manifest tendency of all sovereigns of our time is to take sole charge themselves of the execution of such undertakings; through that they draw populations more tightly each day into a stricter dependence.

On the other hand, as the power of the state increases and its needs augment, it consumes an ever greater quantity of industrial products, which it manufactures ordinarily in its arsenals and factories. Thus it is that in each realm the sovereign becomes the greatest industrialist; it attracts and retains in its service an enormous number of engineers, architects, mechanics, and artisans.

Not only is it the first among industrialists, but it tends more and more to make itself the chief or rather the master of all the others.

As citizens have become weaker in becoming more equal, they can do

---

5. I shall cite some facts in support of this. The natural sources of industrial wealth are found in mines. As industry has been developed in Europe, as the product of the mines has become a more general interest and good exploitation of them more difficult through the division of goods that equality brings, most sovereigns have claimed the right to possess the content of the mines and to oversee their works—something not seen concerning properties of other kinds.

The mines, which were individual properties subject to the same obligations and provided with the same guarantees as other real estate, have thus fallen into the public domain. The state exploits them or contracts them out; the owners have been transformed into users; they hold their rights from the state, and in addition, the state almost everywhere demands the power to direct them; it draws up rules for them, imposes methods on them, subjects them to routine oversight, and, if they resist it, an administrative court dispossesses them; the public administration transfers their privileges to others; in this way the government not only possesses the mines, but holds all the miners in its hands.

Nevertheless, as industry develops, exploitation of old mines increases. New ones are opened. The number of people in the mines expands and enlarges. Each day sovereigns extend their domain under our feet and people it with their servants.

nothing in industry without associating with each other; now, the public power naturally wants to place these associations under its control.

One must recognize that these sorts of collective beings that we name associations are stronger and more formidable than a simple individual can be, and they have less responsibility for their own acts than the latter, as a result of which it seems reasonable to allow to each of them less independence from the social power than one would do for a particular person.

Sovereigns have all the more inclination to act in this way as it suits their tastes. Among democratic peoples it is only by association that the resistance of citizens to the central power can occur; thus the latter never sees but with disfavor associations that are not in its hands; and what is very much worth remarking is that among democratic peoples, citizens often view these same associations, of which they have so much need, with a secret sentiment of fear and jealousy that prevents them from defending them. The power and the duration of these particular little societies in the midst of general weakness and instability astonishes them and makes them anxious, and they are not far from considering as dangerous privileges the free exercise that each of [these societies] makes of its natural faculties.

All these associations born in our day are, moreover, so many new persons whose rights time has not consecrated and who enter the world in a period when the idea of particular rights is weak and when social power is without limits; it is not surprising that they lose their freedom as they are born.

Among all the peoples of Europe, there are certain associations that can only be formed after the state has examined their statutes and authorized their existence. Among several, efforts are being made to extend this rule to all associations. One readily sees where the success of such an undertaking would lead.

Once the sovereign had the general right to authorize associations of every kind under certain conditions, it would not be slow to claim that of overseeing and regulating them, in order that they not be able to deviate from the rule that it had imposed on them. In this manner the state, after having put all those who have the wish to associate with each other in its dependence, would then put there all those who have associated, that is to say, almost all men who live in our day.

Sovereigns thus appropriate more and more and subject to their use the greater part of the new force that industry creates in the world in our time. Industry leads us and they lead it.

I attach so much importance to all that I have just said that I am tormented by the fear of having done harm to my thought while wishing to render it better.

If therefore the reader finds that the examples cited in support of my words are insufficient or badly chosen; if he thinks that I have exaggerated the progress of the social power in some place and that on the contrary I have restricted beyond measure the sphere in which individual independence still moves, I beseech him to leave the book for a moment and to consider for himself in his turn the objects I had undertaken to show him. Should he examine attentively what is taking place daily among us and outside of us; should he interrogate his neighbors; should he finally contemplate himself; I am indeed mistaken if he does not arrive unguided, and by other paths, at the point to which I wanted to lead him.

He will perceive that during the half century that has just elapsed, centralization has grown everywhere in a thousand different ways. Wars, revolutions, conquests have served its development; all men have worked to increase it. In this same period, during which they have succeeded each other with a terrific rapidity to the head of affairs, their ideas, their interests, their passions have varied infinitely; but all have wanted to centralize in some manner. The instinct of centralization has been almost the sole unmovable point in the midst of the singular mobility of their existence and their thoughts.

And when the reader, having examined this detail of human affairs, wishes to embrace the vast picture in its entirety, he will still be astonished.

On the one hand, the firmest dynasties are shaken or destroyed; in all parts peoples violently escape the empire of their laws; they destroy or limit the authority of their lords or of their princes; all nations that are not in revolution at least appear restive and trembling; one and the same spirit of revolt animates them. And on the other hand, in this same time of anarchy and among these same intractable peoples, the social power constantly increases its prerogatives; it becomes more centralized, more enterprising, more absolute, more extensive. At each instant citizens fall under the control of the public administration; they are brought insensibly and almost without their knowing it to sacrifice new parts of their individual independence to it every day, and the same men who from time to time overturn a throne and ride roughshod over kings bend more and more without resistance to the slightest will of a clerk.

So, therefore, two revolutions seem to be operating in our day in contrary directions: one continuously weakens power and the other constantly reinforces it; in no other period of our history has it appeared either so weak or so strong.

But when one finally comes to consider the state of the world more closely, one sees that these two revolutions are intimately bound to one another, that they come from the same source, and that after having had different courses, they finally bring men to the same place.

I will not fear to repeat again for a final time what I have already said or indicated in several places in this book:* one must beware of confusing the fact of equality itself with the revolution that serves to introduce it into the social state and the laws; it is there [in that confusion] that the reason is found for almost all the phenomena that astonish us.

All the old political powers of Europe, the greatest as well as the least, were founded in centuries of aristocracy, and they more or less represented or defended the principle of inequality and privilege. To make prevail in government the new needs and interests suggested by the growing equality, it was therefore necessary that men of our day overturn or constrain the old powers. That led them to make revolutions and inspired in many of them the savage taste for disorder and independence that all revolutions, whatever their object may be, always give birth to.

I do not believe that there is a single land in Europe where the development of equality was not preceded or followed by some violent changes in the state of property and of persons, and almost all these changes have been accompanied by much anarchy and license because they were made by the least well-ordered portion of the nation against that which was the most.

From there have emerged the two contrary tendencies that I previously showed. In the heat of the democratic revolution, men occupied with destroying the old aristocratic powers that were in combat against it showed they were animated by a great spirit of independence; and as the victory of equality became more complete, they abandoned themselves little by little to the natural instincts to which this same equality gives birth, and they reinforced and centralized the social power. They had wanted to be free so as to be able to make themselves equal, and as equality, with the aid of freedom, established itself, it made freedom more difficult for them.

These two states did not always come in succession. Our fathers displayed just how a people could organize an immense tyranny within itself at the very moment when it was escaping the authority of the nobles and defying the power of all kings, teaching the world the way to win its independence and to lose it at the same time.

Men of our time perceive that the old powers are collapsing on all sides; they see all the old influences dying, all the old barriers falling down; this clouds the judgment of the cleverest; they only pay attention to the prodigious revolution that is at work before their eyes, and they believe that the human race is going to fall into anarchy forever. If they pondered the final consequences of this revolution, perhaps they would conceive other fears.

As for me, I confess I do not trust the spirit of freedom that seems to

*DA I Intro.; I 1.5; I 2.10; II 1.1, 10; II 2.3; II 3.5, 11, 19, 21, 23; II 4.4.

animate my contemporaries; I see well that the nations of our day are turbulent; but I do not clearly find that they are liberal, and I fear that sovereigns, at the end of these agitations that make all thrones tremble, will be found more powerful than ever.

{cloud ornament row}

Chapter 6 WHAT KIND OF DESPOTISM DEMOCRATIC NATIONS HAVE TO FEAR

During my stay in the United States I had remarked that a democratic social state like that of the Americans could singularly facilitate the establishment of despotism, and I had seen on my return to Europe how most of our princes had already made use of the ideas, sentiments, and needs to which this same social state had given birth to extend the sphere of their power.

That led me to believe that Christian nations would perhaps in the end come under an oppression similar to that which formerly weighed on several of the peoples of antiquity.

A more detailed examination of the subject and five years of new meditations have not diminished my fears, but they have changed their object.

In past centuries, one never saw a sovereign so absolute and so powerful that it undertook to administer all the parts of a great empire by itself without the assistance of secondary powers; there was none who attempted to subjugate all its subjects without distinction to the details of a uniform rule, nor one that descended to the side of each of them to lord it over him and lead him. The idea of such an undertaking had never presented itself to the human mind, and if any man had happened to conceive of it, the insufficiency of enlightenment, the imperfection of administrative proceedings, and above all the natural obstacles that inequality of conditions gave rise to would soon have stopped him in the execution of such a vast design.

One sees that in the time of the greatest power of the Caesars, the different peoples who inhabited the Roman world still preserved diverse customs and mores: although subject to the same monarch, most of the provinces were administered separately; they were filled with powerful and active municipalities, and although all the government of the empire was concentrated in the hands of the emperor alone and he always remained the arbitrator of all things in case of need, the details of social life and of individual existence ordinarily escaped his control.

It is true that the emperors possessed an immense power without counter-weight, which permitted them to indulge the outlandishness of their penchants freely and to employ the entire force of the state in satisfying them; they often came to abuse this power so as to deprive a citizen of his goods or life arbitrarily: their tyranny weighed enormously on some, but it did not extend over many; it applied itself to a few great principal objects and neglected the rest; it was violent and restricted.

It seems that if despotism came to be established in the democratic nations of our day, it would have other characteristics: it would be more extensive and milder, and it would degrade men without tormenting them.*

I do not doubt that in centuries of enlightenment and equality like ours, sovereigns will come more easily to gather all public powers in their hands alone and to penetrate the sphere of private interests more habitually and more deeply than any of those in antiquity was ever able to do. But the same equality that facilitates despotism tempers it; we have seen how, as men are more alike and more equal, public mores become more humane and milder; when no citizen has either great power or great wealth, tyranny in a way lacks an occasion and a stage. All fortunes being mediocre, passions are naturally contained, imagination bounded, pleasures simple. This universal moderation moderates the sovereign itself and holds the disordered sparks of its desires within certain limits.

Independently of these reasons drawn from the very nature of the social state, I could add many others that I would take from outside my subject, but I want to stay within the bounds I have set for myself.

Democratic governments can become violent and even cruel at certain moments of great excitement and great peril; but these crises will be rare and transient.

When I think of the small passions of men of our day, the softness of their mores, the extent of their enlightenment, the purity of their religion, the mildness of their morality, their laborious and steady habits, the restraint that almost all preserve in vice as in virtue, I do not fear that in their chiefs they will find tyrants, but rather schoolmasters.

I think therefore that the kind of oppression with which democratic peoples are threatened will resemble nothing that has preceded it in the world; our contemporaries would not find its image in their memories. I myself seek in vain an expression that exactly reproduces the idea that I form of it for myself and that contains it; the old words despotism and tyranny are not suitable. The thing is new, therefore I must try to define it, since I cannot name it.

*See AT's note XXVI, page 703.

I want to imagine with what new features despotism could be produced in the world: I see an innumerable crowd of like and equal men who revolve on themselves without repose, procuring the small and vulgar pleasures with which they fill their souls. Each of them, withdrawn and apart, is like a stranger to the destiny of all the others: his children and his particular friends form the whole human species for him; as for dwelling with his fellow citizens, he is beside them, but he does not see them; he touches them and does not feel them; he exists only in himself and for himself alone, and if a family still remains for him, one can at least say that he no longer has a native country.

Above these an immense tutelary power is elevated, which alone takes charge of assuring their enjoyments and watching over their fate. It is absolute, detailed, regular, far-seeing, and mild. It would resemble paternal power if, like that, it had for its object to prepare men for manhood; but on the contrary, it seeks only to keep them fixed irrevocably in childhood; it likes citizens to enjoy themselves provided that they think only of enjoying themselves. It willingly works for their happiness; but it wants to be the unique agent and sole arbiter of that; it provides for their security, foresees and secures their needs, facilitates their pleasures, conducts their principal affairs, directs their industry, regulates their estates, divides their inheritances; can it not take away from them entirely the trouble of thinking and the pain of living?

So it is that every day it renders the employment of free will less useful and more rare; it confines the action of the will in a smaller space and little by little steals the very use of free will from each citizen. Equality has prepared men for all these things: it has disposed them to tolerate them and often even to regard them as a benefit.

Thus, after taking each individual by turns in its powerful hands and kneading him as it likes, the sovereign extends its arms over society as a whole; it covers its surface with a network of small, complicated, painstaking, uniform rules through which the most original minds and the most vigorous souls cannot clear a way to surpass the crowd; it does not break wills, but it softens them, bends them, and directs them; it rarely forces one to act, but it constantly opposes itself to one's acting; it does not destroy, it prevents things from being born; it does not tyrannize, it hinders, compromises, enervates, extinguishes, dazes, and finally reduces each nation to being nothing more than a herd of timid and industrious animals of which the government is the shepherd.

I have always believed that this sort of regulated, mild, and peaceful servitude, whose picture I have just painted, could be combined better than one imagines with some of the external forms of freedom, and that it would not be impossible for it to be established in the very shadow of the sovereignty of the people.

Our contemporaries are incessantly racked by two inimical passions: they feel the need to be led and the wish to remain free. Not being able to destroy either one of these contrary instincts, they strive to satisfy both at the same time. They imagine a unique power, tutelary, all powerful, but elected by citizens. They combine centralization and the sovereignty of the people. That gives them some respite. They console themselves for being in tutelage by thinking that they themselves have chosen their schoolmasters. Each individual allows himself to be attached because he sees that it is not a man or a class but the people themselves that hold the end of the chain.

In this system citizens leave their dependence for a moment to indicate their master, and then reenter it.

In our day there are many people who accommodate themselves very easily to this kind of compromise between administrative despotism and the sovereignty of the people, and who think they have guaranteed the freedom of individuals well enough when they deliver it to the national power. That does not suffice for me. The nature of the master is much less important to me than the obedience.

Nevertheless I shall not deny that such a constitution is infinitely preferable to one which, after having concentrated all powers, would deposit them in the hands of an irresponsible man or body. Of all the different forms that democratic despotism could take, this would surely be the worst.

When the sovereign is elected or closely overseen by a really elected and independent legislature, the oppression it makes individuals undergo is sometimes greater; but it is always less degrading, because each citizen, while he is hindered and reduced to impotence, can still fancy that in obeying he submits only to himself and that it is to one of his wills that he sacrifices all the others.

I understand as well that when the sovereign represents the nation and depends on it, the strength and rights that are taken away from each citizen serve not only the head of state but profit the state itself, and that particular persons get some fruit from the sacrifice of their independence that they have made to the public.

To create a national representation in a very centralized country is therefore to diminish the evil that extreme centralization can produce, but not to destroy it.

I see very well that in this manner one preserves individual intervention in the most important affairs; but one does not suppress it any less in small and particular ones. One forgets that it is above all in details that it is dangerous to enslave men. For my part, I would be brought to believe freedom less necessary in great things than in lesser ones if I thought that one could ever be assured of the one without possessing the other.

Subjection in small affairs manifests itself every day and makes itself felt without distinction by all citizens. It does not make them desperate; but it constantly thwarts them and brings them to renounce the use of their wills. Thus little by little, it extinguishes their spirits and enervates their souls, whereas obedience, which is due only in a few very grave but very rare circumstances, shows servitude only now and then and makes it weigh only on certain men. In vain will you charge these same citizens, whom you have rendered so dependent on the central power, with choosing the representatives of this power from time to time; that use of their free will, so important but so brief and so rare, will not prevent them from losing little by little the faculty of thinking, feeling, and acting by themselves, and thus from gradually falling below the level of humanity.

I add that they will soon become incapable of exercising the great, unique privilege that remains to them. Democratic peoples who have introduced freedom into the political sphere at the same time that they have increased despotism in the administrative sphere have been led to very strange oddities. If one must conduct small affairs in which simple good sense can suffice, they determine that citizens are incapable of it; if it is a question of the government of the whole state, they entrust immense prerogatives in these citizens; they make them alternatively the playthings of the sovereign and its masters, more than kings and less than men. After exhausting all the different systems of election without finding one that suits them, they are astonished and seek again, as if the evil they notice were not due much more to the constitution of the country than to that of the electoral body.

It is in fact difficult to conceive how men who have entirely renounced the habit of directing themselves could succeed at choosing well those who will lead them; and one will not make anyone believe that a liberal, energetic, and wise government can ever issue from the suffrage of a people of servants.

A constitution that was republican at the head and ultramonarchical in all other parts has always seemed to me to be an ephemeral monster. The vices of those who govern and the imbecility of the governed would not be slow to bring it to ruin; and the people, tired of their representatives and of themselves, would create freer institutions or soon return to lying at the feet of a single master.*

*See AT's note XXVII, page 704.

Chapter 7 CONTINUATION OF THE PRECEDING CHAPTERS

I believe that it is easier to establish an absolute and despotic government in a people where conditions are equal than in any other, and I think that if such a government were once established in a people like this, not only would it oppress men, but in the long term it would rob each of them of several of the principal attributes of humanity.

Despotism therefore appears to me particularly to be dreaded in democratic ages.

I would, I think, have loved freedom in all times; but I feel myself inclined to adore it in the time we are in.

I am convinced, on the other hand, that all those in the centuries we are now entering who try to base freedom on privilege and aristocracy will fail. All those who want to attract authority to a single class and retain it there will fail. In our day there is no sovereign clever enough and strong enough to found a despotism by reestablishing permanent distinctions among its subjects; nor is there a legislator so wise and so powerful as to be in a position to maintain free institutions if he does not take equality for his first principle and creed. All those of our contemporaries who want to create or secure the independence and dignity of those like themselves must therefore show themselves as friends of equality; and the only means worthy of them for showing themselves as such is to be such: the success of their holy enterprise depends on it.

Thus there is no question of reconstructing an aristocratic society, but of making freedom issue from the bosom of the democratic society in which God makes us live.

These two first truths seem to me simple, clear and fertile, and they naturally lead me to consider what kind of free government can be established in a people where conditions are equal.

It results from the very constitution of democratic nations and their needs that the power of the sovereign must be more uniform, more centralized, more extended, more penetrating, and more powerful in them than elsewhere. Society there is naturally more active and stronger, the individual more subordinated and weaker: the one does more, the other less; that is mandatory.

One must therefore not expect that the circle of individual independence will ever be as large in democratic lands as in aristocratic countries. But that is not to be wished; for in aristocratic nations, society is often sacrificed to the individual and the prosperity of the greatest number to the greatness of a few.

It is at once necessary and desirable that the central power that directs a democratic people be active and powerful. There is no question of rendering it weak or indolent, but only of preventing it from abusing its agility and force.

What contributed most to securing the independence of particular persons in aristocratic centuries is that the sovereign alone did not take charge of governing and administering citizens; it was obliged to leave this care in part to members of the aristocracy, so that the social power, since it was always divided, never weighed as a whole and in the same manner on each man.

Not only did the sovereign not do everything by itself, but most of the officials who acted in its place, drawing their power from the fact of their birth and not from it, were not constantly in its hands. It could not create them or destroy them at each instant according to its caprices or bend them all uniformly to its least will. That also guaranteed the independence of particular persons.

I well understand that in our day one cannot have recourse to the same means, but I do see democratic procedures that replace them.

Instead of handing over to the sovereign alone all the administrative powers that one takes away from corporations or from the nobles, one can entrust a part of them to secondary bodies formed temporarily of plain citizens; in this manner the freedom of particular persons will be surer without lessening their equality.

Americans, who do not hold to words as much as we do, have preserved the name of county for the largest of their administrative districts; but they have replaced the county in part by a provincial assembly.

I shall admit without difficulty that in a period of equality like ours it would be unjust and unreasonable to institute hereditary officials; but nothing prevents their substitution, in a certain measure, by elective officials. Election is a democratic expedient that secures the independence of the official vis-à-vis the central power as much as and more than heredity can do in aristocratic peoples.

Aristocratic countries are filled with rich and influential particular persons who know how to be self-sufficient and whom one does not oppress easily or secretly; and they maintain power with their general habits of moderation and restraint.

I know well that democratic lands do not naturally present individuals like these; but one can artificially create something analogous there.

I firmly believe that one cannot found an aristocracy anew in the world; but I think that when plain citizens associate, they can constitute very opulent, very influential, very strong beings—in a word, aristocratic persons.

In this manner one would obtain several of the greatest political advantages of aristocracy without its injustices or dangers. A political, industrial, commercial, or even scientific and literary association is an enlightened and powerful citizen whom one can neither bend at will nor oppress in the dark and who, in defending its particular rights against the exigencies of power, saves common freedoms.

In times of aristocracy, each man is always bound in a very tight manner to several of his fellow citizens in such a way that one cannot attack him without having the others rush to his aid. In centuries of equality, each individual is naturally isolated; he has no hereditary friends from whom he can require cooperation, no class whose sympathies are assured him; one easily sets him apart and rides roughshod over him with impunity. In our day a citizen who is oppressed has therefore only one means of defending himself; it is to address the nation as a whole, and if it is deaf to him, the human race; he has only one means of doing it, which is the press. Thus freedom of the press is infinitely more precious in democratic nations than in all others; it alone cures most of the ills that equality can produce. Equality isolates and weakens men, but the press places at the side of each of them a very powerful arm that the weakest and most isolated can make use of. Equality takes away from each individual the support of his neighbors, but the press permits him to call to his aid all his fellow citizens and all who are like him. Printing hastened the progress of equality, and it is one of its best correctives.

I think that men who live in aristocracies can do without freedom of the press if they must; but those who inhabit democratic lands cannot do so. To guarantee the personal independence of the latter, I do not trust in great political assemblies, in parliamentary prerogatives, or in a proclamation of the sovereignty of the people.

All those things are reconcilable, up to a certain point, with individual servitude; but that servitude cannot be complete if the press is free. The press is the democratic instrument of freedom par excellence.

I would say something analogous of judicial power.

It is of the essence of judicial power to be occupied with particular interests and willingly to fix its regard on small objects that are exposed to its view; it is also of the essence of this power not to come of itself to the assistance of those who are oppressed, but to be constantly at the disposition of the most humble among them. However weak one supposes him, he can always force the judge to listen to his complaint and to respond to it: that is due to the very constitution of judicial power.

A power like this is therefore especially applicable to the needs of freedom in a time when the eye and hand of the sovereign are constantly introduced into the slightest details of human actions, and when particular persons, too weak to protect themselves, are too isolated to be able to count on the assistance of their peers. The force of the courts has in all times been the greatest guarantee that can be offered to individual independence, but that is above all true in democratic centuries; rights and particular interests are always in peril then if the judicial power does not grow and extend itself as conditions are equalized.

Equality suggests to men several penchants very dangerous for freedom to which the legislator ought always to keep his eye open. I shall recall only the principal ones.

Men who live in democratic centuries do not readily comprehend the utility of forms; they feel an instinctive disdain for them. I have spoken elsewhere of the reasons for this.* Forms excite their scorn and often their hatred. As they ordinarily aspire only to easy and present enjoyments, they throw themselves impetuously toward the object of each of their desires; the least delays make them despair. This temperament, which they carry into political life, disposes them against the forms that slow them down or stop them every day in some of their designs.

The inconvenience that men in democracies find in forms is, however, what renders them so useful to freedom, their principal merit being to serve as a barrier between strong and weak, he who governs and he who is governed, to slow down the one and to give the other time to recollect himself. Forms are more necessary as the sovereign is more active and more powerful and as particular persons become more indolent and debilitated. Thus democratic peoples naturally have more need of forms than other peoples, and they naturally respect them less. That merits very serious attention.

There is nothing more pathetic than the haughty disdain of most of our contemporaries for questions of form; for the smallest questions of form have acquired an importance in our day that they had not had up to now. Several of the greatest interests of humanity are linked to them.

I think that if statesmen who lived in aristocratic centuries could sometimes scorn forms with impunity and often rise above them, those who lead peoples today must consider the least of them with respect, neglecting it only when an imperious necessity obliges them to do so. In aristocracies, they had a superstition of forms; we must have an enlightened and reflective worship of them.

Another instinct very natural to democratic peoples and very dangerous

---

*DA II 1.1.

is the one that brings them to scorn individual rights and hold them of little account.

Men are generally attached to a right and show respect for it because of its importance or the long use they have made of it. The individual rights that are encountered in democratic peoples are ordinarily of little importance, very recent, and quite unstable; this makes one sacrifice them often without difficulty and violate them almost always without remorse.

Now, it happens that at the same time and in the same nations in which men conceive a natural scorn for the rights of individuals, the rights of society are naturally extended and strengthened; that is to say that men become less attached to particular rights at the moment when it would be most necessary to retain and defend the few that remain to them.

It is therefore above all in the democratic times we are in that the true friends of freedom and human greatness must constantly remain on their feet and ready to prevent the social power from lightly sacrificing the particular rights of some individuals to the general execution of its designs. In these times there is no citizen so obscure that it is not very dangerous to allow him to be oppressed, nor are there individual rights of so little importance that one can deliver them with impunity to arbitrariness. The reason for this is simple: when one violates the particular right of an individual in a time when the human spirit is pervaded by the importance and sanctity of rights of this kind, one does harm only to whomever one strips of it; but to violate a right like this in our day is to corrupt national mores profoundly and to put society as a whole in peril, because the very idea of these sorts of rights constantly tends to be distorted and lost among us.

There are certain habits, certain ideas, and certain vices that are proper to a state of revolution and to which a long revolution cannot fail to give birth and make general, whatever else its character, its object, and its theater may be.

When any nation whatever has changed chiefs, opinions, and laws several times in a short space of time, the men who compose it in the end contract a taste for movement and become habituated to the fact that all movements occur rapidly with the aid of force. They then naturally conceive a scorn for forms, whose impotence they see each day, and only with impatience do they tolerate the empire of a rule that has been evaded so many times before their eyes.

As ordinary notions of equity and morality no longer suffice to explain and justify all the novelties to which the revolution gives birth every day, one becomes attached to the principle of social utility, one creates the dogma of political necessity, and one willingly becomes accustomed to sacrificing particular interests without scruple and to riding roughshod over individual rights in order to attain more promptly the general end that one proposes.

These habits and ideas, which I shall call revolutionary because all revolutions produce them, are displayed within aristocracies as well as in democratic peoples; but in the former, they are often less powerful and always less lasting, because there they encounter habits, ideas, faults, and foibles contrary to them. They therefore fade away by themselves when the revolution is ended, and the nation comes back from them to its former political aspect. It is not always so in democratic lands, where it is always to be feared that revolutionary instincts, mellowing and being regularized without being extinguished, will gradually be transformed into governmental mores and administrative habits.

I therefore do not know of any country in which revolutions are more dangerous than in democratic countries, because independent of the accidental and passing evils that they can never fail to do, they always risk creating permanent and so to speak eternal ones.

I believe that there are honest resistances and legitimate rebellions. I therefore do not say in an absolute manner that men in democratic times ought never to make revolutions; but I think that they have reason to hesitate more than all others before undertaking them and that it is better for them to suffer many discomforts in their present state than to recur to such a perilous remedy.

I shall finish with a general idea that includes within it not only all the particular ideas that have been expressed in this present chapter, but also most of those that this book has the goal of setting forth.

In the centuries of aristocracy that preceded ours, there were very powerful particular persons and a very feeble social authority. The very image of society was obscure and was constantly being lost in the midst of all the different powers that regulated citizens. The principal effort of men in those times should have been brought to enlarging and fortifying the social power, to increasing and securing its prerogatives, and, on the contrary, to compressing individual independence within the narrowest of bounds and subordinating particular interest to the general interest.

Other perils and other cares await men of our day.

In most modern nations, the sovereign, whatever its origin, its constitution, and its name may be, has become almost all-powerful, and particular persons sink more and more into the last degree of weakness and dependence.

All was different in former societies. Unity and uniformity were encountered nowhere in them. In ours, everything threatens to become so alike that the particular shape of each individual will soon be lost entirely in the common physiognomy. Our fathers were always ready to misuse the idea that particular rights are respectable, [whereas] we are naturally brought to exaggerate [the idea] that the interest of one individual ought always to bend before the interest of several.

The political world is changing; henceforth one must seek new remedies for new ills.

To fix extended, but visible and immovable, limits for social power; to give to particular persons certain rights and to guarantee them the uncontested enjoyment of these rights; to preserve for the individual the little independence, force, and originality that remain to him; to elevate him beside society and to sustain him before it: this appears to me to be the first object of the legislator in the age we are entering.

One might say that sovereigns in our time seek only to make great things with men. I should want them to think a little more of making great men; to attach less value to the work and more to the worker, and to remember constantly that a nation cannot long remain strong when each man in it is individually weak, and that neither social forms nor political schemes have yet been found that can make a people energetic by composing it of pusillanimous and soft citizens.

Among our contemporaries, I see two contrary but equally fatal ideas.

Some perceive in equality only the anarchic tendencies to which it gives birth. They dread their free will; they are afraid of themselves.

Others, fewer in number, but more enlightened, have another view. Next to the route that, departing from equality, leads to anarchy, they have finally discovered the path that seems to lead men invincibly toward servitude. They bend their souls in advance to this necessary servitude; and despairing of remaining free, at the bottom of their hearts they already adore the master who will soon come.

The first abandon freedom because they deem it dangerous; the second because they judge it impossible.

If I had had this latter belief, I would not have written the work you have just read; I would have limited myself to groaning in secret about the destiny of those like me.

I wished to expose to broad daylight the perils that equality brings to human independence because I firmly believe that these perils are the most formidable as well as the least foreseen of all those that the future holds. But I do not believe them insurmountable.

Men who live in the democratic centuries we are entering have the taste for independence naturally. They naturally tolerate rule with impatience: the permanence of the very state they prefer tires them. They love power; but they are inclined to scorn and hate whoever exercises it, and they easily escape from its hands because of their very pettiness and mobility.

These instincts will always be found because they come from the foundation of the social state, which will not change. For a long time they will keep any despotism from being able to settle in, and they will furnish new arms to each new generation that wants to struggle in favor of men's freedom.

Let us therefore have that salutary fear of the future that makes one watchful and combative, and not that sort of soft and idle terror that wears hearts down and enervates them.

Chapter 8 GENERAL VIEW OF THE SUBJECT

I should wish, before leaving forever the course I have just traveled, to be able to embrace with one last regard all the diverse features that mark the face of the new world, and finally to judge the general influence that equality will exert on the lot of men; but the difficulty of such an undertaking arrests me; confronted with so great an object I feel my sight becoming blurred and my reason wavering.

The new society that I sought to depict and that I wish to judge is only being born. Time has not yet fixed its form; the great revolution that created it still endures, and in what is happening in our day it is almost impossible to discern what will pass away with the revolution itself and what will remain after it.

The world that is arising is still half entangled in the debris of the world that is falling, and in the midst of the immense confusion that human affairs presents, no one can say what will remain standing of aged institutions and old mores and what of them will in the end disappear.

Although the revolution operating in the social state, the laws, the ideas, the sentiments of men is still very far from being completed, already one cannot compare its works with anything previously seen in the world. I go back century by century to the furthest removed antiquity; I perceive nothing that resembles what is before my eyes. With the past no longer shedding light on the future, the mind advances in darkness.

Nevertheless, in the midst of this picture so vast, so new, so confused, I already glimpse some principal features being sketched and I point them out:

I see that goods and evils are split equally enough in the world. Great wealth is disappearing; the number of small fortunes is increasing; desires and enjoyments are multiplying; there is no longer extraordinary prosperity or irremediable misery. Ambition is a universal sentiment, there are few vast ambitions. Each individual is isolated and weak; society is agile, far-seeing, and strong; particular persons do small things and the state does immense ones.

Souls are not energetic; but mores are mild and legislation humane. If one encounters few great devotions, few very lofty, very brilliant, and very pure virtues, habits are orderly, violence rare, cruelty almost unknown. Men's existence is becoming longer and their property surer. Life is not much adorned, but very easy and very peaceful. There are few very delicate and very coarse pleasures, little politeness in manners, and little brutality in tastes. One scarcely encounters very learned men or very ignorant populations. Genius becomes rarer and enlightenment more common. The human mind is developed by the combined small efforts of all men, and not by the powerful impulsion of some of them. There is less perfection, but more fruitfulness in works. All the bonds of race, of class, of native land slacken; the great bond of humanity draws tighter.

If among all these diverse features I seek the one that appears to me the most general and the most striking, I come to see that what may be remarked in fortunes is represented in a thousand other forms. Almost all extremes become milder and softer; almost all prominent points are worn down to make a place for something middling that is at once less high and less low, less brilliant and less obscure than what used to be seen in the world.

I let my regard wander over this innumerable crowd composed of similar beings, in which nothing is elevated and nothing lowered. The spectacle of this universal uniformity saddens and chills me, and I am tempted to regret the society that is no longer.

When the world was filled with very great and very small men, very rich and very poor, very learned and very ignorant, I turned my regard away from the second and attached it only to the first, and these delighted my view; but I understand that this pleasure was born of my weakness: it is because I cannot see all that surrounds me at the same time that I am permitted to choose in this way and to set apart among so many objects those it pleases me to contemplate. It is not the same with the all-powerful and eternal Being whose eye necessarily envelops the sum of things and who sees distinctly, though at once, the whole human race and each man.

It is natural to believe that what most satisfies the regard of this creator and preserver of men is not the singular prosperity of some, but the greatest well-being of all: what seems to me decadence is therefore progress in his eyes; what wounds me is agreeable to him. Equality is perhaps less elevated; but it is more just, and its justice makes for its greatness and its beauty.

I strive to enter into this point of view of God, and it is from there that I seek to consider and judge human things.

No one on earth can yet assert in an absolute and general manner that the new state of societies is superior to the former state; but it is already easy to see that it is different.

There are certain vices and certain virtues that were attached to the constitution of aristocratic nations and that are so contrary to the genius of the new peoples that one cannot introduce them into their hearts. There are good penchants and bad instincts that were foreign to the first and that are natural to the second; ideas that present themselves to the imagination of the one that the mind of the other rejects. They are, as it were, two distinct humanities, each of which has its particular advantages and inconveniences, its goods and evils that are proper to it.

One must therefore take care in judging the societies being born by ideas one has drawn from those that are no longer. That would be unjust, for these societies, differing enormously between themselves, are not comparable.

It would scarcely be more reasonable to demand of men of our time the particular virtues that flowed from the social state of their ancestors, since that social state itself has fallen and has confusedly carried away in its fall all the goods and all the evils it brought with it.

But these things are still badly understood in our day.

I perceive many of my contemporaries who undertake to make a choice among the institutions, the opinions, the ideas born of the aristocratic constitution of the former society; they willingly abandon some, but they would wish to retain others and carry them into the new world with them.

I think that they are consuming their time and their strength on an honest and sterile work.

It is no longer a question of retaining the particular advantages that inequality of conditions procures for men, but of securing the new goods that equality can offer them.

We ought not to strain to make ourselves like our fathers, but strive to attain the kind of greatness and happiness that is proper to us.

As for myself, having come to the final stage of my course, to discover from afar, but at once, all the diverse objects that I had contemplated separately in advancing, I feel full of fears and full of hopes. I see great perils that it is possible to ward off; great evils that one can avoid or restrain, and I become more and more firm in the belief that to be honest and prosperous, it is still enough for democratic nations to wish it.

I am not unaware that several of my contemporaries have thought that peoples are never masters of themselves here below, and that they necessarily obey I do not know which insurmountable and unintelligent force born of previous events, the race, the soil, or the climate.

Those are false and cowardly doctrines that can never produce any but weak men and pusillanimous nations: Providence has not created the human race either entirely independent or perfectly slave. It traces, it is true, a fatal circle around each man that he cannot leave; but within its vast limits man is powerful and free; so too with peoples.

Nations of our day cannot have it that conditions within them are not equal; but it depends on them whether equality leads them to servitude or freedom, to enlightenment or barbarism, to prosperity or misery.

NOTES

VOLUME ONE, PART ONE

I. Page 21.

On all the localities of the West into which the Europeans have still not penetrated, see the two journeys undertaken by Major Long at the expense of Congress.

Mr. Long says notably, concerning the great American wilderness, that one must draw a line nearly parallel to the 20th degree of longitude ([from] the meridian of Washington),[1] starting from the Red River and [going north,] ending at the Platte River. From this imaginary line to the Rocky Mountains, which are the boundary of the Mississippi valley to the West, extend immense plains, generally covered with sand that resists cultivation or strewn with granite rocks. They are deprived of water in summer. One finds there only great herds of buffalo and wild horses. One also sees some hordes of Indians, but few in number.

Major Long has heard it said that in going beyond the Platte River in the same direction one always encounters the same desert to one's left, but he has not been able to verify for himself the exactness of this report. *Long's Expedition,* vol. 2, p. 361.*

Whatever confidence the account of Major Long merits, one must nevertheless not forget that he did no more than cross the country he speaks of, without making great zigzags outside the line he followed.

---

* *An Account of an Expedition from Pittsburgh to the Rocky Mountains; Performed in the Years 1819 and '20 . . . under the Command of Major Stephen H. Long. From the Notes of Major Long, Mr. T. Say, and Other Gentlemen of the Exploring Party.* Compiled by Edwin James. 2 vols. (Philadelphia, 1823).

1. The 20th degree of longitude, counting from the meridian of Washington, almost corresponds to the 99th degree counting from the meridian of Paris.

II. Page 22.

South America, in its tropical regions, produces with an incredible profusion those climbing plants known by the generic name of creepers. The flora of the West Indies alone presents more than forty different species of them.

Among the most graceful of those shrubs is the passion flower. That pretty plant, says Descourti[l]z in his description of the vegetable kingdom of the West Indies, attaches itself to trees by means of the tendrils with which it is provided and forms moving arcades, colonnades rich and elegant with the beauty of the purple flowers varied with blue that decorate them and that delight the sense of smell with the perfume that they give off; vol. 1, p. 265.*

The great-podded acacia is a very thick creeper that develops rapidly and, running from tree to tree, sometimes covers more than half a league; vol. 3, p. 227.†

III. Page 24.

ON AMERICAN LANGUAGES. The languages that the Indians of America speak, from the Arctic pole to Cape Horn, are all formed, it is said, on the same model, and are subject to the same grammatical rules; from this one can conclude that in all likelihood all the Indian nations issued from the same stock.

Each small tribe on the American continent speaks a different dialect; but the languages properly speaking are very few, which would tend to prove also that the nations of the New World did not have a very old origin.

Finally, the languages of America are extremely regular; it is therefore probable that the peoples who make use of them have still not been subjected to great revolutions and have not been mixed, forcibly or voluntarily, with foreign nations; for it is generally a union of several languages into one that produces irregularities in grammar.

It was not long ago that the American languages, and in particular the languages of North America, attracted the serious attention of philologists. They then discovered for the first time that this idiom of a barbarous people was the product of a very complicated system of ideas and quite learned combinations. They perceived that these languages were quite rich and that in forming them great care had been taken in sparing the delicacy of the ear.

The grammatical system of the Americans differs from all others at several points, but principally in this latter one.

Some peoples of Europe, among them the Germans, have the ability to combine when needed different expressions and thus to give a complex meaning to certain words. The Indians have extended this ability in the most surprising manner, and have come to fix so to speak on a single point a very great number of ideas. This will

---

*Michel Etienne Descourtilz, *Flore pittoresque et médicale des Antilles; ou, Histoire naturelle des plantes usuelles des colonies françaises, anglaises, espagnoles, et portugaises*, 8 vols. (Paris, 1833).
    †Ibid.

be understood without difficulty with the aid of an example cited by Mr. Duponceau in the *Memoirs of the Philosophical Society of America.**

When a Delaware woman plays with a cat or a puppy, he says, one sometimes hears pronounced the word *kuligatschis*. This word is composed in this way: *k* is the sign of the second person and signifies "you" or "your"; *uli*, which one pronounces *ouli*, is a fragment of the word *wulit*, which signifies "beautiful," "pretty"; *gat* is another fragment, of the word *wichgat*, which signifies "paw"; finally *schis*, which one pronounces *chise*, is a diminutive ending that brings with it the idea of smallness. Thus, in a single word, the Indian woman has said: "Your pretty little paw."

Here is another example that shows how happily the savages of North America have composed their words.

"Young man" in Delaware is said *pilape*. This word is formed from *pilsit*, "chaste," "innocent"; and from *lenape*, "man": that is to say, "man in his purity and innocence."

This ability to combine words is above all remarkable in a very strange manner in the formation of verbs. The most complicated action is often rendered by a single verb; almost all the nuances of the idea act on the verb and modify it.

Those who would like to examine in more detail this subject, which I myself have only touched on very superficially, ought to read:

1st, the correspondence of Mr. Duponceau with the Reverend Hecwelder [Heckewelder] relative to Indian tongues. This correspondence is found in the first volume of *Memoirs of the Philosophical Society of America*, published at Philadelphia in 1819, Abraham Small, pp. 356–464.†

2nd, the grammar of the Delaware, or Lenape, language, by Geiberger [Zeisberger], and the preface by Mr. Duponceau, which is joined to it. The whole is found in the same collection, vol. 3.‡

3rd, a very well done summary of these works, contained at the end of volume 6 of the *American Encyclopedia*.§

IV. Page 26.

One finds in Charlevoix,‖ book 1, p. 235, the history of the first war that the French of Canada had to carry on, in 1610, against the Iroquois. The latter, although armed

---

*Peter Stephen Duponceau, "Translator's Preface" to David Zeisberger's "Grammar of the Language of the Lenni Lenape, or Delaware Indians," in *Transactions of the American Philosophical Society*, vol. 3 (Philadelphia, 1830), 82–83. AT takes these examples almost word for word from Duponceau.

†Rev. John Heckewelder, "Correspondence between Mr. Heckewelder and Mr. Duponceau, On the Languages of the American Indians," in *Transactions of the Historical and Literary Committee of the American Philosophical Society*, vol. 1, 351–450.

‡David Zeisberger, "Grammar of the Language of the Lenni Lenape or Delaware Indians," in *Transactions of the American Philosophical Society*, vol. 3 (Philadelphia, 1819), 65–252.

§John Pickering, "Indian Languages of America," Appendix to vol. 6 of *Encyclopædia Americana*, edited by Francis Lieber (Philadelphia, 1829–1833), 581–600.

‖Charlevoix, *Histoire et description générale de la Nouvelle France.*

with arrows and bows, posed a desperate resistance to the French and their allies. Charlevoix, who is not a great portrayer, nevertheless displays very well in this piece the contrast in the mores of the Europeans and those of the savages, as well as the different ways in which the two races understood honor.

"The French," he says, "seized the beaver skins with which the Iroquois, whom they saw stretched out in the place, were covered. [The Hurons, their allies,] were scandalized by this spectacle. The latter, for their part, began to exercise their ordinary cruelties on the prisoners and devoured one of them who had been killed, which was a horror to the French. Thus," adds Charlevoix, "these barbarians gloried in a disinterestedness that they were surprised at not finding in our nation, and did not understand that there was much less evil in despoiling the dead than in feeding on their flesh like ferocious beasts."

The same Charlevoix, in another place, vol. 1, p. 230[–231], portrays in this manner the first torture to which Champlain was witness, and the return of the Hurons to their village.

> After having gone eight leagues, he says, our allies stopped, and, taking one of their captives, they reproached him for all the cruelties that he had exercised on the warriors of their nation who had fallen into his hands and declared to him that he should expect to be treated in the same manner, adding that if he had a heart, he would witness it by singing. He immediately launched into his song of death, then his song of war, and all those that he knew, but in a very sad tone, says Champlain, who still had not had the time to get to know that all the music of the savages is somewhat lugubrious. His torture, accompanied by all the horrors we shall speak of in the sequel, frightened the French, who in vain made every effort to put an end to it. The following night, a Huron having dreamt that he was pursued, the retreat changed into a genuine flight, and the savages did not stop at any spot that was not beyond all danger.
>
> From the moment when they perceived the huts of their village, they cut the long sticks to which they attached the scalps they had shared out and carried them in triumph. At this sight the women ran up, threw themselves in swimming, and, when they reached the canoes, they took the scalps all bloody from the hands of their husbands and attached them to their necks.
>
> The warriors offered one of these horrible trophies to Champlain, and in addition made him a present of several bows and arrows, the sole spoils of the Iroquois that they wanted to take possession of, begging him to show them to the king of France.

Champlain lived alone for a whole winter in the midst of these barbarians without having his person or his property jeopardized for an instant.

V. Page 39.

Although the Puritan rigor that presided at the birth of the English colonies of America has already been much weakened, one still finds some extraordinary traces of it in habits and laws.

In 1792, in the very period when the anti-Christian republic of France began its ephemeral existence, the legislative body of Massachusetts promulgated the law, which you are going to read, to force citizens to observe Sunday. Here are the preamble and the principal provisions of that law, which deserve to get the full attention of the reader:

"Whereas," says the legislator, "the observance of the Lord's Day is highly promotive of the welfare of a community, by affording necessary seasons for relaxation from labour and the cares of business; for moral reflections and conversation on the duties of life, and the frequent errors of human conduct; for public and private worship of the Maker, Governor and Judge of the world; and for those acts of charity which support and adorn a Christian society: And whereas some thoughtless and irreligious persons, inattentive to the duties and benefits of the Lord's Day, profane the same, by unnecessarily pursuing their worldly business and recreations on that day, to their own great damage, as members of a Christian society; to the great disturbance of well-disposed persons, and to the great damage of the community, by producing dissipation of manners and immoralities of life:

"Be it therefore enacted by the Senate and House of Representatives [. . .],

"That no person or persons [. . .] shall keep open his [. . .] shop, ware-house or work-house, nor shall [. . .] do any manner of labour, business or work [. . .] nor be present at any concert of music, dancing, or any public diversion, show or entertainment, nor use any sport, game, play or recreation, on the Lord's Day [. . .] upon penalty of a sum not exceeding twenty shillings, nor less than ten shillings, for every offense.

"That no traveller, drover, waggoner, teamster [. . .] shall travel on the Lord's Day [. . .] (except from necessity or charity) upon the penalty of a sum not exceeding twenty shillings, nor less than ten shillings.

"That no vintner, retailer of strong liquors, innholder [. . .] shall entertain or suffer any of the inhabitants of the respective towns where they dwell [. . .] to abide and remain in their houses [. . .] drinking or spending their time, either idly or at play, or doing any secular business on the Lord's Day [. . .] on penalty of ten shillings, payable by such vintner, retailer or innholder [. . .]; and every person so drinking or abiding [. . .]; and every such licensed person [. . .] having been three times convicted, shall be debarred from renewing his license forever after. [. . .]

"That any person, being able of body and not otherwise necessarily prevented, who shall, for the space of three months together, absent him or herself from the public worship of God, on the Lord's Day [. . .] shall pay a fine of ten shillings.

"That if any person shall, on the Lord's Day, within the walls of any house of public worship, behave rudely or indecently, he or she shall pay a fine not more than forty shillings, nor less than five shillings. [. . .]

"That the tythingmen[2] [. . .] in the several towns and districts, within this Commonwealth, shall be held and obliged to inquire into, and inform of all offences against this Act; [. . .]

"And every tythingman is hereby authorized and empowered, to enter into any of the rooms and other parts of an inn, or public house of entertainment, on the Lord's

---

2. These are annually elected officers, who in their functions approximate both a local policeman [*garde champêtre*] and a police detective [*officier de police judiciaire*] in France.

Day, [...] [and] to examine all persons whom they shall have good cause [...] to suspect of unnecessarily travelling as aforesaid, on the Lord's Day, and to demand of all such persons the cause thereof [...]; and if any person shall refuse to give answer, [...] he shall pay a fine not exceeding five pounds [...]; and if the reason given for such travelling shall not be satisfactory to such tythingman, he shall enter a complaint against the person travelling, before a Justice of the Peace in the county where the offense is committed." *General Laws of Massachusetts*, vol. 1, p. 410.*

On March 11, 1797, a new law raised the rate of fines, half of which was to belong to whoever prosecuted the offender. Same collection, vol. 1, p. 525.†

On February 6, 1816, a new law confirmed these same measures. Same collection, vol. 2, p. 405.‡

Similar provisions exist in the laws of the state of New York, revised in 1827 and 1828. (See *Revised Statutes*,§ part 1, chap. 20, p. 675.) There it says that on Sundays no one shall be able to hunt, fish, gamble, or frequent houses where drink is available. No one shall be able to travel, unless in case of necessity.

This is not the only trace that the religious spirit and austere mores of the first emigrants have left on laws.

One reads in the revised statutes of the state of New York, vol. 1, p. 662,‖ the following article:

"Every person who shall win or lose at play, or by betting at any time, the sum or value of twenty-five dollars" (around 132 francs) "or upwards, within the space of twenty-four hours, shall be deemed guilty of a misdemeanor, and on conviction shall be fined not less than five times the value or sum so lost or won; which [...] shall be paid to the overseers of the poor of the town [...].

"Every person who shall [...] lose at any time or sitting, the sum or value of twenty-five dollars or upwards [...] may [...] sue for and recover the money [...]. In case the person losing such sum or value shall not [...] sue for the sum or value so by him lost [...], the overseers of the poor of the town where the offense was committed, may sue for and recover the sum or value so lost and paid, together with treble the said sum or value, from the winner thereof, for the benefit of the poor."

The laws that we have just cited are very recent; but who could understand them without going back to the very origin of the colonies? I do not doubt that in our day the penal part of this legislation is only very rarely applied; laws preserve their inflexibility when mores have already bent with the movement of time. Nevertheless, observation of Sunday in America is still what strikes the foreigner most vividly.

There is, notably, a great American town in which, from Saturday evening on, social movement is almost suspended. You go through it at the hour that seems to invite the mature to business and youth to pleasures, and you find yourself in profound solitude. Not only does no one work, but no one appears to live. One hears neither the movement of industry nor the accents of joy, not even the confused mur-

---

* *The General Laws of Massachusetts* (Boston, 1823), 3 vols.; vol. 1, 407–409.

†Vol. 1, 535.

‡Vol. 2, 403.

§*Revised Statutes of the State of New York.*

‖Ibid., vol. 1, 662–663.

mur that constantly rises from within a great city. Chains are put up in the vicinity of churches; only with regret do the half-closed shutters of houses allow a ray of sun to penetrate the dwellings of citizens. Now and then you barely perceive an isolated man who glides noiselessly across deserted intersections and along abandoned streets.

At daybreak of the next day, the rumble of vehicles, the noise of hammers, the cries of the population again begin to make themselves heard; the city awakens; a restive crowd hurries toward the hearths of commerce and industry; everything moves, everything is agitated, everything presses around you. To a sort of lethargic drowsiness succeeds a feverish activity; one would say that each has only a single day at his disposal to acquire wealth and enjoy it.

VI. Page 44.

It is needless to say that in the chapter that you are going to read, I have not claimed to do a history of America. My sole aim has been to have the reader himself appreciate the influence that the opinions and mores of the first emigrants exerted on the fate of the different colonies and of the Union in general. I have therefore had to limit myself to citing some detached fragments.

I do not know if I am mistaken, but it seems to me that in advancing on the route that I have only indicated here, one could present pictures of the first age of the American republics that would not be unworthy of attracting the regard of the public and that would doubtless give matter for reflection to statesmen. Not being able to engage in this work myself, I wanted at least to facilitate it for others. I therefore believed I should present a short list and an abridged analysis here of the works from which it appeared to me most useful to draw.

In the number of general documents that one could fruitfully consult I shall place first the work entitled *Historical Collection[s, Consisting] of State Papers and Other Authentic Documents, Intended as Materials for an History of the United States of America, by Ebenezer Hazard.*

The first volume of this compilation, which was printed in Philadelphia in 1792, contains textual copies of all charters granted by the Crown of England to the emigrants, as well as the principal acts of the colonial governments during the first period of their existence. One finds among others a great number of authentic documents on the affairs of New England and Virginia during this period.

The second volume is devoted almost wholly to the acts of the confederation of 1643. That federal pact, which took place among the colonies of New England with the goal of resisting the Indians, was the first example of union that the Anglo-Americans provided. There were also several other confederations of this same nature before the one in 1776 that brought independence to the colonies.

The historical collection of Philadelphia is found in the Bibliothèque Royale.

In addition, each colony has its historical memorials, several of which are very precious. I begin my examination with that of Virginia, which is the oldest populated state.

The first of all the historians of Virginia is its founder, Captain John Smith. Captain Smith has left us one volume in quarto, entitled *The General History of Virginia and New England, by Captain John Smith, Some Time Governor in Those Countries and*

Admiral of New England, printed in London in 1627 [1624]. (This volume is in the Bibliothèque Royale.) Smith's work is adorned with maps and very curious engravings that date from the time when it was printed. The account of the historian extends from the year 1584 to 1626 [1624]. Smith's book is esteemed and deserves to be. The author is one of the most celebrated adventurers who appeared in the century full of adventures at the end of which he lived: the book itself breathes that ardor of discoveries, that spirit of enterprise which characterized men then; one finds in it those chivalrous mores that they mixed with trade and that they made use of in the acquisition of wealth.

But what is above all remarkable in Captain Smith is that he mixes with the virtues of his contemporaries qualities that remained foreign to most of them; his style is simple and clear, his accounts all have the stamp of truth, his descriptions are not adorned.

This author casts precious light on the state of the Indians in the period of the discovery of North America.

The second historian to consult is [Robert] Beverley. Beverley's work, which forms one volume in duodecimo, was translated into French and printed in Amsterdam in 1707.* The author begins his accounts in the year 1585 and ends them in the year 1700. The first part of his book contains historical documents properly speaking, relating to the infancy of the colony. The second contains a curious depiction of the state of the Indians in that distant period. The third gives very clear ideas about the mores, social state, laws, and political habits of the Virginians in the author's time.

Beverley was originally from Virginia, which makes him commence by saying, "If I might be so happy, as to settle my credit with the reader, the next favour I wou'd ask of him, shou'd be, not to criticize too unmercifully upon my style. I am an Indian, and don't pretend to be exact in my language."† Despite this modesty of a colonist, the author gives evidence throughout the whole course of his book that he tolerates with impatience the supremacy of the mother country. One also finds in Beverley's work numerous traces of that spirit of civil freedom that henceforth animated the English colonies of America. One also encounters in it a trace of the divisions that have existed for so long in their midst and that delayed their independence. Beverley detests his Catholic neighbors of Maryland even more than the English government. The style of this author is simple; his accounts are often full of interest and inspire confidence. The French translation of Beverley's history is found in the Bibliothèque Royale.

I saw in America, but I have not been able to find in France, a work that would also deserve to be consulted; it is entitled *History of Virginia, by William Stith.*‡ This book offers curious details, but it appeared to me long and diffuse.

The oldest and best document that one can consult on the history of the Carolinas is a small book in quarto, entitled *The History of Carolina, by John Lawson,* printed in London in 1718.

---

*Beverley, *History and Present State of Virginia* (London: R. Parker, 1705). French edition: *Histoire de la Virginie* (Amsterdam: T. Lombrail, 1707).

†Beverley, 9.

‡Stith, *The History of the First Discovery and Settlement of Virginia* (Williamsburg, Va., 1747).

Lawson's work contains first a voyage of discoveries in the west of Carolina. This voyage is written in the form of a journal; the accounts of the author are confused; his observations are very superficial; one finds in them only a rather striking depiction of the ravages that small pox and brandy caused among the savages of that period and a curious picture of the corruption of mores that reigned among them and that the presence of the Europeans favored.

The second part of Lawson's work is devoted to recounting the physical state of Carolina and to making its products known.

In the third part, the author gives an interesting description of the mores, usages, and government of the Indians of that period.

There is often spirit and originality in that portion of the book.

Lawson's history ends with the charter granted to Carolina in the time of Charles II.

The general tone of this work is light, often licentious, and forms a perfect contrast with the profoundly serious style of works published in that same period in New England.

Lawson's history is an extremely rare document in America and cannot be procured in Europe. There is, however, one copy in the Bibliothèque Royale.

From the southern extremity of the United States I jump immediately to the northern extremity. The intermediate space was populated only later.

I ought first to indicate a very curious compilation entitled *Collection[s] of the Massachusetts Historical Society,* printed for the first time at Boston in 1792, reprinted in 1806. This work is not in the Bibliothèque Royale nor, I think, in any other library.

This collection (which continues) contains a host of very precious documents relative to the history of the different states of New England. One finds in it unedited correspondence and authentic pieces that were buried in provincial archives. The whole work of Gookin relative to the Indians has been inserted in it.*

I have pointed out several times in the course of the chapter to which this note relates the work of Nathaniel Morton entitled *New England's Memorial.*† What I have said about it suffices to prove that it deserves to attract the attention of those who would like to know the history of New England. Nathaniel Morton's book forms one volume in octavo, reprinted in Boston in 1826. It is not in the Bibliothèque Royale.

The most esteemed and most important document that we possess on the history of New England is the work of Rev. Cotton Mather entitled *Magnalia Christi Americana, or the Ecclesiastical History of New-England, 1620–1698,* 2 vol. in octavo, reprinted in Harford [*sic*] in 1820.‡ I do not believe it may be found in the Bibliothèque Royale.

The author has divided his work into seven books.

The first presents the history of whatever prepared and brought about the foundation of New England.

The second contains the lives of the first governors and the principal magistrates who administered that country.

---

*Daniel Gookin, *Historical Collections of the Indians in New England;* in *Collections of the Massachusetts Historical Society* (Boston, 1792), 141–232.

†*New England's Memorial* borrows liberally from William Bradford's *Of Plymouth Plantation,* the manuscript of which was lost until 1858.

‡Cotton Mather, *Magnalia Christi Americana* (Hartford, 1820).

The third is devoted to the lives and works of the evangelical ministers who, during the same period, directed souls.

In the fourth, the author makes known the foundation and development of the University at Cambridge (Massachusetts).*

In the fifth, he sets forth the principles and discipline of the Church of New England.

The sixth is devoted to recounting certain facts that mark, according to Mather, the beneficent action of Providence on the inhabitants of New England.

In the seventh, finally, the author informs us of the heresies and troubles to which the Church of New England has been exposed.

Cotton Mather was an evangelical minister who, after being born in Boston, passed his life there.

All the ardor and all the religious passions that led to the foundation of New England animate and enliven his accounts. One frequently discovers traces of bad taste in his manner of writing; but he attracts [us] because he is full of enthusiasm that in the end is communicated to the reader. He is often intolerant, more often credulous; but one never perceives a desire to deceive in him; sometimes his work presents beautiful passages and true and profound thoughts, such as these:

"Before the arrival of the Puritans," he says, vol. 1, chap. 4, p. 61,† "there were more than a few attempts of the *English*, to people and improve the parts of *New England* [. . .]; but the designs of those attempts being aimed no higher than the advancement of some *worldly interests*, a constant series of disasters has confounded them, until there was a plantation erected upon the nobler designs of *christianity*; and that plantation, though it has had more adversaries than perhaps any one upon earth; yet, *having obtained help from God, it continues to this day.*"

Mather sometimes mixes with the austerity of his pictures images full of sweetness and tenderness: after having spoken of an English lady whom religious ardor had brought to America with her husband, and who soon succumbed to the fatigues and miseries of exile, he adds: "As for her virtuous spouse, Isaac Johnson, he tried to live without her, lik'd it not, and dy'd" (vol. 1, p. 71).

Mather's book makes known admirably the time and the country that he seeks to describe.

Should he want to inform us about the grounds that brought the Puritans to seek asylum beyond the seas, he says:

The God of Heaven served as it were, a *summons* upon the *spirits* of his people in the English nation; stirring up the spirits of thousands which never saw the *faces* of each other, with a most unanimous inclination to leave all the pleasant accommodations of their native country; and go over a terrible *ocean*, into a more terrible *desert*, for the *pure enjoyment of all his ordinances*. It is now reasonable that before we pass any further, the *reasons* of this undertaking should be more exactly made known unto *posterity*, especially unto the *posterity* of

---

*Harvard University.

†Mather, *Magnalia Christi Americana*, vol. 1, 64–65.

those that were the undertakers, lest they come at length to forget and neglect *the true interest of* New England. Wherefore I shall now transcribe some of *them* from a manuscript, wherein they were then tendered unto consideration.

First, It will be a service unto the *Church* of great consequence, to carry the *Gospel* into *those* parts of the world (North America), and raise a bulwark against the kingdom of *antichrist,* which the *Jesuits* labour to rear up in all parts of the world.

Secondly, All other Churches of *Europe* have been brought under *desolations;* and it may be feared that the like judgments are coming upon *us;* and who knows but God hath provided this place (New England) to be a *refuge* for many, whom he means to save out of the *General Destruction.*

Thirdly, The land grows weary of her *inhabitants,* insomuch that *man,* which is the most precious of all creatures, is here more vile and base than the earth he treads upon: *children, neighbours,* and *friends,* especially the *poor,* are counted the greatest *burdens,* which if things were right would be the chiefest earthly *blessings.*

Fourthly, We are grown to that intemperance in all *excess of riot,* as no mean estate almost will suffice a man to keep sail with his *equals,* and he that fails in it, must live in scorn and contempt: hence it comes to pass, that all *arts* and *trades* are carried in that deceitful manner, and unrighteous course, as it is almost impossible for a good upright man to maintain his constant charge, and live comfortably in them.

Fifthly, The *schools* of learning and religion are so corrupted, as [. . .] most children, even the best, wittiest, and of the fairest hopes, are perverted, corrupted, and utterly overthrown, by the multitude of evil examples and licentious behaviours in these *seminaries.*

Sixthly, The *whole earth* is the *Lord's garden,* and he hath given it to the sons of *Adam,* to be tilled and improved by them: why then should we stand starving here for places of habitation, and in the mean time suffer whole countries, as profitable for the use of man, to lie waste without any improvement?

Seventhly, What can be a better or nobler work, and more worthy of a *christian,* than to erect and support a *reformed particular Church* in its infancy, and unite our forces with such a company of faithful people, as by a timely assistance may grow stronger and prosper; but for want of it, may be put to great hazard, if not be wholly ruined.

Eighthly, If any such as are known to be godly, and live in wealth and prosperity here (in England), shall forsake all this to join with this *reformed church,* and with it run the hazard of an hard and mean condition, it will be an example of great use, both for the removing of *scandal,* and to give more *life* unto the *faith* of God's people in their prayers for the plantation, and also to encourage others to join the more willingly in it.

Further on, setting forth the principles of the Church of New England in moral matters, Mather takes up violently against the usage of making toasts at table, which he calls a pagan and abominable habit.

With the same rigor he proscribes all ornaments that women can put in their hair and pitilessly condemns the fashion being established among them, he says, of uncovering their necks and arms.

In another part of his work, he recounts for us at great length several deeds of sorcery that frightened New England. One sees that the visible action of the devil in the affairs of this world seems to him an incontestable and demonstrated truth.

In many places in this same book the spirit of civil freedom and political independence that characterized the contemporaries of the author is revealed. Their principles in the matter of government are shown at each step. Thus, for example, one sees the inhabitants of Massachusetts, from the year 1630 [1636], ten years after the foundation of Plymouth, devoting 400 pounds sterling to the establishment of the University at Cambridge.

If I pass from general documents about the history of New England to those relating to the various states included within its limits, I shall first have to point out the work entitled *The History of the Colony of Massachusetts, by* [Thomas] *Hutchinson*[,] *Lieutenant-Governor of the Massachusetts Province,* 2 vols. in octavo.* A copy of this book is found in the Bibliothèque Royale: it is a second edition, printed in London in 1765.

Hutchinson's history, which I have cited several times in the chapter to which this note relates, commences in the year 1628 and ends in 1750. A great air of veracity reigns in the whole work; its style is simple and without affectation. This history is very detailed.

The best document to consult for Connecticut is Benjamin Trumbull's history, entitled *A Complete History of Connecticut, Civil and Ecclesiastical,* 1630–1764, 2. vols. in octavo, printed in 1818 at New Haven. I do not believe that Trumbull's work is found in the Bibliothèque Royale.

This history contains a clear and cold exposition of all the events occurring in Connecticut during the period indicated in the title. The author has drawn from the best sources, and his accounts preserve the stamp of truth. All that he says of the first times of Connecticut is extremely curious. See, notably, in his work the *Constitution of 1639,* vol. 1, chap. 6, p. 100;† and also the *Penal Laws of Connecticut,* vol. 1, chap. 7, p. 123.‡

One rightly esteems Jeremy Belknap's work, entitled *History of New Hampshire,* 2 vols. in octavo, printed in Boston in 1792. See particularly in the work of Belknap, chapter 3 of the first volume. In that chapter the author gives extremely precious details about the political and religious principles of the Puritans, about the causes of their emigration, and about their laws. One finds in it this curious citation from a sermon pronounced in 1663: "It concerneth New England always to remember, that they are originally a plantation religious, not a plantation of trade. The profession of the purity of doctrine, worship and discipline is written upon her forehead. Let merchants, and such as are increasing cent per cent remember this, and that worldly gain

---

*Thomas Hutchinson, *The History of the Colony of Massachuset's Bay* (London, 1765), 3 vols.

†In *A Complete History of Connecticut,* 100ff.

‡*A Complete History,* 123ff.

was not the end and design of the people of New England but religion. And if any man among us make religion as twelve, and the world as thirteen, such an one hath not the spirit of a true New Englandman."* Readers will encounter in Belknap more general ideas and more force of thought than other American historians have presented up to the present.

I do not know if this book is found in the Bibliothèque Royale.

Among the central states whose existence is already old and that merit our attention, the states of New York and Pennsylvania are distinguished above all. The best history that we have of the state of New York is entitled *History of New York* by William Smith, printed in London in 1757.[†] A French translation of it exists, also printed in London in 1767, 1 vol. in duodecimo. Smith furnishes us with useful details about the wars of the French and English in America. He is of all the American historians the one who best makes known the famous confederation of the Iroquois.

As for Pennsylvania, I cannot do better than point out Proud's work, entitled *The History of Pennsylvania, from the Original Institution and Settlement of That Province, under the First Proprietor and Governor William Penn, in 1681 till after the Year 1742,* by Robert Proud, 2 vols. in octavo, printed in Philadelphia in 1797[–1798].

This particularly deserves to attract the attention of the reader; it contains a host of very curious documents about Penn, the doctrine of the Quakers, the character, mores, and usages of the first inhabitants of Pennsylvania. It is not, I believe, in the Bibliothèque.

I have no need to add that among the most important documents relative to Pennsylvania are the works of Penn[‡] himself and those of Franklin.[§] These works are known to many readers.

Most of the books that I have just cited I had already consulted during my stay in America. The Bibliothèque Royale was very willing to entrust some to me; others were lent to me by Mr. Warden, former consul general of the United States in Paris, author of an excellent work on America.[‖] I do not want to end this note without asking Mr. Warden to accept the expression of my gratitude.

VII. Page 50.

One finds the following in the *Memoirs of Jefferson:* "In the earlier times of the colony [of Virginia], when lands were to be obtained for little or nothing, some provident individuals procured large grants; and, desirous of founding great families for themselves, settled them on their descendants in fee tail. The transmission of this property from generation to generation, in the same name, raised up a distinct set of

---

*From an "Election Sermon" by Rev. Higginson, p. 69.

†William Smith, *The History of the Province of New York from the First Discovery to the Year 1732* (London: Thomas Wilcox, 1757).

‡William Penn (1644–1718).

§Benjamin Franklin (1706–1790).

‖David Bailie Warden (1772–1845), author of *Description statistique, historique et politique des Etats-Unis de l'Amérique septentrionale, depuis l'époque des premiers établissemens jusqu'à nos jours* (Paris: Rey et Gravier, 1820).

families, who, being privileged by law in the perpetuation of their wealth, were thus formed into a Patrician order, distinguished by the splendor and luxury of their establishments. From this order, too, the king habitually selected his counsellors of State." (*Jefferson's Memoirs.*)*

In the United States the principal provisions of English law relative to estates have been universally rejected.

"The first rule of inheritance," says Mr. Kent, "is, that if a person owning real estate, *dies seised,* or as owner, without devising the same, the estate shall descend to his lawful descendants in the direct line of lineal descent; and if there be but one person, then to him or her alone, and if more than one person, and all of equal degree of consanguinity to the ancestor, then the inheritance shall descend to the several persons as tenants in common in equal parts, [. . .] without distinction of sex."[†]

This rule was prescribed for the first time in the state of New York by a statute of February 23, 1786 (see *Revised Statutes,* vol. 3; Appendix, p. 48);[‡] it has since been adopted in the revised statutes of the same state. It now prevails in the whole extent of the United States with the sole exception that in the state of Vermont the male heir takes a double share. *Kent's Commentaries,* vol. 4, p. 370.

Mr. Kent, in the same work, vol. 4, pp. 1–22, gives a history of American legislation relative to entail. It turns out that before the American revolution, English laws of entail formed the common law of the colonies. Entails properly speaking were abolished in Virginia in 1776 (this abolition took place on the motion of Jefferson; see *Jefferson's Memoirs*), in the state of New York in 1786. The same abolition has since taken place in North Carolina, Kentucky, Tennessee, Georgia, Missouri. In Vermont, [and] the states of Indiana, Illinois, South Carolina, and Louisiana, entails have always been uncommon. The states that believed they should preserve English legislation relative to entail modified it in a manner that removes from it its principal aristocratic characteristics.

"The general policy of this country," says Mr. Kent, "does not encourage restraints upon the power of alienation of land."[§]

What singularly strikes the French reader who studies American legislation relative to estates is that our laws on the same matter are still infinitely more democratic than theirs.

American laws partition the goods of the father equally, but only in the case in which his will is not known: "[E]very person," says the law in the state of New York (*Revised Statues,* vol. 3; Appendix, p. 51), "shall have full and free liberty, power and authority to give, dispose, will or devise [his goods], to any person or persons, (except bodies politic and corporate,) by his last will and testament."[‖]

French law makes equal or almost equal partition the rule of the testator.

---

*Conseil, *Mélanges politiques et philosophiques,* 194.

†Kent, *Commentaries,* vol. 4, 371.

‡*Revised Statutes of the State of New York,* 48–50.

§See Kent, *Commentaries,* vol. 4, 17. AT quotes this sentence as follows: "Our general principles in the matter of government tend to favor the free circulation of property."

‖Law of March 3, 1787.

Most of the American republics still accept entails and limit them by restricting their effects.

French law does not permit entails in any case.

If the social state of the Americans is still more democratic than ours, our laws are therefore more democratic than theirs. This may be explained better than one thinks: in France, democracy is still occupied with demolishing; in America, it reigns tranquilly over ruins.

VIII. Page 55.

SUMMARY OF ELECTORAL CONDITIONS IN THE UNITED STATES. All states grant the enjoyment of electoral rights at twenty-one years. In all states, one must have resided for a certain time in the district where one votes. This time varies from three months to two years.

As for the property qualification: in the state of Massachusetts, one must have 3 pounds sterling in revenue or 60 in capital to be an elector.

In Rhode Island one must possess a landed property valued at 133 dollars (704 francs).

In Connecticut one must have a property from which the revenue is 17 dollars (around 90 francs). One year of service in the militia also gives an electoral right.

In New Jersey, the elector must have a fortune of 50 pounds sterling.

In South Carolina and Maryland the elector must possess 50 acres of land.

In Tennessee he must possess any property whatsoever.

In the states of Mississippi, Ohio, Georgia, Virginia, Pennsylvania, Delaware, New York, it suffices, to be an elector, to pay taxes: in most of these states, militia service is equivalent to payment of tax.

In Maine and in New Hampshire it suffices not to be carried on the list of indigents.

Finally, in the states of Missouri, Alabama, Illinois, Louisiana, Indiana, Kentucky, and Vermont, no condition relative to the fortune of the elector is required.

It is, I think, only North Carolina that imposes on electors of the Senate conditions other than those for electors of the House of Representatives. The former must possess a property of 50 acres of land. To be able to elect representatives it suffices to pay a tax.

IX. Page 90.

A system of protective tariffs exists in the United States. The small number of customs officers and the great extent of the coasts make smuggling very easy; nevertheless it is done infinitely less there than elsewhere because each man works to repress it.

As there is no preventive order in the United States, one sees more fires there than in Europe; but generally they are extinguished sooner because the surrounding population does not fail to get rapidly to the site of the danger.

X. Page 92.

It is not correct to say that centralization was born of the French Revolution; the French Revolution perfected it, but did not create it. In France the taste for centralization and the regulatory mania go back to the period when jurists entered the government, which brings us back to the time of Philip the Fair.* Since then, these two things have never ceased to grow. Here is what M. de Malesherbes, speaking in the name of the Cour des Aides, said to King Louis XVI in 1775:[3]

> The right to administer its own affairs remains for each body, for each community of citizens; a right that we do not say is part of the primitive constitution of the kingdom, for it goes back much further: it is natural right, it is the right of reason. Nevertheless, it has been taken away from your subjects, Sire, and we shall not fear to say that in this regard the administration has fallen into excesses that one can call puerile.
>
> Since powerful ministers have made a political principle of not allowing the National Assembly to be convoked, they have gone from one consequence to another as far as to declare null the deliberations of the inhabitants of a village when they were not authorized by an intendant, in a way that if that community has an expenditure to make, it must get the approval of the intendant's subdelegate, thereupon to follow the plan that he has adopted, to employ workers that he favors, to pay them according to his will; and, if the community has a lawsuit to bring, it must also have it authorized by the intendant. It is necessary that the cause be pled in this first tribunal before being brought before justice. And if the opinion of the intendant is contrary to the inhabitants, or if their adversary has credit with the intendancy, the community is deprived of the ability to defend its rights. There, Sire, are the means by which they have worked to stifle all municipal spirit in France, to extinguish, if one could, even the sentiments of citizens; they have so to speak *interdicted* the entire nation and they have given it schoolmasters.

Could one say better of today, when the French Revolution has made what one calls *its conquests* in the matter of centralization?

In 1789, Jefferson wrote from Paris to one of his friends: "Never was there a country where the practice of governing too much had taken deeper root and done more mischief." *Letters to Madison*, August 28, 1789.[†]

---

*Philip IV, King of France (1285–1314).

†Conseil, *Mélanges politiques et philosophiques*, 355–356.

3. See *Mémoires pour servir à l'histoire du droit public de la France en matière d'impôts*, p. 654, printed in Brussels in 1779. [Lamoignon de Malesherbes served under Louis XV and Louis XVI as President of the Cour des Aides, a body responsible for hearing appeals against the decisions of the administrative tribunals of the tax and finance authorities of the Old Regime; it also had the power to issue "Remonstrances" protesting policies that it considered violations of the "fundamental law" of France. The words of Malesherbes quoted by AT are part of a Remonstrance submitted to the King on May 6, 1775.]

The truth is that in France for several centuries the central power has always done everything it could to extend administrative centralization; it has never had any limits on this course other than its strength.

The central power born of the French Revolution has advanced further in this than any of its predecessors because it has been stronger and more skilled than any of them: Louis XIV submitted the details of communal existence to the pleasures of an intendant; Napoleon submitted them to those of a minister. It is still the same principle, extended to more or less distant consequences.

XI. Page 95.

This immutability of the constitution in France is a consequence forced by our laws.

And, to speak first of the most important of all laws, the one that regulates the order of succession to the throne, what is there more immutable in its principle than a political order founded on the natural order of succession of father to son? In 1814, Louis XVIII had this perpetuity of the law of political succession in favor of his family recognized; those who ruled over the consequences of the revolution of 1830 followed his example: only they established the perpetuity of the law to the profit of another family; in this they imitated Chancellor Maupeou,* who, in instituting the new Parlement on the ruins of the former one, took care to declare in the same ordinance that the new magistrates would be irremovable, as their predecessors were.

The laws of 1830 did not indicate, any more than those of 1814, any means of changing the constitution. Now, it is evident that ordinary means of legislation cannot suffice for that.

From whom does the king hold his powers? From the constitution. From whom do the peers? From the constitution. From whom do deputies? From the constitution. How therefore could the king, the peers, and the deputies, in uniting, change something in a law by virtue of which alone they govern? Beyond the constitution they are nothing: on what ground therefore would they place themselves to change the constitution? One of two things: either their efforts are powerless against the charter that continues to exist despite them, and then they continue to reign in its name; or they succeed in changing the charter, and then the law by which they used to exist no longer exists, and they themselves are no longer anything. In destroying the charter, they destroy themselves.

That is still more visible in the laws of 1830 than in those of 1814. In 1814, royal power was placed in a way outside and above the constitution; but in 1830 it is, by its own admission, created by the constitution and is absolutely nothing without it.

So therefore a part of our constitution is immutable because it has been joined to the destiny of one family; and the entirety of the constitution is equally immutable because one perceives no legal means of changing it.

All this is not applicable to England. England not having a written constitution, who can say that anyone is changing its constitution?

*Maupeou (1714–1792), chancellor under Louis XV.

XII. Page 95.

The most esteemed authors who have written on the English constitution almost vie to establish this omnipotence of Parliament.

De Lolme says, chap. 10, p. 77: *It is a fundamental principle with the English lawyers, that Parliament can do every thing, except making a woman a man or a man a woman.*[*]

Blackstone explains more categorically still, if not more energetically, than De Lolme in these terms:

> The power and jurisdiction of parliament, says Sir Edward Coke,[†] is so transcendent and absolute, that it cannot be confined, either for causes or persons, within any bounds. And of this high court, he adds, it may be truly said, *si antiquitatem spectes, est vetustissima; si dignitatem, est honoratissima; si jurisdictionem, est capacissima.*[‡] It hath sovereign and uncontrolable authority in the making, confirming, enlarging, restraining, abrogating, repealing, reviving, and expounding of laws, concerning matters of all possible denominations, ecclesiastical, or temporal, civil, military, maritime, or criminal: this being the place where that absolute despotic power, which must in all governments reside somewhere, is intrusted by the constitution of these kingdoms. All mischiefs and grievances, operations and remedies, that transcend the ordinary course of the laws, are within the reach of this extraordinary tribunal. It can regulate or new-model the succession to the crown; as was done in the reign of Henry VIII and William III. It can alter the established religion of the land; as was done in a variety of instances, in the reigns of king Henry VIII and his three children. *It can change and create afresh even the constitution of the kingdom* and of parliaments themselves; as was done by the act of union, and the several statutes for triennial and septennial elections. It can, in short, do everything that is not naturally impossible; and therefore some have not scrupled to call its power, by a figure rather too bold, the *omnipotence* of parliament.[§]

XIII. Page 104.

There is no matter on which the American [state] constitutions are in greater accord than on political judgment.

All the constitutions that take up this object give the House of Representatives the exclusive right to accuse, with the sole exception of the constitution of North Carolina, which accords this same right to grand juries (article 23).[‖]

Almost all the constitutions give the Senate, or the assembly that takes its place, the exclusive right to judge.

The sole penalties that the political tribunals can pronounce are: removal or bar-

[*]De Lolme, *The Constitution of England,* 84. AT quotes in English.
[†]Coke, *The Fourth Part of the Institutes of the Laws of England* (London: M. Flesher, 1648), 36.
[‡]"If you contemplate antiquity, it is the oldest; if dignity, it is the most honorable; if jurisdiction, it is the most capable."
[§]William Blackstone, *Commentaries on the Laws of England,* vol. 1, 160.
[‖]North Carolina Constitution of 1776.

ring from public office in the future. Only the constitution of Virginia permits them to pronounce all kinds of penalties.

The crimes that can give rise to political judgment are: in the federal constitution (art. 1, sec. 4),* in that of Indiana (art. 3, pp. 23 and 24),† of New York (art. 5),‡ of Delaware (art. 5),§ high treason, corruption, and great crimes or misdemeanors;

In the constitution of Massachusetts (chap. 1, sec. 2),‖ of North Carolina (art. 23),# and of Virginia (p. 252),** bad conduct and bad administration;

In the constitution of New Hampshire (p. 105),†† corruption, guilty maneuvers, and bad administration;

In Vermont (chap. 2, art. 24),‡‡ bad administration;

In South Carolina (art. 5),§§ Kentucky (art. 5),‖‖ Tennessee (art. 4),## Ohio (art. 1, secs. 23, 24),*** Louisiana (art. 5),††† Mississippi (art. 5).‡‡‡ Alabama (art. 6),§§§ Pennsylvania (art. 4),‖‖‖ offenses committed in office.

In the states of Illinois, Georgia, Maine, and Connecticut, no crime is specified.

XIV. Page 160.

It is true that the powers of Europe can make great maritime wars against the Union; but there is always more ease and less danger in sustaining a maritime war than a continental war. Maritime war requires only a single kind of effort. A commercial people that consents to give its government the necessary money is always sure of having fleets. Now, one can much more easily disguise sacrifices of money to nations than sacrifices of men and personal effort. Besides, defeats at sea rarely compromise the existence or independence of the people that experience them.

As for continental wars, it is evident that the peoples of Europe cannot make them dangerous for the American Union.

It is difficult indeed to transport and maintain in America more than 25,000 soldiers; this represents a nation of nearly 2,000,000 men. The greatest European nation in conflict in this manner against the Union is in the same position as would be a

*Art. 2, sec. 4.
†Indiana Constitution of 1816, art. 3, secs. 23 and 24.
‡New York Constitution of 1821, art. 5, secs. 1 and 2.
§Delaware Constitution of 1831.
‖Massachusetts Constitution of 1780, chap. 1, art. 8, sec. 2.
#North Carolina Constitution of 1776.
**Virginia Constitution of 1830, art. 3, sec. 13.
††New Hampshire Constitution of 1792, part 2, sec. 38.
‡‡Vermont Constitution of 1793.
§§South Carolina Constitution of 1790.
‖‖Kentucky Constitution of 1799.
##Tennessee Constitution of 1796.
***Ohio Constitution of 1802.
†††Louisiana Constitution of 1812.
‡‡‡Mississippi Constitution of 1817.
§§§Alabama Constitution of 1819, art. 5.
‖‖‖Pennsylvania Constitution of 1790.

nation of 2,000,000 inhabitants at war against one of 12,000,000. Add to this that the American has within reach all his resources and the European is 1,500 leagues from his, and that the immensity of the territory of the United States would alone present an insurmountable obstacle to conquest.

VOLUME ONE, PART TWO

XV. Page 178.

It was in April 1704 that the first American newspaper appeared. It was published in Boston. See *Collection of the Historical Society of Massachusetts,* vol. 6, p. 66.

One would be wrong to believe that the periodical press has always been entirely free in America; there were attempts to establish something analogous to prior censorship and to surety.

Here is what one finds in the legislative documents of Massachusetts, dated January 14, 1722.

The committee named by the General Assembly (the legislative body of the province) to examine the affair relating to the newspaper entitled *New England Courier,*

> thinks that the tendency of said newspaper is to greet religion derisively and to make it fall into contempt; that the holy authors are treated in a profane and irreverent manner in it; that the conduct of the ministers of the Gospel is interpreted with malice; that the government of His Majesty is insulted, and that the peace and tranquillity of this province are troubled by said newspaper; consequently, the committee is of the opinion that James Franklin, printer and editor, should be forbidden to print and publish said journal or any other writing any more in the future before having submitted them to the secretary of the province. Justices of the peace of the district of Suffolk shall be charged with obtaining from Mr. Franklin a surety that vouches for his good conduct for the coming year.

The proposition of the committee was accepted and became law, but its effect was null. The newspaper eluded the prohibition by putting the name of *Benjamin* Franklin instead of *James* Franklin at the bottom of its columns, and opinion succeeded in doing justice upon the measure.

XVI. Page 260.

In order to be electors in counties (those who represent landed property) before the Reform Bill passed in 1832, one had to have in sole ownership or in lease for life a land-holding bringing 40 shillings net in revenue. This law was made under Henry VI around 1450. It has been calculated that 40 shillings at the time of Henry VI might be the equivalent of 30 pounds sterling in our day. Nevertheless, they allowed this basis adopted in the fifteenth century to continue until 1832, which proves how much the English constitution became democratic with time, even while appearing unmoving. See De Lolme; see also Blackstone, bk. 1, chap. 4.

English jurors are chosen by the county sheriff (De Lolme, 1st bk., chap. 12). The sheriff is generally a considerable man in the county; he fills judicial and administrative posts; he represents the king, and is named by him every year (Blackstone, bk. 1, chap. 9). His position places him above suspicion of corruption by the parties; moreover, if his impartiality is put in doubt, they can recuse the entire jury that he has named, and then another officer is charged with choosing new jurors. See Blackstone, bk. 3, chap. 23.

To have the right to be a juror, one must be the owner of a land-holding of a value of at least 10 shillings in revenue (Blackstone, bk. 3, chap. 23). One will remark that this condition was imposed under the reign of William and Mary, that is to say around 1700, a period when the price of money was infinitely higher than in our day. One sees that the English founded their jury system not on capacity, but on landed property, like all their other political institutions.

In the end they admitted farmers to the jury, but they required that their leases be very long and that they make a net revenue of 20 shillings independently of the rent (Blackstone, idem).

XVII. Page 261.

The federal constitution introduced the jury into the courts of the Union in the same way that the states themselves had introduced it into their particular courts; it did not establish in addition rules of its own for choosing jurors. The federal courts draw jurors from the ordinary list that each state has drawn up for its use. It is therefore the laws of the states that one must examine to learn the theory of jury composition in America. See *Story's Commentaries on the Constitution*, book. 3, chap. 38, pp. 654–659.* *Sergeant's Constitutional Law*, p. 165.[†] See also the federal laws of 1789, 1800, and 1802 on the matter.

In order to make well known the principles of the Americans in regard to the composition of the jury, I have drawn from the laws of states far removed from one another. Here are the general ideas that one can derive from this examination.

In America, all citizens who are voters have the right to be jurors. The great state of New York has nevertheless established a slight difference between the two capacities; but it is in a direction contrary to our laws; that is to say, there are fewer jurors in the state of New York than voters. In general, one can say that in the United States the right to take part in a jury, like the right to elect representatives, extends to everyone; but the exercise of this right is not put indiscriminately in all hands.

Each year a body of municipal or district magistrates, called *selectmen* in New England, *supervisors* in the state of New York, *trustees* in Ohio, *parish sheriffs* in Louisiana, choose for each district a certain number of citizens having the right to be jurors, and in whom they suppose the capacity to be such. These magistrates, being elective themselves, do not arouse distrust; their powers are very extensive and quite

*Story, *Commentary*, 654ff.

†Thomas Sergeant, *Constitutional Law; Being a View of the Practice and Jurisdiction of the Courts of the United States and of the Constitutional Points Decided* (Philadelphia, 1830), 165.

arbitrary, like those of republican magistrates generally, and they often use them, it is said, to turn away unworthy or incapable jurors, above all in New England.

The names of jurors thus chosen are transmitted to the county court, and out of the sum of these names one draws by lot the jury that is to pronounce in each affair.

Furthermore, Americans have sought by all possible means to put the jury within reach of the people, and to make it as little burdensome as possible. Jurors being very numerous, each one's turn comes up scarcely every three years. The sessions are held at each county seat; the county closely corresponds to our *arrondissement*. Thus, the court is located near the jury instead of bringing the jury near it, as in France; finally, the jurors are compensated, either by the state or by the parties. They generally receive a dollar (5.42 F) a day, independent of the expenses of the trip. In America the jury is still regarded as a burden; but it is a burden easy to bear, and to which one submits without trouble.

See *Brevard's Digest of the Public Statute Law of South-Carolina*, 2d vol., p. 338; vol. 1, pp. 454 and 456; vol. 1, p. 218.*

See *The General Laws of Massachusetts Revised and Published by Authority of the Legislature*, vol. 2, pp. 331, 187.

See *The Revised Statutes of the State of New York*, vol. 2, pp. 720, 411, 717, 643.

See *The Statute Law of the State of Tennessee*, vol. 1, p. 209.

See *Acts of the State of Ohio*, pp. 95 and 210.

See *General Digest of the Acts of the Legislature of Louisiana*, vol. 2, p. 55.

XVIII. Page 263.

When one examines closely the constitution of the civil jury among the English, one readily discovers that the jurors never escape the control of the judge.

It is true that the verdict of the jury, civil as well as criminal, generally comprises in a simple statement fact and law. Example: a house is claimed by Peter as having been bought: there is the fact. His adversary opposes to him the incapacity of the seller: there is the right. The jury is limited to saying that the house shall be put back into the hands of Peter; it thus decides fact and right. In introducing the jury into civil matters, the English have not preserved for the jurors' opinion the infallibility that they accord it in criminal matters, when the verdict is favorable.

If the judge thinks that the verdict has made a wrong application of the law, he can refuse to accept it and send the jurors back to deliberate.

If the judge lets the verdict pass without observation, the case is still not entirely closed: there are several avenues of recourse open against the decree. The principal one consists in requesting of the court that the verdict be annulled and that a new jury be assembled. It is true to say that such a request is rarely granted, and never more than twice; nonetheless I have seen the case happen before my eyes. See Blackstone, bk. 3, chap. 24; idem, bk. 3, chap. 25.

---

*Joseph Brevard, *An Alphabetical Digest of the Public Statute Law of South-Carolina* (Charleston, 1814).

VOLUME TWO, PART TWO

XIX. Page 527.

There are, however, aristocracies that have carried on commerce with ardor and cultivated industry with success. The history of the world offers several striking examples of this. But, in general, one should say that aristocracy is not favorable to the development of industry and commerce. It is only aristocracies of money that are the exception to this rule.

Among those, there is scarcely a desire that does not need wealth to be satisfied. The love of wealth becomes so to speak the great road of the human passions. All others end at it or cross through it.

The taste for money and the thirst for consideration and power are then so well confused in the same souls that it becomes difficult to discern whether it is out of ambition that men are greedy or whether it is out of greed that they are ambitious. This is what happens in England, where they want to be wealthy in order to get honors, and where they desire honors as a manifestation of wealth. The human spirit is then seized at all extremes and carried along toward commerce and industry, which are the shortest routes leading to opulence.

This fact, furthermore, seems to me exceptional and transitory. When wealth has become the only sign of aristocracy, it is difficult indeed for the wealthy to maintain themselves alone in power and to exclude all others from it.

Aristocracy of birth and pure democracy are at the two extremities of the social and political state of nations; in the middle is aristocracy of money; this comes close to aristocracy of birth in that it confers great privileges on a few citizens; it is connected to democracy in that the privileges can be acquired by all in turn; it often forms almost a natural transition between these two things, and one cannot say whether it ends in the reign of aristocratic institutions or whether it is already opening the new era of democracy.

VOLUME TWO, PART THREE

XX. Page 567.

In the journal of my voyage I find the following piece that will serve to make known the trials to which the women of America who consent to accompany their spouses to the wilderness are often subjected. There is nothing that recommends this portrait to the reader but its great truth.

... We encounter new clearings from time to time. All these settlements resemble each other. I am going to describe the one where we have stopped this night; it will leave me an image of all the others.

The little bell that the pioneers took care to suspend from the necks of livestock so as to find them in the woods announced to us the approach of the clearing from very far away; soon we heard the noise of the hatchet that brings down the trees of the forest. As we approach, traces of destruction announce the presence of civilized man. Cut branches cover the path; trunks half-charred by fire or mutilated by the ax are still standing along our passage. We continue our advance and we come to a wood in which all the trees seem to have been struck by a sudden death; in the middle of summer they present only the image of winter; in examining them more closely, we perceive that a deep circle has been cut in their bark which, by stopping the circulation of the sap, has quickly made them die; we learn that, in fact, the pioneer ordinarily begins with that. Not being able during the first year to cut all the trees that decorate his new property, he sows corn under their branches and, by striking them dead, he prevents them from putting shade over his harvest. After this field, a rough draft, the first step of civilization into the wilderness, we suddenly perceive the hut of the owner; it is placed in the center of ground more carefully cultivated than the rest, but where man nevertheless still sustains an unequal struggle against the forest; there the trees are cut, but not uprooted, their trunks still decorate and clutter the ground that they formerly shaded. Around this withered debris wheat, offshoots of oaks, plants of all kinds, herbs of every nature grow pell-mell and get larger together on an unruly and half-wild soil. In the midst of this vigorous and varied vegetation rises the house of the pioneer or, as one calls it in that country, the *log-house*. This rustic dwelling, like the field that surrounds it, tells of a new and hasty work; its length does not appear to us to exceed thirty feet, its height fifteen; its walls as well as the roof are formed of unhewn tree trunks between which moss and earth have been placed to prevent the cold and rain from penetrating inside.

Night approaching, we determine to go ask refuge of the owner of the log-house.

At the noise of our steps, the children who were rolling in the midst of the debris get up in a rush and flee toward the house as if frightened at the sight of a man, while two large, half-wild dogs, ears straight and muzzles extended, leave the hut and come growling to cover the retreat of their young masters. The pioneer himself appears at the door of his dwelling; he casts a rapid, scrutinizing glance at us, makes a sign to his dogs to re-enter the home, and sets them his own example without giving evidence that the sight of us excites his curiosity or his anxiety.

We enter into the log-house: the interior does not at all recall the peasant huts of Europe; one finds in it more of the superfluous and less of the necessary.

There is only a single window from which a muslin curtain hangs; in a hearth of trodden earth a great fire crackles that lights the whole inside of the building; above this hearth one perceives a fine scratched rifle, a deerskin, some eagle feathers; to the right of the chimney a map of the United States is spread out, which the wind lifts and agitates as it gets through the chinks in the wall; near to it on a shelf formed of a badly hewn board a few volumes have been placed; I notice on it the Bible, the first six cantos of Milton, and two plays of Shakespeare; along the length of the walls trunks instead of cupboards are placed; in the center is a coarsely worked table, whose feet, formed of wood that is still green and not stripped of bark, seem to have pushed through the ground that it occupies; I see on this table a teapot of English porcelain, some silver spoons, a few chipped cups, and some newspapers.

The master of this dwelling has the angular features and slender limbs that distinguish the inhabitant of New England; it is evident that this man was not born in the solitudes where we encounter him: his physical constitution is enough to tell that his first years were passed in the heart of an intellectual society and that he belongs to the restive, reasoning, and adventurous race that does coldly what only the ardor of the passions explains, and that submits for a time to a wild life in order better to vanquish and civilize the wilderness.

When the pioneer perceives that we have crossed the threshold of his dwelling, he comes to meet us and extends his hand to us, according to usage; but his face remains rigid; he is the first to speak, to interrogate us about what is happening in the world, and when he has satisfied his curiosity, he falls silent; one would believe him worn out by unwelcome visitors and the noise. We interrogate him in our turn, and he gives us all the information that we need; afterwards, he busies himself without hurry, but with diligence, to provide for our needs. Seeing him thus engaged in these benevolent attentions, why, despite ourselves, do we feel our gratitude chill? It is that he himself, in exercising hospitality, seems to submit to a painful necessity of his lot: he sees in it a duty that his position imposes on him, not a pleasure.

At the other end of the hearth a woman is seated who cradles a young child on her knees; without interrupting herself she makes a signal to us with her head. Like the pioneer, this woman is in the flower of age, her appearance seems superior to her condition, her dress even announces a taste for finery still barely extinguished; but her delicate limbs appear diminished, her features are tired, her eye is mild and grave; one sees spread over her whole face a religious resignation, a profound peace of the passions, and a natural and tranquil firmness that confronts all the evils of life without fearing them or braving them.

Her children press around her; they are full of health, turbulence, and energy; they are true sons of the wilderness; from time to time, their mother casts glances full of melancholy and joy at them; to see their strength and her weakness one would say that she has exhausted herself in giving them life and that she does not regret what they have cost her.

The house inhabited by the emigrants has neither interior partition nor attic. In the lone apartment that it contains the entire family comes to seek refuge at night. This dwelling forms, by itself, almost a little world; it is the ark of civilization lost in the middle of an ocean of foliage. A hundred steps further on, the eternal forest extends its shadow around it, and solitude begins again.

XXI. Page 568.

It is not equality of conditions that renders men immoral and irreligious. But when men are immoral and irreligious at the same time that they are equal, the effects of immorality and irreligion are readily produced outwardly, because men have little effect on one another and no class exists that takes charge of policing society. Equality of conditions never creates the corruption of mores, but sometimes allows it to appear.

XXII. Page 585.

If one puts aside all those who do not think and who dare not say what they think, one will still find that the immense majority of Americans appear satisfied with the political institutions that rule them; and, in fact, I believe that they are. I regard these dispositions of public opinion as an index, but not as a proof of the absolute goodness of American laws. National pride, the satisfaction given to certain dominant passions by legislation, fortuitous events, unperceived vices, and more than all that, the interest of a majority that shuts the mouths of opponents can for a long time fool a whole people as well as one man.

Look at England in the whole course of the eighteenth century. Never has a nation lavished itself with more incense; no people has ever been more perfectly content with itself; then, all was well in its constitution, everything in it was even irreproach-able, including its most visible defects. Today a multitude of English seem to be occu-pied only in proving that this same constitution was defective in a thousand places. Who was right, the English people of the last century or the English people of our day?

The same thing happened in France. It is certain that the great mass of the nation under Louis XIV was passionate for the form of government that then ruled society. Those who believe there was debasement in the French character of that time are greatly mistaken. In that century there might have been servitude in France in certain respects, but the spirit of servitude was certainly not there. The writers of the time felt a sort of real enthusiasm in elevating the royal power above all the others, and there was not even an obscure peasant in his humble cottage who did not take pride in the glory of the sovereign and who did not die of joy in crying: "Long live the king!" These same forms have become odious to us. Who was mistaken, the French under Louis XIV or the French of our day?

One must therefore not base oneself on the dispositions of a people alone to judge its laws, since they change from one century to another, but on more elevated grounds and a more general experience.

The love that a people shows for its laws proves only one thing, which is that one must not hasten to change them.

XXIII. Page 629.

In the chapter to which this note relates I have just shown one peril; I want to indicate another one—rarer, but which, if it ever appeared, would be much more to be feared.

If the love of material enjoyments and taste for well-being that equality naturally suggests to men, taking hold of the spirit of a democratic people, came to fill it as a whole, national mores would become so antipathetic to the military spirit that armies themselves would perhaps in the end love peace despite the particular interest that brings them to desire war. Placed in the midst of this universal softness, soldiers would come to think it worth more to rise in peace gradually, but comfortably and without effort, than to buy rapid advancement at the price of the fatigue and the misery of life in a camp. In this spirit the army would take up its arms without ardor and would use them without energy; it would allow itself to be led to the enemy rather than advancing to it itself.

One must not believe that this pacific disposition of the army would drive it away from revolutions, for revolutions, and above all military revolutions, which are ordi-narily very rapid, often bring along great perils, but not long travails; they satisfy ambition at less cost than war; one risks only one's life, which men of democracies cling to less than their ease.

There is nothing more dangerous for the freedom and the tranquillity of a people than an army that fears war, because, when it no longer seeks its greatness and influence on the fields of battle, it wants to find them elsewhere. It could therefore happen that the men who composed a democratic army might lose the interests of the citizen without acquiring the virtue of the soldier, and that the army might cease to be warlike without ceasing to be turbulent.

I shall repeat here what I have already said above. The remedy for such dangers is not in the army, but in the country. A democratic people that preserves virile mores will always find warlike mores in its soldiers as needed.

VOLUME TWO, PART FOUR

XXIV. Page 643.

Men put the greatness of the idea of unity in the means, God in the end; hence it is that the idea of greatness leads us to a thousand [instances] of pettiness. To force all men to march in the same march, toward the same object—that is a human idea. To introduce an infinite variety into actions, but to combine them in a manner so that all these actions lead by a thousand diverse ways toward the accomplishment of one great design—that is a divine idea.

The human idea of unity is almost always sterile, that of God immensely fertile. Men believe they give witness to their greatness in simplifying the means: it is the object of God that is simple, his means vary infinitely.

XXV. Page 645.

A democratic people is brought not only by its tastes to centralize power; the passions of all those who lead it constantly push it toward that.

One can easily foresee that almost all the ambitious and capable citizens that a democratic country contains will work without respite to extend the prerogatives of the social power, because all hope to direct it one day. It is a waste of one's time to want to prove to them that extreme centralization can be harmful to the state, since they centralize for themselves.

Among the public men of democracies there are scarcely any but very disinterested or very mediocre people who want to decentralize power. The former are rare and the latter powerless.

XXVI. Page 662.

I have often wondered what would happen if, in the midst of the softness of democratic mores and as a consequence of the restive spirit of the army, a military government were ever founded in some of the nations of our day.

I think that the government itself would not be far removed from the picture that

I have sketched in the chapter to which this note relates, and that it would not reproduce the savage features of military oligarchy.

I am convinced that in this case a sort of fusion between the habits of the clerk and that of the soldier would be made. The administration would take something from the military spirit and the military some usages from the civil administration. The result of this would be a regular, clear, clean, absolute command; the people having become an image of the army and society kept like a barracks.

XXVII. Page 665.

One cannot say in an absolute and general manner whether the great danger of our day is license or tyranny, anarchy or despotism. Both are equally to be feared and can as easily issue from one and the same cause, which is *general apathy,* the fruit of individualism; it is through this apathy that on the day when the executive power gathers its forces, it is in a position to oppress, and that on the day after, when a party can put thirty men into battle, the latter is equally in a position to oppress. Since neither the one nor the other can found anything lasting, what makes them succeed easily prevents them from succeeding for long. They rise because nothing can resist them, and they fall because nothing sustains them.

What it is important to combat is therefore much less anarchy or despotism than the apathy that can create the one or the other almost indifferently.

SOURCES CITED BY TOCQUEVILLE

Account of an Expedition from Pittsburgh to the Rocky Mountains; Performed in the Years 1819 and '20 . . . under the Command of Major Stephen H. Long. From the Notes of Major Long, Mr. T. Say, and Other Gentlemen of the Exploring Party. Compiled by Edwin James. 2 vols. Philadelphia, 1823.

Acts of a General Nature of the State of Ohio. Columbus, 1831.

Adair, James. *The History of the American Indians: Particularly Those Nations Adjoining to the Mississippi, East and West Florida, Georgia, South and North Carolina, and Virginia; Containing an Account of Their Origin, Language, Manners, Religious and Civil Customs, Laws, Form of Government, Punishments, Conduct in War and Domestic Life; Their Habits, Diet, Agriculture, Manufactures, Disease and Methods of Cure. . . .* London, 1775.

American Almanac and Repository of Useful Knowledge for the Year 1831. Also . . . *for the Year 1832* and . . . *for the year 1834.* Boston: Gray and Bowen, 1831, 1832, 1834.

Beaumont, Gustave de. *Marie; ou, L'esclavage aux Etats-Unis: Tableau de moeurs américaines.* Brussels: Louis Hauman, 1835.

Belknap, Jeremy. *History of New Hampshire.* 2 vols. Boston, 1792.

———. *Queries Respecting the Slavery and Emancipation of the Negroes in Massachusetts, Proposed by the Hon. Judge Tucker of Virginia, and Answered by the Rev. Dr. Belknap,* in *Collections of the Massachusetts Historical Society for the Year 1795.* Boston: Samuel Hall, n.d.

Beverley, Robert. *The History and Present State of Virginia.* London: R. Parker, 1705. French edition: *Histoire de la Virginie.* Amsterdam: T. Lombrail, 1707.

Blackstone, William. *Commentaries on the Laws of England.* London, 1809.

Blosseville, Ernest de. *Histoire des colonies pénales de l'Angleterre dans l'Australie,* Paris: Adrien le Clere, 1831. See also Tanner, John.

Brevard, Joseph. *An Alphabetical Digest of the Public Statute Law of South-Carolina.* Charleston, S.C.: John Hoff, 1814.

Carey, Matthew. *Letters on the Colonization Society and on Its Probable Results.* Philadelphia: Johnson, 1833.

Chalmers, George. *An Introduction to the History of the Revolt of the American Colonies.* London, 1782.

Charlevoix, Pierre-François-Xavier de. *Histoire et description générale de la Nouvelle France.* 6 vols. Paris: Chez Nyon Fils, 1744.

Code of 1650: Being a Compilation of the Earliest Laws and Orders of the General Court of Connecticut: Also, the Constitution, or Civil Compact, Entered Into and Adopted by the Towns of Windsor, Hartford, and Wethersfield in 1638–39: To Which Is Added Some Extracts from the Laws and Judicial Proceedings of New-Haven Colony, Commonly Called Blue Laws. Hartford: S. Andrus, 1830.

Code of Practice in Civil Cases, for the State of Louisiana, in English and French, 1825. Published in Louisiana Legal Archives, vol. 2, 1937.

Coke, Sir Edward. *The Fourth Part of the Institutes of the Laws of England.* London: M. Flesher, 1648.

Collections of the Massachusetts Historical Society. Boston, 1792.

Conseil, Louis. *Mélanges politiques et philosophiques extraits des Mémoirs et de la Correspondance de Thomas Jefferson.* 2 vols. Paris: Paulin, 1833. AT often refers to this abridged edition when he cites *Jefferson's Memoirs.*

Cooper, Thomas. *The Statutes at Large of South Carolina.* Vol. 1. Columbia, S.C., 1836.

Darby, William. *View of the United States: Historical, Geographical, and Statistical.* Philadelphia: H. S. Tanner, 1828.

Descourtilz, Michel Etienne. *Flore pittoresque et médicale des Antilles; ou, Histoire naturelle des plantes usuelles des colonies françaises, anglaises, espagnoles, et portugaises.* 8 vols. Paris, 1833.

Duponceau, Peter Stephen. Translator's Preface to "Grammar of the Language of the Lenni Lenape, or Delaware Indians," by David Zeisberger. In *Transactions of the American Philosophical Society,* vol. 3. Philadelphia, 1830.

Emerson, Gouverneur. *Medical Statistics: Consisting of Estimates Relating to the Population of Philadelphia, with Its Changes as Influenced by the Deaths and Births, during Ten Years.* Philadelphia: Skerret, 1831.

Fischer, Jean-Eberhard. *De l'origine des Américains.* Saint Petersburg, 1771.

Force, Peter. *The National Calendar and Annals of the United States.* Washington, D.C., 1833.

General Laws of Massachusetts. Boston, 1823.

Goodwin, Isaac. *Town Officer; or, Laws of Massachusetts Relative to the Duties of Municipal Officers.* 2d edition. Worcester, Mass., 1829.

Gookin, Daniel. *Historical Collections of the Indians in New England;* in *Collections of the Massachusetts Historical Society.* Boston, 1792.

Hamilton, Alexander, James Madison, and John Jay. *The Federalists on the Constitution Written in the Year 1788.* Washington, D.C., 1831.

Hazard, Ebenezer. *Historical Collection[s, Consisting] of State Papers and Other Authentic Documents Intended as Materials for an History of the United States of America.* Philadelphia, 1792.

Heckewelder, Rev. John. "Correspondence between Mr. Heckewelder and Mr. Duponceau, On the Languages of the American Indians." In *Transactions of the Historical and Literary Committee of the American Philosophical Society,* vol. 1. Philadelphia, 1819.

Humboldt, Alexander von. *Vues des Cordillères, et monumens des peuples indigènes de l'Amérique*. Paris: Chez F. Schoell, 1813.

Hutchinson, Thomas. *The History of the Colony of Massachuset's Bay: From the First Settlement Thereof in 1628 until Its Incorporation with the Colony of Plimouth, Province of Main, &c. by the Charter of King William and Queen Mary, in 1691*. 2d edition. London, 1765.

Indian Treaties and Laws and Regulations Relating to Indian Affairs. Edited by Samuel S. Hamilton. Washington, D.C., 1826.

Jefferson, Thomas. *Notes on the State of Virginia*. AT used a French edition: *Observations sur la Virginie*, trans. Morellet (Paris: Barrois, 1786). Jefferson's friend Charles Thomson, Secretary of Congress, wrote a commentary on the *Notes*, which Jefferson included as an appendix to his work. The edition AT used quietly incorporates both Thomson's comments and Jefferson's own notes directly into the text of *Notes on the State of Virginia*. AT's edition also rearranges Jefferson's work. Cf. Jefferson, *Notes on the State of Virginia*. Chapel Hill, N.C., 1955.

Jefferson's Memoirs. See Conseil, *Mélanges politiques et philosophiques*.

Kent, James. *Commentaries on American Law*. 4 vols. New York: O. Halsted, 1826–1830.

Laws of the Colonial and State Governments Relating to Indians and Indian Affairs from 1633 to 1831 Inclusive. Washington, D.C., 1832.

Lawson, John. *The History of Carolina*. London, 1718.

Lislet, L. Moreau. *A General Digest of the Acts of the Legislature of Louisiana Passed from the Year 1804, to 1827, Inclusive*. 2 vols. New Orleans, 1828.

Lolme, Jean Louis de. *The Constitution of England*. London, 1826.

Malte-Brun, Conrad, ed. *Annales des voyages, de la géographie et de l'histoire*. 24 vols. Paris: Brunet, 1808–1814.

———. *Précis de la géographie universelle; ou, Description de toutes les parties du monde, sur un plan nouveau. . . .* 8 vols. Paris, 1810–1829. English edition: *Universal Geography; or, a Description of All Parts of the World, on a New Plan*, 8 vols. Boston, 1824– .

Marshall, John. *Vie de George Washington*. 5 vols. Paris: Dentu, 1807. English edition: *The Life of George Washington*. London, 1804.

Mather, Cotton. *Magnalia Christi Americana; or, The Ecclesiastical History of New-England*. Hartford, 1820.

Morton, Nathaniel. *New-England's Memorial; or, A Brief Relation of the Most Memorable and Remarkable Passages of the Providence of God, Manifested to the Planters of New-England in America: With Special Reference to the First Colony Thereof, Called New-Plimouth*. Boston, 1826. [This work borrows heavily from William Bradford's *Of Plymouth Plantation*, the manuscript of which was lost until 1858.]

Pickering, John. "Indian Languages of America." Appendix to vol. 6 of *Encyclopædia Americana*, edited by Francis Lieber. Philadelphia, 1829–1833.

Pitkin, Timothy. *A Political and Civil History of the United States of America: From the Year 1763 to the Close of the Administration of President Washington, in March, 1797: Including a Summary View of the Political and Civil State of the North American Colonies Prior to That Period*. 2 vols. New Haven, 1828.

Pratz, Le Page du. *Histoire de la Louisiane, contenant la découverte de ce vaste pays; sa description géographique; un voyage dans les terres; l'histoire naturelle, les moeurs, coutumes et religion des naturels, avec leurs origines; deux voyages dans le nord du nouveau Mexique, dont un jusqu'à la Mer du Sud,* 3 vols. Paris, 1758. English edition: *The History of Louisiana, or of the Western Parts of Virginia and Carolina.* . . . 2 vols. London, 1763.

Proceedings of the Indian Board in the City of New York. [*Documents and Proceedings Relating to the Formation and Progress of a Board in the City of New York for the Emigration, Preservation, and Improvement of the Aborigines of America,* July 22, 1829 (New York: Vanderpool and Cole, 1829).]

Proud, Robert. *The History of Pennsylvania, from the Original Institution and Settlement of That Province, under the First Proprietor and Governor William Penn, in 1681 till after the Year 1742.* 2 vols. Philadelphia, 1797–1798.

Purdon, John. *Digest of the Laws of Pennsylvania.* Philadelphia, 1831.

Revised Statutes of the State of New York, The. 3 vols. Albany, 1829.

Saulnier, Sébastien L. "Nouvelles observations sur les finances des Etats-Unis, en réponse à une brochure publiée par le Général La Fayette." *Revue Britannique* (October 8, 1831): 195–260.

Sergeant, Thomas. *Constitutional Law; Being a View of the Practice and Jurisdiction of the Courts of the United States and of the Constitutional Points Decided.* Philadelphia, 1830.

Smith, John. *The Generall Historie of Virginia, New England, and the Summer Isles: With the Names of the Adventurers, Planters, and Governours from Their First Beginning, Ano: 1584, to This Present 1624.* London: Michael Sparkes, 1624.

Smith, William. *The History of the Province of New York from the First Discovery to the Year 1732.* London: Thomas Wilcox, 1757 (French translation, London, 1767).

Statute Laws of the State of Tennessee, The. Knoxville, 1831.

Stith, William. *The History of the First Discovery and Settlement of Virginia: Being an Essay towards a General History of This Colony.* 8 vols. Williamsburg, Va.: William Parks, 1747.

Story, Joseph. *Commentary on the Constitution of the United States.* Boston, 1833. This is the abridged edition used by AT.

———. *Public and General Statutes Passed by the Congress of the United States, 1789–1827.* Boston, 1828.

Tanner, John. *A Narrative of the Captivity and Adventures of John Tanner, during Thirty Years Residence among the Indians in the Interior of North America.* New York: G. & C. & H. Carvill, 1830. French translation: *Mémoires de John Tanner; ou, Trente années dans les déserts de l'Amérique du Nord.* Translated by Ernest de Blosseville. Paris: A. Bertrand, 1835.

Trumbull, Benjamin. *A Complete History of Connecticut, Civil and Ecclesiastical.* 2 vols. New Haven, 1818.

U.S. Congress. House. "Cherokee Indians, Memorial of, by the Delegation of." 21st Cong., 1st sess., 1829–1830. H. Rep. 311, serial 201.

U.S. Congress. House. "Commerce and Navigation of U.S." 21st Cong., 2d sess., 1830. H. Doc. 140, serial 209.

U.S. Congress. House. "Indians, Laws of Colonial and State Governments Relating to." 21st Cong., 1st sess., 1829–1830. H. Rep. 319, serial 201.

U.S. Congress. House. "Intrusions on Cherokee Lands." 21st Cong., 1st sess., 1830. H. Doc. 89, serial 197.

U.S. Congress. House. "On Indian Affairs." 20th Cong., 2d sess., 1829. H. Doc. 117, serial 186.

U.S. Congress. House. "Removal of the Indians." 21st Cong., 1st sess., 1830. H. Rep. 227, serial 200.

U.S. Congress. House. 20th Cong., 2d sess., 1828–1829. H. Rep. 87, serial 190.

U.S. Congress. Senate. "Presidential Message with Proclamations, Proceedings, and Documents, on Measures of South Carolina and General Government on Nullification." 22d Cong., 2d sess., 1832–1833. Sen. Doc. 30, serial 230.

Volney, Constantin F. *Tableau du climat et du sol des Etats-Unis d'Amérique.* Paris: Boussangue Frères, 1822.

Warden, David Bailie. *Description statistique, historique et politique des Etats-Unis de l'Amérique septentrionale, depuis l'époque des premiers établissemens jusqu'à nos jours.* Paris: Rey et Gravier, 1820.

Williams, Edwin. *The New York Annual Register.* New York, 1832.

I N D E X

Abolition: and civil war, 346; effects on prejudice, 328–30, 343–45; effects on slaves,
335–37; obstacles to, in the South, 337–41,
345–48. *See also* Slavery

Adair, James, 24n

Adams, John Quincy, 126

Administration: centralization of, 79n, 82–85,
250–51, 380, 494; in China, 86n; in counties, 66, 76–78, 88; and court of sessions,
73–74, 76; and crime, 91; decentralization
of, 82–93; and democratic despotism,
661–65; in England, 83; in Europe, 85, 87–
89, 652–55; and executive power, 82; in
France, 83, 92; general ideas about, 75–79;
hierarchy in, 73, 77–78; instability of, 198–
99, 239; and justices of the peace, 78, 82;
and legislative power, 80; in New England, 66–75; and omnipotence of the majority, 238–39; outside of New England,
76–80; political effects of, 90; and townships, 58–59, 63, 78. *See also* Centralization; Decentralization

Aesop, 327n

Africa, 304, 344–45. *See also* Liberia

Agriculture, 338–39, 529, 553–55; in democracies, 526–27; in France, 556

Alabama, 306, 321n, 691

Alexander the Great, 630

Allegheny Mountains, 20–21, 355–56, 364

Ambassadors, 135

Ambition: in aristocracies, 603–5; in democracies, 594, 599–605, 624; and elections, 120,

195; of magistrates, 259n; military, 618–21;
and parties, 169; in republics, 150–51, 153;
and revolutions, 600; in townships,
64–65; and wealth, love of, 293, 594

Amphictyons, 148n

Anarchy: and apathy, 704; and association,
freedom of, 184, 500; and decentralization, 67, 85; and elections, 85, 123–24; and
equality, development of, 660; fear of,
causing concentration of power, 639–40,
644, 649, 659, 672; fear of, used by Federalists, 168; and federal system, 148; influence on Anglo-American development,
393–94; intellectual, 407, 612; and judicial
power, expansion of, 70; in Mexico, 156;
in Middle Ages, 592; and nullification,
375; and religion, 281; and Supreme
Court, corrupt, 142; and township spirit,
64; and tyranny of the majority, 248–49;
and the Union, 368, 370

Antiquity: republics of, 201, 266–67, 289; slavery in, 327–28, 334, 346–47, 413; tyranny
in, 301. *See also* Greeks; Rome

Apathy, 631, 704

Aristocracies: ambition in, 603–5; armies of,
618, 624, 627, 630, 633–34; arts in, 439–40;
class interests in, 224; corruption in,
210–12; crime in, 91; eloquence in, 472–73,
476; and estate laws, 46–47; and expenditures, 201–5; and external affairs, 219–20;
family in, 561–63; and greatness, 615; happiness in, 8–10; historians in, 469–72;

e suivant Darby

AMÉRIQUE

Montagnes

RÉPUB

ligne qui indique la

Misouri R.

QUE

R. Rouge

Rocheuses

DE

P.A. 13.0

Arkansas R.

Limites du grand desert suivant M.r Long
Plaines couvertes de sable, ou reste à la
culture, parcourues de pers ou quelquefois
prairies d'une côte on n'y rencontre que la
grande tonpeurse de Buffles et de chevaux
sauvages, on y trouve aussi quelques hordes
d'indiens, mais en petit nombre.

R. Roug

M E

P.A. 6,2

ULÉ

ÉRIQUE

e